HISTORY
OF
JEFFERSON COUNTY,

ILLINOIS.

EDITED BY WILLIAM HENRY PERRIN.

ILLUSTRATED.

Southern Historical Press, Inc.
Greenville, South Carolina

This volume was reproduced
from a personal copy located in
the Publishers private library

All rights reserved. No part of this publication may be reproduced,
stored in a retrieval system, transmitted in any form, posted
on the web in any form or by any means without the
prior written permission of the publisher.

Please direct all correspondence and book orders to:
SOUTHERN HISTORICAL PRESS, Inc.
1071 Park West Blvd.
Greenville, SC 29611

Published 1883 by:
  Globe Publishing Company
New material Copyright 2025 by:
  Southern Historical Press, Inc.
ISBN #978-1-63914-656-7
Printed in the United States of America

PREFACE.

THE history of Jefferson County, after months of persistent toil and research, is now completed, and it is believed that no subject of universal public importance or interest has been omitted, save where protracted effort failed to secure reliable results. We are well aware of our inability to furnish a perfect history from meager public documents and numberless conflicting traditions, but claim to have prepared a work fully up to the standard of our promises. Through the courtesy and assistance generously afforded by the residents of the county, we have been enabled to trace out and put on record the greater portion of the important events that have transpired in Jefferson up to the present time. And we feel assured that all thoughtful people in the county, now and in future, will recognize and appreciate the importance of the work and its permanent value. A dry statement of events has, as far as possible, been avoided, and incidents and anecdotes have been interwoven with facts and statistics, forming a narrative at once instructive and entertaining.

We are indebted to George M. Haynes, Esq., for his very able history of the Bench and Bar; to Dr. A. Clark Johnson for the history of Mount Vernon, and to other prominent citizens for interesting and important facts and data in the compilation of the work.

THE PUBLISHERS.

NOVEMBER, 1883.

CONTENTS.

PART I.

	PAGE.
Northwest Territory	1
Early History of Illinois	51

PART II.
GENERAL HISTORY.

CHAPTER I.—Introductory—Geology and Its Practical Value—How Thoroughly to Educate the Farmers—Why They Should Understand the Geological Formations of the Land They Till—Age of the Earth According to the Research of the Geologists—Local Geology—Configuration—Soils and Timber—Minerals and Mineral Springs—Building Materials, etc............ 101

CHAPTER II.—The Pre-historic Races—Mound-Builders—Their Occupation of the Country—Relics Left by Them—The Indians—Speculations as to Their Origin—Ultimate Extinction of the Race—Something of the Tribes of Southern Illinois—What Became of Them—Local Traditions and Incidents—The Black Hawk War, etc., etc................ 110

CHAPTER III.—Settlement of the County by White People—Who the Pioneers Were, and Where They Came From—Andrew Moore—His Murder by the Indians—Moore's Prairie, and the People Who Settled It—The Wilkeys, Crenshaws, Atchisons, etc.—Settlement at Mount Vernon—Other Pioneers—Hardships, Trials, Privations, Manners, Customs, etc., etc............ 121

CHAPTER IV.—Illinois a County of Virginia—John Todd, the First Civil Governor—Organization of Jefferson County—The Legislative Act Creating It—Location of the Seat of Justice—First Officials—The Courts—Public Buildings—Census—The County Divided Into Districts—County Officers—J. R. Satterfield—Township Organization, etc................ 130

CHAPTER V.—Some of the Pioneer Families of the County—The Caseys—Their Emigration to America—How They Served in the Revolution—Facts and Incidents of Their Residence Here—The Maxeys, Another Old Family—Their Welsh Descent—Where and When They Settled—The Johnsons—They are an Old Family, Too—Something of Them and Their Descendants—Other Pioneers—Incidents, etc., etc............ 142

CHAPTER VI.—The Bench and Bar—Supreme Court—Its Location at Mount Vernon—The Judges of the Same—Breeze and Scates—Other Luminaries—The Appellate Court—Some of Its Great Lights—Circuit Court—Judge Tanner and Others—Early Cases Tried in the Courts—Marshall, Baugh, etc.—Present Members of the Bar, etc., etc................ 153

CHAPTER VII.—Political History—Birth of the Whig and Democratic Organizations—Party Strife and Scramble for Office—Joel Pace, First Clerk of the County—Politicians of the Times—Zadok Casey—His Life and Official Services—Gov. Anderson—Sketch of His Public Career—Noah Johnston and Other Distinguished Characters—Senators and Representatives, etc............ 179

CHAPTER VIII.—Something More About the Pioneers—Those Who Came In Later—Their Settlement—Game and Wild Animals—Pioneer Incidents—Mrs. Robinson and the Panther—Some Rattling Snake Stories—Female Fashion and Dress—Woman's Life in the Wilderness—Hard Times, Financial Difficulties, etc............ 196

CHAPTER IX.—Internal Improvements—Early Roads and Trails—Saline and Walnut Hill Road—The Vandalia Road—Other Highways and Bridges—Railroads—How They Grew Out of the Old Improvement System—Jefferson County's Efforts for Railroads—St. Louis Southeastern—The Air Line—Projected Roads, Some of which will be Built, etc................ 208

CHAPTER X.—Educational—Early Efforts at Free Schools—The Duncan Law—Education at Present—Statistics—The Press—Editor John S. Bogan—First Newspapers—Mount Vernon a Newspaper Graveyard—The Press of To-day—Religious History—Old-Time Christianity—Pioneer Ministers—Churches Organized—Rev. John Johnson, etc................ 218

CHAPTER XI.—Agriculture—Its Rank Among the Sciences—How to Keep the Boys Upon the Farm—Educate Them To It—Progress of Agriculture in the County—Some Statistical Information—County Fairs and Associations—Officials of the Same—Horticulture—Value of Fruit Growing—Statistics—The Forests, etc................ 236

CHAPTER XII.—War History—The Revolution and the War of 1812—What We Gained By Them—The Mexican War—Jefferson County's Part in It—Her Officers and Soldiers—The Late Civil War—Sketches of the Regiments in which the County was Represented—Gen. Anderson, Col. Hicks and Other Veterans—Incidents, etc., etc................ 245

CHAPTER XIII.—Odds and Ends—De Omnibus Rebus Et Quibusdam Aliis—A Brief Retrospection—Millers and Mills—Blacksmiths and Other Mechanics—Births, Marriages, Deaths—A Batch of Incidents—Buck Casey Playing Bull Calf—Donnybrook Fights—Forest Fires—A Runaway Negro—Counterfeiting—The Poor Farm, etc., etc................ 264

CONTENTS

PART III.

HISTORY OF THE TOWNSHIPS.

PAGE.

CHAPTER I.—Mount Vernon Township—Description, Topography, etc.—Early Settlement—Old Surveys and Land Entries—A Closer Acquaintance With the Pioneers—Who They Were and Where They Located—Their Good Traits and Peculiarities—The Selecting of a Site for a Town—Mount Vernon Chosen as the County Seat, etc.. 275

CHAPTER II.—City of Mount Vernon—The Laying-out and Beginning of the Town—Sale of Lots—Erection of Public Buildings—The First Court House—Stray Pound, Gaol and Clerk's Office—Stick Chimneys, Court House Lock, etc.—The Pioneers and First Settlers in the Town—Their Genealogical Trees, etc.......................... 283

CHAPTER III.—City of Mount Vernon—More About Its Early Citizens—Some Pen Photographs—The Second Court House—Mount Vernon From 1824 to 1830—A Few of the Old Houses—Relics of a By-gone Period—More Township Items, and a Triple Wedding—Later Settlers—County Roads—The First Churches Outside of Town, etc., etc.. 290

CHAPTER IV.—City of Mount Vernon—The Decade From 1830 to 1840—Growth of the Town—New Buildings and New Business—A Look Beyond the Town—Brief Retrospect—Another Court House—Some of the Business Men and What They Did—Still Another Court House—The Jail—Organization of Mount Vernon Township—Officials, etc.. 300

CHAPTER V.—Mount Vernon—Its Religious History—The Methodists, the Pioneers of Christianity in the County—A List of Ministers—The First Church—Presbyterian Church—Baptists—Catholics and Other Denominations—Churches of the Township—Schools In and Out of the City, etc., etc.. 310

CHAPTER VI.—Mount Vernon—Town Surveys and Additions—"More Than Any Man Can Number"—Casey's Addition—Green's, Strattan's and Several Others—The Number of Acres Covered by the City—Municipal Government—City Officials, etc., etc............................. 326

CHAPTER VII.—Mount Vernon—Temperance Movements—Their Good Work in the Community—Village of East Mount Vernon—Mystic Orders—Masons, Odd Fellows, etc.—Miscellaneous—Which Comprises Fires, Fire Department, and Many Other Local Items—Births, Deaths, etc., etc.. 335

CHAPTER VIII.—Shiloh Township—General Description—Topography and Boundaries—Early Settlement—Pioneer Hardships and Privations—Mills, etc.—An Incident—Births, Deaths and Marriages—Roads and Bridges—Stock-raising—Schools and Churches—Woodlawn Village, etc., etc.. 344

CHAPTER IX.—Pendleton and Moore's Prairie Townships—General Description and Topography—The First Settlers—Moore's Prairie a Historical Spot—Pioneer Hardships and Difficulties—Early Industries and Customs—Township Officers—Churches and Schools—Lynchburg—Belle Rive and Opdyke—Their Growth, Business, etc., etc.. 352

CHAPTER X.—Rome Township—Topographical and Physical Features—Occupation by White People—Who the Pioneers Were—The Maxwells and Others—Hardships and Trials—Mills and Other Improvements—Township Officers—Schools and Churches—Village of Rome—Growth, Improvement, etc.................................. 360

CHAPTER XI.—Spring Garden Township—General Description and Topography—Settlement of the Whites—Their Early Trials and Tribulations—Roads, Mills, etc., etc.—Schools and Churches—Township Officials—Spring Garden Village—Its Growth, Development, etc., etc......... 365

CHAPTER XII.—Webber Township—Introduction and Description—Boundaries, Topography, By-gone, etc.—Early Settlement—Pioneer Life and Trials—Pigeon Post Office—A Law Suit—Township Officials—Schools and Churches—Marlow, Bluford, etc.. etc................................... 372

CHAPTER XIII—Elk Prairie Township—Topography and Physical Features—Coming of the Pale Faces—Incidents of their Settlement—Hard Times, etc.—Roads, Mills and Bridges—Schools and Schoolhouses—Churches, etc.—Township Officials—Villages, etc., etc............... 376

CHAPTER XIV.—Farrington Township—General Topography, Boundaries, etc.—Settlement of White People—Early Industries—Schools and Churches—Township Officers—Villages—Stock-raising, etc........................ 380

CHAPTER XV.—Grand Prairie Township—Boundaries and Topography—Early Settlement, Hardships of the People, etc.—First Mills and Roads—Birth, Death and Marriage—An Incident—First Voting Place—Township Officials, etc.—Schools and Schoolhouses—Churches, etc.......... 387

CHAPTER XVI.—McClellan Township—Introduction and Description—Topography—Early Settlement—Trials, Hardships and Good Times—Pioneer Improvements—Roads, Bridges and Mills—Education, Schoolhouses and Teachers—Early Churches—Township Officials, etc., etc. 391

CHAPTER XVII.—Field Township—Topographical, Geographical, Physical, etc.—Settlement by White People—Life on the Border—Educational Facilities—Churches and Church Buildings—An Incident—Township Officers—Summary, etc., etc.. 396

CHAPTER XVIII.—Casner Township—Topography and Physical Features—Early Settlement—Rough Fare of the Pioneers—Schools and Churches—List of Township Officers—Politics, etc.—Roachville Village, the Chicago of the County, etc., etc.................................... 399

CHAPTER XIX.—Dodds Township—Description and Topography—Coming of the Whites—Early Facts and Incidents—The Main Settlement—Roads—First Mills, etc.—Early Schools—Mode of Paying the Teachers—First Preachers and Churches—Township Officers, etc., etc..... 405

CHAPTER XX.—Blissville Township—Description and Topography—Knob Prairie—Settlement—How the People Lived—Name of Township, and Its List of Officials—Roads, Bridges, etc.—The Village of Williamsburg—Churches and Schools—Retrospection, etc., etc.............. 411

CHAPTER XXI.—Bald Hill Township—Its Geographical and Physical Features—Advent of the Pioneers—Their Trials, Tribulations, etc.—Mills and Roads—Organization of the Township, and the List of Officials—Schools, Churches, etc., etc..................................... 416

PART IV.

BIOGRAPHICAL.

	PAGE.
Mount Vernon—City and Township	3
Pendleton Township	45
Shiloh Township	62
Webber Township	73
Rome Township	78
Dodds Township	87
Blissville Township	93
Spring Garden Township	102
Grand Prairie Township	111
Field Township	119
Moore's Prairie Township	123
Casner Township	130
Farrington Township	135
Elk Prairie Township	138
McClellan Township	144
Bald Hill Township	147
Sketch of C. T. Stratton	149

PORTRAITS.

	PAGE.
Anderson, W. B.	259
Baldridge, J. C.	115
Bruce, M. D.	133
Carpenter, S. W.	169
Dees, J. A.	187
Garrison, W. J.	205
Gilbert, Eli	223
Hails, J. W.	241
Hicks, S. G.	151
Holland, T. G.	295
Jones, G. D.	313
Moss, J. R.	331
Norris, O. P.	349
Plummer, H. S.	277

APPENDIX.

THE NORTHWEST TERRITORY,

INCLUDING A BRIEF

HISTORY OF ILLINOIS.

GEOGRAPHICAL POSITION.

WHEN the Northwestern Territory was ceded to the United States by Virginia in 1784, it embraced only the territory lying between the Ohio and the Mississippi Rivers, and north to the northern limits of the United States. It coincided with the area now embraced in the States of Ohio, Indiana, Michigan, Illinois, Wisconsin, and that portion of Minnesota lying on the east side of the Mississippi River. The United States itself at that period extended no farther west than the Mississippi River; but by the purchase of Louisiana in 1803, the western boundary of the United States was extended to the Rocky Mountains and the Northern Pacific Ocean. The new territory thus added to the National domain, and subsequently opened to settlement, has been called the "New Northwest," in contradistinction from the old "Northwestern Territory."

In comparison with the old Northwest this is a territory of vast magnitude. It includes an area of 1,887,850 square miles; being greater in extent than the united areas of all the Middle and Southern States, including Texas. Out of this magnificent territory have been erected eleven sovereign States and eight Territories, with an aggregate population, at the present time, of 13,000,000 inhabitants, or nearly one-third of the entire population of the United States.

Its lakes are fresh-water seas, and the larger rivers of the continent flow for a thousand miles through its rich alluvial valleys and far-stretching prairies, more acres of which are arable and productive of the highest percentage of the cereals than of any other area of like extent on the globe.

For the last twenty years the increase of population in the Northwest has been about as three to one in any other portion of the United States.

EARLY EXPLORATIONS.

In the year 1541, De Soto first saw the Great West in the New World. He, however, penetrated no farther north than the 35th parallel of latitude. The expedition resulted in his death and that of more than half his army, the remainder of whom found their way to Cuba, thence to Spain, in a famished and demoralized condition. De Soto founded no settlements, produced no results, and left no traces, unless it were that he awakened the hostility of the red man against the white man, and disheartened such as might desire to follow up the career of discovery for better purposes. The French nation were eager and ready to seize upon any news from this extensive domain, and were the first to profit by De Soto's defeat. Yet it was more than a century before any adventurer took advantage of these discoveries.

In 1616, four years before the pilgrims "moored their bark on the wild New England shore," Le Caron, a French Franciscan, had penetrated through the Iroquois and and Wyandots (Hurons) to the streams which run into Lake Huron; and in 1634, two Jesuit missionaries founded the first mission among the lake tribes. It was just one hundred years from the discovery of the Mississippi by De Soto (1541) until the Canadian envoys met the savage nations of the Northwest at the Falls of St. Mary, below the outlet of Lake Superior. This visit led to no permanent result, yet it was not until 1659 that any of the adventurous fur traders attempted to spend a winter in the frozen wilds about the great lakes, nor was it until 1660 that a station was established upon their borders by Mesnard, who perished in the woods a few months after. In 1665, Claude Allouez built the earliest lasting habitation of the white man among the Indians of the Northwest. In 1668, Claude Dablon and James Marquette founded the mission of Sault Ste. Marie at the Falls of St. Mary, and two years afterward, Nicholas Perrot, as agent for M. Talon, Governor General of Canada, explored Lake Illinois (Michigan) as far south as the present City of Chicago, and invited the Indian nations to meet him at a grand council at Sault Ste. Marie the following spring, where they were taken under the protection of the king, and formal possession was taken of the Northwest. This same year Marquette established a mission at Point St. Ignatius, where was founded the old town of town of Michillimackinac.

During M. Talon's explorations and Marquette's residence at St. Ignatius, they learned of a great river away to the west, and fancied—as all others did then—that upon its fertile banks whole tribes of God's children resided, to whom the sound of the Gospel had never come. Filled with a wish to go and preach to them, and in compliance with a request of M. Talon, who earnestly desired to extend the domain of his king, and to ascertain whether the river flowed into the Gulf of Mexico or the Pacific Ocean, Marquette with Joliet, as commander of the expedition, prepared for the undertaking.

On the 13th of May, 1673, the explorers, accompanied by five assistant French Canadians, set out from Mackinaw on their daring voyage of discovery. The Indians, who gathered to witness their departure, were astonished at the boldness of the undertaking, and endeavored to dissuade them from their purpose by representing the tribes on the Mississippi as exceedingly savage and cruel, and the river itself as full of all sorts of frightful monsters ready to swallow them and their canoes together. But, nothing daunted by these terrific descriptions, Marquette told them he was willing not only to encounter all the perils of the unknown region they were about to explore, but to lay down his life in a cause in which the salvation of souls was involved; and having prayed together they separated. Coasting along the northern shore of Lake Michigan, the adventurers entered Green Bay, and passed thence up the Fox River and Lake Winnebago to a village of the Miamis and Kickapoos. Here Marquette was delighted to find a beautiful cross planted in the middle of the town, ornamented with white skins, red girdles and bows and arrows, which these good people had offered to the great Manitou, or God, to thank him for the pity he had bestowed on them during the winter in giving them an abundant "chase." This was the farthest outpost to which Dablon and Allouez had extended their missionary labors the year previous. Here Marquette drank mineral waters and was instructed in the secret of a root which cures the bite of the venomous rattlesnake. He assembled the chiefs and old men of the village, and, pointing to Joliet, said: " My friend is an envoy of France, to discover new countries, and I am an ambassador from God to enlighten them with the truths of the Gospel." Two Miami guides were here furnished to conduct them to the Wisconsin River, and they set out from the Indian village on the 10th of June, amidst a great crowd of natives who had assembled to witness their departure into a region where no white man had ever yet ventured. The guides, having conducted them across the portage, returned. The explorers launched their canoes upon the Wisconsin which they descended to the Mississippi and proceeded down its unknown waters. What emotions must have swelled their breasts as they struck out into the broadening current and became conscious that they were now upon the bosom of the Father of Waters. The mystery was about to be lifted from the long-sought river. The scenery in that locality is beautiful, and on that delightful seventeenth of June must have been clad in all its primeval loveliness as it had been adorned by the hand of Nature. Drifting rapidly, it is said that the bold bluffs on either hand "reminded them of the castled shores of their own beautiful rivers of France." By-and-by, as they drifted along, great herds of buffalo appeared on the banks. On going to the heads of the valley they could see a country of the greatest beauty and fertility, apparently destitute of inhabitants yet presenting the appearance of extensive manors, under the fastidious cultivation of lordly proprietors.

On June 25th, they went ashore and found some fresh traces of men upon the sand, and a path which led to the prairie. The men remained in the boat, and Marquette and Joliet followed the path till they discovered a village on the banks of a river, and two other villages on a hill, within a half league of the first, inhabited by Indians. They were received most hospitably by these natives, who had never before seen a white person. After remaining a few days they re-embarked and descended the river to about latitude 33°, where they found a village of the Arkansas, and being satisfied that the river flowed into the Gulf of Mexico, turned their course up the river, and ascending the stream to the mouth of the Illinois, rowed up that stream to its source, and procured guides from that point to the lakes. "No where on this journey," says Marquette, "did we see such grounds, meadows, woods, stags, buffaloes, deer, wildcats, bustards, swans, ducks, parroquets, and even beavers, as on the Illinois River." The party, without loss or injury, reached Green Bay in September, and reported their discovery—one of the most important of the age, but of which no record was preserved save Marquette's, Joliet losing his by the upsetting of his canoe on his way to Quebec. Afterward Marquette returned to the Illinois Indians by their request, and ministered to them until 1675. On the 18th of May, in that year, as he was passing the mouth of a stream—going with his boatmen up Lake Michigan—he asked to land at its mouth and celebrate mass. Leaving his men with the canoe, he retired a shore distance and began his devotions. As much time passed and he did not return, his men went in search of him, and found him upon his knees, dead. He had peacefully passed away while at prayer. He was buried at this spot. Charlevoix, who visited the place fifty years after, found the waters had retreated from the grave, leaving the beloved missionary to repose in peace. The river has since been called Marquette.

While Marquette and his companions were pursuing their labors in the West, two men, differing widely from him and each other, were preparing to follow in his footsteps and perfect the discoveries so well begun by him. These were Robert de La Salle and Louis Hennepin.

After La Salle's return from the discovery of the Ohio River (see the narrative elsewhere), he established himself again among the French trading posts in Canada. Here he mused long upon the pet project of those ages—a short way to China and the East, and was busily planning an expedition up the great lakes, and so across the continent to the Pacific, when Marquette returned from the Mississippi. At once the vigorous mind of La Salle received from his and his companions' stories the idea that by following the Great River northward, or by turning up some of the numerous western tributaries, the object could easily be gained. He applied to Frontenac, Governor General of Canada, and laid before him the plan, dim but gigantic. Frontenac entered warmly into his plans, and saw that La Salle's idea to connect the great lakes by a chain of forts with the Gulf of Mexico would bind the country so wonderfully together, give unmeasured power to France, and glory to himself, under whose administration he earnestly hoped all would be realized.

La Salle now repaired to France, laid his plans before the King, who warmly approved of them, and made him a Chevalier. He also received from all the noblemen the warmest wishes for his success. The Chevalier returned to Canada, and busily entered upon his work. He at once rebuilt Fort Frontenac and constructed the first ship to sail on these fresh-water seas. On the 7th of August, 1679, having been joined by Hennepin, he began his voyage in the Griffin up Lake Erie. He passed over this lake, through the straits beyond, up Lake St. Clair and into Huron. In this lake they encountered heavy storms. They were some time at Michillimackinac, where La Salle founded a fort, and passed on to Green Bay, the "Baie des Puans" of the French, where he found a large quantity of furs collected for him. He loaded the Griffin with these, and placing her under the care of a pilot and fourteen sailors, started her on her return voyage. The vessel was never afterward heard of. He remained about these parts until early in the winter, when, hearing nothing from the Griffin, he collected all his men—thirty working men and three monks—and started again upon his great undertaking.

By a short portage they passed to the Illinois or Kankakee, called by the Indians, "Theakeke," *wolf*, because of the tribes of Indians called by that name, commonly known as the Mahingans, dwelling there. The French pronounced it *Kiakiki*, which became corrupted to Kankakee. "Falling down the said river by easy journeys, the better to observe the country," about the last of December they reached a village of the Illinois Indians, containing some five hundred cabins, but at that moment no inhabitants. The Seur de La Salle being in want of some breadstuffs, took advantage of the absence of the Indians to help himself to a sufficiency of maize, large quantities of which he found concealed in holes under the wigwams. This village was situated near the present village of Utica in La Salle County, Illinois. The corn being securely stored, the voyagers again betook themselves to the stream, and toward evening on the 4th day of January, 1680, they came into a lake, which must have been the lake of Peoria. This was called by the Indians *Pim-i-te-wi*, that is *a place where there are many fat beasts*. Here the natives were met with in large numbers, but they were gentle and kind, and having spent some time with them, La Salle determined to erect another fort in that place, for he had heard rumors that some of the adjoining tribes were trying to disturb the good feeling which existed, and some of his men were disposed to complain, owing to the hardships and perils of the travel. He called this fort "*Crevecœur*" (broken-heart), a name expressive of the very natural sorrow and anxiety which the pretty certain loss of his ship, Griffin, and his consequent impoverishment, the danger of hostility on the part of the Indians, and of mutiny among his own men, might well cause him. His fears were not entirely groundless. At one time poison was placed in his food, but fortunately was discovered.

While building this fort, the winter wore away, the prairies began to look green, and La Salle, despairing of any reinforcements, concluded to return to Canada, raise new means and new men, and embark anew in the enterprise. For this purpose he made Hennepin the leader of a party to explore the head waters of the Mississippi, and he set out on his journey. This journey was accomplished with the aid of a few persons, and was successfully made, though over an almost unknown route, and in a bad season of the year. He safely reached Canada, and set out again for the object of his search.

Hennepin and his party left Fort Crevecœur on the last of February, 1680. When La Salle reached this place on his return expedition, he found the fort entirely deserted, and he was obliged to return again to Canada. He embarked the third time, and succeeded. Seven days after leaving the fort, Hennepin reached the Mississippi, and paddling up the icy stream as best he could, reached no higher than the Wisconsin River by the 11th of April. Here he and his followers were taken prisoners by a band of Northern Indians, who treated them with great kindness. Hennepin's comrades were Anthony Anguel and Michael Ako. On this voyage they found several beautiful lakes, and "saw some charming prairies." Their captors were the Isaute or Sauteurs, Chippewas, a tribe of the Sioux nation, who took them up the river until about the first of May, when they reached some falls, which Hennepin christened Falls of St. Anthony in honor of his patron saint. Here they took the land, and traveling nearly two hundred miles to the northwest, brought them to their villages. Here they were kept about three months, were treated kindly by their captors, and at the end of that time, were met by a band of Frenchmen, headed by one Seur de Luth, who, in pursuit of trade and game, had penetrated thus far by the route of Lake Superior; and with these fellow-countrymen Hennepin and his companions were allowed to return to the borders of civilized life in November, 1680, just after La Salle had returned to the wilderness on his second trip. Hennepin soon after went to France, where he published an account of his adventures.

The Mississippi was first discovered by De Soto in April, 1541, in his vain endeavor to find gold and precious gems. In the following spring, De Soto, weary with hope long deferred, and worn out with his wanderings, fell a victim to disease, and on the 21st of May, died. His followers, reduced by fatigue and disease to less than three hundred men, wandered about the country nearly a year, in the vain endeavor to rescue themselves by land, and finally constructed seven small vessels, called brigantines, in which they embarked, and descending the river, supposing it would lead them to the sea, in July they came to the sea (Gulf of Mexico), and by September reached the Island of Cuba.

They were the first to see the great outlet of the Mississippi; but, being so weary and discouraged, made no attempt to claim the country, and hardly had an intelligent idea of what they had passed through.

To La Salle, the intrepid explorer, belongs the honor of giving the first account of the mouths of the river. His great desire was to possess this entire country for his king, and in January, 1682, he and his band of explorers left the shores of Lake Michigan on their third attempt, crossed the portage, passed down the Illinois River, and on the 6th of February, reached the banks of the Mississippi.

On the 13th they commenced their downward course, which they pursued with but one interruption, until upon the 6th of March they discovered the three great passages by which the river discharges its waters into the gulf. La Salle thus narrates the event:

"We landed on the bank of the most western channel, about three leagues (nine miles) from its mouth. On the seventh, M. de La Salle went to reconnoiter the shores of the neighboring sea, and M. de Tonti meanwhile examined the great middle channel. They found the main outlets beautiful, large and deep. On the 8th we reascended the river, a little above its confluence with the sea, to find a dry place beyond the reach of inundations. The elevation of the North Pole was here about twenty-seven degrees. Here we prepared a column and a cross, and to the column were affixed the arms of France with this inscription:

Louis LeGrand, Roi De France et de Navarre, regne; Le neuvieme Avril 1682.

The whole party, under arms, chanted the *Te Deum*, and then, after a salute and cries of "*Vive le Roi*," the column was erected by M. de La Salle, who, standing near it, proclaimed in a loud voice the authority of the King of France. La Salle returned and laid the foundations of the Mississippi settlements in Illinois, thence he proceeded to France, where another expedition was fitted out, of which he was commander, and in two succeeding voyages failed to find the outlet of the river by sailing along the shore of the gulf. On his third voyage he was killed, through the treachery of his followers, and the object of his expeditions was not accomplished until 1699, when D'Iberville, under the authority of the crown, discovered, on the second of March, by way of the sea, the mouth of the "Hidden River." This majestic stream was called by the natives "*Malbouchia*," and by the Spaniards, "*la Palissade,*" from the great number of trees about its mouth. After traversing the several outlets, and satisfying himself as to its certainty, he erected a fort near its western outlet and returned to France.

An avenue of trade was now opened out, which was fully improved. In 1718, New Orleans was laid out and settled by some European colonists. In 1762, the colony was made over to Spain, to be regained by France under the consulate of Napoleon. In 1803, it was purchased by the United States for the sum of fifteen million dollars, and the territory of Louisiana and commerce of the Mississippi River came under the charge of the United States. Although La Salle's labors ended in defeat and death, he had not worked and suffered in vain. He had thrown open to France and the world an immense and most valuable country; had established several ports, and laid the foundations of more than one settlement there. "Peoria, Kaskaskia and Cahokia, are to this day monuments of La Salle's labors; for, though he had founded neither of them (unless Peoria, which was built nearly upon the site of Fort Crevecœur,) it was by those whom he led into the West that these places were peopled and civilized. He was, if not the discoverer, the first settler of the Mississippi Valley, and as such deserves to be known and honored."

The French early improved the opening made for them. Before the year 1698, the Rev. Father Gravier began a mission among the Illinois, and founded Kaskaskia. For some time this was merely a missionary station, where none but natives resided, it being one of three such villages, the other two being Cahokia and Peoria. What is known of these missions is learned from a letter written by Father Gabriel Marest, dated "Aux Cascaskias, autrement dit de l'Immaculate Conception de la Sainte Vierge, le 9 Novembre, 1712." Soon after the founding of Kaskaskia, the missionary, Pinet, gathered a flock at Cahokia, while Peoria arose near the ruins of Fort Crevecœur. This must have been about a year 1700. The post at Vincennes on the Oubache river, (pronounced Wa-ba, meaning *summer cloud moving swiftly*) was established in 1702, according to the best authorities.* It is altogether probable that

* There is considerable dispute about this date, some asserting it was founded as late as 1742. When the new court house at Vincennes was erected, all authorities on the subject were carefully examined, and 1702 fixed upon as the correct date. It was accordingly engraved on the corner-stone of the court house.

on La Salle's last trip he established the stations at Kaskaskia and Cahokia. In July, 1701, the foundations of Fort Ponchartrain were laid by De la Motte Cadillac on the Detroit River. These stations, with those established further north, were the earliest attempts to occupy the Northwest Territory. At the same time efforts were being made to occupy the Southwest, which finally culminated in the settlement and founding of the City of New Orleans by a colony from England in 1718. This was mainly accomplished through the efforts of the famous Mississippi Company, established by the notorious John Law, who so quickly arose into prominence in France, and who with his scheme so quickly and so ignominiously passed away.

From the time of the founding of these stations for fifty years the French nation were engrossed with the settlement of the lower Mississippi, and the war with the Chicasaws, who had, in revenge for repeated injuries, cut off the entire colony at Natchez. Although the company did little for Louisiana, as the entire West was then called, yet it opened the trade through the Mississippi River, and started the raising of grains indigenous to that climate. Until the year 1750, but little is known of the settlements in the Northwest, as it was not until this time that the attention of the English was called to the occupation of this portion of the New World, which they then supposed they owned. Vivier, a missionary among the Illinois, writing from "Aux Illinois," six leagues from Fort Chartres, June 8, 1750, says: "We have here whites, negroes and Indians, to say nothing of cross-breeds. There are five French villages, and three villages of the natives, within a space of twenty-one leagues situated between the Mississippi and another river called the Karkadaid (Kaskaskias). In the five French villages are, perhaps, eleven hundred whites, three hundred blacks and some sixty red slaves or savages. The three Illinois towns do not contain more than eight hundred souls all told. Most of the French till the soil; they raise wheat, cattle, pigs and horses, and live like princes. Three times as much is produced as can be consumed; and great quantities of grain and flour are sent to New Orleans." This city was now the seaport town of the Northwest, and save in the extreme northern part, where only furs and copper ore were found, almost all the products of the country found their way to France by the mouth of the Father of Waters. In another letter, dated November 7, 1750, this same priest says: "For fifteen leagues above the mouth of the Mississippi one sees no dwellings, the ground being too low to be habitable. Thence to New Orleans, the lands are only partially occupied. New Orleans contains black, white and red, not more, I think, than twelve hundred persons. To this point come all lumber, bricks, salt-beef, tallow, tar, skins and bear's grease; and above all, pork and flour from the Illinois. These things create some commerce, as forty vessels and more have come hither this year. Above New Orleans, plantations are again met with; the most considerable is a colony of Germans, some ten leagues up the river. At Point Coupee, thirty-five leagues above the German settlement, is a fort. Along here, within five or six leagues, are not less than sixty habitations. Fifty leagues farther up is the Natchez post, where we have a garrison, who are kept prisoners through fear of the Chicasaws. Here and at point Coupee, they raise excellent tobacco. Another hundred leagues brings us to the Arkansas, where we have also a fort and a garrison for the benefit of the river traders. * * * From the Arkansas to the Illinois, nearly five hundred leagues, there is not a settlement. There should be, however, a fort at the Oubache (Ohio), the only path by which the English can reach the Mississippi. In the Illinois country are numberless mines, but no one to work them as they deserve." Father Marest, writing from the post at Vincennes, in 1812, makes the same observation. Vivier also says: "Some individuals dig lead near the surface and supply the Indians and Canada. Two Spaniards now here, who claim to be adepts, say that our mines are like those of Mexico, and that if we would dig deeper, we should find silver under the lead; and at any rate the lead is excellent. There is also in this country, beyond doubt, copper ore, as from time to time large pieces are found in the streams."

At the close of the year 1750, the French occupied, in addition to the lower Mississippi posts and those in Illinois, one at Du Quesne, one at the Maumee in the country of the Miamis, and one at Sandusky, in what may be termed the Ohio Valley. In the northern part of the Northwest they had stations at St. Joseph's on the St. Joseph's of Lake Michigan, at Fort Ponchartrain (Detroit), at Michillimackanac or Massillimacanac, Fox River of Green Bay, and at Sault Ste. Marie. The fondest dreams of La Salle were now fully realized. The French alone were possessors of this vast realm, basing their claim on discovery and settlement. Another nation, however, was now turning its attention to this extensive country, and hearing of its wealth, began to lay plans for occupying it and for securing the great profits arising therefrom.

The French, however, had another claim to this country, namely, the

DISCOVERY OF THE OHIO.

This "Beautiful" river was discovered by Robert Cavalier de La Salle in 1669, four years before the discovery of the Mississippi by Joliet and Marquette.

While La Salle was at his trading post on the St. Lawrence, he found leisure to study nine Indian dialects, the chief of which was the Iroquois. He not only desired to facilitate his intercourse in trade, but he longed to travel and explore the unknown regions of the West. An incident soon occurred which decided him to fit out an exploring expedition.

While conversing with some Senecas, he learned of a river called the Ohio, which rose in their country and flowed to the sea, but at such a distance that it required eight months to reach its mouth. In this statement the Mississippi and its tributaries were considered as one stream. La Salle, believing, as most of the French at that period did, that the great rivers flowing west emptied into the Sea of California, was anxious to embark in the enterprise of discovering a route across the continent to the commerce of China and Japan.

He repaired at once to Quebec to obtain the approval of the Governor. His eloquent appeal prevailed. The Governor and the Intendant, Talon, issued letters patent authorizing the enterprise, but made no provision to defray the expenses. At this juncture the seminary of St. Sulpice decided to send out missionaries in connection with the expedition, and La Salle offering to sell his improvements at La Chine to raise money, the offer was accepted by the Superior, and two thousand eight hundred dollars were raised, with which La Salle purchased four canoes and the necessary supplies for the outfit.

On the 6th of July, 1669, the party, numbering twenty-four persons, embarked in seven canoes on the St. Lawrence; two additional canoes carried the Indian guides. In three days they were gliding over the bosom of Lake Ontario. Their guides conducted them directly to the Seneca village on the bank of the Genesee, in the vicinity of the present City of Rochester, New York. Here they expected to procure guides to conduct them to the Ohio, but in this they were disappointed.

The Indians seemed unfriendly to the enterprise. La Salle suspected that the Jesuits had prejudiced their minds against his plans. After waiting a month in the hope of gaining their object, they met an Indian from the Iroquois colony at the head of Lake Ontario, who assured them that they could there find guides, and offered to conduct them thence.

On their way they passed the mouth of the Niagara River, when they heard for the first time the distant thunder of the cataract. Arriving among the Iroquois, they met with a friendly reception, and learned from a Shawanee prisoner that they could reach the Ohio in six weeks. Delighted with the unexpected good fortune, they made ready to resume their journey; but just as they were about to start they heard of the arrival of two Frenchmen in a neighboring village. One of them proved to be Louis Joliet, afterward famous as an explorer in the West. He had been sent by the Canadian Government to explore the copper mines on Lake Superior, but had failed, and was on his way back to Quebec. He gave the missionaries a map of the country he had explored in the lake region, together with an account of the condition of the Indians in that quarter. This induced the priests to determine on leaving the expedition and going to Lake Superior. La Salle warned them that the Jesuits were probably occupying that field, and that they would meet with a cold reception. Nevertheless they persisted in their purpose, and after worship on the lake shore parted from La Salle. On arriving at Lake Superior, they found, as La Salle had predicted, the Jesuit Fathers, Marquette and Dablon, occupying the field.

These zealous disciples of Loyola informed them that they wanted no assistance from St. Sulpice, nor from those who made him their patron saint; and thus repulsed, they returned to Montreal the following June without having made a single discovery or converted a single Indian.

After parting with the priests, La Salle went to the chief Iroquois village at Onondaga, where he obtained guides, and passing thence to a tributary of the Ohio south of Lake Erie, he descended the latter as far as the falls at Louisville. Thus was the Ohio discovered by La Salle, the persevering and successful French explorer of the West, in 1669.

The account of the latter part of his journey is found in an anonymous paper, which purports to have been taken from the lips of La Salle himself during a subsequent visit to Paris. In a letter written to Count Frontenac in 1667, shortly after the discovery, he himself says that he discovered the Ohio and descended it to the falls. This was regarded as an indisputable fact by the French authorities, who claimed the Ohio Valley upon another ground. When Washington was sent by the colony of Virginia in 1753, to demand of Gordeur de St. Pierre why the French had built a fort on the Monongahela, the haughty commandant at Quebec replied: "We claim the country on the Ohio by virtue of the discoveries of La Salle, and will not give it up to the English. Our orders are to make prisoners of every Englishman found trading in the Ohio Valley."

ENGLISH EXPLORATIONS AND SETTLEMENTS.

When the new year of 1750 broke in upon the Father of Waters and the Great Northwest, all was still wild save at the French posts already described. In 1749, when the English first began to think seriously about sending men into the West, the greater portion of the States of Indiana, Ohio, Illinois, Michigan, Wisconsin, and Minnesota were yet under the dominion of the red men. The English knew, however, pretty conclusively of the nature of the wealth of these wilds. As early as 1710, Governor Spotswood, of Virginia, had commenced movements to secure the country west of the Alleghanies to the English crown. In Pennsylvania, Governor Keith and James Logan, secretary of the province, from 1719 to 1731, represented to the powers of England the necessity of securing the Western lands. Nothing was done, however, by that power save to take some diplomatic steps to secure the claims of Britain to this unexplored wilderness.

England had from the outset claimed from the Atlantic to the Pacific, on the ground that the discovery of the seacoast and its possession was a discovery and possession of the country, and, as is well known, her grants to the colonies extended "from sea to sea." This was not all her claim. She had purchased from the Indian tribes large tracts of land. This latter was also a strong argument. As early as 1684, Lord Howard, Governor of Virginia, held a treaty with the six nations. These were the great Northern Confederacy, and comprised at first the Mohawks, Oneidas, Onondagas, Cayugas, and Senecas. Afterward the Tuscaroras were taken into the confederacy, and it became known as the SIX NATIONS. They came under the protection of the mother country, and again in 1701, they repeated the agreement, and in September, 1726, a formal deed was drawn up and signed by the chiefs. The validity of this claim has often been disputed, but never successfully. In 1744, a purchase was made at Lancaster, Pennsylvania, of certain lands within the "Colony of Virginia," for which the Indians received £200 in gold and a like sum in goods, with a promise that, as settlements increased, more should be paid. The Commissioners from Virginia were Colonel Thomas Lee and Colonel William Beverley. As settlements extended, the promise of more pay was called to mind, and Mr. Conrad Weiser was sent across the mountains with presents to appease the savages. Col. Lee, and some Virginians accompanied him with the intention of sounding the Indians upon their feelings regarding the English. They were not satisfied with their treatment, and plainly told the Commissioners why. The English did not desire the cultivation of the country, but the monopoly of the Indian trade. In 1748, the Ohio Company was formed, and petitioned the king for a grant of land beyond the Alleghenies. This was granted, and the government of Virginia was ordered to grant to them a half million acres, two hundred thousand of which were to be located at once. Upon the 12th of June, 1749, 800,000 acres from the line of Canada north and west was made to the Loyal Company, and on the 29th of October, 1751, 100,000 acres were given to the Greenbriar Company. All this time the French were not idle. They saw that, should the British gain a foothold in the West, especially upon the Ohio, they might not only prevent the French settling upon it, but in time would come to the lower posts and so gain possession of the whole country. Upon the 10th of May, 1774, Vaudreuil, Governor of Canada and the French possessions, well knowing the consequences that must arise from allowing the English to build trading posts in the Northwest, seized some of their frontier posts, and to further secure the claim of the French to the West, he, in 1749, sent Louis Celeron with a party of soldiers to plant along the Ohio River, in the mounds and at the mouths of its principal tributaries, plates of lead, on which were inscribed the claims of France. These were heard of in 1752, and within the memory of residents now living along the "Oyo," as the beautiful river was called by the French. One of these plates was found with the inscription partly defaced. It bears date August 16, 1749, and a copy of the inscription with particular account of the discovery of the plate, was sent by DeWitt Clinton to the American Antiquarian Society, among whose journals it may now be found.* These measures did not, however, deter the English from going on with their explorations, and though neither party resorted to arms, yet the conflict was gathering, and it was only a question of time when the storm would burst upon the frontier settlements. In 1750, Christopher Gist was sent by the Ohio Company to examine its lands. He went to a village of the Twigtwees, on the Miami, about one hundred and fifty miles above its mouth. He afterward spoke of it as very populous. From there he went down the Ohio River nearly to the falls at the present City of Louisville, and in November he commenced a survey of the company's lands. During the winter, General Andrew Lewis performed a similar work for the Greenbriar Company. Meanwhile the French were busy in preparing their forts for defense, and in opening roads, and also sent a small party of soldiers to keep the Ohio clear. This party, having heard of the English post on the Miami

* The following is a translation of the inscription on the plate: "In the year 1749, reign of Louis XV., King of France, we, Celeron, commandant of a detachment by Monsieur the Marquis of Gallisoniere, commander-in-chief of New France, to establish tranquility in certain Indian villages of these cantons, have buried this plate at the confluence of the Toradakoin, this twenty-ninth of July, near the river Ohio, otherwise Beautiful River, as a monument of renewal of possession which we have taken of the said river, and all its tributaries; inasmuch as the preceding Kings of France have enjoyed it, and maintained it by their arms a 1 treaties; esp cially by those of Ryswick, Utrecht, and Aix La Chapelle."

River, early in 1652, assisted by the Ottawas and Chippewas, attacked it, and, after a severe battle, in which fourteen of the natives were killed and others wounded, captured the garrison. (They were probably garrisoned in a block house). The traders were carried away to Canada, and one account says several were burned. This fort or post was called by the English Pickawillany. A memorial of the king's ministers refers to it as "Pickawillanes, in the center of the territory between the Ohio and the Wabash. The name is probably some variation of Pickaway or Picqua, in 1773, written by Rev. David Jones, Pickaweke."

This was the first blood shed between the French and English, and occurred near the present City of Piqua, Ohio, or at least at a point about forty-seven miles north of Dayton. Each nation became now more interested in the progress of events in the Northwest. The English determined to purchase from the Indians a title to the lands they wished to occupy, and Messrs. Fry (afterward Commander-in-chief over Washington at the commencement of the French War of 1775-1763), Lomax and Patton were sent in the spring of 1752 to hold a conference with the natives at Logstown to learn what they objected to in the treaty of Lancaster already noticed and to settle all difficulties. On the 9th of June, these Commissioners met the red men at Logstown, a little village on the north bank of the Ohio, about seventeen miles below the site of Pittsburgh. Here had been a trading point for many years, but it was abandoned by the Indians in 1750. At first the Indians declined to recognize the treaty of Lancaster, but, the Commissioners taking aside Montour, the interpreter, who was a son of the famous Catharine Montour, and a chief among the Six Nations, induced him to use his influence in their favor. This he did, and upon the 13th of June they all united in signing a deed, confirming the Lancaster treaty in its full extent, consenting to a settlement of the southeast of the Ohio, and guaranteeing that it should not be disturbed by them. These were the means used to obtain the first treaty with the Indians in the Ohio Valley.

Meanwhile the powers beyond the sea were trying to out-maneuver each other, and were professing to be at peace. The English generally outwitted the Indians, and failed in many instances to fulfill their contracts. They thereby gained the ill-will of the red men, and further increased the feeling by failing to provide them with arms and ammunition. Said an old chief, at Easton, in 1758: "The Indians on the Ohio left you because of your own fault. When we heard the French were coming, we asked you for help and arms, but we did not get them. The French came, they treated us kindly, and gained our affections. The Governor of Virginia settled on our lands for his own benefit, and, when we wanted help, forsook us."

At the beginning of 1653, the English thought they had secured by title the lands in the West, but the French had quietly gathered cannon and military stores to be in readiness for the expected blow. The English made other attempts to ratify these existing treaties, but not until the summer could the Indians be gathered together to discuss the plans of the French. They had sent messages to the French, warning them away; but they replied that they intended to complete the chain of forts already begun, and would not abandon the field.

Soon after this, no satisfaction being obtained from the Ohio regarding the positions and purposes of the French, Governor Dinwiddie of Virginia determined to send to them another messenger and learn from them, if possible, their intentions. For this purpose he selected a young man, a surveyor, who, at the early age of nineteen, had received the rank of major, and who was thoroughly posted regarding frontier life. This personage was no other than the illustrious George Washington, who then held considerable interest in Western lands. He was at this time just twenty-two years of age. Taking Gist as his guide, the two, accompanied by four servitors, set out on their perilous march. They left Will's Creek on the 10th of November, 1753, and on the 22d reached the Monongahela, about ten miles above the fork. From there they went to Logstown, where Washington had a long conference with the chiefs of the Six Nations. From them he learned the condition of the French, and also heard of their determination not to come down the river till the following spring. The Indians were non-committal, as they were afraid to turn either way, and, as far as they could, desired to remain neutral. Washington, finding nothing could be done with them, went on to Venango, an old Indian town at the mouth of French Creek. Here the French had a fort, called Fort Machault. Through the rum and flattery of the French, he nearly lost all his Indian followers. Finding nothing of importance here, he pursued his way amid great privations, and on the 11th of December reached the fort at the head of French Creek. Here he delivered Governor Dinwiddie's letter, received his answer, took his observations, and on the 16th set out upon his return journey with no one but Gist, his guide, and a few Indians who still remained true to him, notwithstanding the endeavors of the French to retain them. Their homeward journey was one of great peril and suffering from the cold, yet they reached home in safety on the 6th of January, 1754.

From the letter of St. Pierre, commander of the French fort, sent by Washington to Governor Dinwiddie, it was learned that the French would not give up without a struggle. Active preparations were at once made in all the English colonies for the coming conflict, while the French finished the fort at Venango and strengthened their lines of fortifications, and gathered their forces to be in readiness.

The Old Dominion was all alive. Virginia was the center of great activities; volunteers were called for, and from all the neighboring colonies men rallied to the conflict, and everywhere along the Potomac men were enlisting under the governor's proclamation—which promised two hundred thousand acres on the Ohio. Along this river they were gathering as far as Will's Creek, and far beyond this point, whither Trent had come for assistance for his little band of forty-one men, who were working away in hunger and want, to fortify that point at the fork of the Ohio, to which both parties were looking with deep interest.

"The first birds of spring filled the air with their song; the swift river rolled by the Allegheny hillsides. swollen by the melting snows of spring and the April showers. The leaves were appearing; a few Indian scouts were seen, but no enemy seemed near at hand; and all was so quiet, that Frazier, an old Indian scout and trader, who had been left by Trent in command, ventured to his home at the mouth of Turtle Creek, ten miles up the Monongahela. But, though all was so quiet in that wilderness, keen eyes had seen the low intrenchment rising at the fork, and swift feet had borne the news of it up the river; and upon the morning of the 17th of April, Ensign Ward, who then had charge of it, saw upon the Allegheny a sight that made his heart sink--sixty batteaux and three hundred canoes filled with men, and laden deep with cannon and stores. * * * That evening he supped with his captor, Contrecœur, and the next day he was bowed off by the Frenchman, and with his men and tools, marched up the Monongahela."

The French and Indian war had begun. The treaty of Aix la Chapelle, in 1748, had left the boundaries between the French and English possessions unsettled, and the events already narrated show the French were determined to hold the country watered by the Mississippi and its tributaries; while the English laid claims to the country by virtue of the discoveries of the Cabots, and claimed all the country from Newfoundland to Florida, extending from the Atlantic to the Pacific. The first decisive blow had now been struck, and the first attempt of the English, through the Ohio Company, to occupy these lands, had resulted disastrously to them. The French and Indians immediately completed the fortifications begun at the Fork, which they had so easily captured, and when completed gave to the fort the name of Du Quesne.

Washington was at Will's Creek when the news of the capture of the fort arrived. He at once departed to recapture it. On his way he entrenched himself at a place called the "Meadows," where he erected a fort called by him Fort Necessity. From there he surprised and captured a force of French and Indians marching against him, but was soon after attacked in his fort by a much superior force, and was obliged to yield on the morning of July 4th. He was allowed to return to Virginia.

The English Government immediately planned four campaigns; one against Fort Du Quesne; one against Nova Scotia; one against Fort Niagara, and one against Crown Point. These occurred during 1755-6, and were not successful in driving the French from their possessions. The expedition against Fort Du Quesne was led by the famous General Braddock, who, refusing to listen to the advice of Washington and those acquainted with Indian warfare, suffered such an inglorious defeat. This occurred on the morning of July 9th, and is generally known as the battle of Monongahela, or "Braddock's Defeat." The war continued with various vicissitudes through the years 1756-7; when, at the commencement of 1758 in accordance with the plans of William Pitt, then Secretary of State, afterward Lord Chatham, active preparations were made to carry on the war. Three expeditions were planned for this year: one, under General Amherst, against Louisburg; another, under Abercrombie, against Fort Ticonderoga; and a third, under General Forbes, against Fort Du Quesne. On the 26th of July, Louisburg surrendered after a desperate resistance of more than forty days, and the eastern part of the Canadian possessions fell into the hands of the British. Abercrombie captured Fort Frontenac, and when the expedition against Fort Du Quesne, of which Washington had the active command, arrived there, it was found in flames and deserted. The English at once took possession, rebuilt the fort, and in honor of their illustrious statesman, changed the name to Fort Pitt.

The great object of the campaign of 1759, was the reduction of Canada. General Wolfe was to lay siege to Quebec; Amherst was to reduce Ticonderoga and Crown Point, and General Prideaux was to capture Niagara. This latter place was taken in July, but the gallant Prideaux lost his life in the attempt. Amherst captured Ticonderoga and Crown Point without a blow; and Wolfe, after making the memorable ascent to the plains of Abraham, on September 13th, defeated Montcalm, and on the 18th, the city capitulated. In this engagement Montcalm and Wolfe both lost their lives. De Levi, Montcalm's successor, marched to Sillery, three miles above the city, with the purpose of defeating the English, and there, on the 28th of the following April, was fought one of the bloodiest battles of the French and Indian war. It resulted in the defeat of the French, and the fall of the city of Montreal. The Governor signed a capitulation, by which the whole of Canada was surrendered to the English. This practically concluded the war, but it was not until 1763 that the treaties of peace between France and England were signed. This was done on the 10th of February of that year, and under its provisions all the country east of the Mississippi and north of the Iberville river, in Louisiana, were ceded to England. At the same time Spain ceded Florida to Great Britain.

On the 13th of September, 1760, Major Robert Rogers was sent from Montreal to take charge of Detroit, the only remaining French post in the territory. He arrived there on the 19th of November, and summoned the place to surrender. At first the commander of the post, Beletre, refused, but on the 29th, hearing of the continued defeat of the French arms, surrendered. Rogers remained there until December 23d, under the personal protection of the celebrated chief, Pontiac, to whom, no doubt, he owed his safety. Pontiac had come here to inquire the purposes of the English in taking possession of the country. He was assured that they came simply to trade with the natives, and did not desire their country. This answer conciliated the savages, and did much to insure the safety of Rogers and his party during their stay, and while on their journey home.

Rogers set out for Fort Pitt on December 23d, and was just one month on the way. His route was from Detroit to Maumee, thence across the present State of Ohio directly to the fort. This was the common trail of the Indians in their journeys from Sandusky to the Fork of the Ohio. It went from Fort Sandusky, where Sandusky city now is, crossed the Huron river, then called Bald Eagle Creek, to "Mohickon John's Town" Creek, on Mohikon Creek, the northern branch of White Woman's river, and then crossed to Beaver's town, a Delaware town on what is now Sandy Creek. At Beaver's town were probably one hundred ar ' fifty warriors, and not less than three thousand acres of cleared land. From there the track went up Sandy Creek to and across Big Beaver, and up the Ohio to Logstown, thence on to the fork.

The Northwest Territory was now entirely under the English rule. New settlements began to be rapidly made, and the promise of a large trade was speedily manifested. Had the British carried out their promises with the natives, none of those savage butcheries would have been perpetrated, and the country would have been spared their recital.

The renowned chief, Pontiac, was one of the leading spirits in these atrocities. We will now pause in our narrative, and notice the leading events in his life. The earliest authentic information regarding this noted Indian chief, is learned from an account of an Indian trader named Alexander Henry, who, in the spring of 1761, penetrated his domains as far as Missillimacnac. Pontiac was then a great friend of the French, but a bitter foe of the English, whom he considered as encroaching on his hunting grounds. Henry was obliged to disguise himself as a Canadian to insure safety, but was discovered by Pontiac, who bitterly reproached him, and the English for their attempted subjugation of the West. He declared that no treaty had been made with them; no presents sent them, and that he would resent any possession of the West by that nation. He was at the time about fifty years of age, tall and dignified, and was civil and military ruler of the Ottawas, Ojibwas and Pottawatomies.

The Indians, from Lake Michigan to the borders of North Carolina, were united in this feeling, and at the time of the treaty of Paris, ratified February 10, 1763, a general conspiracy was formed to fall suddenly upon the frontier British posts, and with one blow strike every man dead. Pontiac was the marked leader in all this, and was the commander of the Chippewas, Ottawas, Wyandots, Miamis, Shawanese, Delawares and Mingoes, who had, for the time, laid aside their local quarrels to unite in this enterprise.

The blow came, as near as can be ascertained, on May 7, 1763. Nine British posts fell, and the Indians drank, "scooped up in the hollow of joined hands," the blood of many a Briton.

Pontiac's immediate field of action, was the garrison at Detroit. Here, however, the plans were frustrated by an Indian woman disclosing the plot the evening previous to his arrival. Everything was carried out, however, according to Pontiac's plans until the moment of action, when Major Gladwyn, the commander of the post, stepping to one of the Indian chiefs, suddenly drew aside his blanket and disclosed the concealed musket. Pontiac though a brave man, turned pale and trembled. He saw his plan was known and that the garrison were prepared. He endeavored to exculpate himself from any such intentions; but the guilt was evident, and he and his followers were dismissed with a severe reprimand, and warned never to again enter the walls of the post.

Pontiac at once laid siege to the fort, and until the treaty of peace between the British and the Western Indians, concluded in August, 1764, continued to harass and besiege the fortress. He organized a regular commissariat department, issued bills of credit written out on bark, which to his credit, it may be stated, were punctually redeemed. At the conclusion of the treaty, in which it seems he took no part, he went farther south, living many years among the Illinois.

He had given up all hope of saving his country and race. After a time he endeavored to unite the Illinois tribe and those about St. Louis in a war with the whites. His efforts were fruitless, and only ended in a quarrel between himself and some Kaskaskia Indians, one of whom soon afterward killed him. His death was, however, avenged by the northern Indians, who nearly exterminated the Illinois in the wars which followed.

Had it not been for the treachery of a few of his followers, his plan for the extermination of the whites, a masterly one, would undoubtedly have been carried out.

It was in the spring of the year following Rogers' visit that Alexander Henry went to Missillimacnac, and everywhere found the strongest feelings against the English who had not carried out their promises, and were doing nothing to conciliate the natives. Here he met the chief, Pontiac, who after conveying to him in a speech the idea that their French father would awake soon and utterly destroy his enemies, said: "Englishman, although you have conquered the French, you have not yet conquered us! We are not your slaves! These lakes, these woods, these mountains, were left us by our ancestors. They are our inheritance, and we will part with them to none. Your nation supposes that we, like the white people, can not live without bread and pork and beef. But you ought to know that He, the Great Spirit and Master of Life, has provided food for us upon these broad lakes and in these mountains."

He then spoke of the fact that no treaty had been made with them, no presents sent them, and that he and his people were yet for war. Such were the feelings of the Northwestern Indians immediately after the English took possession of their country. These feelings were no doubt encouraged by the Canadians and French, who hoped that yet the French arms might prevail. The treaty of Paris, however, gave to the English the right to this vast domain, and active preparations were going on to occupy it and enjoy its trade and emoluments.

In 1762, France, by a secret treaty, ceded Louisiana to Spain, to prevent it falling into the hands of the English, who were becoming masters of the entire West. The next year the treaty of Paris, signed at Fontainbleau, gave to the English the domain of the country in question. Twenty years after, by the treaty of peace between the United States and England, that part of Canada lying south and west of the Great Lakes, comprehending a large territory which is the subject of these sketches, was acknowledged to be a portion of the United States; and twenty years still later, in 1803, Louisiana was ceded by Spain back to France, and by France sold to the United States.

In the half century, from the building of the Fort of Crevecœur by La Salle, in 1680, up to the erection of Fort Chatres, many French settlements had been made in that quarter. These have already been noticed, being those at St. Vincent (Vincennes), Kohokia or Cahokia, Kaskaskia and Prairie du Rocher, on the American

Bottom, a large tract of rich alluvial soil in Illinois, on the Mississippi, opposite the site of St. Louis.

By the treaty of Paris, the regions east of the Mississippi, including all these and other towns of the Northwest, were given over to England, but they do not appear to have been taken possession of until 1765, when Captain Stirling, in the name of the Majesty of England, established himself at Fort Chartres bearing with him the proclamation of General Gage, dated December 30, 1764, which promised religious freedom to all Catholics who worshipped here, and a right to leave the country with their effects if they wished, or to remain with the privileges of Englishmen. It was shortly after the occupancy of the West by the British that the war with Pontiac opened. It is already noticed in the sketch of that chieftain. By it many a Briton lost his life, and many a frontier settlement in its infancy ceased to exist. This was not ended until the year 1764, when, failing to capture Detroit, Niagara and Fort Pitt, his confederacy became disheartened, and, receiving no aid from the French, Pontiac abandoned the enterprise and departed to the Illinois, among whom he afterward lost his life.

As soon as these difficulties were definitely settled, settlers began rapidly to survey the country, and prepare for occupation. During the year 1770, a number of persons from Virginia and other British provinces explored and marked out nearly all the valuable lands on the Monongahela and along the banks of the Ohio, as far as the Little Kanawha. This was followed by another exploring expedition, in which George Washington was a party. The latter, accompanied by Dr. Craik, Capt. Crawford and others, on the 20th of October, 1770, descended the Ohio from Pittsburgh to the mouth of the Kanawha; ascended that stream about fourteen miles, marked out several large tracts of land, shot several buffalo, which were then abundant in the Ohio valley, and returned to the fort.

Pittsburgh was at this time a trading post, about which was clustered a village of some twenty houses, inhabited by Indian traders. This same year, Capt. Pittman visited Kaskaskia and its neighboring villages. He found there about sixty-five resident families, and at Cahokia only forty-five dwellings. At Fort Chartres was another small settlement, and at Detroit the garrison were quite prosperous and strong. For a year or two settlers continued to locate near some of these posts, generally Fort Pitt or Detroit, owing to the fears of the Indians, who still maintained some feelings of hatred to the English. The trade from the posts was quite good, and from those in Illinois large quantities of pork and flour found their way to the New Orleans market. At this time the policy of the British Government was strongly opposed to the extension of the colonies west. In 1763, the King of England forbade, by royal proclamation, his colonial subjects from making a settlement beyond the sources of the rivers which fall into the Atlantic Ocean. At the instance of the Board of Trade, measures were taken to prevent the settlement without the limits prescribed, and to retain the commerce within easy reach of Great Britain.

The commander-in-chief of the king's

forces wrote in 1769: "In the course of a few years necessity will compel the colonists, should they extend their settlements west, to provide manufactures of some kind for themselves, and when all connection upheld by commerce with the mother country ceases, an *independency* in their government will soon follow."

In accordance with this policy, Gov. Gage issued a proclamation in 1772, commanding the inhabitants of Vincennes to abandon their settlements and join some of the Eastern English colonies. To this they strenuously objected, giving good reasons therefor, and were allowed to remain. The strong opposition to this policy of Great Britain led to its change, and to such a course as to gain the attachment of the French population. In December, 1773, influential citizens of Quebec petitioned the king for an extension of the boundary lines of that province, which was granted, and Parliament passed an act on June 2, 1774, extending the boundary so as to include the territory lying within the present states of Ohio, Indiana, Illinois and Michigan.

In consequence of the liberal policy pursued by the British Government toward the French settlers in the West, they were disposed to favor that nation in the war which soon followed with the colonies; but the early alliance between France and America soon brought them to the side of the war for independence.

In 1774, Gov. Dunmore, of Virginia, began to encourage emigration to the Western lands. He appointed magistrates at Fort Pitt, under the pretense that the fort was under the government of that commonwealth. One of these justices, John Connelly, who possessed a tract of land in the Ohio Valley, gathered a force of men and garrisoned the fort, calling it Fort Dunmore. This and other parties were formed to select sites for settlements, and often came in conflict with the Indians, who yet claimed portions of the valley, and several battles followed. These ended in the famous battle of Kanawha, in July, where the Indians were defeated and driven across the Ohio.

During the years 1775 and 1776, by the operations of land companies and the perseverance of individuals, several settlements were firmly established between the Alleghenies and the Ohio River, and western land speculators were busy in Illinois and on the Wabash. At a council held in Kaskaskia, on July 5, 1773, an association of English traders, calling themselves the "Illinois Land Company," obtained from ten chiefs of the Kaskaskia, Cahokia and Peoria tribes two large tracts of land lying on the east side of the Mississippi River south of the Illinois. In 1775, a merchant from the Illinois country, named Viviat, came to Post Vincennes as the agent of the association called the "Wabash Land Company." On the 8th of October he obtained from eleven Piankeshaw chiefs, a deed for 37,497,600 acres of land. This deed was signed by the grantors, attested by a number of the inhabitants of Vincennes, and afterward recorded in the office of a notary public at Kaskaskia. This and other land companies had extensive schemes for the colonization of the West; but all were frustrated by the breaking out of the Revolution. On the 20th of April, 1780, the two companies named consolidated under the name of the "United Illinois and Wabash

Land Company." They afterward made strenuous efforts to have these grants sanctioned by Congress, but all signally failed.

When the War of the Revolution commenced, Kentucky was an unorganized country, though there were several settlements within her borders.

In Hutchins' Topography of Virginia, it is stated that at that time "Kaskaskia contained 80 houses, and nearly 1,000 white and black inhabitants—the whites being a little the more numerous. Cahokia contains 50 houses and 300 white inhabitants and 80 negroes. There were east of the Mississippi River, about the year 1771"—when these observations were made—"300 white men capable of bearing arms, and 230 negroes."

From 1775 until the expedition of Clark, nothing is recorded and nothing known of these settlements, save what is contained in a report made by a committee to Congress in June, 1778. From it the following extract is made:

"Near the mouth of the River Kaskaskia, there is a village which appears to have contained nearly eighty families from the beginning of the late revolution. There are twelve families in a small village at la Prairie du Rochers, and near fifty families at the Kahokia Village. There are also four or five families at Fort Chartres and St. Phillips, which is five miles farther up the river."

St. Louis had been settled in February, 1764, and at this time contained, including its neighboring towns, over six hundred whites and one hundred and fifty negroes. It must be remembered that all the country west of the Mississippi was now under French rule, and remained so until ceded again to Spain, its original owner, who afterwards sold it and the country including New Orleans to the United States. At Detroit there were, according to Capt. Carver, who was in the northwest from 1766 to 1768, more than one hundred houses and the river was settled for more than twenty miles, although poorly cultivated—the people being engaged in the Indian trade. This old town has a history, which we will here relate.

It is the oldest town in the Northwest, having been founded by Antoine Lademotte Cadillac, in 1701. It was laid out in the form of an oblong square, of two acres in length and an acre and a half in width. As described by A. D. Frazer, who first visited it and became a permanent resident of the place, in 1778, it comprised within its limits that space between Mr. Palmer's store (Conant Block) and Capt. Perkins' house (near the Arsenal building), and extended back as far as the public barn, and was bordered in front by the Detroit River. It was surrounded by oak and cedar pickets, about fifteen feet long, set in the ground, and had four gates—east, west, north and south. Over the first three of these gates were block houses provided with four guns apiece, each a six pounder. Two six-gun batteries were planted fronting the river, and in a parallel direction with the block houses. There were four streets running east and west, the main street being twenty feet wide and the rest fifteen feet, while the four streets crossing these at right angles were from ten to fifteen feet in width.

At the date spoken of by Mr. Frazer, there was no fort within the enclosure, but a citadel on the ground corresponding to the present northwest corner of Jefferson Avenue and Wayne Street. The citadel was inclosed by pickets, and within it were erected barracks of wood, two stories high, sufficient to contain ten officers, and also barracks sufficient to contain four hundred men, and a provision store built of brick. The citadel also contained a hospital and a guard-house. The old town of Detroit, in 1778, contained about sixty houses, most of them one story, with a few a story and a half in height. They were all of logs, some hewn and some round. There was one building of splendid appearance, called the "King's Palace," two stories high, which stood near the east gate. It was built for Governor Hamilton, the first governor commissioned by the British. There were two guard-houses, one near the west gate and the other near the Government House. Each of the guards consisted of twenty-four men and a subaltern, who mounted regularly every morning between nine and ten o'clock. Each furnished four sentinels, who were relieved every two hours. There was also an officer of the day, who performed strict duty. Each of the gates was shut regularly at sunset; even wicket gates were shut at nine o'clock, and all the keys were delivered into the hands of the commanding officer. They were opened in the morning at sunrise. No Indian or squaw was permitted to enter town with any weapon, such as a tomahawk or a knife. It was a standing order that the Indians should deliver their arms and instruments of every kind before they were permitted to pass the sentinel, and they were restored to them on their return. No more than twenty-five Indians were allowed to enter the town at any one time, and they were admitted only at the east and west gates. At sundown the drums beat, and all the Indians were required to leave town instantly. There was a council house near the water side for the purpose of holding council with the Indians. The population of the town was about sixty families, in all about two hundred males and one hundred females. This town was destroyed by fire, all except one dwelling, in 1805. After which the present "new" town was laid out.

On the breaking out of the Revolution, the British held every post of importance in the West. Kentucky was formed as a component part of Virginia, and the sturdy pioneers of the West, alive to their interests, and recognizing the great benefits of obtaining the control of the trade in this part of the New World, held steadily to their purposes, and those within the commonwealth of Kentucky proceeded to exercise their civil privileges, by electing John Todd and Richard Calloway, burgesses to represent them in the Assembly of the parent state. Early in September of that year (1777) the first court was held in Harrodsburg, and Col. Bowman, afterward major, who had arrived in August, was made the commander of a militia organization which had been commenced the March previous. Thus the tree of loyalty was growing. The chief spirit in this far-out colony, who had represented her the year previous east of the mountains, was now meditating a move unequaled in its boldness. He had been watching the movements of the British throughout the Northwest, and understood their whole plan. He saw it was through their possession of the posts at Detroit, Vincennes, Kaskaskia, and other places, which would give them constant and easy access to the various Indian tribes in the Northwest, that the British intended to penetrate the country from the north and south, and annihilate the frontier fortresses. This moving, energetic man was Colonel, afterward General, George Rogers Clark. He knew the Indians were not unanimously in accord with the English, and he was convinced that, could the British be defeated and expelled from the Northwest, the natives might be easily awed into neutrality; and by spies sent for the purpose, he satisfied himself that the enterprise against the Illinois settlements might easily succeed. Having convinced himself of the certainty of the project, he repaired to the Capital of Virginia, which place he reached on November 5th. While he was on his way, fortunately, on October 17th, Burgoyne had been defeated, and the spirits of the colonists greatly encouraged thereby. Patrick Henry was Governor of Virginia, and at once entered heartily into Clark's plans. The same plan had before been agitated in the Colonial Assemblies, but there was no one until Clark came who was sufficiently acquainted with the condition of affairs at the scene of action to be able to guide them.

Clark, having satisfied the Virginia leaders of the feasibility of his plan, received, on the 2d of January, two sets of instructions—one secret, the other open—the latter authorized him to proceed to enlist seven companies to go to Kentucky, subject to his orders, and to serve three months from their arrival in the West. The secret order authorized him to arm these troops, to procure his powder and lead of General Hand at Pittsburgh, and to proceed at once to subjugate the country.

With these instructions Clark repaired to Pittsburgh, choosing rather to raise his men west of the mountains, as he well knew all were needed in the colonies in the conflict there. He sent Col. W. B. Smith to Holston for the same purpose, but neither succeeded in raising the required number of men. The settlers in these parts were afraid to leave their own firesides exposed to a vigilant foe, and but few could be induced to join the proposed expedition. With three companies and several private volunteers, Clark at length commenced his descent of the Ohio, which he navigated as far as the Falls, where he took possession of and fortified Corn Island, a small island between the present cities of Louisville, Kentucky, and New Albany, Indiana. Remains of this fortification may yet be found. At this place he appointed Col. Bowman to meet him with such recruits as had reached Kentucky by the southern route, and as many as could be spared from the station. Here he announced to the men their real destination. Having completed his arrangements, and chosen his party, he left a small garrison upon the island, and on the 24th of June, during a total eclipse of the sun, which to them augured no good, and which fixes beyond dispute the date of starting, he with his chosen band, fell down the river. His plan was to go by water as far as Fort Massac or Massacre, and thence march direct to Kaskaskia. Here he intended to surprise the garrison, and after its capture go to Cahokia, then to Vincennes, and lastly to Detroit. Should he fail, he intended to march directly to the Mississippi River and cross it into the Spanish country. Before his start he received two good items of information; one that the alliance had been formed between France and the United States; and the other that the Indians throughout the Illinois country and the inhabitants, at the various frontier posts, had been led to believe by the British that the "Long Knives" or Virginians, were the most fierce, bloodthirsty and cruel savages that ever scalped a foe. With this impression on their minds, Clark saw that proper management would cause them to submit at once from fear, if surprised, and then from gratitude would become friendly if treated with unexpected leniency.

The march to Kaskaskia was accomplished through a hot July sun, and the town reached on the evening of July 4. He captured the fort near the village, and soon after the village itself by surprise, and without the loss of a single man or by killing any of the enemy. After sufficiently working upon the fears of the natives, Clark told them they were at perfect liberty to worship as they pleased, and to take whichever side of the great conflict they would, also, he would protect them from any barbarity from British or Indian foe. This had the desired effect, and the inhabitants, so unexpectedly and so gratefully surprised by the unlooked-for turn of affairs, at once swore allegiance to the American arms, and when Clark desired to go to Cahokia on the 6th of July, they accompanied him, and through their influence the inhabitants of the place surrendered, and gladly placed themselves under his protection. Thus the two important posts in Illinois passed from the hands of the English into the possession of Virginia.

In the person of the priest at Kaskaskia, M. Gibault, Clark found a powerful ally and generous friend. Clark saw that, to retain possession of the Northwest and treat successfully with the Indians within its boundaries, he must establish a government for the colonies he had taken. St. Vincent, the next important post to Detroit, remained yet to be taken before the Mississippi Valley was conquered. M. Gibault told him that he would alone, by persuasion, lead Vincennes to throw off its connection with England. Clark gladly accepted his offer, and on the 14th of July, in company with a fellow-townsman, M. Gibault started on his mission of peace and on the 1st of August returned with the cheerful intelligence that the post on the "Oubache" had taken the oath of allegiance to the Old Dominion. During this interval, Clark established his courts, placed garrisons at Kaskaskia and Cahokia, successfully re-enlisted his men, sent word to have a fort, which proved the germ of Louisville, erected at the Falls of the Ohio, and dispatched M. Rocheblave, who had been commander at Kaskaskia, as a prisoner of war to Richmond. In October the County of Illinois was established by the Legislature of Virginia, John Todd appointed Lieutenant Colonel and Civil Governor, and in November General Clark and his men received the thanks of the Old Dominion through their Legislature.

In a speech a few days afterward, Clark made known fully to the natives his plans, and at its close all came forward and swore allegiance to the Long Knives. While he was doing this Governor Hamilton, having made his various arrangements, had left Detroit and moved down the Wabash to

Vincennes intending to operate from that point in reducing the Illinois posts, and then proceed on down to Kentucky and drive the rebels from the West. Gen. Clark had, on the return of M. Gibault, dispatched Captain Helm, of Fauquier County, Virginia, with an attendant named Henry, across the Illinois prairies to command the fort. Hamilton knew nothing of the capitulation of the post, and was greatly surprised on his arrival to be confronted by Capt. Helm, who, standing at the entrance of the fort by a loaded cannon ready to fire upon his assailants, demanded upon what terms Hamilton demanded possession of the fort. Being granted the rights of a prisoner of war, he surrendered to the British General, who could scarcely believe his eyes when he saw the force in the garrison.

Hamilton, not realizing the character of the men with whom he was contending, gave up his intended campaign for the winter, sent his four hundred Indian warriors to prevent troops from coming down the Ohio, and to annoy the Americans in all ways, and sat quietly down to pass the winter. Information of all these proceedings having reached Clark, he saw that immediate and decisive action was necessary, and that unless he captured Hamilton, Hamilton would capture him. Clark received the news on the 29th of January, 1779, and on February 4th, having sufficiently garrisoned Kaskaskia and Cahokia, he sent down the Mississippi a "battoe," as Major Bowman writes it, in order to ascend the Ohio and Wabash, and operate with the land forces gathering for the fray.

On the next day, Clark, with his little force of one hundred and twenty men, set out for the post, and after incredible hard marching through much mud, the ground being thawed by the incessant spring rains, on the 22nd reached the fort, and being joined by his "battoe," at once commenced the attack on the post. The aim of the American backwoodsmen was unerring, and on the 24th the garrison surrendered to the intrepid boldness of Clark. The French were treated with great kindness, and gladly renewed their allegiance to Virginia. Hamilton was sent as a prisoner to Virginia, where he was kept in close confinement. During his command of the British frontier posts, he had offered prizes to the Indians for all the scalps of Americans they would bring to him, and had earned in consequence thereof, the title "Hair-buyer General," by which he was ever afterward known.

Detroit was now without doubt within easy reach of the enterprising Virginian, could he but raise the necessary force. Governor Henry being apprised of this, promised him the needed reinforcement, and Clark concluded to wait until he could capture and sufficiently garrison the posts. Had Clark failed in this bold undertaking, and Hamilton succeeded in uniting the western Indians for the next spring's campaign, the West would indeed have been swept from the Mississippi to the Allegheny Mountains, and the great blow struck, which had been contemplated from the commencement, by the British.

"But for this small army of dripping, but fearless Virginians, the union of all the tribes from Georgia to Maine against the colonies might have been effected, and the whole current of our history changed."

At this time some fears were entertained by the Colonial Governments that the Indians in the North and Northwest were inclining to the British, and under the instructions of Washington, now Commander-in-Chief of the Colonial army, and so bravely fighting for American independence, armed forces were sent against the Six Nations, and upon the Ohio frontier, Col. Bowman, acting under the same general's orders, marched against Indians within the present limits of that State. These expeditions were in the main successful, and the Indians were compelled to sue for peace.

During the same year (1779) the famous "Land Laws" of Virginia were passed. The passage of these laws was of more consequence to the pioneers of Kentucky and the Northwest than the gaining of a few Indian conflicts. These laws confirmed in main all grants made, and guaranteed to all actual settlers their rights and privileges. After providing for the settlers, the laws provided for selling the balance of the public lands at forty cents per acre. To carry the Land Laws into effect, the Legislature sent four Virginians westward to attend to the various claims, over many of which great confusion prevailed concerning their validity. These gentlemen opened their court on October 13, 1779, at St. Asaphs, and continued until April 26, 1780, when they adjourned, having decided three thousand claims. They were succeeded by the surveyor, who came in the person of Mr. George May, and assumed his duties on the 10th day of the month whose name he bore. With the opening of the next year (1780) the troubles concerning the navigation of the Mississippi commenced. The Spanish Government exacted such measures in relation to its trade as to cause the overtures made to the United States to be rejected. The American Government considered they had a right to navigate its channel. To enforce their claims, a fort was erected below the mouth of the Ohio on the Kentucky side of the river. The settlements in Kentucky were being rapidly filled by emigrants. It was during this year that the first seminary of learning was established in the West in this young and enterprising Commonwealth.

The settlers here did not look upon the building of this fort in a friendly manner, as it aroused the hostility of the Indians. Spain had been friendly to the Colonies during their struggle for independence, and though for a while this friendship appeared in danger from the refusal of the free navigation of the river, yet it was finally settled to the satisfaction of both nations.

The winter of 1779-80 was one of the most unusually severe ones ever experienced in the West. The Indians always referred to it as the "Great Cold." Numbers of wild animals perished, and not a few pioneers lost their lives. The following summer a party of Canadians and Indians attacked St. Louis, and attempted to take possession of it in consequence of the friendly disposition of Spain to the revolting Colonies. They met with such a determined resistance on the part of the inhabitants, even the women taking part in the battle, that they were compelled to abandon the contest. They also made an attack on the settlements in Kentucky, but, becoming alarmed in some unaccountable manner, they fled the country in great haste.

About this time arose the question in the Colonial Congress concerning the western lands claimed by Virginia, New York, Massachusetts and Connecticut. The agitation concerning this subject finally led New York, on the 19th of February, 1780, to pass a law giving to the delegates of that State in Congress the power to cede her western lands for the benefit of the United States. This law was laid before Congress during the next month, but no steps were taken concerning it until September 6th, when a resolution passed that body calling upon the States claiming western lands to release their claims in favor of the whole body. This basis formed the union, and was the first after all of those legislative measures which resulted in the creation of the States of Ohio, Indiana, Illinois, Michigan, Wisconsin and Minnesota. In December of the same year, the plan of conquering Detroit again arose. The conquest might have easily been effected by Clark had the necessary aid been furnished him. Nothing decisive was done, yet the heads of the Government knew that the safety of the Northwest from British invasion lay in the capture and retention of that important post, the only unconquered one in the territory.

Before the close of the year, Kentucky was divided into the Counties of Lincoln, Fayette and Jefferson, and the act establishing the Town of Louisville was passed. This same year is also noted in the annals of American history as the year in which occurred Arnold's treason to the United States.

Virginia, in accordance with the resolution of Congress, on the 2d day of January, 1781, agreed to yield her western lands to the United States upon certain conditions, which Congress would not accede to, and the act of Cession, on the part of the Old Dominion, failed, nor was anything further done until 1783. During all that time the Colonies were busily engaged in the struggle with the mother country, and in consequence thereof but little heed was given to the western settlements. Upon the 16th of April, 1781, the first birth north of the Ohio River of American parentage occurred, being that of Mary Heckewelder, daughter of the widely known Moravian missionary, whose band of Christian Indians suffered in after years a horrible massacre by the hands of the frontier settlers, who had been exasperated by the murder of several of their neighbors, and in their rage committed, without regard to humanity, a deed which forever afterward cast a shade of shame upon their lives. For this and kindred outrages on the part of the whites, the Indians committed many deeds of cruelty which darken the years of 1771 and 1772 in the history of the Northwest.

During the year 1782 a number of battles among the Indians and frontiersmen occurred, and between the Moravian Indians and the Wyandots. In these, horrible acts of cruelty were practiced on the captives, many of such dark deeds transpiring under the leadership of the notorious frontier outlaw, Simon Girty, whose name, as well as those of his brothers, was a terror to women and children. These occurred chiefly in the Ohio valleys. Contemporary with them were several engagements in Kentucky, in which the famous Daniel Boone engaged, and who often, by his skill and knowledge of Indian warfare, saved the outposts from cruel destruction. By the close of the year victory had perched upon the American banner, and on the 30th of November, provisional articles of peace had been arranged between the Commissioners of England, and her unconquerable Colonies. Cornwallis had been defeated on the 19th of October preceding, and the liberty of America was assured. On the 19th of April following, the anniversary of the battle of Lexington, peace was proclaimed to the army of the United States, and on the 3d of the next September, the definite treaty which ended our revolutionary struggle, was concluded. By the terms of that treaty, the boundaries of the West were as follows: On the north the line was to extend along the center of the Great Lakes; from the western point of Lake Superior to Long Lake; thence to the Lake of the Woods; thence to the head of the Mississippi River, down its center to the 31st parallel of latitude, then on that line east to the head of the Appalachicola River; down its center to its junction with the Flint; thence straight to the head of St. Mary's River, and thence down along its center to the Atlantic Ocean.

Following the cessation of hostilities with England, several posts were still occupied by the British in the North and West. Among these was Detroit, still in the hands of the enemy. Numerous engagements with the Indians throughout Ohio and Indiana occurred, upon whose lands adventurous whites would settle ere the title had been acquired by the proper treaty.

To remedy this latter evil, Congress appointed commissioners to treat with the natives and purchase their lands, and prohibited the settlement of the territory until this could be done. Before the close of the year another attempt was made to capture Detroit, which was, however, not pushed, and Virginia, no longer feeling the interest in the Northwest she had formerly done, withdrew her troops, having on the 20th of December preceding authorized the whole of her possessions to be deeded to the United States. This was done on the 1st of March following, and the Northwest Territory passed from the control of the Old Dominion. To Gen. Clark and his soldiers, however, she gave a tract of one hundred and fifty thousand acres of land, to be situated anywhere north of the Ohio wherever they chose to locate them. They selected the region opposite the falls of the Ohio, where is now the dilapidated village of Clarksville, about midway between the Cities of New Albany and Jeffersonville, Indiana.

While the frontier remained thus, and Gen. Haldimand at Detroit refused to evacuate, alleging that he had no orders from his King to do so, settlers were rapidly gathering about the inland forts. In the spring of 1784, Pittsburgh was regularly laid out, and from the journal of Arthur Lee, who passed through the town soon after on his way to the Indian council at Fort McIntosh, we suppose it was not very prepossessing in appearance. He says:

" Pittsburgh is inhabited almost entirely by Scots and Irish, who live in paltry log houses, and are as dirty as if in the north of Ireland or even Scotland. There is a great deal of trade carried on, the goods being brought at the vast expense of forty-five shillings per pound from Philadelphia and Baltimore. They take in the shops flour, wheat, skins and money. There are in the town four attorneys, two doctors, and not a priest of any persuasion, nor church nor chapel."

Kentucky at this time contained thirty thousand inhabitants, and was beginning to discuss measures for a separation from Virginia. A land office was opened at Louisville, and measures were adopted to take defensive precaution against the Indians who were yet, in some instances, incited to deeds of violence by the British. Before the close of this year, 1784, the military claimants of land began to occupy them, although no entries were recorded until 1787.

The Indian title to the Northwest was not yet extinguished. They held large tracts of lands, and in order to prevent bloodshed Congress adopted means for treaties with the original owners and provided for the surveys of the lands gained thereby, as well as for those north of the Ohio, now in its possession. On January 31, 1786, a treaty was made with the Wabash Indians. The treaty of Fort Stanwix had been made in 1784. That at Fort McIntosh in 1785, and through these much land was gained. The Wabash Indians, however, afterward refused to comply with the provisions of the treaty made with them, and in order to compel their adherence to its provisions, force was used. During the year 1786, the free navigation of the Mississippi came up in Congress, and caused various discussions, which resulted in no definite action, only serving to excite speculation in regard to the western lands. Congress had promised bounties of land to the soldiers of the Revolution, but owing to the unsettled condition of affairs along the Mississippi respecting its navigation, and the trade of the Northwest, that body had, in 1783, declared its inability to fulfill these promises until a treaty could be concluded between the two Governments. Before the close of the year 1786, however, it was able, through the treaties with the Indians, to allow some grants and the settlement thereon, and on the 14th of September, Connecticut ceded to the General Government the tract of land known as the "Connecticut Reserve," and before the close of the following year a large tract of land north of the Ohio was sold to a company, who at once took measures to settle it. By the provisions of this grant, the company were to pay the United States one dollar per acre, subject to a deduction of one-third for bad lands and other contingencies. They received 750,000 acres, bounded on the south by the Ohio, on the east by the seventh range of townships, on the west by the sixteenth range, and on the north by a line so drawn as to make the grant complete without the reservations. In addition to this, Congress afterward granted 100,000 acres to actual settlers, and 214,285 acres as army bounties under the resolutions of 1789 and 1790.

While Dr. Cutler, one of the agents of the company, was pressing its claims before Congress, that body was bringing into form an ordinance for the political and social organization of this Territory. When the cession was made by Virginia, in 1784, a plan was offered, but rejected. A motion had been made to strike from the proposed plan the prohibition of slavery, which prevailed. The plan was then discussed and altered, and finally passed unanimously, with the exception of South Carolina. By this proposition, the Territory was to have been divided into states by parallels and meridian lines. This, it was thought, would make ten states, which were to have been named as follows—beginning at the northwest corner and going southwardly: Savlynia, Michigania, Chersonesus, Assenisipia, Metropotamia, Illenoia, Saratoga, Washington, Polypotamia and Pelisipia.

There was a more serious objection to this plan than its category of names,—the boundaries. The root of the difficulty was in the resolution of Congress passed in October, 1780, which fixed the boundaries of the ceded lands to be from one hundred to one hundred and fifty miles square. These resolutions being presented to the Legislatures of Virginia and Massachusetts, they desired a change, and in July, 1786, the subject was taken up in Congress, and changed to favor a division into not more than five states, and not less than three. This was approved by the State Legislature of Virginia. The subject of the Government was again taken up by Congress in 1786, and discussed throughout that year and until July, 1787, when the famous "Compact of 1787" was passed, and the foundation of the government of the Northwest laid. This compact is fully discussed and explained in the history of Illinois in this book, and to it the reader is referred.

The passage of this act and the grant to the New England Company was soon followed by an application to the Government by John Cleves Symmes, of New Jersey, for a grant of the land between the Miamis. This gentleman had visited these lands soon after the treaty of 1786, and, being greatly pleased with them offered similar terms to those given to the New England Company. The petition was referred to the Treasury Board with power to act, and a contract was concluded the following year. During the autumn the directors of the New England Company were preparing to occupy their grant the following spring, and upon the 23d of November made arrangements for a party of forty-seven men, under the superintendency of Gen. Rufus Putnam, to set forward. Six boat-builders were to leave at once, and on the first of January the surveyors and their assistants, twenty-six in number, were to meet at Hartford and proceed on their journey westward; the remainder to follow as soon as possible. Congress, in the mean time, upon the 3d of October, had ordered seven hundred troops for defense of the western settlers, and to prevent unauthorized intrusions; and two days later appointed Arthur St. Clair Governor of the Territory of the Northwest.

AMERICAN SETTLEMENTS.

The civil organization of the Northwest Territory was now complete, and notwithstanding the uncertainty of Indian affairs, settlers from the East began to come into the country rapidly. The New England Company sent their men during the winter of 1787-8 pressing on over the Alleghenies by the old Indian path which had been opened into Braddock's road and which has since been made a national turnpike from Cumberland westward. Through the weary winter days they toiled on, and by April were all gathered on the Yohiogany, where boats had been built, and at once started for the Muskingum. Here they arrived on the 7th of that month, and unless the Moravian missionaries be regarded as the pioneers of Ohio, this little band can justly claim that honor.

General St. Clair, the appointed Governor of the Northwest, not having yet arrived, a set of laws were passed, written out, and published by being nailed to a tree in the embryo town, and Jonathan Meigs appointed to administer them.

Washington in writing of this, the first American settlement in the Northwest, said: "No colony in America was ever settled under such favorable auspices as that which has just commenced at Muskingum. Information, property and strength will be its characteristics. I know many of its settlers personally, and there never were men better calculated to promote the welfare of such a community."

On the 2d of July a meeting of the directors and agents was held on the banks of the Muskingum, "for the purpose of naming the new-born city and its squares." As yet the settlement was known as the "Muskingum," but that was now changed to the name Marietta, in honor of Marie Antoinette. The square upon which the block-houses stood was called "*Campus Martius*," square number 19, "*Capitolium*," square number 61, "*Cecilia*," and the great rough road through the covert way, "*Sacra Via*." Two days after, an oration was delivered by James M. Varnum, who with S. H. Parsons and John Armstrong had been appointed to the judicial bench of the Territory on the 16th of October, 1787. On July 9, Gov. St. Clair arrived, and the Colony began to assume form. The act of 1787 provided two distinct grades of government for the Northwest, under the first of which the whole power was invested in the hands of a governor and three district judges. This was immediately formed upon the governor's arrival, and the first laws of the Colony passed on the 25th of July. These provided for the organization of the militia, and on the next day appeared the Governor's proclamation, erecting all that country that had been ceded by the Indians east of the Scioto River into the County of Washington. From that time forward, notwithstanding the doubts yet existing as to the Indians, all Marietta prospered, and on the 2d of September the first court of the Territory was held with imposing ceremonies.

The emigration westward at this time was very great. The commander at Fort Harmar, at the mouth of the Muskingum, reported four thousand five hundred persons as having passed that post between February and June, 1788—many of whom would have purchased of the "Associates," as the New England Company was called, had they been ready to receive them.

On the 26th of November, 1787, Symmes issued a pamphlet stating the terms of his contract and the plan of sale he intended to adopt. In January, 1788, Matthias Denman, of New Jersey, took an active interest in Symmes' purchase, and located among other tracts the sections upon which Cincinnati has been built. Retaining one-third of this locality, he sold the other two-thirds to Robert Patterson and John Filson, and the three, about August, commenced to lay out a town on the spot, which was designated as being opposite Licking River, to the mouth of which they proposed to have a road cut from Lexington. The naming of the town is thus narrated in the "Western Annals": "Mr.

Filson, who had been a schoolmaster, was appointed to name the town, and in respect to its situation, and as if with a prophetic perception of the mixed races that were to inhabit it in after days, he named it Losantiville, which being interpreted, means: *ville*, the town; *anti*, against or opposite to; *os*, the mouth; *L.* of Licking."

Meanwhile, in July, Symmes got thirty persons and eight four-horse teams under way for the West. These reached Limestone (now Maysville) in September, where were several persons from Redstone. Here Mr. Symmes tried to found a settlement, but the great freshet of 1789 caused the "Point," as it was and is yet called, to be fifteen feet under water, and the settlement to be abandoned. The little band of settlers removed to the mouth of the Miami. Before Symmes and his colony left the "Point," two settlements had been made on his purchase. The first was by Mr. Stiltes, the original projector of the whole plan, who, with a colony of Redstone people, had located at the mouth of the Miami, whither Symmes went with his Maysville colony. Here a clearing had been made by the Indians owing to the great fertility of the soil. Mr. Stiltes with his colony came to this place on the 18th of November, 1788, with twenty-six persons, and, building a block house, prepared to remain through the winter. They named the settlement Columbia. Here they were kindly treated by the Indians, but suffered greatly from the flood of 1789.

On the 4th of March, 1789, the Constitution of the United States went into operation, and on April 30th, George Washington was inaugurated President of the American people, and during the next summer, an Indian war was commenced by the tribes north of the Ohio. The President at first used pacific means; but these failing, he sent General Harmar against the hostile tribes. He destroyed several villages, but was defeated in two battles, near the present City of Fort Wayne, Indiana. From this time till the close of 1795, the principal events were the wars with the various Indian tribes. In 1796, General St. Clair was appointed in command, and marched against the Indians; but while he was encamped on a stream, the St. Mary, a branch of the Maumee, he was attacked and defeated with the loss of six hundred men.

General Wayne was now sent against the savages. In August, 1794, he met them near the rapids of the Maumee, and gained a complete victory. This success, followed by vigorous measures, compelled the Indians to sue for peace, and on the 30th of July, the following year, the treaty of Greenville was signed by the principal chiefs, by which a large tract of country was ceded to the United States.

Before proceeding in our narrative, we will pause to notice Fort Washington, erected in the early part of this war on the site of Cincinnati. Nearly all of the great cities of the Northwest, and indeed of the whole country, have had their *nuclei* in those rude pioneer structures, known as forts or stockades. Thus Forts Dearborn, Washington, Ponchartrain, mark the original sites of the now proud cities of Chicago, Cincinnati and Detroit. So of most of the flourishing cities east and west of the Mississippi. Fort Washington erected by Doughty in 1790, was a rude but highly interesting structure. It was composed of a number of strongly-built hewed log cabins. Those designed for soldiers' barracks were a story and a half high, while those composing the officers' quarters were more imposing and more conveniently arranged and furnished. The whole were so placed as to form a hollow square, enclosing about an acre of ground, with a block house at each of the four angles.

The logs for the construction of this fort were cut from the ground upon which it was erected. It stood between Third and Fourth Streets of the present city (Cincinnati) extending east of Eastern Row, now Broadway, which was then a narrow alley, and the eastern boundary of the town as it was originally laid out. On the bank of the river, immediately in front of the fort, was an appendage of the fort, called the Artificer's Yard. It contained about two acres of ground, enclosed by small contiguous buildings, occupied by workshops and quarters of laborers. Within this enclosure there was a large two-story frame house, familiarly called the "Yellow House," built for the accommodation of the Quartermaster General. For many years this was the best finished and most commodious edifice in the Queen City. Fort Washington was for some time the headquarters of both the civil and military governments of the Northwestern Territory.

Following the consummation of the treaty, various gigantic land speculations were entered into by different persons, who hoped to obtain from the Indians in Michigan and northern Indiana, large tracts of lands. These were generally discovered in time to prevent the outrageous schemes from being carried out, and from involving the settlers in war. On October 27, 1795, the treaty between the United States and Spain was signed, whereby the free navigation of the Mississippi was secured.

No sooner had the treaty of 1795 been ratified, than settlements began to pour rapidly into the West. The great event of the year 1796 was the occupation of that part of the Northwest including Michigan, which was this year, under the provisions of the treaty, evacuated by the British forces. The United States, owing to certain conditions, did not feel justified in addressing the authorities in Canada in relation to Detroit and other frontier posts. When at last the British authorities were called to give them up, they at once complied, and General Wayne, who had done so much to preserve the frontier settlements, and who, before the year's close, sickened and died near Erie, transferred his headquarters to the neighborhood of the lakes, where a county named after him was formed, which included the northwest of Ohio, all of Michigan, and the northeast of Indiana. During this same year settlements were formed at the present City of Chillicothe, along the Miami from Middletown to Piqua, while in the more distant West, settlers and speculators began to appear in great numbers. In September, the City of Cleveland was laid out, and during the summer and autumn, Samuel Jackson and Jonathan Sharpless erected the first manufactory of paper—the "Redstone Paper Mill"—in the West. St. Louis contained some seventy houses, and Detroit over three hundred, and along the river, contiguous to it, were more than three thousand inhabitants, mostly French Canadians, Indians and half-breeds, scarcely any Americans venturing yet into that part of the Northwest.

The election of representatives for the Territory had taken place, and on the 4th of February, 1799, they convened at Losantiville—now known as Cincinnati, having been named so by Gov. St. Clair, and considered the capital of the Territory—to nominate persons from whom the members of the legislature were to be chosen in accordance with a previous ordinance. These nominations being made, the Assembly adjourned until the 16th of the following September. From those named, the President selected as members of the council, Henry Vandenbnrg, of Vincennes, Robert Oliver, of Marietta, James Findlay and Jacob Burnett, of Cincinnati, and David Vance, of Vanceville. On the 16th of September the Territorial Legislature met, and on the 24th the two houses were duly organized, Henry Vandenburg being elected President of the Council.

The message of Gov. St. Clair was addressed to the Legislature September 20h, and on October 13th that body elected as a delegate to Congress, Gen. Wm. Henry Harrison, who received eleven of the votes cast, being a majority of one over his opponent, Arthur St. Clair, son of Gen. St. Clair.

The whole number of acts passed at this session, and approved by the Governor, were thirty-seven—eleven others were passed, but received his veto. The most important of those passed, related to the militia, to the administration, and to taxation. On the 19th of December, this protracted session of the first Legislature in the West was closed, and on the 30th of December, the President nominated Charles Willing Bryd to the office of Secretary of the Territory *vice* Wm. Henry Harrison, elected to Congress. The Senate confirmed his nomination the next day.

DIVISION OF THE NORTHWEST TERRITORY.

The increased emigration to the Northwest, the extent of the domain, and the inconvenient modes of travel, made it very difficult to conduct the ordinary operations of government, and rendered the efficient action of courts almost impossible. To remedy this, it was deemed advisable to divide the territory for civil purposes. Congress, in 1800, appointed a committee to examine the question and report some means for its solution. This committee, on the 3d of March, reported that:

"In the three western countries, there has been but one court having cognizance of crimes, in five years, and the immunity which offenders experience attracts, as to an asylum, the most vile and abandoned criminals, and at the same time deters useful citizens from making settlements in such society. The extreme necessity of judiciary attention and assistance is experienced in civil as well as in criminal cases. * * * * To minister a remedy to these and other evils, it occurs to this committee that it is expedient that a division of said territory into two distinct and separate governments should be made; and that such division be made by a line beginning at the mouth of the Great Miami River, running directly north until it intersects the boundary between the United States and Canada."

The report was accepted by Congress, and, in accordance with its suggestions, that body passed an act extinguishing the

Northwest Territory, which act was approved May 7th. Among its provisions were these:

"That from and after July 4th next, all that part of the territory of the United States, northwest of the Ohio River, which lies to the westward of a line beginning at a point on the Ohio, opposite to the mouth of the Kentucky River, and running thence to Fort Recovery, and thence north until it shall intersect the territorial line between the United States and Canada, shall, for the purpose of temporary government, constitute a separate territory, and be called the Indiana Territory."

After providing for the exercise of the civil and criminal powers of the Territories, and other provisions, the act further provides:

"That until it shall otherwise be ordered by the Legislatures of the said Territories, respectively, Chillicothe on the Scioto River shall be the seat of government of the Territory of the United States northwest of the Ohio River; and that St. Vincennes on the Wabash River shall be the seat of government for the Indiana Territory."

Gen. Wm. Henry Harrison was appointed Governor of the Indiana Territory, and entered upon his duties about a year later. Connecticut also about this time released her claims to the reserve, and in March a law was passed accepting this cession. Settlements had been made upon thirty-five of the townships in the reserve, mills had been built, and seven hundred miles of road cut in various directions. On the 3d of November, the General Assembly met at Chillicothe. Near the close of the year, the first missionary of the Connecticut Reserve came, who found no township containing more than eleven families. It was upon the first of October that the secret treaty had been made between Napoleon and the King of Spain, whereby the latter agreed to cede to France the province of Louisiana.

In January, 1802, the assembly of the Northwestern Territory chartered the college at Athens. From the earliest dawn of the western colonies, education was promptly provided for, and as early as 1787, newspapers were issued from Pittsburgh and Kentucky, and largely read throughout the frontier settlements. Before the close of this year, the Congress of the United States granted to the citizens of the Northwestern Territory, the formation of a State government. One of the provisions of the "compact of 1787" provided that whenever the number of inhabitants within prescribed limits exceeded 45,000, they should be entitled to a separate government. The prescribed limits of Ohio contained, from a census taken to ascertain the legality of the act, more than that number, and on the 30th of April, 1802, Congress passed the act defining its limits, and on the 29th of November the Constitution of the new State of Ohio, so named from the beautiful river forming its southern boundary, came into existence. The exact limits of Lake Michigan were not then known, but the territory now included within the State of Michigan was wholly within the territory of Indiana.

General Harrison, while residing at Vincennes, made several treaties with the Indians, thereby gaining large tracts of lands. The next year is memorable in the history of the West for the purchase of

Louisiana from France by the United States for $15,000,000. Thus by a peaceful mode, the domain of the United States was extended over a large tract of country west of the Mississippi, and was for a time under the jurisdiction of the Northwest government, and as has been mentioned in the early part of this narrative, was called the "New Northwest." The limits of this history will not allow a description of its territory. The same year large grants of land were obtained from the Indians, and the House of Representatives of the new State of Ohio signed a bill respecting the college township in the district of Cincinnati.

Before the close of the year, General Harrison obtained additional grants of lands from the various Indian nations in Indiana and the present limits of Illinois, and on the 18th of August, 1804, a treaty at St. Louis, whereby over 51,000,000 acres of lands were obtained from the aborigines. Measures were also taken to learn the condition of affairs in and about Detroit.

C. Jouette, the Indian agent in Michigan, still a part of Indiana Territory, reported as follows upon the condition of matters at that post:

"The Town of Detroit.—The charter, which is for fifteen miles square, was granted in the time of Louis XIV of France, and is now, from the best information I have been able to get, at Quebec. Of those two hundred and twenty-five acres, only four are occupied by the town and Fort Lenault. The remainder is a common, except twenty-four acres, which were added twenty years ago to a farm belonging to Wm. Macomb. * * * *
A stockade encloses the town, fort and citadel. The pickets, as well as the public houses, are in a state of gradual decay. The streets are narrow, straight and regular, and intersect each other at right angles. The houses are for the most part low and inelegant."

During this year Congress granted a township of land for the support of a college, and began to offer inducements for settlers in these wilds, and the country now comprising the State of Michigan began to fill rapidly with settlers along its southern borders. This same year, also, a law was passed organizing the Southwest Territory, dividing it into two portions, the Territory of New Orleans, which city was made the seat of government, and the District of Louisiana, which was annexed to the domain of Gen. Harrison.

On the 11th of January, 1805, the Territory of Michigan was formed. Wm. Hull was appointed governor with headquarters at Detroit, the change to take effect on June 30th. On the 11th of that month, a fire occurred at Detroit, which destroyed almost every building in the place. When the officers of the new Territory reached the post, they found it in ruins, and the inhabitants scattered throughout the country. Rebuilding, however, soon commenced, and ere long the town contained more houses than before the fire, and many of them much better built.

While this was being done, Indiana had passed to the second grade of government, and through her General Assembly had obtained large tracts of land from the Indian tribes. To all this the celebrated Indian, Tecumthe or Tecumseh, vigorously protested, and it was the main cause of his attempts to unite the various Indian tribes in a conflict with the settlers. To obtain a full account of these attempts, the workings of the British, and the signal failure, culminating in the death of Tecumseh at the battle of the Thames, and the close of the war of 1812 in the Northwest, we will step aside in our story, and relate the principal events of his life, and his connection with this conflict.

TECUMSEH, AND THE WAR OF 1812.

This famous Indian chief was born about the year 1768, not far from the site of the present City of Piqua, Ohio. His father, Puckeshinwa, was a member of the Kisopok tribe of the Shawanoese nation, and his mother, Methontaske, was a member of the Turtle tribe of the same people. They removed from Florida about the middle of the last century to the birthplace of Tecumseh. In 1774, his father, who had risen to be chief, was slain at the battle of Point Pleasant, and not long after, Tecumseh, by his bravery, became the leader of his tribe. In 1795 he was declared chief, and then lived at Deer Creek, near the site of the present City of Urbana. He remained here about one year, when he returned to Piqua, and in 1798, he went to White River, Indiana. In 1805, he and his brother, Laulewasikan (Open Door), who had announced himself as a prophet, went to a tract of land on the Wabash River, given them by the Pottawatomies and Kickapoos. From this date the chief comes into prominence. He was now about thirty-seven years of age, was five feet and ten inches in height, was stoutly built, and possessed of enormous powers of endurance. His countenance was naturally pleasing, and he was, in general, devoid of those savage attributes possessed by most Indians. It is stated he could read and write, and had a confidential secretary and adviser, named Billy Caldwell, a half-breed, who afterward became chief of the Pottawatomies. He occupied the first house built on the site of Chicago. At this time, Tecumseh entered upon the great work of his life. He had long objected to the grants of land made by the Indians to the whites, and determined to unite all the Indian tribes into a league, in order that no treaties or grants of land could be made save by the consent of this confederation.

He traveled constantly, going from north to south; from the south to the north, everywhere urging the Indians to this step. He was a matchless orator, and his burning words had their effect.

Gen. Harrison, then Governor of Indiana, by watching the movement of the Indians, became convinced that a grand conspiracy was forming, and made preparations to defend the settlements. Tecumseh's plan was similar to Pontiac's, elsewhere described, and to the cunning artifice of that chieftain was added his own sagacity.

During the year 1809, Tecumseh and the prophet were actively preparing for the work. In that year, Gen. Harrison entered into a treaty with the Delawares, Kickapoos, Pottawatomies, Miamis, Eel River Indians and Weas, in which these tribes ceded to the whites certain lands upon the Wabash, to all of which Tecumseh entered a bitter protest, averring as one principal reason that he did not want the Indians to give up any lands north and west of the Ohio River.

Tecumseh, in August, 1810, visited the General at Vincennes and held a council relating to the grievances of the Indians. Becoming unduly angry at this conference he was dismissed from the village, and soon after departed to incite the Southern Indian tribes to the conflict.

Gen. Harrison determined to move upon the chief's headquarters at Tippecanoe, and for this purpose went about sixty-five miles up the Wabash, where he built Fort Harrison. From this place he went to the prophet's town, where he informed the Indians he had no hostile intentions, provided they were true to the existing treaties. He encamped near the village early in October, and on the morning of November 7th, he was attacked by a large force of the Indians, and the famous battle of Tippecanoe occurred. The Indians were routed and their town broken up. Tecumseh returning not long after, was greatly exasperated at his brother, the prophet, even threatening to kill him for rashly precipitating the war, and foiling his (Tecumseh's) plans.

Tecumseh sent word to General Harrison that he was now returned from the South, and was ready to visit the President, as had at one time previously been proposed. Gen. Harrison informed him he could not go as a chief, which method Tecumseh desired, and the visit was never made.

In June of the following year, he visited the Indian agent at Fort Wayne. Here he disavowed any intention to make a war against the United States, and reproached Gen. Harrison for marching against his people. The agent replied to this; Tecumseh listened with a cold indifference, and after making a few general remarks, with a haughty air drew his blanket about him, left the council house, and departed for Fort Malden, in upper Canada, where he joined the British standard.

He remained under this Government, doing effective work for the Crown while engaged in the war of 1812 which now opened. He was, however, always humane in his treatment of the prisoners, never allowing his warriors to ruthlessly mutilate the bodies of those slain, or wantonly murder the captive.

In the summer of 1813, Perry's victory on Lake Erie occurred, and shortly after active preparations were made to capture Malden. On the 27th of September, the American army, under Gen. Harrison, set sail for the shores of Canada, and in a few hours stood around the ruins of Malden, from which the British army, under Proctor, had retreated to Sandwich, intending to make its way to the heart of Canada by the Valley of the Thames. On the 29th Gen. Harrison was at Sandwich, and Gen. McArthur took possession of Detroit and the Territory of Michigan.

On the 2d of October, the Americans began their pursuit of Proctor, whom they overtook on the 5th, and the battle of the Thames followed. Early in the engagement, Tecumseh who was at the head of the column of Indians was slain, and they, no longer hearing the voice of their chieftain, fled. The victory was decisive, and practically closed the war in the Northwest.

Just who killed the great chief has been a matter of much dispute; but the weight of opinion awards the act to Col. Richard M. Johnson, who fired at him with a pistol, the shot proving fatal.

In 1805 occurred Burr's Insurrection. He took possession of a beautiful island in the Ohio, after the killing of Hamilton, and is charged by many with attempting to set up an independent government. His plans were frustrated by the general government, his property confiscated and he was compelled to flee the country for safety.

In January, 1807, Governor Hull, of Michigan Territory, made a treaty with the Indians, whereby all that peninsula was ceded to the United States. Before the close of the year, a stockade was built about Detroit. It was also during this year that Indiana and Illinois endeavored to obtain the repeal of that section of the compact of 1787, whereby slavery was excluded from the Northwest Territory. These attempts, however, all signally failed.

In 1809 it was deemed advisable to divide the Indiana Territory. This was done, and the Territory of Illinois was formed from the western part, the seat of government being fixed at Kaskasia. The next year, the intentions of Tecumseh manifested themselves in open hostilities, and then began the events already narrated.

While this war was in progress, emigration to the West went on with surprising rapidity. In 1811, under Mr. Roosevelt of New York, the first steamboat trip was made on the Ohio, much to the astonishment of the natives, many of whom fled in terror at the appearance of the "monster." It arrived at Louisville on the tenth day of October. At the close of the first week of January, 1812, it arrived at Natchez, after being nearly overwhelmed in the great earthquake which occurred, while on its downward trip.

The battle of the Thames was fought on October 6th, 1813. It effectually closed hostilities in the Northwest, although peace was not fully restored until July 22d, 1814, when a treaty was formed at Greenville, under the direction of General Harrison, between the United States and the Indian tribes, in which it was stipulated that the Indians should cease hostilities against the Americans if the war were continued. Such, happily, was not the case, and on the 24th of December, the treaty of Ghent was signed by the representatives of England, and the United States. This treaty was followed the next year by treaties with various Indian tribes throughout the West and Northwest, and quiet was again restored in this part of the new world.

On the 18th of March, 1816, Pittsburgh was incorporated as a city. It then had a population of 8,000 people, and was already noted for its manufacturing interests. On April 19th, Indiana Territory was allowed to form a State government. At that time there were thirteen counties organized, containing about sixty-three thousand inhabitants. The first election of State officers was held in August, when Jonathan Jennings was chosen Governor. The officers were sworn in on November 7th, and on December 11th, the State was formally admitted into the Union. For some time the seat of government was at Corydon, but a more central location being desirable, the present capital, Indianapolis (City of Indiana), was laid out January 1, 1825.

On the 28th of December, the Bank of Illinois, at Shawneetown, was chartered, with a capital of $300,000. At this period all banks were under the control of the States, and were allowed to establish branches at different convenient points.

Until this time Chillicothe and Cincinnati had in turn enjoyed the privileges of being the capital of Ohio. But the rapid settlement of the northern and eastern portions of the State demanded, as in Indiana, a more central location, and before the close of the year, the site of Columbus was selected and surveyed as the future capital of the State. Banking had begun in Ohio as early as 1808, when the first bank was chartered at Marietta, but here as elsewhere it did not bring to the State the hoped-for assistance. It and other banks were subsequently unable to redeem their currency, and were obliged to suspend.

In 1818, Illinois was made a State, and all the territory north of her northern limits was erected into a separate territory and joined to Michigan for judicial purposes. By the following year, navigation of the lakes was increasing with great rapidity and affording an immense source of revenue to the dwellers in the Northwest, but it was not until 1826, that the trade was extended to Lake Michigan, or that steamships began to navigate the bosom of that inland sea.

Until the year 1832, the commencement of the Black Hawk War, but few hostilities were experienced with the Indians. Roads were opened, canals were dug, cities were built, common schools were established, universities were founded, many of which, especially the Michigan University, have achieved a world-wide reputation. The people were becoming wealthy. The domains of the United States had been extended, and had the sons of the forest been treated with honesty and justice, the record of many years would have been that of peace and continuous prosperity.

BLACK HAWK AND THE BLACK HAWK WAR.

This conflict, though confined to Illinois, is an important epoch in the Northwestern history, being the last war with the Indians in this part of the United States.

Ma-ka-tai-me-she-kia-kiah, or Black Hawk, was born in the principal Sac village, about three miles from the junction of Rock River with the Mississippi, in the year 1767. His father's name was Py-e-sa or Pahaes; his grandfather's, Na-na-ma-kee, or the Thunderer. Black Hawk early distinguished himself as a warrior, and at the age of fifteen was permitted to paint, and was ranked among the braves. About the year 1783, he went on an expedition against the enemies of his nation, the Osages, one of whom he killed and scalped, and for this deed of Indian bravery he was permitted to join in the scalp dance. Three or four years after, he, at the head of two hundred braves, went on another expedition against the Osages, to avenge the murder of some women and children belonging to his own tribe. Meeting an equal number of Osage warriors, a fierce battle ensued, in which the latter tribe lost one-half their number. The Sacs lost only about nineteen warriors. He next attacked the Cherokees for a similar cause. In a severe battle with them, near the present City of St. Louis, his father was slain, and Black Hawk, taking possession of the "Medicine Bag," at once announced himself chief of the Sac nation. He had now conquered the Cherokees, and about the year 1800, at the head of five hundred Sacs and Foxes, and a hundred Iowas, he waged war against the Osage nation and subdued it. For two years he battled successfully with other Indian tribes, all of whom he conquered.

Black Hawk does not at any time seem to have been friendly to the Americans. When on a visit to St Louis to see his "Spanish Father," he declined to see any of the Americans, alleging as a reason, he did not want *two* fathers.

The treaty at St. Louis was consummated in 1804. The next year the United States Government erected a fort near the head of the Des Moines Rapids, called Fort Edwards. This seemed to enrage Black Hawk, who at once determined to capture Fort Madison, standing on the west side of the Mississippi above the mouth of the Des Moines River. The fort was garrisoned by about fifty men. Here he was defeated. The difficulties with the British Government arose about this time, and the War of 1812 followed. That government, extending aid to the Western Indians, by giving them arms and ammunition, induced them to remain hostile to the Americans. In August, 1812, Black Hawk, at the head of about five hundred braves, started to join the British forces at Detroit, passing on his way the site of Chicago, where the famous Fort Dearborn Massacre had a few days before occurred. Of his connection with the British Government but little is known. In 1813, he with his little band descended the Mississippi, and attacking some United States troops at Fort Howard, was defeated.

In the early part of 1815, the Indian tribes west of the Mississippi were notified that peace had been declared between the United States and England, and nearly all hostilities had ceased. Black Hawk did not sign any treaty, however, until May of the following year. He then recognized the validity of the treaty at St. Louis in 1804. From the time of signing this treaty in 1816, until the breaking out of the war in 1832, he and his band passed their time in the common pursuits of Indian life.

Ten years before the commencement of this war, the Sac and Fox Indians were urged to join the Iowas on the west bank of the Father of Waters. All were agreed, save the band known as the British Band, of which Black Hawk was leader. He strenuously objected to the removal, and was induced to comply only after being threatened with the power of the Government. This and various actions on the part of the white settlers provoked Black Hawk and his band to attempt the capture of his native village now occupied by the whites. The war followed. He and his actions were undoubtedly misunderstood, and had his wishes been acquiesced in at the beginning of the struggle, much bloodshed would have been prevented.

Black Hawk was chief now of the Sac and Fox nations, and a noted warrior. He and his tribe inhabited a village on Rock River, nearly three miles above its confluence with the Mississippi, where the tribe had lived many generations. When that portion of Illinois was reserved to them, they remained in peaceable possession of their reservation, spending their time in the enjoyment of Indian life. The fine situation of their village and the quality of their lands incited the more lawless white settlers, who from time to time began to encroach upon the red men's domain. From one pretext to another, and from one step to another, the crafty white men gained a foothold, until through whisky and artifice they obtained deeds from many of the Indians for their possessions. The Indians were finally induced to cross over the Father of Waters and locate among the Iowas. Black Hawk was strenuously opposed to all this, but as the authorities of Illinois and the United States thought this the best move, he was forced to comply. Moreover other tribes joined the whites and urged the removal. Black Hawk would not agree to the terms of the treaty made with his nation for their lands, and as soon as the military, called to enforce his removal, had retired, he returned to the Illinois side of the river. A large force was at once raised and marched against him. On the evening of May 14, 1832, the first engagement occurred between a band from this army and Black Hawk's band, in which the former were defeated.

This attack and its result aroused the whites. A large force of men was raised, and Gen. Scott hastened from the seaboard, by way of the lakes, with United States troops and artillery to aid in the subjugation of the Indians. On the 24th of June, Black Hawk, with 200 warriors, was repulsed by Major Demont between Rock River and Galena. The American army continued to move up Rock River toward the main body of the Indians, and on the 21st of July came upon Black Hawk and his band, and defeated them near the Blue Mounds.

Before this action, Gen. Henry, in command, sent word to the main army by whom he was immediately rejoined, and the whole crossed the Wisconsin in pursuit of Black Hawk and his band who were fleeing to the Mississippi. They were overtaken on the 2d of August, and in the battle which followed the power of the Indian chief was completely broken. He fled, but was seized by the Winnebagoes and delivered to the whites.

On the 21st of September, 1832, Gen. Scott and Gov. Reynolds concluded a treaty with the Winnebagoes, Sacs and Foxes, by which they ceded to the United States a vast tract of country, and agreed to remain peaceable with the whites. For the faithful performance of the provisions of this treaty on the part of the Indians, it was stipulated that Black Hawk, his two sons, the prophet Wabokieshiek, and six other chiefs of the hostile bands should be retained as hostages during the pleasure of the President. They were confined at Fort Barracks and put in irons.

The next spring, by order of the Secretary of War, they were taken to Washington. From there they were removed to Fortress Monroe, "there to remain until the conduct of their nation was such as to justify their being set at liberty." They were retained here until the 4th of June, when the authorities directed them to be taken to the principal cities so that they might see the folly of contending against the white people. Everywhere they were observed by thousands, the name of the old chief being extensively known. By the middle of August they reached Fort Armstrong on Rock Island, where Black Hawk was soon after released to go to his countrymen. As he passed the site of his birthplace, now the home of the white man, he was deeply moved. His village where he was born, where he had so happily lived, and where he had hoped to die, was now another's dwelling place, and he was a wanderer.

On the next day after his release, he went at once to his tribe and his lodge. His wife was yet living, and with her he passed the remainder of his days. To his credit it may be said that Black Hawk always remained true to his wife, and served her with a devotion uncommon among the Indians, living with her upward of forty years.

Black Hawk now passed his time hunting and fishing. A deep melancholy had settled over him from which he could not be freed. At all times when he visited the whites he was received with marked attention. He was an honored guest at the old settlers' reunion in Lee County, Illinois, at some of their meetings, and received many tokens of esteem. In September, 1838, while on his way to Rock Island to receive his annuity from the Government, he contracted a severe cold which resulted in a fatal attack of bilious fever which terminated his life on October 3d. His faithful wife, who was devotedly attached to him, mourned deeply during his sickness. After his death he was dressed in the uniform presented to him by the President while in Washington. He was buried in a grave six feet in depth, situated upon a beautiful eminence. "The body was placed in the middle of the grave, in a sitting posture, upon a seat constructed for the purpose. On his left side, the cane, given him by Henry Clay, was placed upright, with his right hand resting upon it. Many of the old warrior's trophies were placed in the grave, and some Indian garments, together with his favorite weapons.

No sooner was the Black Hawk war concluded than· settlers began rapidly to pour into the northern parts of Illinois, and into Wisconsin, now free from Indian depredations. Chicago, from a trading post, had grown to a commercial center, and was rapidly coming into prominence. In 1835, the formation of a State Government in Michigan was discussed, but did not take active form until two years later, when the State became a part of the Federal Union.

The main attraction to that portion of the Northwest lying west of Lake Michigan, now included in the State of Wisconsin, was its alluvial wealth. Copper ore was found about Lake Superior. For some time this region was attached to Michigan for judiciary purposes, but in 1836 was made a Territory, then including Minnesota and Iowa. The latter State was detached two years later. In 1848, Wisconsin was admitted as a State, Madison being made the capital. We have now traced the various divisions of the Northwest Territory (save a little in Minnesota) from the time it was a unit comprising this vast territory, until circumstances compelled its present division.

OTHER INDIAN TROUBLES.

Before leaving this part of the narrative, we will narrate briefly the Indian troubles in Minnesota and elsewhere by the Sioux Indians.

In August, 1862, the Sioux Indians living on the western borders of Minnesota fell upon the unsuspecting settlers, and in a few hours massacred ten or twelve hundred persons. A distressful panic was the immediate result, fully thirty thousand persons fleeing from their homes to districts supposed to be better protected. The military authorities at once took active measures to punish the savages, and a large number were killed and captured. About a year after, Little Crow, the chief, was killed by a Mr. Lampson near Scattered Lake. Of those captured thirty were hung at Mankato, and the remainder, through fears of mob violence, were removed to Camp McClellan, on the outskirts of the City of Davenport. It was here that Big Eagle came into prominence and secured his release by the following order:

"Special Order, No. 430. "WAR DEPARTMENT,
   "ADJUTANT GENERAL'S OFFICE,
        "WASHINGTON, Dec. 8, 1864.
"Big Eagle, an Indian now in confinement at Davenport, Iowa, will, upon the receipt of this order, be immediately released from confinement and set at liberty.
"By order of the President of the United States.
"Official: "E. D. TOWNSEND,
                       Ass't Adj't Gen.
"CAPT. JAMES VANDERVENTER,
                Com'y Sub. Vols.
"Through Com'g Gen'l, Washington, D. C."

Another Indian who figures more prominently than Big Eagle, and who was more cowardly in his nature, with his band of Modoc Indians, is noted in the annals of the New Northwest: we refer to Captain Jack. This distinguished Indian, noted for his cowardly murder of Gen. Canby, was a chief of a Modoc tribe of Indians inhabiting the border lands between California and Oregon. This region of country comprises what is known as the "Lava Beds," a tract of land described as utterly impenetrable, save by those savages who had made it their home.

The Modocs are known as an exceedingly fierce and treacherous race. They had, according to their own traditions, resided here for many generations, and at one time were exceedingly numerous and powerful. A famine carried off nearly half their numbers, and disease, indolence and the vices of the white man have reduced them to a poor, weak and insignificant tribe.

Soon after the settlement of California and Oregon, complaints began to be heard of massacres of emigrant trains passing through the Modoc country. In 1847, an emigrant train, comprising eighteen souls, was entirely destroyed at a place since known as "Bloody Point." These occurrences caused the United States Government to appoint a peace commission, who, after repeated attempts, in 1864, made a treaty with the Modocs, Snakes and Klamaths, in which it was agreed on their part to remove to a reservation set apart for them in the southern part of Oregon.

With the exception of Captain Jack and a band of his followers, who remained at Clear Lake, about six miles from Klamath, all the Indians complied. The Modocs who went to the reservation were under chief Schonchin. Captain Jack remained at the lake without disturbance until 1869, when he was also induced to remove to the reservation. The Modocs and the Klamaths soon became involved in a quarrel, and Captain Jack and his band returned to the Lava Beds.

Several attempts were made by the Indian Commissioners to induce them to return to the reservation, and finally becoming involved in a difficulty with the commissioner and his military escort, a fight ensued, in which the chief and his band were routed. They were greatly enraged and on their retreat, before the day closed, killed eleven inoffensive whites.

The nation was aroused and immediate action demanded. A commission was at once appointed by the Government to see what could be done. It comprised the following persons: Gen. E. R. S. Canby, Rev. Dr. E. Thomas, a leading Methodist divine of California; Mr. A. B. Meacham, Judge Rosborough, of California, and a Mr.

Dyer, of Oregon. After several interviews, in which the savages were always aggressive, often appearing with scalps in their belts, Bogus Charley came to the commission on the evening of April 10, 1873, and informed them that Capt. Jack and his band would have a "talk" to-morrow at a place near Clear Lake, about three miles distant. Here the Commissioners, accompanied by Charley, Riddle, the interpreter, and Boston Charley, repaired. After the usual greeting the council proceedings commenced. On behalf of the Indians there were present: Capt. Jack, Black Jim, Schac Nasty Jim, Ellen's Man, and Hooker Jim. They had no guns, but carried pistols. After short speeches by Mr. Meacham, Gen. Canby and Dr. Thomas, Chief Schonchin arose to speak. He had scarcely proceeded when, as if by a preconcerted arrangement, Capt. Jack drew his pistol and shot Gen. Canby dead. In less than a minute a dozen shots were fired by the savages, and the massacre completed. Mr. Meacham was shot by Schonchin, and Dr. Thomas by Boston Charley. Mr. Dyer barely escaped, being fired at twice. Riddle, the interpreter, and his squaw escaped. The troops rushed to the spot where they found Gen. Canby and Dr. Thomas dead, and Mr. Meacham badly wounded. The savages had escaped to their impenetrable fastnesses and could not be pursued.

The whole country was aroused by this brutal massacre; but it was not until the following May that the murderers were brought to justice. At that time Boston Charley gave himself up, and offered to guide the troops to Capt. Jack's stronghold. This led to the capture of his entire gang, a number of whom were murdered by Oregon volunteers while on their way to trial. The remaining Indians were held as prisoners until July, when their trial occurred, which led to the conviction of Capt. Jack, Schonchin, Boston Charley, Hooker Jim, Broncho, *alias* One-Eyed Jim, and Slotuck, who were sentenced to be hanged. These sentences were approved by the President, save in the case of Slotuck and Broncho whose sentences were commuted to imprisonment for life. The others were executed at Fort Klamath, October 3, 1873.

These closed the Indian troubles for a time in the Northwest, and for several years the borders of civilization remained in peace. They were again involved in a conflict with the savages about the country of the Black Hills, in which war the gallant Gen. Custer lost his life. Just now the borders of Oregon and California are again in fear of hostilities; but as the Government has learned how to deal with the Indians, they will be of short duration. The red man is fast passing away before the march of the white man, and a few more generations will read of the Indians as one of the nations of the past.

The Northwest abounds in memorable places. We have generally noticed them in the narrative, but our space forbids their description in detail, save of the most important places. Detroit, Cincinnati, Vincennes, Kaskaskia and their kindred towns have all been described. But ere we leave the narrative we will present our readers with an account of the Kinzie house, the old landmark of Chicago, and the discovery of the source of the Mississippi River, each of which may well find a place in the annals of the Northwest.

Mr. John Kinzie, of the Kinzie house,

established a trading house at Fort Dearborn in 1804. The stockade had been erected the year previous, and named Fort Dearborn in honor of the Secretary of War. It had a block house at each of the two angles, on the southern side a sallyport, a covered way on the north side, that led down to the river, for the double purpose of providing means of escape, and of procuring water in the event of a siege.

Fort Dearborn stood on the south bank of the Chicago River, about half a mile from its mouth. When Major Whistler built it, his soldiers hauled all the timber, for he had no oxen, and so economically did he work that the fort cost the Government only fifty dollars. For a while the garrison could get no grain, and Whistler and his men subsisted on acorns. Now Chicago is the greatest grain center in the world.

Mr. Kinzie bought the hut of the first settler, Jean Baptiste Point au Sable, on the site of which he erected his mansion. Within an inclosure in front he planted some Lombardy poplars, and in the rear he soon had a fine garden and growing orchard.

In 1812 the Kinzie house and its surroundings became the theater of stirring events. The garrison of Fort Dearborn consisted of fifty-four men, under the charge of Capt. Nathan Heald, assisted by Lieutenant Lenai T. Helm (son-in-law to Mrs. Kinzie), and ensign Ronan. The surgeon was Dr. Voorhees. The only residents at the post at that time were the wives of Capt. Heald and Lieutenant Helm and a few of the soldiers, Mr. Kinzie and his family, and a few Canadian voyageurs with their wives and children. The soldiers and Mr. Kinzie were on the most friendly terms with the Pottawatomies and the Winnebagoes, the principal tribes around them, but they could not win them from their attachment to the British.

After the battle of Tippecanoe it was observed that some of the leading chiefs became sullen, for some of their people had perished in that conflict with American troops.

One evening in April 1812, Mr. Kinzie sat playing his violin and his children were dancing to the music, when Mrs. Kinzie came rushing into the house pale with terror, exclaiming, "The Indians! the Indians!" "What? Where?" eagerly inquired Mr. Kinzie. "Up at Lee's, killing and scalping," answered the frightened mother, who, when the alarm was given, was attending Mrs. Burns, a newly-made mother, living not far off. Mr. Kinzie and his family crossed the river in boats, and took refuge in the fort, to which place Mrs. Burns and her infant, not a day old, were conveyed in safety to the shelter of the guns of Fort Dearborn, and the rest of the white inhabitants fled. The Indians were a scalping party of Winnebagoes, who hovered around the fort some days, when they disappeared, and for several weeks the inhabitants were not disturbed by alarms.

Chicago was then so deep in the wilderness, that the news of the declaration of war against Great Britain, made on the 19th of June, 1812, did not reach the commander of the garrison at Fort Dearborn till the 7th of August. Now the fast mail train will carry a man from New York to Chicago in twenty-seven hours, and such a declaration might be sent, every word, by the telegraph in less than the same number of minutes.

PRESENT CONDITION OF THE NORTHWEST.

Preceding chapters have brought us to the close of the Black Hawk war, and we now turn to the contemplation of the growth and prosperity of the northwest under the smile of peace and the blessings of our civilization. The pioneers of this region date events back to the deep snow of 1831, no one arriving here since that date taking first honors. The inciting cause of the immigration which overflowed the prairies early in the '30s was the reports of the marvelous beauty and fertility of the region distributed through the East by those who had participated in the Black Hawk campaign with Gen. Scott. Chicago and Milwaukee then had a few hundred inhabitants, and Gurdon S. Hubbard's trail from the former city to Kaskaskia led almost through a wilderness. Vegetables and clothing were largely distributed through the regions adjoining the lakes by steamers from the Ohio towns. There are men now living in Illinois who came to the State when barely an acre was in cultivation, and a man now prominent in the business circles of Chicago looked over the swampy, cheerless site of that metropolis in 1818 and went southward into civilization. Emigrants from Pennsylvania in 1830 left behind them but one small railway in the coal regions thirty miles in length, and made their way to the Northwest mostly with ox teams, finding in Northern Illinois petty settlements scores of miles apart, although the southern portion of the state was fairly dotted with farms. The water courses of the lakes and rivers furnished transportation to the second great army of immigrants, and about 1850 railroads were pushed to that extent that the crisis of 1837 was precipitated upon us, from the effects of which the Western country had not fully recovered at the outbreak of the war. Hostilities found the colonists of the prairies fully alive to the demands of the occasion, and the honor of recruiting the vast armies of the Union fell largely to Gov. Yates, of Illinois, and Gov. Morton, of Indiana. To recount the share of the glories of the campaign won by our Western troops is a needless task, except to mention the fact that Illinois gave to the nation the President who saved it, and sent out at the head of one of its regiments the general who led its armies to the final victory at Appomattox. The struggle, on the whole, had a marked effect for the better on the new Northwest, giving it an impetus which twenty years of peace would not have produced. In a large degree this prosperity was an inflated one, and with the rest of the Union we have since been compelled to atone therefor. Agriculture, still the leading feature in our industries, has been quite prosperous through all these years, and the farmers have cleared away many incumbrances resting over them from the period of fictitious values. The population has steadily increased, the arts and sciences are gaining a stronger foothold, the trade area of the region is becoming daily more extended, and we have been largely exempt from the financial calamities.

At the present period there are no great schemes broached for the Northwest, no propositions for government subsidies or national works of improvement, but the capital of the world is attracted hither for the purchase of our products or the expansion of our capacity for serving the nation at large. A new era is dawning as to transportation, and we bid fair to deal almost exclusively with the increasing and expanding lines of steel rail running through every few miles of territory on the prairies. The lake marine will no doubt continue to be useful in the warmer season, and to serve as a regulator of freight rates; but experienced navigators forecast the decay of the system in moving to the seaboard the enormous crops of the West. Within the past few years it has become quite common to see direct shipments to Europe and the West Indies going through from the second-class towns along the Mississippi and Missouri.

As to popular education, the standard has of late risen very greatly, and our schools would be creditable to any section of the Union.

More and more as the events of the war pass into obscurity will the fate of the Northwest be linked with that of the Southwest.

Our public men continue to wield the full share of influence pertaining to their rank in the national autonomy, and seem not to forget that for the past sixteen years they and their constituents have dictated the principles which should govern the country.

In a work like this, destined to lie on the shelves of the library for generations, and not doomed to daily destruction like a newspaper, one can not indulge in the same glowing predictions, the sanguine statements of actualities that fill the columns of ephemeral publications. Time may bring grief to the pet projects of a writer, and explode castles erected on a pedestal of facts. Yet there are unmistakable indications before us of the same radical change in our great Northwest which characterizes its history for the past thirty years. Our domain has a sort of natural geographical border, save where it melts away to the southward in the cattle raising districts of the Southwest.

Our prime interest will for some years doubtless be the growth of the food of the world, in which branch it has already outstripped all competitors, and our great rival in this duty will naturally be the fertile plains of Kansas, Nebraska and Colorado, to say nothing of the new empire so rapidly growing up in Texas. Over these regions there is a continued progress in agriculture and in railway building, and we must look to our laurels. Intelligent observers of events are fully aware of the strides made in the way of shipments of fresh meats to Europe, many of these ocean cargoes being actually slaughtered in the West and transported on ice to the wharves of the seaboard cities. That this new enterprise will continue there is no reason to doubt. There are in Chicago several factories for the canning of prepared meats for European consumption, and the orders for this class of goods are already immense. English capital is becoming daily more and more and more dissatisfied with railway loans and investments, and is gradually seeking mammoth outlays in lands and live stock. The stock yards in Chicago, Indianapolis and East St. Louis are yearly increasing their facilities, and their plant steadily grows more valuable. Importations of blooded animals from the progressive countries of Europe are destined to greatly improve the quality of our beef and mutton. Nowhere is there to be seen a more enticing display in this line than at our state and county fairs, and the interest in the matter is on the increase.

To attempt to give statistics of our grain production would be useless, so far have we surpassed ourselves in the quantity and quality of our product. We are too liable to forget that we are giving the world its first article of necessity—its food supply. An opportunity to learn this fact so it never can be forgotten was afforded at Chicago at the outbreak of the great panic of 1873, when Canadian purchasers, fearing the prostration of business might bring about an anarchical condition of affairs, went to that city with coin in bulk and foreign drafts to secure their supplies in their own currency at first hands. It may be justly claimed by the agricultural community that their combined efforts gave the nation its first impetus toward a restoration of its crippled industries, and their labor brought the gold premium to a lower depth than the government was able to reach by its most intense efforts of legislation and compulsion. The hundreds of millions about to be disbursed for farm products have already, by the anticipation common to all commercial nations, set the wheels in motion, and will relieve us from the perils so long shadowing our efforts to return to a healthy tone.

Manufacturing has attained in the chief cities a foothold which bids fair to render the Northwest independent of the outside world. Nearly our whole region has a distribution of coal measures which will in time support the manufactures necessary to our comfort and prosperity. Asns transportation, the chief factor in the production of all articles except food, no section is so magnificently endowed, and our facilities are yearly increasing beyond those of any other region.

The period from a central point of the war to the outbreak of the panic was marked by a tremendous growth in our railway lines, but the depression of the times caused almost a total suspension of operations. Now that prosperity is returning to our stricken country we witness its anticipation by the railroad interest in a series of projects, extensions, and leases which bid fair to largely increase our transportation facilities. The process of foreclosure and sale of incumbered lines is another matter to be considered. In the case of the Illinois Central road, which formerly transferred to other lines at Cairo the vast burden of freight destined for the Gulf region, we now see the incorporation of the tracts connecting through to New Orleans, every mile co-operating in turning toward the northwestern metropolis the weight of the interstate commerce of a thousand miles or more of fertile plantations. Three competing routes to Texas have established in Chicago their general freight and passenger agencies. Four or five lines compete for all Pacific freights to a point as far as the interior of Nebraska. Half a dozen or more splendid bridge structures have been thrown across the Missouri and Mississippi Rivers by the railways. The Chicago and Northwestern line has become an aggregation of over two thousand miles of rail, and the Chicago, Milwaukee and St. Paul is its close rival in extent and importance. The three lines running to Cairo *via* Vincennes form a through route for all traffic with the States to the southward. The trunk lines being mainly in operation, the progress made in the way of shortening tracks, making air-line branches, and running extensions does not show to the advantage it deserves, as this process is constantly adding new facilities to the established order of things. The panic reduced the price of steel to a point where the railways could hardly afford to use iron rails, and all our northwestern lines report large relays of Bessemer track. The immense crops now being moved have given a great rise to the value of railway stocks, and their transportation must result in heavy pecuniary advantages.

Few are aware of the importance of the wholesale and jobbing trade of Chicago. In boots and shoes and in clothing, twenty or more great firms from the East have placed here their distributing agents or their factories; and in groceries Chicago supplies the entire Northwest at rates presenting advantages over New York.

Chicago has stepped in between New York and the rural banks as a financial center, and scarcely a banking institution in the grain or cattle regions but keeps its reserve funds in the vaults of our commercial institutions. Accumulating here throughout the spring and summer months, they are summoned home at pleasure to move the products of the prairies. This process greatly strengthens the northwest in its financial operations, leaving home capital to supplement local operations on behalf of home interests.

It is impossible to forecast the destiny of this grand and growing section of the Union. Figures and predictions made at this date might seem ten years hence so ludicrously small as to excite only derision.

EARLY HISTORY OF ILLINOIS.

The name of this beautiful Prairie State is derived from *Illini*, a Delaware word signifying Superior Men. It has a French termination, and is a symbol of how the two races—the French and the Indians—were intermixed during the early history of the country.

The appellation was no doubt well applied to the primitive inhabitants of the soil whose prowess in savage warfare long withstood the combined attacks of the fierce Iroquois on the one side, and the no less savage and relentless Sacs and Foxes on the other. The Illinois were once a powerful confederacy, occupying the most beautiful and fertile region in the great Valley of the Mississippi, which their enemies coveted, and struggled long and hard to wrest from them. By the fortunes of war, they were diminished in numbers, and finally destroyed. "Starved Rock," on the Illinois River, according to tradition, commemorates their last tragedy, where, it is said, the entire tribe starved rather than surrender.

EARLY DISCOVERIES.

The first European discoveries in Illinois date back over two hundred years. They are a part of that movement which, from the beginning to the middle of the seventeenth century, brought the French Canadian missionaries and fur traders into the Valley of the Mississippi, and which at a later period established the civil and ecclesiastical authority of France, from the Gulf of St. Lawrence to the Gulf of Mexico, and from the foot-hills of the Alleghenies to the Rocky Mountains.

The great river of the West had been discovered by De Soto, the Spanish conqueror of Florida, three quarters of a century before the French founded Quebec in 1608, but the Spanish left the country a wilderness, without further exploration or settlement within its borders, in which condition it remained until the Mississippi was discovered by the agents of the French Canadian government, Joliet and Marquette, in 1673. These renowned explorers were not the first white visitors to Illinois In 1671—two years in advance of them—came Nicholas Perrot to Chicago. He had been sent by Talon as an agent of the Canadian government to call a great peace convention of Western Indians at Green Bay, preparatory to the movement for the discovery of the Mississippi. It was deemed a good stroke of policy to secure, as far as possible, the friendship and co-operation of the Indians, far and near, before venturing upon an enterprise which their hostility might render disastrous, and which their friendship and assistance would do so much to make successful; and to this end Perrot was sent to call together in council, the tribes throughout the Northwest, and to promise them the commerce and protection of the French government. He accordingly arrived at Green Bay in 1671, and procuring an escort of Pottawatomies, proceeded in a bark canoe upon a visit to the Miamis, at Chicago. Perrot was therefore the first European to set foot upon the soil of Illinois.

Still there were others before Marquette. In 1672, the Jesuit missionaries, Fathers Claude Allouez and Claude Dablon, bore the standard of the Cross from their mission at Green Bay through western Wisconsin and northern Illinois, visiting the Foxes on Fox River, and the Masquotines and Kickapoos at the mouth of the Milwaukee. These missionaries penetrated on the route afterwards followed by Marquette as far as the Kickapoo village at the head of Lake Winnebago, where Marquette, in his journey, secured guides across the portage to the Wisconsin.

The oft repeated story of Marquette and Joliet is well known. They were the agents employed by the Canadian government to discover the Mississippi. Marquette was a native of France, born in 1637, a Jesuit priest by education, and a man of simple faith and of great zeal and devotion in extending the Roman Catholic religion among the Indians. Arriving in Canada in 1666, he was sent as a missionary to the far Northwest, and, in 1668, founded a mission at Sault Ste. Marie. The following year he moved to La Pointe, in Lake Superior, where he instructed a branch of the Hurons till 1670, when he removed south and founded the mission at St. Ignace, on the Straits of Mackinaw. Here he remained, devoting a portion of his time to the study of the Illinois language under a native teacher who had accompanied him to the mission from La Pointe, till he was joined by Joliet in the spring of 1673. By the way of Green Bay and the Fox and Wisconsin Rivers, they entered the Mississippi, which they explored to the mouth of the Arkansas, and returned by the way of the Illinois and Chicago Rivers to Lake Michigan.

On his way up the Illinois, Marquette visited the great village of the Kaskaskias, near what is now Utica, in the county of La Salle. The following year he returned and established among them the mission of the Immaculate Virgin Mary, which was the first Jesuit mission founded in Illinois and in the Mississippi Valley. The intervening winter he had spent in a hut which his companions erected on the Chicago River, a few leagues from its mouth. The founding of this mission was the last act of Marquette's life. He died in Michigan, on his way back to Green Bay, May 18, 1675.

FIRST FRENCH OCCUPATION.

The first French occupation of the territory now embraced in Illinois was effected by La Salle in 1680, seven years after the time of Marquette and Joliet. La Salle, having constructed a vessel, the "Griffin," above the falls of Niagara, which he sailed to Green Bay, and having passed thence in canoes to the mouth of the St. Joseph River, by which and the Kankakee he reached the Illinois, in January, 1680, erected Fort Crevecœur, at the lower end of Peoria Lake, where the city of Peoria is now situated. The place where this ancient fort stood may still be seen just below the outlet of Peoria Lake. It was destined, however, to a temporary existence. From this point, La Salle determined to descend the Mississippi to its mouth, but did not accomplish this purpose till two years later —in 1682. Returning to Fort Frontenac for the purpose of getting materials with which to rig his vessel, he left the fort in charge of Tonti, his lieutenant, who during his absence was driven off by the Iroquois Indians. These savages had made a raid upon the settlement of the Illinois, and had left nothing in their track but ruin and desolation. Mr. Davidson, in his History of Illinois, gives the following graphic account of the picture that met the eyes of La Salle and his companions on their return:

"At the great town of the Illinois they were appalled at the scene which opened to their view. No hunter appeared to break its death-like silence with a salutatory whoop of welcome. The plain on which the town had stood was now strewed with charred fragments of lodges, which had so recently swarmed with savage life and hilarity. To render more hideous the picture of desolation, large numbers of skulls had been placed on the upper extremities of lodge-poles which had escaped the devouring flames. In the midst of these horrors was the rude fort of the spoilers, rendered frightful by the same ghastly relics. A near approach showed that the graves had been robbed of their bodies, and swarms of buzzards were discovered glutting their loathsome stomachs on the reeking corruption. To complete the work of destruction, the growing corn of the village had been cut down and burned, while the pits containing the products of previous years, had been rifled and their contents scattered with wanton waste. It was evident the suspected blow of the Iroquois had fallen with relentless fury."

Tonti had escaped, La Salle knew not whither. Passing down the lake in search of him and his men, La Salle discovered that the fort had been destroyed, but the vessel which he had partly constructed was still on the stocks, and but slightly injured. After further fruitless search, failing to find Tonti, he fastened to a tree a painting representing himself and party sitting in a canoe and bearing a pipe of peace, and to the painting attached a letter addressed to Tonti.

Tonti had escaped, and after untold privations, taken shelter among the Pottawattomies near Green Bay. These were friendly to the French. One of their old chiefs used to say, "There were but three great captains in the world, himself, Tonti and La Salle."

GENIUS OF LA SALLE.

We must now return to La Salle, whose exploits stand out in such bold relief. He was born in Rouen, France, in 1643. His father was wealthy but he renounced his patrimony on entering a college of the Jesuits, from which he separated and came to Canada a poor man in 1666. The priests of St. Sulpice, among whom he had a brother, were then the proprietors of Montreal, the nucleus of which was a seminary or convent founded by that order. The Superior granted to La Salle a large tract of land at La Chine, where he established himself in the fur trade. He was a man of daring genius, and outstripped all his competitors in exploits of travel and commerce with the Indians. In 1669, he visited the headquarters of the great Iroquois confederacy, at Onondaga, in the heart of New York, and obtaining guides, explored the Ohio River to the falls at Louisville.

In order to understand the genius of La Salle, it must be remembered that for many years prior to his time the missionaries and traders were obliged to make their way to the Northwest by the Ottawa River (of Canada) on account of the fierce hostility of the Iroquois along the lower lakes and Niagara River, which entirely closed this latter route to the Upper Lakes. They carried on their commerce chiefly by canoes, paddling them through the Ottawa to Lake Nipissing, carrying them across the portage to French River, and descending that to Lake Huron. This being the route by which they reached the Northwest accounts for the fact that all the earliest Jesuit missions were established in the neighborhood of the Upper Lakes. La Salle conceived the grand idea of opening the route by Niagara River and the Lower Lakes to Canadian commerce by sail vessels connecting it with the navigation of the Mississippi, and thus opening a magnificent water communication from the Gulf of St. Lawrence to the Gulf of Mexico. This truly grand and comprehensive purpose seems to have animated him in all his wonderful achievements and the matchless difficulties and hardships he surmounted. As the first step in the accomplishment of this object he established himself on Lake Ontario, and built and garrisoned Fort Frontenac, the site of the present city of Kingston, Canada. Here he obtained a grant of land from the French crown, and a body of troops by which he beat back the invading Iroquois and cleared the passage to Niagara Falls. Having by this masterly stroke made it safe to attempt a hitherto untried expedition, his next step, as we have seen, was to advance to the Falls with all his outfit for building a ship with which to sail the lakes. He was successful in this undertaking, though his ultimate purpose was defeated by a strange combination of untoward circumstances. The Jesuits evidently hated La Salle and plotted against him, because he had abandoned them and co-operated with a rival order. The fur traders were also jealous of his superior success in opening new channels of commerce. At La Chine he had taken the trade of Lake Ontario, which but for his presence there would have gone to Quebec. While they were plodding with their bark canoes through the Ottawa he was constructing sailing vessels to command the trade of the lakes and the Mississippi. These great plans excited the jealousy and envy of the small traders, introduced treason and revolt into the ranks of his own companions, and finally led to the foul assassination by which his great achievements were prematurely ended.

In 1682, La Salle, having completed his vessel at Peoria, descended the Mississippi to its confluence with the Gulf of Mexico. Erecting a standard on which he inscribed the arms of France, he took formal possession of the whole valley of the mighty river, in the name of Louis XIV, then reigning, in honor of whom he named the country LOUISIANA.

La Salle then went to France, was appointed Governor, and returned with a fleet and immigrants, for the purpose of planting a colony in Illinois. They arrived in due time in the Gulf of Mexico, but failing to find the mouth of the Mississippi, up which La Salle intended to sail, his supply ship, with the immigrants, was driven ashore and wrecked on Matagorda Bay. With the fragments of the vessel he constructed a stockade and rude huts on the shore for the protection of the immigrants, calling the post Fort St. Louis. He then made a trip into New Mexico, in search of silver mines, but, meeting with disappointment, returned to find his little colony reduced to forty souls. He then resolved to travel on foot to Illinois, and, starting with his companions, had reached the valley of the Colorado, near the mouth of Trinity river, when he was shot by one of his men. This occurred on the 19th of March, 1687.

Dr. J. W. Foster remarks of him: "Thus fell, not far from the banks of the Trinity, Robert Cavalier de la Salle, one of the grandest characters that ever figured in American history—a man capable of originating the vastest schemes, and endowed with a will and a judgment capable of carrying them to successful results. Had ample facilities been placed by the King of France at his disposal, the result of the colonization of this continent might have been far different from what we now behold."

EARLY SETTLEMENTS.

A temporary settlement was made at Fort St. Louis, or the old Kaskaskia village, on the Illinois River, in what is now La Salle County, in 1682. In 1690, this was removed, with the mission connected with it, to Kaskaskia, on the river of that name, emptying into the lower Mississippi in St. Clair County. Cahokia was settled about the same time, or at least, both of these settlements began in the year 1690, though it is now pretty well settled that Cahokia is the older place, and ranks as the oldest permanent settlement in Illinois, as well as in the Mississippi Valley. The reason for the removal of the old Kaskaskia settlement and mission, was probably because the dangerous and difficult route by Lake Michigan and the Chicago portage had been almost abandoned, and travelers and traders passed down and up the Mississippi by the Fox and Wisconsin River route. They removed to the vicinity of the Mississippi in order to be in the line of travel from Canada to Louisiana, that is, the lower part of it, for it was all Louisiana then south of the lakes.

During the period of French rule in Louisiana, the population probably never exceeded ten thousand, including whites and blacks. Within that portion of it now included in Indiana, trading posts were established at the principal Miami villages which stood on the head waters of the Maumee, the Wea villages situated at Ouiatenon, on the Wabash, and the Piankeshaw villages at Post Vincennes; all of which were probably visited by French traders and missionaries before the close of the seventeenth century.

In the vast territory claimed by the French, many settlements of considerable importance had sprung up. Biloxi, on Mobile Bay, had been founded by D'Iberville, in 1699; Antoine de Lamotte Cadillac had founded Detroit in 1701; and New Orleans had been founded by Bienville, under the auspices of the Mississippi Company, in 1718. In Illinois also, considerable settlements had been made, so that in 1730 they embraced one hundred and forty French families, about six hundred "converted Indians," and many traders and voyageurs. In that portion of the country, on the east side of the Mississippi, there were five distinct settlements, with their respective villages, viz.: Cahokia, near the mouth of Cahokia Creek and about five miles below the present city of St. Louis; St. Philip, about forty-five miles below Cahokia, and four miles above Fort Chartres; Fort Chartres, twelve miles above Kaskaskia; Kaskaskia, situated on the Kaskaskia River, five miles above its confluence with the Mississippi; and Prairie du Rocher, near Fort Chartres. To these must be added St. Genevieve and St. Louis, on the west side of the Mississippi. These with the exception of St. Louis, are among the oldest French towns in the Mississippi Valley. Kaskaskia, in its best days, was a town of some two or three thousand inhabitants. After it passed from the crown of France its population for many years did not exceed fifteen hundred. Under British rule, in 1773, the population had decreased to four hundred and fifty. As early as 1721 the Jesuits had established a college and a monastery in Kaskaskia.

Fort Chartres was first built under the direction of the Mississippi Company, in 1718, by M. de Boisbraint, a military officer, under command of Bienville. It stood on the east bank of the Mississippi, about eighteen miles below Kaskaskia, and was for some time the headquarters of the military commandants of the district of Illinois.

In the Centennial Oration of Dr. Fowler, delivered at Philadelphia, by appointment of Gov. Beveridge, we find some interesting facts with regard to the State of Illinois, which we appropriate in this history:

In 1682 Illinois became a possession of the French crown, a dependency of Canada, and a part of Louisiana. In 1765 the English flag was run up on old Fort Chartres, and Illinois was counted among the treasures of Great Britain.

In 1779 it was taken from the English by Col. George Rogers Clark. This man was resolute in nature, wise in council, prudent in policy, bold in action, and heroic in danger. Few men who have figured in the history of America are more deserving than this colonel. Nothing short of first-class ability could have rescued Vincennes and all Illinois from the English. And it is not possible to over-estimate the influence of this achievement upon the republic. In 1779 Illinois became a part of Virginia. It was soon known as Illinois County. In 1784 Virginia ceded all this territory to the general government, to be cut into States, to be republican in form, with "the same right of sovereignty, freedom, and independence as the other States."

In 1787 it was the object of the wisest and ablest legislation found in any merely human records. No man can study the secret history of

THE "COMPACT OF 1787,"

and not feel that Providence was guiding with sleepless eye these unborn States. The ordinance that on July 13, 1787, finally became the incorporating act, has a most marvelous history. Jefferson had vainly tried to secure a system of government for the northwestern territory. He was an emancipationist of that day, and favored the exclusion of slavery from the territory Virginia had ceded to the general government; but the South voted him down as often as it came up. In 1787, as late as July 10th, an organizing act without the anti-slavery clause was pending. This concession to the South was expected to carry it. Congress was in session in New York City. On July 5th, Rev. Dr. Mannasseh Cutler, of Massachusetts, came into New York to lobby on the northwestern territory. Everything seemed to fall into his hands. Events were ripe.

The state of the public credit, the growing of Southern prejudice, the basis of his mission, his personal character, all combined to complete one of those sudden and marvelous revolutions of public sentiment that once in five or ten centuries are seen to sweep over a country like the breath of the Almighty. Cutler was a graduate of Yale—received his A. M. from Harvard, and his D. D. from Yale. He had studied and taken degrees in the three learned professions, medicine, law, and divinity. He had thus America's best indorsement. He had published a scientific examination of the plants of New England. His name stood second only to that of Franklin as a scientist in America. He was a courtly gentleman of the old style, a man of commanding presence, and of inviting face. The Southern members said they had never seen such a gentleman in the North. He came representing a company that desired to purchase a tract of land now included in Ohio, for the purpose of planting a colony. It was a speculation. Government money was worth eighteen cents on the dollar. This Massachusetts company had collected enough to purchase 1,500,000 acres of land. Other speculators in New York made Dr. Cutler their agent (lobbyist). On the 12th he represented a demand for 5,500,000 acres. This would reduce the national debt. Jefferson and Virginia were regarded as authority concerning the land Virginia had just ceded. Jefferson's policy wanted to provide for the public credit, and this was a good opportunity to do something.

Massachusetts then owned the Territory of Maine, which she was crowding on the market. She was opposed to opening the northwestern region. This fired the zeal of Virginia. The South caught the inspiration, and all exalted Dr. Cutler. The English minister invited him to dine with some of the Southern gentlemen. He was the center of interest.

The entire South rallied round him, Massachusetts could not vote against him, because many of the constituents of her members were interested personally in the western speculation. Thus Cutler, making friends with the South, and, doubtless, using all the arts of the lobby, was enabled to command the situation. True to deeper convictions, he dictated one of the most compact and finished documents of wise statesmanship that has ever adorned any human law book. He borrowed from Jefferson the term "Articles of Compact," which, preceding the Federal constitution, rose into the most sacred character. He then followed very closely the constitution of Massachusetts, adopted three years before. Its most marked points were:

1. The exclusion of slavery from the territory forever.

2. Provision for public schools, giving one township for a seminary, and every section numbered 16 in each township; that

is, one thirty-sixth of all the land, for public schools.

3. A provision prohibiting the adoption of any constitution or the enactment of any law that should nullify pre-existing contracts.

Be it forever remembered that this compact declared that "Religion, morality and knowledge being necessary to good government and the happiness of mankind, schools and the means of education shall always be encouraged."

Dr. Cutler planted himself on this platform and would not yield. Giving his unqualified declaration that it was that or nothing—that unless they could make the land desirable they did not want it—he took his horse and buggy, and started for the constitutional convention in Philadelphia. On July 13, 1787, the bill was put upon its passage, and was unanimously adopted, every Southern member voting for it, and only one man, Mr. Yates, of New York, voting against it. But as the States voted as States, Yates lost his vote, and the compact was put beyond repeal.

Thus the great States of Ohio, Indiana, Illinois, Michigan and Wisconsin—a vast empire, the heart of the great valley—were consecrated to freedom, intelligence and honesty. Thus the great heart of the nation was prepared for a year and a day and an hour. In the light of these eighty-nine years I affirm that this act was the salvation of the republic and the destruction of slavery. Soon the South saw their great blunder, and tried to repeal the compact. In 1803, Congress referred it to a committee of which John Randolph was chairman. He reported that this ordinance was a compact, and opposed repeal. Thus it stood a rock, in the way of the on-rushing sea of slavery.

With all this timely aid, it was, after all, a most desperate and protracted struggle to keep the soil of Illinois sacred to freedom. It was the natural battle-field for the irrepressible conflict. In the southern end of the State, slavery preceded the compact. It existed among the old French settlers, and was hard to eradicate. The southern part of the State was settled from the slave States, and this population brought their laws, customs and institutions with them. A stream of population from the North poured into the northern part of the State. These sections misunderstood and hated each other perfectly. The Southerners regarded the Yankees as a skinning, tricky, penurious race of peddlers, filling the country with tinware, brass clocks and wooden nutmegs. The Northerner thought of the Southerner as a lean, lank, lazy creature, burrowing in a hut, and rioting in whisky, dirt and ignorance. These causes aided in making the struggle long and bitter. So strong was the sympathy with slavery, that in spite of the ordinance of 1787, and in spite of the deed of cession, it was determined to allow the old French settlers to retain their slaves. Planters from the slave States might bring their slaves, if they would give them a chance to choose freedom or years of service and bondage for their children till they should become thirty years of age. If they chose freedom they must leave the State in sixty days or be sold as fugitives. Servants were whipped for offenses for which white men are fined. Each lash paid forty cents of the fine. A negro ten miles from home without a pass was whipped. These famous laws were imported from the slave States just as they imported laws for the inspection of flax and wool when there was neither in the State.

These Black Laws are now wiped out. A vigorous effort was made to protect slavery in the State Constitution of 1817. It barely failed. It was renewed in 1825, when a convention was asked to make a new constitution. After a hard fight the convention was defeated. But slaves did not disappear from the census of the State until 1850. There were mobs and murders in the interest of slavery. Lovejoy was added to the list of martyrs—a sort of first fruits of that long life of immortal heroes who saw freedom as the one supreme desire of their souls, and were so enamored of her, that they preferred to die rather than survive her.

The population of 12,282 that occupied the Territory in A. D. 1800, increased to 45,000 in A. D. 1818, when the State Constitution was adopted, and Illinois took her place in the Union, with a star on the flag and two votes in the Senate.

Shadrach Bond was the first Governor, and in his first message he recommended the construction of the Illinois and Michigan Canal.

The simple economy in those days is seen in the fact the entire bill for stationery for the first Legislature was only $13.50. Yet this simple body actually enacted a very superior code.

There was no money in the Territory before the war of 1812. Deer skins and coon skins were the circulating medium. In 1821, the Legislature ordained a State Bank on the credit of the State. It issued notes in the likeness of bank bills. These notes were made a legal tender for every thing, and the bank was ordered to loan to the people $100 on personal security, and more on mortgages. They actually passed a resolution requesting the Secretary of the Treasury of the United States to receive these notes for land. The old French Lieutenant Governor, Col. Menard, put the resolution as follows: "Gentlemen of the Senate: It is moved and seconded *dat de notes of dis bank* be made land office money. All in favor of dat motion say aye; all against it say no. It is decided in de affirmative. Now, gentlemen, I bet you one hundred dollar he never be land-office money!" Hard sense, like hard money, is always above par.

This old Frenchman presents a fine figure up against the dark background of most of his nation. They made no progress. They clung to their earliest and simplest implements. They never wore hats or caps. They pulled their blankets over their heads in the winter like the Indians, with whom they freely intermingled.

Demagogism had an early development. One John Grammar (only in name), elected to the Territorial and State Legislatures of 1816 and 1836, invented the policy of opposing every new thing, saying, "If it succeeds, no one will ask who voted against it. If it proves a failure, he could quote its record." In sharp contrast with Grammar was the character of D. P. Cook, after whom the county containing Chicago was named. Such was his transparent integrity and remarkable ability that his will was almost the law of the State. In Congress, a young man, and from a poor State, he was made Chairman of the Ways and Means Committee. He was pre-eminent for standing by his committee, regardless of consequences. It was his integrity that elected John Quincy Adams to the Presidency. There were four candidates in 1824, Jackson, Clay, Crawford, and John Quincy Adams. There being no choice by the people, the election was thrown into the House. It was so balanced that it turned on his vote, and that he cast for Adams, electing him; then went home to face the wrath of the Jackson party in Illinois. It cost him all but character and greatness. It is a suggestive comment on the times, that there was no legal interest till 1830. It often reached 150 per cent., usually 50 per cent. Then it was reduced to 12, and now to 10 per cent.

PHYSICAL FEATURES OF THE PRAIRIE STATE.

In area the State has 55,410 square miles of territory. It is about 150 miles wide and 400 miles long, stretching in latitude from Maine to North Carolina. It embraces wide variety of climate. It is tempered on the north by the great inland, saltless, tideless sea, which keeps the thermometer from either extreme. Being a table land, from 600 to 1,200 feet above the level of the sea, one is prepared to find on the health maps, prepared by the general government, an almost clean and perfect record. In freedom from fever and malarial diseases and consumptions, the three deadly enemies of the American Saxon, Illinois, as a State, stands without a superior. She furnishes one of the essential conditions of a great people— sound bodies. I suspect that this fact lies back of that old Delaware word, Illini, superior men.

The great battles of history that have been determinative of dynasties and destinies have been strategical battles, chiefly the question of position. Thermopylæ has been the war-cry of freemen for twenty-four centuries. It only tells how much there may be in position. All this advantage belongs to Illinois. It is in the heart of the greatest valley in the world, the vast region between the mountains—a valley that could feed mankind for one thousand years. It is well on toward the center of the continent. It is in the great temperate belt, in which have been found nearly all the aggressive civilizations of history. It has sixty-five miles of frontage on the head of the lake. With the Mississippi forming the western and southern boundary, with the Ohio running along the southeastern line, with the Illinois river and canal dividing the State diagonally from the lake to the lower Mississippi, and with the Rock and Wabash rivers, furnishing altogether 2,000 miles of water front, connecting with, and running through, in all about 12,000 miles of navigable water.

But this is not all. These waters are made most available by the fact that the lake and the State lie on the ridge running into the great valley from the east. Within cannon-shot of the lake, the water runs away from the lake to the gulf. The lake now empties at both ends, one into the Atlantic and one into the gulf of Mexico. The lake thus seems to hang over the land. This makes the dockage most serviceable; there are no steep banks to damage it. Both lake and river are made for use.

The climate varies from Portland to Richmond; it favors every product of the continent, including the tropics, with less than half a dozen exceptions. It produces every great nutriment of the world except bananas and rice. It is hardly too much to say that it is the most productive spot known to civilization. With the soil full of bread and the earth full of minerals; with an upper surface of food and an under layer of fuel; with perfect natural drainage, and abundant springs and streams and navigable rivers; half way between the forests of the north and the fruits of the south; within a day's ride of the great deposits of iron, coal, copper, lead and zinc; containing and controlling the great grain, cattle, pork and lumber markets of the world, it is not strange that Illinois has the advantage of position.

This advantage has been supplemented by the character of the population. In the early days when Illinois was first admitted to the union, her population were chiefly from Kentucky and Virginia. But, in the conflict of ideas concerning slavery, a strong tide of emigration came in from the East, and soon changed this composition. In 1870 her non-native population were from colder soils. New York furnished 133,290; Ohio gave 162,623; Pennsylvania sent on 98,352; the entire South gave us only 206,734. In all her cities, and in all her German and Scandinavian and other foreign colonies, Illinois has only about one-fifth of her people of foreign birth.

PROGRESS OF DEVELOPMENT.

One of the greatest elements in the early development of Illinois is the Illinois and Michigan Canal, connecting the Illinois and Mississippi Rivers with the lakes. It was of the utmost importance to the State. It was recommended by Gov. Bond, the first governor, in his first message. In 1821, the Legislature appropriated $10,000 for surveying the route. Two bright young engineers surveyed it, and estimated the cost at $600,000 or $700,000. It finally cost $8,000,000. In 1825, a law was passed to incorporate the Canal Company, but no stock was sold. In 1826, upon the solicitation of Cook, Congress gave 800,000 acres of land on the line of the work. In 1828, another law—commissioners appointed, and work commenced with new survey and new estimates. In 1834–35, George Farquhar made an able report on the whole matter. This was, doubtless, the ablest report ever made to a western legislature, and it became the model for subsequent reports and action. From this, the work went on till it was finished in 1848. It cost the State a large amount of money; but it gave to the industries of the State an impetus that pushed it up into the first rank of greatness. It was not built as a speculation any more than a doctor is employed on a speculation. But it has paid into the treasury of the State an average annual net sum of over $111,000.

Pending the construction of the canal, the land and town-lot fever broke out in the State, in 1834–35. It took on the malignant type in Chicago, lifting the town up into a city. The disease spread over the entire State and adjoining States. It was epidemic. It cut up men's farms without regard to locality, and cut up the purses of the purchasers without regard to consequences. It is estimated that building lots enough were sold in Indiana alone to accommodate every citizen then in the United States.

Towns and cities were exported to the Eastern market by the ship-load. There was no lack of buyers. Every up-ship came freighted with speculators and their money.

This distempter seized upon the Legislature in 1836-37, and left not one to tell the tale. They enacted a system of internal improvement without a parallel in the grandeur of its conception. They ordered the construction of 1,300 miles of railroad, crossing the State in all directions. This was surpassed by the river and canal improvements. There were a few counties not touched by either railroad or river or canal, and those were to be comforted and compensated by the free distribution of $200,000 among them. To inflate this balloon beyond credence, it was ordered that work should be commenced on both ends of each of these railroads and rivers, and at each river crossing, all at the same time. The appropriations for these vast improvements were over $12,000,000, and commissioners were appointed to borrow the money on the credit of the State. Remember that all this was in the early days of railroading, when railroads were luxuries; that the State had whole counties with scarcely a cabin; and that the population of the State was less than 400,000, and you can form some idea of the vigor with which these brave men undertook the work of making a great State. In the light of history I am compelled to say that this was only a premature throb of the power that actually slumbered in the soil of the State. It was Hercules in the cradle.

At this juncture the State Bank loaned its funds largely to Godfrey Gilman & Co. and to other leading houses, for the purpose of drawing trade from St. Louis to Alton. Soon they failed and took down the bank with them.

In 1840, all hope seemed gone. A population of 480,000 were loaded with a debt of $14,000,000. It had only six small cities, really only towns, namely: Chicago, Alton, Springfield, Quincy, Galena, Nauvoo. This debt was to be cared for when there was not a dollar in the treasury, and when the State had borrowed itself out of all credit, and when there was not good money enough in the hands of all the people to pay the interest of the debt for a single year. Yet, in the presence of all these difficulties, the young State steadily refused to repudiate. Gov. Ford took hold of the problem and solved it, bringing the State through in triumph.

Having touched lightly upon some of the more distinctive points in the history of the development of Illinois, let us next briefly consider the

MATERIAL RESOURCES OF THE STATE.

It is a garden four hundred miles long and one hundred and fifty miles wide. Its soil is chiefly a black sandy loam, from six inches to sixty feet thick. On the American bottoms it has been cultivated for one hundred and fifty years without renewal.

About the old French towns it has yielded corn for a century and a half without rest or help. It produces nearly everything green in the temperate and tropical zones. She leads all other States in the number of acres actually under plow. Her products from 25,000,000 of acres are incalculable. Her mineral wealth is scarcely second to her agricultural power. She has coal, iron, lead, copper, zinc, many varieties of building stone, fire clay, cuma clay, common brick clay, sand of all kinds, gravel, mineral paint—everything needed for a high civilization. Left to herself, she has the elements of all greatness. The single item of coal is too vast for an appreciative handling in figures. We can handle it in general terms like algebraical signs, but long before we get up into the millions and billions the human mind drops down from comprehension to mere symbolic apprehension.

When I tell you that nearly four-fifths of the entire State is underlaid with a deposit of coal more than forty feet thick on the average (now estimated by recent surveys, at seventy feet thick), you can get some idea of its amount, as you do of the amount of the national debt. There it is! 41,000 square miles—one vast mine into which you could put any of the States; in which you could bury scores of European and ancient empires, and have room all round to work without knowing that they had been sepulchered there.

Put this vast coal-bed down by the other great coal deposits of the world, and its importance becomes manifest. Great Britain has 12,000 square miles of coal; Spain, 3,000; France, 1719; Belgium, 578; Illinois about twice as many square miles as all combined. Virginia has 20,000 square miles; Pennsylvania, 16,000; Ohio, 12,000. Illinois has 41,000 square miles. One-seventh of all the known coal on this continent is in Illinois.

Could we sell the coal in this single State for one-seventh of one cent a ton, it would pay the national debt. Converted into power, even with the wastage in our common engines, it would do more work than could be done by the entire race, beginning at Adam's wedding and working ten hours a day through all the centuries till the present time, and right on into the future at the same rate for the next 600,000 years.

Great Britain uses enough mechanical power to-day to give to each man, woman, and child in the kingdom, the help and service of nineteen untiring servants. No wonder she has leisure and luxuries. No wonder the home of the common artisan has in it more luxuries than could be found in the palace of good old King Arthur. Think if you can conceive of it, of the vast army of servants that slumber in the soil of Illinois, impatiently awaiting the call of Genius to come forth to minister to our comfort.

At the present rate of consumption England's coal supply will be exhausted in 250 years. When this is gone she must transfer her dominion either to the Indies, or to British America, which I would not resist; or to some other people, which I would regret as a loss to civilization.

COAL IS KING.

At the same rate of consumption (which far exceeds our own), the deposit of coal in Illinois will last 120,000 years. And her kingdom shall be an everlasting kingdom.

Let us turn now from this reserve power to the *annual products* of the State. We shall not be humiliated in this field. Here we strike the secret of our national credit. Nature provides a market in the constant appetite of the race. Men must eat, and if we can furnish the provisions we can command the treasure. All that a man hath will he give for his life.

According to the last census Illinois produced 30,000,000 of bushels of wheat. That is more wheat than was raised by any other State in the union. She raised in 1875, 130,000,000 of bushels of corn—twice as much as any other State, and one-sixth of all the corn raised in the United States. She harvested 2,747,000 tons of hay, nearly one-tenth of all the hay in the republic. It is not generally appreciated, but it is true that the hay crop of the country is worth more than the cotton crop. The hay of Illinois equals the cotton of Louisiana. Go to Charleston, S. C., and see them peddling handfuls of hay or grass, almost as a curiosity, as we regard Chinese gods or the cryolite of Greenland; drink your coffee and *condensed milk;* and walk back from the coast for many a league through the sand and burs till you get up into the better atmosphere of the mountains, without seeing a waving meadow or a grazing herd; then you will begin to appreciate the meadows of the Prairie State, where the grass often grows sixteen feet high.

The value of her farm implements is $211,000,000, and the value of her live stock is only second to the great State of New York. In 1875 she had 25,000,000 hogs, and packed 2,113,845, about one-half of all that were packed in the United States. This is no insignificant item. Pork is a growing demand of the old world. Since the laborers of Europe have gotten a taste of our bacon, and we have learned how to pack it dry in boxes, like dry goods, the world has become the market.

The hog is on the march into the future. His nose is ordained to uncover the secrets of dominion, and his feet shall be guided by the star of empire.

Illinois marketed $57,000,000 worth of slaughtered animals—more than any other State, and a seventh of all the States.

Be patient with me, and pardon my pride, and I will give you a list of some of the things in which Illinois excels all other States.

Depth and richness of soil; per cent. of good ground; acres of improved land; large farms—some farms contain from 40,000 to 60,000 acres of cultivated land, 40,000 acres of corn on a single farm; number of farmers; amount of wheat, corn, oats and honey produced; value of animals for slaughter; number of hogs; amount of pork; number of horses—three times as many as Kentucky, the horse State.

Illinois excels all other States in miles of railroads and in miles of postal service, and in money orders sold per annum, and in the amount of lumber sold in her markets.

Illinois is only second in many important matters. This sample list comprises a few of the more important: Permanent school fund (good for a young State); total income for educational purposes; number of publishers of books, maps, papers, etc.; value of farm products and implements, and of live stock; in tons of coal mined.

The shipping of Illinois is only second to New York. Out of one port during the business hours of the season of navigation she sends forth a vessel every ten minutes. This does not include canal boats, which go one every five minutes. No wonder she is only second in number of bankers and brokers or in physicians and surgeons.

She is third in colleges, teachers and schools; cattle, lead, hay, flax, sorghum and beeswax.

She is fourth in population, in children enrolled in public schools, in law schools, in butter, potatoes and carriages.

She is fifth in value of real and personal property, in theological seminaries and colleges exclusively for women, in milk sold, and in boots and shoes manufactured, and in book-binding.

She is only seventh in the production of wood, while she is the twelfth in area. Surely that is well done for the Prairie State. She now has much more wood and growing timber than she had thirty years ago.

A few leading industries will justify emphasis. She manufactures $205,000,000 worth of goods, which places her well up toward New York and Pennsylvania. The number of her manufacturing establishments increased from 1860 to 1870, 300 per cent.; capital employed increased 350 per cent., and the amount of product increased 400 per cent. She issued 5,500,000 copies of commercial and financial newspapers—only second to New York. She has 6,759 miles of railroad, thus leading all other States, worth $636,458,000, using 3,245 engines, and 67,712 cars, making a train long enough to cover one-tenth of the entire roads of the State. Her stations are only five miles apart. More than two-thirds of her land is within five miles of a railroad, and less than two per cent is more than fifteen miles away.

The State has a large financial interest in the Illinois Central railroad. The road was incorporated in 1850, and the State gave each alternate section for six miles on each side, and doubled the price of the remaining land, so keeping herself good. The road received 2,595,000 acres of land, and pays to the State one-seventh of the gross receipts. Add to this the annual receipts from the canal, $111,000, and a large per cent. of the State tax is provided for.

THE RELIGION AND MORALS

of the State keep step with her productions and growth. She was born of the missionary spirit. It was a minister who secured for her the ordinance of 1787, by which she has been saved from slavery, ignorance, and dishonesty. Rev. Mr. Wiley, pastor of a Scotch congregation in Randolph County, petitioned the Constitutional Convention of 1818 to recognize Jesus Christ as king, and the scriptures as the only necessary guide and book of law. The convention did not act in the case, and the old covenanters refused to accept citizenship. They never voted until 1824, when the slavery question was submitted to the people; then they all voted against it and cast the determining votes. Conscience has predominated whenever a great moral question has been submitted to the people.

But little mob violence has ever been felt in the State. In 1817 regulators disposed of a band of horse-thieves that infested the Territory. The Mormon indignities finally awoke the same spirit. Alton was also the scene of a pro-slavery mob, in which Lovejoy was added to the list of martyrs. The moral sense of the people makes the law supreme, and gives to the State unruffled peace.

With $22,300,000 in church property, and 4,298 church organizations, the State has that divine police, the sleepless patrol of moral ideas, that alone is able to secure perfect safety. Conscience takes the knife from the assassin's hand and the bludgeon from the grasp of the highwayman. We sleep in safety, not because we are behind bolts and bars—these only fence against the innocent; not because a lone officer drowses on a distant corner of a street; not because a sheriff may call his posse from a remote part of the county; but because *conscience* guards the very portals of the air and stirs in the deepest recesses of the public mind. This spirit issues within the State 9,500,000 copies of religious papers annually, and receives still more from without. Thus the crime of the State is only one fourth that of New York and one half that of Pennsylvania.

Illinois never had but one duel between her own citizens. In Belleville, in 1820, Alphonso Stewart and William Bennett arranged to vindicate injured honor. The seconds agreed to make it a sham, and make them shoot blanks. Stewart was in the secret. Bennett mistrusted something, and unobserved, slipped a bullet into his gun and killed Stewart. He then fled the State. After two years he was caught, tried, convicted, and, in spite of friends and political aid, was hung. This fixed the code of honor on a Christian basis, and terminated its use in Illinois.

The early preachers were ignorant men, who were accounted eloquent according to the strength of their voices. But they set the style for all public speakers. Lawyers and political speakers followed this rule. Gov. Ford says: "Nevertheless, these first preachers were of incalculable benefit to the country. They inculcated justice and morality. To them are we indebted for the first Christian character of the Protestant portion of the people."

In education Illinois surpasses her material resources. The ordinance of 1787 consecrated one thirty-sixth of her soil to common schools, and the law of 1818, the first law that went upon her statutes, gave three per cent of all the rest to

EDUCATION.

The old compact secures this interest forever, and by its yoking morality and intelligence it precludes the legal interference with the Bible in the public schools. With such a start it is natural that we should have 11,050 schools, and that our illiteracy should be less than New York or Pennsylvania, and only about one half of Massachusetts. We are not to blame for not having more than one half as many idiots as the great States. These public schools soon made colleges inevitable. The first college, still flourishing, was started in Lebanon in 1828, by the M. E. church, and named after Bishop McKendree. Illinois College, at Jacksonville, supported by the Presbyterians, followed in 1830. In 1832 the Baptists built Shurtleff College, at Alton. Then the Presbyterians built Knox College, at Galesburg, in 1838, and the Episcopalians built Jubilee College, at Peoria, in 1847. After these early years, colleges have rained down. A settler could hardly encamp on the prairie but a college would spring up by his wagon. The State now has one very well endowed and equipped university, namely, the Northwestern University, at Evanston, with six colleges, ninety instructors, over 1,000 students, and $1,500,000 endowment.

Rev. J. M. Peck was the first educated Protestant minister in the State. He settled at Rock Spring, in St. Clair County,

1820, and left his impress on the State. Before 1837 only party papers were published, but Mr. Peck published a Gazetteer of Illinois. Soon after John Russell, of Bluffdale, published essays and tales showing genius. Judge James Hall published *The Illinois Monthly Magazine* with great ability, and an annual called *The Western Souvenir*, which gave him an enviable fame all over the United States. From these beginnings, Illinois has gone on till she has more volumes in public libraries even than Massachusetts, and of the 44,500,000 volumes in all the public libraries of the United States, she has one thirteenth. In newspapers she stands fourth. Her increase is marvelous.

This brings us to a record unsurpassed in the history of any age.

THE WAR RECORD OF ILLINOIS.

I hardly know where to begin, or how to advance, or what to say. I can at best give you only a broken synopsis of her deeds, and you must put them in the order of glory for yourself. Her sons have always been foremost on fields of danger. In 1832-33, at the call of Gov. Reynolds, her sons drove Blackhawk over the Mississippi.

When the Mexican war came, in May, 1846, 8,370 men offered themselves when only 3,720 could be accepted. The fields of Buena Vista and Vera Cruz, and the storming of Cerro Gordo, will carry the glory of Illinois soldiers long after the causes that led to that war have been forgotten. But it was reserved till our day for her sons to find a field and cause and foemen that could fitly illustrate their spirit and heroism. Illinois put into her own regiments for the United States government 256,000 men, and into the army through other States enough to swell the number to 290,000. This far exceeds all the soldiers of the Federal government in all the war of the Revolution. Her total years of service were over 600,000. She enrolled men from eighteen to forty-five years of age when the law of Congress in 1864—the test time—only asked for those from twenty to forty-five. Her enrollment was otherwise excessive. Her people wanted to go, and did not take the pains to correct the enrollment. Thus the basis of fixing the quota was too great, and then the quota itself, at least in the trying time, was far above any other State.

Thus the demand on some counties, as Monroe, for example, took every able-bodied man in the county, and then did not have enough to fill the quota. Moreover, Illinois sent 20,844 men for ninety or one hundred days, for whom no credit was asked. When Mr. Lincoln's attention was called to the inequality of the quota compared with other States, he replied: "The country needs the sacrifice. We must put the whip on the free horse." In spite of all these disadvantages Illinois gave to the country 73,000 years of service above all calls. With one thirteenth of the population of the loyal States, she sent regularly one tenth of all the soldiers, and in the peril of the closing calls, when patriots were few and weary, she then sent one eighth of all that were called for by her loved and honored son in the White House. Her mothers and daughters went into the fields to raise the grain and keep the children together, while the fathers and older sons went to the harvest fields of the world. I knew a father and four sons who agreed that one of them must stay at home; and they pulled straws from a stack to see who might go. The father was left. The next day he came into the camp, saying: "Mother says she can get the crops in, and I am going, too." I know large Methodist churches from which every male member went to the army. Do you want to know what these heroes from Illinois did in the field? Ask any soldier with a good record of his own, who is able to judge, and he will tell you that the Illinois men went in to win. It is common history that the greater victories were won in the West. When everything else looked dark Illinois was gaining victories all down the river, and dividing the Confederacy. Sherman took with him on his great march forty-five regiments of Illinois infantry, three companies of artillery, and one company of cavalry. He could not avoid

GOING TO THE SEA.

If he had been killed, I doubt not the men would have gone right on. Lincoln answered all rumors of Sherman's defeat with, "It is impossible; there is a mighty sight of fight in 100,000 Western men." Illinois soldiers brought home 300 battle-flags. The first United States flag that floated over Richmond, was an Illinois flag. She sent messengers and nurses to every field and hospital, to care for her sick and wounded sons. She said, "these suffering ones are my sons, and I will care for them."

When individuals had given all, then cities and towns came forward with their credit to the extent of many millions, to aid these men and their families.

Illinois gave the country the great general of the war—Ulysses S. Grant— since honored with two terms of the Presidency of the United States.

One other name from Illinois comes up in all minds, embalmed in all hearts, that must have the supreme place in this story of our glory and of our nation's honor; that name is Abraham Lincoln, of Illinois.

The analysis of Mr. Lincoln's character is difficult on account of its symmetry.

In this age we look with admiration at his uncompromising honesty. And well we may, for this saved us. Thousands throughout the length and breadth of our country, who knew him only as "Honest Old Abe," voted for him on that account; and wisely did they choose, for no other man could have carried us through the fearful night of the war. When his plans were too vast for our comprehension, and his faith in the cause too sublime for our participation; when it was all night about us, and all dread before us, and all sad and desolate behind us; when not one ray shone upon our cause; when traitors were haughty and exultant at the South, and fierce and blasphemous at the North; when the loyal men here seemed almost in the minority; when the stoutest heart quailed, the bravest cheek paled, when generals were defeating each other for place, and contractors were leeching out the very heart's blood of the prostrate republic; when every thing else had failed us, we looked at this calm, patient man, standing like a rock in the storm, and said: "Mr. Lincoln is honest, and we can trust him still." Holding to this single point with the energy of faith and despair we held together, and, under God, he brought us through to victory.

His practical wisdom made him the

wonder of all lands. With such certainty did Mr. Lincoln follow causes to their ultimate effects, that his foresight of contingencies seemed almost prophetic.

He is radiant with all the great virtues, and his memory shall shed a glory upon this age, that shall fill the eyes of men as they look into history. Other men have excelled him in some point, but, taken at all points, all in all, he stands head and shoulders above every other man of 6,000 years. An administrator, he saved the nation in the perils of unparalleled civil war. A statesman, he justified his measures by their success. A philanthropist, he gave liberty to one race and salvation to another. A moralist, he bowed from the summit of human power to the foot of the Cross, and became a Christian. A mediator, he exercised mercy under the most absolute abeyance to law. A leader, he was no partisan. A commander, he was untainted with blood. A ruler in desperate times, he was unsullied with crime. A man, he has left no word of passion, no thought of malice, no trick of craft, no act of jealousy, no purpose of selfish ambition. Thus perfected, without a model and without a peer, he was dropped into these troubled years to adorn and embellish all that is good and all that is great in our humanity, and to present to all coming time the representative of the divine idea of free government.

It is not too much to say that away down in the future, when the republic has fallen from its niche in the wall of time; when the great war itself shall have faded out in the distance like a mist on the horizon; when the Anglo Saxon language shall be spoken only by the tongue of the stranger; then the generations looking this way shall see the great president as the supreme figure in this vortex of history.

CHICAGO.

It is impossible in our brief space to give more than a meager sketch of such a city as Chicago, which is in itself the greatest marvel of the Prairie State. This mysterious, majestic, mighty city, born first of water, and next of fire; sown in weakness, and raised in power; planted among the willows of the marsh, and crowned with the glory of the mountains, sleeping on the bosom of the prairie, and rocked on the bosom of the sea; the youngest city of the world, and still the eye of the prairie, as Damascus, the oldest city of the world, is the eye of the desert. With a commerce far exceeding that of Corinth on her isthmus, in the highway to the East; with the defenses of a continent piled around her by the thousand miles, making her far safer than Rome on the banks of the Tiber; with schools eclipsing Alexandria and Athens; with liberties more conspicuous than those of the old republics; with a heroism equal to the first Carthage, and with a sanctity scarcely second to that of Jerusalem—set your thoughts on all this, lifted into the eyes of all men by the miracle of its growth, illuminated by the flame of its fall, and transfigured by the divinity of its resurrection, and you will feel, as I do, the utter impossibility of compassing this subject as it deserves. Some impression of her importance is received from the shock her burning gave to the civilized world.

When the doubt of her calamity was removed, and the horrid fact was accepted, there went a shudder over all cities, and a quiver over all lands. There was scarcely a town in the civilized world that did not shake on the brink of this opening chasm. The flames of our homes reddened all skies. The city was set upon a hill, and could not be hid. All eyes were turned upon it. To have struggled and suffered amid the scenes of its fall is as distinguishing as to have fought at Thermopylæ, or Salamis, or Hastings, or Waterloo, or Bunker Hill.

Its calamity amazed the world, because it was felt to be the common property of mankind.

The early history of the city is full of interest, just as the early history of such a man as Washington or Lincoln becomes public property, and is cherished by every patriot.

Starting with 560 acres in 1833, it embraced and occupied 23,000 acres in 1869, and having now a population of more than 600,000, it commands general attention.

The first settler—Jean Baptiste Pointe au Sable, a mulatto from the West Indies —came and began trade with the Indians in 1796. John Kinzie became his successor in 1804, in which year Fort Dearborn was erected.

A mere trading-post was kept here from that time till about the time of the Blackhawk war, in 1832. It was not the city. It was merely a cock crowing at midnight. The morning was not yet. In 1833 the settlement about the fort was incorporated as a town. The voters were divided on the propriety of such corporation, twelve voting for it and one against it. Four years later it was incorporated as a city, and embraced 560 acres.

The produce handled in this city is an indication of its power. Grain and flour were imported from the East till as late as 1837. The first exportation by way of experiment was in 1839. Exports exceeded imports first in 1842. The Board of Trade was organized in 1848, but it was so weak that it needed nursing till 1855. Grain was purchased by the wagon-load in the street.

I remember sitting with my father on a load of wheat, in the long line of wagons along Lake street, while the buyers came and untied the bags, and examined the grain, and made their bids. That manner of business had to cease with the day of small things. One tenth of all the wheat in the United States is handled in Chicago. Even as long ago as 1853 the receipts of grain in Chicago exceeded those of the goodly city of St. Louis, and in 1854 the exports of grain from Chicago exceeded those of New York and doubled those of St. Petersburg, Archangel, or Odessa, the largest grain markets in Europe.

The manufacturing interests of the city are not contemptible. In 1873 manufactories employed 45,000 operatives; in 1876, 60,000. The manufactured product in 1875 was worth $177,000,000.

No estimate of the size and power of Chicago would be adequate that did not put large emphasis on the railroads. Before they came thundering along our streets, canals were the hope of our country. But who ever thinks now of traveling by canal packets? In June, 1852, there were only forty miles of railroad connected with the city. The old Galena division of the Northwestern ran out to Elgin. But now, who can count the trains and measure the roads that seek a terminus or connection in this city? The lake stretches away to the north, gathering into this center all the harvests that might otherwise pass to the north of us. If you will take a map and look at the adjustment of railroads, you will see, first, that Chicago is the great railroad center of the world, as New York is the commercial city of this continent; and, second, that the railroad lines form the iron spokes of a great wheel whose hub is this city. The lake furnishes the only break in the spokes, and this seems simply to have pushed a few spokes together on each shore. See the eighteen trunk lines, exclusive of eastern connections.

Pass round the circle, and view their numbers and extent. There is the great Northwestern, with all its branches, one branch creeping along the lake shore, and so reaching to the north, into the Lake Superior regions, away to the right, and on to the Northern Pacific on the left, swinging around Green Bay for iron and copper and silver, twelve months in the year, and reaching out for the wealth of the great agricultural belt and isothermal line traversed by the Northern Pacific. Another branch, not so far north, feeling for the heart of the Badger State. Another pushing lower down the Mississippi—all these make many connections, and tapping all the vast wheat regions of Minnesota, Wisconsin, Iowa, and all the regions this side of sunset. There is that elegant road, the Chicago, Burlington & Quincy, running out a goodly number of branches, and reaping the great fields this side of the Missouri River. I can only mention the Chicago, Alton & St. Louis, *our* Illinois Central, described elsewhere, and the Chicago & Rock Island. Further around we come to the lines connecting us with all the Eastern cities. The Chicago, Indianapolis & St. Louis, the Pittsburg, Fort Wayne & Chicago, the Lake Shore & Michigan Southern, and the Michigan Central and Great Western, give us many highways to the seaboard. Thus we reach the Mississippi at five points, from St. Paul to Cairo and the Gulf itself by two routes. We also reach Cincinnati and Baltimore, and Pittsburg and Philadelphia, and New York. North and south run the water courses of the lakes and the rivers, broken just enough at this point to make a pass. Through this, from east to west, run the long lines that stretch from ocean to ocean.

This is the neck of the glass, and the golden sands of commerce must pass into our hands. Altogether we have more than 10,000 miles of railroad, directly tributary to this city, seeking to unload their wealth in our coffers. All these roads have come themselves by the infallible instinct of capital. Not a dollar was ever given by the city to secure one of them, and only a small per cent. of stock taken originally by her citizens, and that taken simply as an investment. Coming in the natural order of events, they will not be easily diverted.

There is still another showing to all this. The connection between New York and San Francisco is by the middle route. This passes inevitably through Chicago. St. Louis wants the Southern Pacific or Kansas Pacific, and pushes it out through Denver, and so on up to Cheyenne. But before the road is fairly under way, the Chicago roads shove out to Kansas City, making even the Kansas Pacific a feeder, and actually leaving St. Louis out in the cold. It is not too much to expect that Dakota, Montana, and Washington Territory will find their great market in Chicago.

But these are not all. Perhaps I had better notice here the ten or fifteen new roads that have just entered, or are just entering, our city. Their names are all that is necessary to give. Chicago & St. Paul, looking up the Red River country to the British possessions; the Chicago, Atlantic & Pacific; the Chicago, Decatur & State line; the Baltimore & Ohio; the Chicago, Danville & Vincennes; the Chicago & La Salle Railroad; the Chicago, Pittsburgh & Cincinnati; the Chicago and Canada Southern; the Chicago and Illinois River Railroad. These, with their connections, and with the new connections of the old roads, already in process of erection, give to Chicago not less than 10,000 miles of new tributaries from the richest land on the continent. Thus there will be added to the reserve power, to the capital within reach of this city, not less than $1,000,000,000.

Add to all this transporting power the ships that sail one every nine minutes of the business hours of the season of navigation; add, also, the canal boats that leave one every five minutes during the same time—and you will see something of the business of the city.

THE COMMERCE OF THIS CITY

has been leaping along to keep pace with the growth of the country around us. In 1852, our commerce reached the hopeful sum of $20,000,000. In 1870 it reached $400,000,000. In 1871 it was pushed up above $450,000,000, and in 1875 it touched nearly double that.

One half of our imported goods come directly to Chicago. Grain enough is exported directly from our docks to the old world to employ a semi-weekly line of steamers of 3,000 tons capacity. This branch is not likely to be greatly developed. Even after the great Welland Canal is completed we shall have only fourteen feet of water. The great ocean vessels will continue to control the trade.

The schools of Chicago are unsurpassed in America. Out of a population of 300,000, there were only 186 persons between the ages of six and twenty-one unable to read. This is the best known record.

In 1831 the mail system was condensed into a half-breed, who went on foot to Niles, Mich., once in two weeks, and brought back what papers and news he could find. As late as 1846 there was often only one mail a week. A post-office was established in Chicago in 1833, and the post-master nailed up old boot-legs on one side of his shop to serve as boxes for the nabobs and literary men.

The improvements that have characterized the city are as startling as the city itself. In 1831, Mark Beaubien established a ferry over the river, and put himself under bonds to carry all the citizens free for the privilege of charging strangers. Now there are twenty-four large bridges and two tunnels.

In 1833 the government expended $30,000 on the harbor. Then commenced that series of maneuvers with the river that has made it one of the world's curiosities. It used to wind around in the lower end of the town, and make its way rippling over the sand into the lake at the foot of Madison street. They took it up and put it down where it now is. It was a narrow stream, so narrow that even moderately small crafts had to go up through the willows and cat's tails to the point near Lake street bridge, and back up one of the branches to get room enough in which to turn around.

In 1844 the quagmires in the streets were first pontooned by plank roads, which acted in wet weather as public squirt-guns. Keeping you out of the mud, they compromised by squirting the mud over you. The wooden-block pavements came to Chicago in 1857. In 1840 water was delivered by peddlers in carts or by hand. Then a twenty-five horse-power engine pushed it through hollow or bored logs along the streets till 1854, when it was introduced into the houses by new works. The first fire-engine was used in 1835, and the first steam fire-engine in 1859. Gas was utilized for lighting the city in 1850. The Young Men's Christian Association was organized in 1858, and horse railroads carried them to their work in 1859. The alarm telegraph adopted in 1864. The opera-house built in 1865. The city grew from 560 acres in 1833 to 23,000 in 1869. In 1834, the taxes amounted to $48.90, and the trustees of the town borrowed $60 more for opening and improving streets. In 1835, the Legislature authorized a loan of $2,000, and the treasurer and street commissioners resigned rather than plunge the town into such a gulf.

One third of the city has been raised up an average of eight feet, giving good pitch to the 263 miles of sewerage. The water of the city is above all competition. It is received through two tunnels extending to a crib in the lake two miles from shore. The first tunnel is five feet two inches in diameter and two miles long, and can deliver 50,000,000 of gallons per day. The second tunnel is seven feet in diameter and six miles long, running four miles under the city, and can deliver 100,000,000 of gallons per day. This water is distributed through 410 miles of watermains.

The three grand engineering exploits of the city are: First, lifting the city up on jack-screws, whole squares at a time, without interrupting the business, thus giving us good drainage; second, running the tunnels under the lake, giving us the best water in the world; and third, the turning the current of the river in its own channel, delivering us from the old abominations, and making decency possible. They redound about equally to the credit of the engineering, to the energy of the people, and to the health of the city.

That which really constitutes the city, its indescribable spirit, its soul, the way it lights up in every feature in the hour of action, has not been touched. In meeting strangers, one is often surprised how some homely women marry so well. Their forms are bad, their gait uneven and awkward, their complexion is dull, their features are misshapen and mismatched, and when we see them there is no beauty that we should desire them. But when once they are aroused on some subject, they put on new proportions. They light up into great power. The real person comes out from its unseemly ambush, and captures us at will. They have power. They have ability to cause things to come to pass. We no longer wonder why they are in such high demand. So it is with our city.

There is no grand scenery except the two seas, one of water, the other of prairie. Nevertheless, there is a spirit about it, a push, a breadth, a power, that soon makes it a place never to be forsaken. One soon ceases to believe in impossibilities. Balaams are the only prophets that are disappointed. The bottom that has been on the point of falling out has been there so long that it has grown fast. It can not fall out. It has all the capital of the world itching to get inside the corporation.

The two great laws that govern the growth and size of cities are, first, the amount of territory for which they are the distributing and receiving points; second, the number of medium or moderate dealers that do this distributing. Monopolists build up themselves, not the cities. They neither eat, wear, nor live in proportion to their business. Both these laws help Chicago.

The tide of trade is eastward—not up or down the map, but across the map. The lake runs up a wingdam for 500 miles to gather in the business. Commerce can not ferry up there for seven months in the year and the facilities for seven months can do the work for twelve. Then the great region west of us is nearly all good, productive land. Dropping south into the trail of St. Louis, you fall into vast deserts and rocky districts, useful in holding the world together. St. Louis and Cincinnati, instead of rivaling and hurting Chicago, are her greatest sureties of dominion. They are far enough away to give sea-room—farther off than Paris is from London—and yet they are near enough to prevent the springing up of any other great city between them.

St. Louis will be helped by the opening of the Mississippi, but also hurt. That will put New Orleans on her feet, and with a railroad running over into Texas and so West, she will tap the streams that now crawl up the Texas and Missouri road. The current is East, not North, and a seaport at New Orleans can not permanently help St. Louis.

Chicago is in the field almost alone, to handle the wealth of one fourth of the territory of this great republic. This strip of seacoast divides its margins between Portland, Boston, New York, Philadelphia, Baltimore and Savannah or some other great port to be created for the South in the next decade. But Chicago has a dozen empires casting their treasures into her lap. On a bed of coal that can run all the machinery of the world for 500 centuries; in a garden feed the race by the thousand years; at the head of the lakes that give her a temperature as a summer resort equaled by no great city in the land; with a climate that insures the health of her citizens; surrounded by all the great deposits of natural wealth in mines and forests and herds, Chicago is the wonder of to-day, and will be *the city of the future.*

MASSACRE AT FORT DEARBORN.

During the war of 1812, Fort Dearborn became the theater of stirring events. The garrison consisted of fifty-four men under command of Captain Nathan Heald, assisted by Lieutenant Helm (son-in-law of Mrs. Kinzie) and Ensign Ronan. Dr. Voorhees was surgeon. The only residents at the post at that time were the wives of Captain Heald and Lieutenant Helm, and a few of the soldiers, Mr. Kinzie and his family, and a few Canadian *voyageurs*, with their wives and children. The soldiers and Mr. Kinzie were on most friendly terms with the Pottawatomies and Winnebagoes, the principal tribes around them, but they could not win them from their attachment to the British.

One evening in April, 1812, Mr. Kinzie sat playing on his violin and his children were dancing to the music, when Mrs. Kinzie came rushing into the house pale with terror, and exclaiming: "The Indians! the Indians!" "What? where?" eagerly inquired Mr. Kinzie. "Up at Lee's, killing and scalping," answered the frightened mother, who, when the alarm was given, was attending Mrs. Barnes (just confined) living not far off. Mr. Kinzie and his family crossed the river and took refuge in the fort, to which place Mrs. Barnes and her infant not a day old, were safely conveyed. The rest of the inhabitants took shelter in the fort. This alarm was caused by a scalping party of Winnebagoes, who hovered about the fort several days, when they disappeared, and for several weeks the inhabitants were undisturbed.

On the 7th of August, 1812, General Hull, at Detroit, sent orders to Captain Heald to evacuate Fort Dearborn, and to distribute all the United States property to the Indians in the neighborhood—a most insane order. The Pottawatomie chief who brought the dispatch had more wisdom than the commanding general. He advised Captain Heald not to make the distribution. Said he: "Leave the fort and stores as they are, and let the Indians make distribution for themselves; and while they are engaged in the business, the white people may escape to Fort Wayne."

Captain Heald held a council with the Indians on the afternoon of the 12th, in which his officers refused to join, for they had been informed that treachery was designed—that the Indians intended to murder the white people in the council, and then destroy those in the fort. Captain Heald, however, took the precaution to open a port-hole displaying a cannon pointing directly upon the council, and by that means saved his life.

Mr. Kinzie, who knew the Indians well, begged Captain Heald not to confide in their promises, nor distribute the arms and munitions among them, for it would only put power into their hands to destroy the whites. Acting upon this advice, Heald resolved to withhold the munitions of war; and on the night of the 13th after the distribution of the other property had been made, the powder, ball and liquors were thrown into the river, the muskets broken up and destroyed.

Black Partridge, a friendly chief, came to Captain Heald and said: "Linden birds have been singing in my ears to-day; be careful on the march you are going to take." On that night vigilant Indians had crept near the fort and discovered the destruction of their promised booty going on within. The next morning the powder was seen floating on the surface of the river. The savages were exasperated and made loud complaints and threats.

On the following day when preparations were making to leave the fort, and all the inmates were deeply impressed with a sense of impending danger, Capt. Wells, an uncle of Mrs. Heald, was discovered upon the Indian trail among the sand hills on the borders of the lake, not far distant, with a band of mounted Miamis, of whose tribe he was chief, having been adopted by the famous Miami warrior, Little Turtle.

When news of Hull's surrender reached Fort Wayne, he had started with this force to assist Heald in defending Fort Dearborn. He was too late. Every means for its defense had been destroyed the night before, and arrangements were made for leaving the fort on the morning of the 15th.

It was a warm, bright morning in the middle of August. Indications were positive that the savages intended to murder the white people; and when they moved out of the southern gate of the fort, the march was like a funeral procession. The band, feeling the solemnity of the occasion, struck up the Dead March in Saul.

Capt. Wells, who had blackened his face with gun-powder in token of his fate, took the lead with his band of Miamis, followed by Captain Heald with his wife by his side on horseback. Mr. Kinzie hoped by his personal influence to avert the impending blow, and therefore accompanied them, leaving his family in a boat in charge of a friendly Indian, to be taken to his trading station at the site of Niles, Michigan, in the event of his death.

The procession moved slowly along the lake shore till they reached the sand hills between the prairie and the beach, when the Pottawatomie escort, under the leadership of Blackbird, filed to the right, placing those hills between them and the white people. Wells, with his Miamis, had kept in the advance. They suddenly came rushing back, Wells exclaiming, "They are about to attack us; form instantly." These words were quickly followed by a storm of bullets which came whistling over the little hills which the treacherous savages had made the covert for their murderous attack. The white troops charged upon the Indians, drove them back to the prairie, and then the battle was waged between fifty-four soldiers, twelve civilians and three or four women (the cowardly Miamis having fled at the outset) against five hundred Indian warriors. The white people, hopeless, resolved to sell their lives as dearly as possible. Ensign Ronan wielded his weapon vigorously, even after falling upon his knees weak from the loss of blood. Capt. Wells, who was by the side of his niece, Mrs. Heald, when the conflict began, behaved with the greatest coolness and courage. He said to her, "We have not the slightest chance for life. We must part to meet no more in this world. God bless you." And then he dashed forward. Seeing a young warrior, painted like a demon, climb into a wagon in which were twelve children, and tomahawk them all, he cried out, unmindful of his personal danger, "If that is your game, butchering women and children, I will kill too." He spurred his horse towards the Indian camp, where they had left their squaws and papooses, hotly pursued by swift-footed young warriors, who sent bullets whistling after him. One of these killed his horse and wounded him severely in the leg. With a yell the young braves rushed to make him their prisoner and reserve him for torture. He resolved not to be made a captive, and by the use of the most provoking epithets tried to induce them to kill him instantly. He called a fiery young chief a *squaw*, when the enraged warrior killed Wells instantly with his tomahawk, jumped upon his body, cut out his heart, and ate a portion of the warm morsel with savage delight!

In this fearful combat women bore a

conspicuous part. Mrs. Heald was an excellent equestrian and an expert in the use of the rifle. She fought the savages bravely, receiving several severe wounds. Though faint from the loss of blood, she managed to keep her saddle. A savage raised his tomahawk to kill her, when she looked him full in the face, and with a sweet smile and in a gentle voice said, in his own language, "Surely you will not kill a squaw!" The arm of the savage fell, and the life of the heroic woman was saved.

Mrs. Helm, the step-daughter of Mr. Kinzie, had an encounter with a stout Indian, who attempted to tomahawk her. Springing to one side, she received the glancing blow on her shoulder, and at the same instant seized the savage round the neck with her arms and endeavored to get hold of his scalping knife, which hung in a sheath at his breast. While she was thus struggling she was dragged from her antagonist by another powerful Indian, who bore her, in spite of her struggles, to the margin of the lake and plunged her in. To her astonishment she was held by him so that she would not drown, and she soon perceived that she was in the hands of the friendly Black Partridge, who had saved her life.

The wife of Sergeant Holt, a large and powerful woman, behaved as bravely as an Amazon. She rode a fine, high-spirited horse, which the Indians coveted, and several of them attacked her with the butts of their guns, for the purpose of dismounting her; but she used the sword which she had snatched from her disabled husband so skillfully that she foiled them; and, suddenly wheeling her horse, she dashed over the prairie, followed by the savages shouting, "The brave woman! the brave woman! Don't hurt her!" They finally overtook her, and while she was fighting them in front, a powerful savage came up behind her, seized her by the neck and dragged her to the ground. Horse and woman were made captive. Mrs. Holt was a long time a captive among the Indians, but was afterward ransomed.

In this sharp conflict two thirds of the white people were slain and wounded, and all their horses, baggage and provision were lost. Only twenty-eight straggling men now remained to fight five hundred Indians rendered furious by the sight of blood. They succeeded in breaking through the ranks of the murderers and gaining a slight eminence on the prairie near the Oak Woods. The Indians did not pursue, but gathered on their flanks, while the chiefs held a consultation on the sand-hills, and showed signs of willingness to parley. It would have been madness on the part of the whites to renew the fight; and so Capt. Heald went forward and met Blackbird on the open prairie, where terms of surrender were agreed upon. It was arranged that the white people should give up their arms to Blackbird, and that the survivors should become prisoners of war, to be exchanged for ransoms as soon as practicable. With this understanding captives and captors started for the Indian camp near the fort, to which Mrs. Helm had been taken bleeding and suffering by Black Partridge, and had met her step-father and learned that her husband was safe.

A new scene of horror was now opened at the Indian camp. The wounded, not being included in the surrender, as it was interpreted by the Indians, and the British general, Proctor, having offered a liberal bounty for American scalps, delivered at Malden, nearly all the wounded men were killed and scalped, and price of the trophies was afterward paid by the British government.

This celebrated Indian chief, Shabbona, deserves more than a passing notice. Although he was not so conspicuous as Tecumseh or Black Hawk, yet in point of merit he was superior to either of them.

Shabbona was born at an Indian village on the Kankakee River, now in Will County about the year 1775. While young he was made chief of the band, and went to Shabbona Grove, now De Kalb County, where they were found in the early settlement of the county.

In the war of 1812, Shabbona, with his warriors, joined Tecumseh, was aid to that great chief, and stood by his side when he fell at the battle of the Thames. At the time of the Winnebago war, in 1827, he visited almost every village among the Pottawatomies, and by his persuasive arguments prevented them from taking part in the war. By request of the citizens of Chicago, Shabbona, accompanied by Billy Caldwell (Sauganash), visited Big Foot's village at Geneva Lake, in order to pacify the warriors, as fears were entertained that they were about to raise the tomahawk against the whites. Here Shabbona was taken prisoner by Big Foot, and his life threatened, but on the following day was set at liberty. From that time the Indians (through reproach) styled him "the white man's friend," and many times his life was endangered.

Before the Black Hawk war, Shabbona met in council at two different times, and by his influence prevented his people from taking part with the Sacs and Foxes. After the death of Black Partridge and Senachwine, no chief among the Pottawatomies exerted so much influence as Shabbona. Black Hawk, aware of this influence, visited him at two different times, in order to enlist him in his cause, but was unsuccessful. While Black Hawk was a prisoner at Jefferson Barracks, he said, had it not been for Shabbona the whole Pottawatomie nation would have joined his standard, and he could have continued the war for years.

To Shabbona many of the early settlers of Illinois owe the preservation of their lives, for it is a well-known fact, had he not notified the people of their danger, a large portion of them would have fallen victims to the tomahawk of savages. By saving the lives of whites he endangered his own, for the Sacs and Foxes threatened to kill him, and made two attempts to execute their threats. They killed Pypeogee, his son, and Pyps, his nephew, and hunted him down as though he was a wild beast.

Shabbona had a reservation of two sections of land at his Grove, but by leaving it and going West for a short time, the Government declared the reservation forfeited, and sold it the same as other vacant land. On Shabbona's return, and finding his possessions gone, he was very sad and broken down in spirit, and left the Grove forever. The citizens of Ottawa raised money and bought him a tract of land on the Illinois River, above Seneca, in Grundy County, on which they built a house, and supplied him with means to live on. He lived here until his death, which occurred on the 17th of July, 1859, in the eighty-fourth year of his age, and was buried with great pomp in the cemetery at Morris. His squaw, Pokanoka, was drowned in Mazon Creek, Grundy County, on the 30th of November, 1864, and was buried by his side.

In 1861 subscriptions were taken up in many of the river towns, to erect a monument over the remains of Shabbona, but the war breaking out, the enterprise was abandoned. Only a plain marble slab marks the resting-place of this friend of the white man.

PART II.

HISTORY OF JEFFERSON COUNTY.

PART II.

HISTORY OF JEFFERSON COUNTY.

CHAPTER I.*

INTRODUCTORY—GEOLOGY AND ITS PRACTICAL VALUE—HOW THOROUGHLY TO EDUCATE THE FARMERS—WHY THEY SHOULD UNDERSTAND THE GEOLOGICAL FORMATIONS OF THE LAND THEY TILL—AGE OF THE EARTH ACCORDING TO THE RESEARCH OF THE GEOLOGISTS—LOCAL GEOLOGY—CONFIGURATION— SOILS AND TIMBER—MINERALS AND MINERAL SPRINGS—BUILDING MATERIALS, ETC.

"The little fields made green
By husbandry of many thrifty years."

THERE is no question of such deep interest as the geological history of that particular portion of the country in which we make our homes. The people of Southern Illinois are an agricultural people in their pursuits. Their first care is the soil and climate, and it is in them they may find an almost inexhaustible fund of knowledge, that will ever put money in their coffers. All mankind are deeply interested in the soil. From it comes all life, all beauty, pleasure, wealth and enjoyment. Of itself, it may not be a beautiful thing, but from it comes the fragrant flower, the golden fields, the sweet blush of the maiden's cheek, the flash of the lustrous eye, that is more powerful to subdue the heart of obdurate man than an army with banners. From it spring the great, rich cities, whose towers, and temples, and minarets kiss the early morning sun, and whose ships, with their precious cargoes, fleck every sea. In short, it is the nourishing mother whence comes our high civilization—the wealth of nations, the joys and exalted pleasures of life.

The corner-stone upon which all life rests is the farmer, who tickles the earth, and it laughs with the rich harvests that so bountifully bless mankind. Who, then, should be so versed in the knowledge of the soil as the farmer? What other information can be so valuable to him as the mastery of the science of geology, that much of it, at least, as applies to the portion of the earth where he has cast his fortunes and cultivates the soil? We talk of educating the farmer, and ordinarily this means to send the boys to college, to acquire what is termed a classical education, and they come back, perhaps, as graduates, as incapable of telling the geological story of their father's farm as of describing the color and shape of last year's clouds. How much more of practical value it would have been to the young man had he never looked into the classics, and instead thereof

---

* By W. H. Perrin.

had taken a few practical lessons in the local geology that would have told him the story of the soil around him, and enabled him to comprehend how it was formed, its different qualities and from whence it came and its constituent elements. The farmer grows to be an old man, and he will tell you he has learned to be a good farmer only by a long life of laborious experiments; and if you should tell him that these experiments had made him a scientific farmer, he would look with a good deal of contempt upon your supposed effort to poke ridicule at him. He has taught himself to regard the word "science" as the property only of bookworms and cranks. He does not realize that every step in farming is a purely scientific operation, because science is made by experiments and investigations. An old farmer may examine a soil and tell you that it is adapted to wheat or corn, that it is warm, or cold and heavy, or a few other facts that this long experience has taught him, and to that extent he is a scientific farmer. He will tell you that his knowledge has cost him much labor, and many sore disappointments. Suppose that in his youth a well-digested chapter on the geological history, that would have told him in the simplest terms, all about the land he was to cultivate, how invaluable the lesson would have been, and how much in money value it would have proved to him. In other words, if you could give your boys a practical education, made up of a few lessons pertaining to those subjects that immediately concern their lives, how invaluable such an education might be, and how many men would thus be saved the pangs and penalties of ill-directed lives.

The parents often spend much money in the education of their children, and from this they build great hopes upon their future that are often blasted, not through the fault, always, of the child, but through the error of the parent in not being able to know in what real, practical education consists. If the schools of the country, for instance, could devote one of the school months in each year to rambling over the hills and the fields, and gathering practical lessons in the geology and botany of the section of country in which the children were born and reared, how incomparably more valuable and useful the time thus spent would be to them in after life, than would the present mode of shutting out the sunshine of life, and spending both life and vitality in studying metaphysical mathematics, or the most of the other text-books, that impart nothing that is worth the carrying home to the child's stock of knowledge. At all events, the chapter in the county's history, or in the history of any community or country, that tells its geological formation, is of first importance to all its people, and if properly prepared it will become a source of great interest to all, and do much to disseminate a better education among the people, and thus be a perpetual blessing to the community.

The permanent effects of the soil on the people are as strong and certain as they are upon the vegetation that springs from it. It is a maxim in geology that the soil and its underlying rocks forecast unerringly to the trained eye the character of the people, the number and the quality of the civilization of those who will, in the coming time, occupy it. Indeed, so close are the relations of the geology and the people that this law is plain and fixed, that a new country may have its outlines of history written when first looked upon; and it is not, as so many suppose, one of those deep, abstruse subjects that are to be given over solely to a few great investigators and thinkers, and to the masses must forever remain a sealed book. Our youths may learn the important outlines of the geology of their country with no more difficulty than they meet in mastering the multiplication table or the simple rule of three. And we make no question that a youth need not possess one-half of the mental activity and shrewdness in making a fair geologist of himself that he would find was required of him to become a skillful manipulator of cards or a successful jockey.

On the geological structure of a country depend the pursuits of its inhabitants, and the genius of its civilization. Agriculture is the outgrowth of a fertile soil; mining results from mineral resources, and from navigable rivers spring navies and commerce. Every great branch of industry requires, for its successful devolopment, the cultivation of kindred arts and sciences. Phases of life and modes of thought are thus induced, which give to different communities and States characters as various as the diverse rocks that underlie them. In like manner it may be shown that their moral and intellectual qualities depend on material conditions. Where the soil and subjacent rocks are profuse in the bestowal of wealth, man is indolent and effeminate; where effort is required to live, he becomes enlightened and virtuous. A perpetually mild climate and bread growing upon the trees will produce only ignorant savages. The heaviest misfortune that has so long environed poor, persecuted Ireland has been her ability to produce the potato, and thus subsist wife and children upon a small patch of ground. Statistics tell us that the number of marriages are regulated by the price of corn, and the true philosopher has discovered that the invention of gunpowder did more to civilize the world than any one thing in its history.

Geology traces the history of the earth back through successive stages of development to its rudimental condition in a state of fusion. The sun, and the planetary system that revolves around it, were originally a common mass, that became separated in a gaseous state, and the loss of heat in a planet reduced it to an elastic state, and thus it commenced to write its own history, and place its records upon these imperishable books, where the geologist may go and read the strange, eventful story. The earth was a wheeling ball of fire, and the cooling eventually formed the exterior crust, and in the slow process of time prepared the way for the animal and vegetable life it now contains. In its center, the fierce flames still rage with undiminished energy. Volcanoes are outlets for these deep-seated fires, where are generated those tremendous forces, an illustration of which is given in the eruptions of Vesuvius, which has thrown a jet of lava, resembling a column of flame, 10,000 feet high. The amount of lava ejected at a single eruption from one of the volcanoes of Iceland has been estimated at 40,000,000,000 tons, a quantity sufficient to cover a large city with a mountain as high as the tallest Alps. Our world is yet constantly congealing, just as the process has been constantly going on for billions of years, and yet the rocky crust that rests upon this internal fire is estimated to be only between thirty and forty miles in thickness. In the silent depths of the stratified rocks are the former creation of plants and animals, which lived and died during the slow, dragging centuries of their formation. These fossil remains are fragments of history, which enable the geologist to extend his researches far back into the realms of the past, and not only determine their former modes of life, but study the contemporaneous history of their rocky beds, and group them into systems. And such has been the profusion of life, that the great limestone formations of the globe consist mostly of animal remains, cemented by the infusion of animal matter. A large part of the soil spread over the earth's surface has been elaborated in animal organisms. First, as nourishment, it enters into the structure of plants, and forms vegetable tissue; passing thence, as food, into the animal, it becomes endowed with life, and when death occurs it returns into the soil and imparts to it additional elements of fertility.

The realization of great defects in the education of our young farmers and of their losses and disappointments, and even disasters, in the pursuit of their occupation of tilling the earth, that come of their neglect in early education and training, prompts us to present a subject that many of our readers will consider dry and uninteresting. The views of the writer are not visionary, or mere theories drawn from books. Born and reared on a farm, with nearly a quarter of a century's experience in tilling the soil, qualifies him to tell, with as much facility as Horace Greeley, what "he knows about farming." The most inportant subject to all mankind to-day is how to get for the young people the best education; how to fit our youths for the life struggle before them. Agassiz was once appealed to by some New England horse-breeders in regard to developing horses, and told them it was not a question of equestrianism, but one of *rocks*. To most men the reply would have been almost meaningless, yet it was full of wisdom. It signified that certain rock formations that underlie the soil would insure a certain growth of grasses and water, and the secret of the perfect horse lay here.

That the reader may gather here lessons in the knowledge of the rocks that are spread out over the earth, we give in their order the different groups and systems in the simplest form we can present them, as gathered from the geologists. We only deem it necessary to explain that all rocks are either igneous or stratified; the former meaning melted by fire, and the latter, sediment deposited in water. Their order, commencing with the lowest stratified rocks and ascending, are as follows:

The Laurentian system is the lowest and oldest of the stratified rocks. From the effects of great heat, it has assumed, to some extent, the character of the igneous rocks below, but still retains its original lines of stratification. A principal effect of the great heat to which its rocks were exposed is crystallization. The Laurentian system was formerly believed to be destitute of organic remains, but recent investigations have led to the discovery of animals, so low in the scale of organization as to be regarded as the first appearance of sentient existence. This discovery, as it extends the origin of life backward through 30,000 feet of strata, may be regarded as one of the most important advances made in American geology.

The Huronian system, like the one that precedes it, and on which it rests, is highly crystalline. Although fossils have not been found in it, yet from its position, the inference is they once existed, and if they do not now, the great transforming power of heat has caused their obliteration. This, and the subjacent system, extend from Labrador southwesterly to the great lakes, and thence northwesterly toward the Arctic Ocean. They derive their names from the St. Lawrence and Lake Huron, on the banks of which are found their principal outcrops. Their emergence from the ocean was the birth of the North American Continent. One face of the uplift looked toward the Atlantic and the other toward the Pacific, thus prefiguring the future shores of this great divison of the globe of which they are the germ.

The Silurian age, compared with the more stable formations of subsequent times, was one of commotion, in which fire and water played a conspicuous part. Earthquakes and volcanoes furrowed the yielding crust with ridges, and threw up islands whose craggy summits, here and there, stood like sentinels above the murky deep which dashed against their shores. The present diversities of climate did not exist, as the temperature was mostly due to the escape of internal heat, which was the same over every part of the surface. As the radiation of heat, in future ages, declined, the sun became the controlling power, and zones of climate appeared as the result of solar domination. Uniform thermal conditions imparted a corresponding character to vegetable and animal life, and one universal fauna and flora extended from the equator to the poles. During the Silurian age, North America, like its inhabitants, was mostly submarine, as proved by wave-lines on the emerging lands.

The Devonian age is distinguished for the introduction of vertebrates, or the fourth sub-kingdom of animal life, and the beginning of terrestrial vegetation. The latter appeared in two classes, the highest of the flowerless and the lowest of the flowering plants. The Lepidodendron, a noted instance of the former, was a majestic, upland forest tree, which, during the coal period, grew to a height of eighty feet, and had a base of more than three feet in diameter. Its description is quite poetical, and is as follows: Beautiful spiral flutings, coiling in opposite directions and crossing each other at fixed angles, carved the trunks and branches into rhomboidal eminences, each of which was scarred with the mark of a falling leaf. At an altitude of sixty feet, it sent off arms, each separating into branchlets, covered with a needle-like foliage destitute of flowers. It grew, not by internal or external accretions, as plants of the present day, but, like the building of a monument, by additions to the top of its trunk. Mosses, rushes and other diminutive flowerless plants are now the only representatives of this cryptogamic vegetation, which so largely predominated in the early botany of the globe. Floral beauty and fragrance were not characteristic of the old Devonian woods. No bird existed to enliven their silent groves with song; no serpent to hiss in the fenny brakes, nor beast to pursue, with hideous yells, its panting prey.

The vertebrates consisted of fishes, of which the Ganoids and Placoids were the principal groups. The former were the forerunners of the reptile, which in many respects they closely resemble. They embraced a large number of species, many of which grew to a gigantic size; but, with the exception of the gar and sturgeon, they have no living representative. The Placoids, structurally formed for advancement, still remain among the highest types of the present seas. The shark, a noted instance, judging from its fossil remains, must have attained 100 feet in length. Both groups lived in the sea, and if any fresh water animals existed, their remains have either perished or not been found. So numerous were the inhabitants of the ocean, that the Devonian has been styled the age of fishes. In their anatomical structure was foreshadowed the organization of man; reptiles, birds and mammals being the intermediate gradations.

The Carboniferous age opened with the deposition of widely extended marine formations. Added to the strata previously deposited, the entire thickness in the region of the Alleghanies, now partially elevated, amounted to seven miles. The most prominent feature of the Carboniferous age was the formation of coal. Being carbonized vegetable tissue, the material furnished for this purpose was the vast forest accumulation peculiar to the period. The coal-fields of Europe are estimated at 18,000 square miles, those of the United States at 150,000. In Illinois, three-fourths of the surface are underlaid by beds of coal, and the State, consequently, has a greater area than any other member of the Union. The entire carboniferous system, including the coal beds and the intervening strata, in Southern Illinois, is 27,000 feet in thickness and in the northern part only 500 feet.

The Reptilian age came next, and is distinguished for changes in the continental borders, which generally ran within their present limits.

The Mammalian age witnessed the increase of the mass of the earth above the ocean's level threefold, and next in regular succession was the age of Man, which commenced with the present geological conditions. These are the order of the earth's formation, simply given, to the time of the coming of man. Though the absolute time of his coming cannot be determined, he was doubtless an inhabitant of the earth many thousands of years before he was sufficiently intelligent to preserve the records of his own history.

The present age still retains, in a diminished degree of activity, the geological action we have briefly sketched. The oscillations of the earth's crust are still going on, perhaps as they ever have. As an evidence of this, it is a well-known fact that the coast of Greenland, on the western side, for a distance of 600 miles, has been slowly sinking for the past four hundred years. Thus constantly have the bottoms of the oceans been lifted above the waters and the mountains sunk and became the beds of the sea. In the science of geology, this solid old earth and its fixed and eternal mountains are as unstable as the floating waves of the water.

Jefferson County is situated southeast of the intersection of the Ohio & Mississippi and the Illinois Central Railroads, and is bounded on the north by Marion County, on the east by Wayne and Hamilton, on the south by Franklin, on the west by Perry and Washington, and has an area of 576 square miles. It is estimated that at least four-fifths of this territory is timbered land, while only about one-fifth is prairie. The prairies invariably occupy the more or less elevated lands between the water-courses, and have generally a considerable depth of quaternary deposits, sometimes underlaid with shales. It is seldom that rocks are found in the prairies, even by digging to some depth, though at some places timbered hills occur in the prairie, which are underlaid with solid rocky strata, and rise above the level of the prairie either within its bounds or at its edge. Knob Prairie has its name from such a hill or knob. The timbered portion of the county is partly flat, but most of it is undulating or broken, in consequence of the numerous water-courses which traverse the county in every direction. It has some post-oak flats, also some wet flats at the edge of prairies, in which water-oak predominates, but more oak barrens, with a growth of black oak, white oak, post oak, hickory, etc. The timber in the creek bottoms is generally quite heavy, and consists of swamp white oak, water oak, sugar maple, sycamore, black walnut, white walnut, etc. In the extreme southeast part of the county, however, are occasional trees of more southern affinity, such as the sweet gum.

The county is well supplied with running water, principally by the branches of Big Muddy River, which head near the north line of the county and traverse it in a southerly direction, with many smaller creeks which empty into them, both from the west and east. The main branch of Big Muddy River heads near the northwest corner of the county, some miles southeast of Centralia, while some other ravines near by run westward toward Crooked Creek and the Kaskaskia River. The Little Muddy River passes through the southwest corner of the county. In the northeast part of the county is Horse Creek, a tributary of the Little Wabash River, and all the branches on the east line of the county take their course eastward, toward the Little Wabash.

The geological formation of Jefferson County, like those of all the adjoining counties, are members of the coal formation. All over the county, with the exception of a limited area in the southwest corner, is found the same strata traced all over the county of Marion—a subdivision of the upper coal measures, including a coal seam which varies from six to twenty-four inches in thickness. At a greater depth may be found the Du Quoin coal bed, and the sandstones overlying this coal and its associated limestones, have been traced over a large area east of the outcrop of the coal, and attain a considerable but variable thickness, sometimes amounting to more than two hundred feet, and appear to pass across the extreme southeast corner of this county.*

The Shoal Creek limestone has no great thickness. It varies between seven and fifteen feet; but being the only prominent limestone between two heavy bodies of sandstone, it forms a well marked horizon, and can be readily traced over a long distance. In Perry County, only a quarter of a mile from the Jefferson County line, on Little Muddy River, just before it enters the latter county, is an outcrop of evidently the same limestone. Here five feet of it are exposed, covered with soil. It rests on one foot of shales and three feet of black, laminated slates, which reach to the water level. Coal, probably fifteen inches thick, has been dug from the bed of the creek. From this point, the Shoal Creek limestone must pass into Jefferson County; but the county is mostly covered with heavy quaternary deposits, and is thinly settled, so that artificial deposits are wanting. Higher up these creeks and in the barrens, sandstones crop out at a few points. The rest of the county is occupied by the higher sandstone formation, the same which covers the whole of Marion County. Almost everywhere single layers of the sandstone can be found of sufficient hardness for building purposes. This formation being part of the coal measure system, it may be expected to contain some stone coal, but it is not rich in this mineral. It is found at numerous points, however, throughout Jefferson and Marion Counties, and it undoubtedly extends much further. It is of considerable local importance, being used extensively in this district, and has been opened at numerous points. At some places, this coal is quite pure and free from sulphur, but at others it contains much sulphuret of iron.

The slaty, fossiliferous limestone, which is a certain indication of the coal, has been noticed north of the "Limestone Branch." In Jordan's Prairie, at Rome, the coal is struck in every well, only ten feet below the surface, and is probably ten inches thick. At the edge of the prairie southeast from Rome, the coal has been mined to some extent, especially in the southwest part of Section 18. At that point the bed is fourteen inches thick, of which at least ten is good coal. The coal has likewise been found near the middle of the north line of the northeast

---

* Most of the local geology, and the facts pertaining to it, are compiled from the official survey of the State.

quarter of Section 24 and farther east, and at other points in this portion of the county. In all places it was from ten to twelve inches thick, and accompanied with shales, the calcareous slate and sandstone.

The official survey, and a description of all the noteworthy discoveries in the county leads to the conclusion that all the coal which is near the surface in the county, with the exception of that in the southwest corner, belongs to one stratum, which, is in some places divided in two by a parting of shale, and which is the same that extends all over the adjoining county of Marion. The stratum, at a few points, exceeds one and a half feet in thickness of good coal, and is frequently thinner. Where it is thicker, it generally contains impure portions. It is at many points of a very good quality, and, as the country is broken, it can be profitably worked in numerous localities by stripping along the outcropping edges. It is, therefore, well adapted to supply the local demand for coal throughout the county at a very moderate cost. The coal and accompanying strata are neither horizontal nor dipping in one direction, but they form waves which follow more or less the surface configuration of the country. A question arises whether there is a lower coal bed, of greater thickness, at an available depth. The next lower coal seam is that underneath the Shoal Creek limestone; but this coal, where it is known on Little Muddy River, near the west line of the county, is too thin to pay the expenses of deep mining. This seam may become of some local importance in the southwest corner of the county, where it can be worked by stripping along its outcrop on a limited area, but further on it is covered by a considerable thickness of the higher strata. The only remaining coal bed of good promise is, then, the one worked in the coal shaft at Tamaroa, on the Illinois Central Railroad, at a depth of about two hundred feet below the surface, which is the Du Quoin coal. Tamaroa is a little over four miles west of the southwest corner of the county, and it would seem, therefore, as if this coal bed, in the nearest part of the county, could not be much, if any, deeper. From the same formations, however, in the adjoining counties, it is believed that this coal dips rapidly downward from Tamaroa, and in most parts of Jefferson County lies at a considerable depth. It would probably be found at the least depth in the southwest corner of the county, but even there it would hardly be reached under several hundred feet.

The coal near the surface in this county is the same as the vein near the surface at Central City. If a great demand for coal should arise, this lower coal bed might supply it. Its depth, at least, would not be greater than that of many coal pits in other countries, and the only question would be as to its thickness, which at Tamaroa amounts to five feet eight inches.

The shales accompanying the coal bed contain generally much kidney-iron ore—an impure carbonate of iron in sub-globular concretions, or in flat bodies or sheets. The aggregate quantity of this ore is large, but it is probably not concentrated at any one point in sufficient quantity and of sufficient purity to be, for the present, of practical value for the production of iron. Some pieces of galena have been found scattered over the country, such as occur in the drift in many other counties of the State. The water in some parts of the county is impregnated with salts, originating principally from the decomposition of the sulphate of iron contained in the coal or shales, and from the action of the sulphate of iron thus produced upon the strata which it percolates. Thus, other and more complex combinations of salts are formed, such as magnesia salts, alums, etc. As the coal seam is near the surface in many neighborhoods, wells are frequently sunk down to it or the accompanying strata, and this well-water contains these salts in variable quantities, which are often sufficiently large to prevent the use of the water for household purposes. Thus it is at Mount Vernon, at Rome, in some parts of Horse Prairie, especially at the Stone-Coal branch, and at other places.

The strongest mineral water, probably, in the county is the springs of Dr. William Duff Green, in the southeastern part of the city of Mount Vernon. There are several of these springs. They issue from the side of a shallow ravine, at the same level, a few feet from each other, from a highly ferruginous stratum, which is apparently the slaty shale, with the iron ore above the coal seam here changed beyond recognition by the long-continued influence of the mineral water. These springs all contain a considerable quantity of iron combined with other salts. A remarkable fact is that the water of all of them is not quite the same. The difference consists, however, principally in the relative quantity of the salts. The springs evidently emanate from the same stratum, but, passing through different portions of the rock, the water may come in contact with slightly different mineral substances.

The temperature of the running springs is the mean temperature of the earth in this latitude, or, what is the same, that of a deep, cool cellar; but one spring, which is by Dr. Green called "Tepid Spring," differs from the others in various respects. It is warmer than the others, at least in summer, because, not running as freely as they do, its water is stationary; and assumes the temperature of the air. It does not freeze in winter, which is, apparently, not a consequence of intrinsic heat, but of its saline character. Its water has a milky hue, because the iron salts which it contains begin to decompose in the orifice of the spring, where they are long exposed to the oxidizing influence of the air, without being discharged. Such is the simple explanation, based on the teaching of science, of some facts which have been regarded as wonderful mysteries. Nature's works seem mysterious, but all conform to definite laws, which, when the principles are once understood, appear clear and plain as daylight. A small quantity of gas is devolved in the springs, either through the action of sulphates upon carbonates in the strata or perhaps altogether by a vegetation of a low order, which rapidly grows and coats the orifice of the springs, and, under the direct action of the sun's rays, exhales oxygen. Although originally similar, the waters of these different springs now, very probably, have a different medicinal effect upon the system.

Building material is found in the county in large quantities. Sandstone, for foundations, the walling of wells and for all ordinary and heavy masonry, can be readily obtained in nearly all parts of the county. Good quarries are already known in large numbers, and with little labor many new ones might be opened in convenient locations, as sandstones form the principal substrata of the county. The limestone is generally impure, siliceous or argillaceous. At some points it can be burnt and used for making mortar, and if the demand were sufficient, better quarries might be opened, and a better article might be obtained. The fossiliferous, slaty limestone, or calcareous slate, is undoubtedly a superior fertilizer, but has not yet been used as such. Its wide distribution over the county will render it valuable in future times. Brick may be manufactured wherever needed; and of fine timber of various kinds—white oak, black oak, post oak, black walnut, etc.—there is an excellent supply.

The agricultural excellence of the county, which is fully up to the standard of any of the counties in this portion of the State, will be treated of further along in this work.

CHAPTER II.*

THE PRE-HISTORIC RACES—MOUND-BUILDERS—THEIR OCCUPATION OF THE COUNTRY—RELICS LEFT BY THEM—THE INDIANS—SPECULATIONS AS TO THEIR ORIGIN—ULTIMATE EXTINCTION OF THE RACE—SOMETHING OF THE TRIBES OF SOUTHERN ILLINOIS—WHAT BECAME OF THEM—LOCAL TRADITIONS AND INCIDENTS—THE BLACK HAWK WAR, ETC., ETC.

"Wrapped in clouds and darkness, and defying historic scrutiny."

THROUGHOUT the Ohio and Mississippi Valleys, as well as many portions of North America, and extending into South America, are found the remains of a former race of inhabitants, of whose origin and history we have no record, and who are only known to us by the relics that are found in the tumuli which they have left. The Mound-Builders were a numerous people, entirely distinct from the North American Indians, and they lived so long before the latter that they are not known to them by tradition. They were evidently industrious and domestic in their habits, and the finding of large sea shells in the Illinois mounds, which must have been brought from the Gulf of Mexico, if not from more distant shores, proves that they had communication and trade with other tribes. Perhaps the most interesting fact connected with this ancient people is that they had a written language. This is proved by some inscribed tablets that have been discovered in the mounds, the most important of which belong to the Davenport Academy of Sciences. These tablets have attracted great attention from archæologists, and it is thought they will some time prove of great value as records of the people who wrote them. It is still uncertain whether the language was generally understood by the Mound-Builders, or whether it was confined to a few persons of high rank. In the mound where two of these tablets were discovered, the bones of a child were found, partially preserved by contact with a large number of copper beads, and as copper was a rare and precious metal with them, it would seem that the mound in question was used for burial of persons of high rank. The inscriptions have not been deciphered, for no key to them has yet been found; we are totally ignorant of the derivation of the language, or its affinities with other written languages.

The Mound-Builders lived while the mammoth and mastodon were upon the earth, as is clearly proved by the carvings upon some of their elaborate stone pipes. From the size and other peculiarities of the pipes, it is inferred that smoking was not habitual with them, but that it was reserved as a sort of ceremonial observance. Our knowledge of the habits and customs of the Mound-Builders

* By W. H. Perrin.

is very incomplete, but it is sufficient to show that at least a part of this country was once inhabited by a people who have passed away without leaving so much as a tradition of their existence, and who are only known to us through the silent relics which have been interred for centuries. A people utterly forgotten, a civilization totally lost! Oblivion has drawn her impenetrable veil over their history. No printed page intelligible to us, or sculptured monument, inform us who they were, whence they came or whither they went. In vain has science sought to penetrate the gloom and solve the problem locked in the breast of the voiceless past, but every theory advanced, every reason assigned ends where it began, in speculation.

"Ye moldering relics of departed years,
  Your names have perished; not a trace remains,
  Save where the grass-grown mound its summit rears
  From the green bosom of your native plains.
  Say, do your spirits wear oblivion's chains?
  Did death forever quench your hopes and fears?"

There are no traces of the Mound-Builders to be found in Jefferson County. From the relics they have left of their existence, it seems they kept near the water, as the most extensive mounds and earthworks are found in the vicinity of the lakes of the North and along our great rivers. Two of the largest mounds in the United States are located in Illinois and West Virginia—the great mound in the American Bottom between Alton and East St. Louis, denominated the "Monarch of all similar structures in the United States," and that located near the junction of Grave Creek with the Ohio River in West Virginia. Along the Illinois and Wabash Rivers, many of these mounds may still be seen, though hundreds of the smaller ones have been leveled with the earth by the plowshare. At Palestine and Hutsonville, Ill., and at Merom, Ind., on the Wabash River, are extensive groups. The Hutsonville group contains fifty-nine mounds, and vary in size from eighteen to fifty feet in diameter at the base: They were scientifically examined a few years ago by Prof. Putnam, of Boston, who made an extended report of them to the Boston Historical Society.

The Indians.—Of the Red Indians, but little is known of them prior to the discovery of the country by the Europeans. They were found here, but how long they had been in posssssion historians have no definite means of knowing. Their origin is a question that has long interested archæologists, and is one of the most difficult they have been called on to answer. Many theories upon the subject are entertained, but all, alike, are more or less unsatisfactory. It is believed by some that they were an original race, indigenous to the Western Hemisphere. A more common supposition, however, is that they are a derivative race, and sprang from one or more of the ancient peoples of Asia. In the absence of all authentic history, and even when tradition is wanting, any attempt to point the particular theater of their origin must prove unsuccessful. For centuries they have lived without progress, while the Caucasian variety of the race, under the transforming power of art, science and improved systems of civil polity, have made the most rapid advancement.

The advent of the whites upon the shores of the western continent engendered in the red man's bosom a spark of jealousy, which, by the impolitic course of the former, was soon fanned into a blaze, and a contest was thereby inaugurated that sooner or later must end in the utter extermination of the latter. But the struggle was long and bitter. Many a campaign was planned by warriors worthy and fit to command armies, for the destruction of the pale-faced invaders.

When King Philip struck the blow which he hoped would forever crush the growing power of the white men, both sides recognized the supreme importance of the contest, and the courage and resources of the New England colonists were taxed to the utmost to avoid a defeat which meant destruction final and complete. When Tecumseh organized the tribes of the West for a last and desperate effort to hold their own against the advancing tide of civilization, it was a duel to the death, and the conquerors were forced to pay dearly for the victory which to them was salvation. When the Creeks challenged the people of the South to mortal combat, it required the genius of a Jackson and soldiers worthy of such a chief to avert an overwhelming calamity, and the laurels gathered by the heroes of Talledega, Emuckfau, and Tohopeka lost little of their luster when with them were twined the laurels of Chalmette. But since the decisive battle of Tohopeka, March 27, 1814, there has been no Indian war of any considerable magnitude, none certainly which threatened the supremacy of the whites upon the continent, or even seriously jeopardized the safety of the States or Territories where they occurred. The Black Hawk war, about the last organized effort, required but a few weeks service of raw militia to quell. Since then, campaigns have dwindled into mere raids, battles into mere skirmishes, and the massacre of Dade's command in Florida and Custer's in Montana were properly regarded as accidents of no permanent importance. A dozen such, melancholy as they might be, would not, in the least, alarm the country, and Indian fighting, though not free from peril, now serves a useful purpose as a training school for the young graduates of West Point, who might otherwise go to their graves at a good old age without ever having smelled hostile gun-powder.

The Indians as a race are doomed by the inexorable laws of humanity to speedy and everlasting extinguishment. Accepting the inevitable with the stoical indifference which the instinct of self-preservation or the prompting of revenge seldom disturb, they excite pity rather than fear. The recent Apache uprising, which Gen. Crook suppressed so quickly and cheaply, is the utmost the red man can now do in the way of warlike enterprise. Discouraged and demoralized, helpless and hopeless, he sits down to await a swiftly approaching fate; and if now and then he treads the war path and takes a few white scalps, it is more from force of habit than from any expectation of crippling the power that is sweeping him and his out of existence.

Two hundred years ago, however, the white man lived in America only by the red man's consent, and less than a hundred years ago the combined strength of the red man might have driven the white into the sea. Along our Atlantic coast are still to be seen the remains of the rude fortifications which the early settlers built to protect themselves from the host of enemies around; but to find the need of such protection now one must go beyond the Mississippi, beyond the Rocky Mountains, to a few widely scattered points in Arizona, New Mexico and Oregon. The enemy that once camped in sight of the Atlantic has retreated almost to the shores of the Pacific, and from that long retreat there can be no returning advance. East of the stream which he called the "Father of Waters," nothing is left of the Indian except the names he gave and the graves of his dead, with here and there the degraded remnants of a once powerful tribe dragging out a miserable life by the sufferance of their conquerors. Fifty years hence, if not in a much shorter period, he will live only in the pages of history and the brighter immortality of romantic song and story. He will leave nothing behind him but a memory, for he has done nothing and been nothing. He has resisted and will continue to resist every attempt to civilize him—every attempt to inject the white man's ideas into the red man's brain. He does not want and will not have our manners, our morals or our religion, clinging to his own and perishing with them. The greatest redeeming feature in his career, so far as that career is known to us, is that he has always preferred the worst sort of freedom to the best sort of slavery. Had he consented to become a hewer of wood and drawer of water for the superior race, he might, like our Americanized Africans, be enjoying the blessings of Bible and breeches, sharing the honors of citizenship and the delights of office, seeking and receiving the bids of rival political parties. Whether his choice was a wise one, we leave our readers to determine; but it is impossible not to feel some admiration for the indomitable spirit that has never bowed its neck to the yoke, never called any man "master." The Indian is a savage, but he never was, never will be a slave.

If the treatment of the red man by the white had been uniformly or even generally honest and honorable, the superior race might contemplate the decay and disappearance of the inferior without remorse, if not without regret. But unfortunately that treatment has been, on the whole, dishonest and dishonorable. In a speech in New York City, not long before his death, Gen. Sam Houston, an indisputable authority in such matters, declared with solemn emphasis that "there never was an Indian war in which the white man was not the agressor." The facts sustain an assertion which carries its own comment. But aggression leading to war is not the heaviest sin against the Indian. He has been deceived, he has been cheated, he has been robbed; and the deception, cheating and robbery has taught him that the red man has no rights which the white man feels bound to respect. Whatever else he may be, he is no fool, and with the dismal experience of more than 250 years burning his soul, is it any wonder that they will have none of our manners, our morals, or our religion? "My son," said the mother of a too often whipped boy, "why will you not behave like a gentleman?" "If you did not treat me like a dog, I might," was the reply. We have treated the Indian like a dog and are surprised that he has developed into a dog and not into a Christian citizen. There is no reason to suppose that the Indian is capable of a high degree of civilization, but that he is what he is may be largely ascribed to white influences and examples, and to what he has suffered from the whites since the first European landed on American soil. Every spark of genuine manhood has been literally ground out of him by the heel of relentless oppression, and outrage. He was always a barbarian, but we have made him a brute. He might, perhaps, have been gradually transformed into a humble and harmless member of civilized society. We have made him a nuisance and a curse whose extermination the interests of society imperatively demand—and are rapidly accomplshing. The crimes of the Indian have been blazoned in a hundred histories; his wrongs are written only in the records of that court of final appeal, before which oppressors and oppressed must stand for judgment.

But few people, and particularly the pioneers of the country, will agree with any defense, be it ever so feeble, of the Indian. Their hatred of him, often on general principles, is intense, and always was so, and the greatest wrongs have been heaped upon him merely because he was an Indian, utterly regardless of the fact that he was a human being. When resenting the encroachments of the whites upon his hunting grounds, he has been characterized as a fiend, a savage and a barbarian, and one who might be robbed, mistreated, and even murdered without any compunction. This whole broad land was the Indian's birthright. How he came to possess it is no business of ours, nor is it pertinent to the subject. It is our own now, and it is a matter of grave doubt whether we attained it more honorably than did the Indian before us. Were our title to be challenged by another race of people, we doubtless should do as the Indians did, contest our rights step by step to the bitter end, and with all our boasted civilization and refinement, it is not improbable that we might inaugurate as great barbarities and cruelties as they did, rather than yield our homes and firesides.

Tribes of Southern Illinois.—The Indians occupying Southern Illinois when first known to the whites were the Delawares, the Kickapoos, the Shawnees and the Piankeshaws, with occasional fragmentary bands from the tribes who came to hunt. The Delawares were once a powerful tribe, one of the most powerful of North America. They called themselves Lenno Lenape, which signifies "original" or "unmixed" men. When first met with by Europeans, they occupied a district of country bounded easterly by the Hudson River and the Atlantic, on the west their territories extended to the ridge separating the flow of the Delaware from the other streams emptying into the Susquehanna River and Chesapeake Bay. The Delawares had been a migratory people. According to their own traditions, many hundred years had elapsed since they had resided in the western part of the continent; thence, by slow emigration, they reached the Alleghany River, so called from a nation of giants, the "Allegewi," against whom they (the Delawares) and the Iroquois (the latter also emigrants from the West) carried on successful war; and still proceeding eastward, settled on the Delaware, Hudson, Susquehanna and Potomac Rivers, making the Delaware the center of their possessions. By the other Algonquin tribes, the Delawares were regarded with the utmost respect and veneration. They were called "fathers," "grandfathers," etc.*

A paper addressed to Congress, May 10, 1779, establishes the territory of the Delawares subsequent to their being driven westward from their former possessions by their old enemies, the Iroquois, in the following described boundaries: "From the mouth of the Alleghany River at Fort Pitt to the Venango, and thence up French Creek and by Le Bœuf (the present site of Waterford, Penn.) along the old road to Presque Isle on the east; the Ohio River, including all the islands in it, from Fort Pitt to the Oubache (Wabash), on the south; thence up the Oubache River to that branch, Ope-co-mee-cah (the Indian name of White River, Indiana), and up the same to the head thereof; from thence to the head-waters and springs of the Great Miami, or Rocky River; thence across to the head-waters of the most northeastern branches of the Scioto River; thence to the westermost springs of the Sandusky River; thence down said river, including the islands in it and in the little lake (Sandusky Bay), to Lake Erie on the west and northwest, and Lake Erie on the north." These boundaries contain the cessions of lands made to the Delaware nation by the Wyandots, the Hurons and the

---

*Taylor's History.

Iroquois. The Delawares, after Gen. Wayne's signal victory in 1794, came to realize that further contests with the American colonies would be worse than useless. They therefore submitted to the inevitable, acknowledged the supremacy of the whites and desired to make peace with the victors. At the close of the treaty at Greenville, made in 1795, by Gen. Wayne, Bu-kon-ge-he-las, a Delaware chief of great influence in his tribe, spoke as follows: "Father, your children all well understand the sense of the treaty which is now concluded. We experience daily proofs of your increasing kindness. I hope we may all have sense enough to enjoy our dawning happiness. All who know me, know me to be a man and a warrior, and I now declare that I will for the future be as steady and true friend to the United States as I have, heretofore, been an active enemy."

This promise of Bu-kon-ge-he-las was faithfully kept by his people. They evaded all the efforts of the Shawnee prophet, Tecumseh, and the British, who endeavored to induce them by threats or bribes to violate it. They remained faithful to the United States during the war of 1812, and, with the Shawnees, furnished some very able warriors and scouts who rendered valuable services to the United States during the war. After the Greenville treaty, the great body of the Delawares removed to their lands on White River, Indiana, whither some of their people had preceded them, while a large fragment of the tribe crossed the Wabash into Southern Illinois. Now and then predatory bands committed outrages on the scattered settlers, but on a small scale. They continued to reside on White River and the Wabash and their tributaries until 1819, when most of them emigrated to Missouri and located on the tract of land granted by the Spanish authorities in 1793, jointly to them and the Shawnees. Others of their tribe, who remained in Illinois, finally scattered themselves among the Miamis, Pottawatomies and Kickapoos, and a few, including the Moravian converts, went to Canada, and their identity as part of a distinct tribe is lost.

The largest part of the Delaware nation in 182, settled on the Kansas and Missouri Rivers. They numbered 1,000, were brave, enterprising hunters, cultivated lands and were friendly to the whites. In 1853, they sold the Government all the lands granted them, excepting a reservation in Kansas. During the late civil war, they sent to the United States Army 170 out of their 200 able-bodied men. Like their ancestors, they proved valiant and trustworthy soldiers.

The Shawnese or Shawanese were an erratic tribe of the Algonquin family. A tradition recently originated makes them primarily one with the Kickapoo nation. They were driven southward by the warlike Iroquois and wandered into the Carolinas and some of them into Florida. But toward the close of the seventeenth century a large band of them went North and was among the tribes occupying Pennsylvania when it was granted to Penn. The Iroquois claimed sovereignty over the Shawnees and drove them to the West. They took part in the conspiracy of Pontiac, and afterward participated in the campaigns against Gens. Harmar and St. Clair in Ohio. For many years they were bitter and relentless foes of the whites. They submitted under the treaty of Gen. Wayne at Greenville in 1795, but in the war of 1812 some of the petty tribes of the Shawnees joined the British. A fragment of the tribe drifted to Southern Illinois, and had their village at Shawneetown, which place now bears their name. Some of them went

West after the Greenville treaty, and a few years after the close of the war of 1812 most of those remaining crossed the Father of Waters. In 1854, there were about 900 Shawnees in Kansas, and in 1876 there were some 750 in the Indian Territory.

The Kickapoos were also a tribe of the Algonquin family, and were found by the French missionaries toward the close of the seventeenth century on the Wisconsin River. They were closely allied to the Miamis, but roved in bands over a large territory. They were more civilized, industrious, energetic and cleanly than the neighboring tribes, and, it may also be added, more implacable in their hatred of the Americans. They were among the first to commence battle and the last to enter into treaties. Unappeasable enmity led them into the field against Harmar, St. Clair and Wayne, and a like spirit placed them first in all the bloody charges on the field of Tippecanoe. In the treaties of Portage des Sioux in 1815, Fort Harrison, 1816, and Edwardsville, 1819, they ceded a large part of the land they claimed. Many of the tribes had already gone beyond the Mississippi, and the United States assigned them a large tract on the Osage. But they still retained their old enmity to the Americans, and when removed from Illinois a part of them went to Texas, then a province of Mexico, to get beyond the jurisdiction of the United States. In 1822, about 1,800 had removed, leaving only 400 remaining in Illinois. Some few of these settled down to cultivate the ground, but more of them rambled off to hunt on the grounds of Southern tribes. They plundered on all sides and made constant inroads, killing and horse-stealing. During the years 1810 and 1811, and prior to the emigration of any of them to the West, they committed so many thefts and murders on the frontier settlements in conjunction with the Chippewas, Pottawatomies and Ottawas, that Gov Edwards was compelled to employ military force to suppress them.

The Piankeshaws were a weak, petty tribe, and supposed to have been an offshoot of the Shawnees. They at one time inhabited and claimed the country for some distance on both sides of the Wabash River toward its mouth, and northwest to the head-waters of the Káskaskia River. This comprises a brief sketch of the different tribes of the "noble red men" who inhabited Southern Illinois, and who doubtless have chased the deer and hunted the game through the woodland groves and prairies of Jefferson County. The Piankeshaws, however, seem to have been the Indians who held a kind of claim on this immediate section of the country. "But what is remarkable," says Mr. Johnson, "they have not left a single name of prairie, town or stream that may remain as a monument to tell the world that such a tribe ever existed." All the Indians of Southern Illinois were driven back finally by stronger tribes coming down from the North. They lost the proud spirit characteristic of their race, cowered around the white settlements for protection and abandoned themselves to indolence and drunkenness.

From the time of the first white settlements in this county, occasional bands of Indians made incursions for hunting and traffic. They carried their pelts to Shawneetown, Kaskaskia and St. Louis, and in return brought back a variety of articles which they bartered away among the white settlers. In 1819–20, the Delawares came through the county on their way to their Western reservation. From some cause or other, they remained here a considerable time. A large number of them were encamped on the creek near where John Pearcy lives, under a

County took part in the battle of Kellogg's Grove, in which, as already stated, one man was killed and two others wounded.

The war ended with the battle of August 2, 1832, at the mouth of Bad Axe, a creek which empties into the Mississippi near Prairie Du Chien. A treaty was made in the following September, which ended the Indian troubles in this State. Black Hawk had been captured, and upon regaining his liberty ever after remained friendly to the whites.

CHAPTER III.*

SETTLEMENT OF THE COUNTY BY WHITE PEOPLE—WHO THE PIONEERS WERE, AND WHERE THEY CAME FROM—ANDREW MOORE—HIS MURDER BY THE INDIANS—MOORE'S PRAIRIE, AND THE PEOPLE WHO SETTLED IT—THE WILKEYS, CRENSHAWS, ATCHISONS, ETC.— SETTLEMENT AT MOUNT VERNON—OTHER PIONEERS—HARDSHIPS, TRIALS, PRIVATIONS, MANNERS, CUSTOMS, ETC., ETC.

——"the westward tide should overflow
The mountain barriers to this unknown clime,
To change the wilderness and barren waste,
Where savage and the deer in turn were chased,
And there to found in this broad valley home
A richer, vaster empire than was ruled by ancient
    Rome."—*Byers*.

THE first white people, according to authentic history, who ever traversed the plains of Illinois or navigated its streams were the French. The importance which attaches to all that is connected with the explorations and discoveries of the early French travelers in the Northwest, but increases in interest as time rolls on. Two hundred years or more ago, settlements were made by the French in what is now the State of Illinois, among which were Fort Chartres, Kaskaskia, Cahokia and other places; also at Vincennes on the east side of the Wabash River. Marquette, Lasalle, De Frontenac, Joliet, Hennepin and Tonti were Frenchmen whose names are familiar in the early history of Illinois. From the year 1680 until the close of the "Old French and Indian war" between France and England, Illinois was under French dominion. At the treaty of Paris, February 16, 1763, France relinquished to England all the territory she claimed east of the Mississippi River, from its source to Bayou Iberville. Less than a quarter of a century passed, and it was wrested from Great Britain by her American colonies. In 1778, Gen. George Rogers Clark, with a handful of the ragged soldiers of freedom, under commission from the Governor of Virginia, conquered the country, and the banner of the thirteen colonies floated in the breeze for the first time on the banks of the Mississippi. The conquest of Clark made Illinois a county of Virginia, as noticed in a subsequent chapter. This acquisition of territory brought many adventurous individuals hither, and Southern Illinois at once became the center of attraction.

There is but little doubt that Andrew Moore was the first white man to make a settlement within the present confines of Jefferson County. Mr. Johnson, in his pioneer sketches of the county, notices a settlement made in 1808–09 in what is now Franklin County, by Thomas and Francis Jordan. They settled some eight or nine miles from the present town of Frankfort, and with the assistance of a company of

*By W. H. Perrin.

The different tribes not only commenced a warfare among themselves, in regard to their respective boundaries, but they extended their hostilites to the white settlements. A treaty of peace, in which the whites acted more as mediators than as a party, had been signed at Prairie Du Chien on the 29th of August, 1825, by the terms of which the boundaries between the Winnebagoes and Sioux, Chippewas, Sacs, Foxes and other tribes, were defined, but it failed to keep them quiet. Their depredations and murders continued frequent, and in the summer of 1827 their conduct particularly of the Winnebagoes, became very alarming. There is little doubt, however, that the whites, who at this period were immigrating in large numbers to the Northwest and earnestly desired their removal further westward, purposely exasperated the Indians, at the same time that they greatly exaggerated the hostlities committed. The Indians thus maddened and rendered insanely jealous of the encroachments of the whites and the insults and injuries heaped upon them, finally broke out into open war.

Black Hawk, in the spring of 1831, came over from west of the Mississippi River with 300 warriors of his "old guard," and ordered the whites to leave, committed numerous depredations and threatened more serious results if his orders were not immediately complied with. Gens. Gaines and Duncan were ordered to quell the Indians, and marched to the scene with a hastily collected army. The clouds of war soon disappeared, however, by Black Hawk and his warriors suing for peace, and the former treaty of 1804 was ratified.

This peace was not destined to remain long unbroken. Early in the spring of 1832, Black Hawk again prepared to assert his right to the disputed territory. He recrossed the Mississippi River, proceeded toward Rock River and began to collect an army.

Gov. Reynolds called for troops and promptly the State responded. Jefferson County furnished a full company, besides a number of men scattered through other companies and battalions. From the report of the Adjutant General of the State, for the Black Hawk and Mexican wars, we give the roster of this company, as follows: James Bowman, Captain; Franklin S. Casey, First Lieutenant; Green Deprist, Second Lieutenant; Stephen G. Hicks, Eli D. Anderson, John R. Satterfield and Littleton Daniels, Sergeants; George Bullock, James Bullock, Isaac S. Casey and Isaac Deprist, Corporals; Privates, S. H. Anderson, G. W. Atchison, Ignatius Atchison, Samuel Bullock, William Bingaman, Joseph Bradford, M. D. Bruce, P. C. Buffington, John Baugh, S. W. Carpenter, Zadok Casey, John Darnall, William Deweeze, Gasaway Elkin, Robert Elkin, Isaac Faulkenburg, William D. Gastin, Willis B. Holder, William B. Hays, James Ham, Joel Harlow, John Isam, John Jenkins, David Kitrell, James C. Martin, Nathaniel Morgan, James F. Miner, John E. McBrian, H. B. Newby, J. R. Owens, Peter Owens, Wyatt Parrish, George W. Pace, James Rhea, Jacob Reynolds, William Thomason and Joseph Thomason. Killed, William Allen, at Kellogg's Grove, June 25, 1832; James B. Bond, James Black and Abram Bradford, died of disease; Robert Meek and Marcus Randolph wounded at Kellogg's Grove.

The men elected their own officers and each man furnished his own horse and gun. These were to be valued when the men were mustered in, and paid for if lost when the men should be discharged. By the 15th of June the troops had arrived at their place of rendezvous and amounted to over 3,000 men. They were formed into three brigades, commanded respectively by Gens. Posey, Alexander and Henry. The company from Jefferson

County took part in the battle of Kellogg's Grove, in which, as already stated, one man was killed and two others wounded.

The war ended with the battle of August 2, 1832, at the mouth of Bad Axe, a creek which empties into the Mississippi near Prairie Du Chien. A treaty was made in the following September, which ended the Indian troubles in this State. Black Hawk had been captured, and upon regaining his liberty ever after remained friendly to the whites.

CHAPTER III.*

SETTLEMENT OF THE COUNTY BY WHITE PEOPLE—WHO THE PIONEERS WERE, AND WHERE THEY CAME FROM—ANDREW MOORE—HIS MURDER BY THE INDIANS—MOORE'S PRAIRIE, AND THE PEOPLE WHO SETTLED IT—THE WILKEYS, CRENSHAWS, ATCHISONS, ETC.— SETTLEMENT AT MOUNT VERNON—OTHER PIONEERS—HARDSHIPS, TRIALS, PRIVATIONS, MANNERS, CUSTOMS, ETC., ETC.

——"the westward tide should overflow
The mountain barriers to this unknown clime,
To change the wilderness and barren waste,
Where savage and the deer in turn were chased,
And there to found in this broad valley home
A richer, vaster empire than was ruled by ancient Rome."—*Byers*.

THE first white people, according to authentic history, who ever traversed the plains of Illinois or navigated its streams were the French. The importance which attaches to all that is connected with the explorations and discoveries of the early French travelers in the Northwest, but increases in interest as time rolls on. Two hundred years or more ago, settlements were made by the French in what is now the State of Illinois, among which were Fort Chartres, Kaskaskia, Cahokia and other places; also at Vincennes on the east side of the Wabash River. Marquette, Lasalle, De Frontenac, Joliet, Hennepin and Tonti were Frenchmen whose names are familiar in the early history of Illinois. From the year 1680 until the close of the "Old French and Indian war" between France and England, Illinois was under French dominion. At the treaty of Paris, February 16, 1763, France relinquished to England all the territory she claimed east of the Mississippi River, from its source to Bayou Iberville. Less than a quarter of a century passed, and it was wrested from Great Britain by her American colonies. In 1778, Gen. George Rogers Clark, with a handful of the ragged soldiers of freedom, under commission from the Governor of Virginia, conquered the country, and the banner of the thirteen colonies floated in the breeze for the first time on the banks of the Mississippi. The conquest of Clark made Illinois a county of Virginia, as noticed in a subsequent chapter. This acquisition of territory brought many adventurous individuals hither, and Southern Illinois at once became the center of attraction.

There is but little doubt that Andrew Moore was the first white man to make a settlement within the present confines of Jefferson County. Mr. Johnson, in his pioneer sketches of the county, notices a settlement made in 1808–09 in what is now Franklin County, by Thomas and Francis Jordan. They settled some eight or nine miles from the present town of Frankfort, and with the assistance of a company of

---
*By W. H. Perrin.

soldiers' from the salt-works, erected two forts or block-houses there for their protection. This settlement was some fifteen or twenty miles from the south line of Jefferson County. In 1810, Andrew Moore came from the Goshen settlement, and located in what is now Moore's Prairie Township, in this county. The nearest settlement to him was the Jordan settlement, and that was distant, as we have said, some fifteen or twenty miles. At the edge of a hickory grove, on the old Goshen road, he reared his lone cabin. It was a double cabin, and composed of round hickory poles, with a chimney and fire-place in the middle. Here he lived with his family for several years—Gov. Reynolds says until 1812; other authorities until 1814–15. All the while they were alone, except an occasional adventurous traveler who chanced to pass, or a company on their way to the Saline for salt. With these exceptions, they saw none of their kind. Crusoe on his desert island was not more alone than this first family of Jefferson County—these lone mariners of the desert.

Andrew Moore, from all that is known of him, was a pioneer of the true type. He was a self-exile from civilization, as it were, and by choice a roving nomad, who sought the solitudes of the pathless woods, the dreariness of the desert waste, in exchange for the trammels of civilized society. Of the latter he could not endure its restraints, and he despised its comforts and pleasures. He yearned for freedom—freedom in its fullest sense, applied to all property, life and everything, here and hereafter. He had branched out into the wilderness, cut loose from his kind, and he did not burn the bridges behind him, because there were none to burn. He hunted, fished, cut bee trees, and cultivated a small patch in the way of a farm. He lived and moved without fear of the Indians, and felt as secure in his cabin as though it had been a fortified castle; but in everything—every perilous act, every

dangerous feat—there must be a last one. The pitcher went once too often to the fountain, and Moore finally made his last excursion.

Mr. Johnson thus tells the story of his tragic death: "Moore and his son, a boy some eight or ten years of age, went one day on horseback to Jordan's settlement, to mill, expecting to return the same evening or the next day. But the next day passed without bringing the absent ones, and after a night of fear and apprehension, Mrs. Moore took her children and set off down the path to meet her husband. They plodded along until they finally reached the mill, when, to their great grief, they learned from Jordan that Moore and his boy had got their grinding, and had started home in due time. The anguish of the poor woman at this dismal news was most distressing. She begged for help to look for her husband and child, and as many as dared leave the settlement at once turned out and engaged in the search. For several days they scoured the woods along the trail, but found no trace of the missing, and finally the search was reluctantly abandoned. Mrs. Moore, desolate and heart-broken, returned to her cabin, gathered together her few possessions, and removed down into the neighborhood of the Saline. A few years later, a brother of Mrs. Moore, named Bales, his son-in-law, a Mr. Fannin, and a Mr. Fipps, a son-in-law of Mrs. Moore, moved up to the prairie, and Mrs. Moore returned with them. A hunting party some years afterward found a human skull stuck upon a snag or broken limb of an elm tree, near the creek, and but a mile or two south of where Moore had lived. When Mrs. Moore heard of this, she said that if it was her husband's, it would be known by his having lost a certain tooth from his upper jaw. Upon examination it was found that that tooth, and no other, was lacking. Fully persuaded now that it was the scull of her poor, unfortunate husband, she took it to her home, and kept it sacredly as long as she lived." There is a comfort and a blessing in the sweet recollection of having once been all the world to another, and with a love such as only a true woman knows, Mrs. Moore preserved the ghastly relic, cherished it and wept over it, and to her last days seemed to take a sad and mournful pleasure in showing it to her friends. She finally returned to the old town of Equality, and died there.

No other intelligence of Moore's fate or that of his son was ever received by his family or friends. It was the generally accepted theory that the Indians surprised them, killed the father, and to satisfy their fiendish cruelty, cut off his head, placed it where it was found, and carried the boy away into captivity, taking the horses and meal with them. The body of the murdered man, no doubt, was devoured by wild animals.

Such was the first attempt at a settlement in the county, and its tragic and melancholy termination. The next attempt, and what may perhaps, be termed the first permanent settlement, was in 1816, by Carter Wilkey. About the same time or very soon after, Daniel Crenshaw and Robert Cook came to the country. All these settled in Moore's Prairie, which received its name from Andrew Moore, whose settlement is above noticed. Crenshaw moved into Moore's deserted cabin, and Wilkey, who was single, boarded at Crenshaw's. Cook settled in the lower end of the prairie, where Mr. Brookins afterward lived. Wilkey was a native of Georgia, but removed from that State to Tennessee, where he enlisted in the war of 1812. Being under age, his mother succeeded in getting him out of the army after a few months' service. Both he and Robert Cook were connected with a surveying party, engaged in surveying the lands in this part of the State. A Mr. Berry was the surveyor, and Cook was attached to his party as "baggage master," having in charge the tent, camp equipage, etc. Carter Wilkey was the "commissary"—the huntsman, who furnished the game for the use of the party. This surveying was done in 1815, and the next spring Wilkey came back to stay, as already noted. Crenshaw repaired Moore's cabin, and cultivated his improvement, while Wilkey raised a crop during the summer of 1816, in the prairie about a quarter of a mile west of Crenshaw's. In the fall, Barton Atchison came and bought Wilkey's crop, and settled near Cook's. Next came Mrs. Wilkey—the mother of Carter—and her family, Maxey Wilkey—an older brother of Carter's—and his wife and child. They all arrived at Crenshaw's on the 22d of October, 1816, and spent the winter in one of his cabins—Crenshaw's wife was Mrs. Wilkey's niece. Thus, at the close of the year 1816, the population of the region of country now embraced within the limits of Jefferson County consisted of five families—the Wilkeys, Crenshaws, Cook and Atchison and Carter Wilkey, who, though single, was not "his own man"—probably less than twenty souls.

A modern writer refers to the first inhabitants of the Great West as men and women of that "hardy race of pioneers to whom the perils of the wilderness are as nothing, if only that wilderness be free." The eulogium is scarcely less creditable to the writer than to the subjects of it. While like produces like, heroic men and women will spring from heroic ancestors. And the people of the West, the pioneers who peopled this broad domain, were as much heroes as though they had swayed the destinies of an empire, or commanded the armies of the world. Of the first settlers of the county, whom we have already mentioned, a few words additional are not out of place.

Maxey Wilkey was a soldier of the war of 1812, and served in the armies of the North until peace was made. He claimed to have been at the death of Tecumseh, who was killed at the battle of the Thames. This is not unlike the story of Washington's servant, inasmuch as the men who saw the great warrior pass to the happy hunting-grounds are about as numerous as Washington's body servants. Though it is not improbable that Mr. Wilkey witnessed it, as he claims to have been in the battle of the Thames. The following upon the subject is from Johnson's sketches: "He says the Indian was wounded in the thigh, fell from his horse, and was surrounded and taken. It was believed that the prisoner was Tecumseh, but he refused to speak. Gen. Harrison was called to the spot, recognized the chief, but could get no answer from him, and left him to his fate. The soldiers took charge of him, and he soon after died. The old man tells me that he saw two razor strops taken off the dead Indian's back, and a third from his thigh, that is, strips of skin about two by twelve inches in size." This story is not only a little "wild," but contradictory of recognized history. That the old soldier witnessed the circumstance he relates may not be at all untrue, but that the Indian was Tecumseh is most improbable.

After the close of the war and his discharge from the army, Maxey Wilkey married a Miss Caldwell, and came to Illinois, as already stated, in the fall of 1816. He was a great hunter, and thought far more of the excitement of the chase than of the accumulation of worldly wealth, hence he remained comparatively poor. He was an extraordinary man in many respects, and his wife was an extraordinary woman. She was the mother of eighteen children, and in that respect she was more extraordinary than many of her pioneer lady friends. Mr. Johnson relates the following of an interview he had with Wilkey a short time before his death: "His present homestead adjoins the lands on which he settled, and he and his aged wife live nearly alone, both, however, are stout and vigorous for people of their age. The old man is as erect as a General, and looks about fifty years of age, though upward of eighty. His wife, at the time of my visit, was just recovering from a severe illness. In the course of our conversation, he remarked, in his characteristic style, 'That woman, sir, that you see lying upon her bunk, is the mother of eighteen children. twelve sons and six daughters, and six of the sons are still living.' He also stated that he was one of the little party that opened out the old 'Goshen Trail,' and made it a wagon-road."

Carter Wilkey, the younger of the two Wilkeys, and the first one to come to the county, after a few years returned to Tennessee, where he learned the carpenter's trade. When he came back to Illinois, he still made his home with Crenshaw. A great emigration had now sprung up from Kentucky and Tennessee to the "Sangamo country." Emigrations to the middle or northern part of the State were termed going to the "Sangamo," and it was no uncommon sight to see a hundred wagons in a single company going north. Crenshaw's was the great camping-place for emigrants on their way to the new promised land. Carter Wilkey long followed the business of going to Carmi, a distance of forty miles, with two or three packhorses, and bringing back meal to sell to these "movers." This would seem a small business in this day of railroads, as he could only bring two or three sacks of meal at a time, but as he sold it at $2 a bushel, it was a lucrative business for that early day. In the meantime, Dempsey Wood had moved into the settlement with four stalwart sons—John, Ben, Lawson and Aleck. Ben was a carpenter, and he and Carter Wilkey at once began to work at the business in partnership. They built many of the first houses (we do not mean cabins) in the country. They built the first house on Jordan's Prairie; they built the Clerk's office in McLeansboro, the first house erected in that town; they built or helped to build the first bridge over Casey's Fork of Muddy Creek. They agreed to furnish the lumber for the bridge floor by a certain Saturday, and it was Monday morning when they went to work. The amount required was 1,660 feet, 2x10 inch-stuff, and all had to be sawed by hand with a whip-saw. They sawed the lumber, and had it on the ground by 10 o'clock on Saturday morning.

Wilkey afterward went to Burlington, Iowa, where he was engaged for some time in the provision and grocery business, then as a druggist, and finally studied medicine under Dr. Hasbrook of that city. He practiced medicine for many years, and was a very active and energetic business man. He used to trade in horses and cattle, and bought up and took many hundred of them to the southern markets. He was married in 1821 to Miss Brunetta Casey, a daughter of Isaac Casey. Of the others of the Wilkey family, a daughter married Abel Allen, another one married Jacob Weldon, and another a Mr. Robinson. Dick Wilkey, as he was called, married a Kirkendale.

Crenshaw sold out in 1822, and went to Adams County, where he afterward died. He was a good man and got along well. Not strictly religious, but honest and upright, free and liberal in his views, and believed in the young people enjoying themselves, on the principle that "all work and no play makes Jack a dull boy." His cabin was always open to the wandering minister of Christ, the frontier missionary, who received a warm welcome when he called, and was pressed to stay and preach to the neighbors, who were hastily summoned from the highways and by-ways of the wilderness. The young people always found equally as warm a welcome when they met there for a backwoods frolic and dance. Crenshaw's trade was the making of "saddle-trees," and he used to make saddles, bringing his materials from Carmi.

Barton Atchison was also in the war of 1812, and was a character in his way. He was a man who moved everything by his own promptings; he knew little or nothing of the rules of society and he cared less. He was an honest man, and as rough of speech as rough could be —a genuine rough diamond. He was long a County Commissioner, and held other offices to the satisfaction of the people. He was a great story-teller, and delighted to relate his adventures in the army and elsewhere. Mr. Johnson tells the following as one of his army stories: "The army was encamped for some time at a certain point, and during their stay there, he and a companion went out one evening to take a hunt. It soon began to snow, and as they wandered in the pathless woods they became bewildered, and night overtook them before they reached camp. To lie down was to freeze, and to walk on was to risk getting farther away, of rushing into unknown dangers, and of finally perishing in the snow. At length, to their great joy, they came to an old unoccupied cabin, and they hastened to take shelter beneath its friendly roof. They shook off the snow, and were about to wrap their mantles around them and lie down to pleasant dreams, otherwise roll up in their army blankets, prepare to pass the night, when Atchison bethought him that, perchance, the inclemency of the weather might bring other company, either wild beast or Indian, to the cabin, and it prove, after all, a dangerous resting place. So finding a part of a loft, two courses of boards laid on poles, they climbed up and made their beds. The wisdom of his suggestion was soon apparent, as in a little while a band of Indians came in and took possession of the cabin, one of whom was the tallest Indian they had ever seen. The new-comers kindled a fire, roasted a little meat and began a night carousal. After some time Atchison shifted his position in order to see a little better, when the boards tipped up, and he and his companion and the loft all came clattering down on the Indians' heads. This was too much for a people both cowardly and superstitious, and they fled in terror and confusion."

Atchison, as we have said, was an active man, and took considerable interest in county affairs. He raised a large family, and still has many living descendants in the county, of whom much will be said in other chapters of this work. He died a few years ago at an advanced age, leaving many warm friends to mourn his death. At one time and another he held many county offices, and in each and all he was ever honest and faithful. His learning, so far as the schoolbooks go, was limited and meager, but his practical education was good, and was gained by daily experience with men and things. Such were the men and the families who made the first settlement in this county. We deem no excuse necessary for the extended sketch given of these, the first settlers—the advance guard, as it were, of the grand army of emigrants who have followed, and in the years that have come and gone, have given to Jefferson County a population not surpassed by any county in the State.

The next settlement made after those already described was made in the fall of 1816 by a man named Thompson. He did not remain long, however, and of him very little is known. In the winter following (1816–17), several families moved into the new settlement. Of these were Theophilus Cook, the Widow Hicks and a few others. Cook settled near Sloo's Point.*

He had served in the war of 1812, and was a man whom everybody that knew him loved and honored him. His Christian character was pure, and so far as man can judge, without spot or blemish. As a husband, father, neighbor, friend, he lived above reproach. He left a family of five sons and six daughters, several of whom are still living.

Mrs. Hicks was the widow of John Hicks, one of the seven men who fell in the battle of New Orleans January 8, 1815. Hicks was standing by the side of Theophilus Cook when he received his death wound. He left three children, Stephen G. and two daughters. After the war was over, Carter Wilkey, who was a brother of Mrs. Hicks, visited her in Georgia, where she lived, and induced her to remove with her family to Illinois. It was a terrible journey to be made in winter in that early day, and rendered doubly so by the hostile demonstrations frequently made by the faithless Indians. They finally arrived, however, in safety. It was about this time that a man named Hodge moved in and settled on the place where Abraham Irvin afterward lived for many years. Mrs. Robinson came about the same time, as also Fannin, Fipps, Bales and Mrs. Moore, widow of Andrew Moore (whose murder by the Indians has already been noticed), moved back to Moore's Prairie.

The settlements so far described were made in that portion of Jefferson County originally belonging to White County. The northern line of White County then ran about four miles south of the present city of Mount Vernon, dividing Township 3 south, and extending west to the Third Principal Meridian, and all north of that line was in Edwards County. Moore's Prairie, where the first settlement of the county began, was in the northwest part of White County. The next settlement we shall notice sprang up in what was then the southwestern part of Edwards County, and was in the immediate vicinity of Mount Vernon.

The circumstances which led to the second settlement were somewhat as follows: Some time about the spring of 1816, a man of the name of Black came up from Pope County, on a hunt, and upon his return told fabulous stories of the country he had seen, and especially of a beautiful prairie where perennial flowers seemed to bloom, and the richest luxuriance gave token of an earthly paradise. His description of the fruitful lands he had visited excited in his neighbors and friends a

---

* Regarding the name of Sloo's Point, Mr. Johnson, in his sketches, says: "Almost as soon as this county was surveyed, Thomas Sloo of Shawneetown, came in and entered about one hundred quarter-sections of land in different parts of what is now Jefferson County. John T. Johnson lives on one of these quarter-sections; on the southeastern part of Moore's Prairie was a long point of timber, lying on the waters of Ochshire's Creek; and Sloo had entered a good deal of the land in this vicinity—hence the name. Among other entries, I believe, was the land on which William Scrivner lives."

burning desire to see and learn for themselves. Among others to whom he related his wonderful stories were the Caseys, who lived near Cave-in-Rock, and they at once determined to visit this fabled land. In the fall following the trip of Black to this section, the Caseys came on a tour inspection. This was the first sight any of the Caseys had of what is now Jefferson County.

Isaac Casey and two sons, William and Thomas, in the autumn of 1816, started out to visit Black's Prairie, of which he had given so glowing an account. They missed it, however, nor did they strike any prairie until they came to the small one in which Mount Vernon was afterward built. They stopped at Crenshaw's, and he, glad to meet new-comers, as all pioneers were, accompanied them in their search of locations. They went a few miles beyond where Mount Vernon is situated, and then returned to Crenshaw's and finally home. The following spring, Isaac Casey came back, and his son William, his daughter Katy, and his son-in-law, Isaac Hicks, came with him for the purpose of founding a settlement. They built a cabin or camp in the open prairie, and cultivated a small patch of ground near where the Methodist Church now stands. While thus encamped in the prairie, they had no trouble in procuring meat, as game was abundant; honey, too, was more abundant still. But bread was a serious matter, and to procure it Mr. Casey and his daughter would go on horseback to the Wabash bottoms beyond Carmi for meal. He would ride one horse and lead one, while his daughter would ride another, and thus three "turns" of meal would be brought back. In the fall, they all returned to the Ohio River, where they had come from, and brought out the rest of their families, their stock and such other property as they possessed. William Casey moved into the camp or cabin above referred to, Isaac Casey erected his cabin near by and Isaac Hicks located near the place where he died; other families followed soon after. Kelly settled on the hill and remained there until the capital of the State was moved to Vandalia. He then moved to that place and became an officer in the first bank ever established there. An old man named Hynes settled a little west of Kelly, out on the Goshen road, where for some years he kept a public house; afterward he moved up North, where he died. Further up the Goshen road, William Goings settled. He was considered a bad man; he made millstones, and it was believed that he made counterfeit money, too. He was finally, after the settlement had increased a little more, given warning to leave the country, a warning he obeyed with alacrity, and in his vacant house many relics of the counterfeiting business, it is said, were found. James and John Abbott, John Utesler, Mr. Stull and Archibald Harris came in during the latter part of the year 1817. They were from Orange County, Ind., and upon their arrival here they settled in the neighborhood above noticed.

Zadok Casey, of whom we shall have more to say hereafter, came in the spring of 1817 and settled on the place where Mr. J. R. Moss now lives. He reared his cabin on a slight elevation of land, which he called Red Bud Hill. Abraham Casey, his brother, came the next year, and settled near where Joseph Pace lives. A son, Clark Casey, came with him and settled on what is called the "Mulberry Hill." Lewis Watkins settled about a mile south of the Atchison place, where he sold goods for a time. Thomas Jordan located in the edge of the prairie which was named for him. The place is now known as the McConnell place, and his brother William settled in the edge of Moore's Prairie. William Jordan, Jr., settled on Seven Mile Creek, and Oliver Morris settled near Joseph Jordan's first location.

While these accessions were being made to the new settlements, another, and a quite important one, was on the way. This was a Tennessee colony of six families, consisting of William Maxey, James E. Davis, James Johnson, Nathaniel Parker, John Wilkerson and H. B. Maxey. They organized themselves into a colony, and all started from William Maxey's, in Tennessee, and quite a lively trip they had of it. Fipps, who lived in Knight's Prairie, was the only man they found between the Saline and Crenshaw's, where they stopped. They arrived May 9, 1818, and camped in the edge of Moore's Prairie. Here they raised a small crop in the edge of the prairie, inclosed with a brush fence, and in the fall they moved up to the other settlement—all except Parker, who did not relish the gloomy aspect of the country, and moved back to Allen County, Ky. James Johnson settled near the place where he died; Wilkerson, where Simon King afterward lived; William Maxey, at the old Maxey place, and H. B. Maxey in the little prairie where Ward now lives. James E. Davis settled where Sam Edwards afterward lived. In September following the arrival of this colony, Edward Maxey moved into the settlement. He came from Allen County, Ky., and settled on the branch, northeast of what is now Judge Satterfield's farm, on the present Richview road. About the same time, Fleming Greenwood came; his son-in-law lived near what is now Thomas McMeen's place. James and William Hicks also came during the fall or winter. James bought Clark Casey's place on Mulberry Hill; William was single, but afterward married the Widow Dodds.

According to the historical sketches of Mr. Johnson, from which we have so often quoted, and which are considered by the old citizens generally to be substantially correct, the foregoing is believed to comprise a very full and complete list of the families who settled within the present limits of the territory of Jefferson prior to its organization as a distinct and independent county. There may have been a few who came and remained but a short time, and then left, but as to permanent settlers, the list, perhaps, is as nearly correct as it is possible to make now, after all these years.

Illinois was still a Territory when the first white people came to Jefferson County. These early settlers were men inured to toil and danger. They had been reared, many of them, amid scenes of peril and savage warfare, where the howl of the wolf, the scream of the panther, and the yell of the Indian were familiar music to their ears. Some of them had not reached life's meridian, but they were hopeful, courageous and determined. They were poor in actual worth, but rich in possibilities, and were ready to face danger and endure cold and hunger, if a home stood at the end of their journey beckoning them on. For the grand simplicity of their lives and their sturdy virtue, these early settlers achieved recognition and fame, as Enoch Arden did—after death. It was their lot to plant civilization here, and in doing it they displayed virtues which render modern civilization a boast and a blessing. In their little space of time they made greater progress than ten centuries had witnessed before. The work thirty generations had left undone they performed, and the abyss between us of to-day and the pioneers of Jefferson County is wider and more profound than the chasm between 1815 and the battle of Hastings. They did so much that it is hard to recognize the doers. "They builded wiser than they knew," and the monuments to their energy and industry still stand in perpetuation of their memory.

The first settlements of the county were made under difficulties, and amid hardships and dangers. As we have said, the people were poor. They had come here with a meager outfit of this world's goods, expecting to increase their stores and provide homes for their children. Some of their experiences in their new homes are thus detailed by Mr. Johnson, the faithful chronicler of the early history of the county:

"The farms, as in most new countries, were

mere patches, inclosed with rails or brush, and sometimes not inclosed at all. The houses were round-pole cabins, but in rare cases made of small logs—"skelped down," or very slightly hewn, sometimes of split logs smoothed a little on the face. Some of the cracks in the wall were chinked and daubed, while some were left open to admit light and serve as windows. Some of the cabins had cracks all around that a dog could jump through. If the floor was anything else than the bare ground, it was made of puncheons or slabs, fastened down with wooden pins, or not fastened at all. * * * * * Shelves resting on long pins in the walls answered for cupboard, pantry, bureau and wardrobe. There were but few bedsteads in the county. Bed scaffolds were made on two rails or pieces driven into the walls, one for the side and one for the end, in the corner of the cabin, the other end of these rails being let into a post—the entire structure frequently having but one bed-post. Boards were laid across from the long rail to the wall, and on these the bed, if the happy family had any, was laid. The table was either made of boards nailed to a rough, unwieldy frame, or it was made on stakes driven into the (ground) floor. The well-to-do had a pot and a skillet; some broiled their meat on the coals, and cooked their "Johnny-cake" on a board. The cook-stove is a modern invention, and was then unknown in the West.

"Isaac and William Casey constructed a little hand-mill that would grind a bushel or two a day, and they did well. But many of the first settlers had to beat their meal in a mortar, which was generally a stump with a basin burnt out in the top of it. The meal thus made was sifted through a sieve made by punching a piece of deer-skin full of holes with a hot wheel-spindle, and stretching it (the deer-skin, not the spindle) over a hoop. In the early autumn, meal was grated, and the bread made of this meal and baked in the ashes, or on a board, was as delicious as heart could wish.

* * * * * * *

"Most of the hats and caps were made of skins, often of the most fantastic shape. After the original supply of clothing was exhausted, the first resource was to make clothing of deer-skins. These in the hands of the Indians made excellent clothing; but our first settlers were not such good tanners, and the clothes did not do so well. The breeches soon got a tremendous knee, that was a permanent thing. When "Aunt Franky" Johnson was coming out, she saw a boy in Moore's Prairie dressed in buck-skin, and she exclaimed in the sincerity of her kind heart: "Why, la me, honey, just look at that poor crippled boy!" When the men or boys, in their buckskin suits, went out in the dewy grass, their breeches' legs would soon be dangling around their feet, nearly a foot too long; and then about ten o'clock, when they became dry again, they crackled and rustled about their legs nearly a foot too short. After the first year or two, however, when people had time to raise cotton, buckskin gave way to cotton goods, the latter being died with copperas, the copperas being mingled with white when variety was desired. People made their own indigo. The plant they used was bruised and kept in soak for some time, then wrung out; the fluid was churned with a basket to cut the indigo, then left to settle, and afterward dried in the sun. The article to "set" the dye was such as to make it an unpleasant process, and such as to sometimes draw the buffalo gnats around one's Sunday clothes in a most provoking manner." * * * * *

Such was the life, and such the trials of the first settlers of Jefferson County—men who wrought for their successors the richest and most enduring legacy in all the world. Most of them have served out their day and generation, and have passed away. Their graves, many of them, are unmarked and unknown, and their fast receding memories are unhonored and unsung. They deserve better than this. Justice demands that a meed of praise be awarded those great lives whose works will ripen, and are ripening into the noblest civilization the world has ever known.

In a subsequent chapter we shall give extended sketches of these pioneer families, whose settlements have been here noticed. Many of the men who came here in that early day were giants, and it is meet that they should receive their deserts from the pen of the historian. Their country's history demands that their names, their acts and their deeds shall be placed on record, and preserved for the generations to come.

It has been said that the American people take as naturally to self-government as a babe turns to the maternal fount for nourishment. The truthfulness of the remark is evidenced in the fact that new counties are formed when their area contain but a few hundred inhabitants. Thus far we have shown the number of families locating in Jefferson County prior to its organization, and with which we will close this chapter. In a new chapter we will give the formation of the county, and the circumstances which led to the same.

CHAPTER IV.*

ILLINOIS A COUNTY OF VIRGINIA—JOHN TODD, THE FIRST CIVIL GOVERNOR—ORGANIZATION OF JEFFERSON COUNTY—THE LEGISLATIVE ACT CREATING IT—LOCATION OF THE SEAT OF JUSTICE—FIRST OFFICIALS—THE COURTS—PUBLIC BUILDINGS—CENSUS—THE COUNTY DIVIDED INTO DISTRICTS—COUNTY OFFICERS—J. R. SATTERFIELD—TOWNSHIP ORGANIZATION, ETC.

THAT Illinois, now one of the greatest States of the Federal Union, once formed a county of Virginia is a fact unknown, perhaps, to a majority of our readers. In October, 1778, the General Assembly of Virginia passed an act for "establishing the county of Illinois, and for the more effectual protection and defense thereof." A clause of the act reads: "That all the citizens of this commonwealth, who are already settled, or shall hereafter settle on the western side of the Ohio and east of the Mississippi, shall be included in a distinct county, which shall be called Illinois County." By the provisions of the act, the Governor of Virginia was to appoint "a County Lieutenant or Commandant in Chief," who should "appoint and commission so many Deputy Commandants, Militia officers and Commissaries," as he should deem expedient, for the enforcement of law and order. The civil officers were to be chosen by a majority of the people, and were to "exercise their several jurisdictions and conduct themselves agreeable to the laws which the present settlers are now accustomed to."

Patrick Henry, the first Governor of Virginia after the colonies had thrown off the galling yoke of Britain, appointed John Todd the County Lieutenant Commandant of Illinois. At Williamsburg, the capital then of Virginia, and in the very mansion of the royal rulers of the whilom colony, Gov. Henry indicted his letter of appointment to Todd on the 12th of December, 1778. It

---

*By W. H. Perrin.

occupies the first five pages of the record book of John Todd's official acts while exercising authority over the county of Illinois, and is in Patrick Henry's own handwriting. This old book, a valuable relic of the early history of Illinois, is now in the possession of the Chicago Historical Society. From its pages, browned by time and dimmed with age, some interesting facts are gleaned. The following, of the first civil Governor of Illinois, is not out of place in this connection:

Todd was not unknown on the frontier. Born in Pennsylvania and educated in Virginia, he had practiced law in the latter colony for several years, when, in 1775, he removed to Kentucky, which was then, also, a county of Virginia. He became very prominent in the councils of its House of Delegates, or Representatives, the first legislative body organized west of the Alleghany Mountains. Early in 1777, the first court in Kentucky convened at Harrodsburg, and Todd was one of the Justices. Shortly after, he was chosen one of the Representatives of Kentucky in the Legislature of Virginia, and proceeded to the capital to fulfill this duty. The following year he accompanied Gen. George Rogers Clark in his expedition to "the Illinois," and was the first man to enter Fort Gage, at Kaskaskia, when it was taken from the British, and was present at the final capture of Vincennes.

The record book already referred to of itself forms an interesting chapter in the history of Illinois. After Gov. Henry had indicted upon its pages his letter to Todd, it was intrusted to a faithful messenger, who, on foot, carried it from tide water across the mountains to Fort Pitt, thence down the Ohio until he met with its destined recipient and delivered to him his credentials. It is supposed that Todd received it at Vincennes, then known to Virginians as St. Vincent, not long after the surrender of that place to Clark on the 24th of February, 1779, and that he at once assumed his new duties as Governor, or "Lieutenant Commandant." This position he held until the time of his death, although his many duties called him frequently to Kentucky. In the spring of 1780, he was elected a Delegate from the county of Kentucky to the Legislature of Virginia. In November following, Kentucky was divided into three counties, viz., Fayette, Lincoln and Jefferson, and in 1781 Thomas Jefferson, who, in the meantime, had become Governor of Virginia, appointed Todd Colonel of Fayette County, and Daniel Boone, Lieutenant Colonel. In the summer of 1782, Todd visited Richmond, Va., on business connected with the Illinois country, where, it is said, he had determined to permanently reside, and on his return he stopped over at Lexington, Ky., and while there met his untimely death. An Indian attack on a frontier settlement (Bryant Station) aroused the militia to arms, and Todd, as Senior Colonel, took command of the little army sent in pursuit of the retreating savages. It included Boone and many other pioneers whose names rank high in the history of the dark and bloody ground. At the Blue Licks, on the 18th of August, 1782, they came up with the enemy, but the headlong courage of those who would not heed the prudent counsels of Todd and Boone precipitated an action which proved more disastrous to the whites than any ever fought in Kentucky soil—that sanguinary theater of savage warfare. More than one-third of those who entered the fight were killed outright and many others wounded. Among the slain was Todd, who fell, like the brave man that he was, with his face to the foe, gallantly fighting at the head of his troops. On the brow of a small hill overlooking Blue

Licks, and near the spot where he fell, still repose the mortal remains of the first civil Governor of Illinois. August 18, 1882, the centennial of the disastrous battle of Blue Licks was held on the field where it was fought, and a resoluton adopted to erect a monument to the heroes that there fell in defense of their country.

John Todd was a soldier and a statesman. He was a soldier fit to stand by the mightiest and give command. He was a statesman tried and true, and marvelously adapted to the times and surroundings amid which he lived. Just such as he was he had to be, to fulfill the mission to which far-seeing wisdom had appointed him, and to blaze out the way for the coming hosts of civilization who were to people this great Northwest. His tragic death, in the prime of life, was a calamity to the nation just struggling up from the fires of a mighty revolution, and a loss not easily repaired in that early period of our history.

Upon the organization of the Northwest Territory, Gen. Arthur St. Clair was appointed Governor. In the spring of 1790, in company with the Territorial Judges, he went to Cahokia, where, by proclamation, he organized the county of St. Clair, the first individual county formed in what is now the State of Illinois, and its seat of justice was fixed at Kaskaskia. Randolph was the next county created in Illinois; and the date of its organization extends back to 1795. These were the only counties formed until after the dawning of the nineteenth century. At the session of the Territorial Legislature of 1811-12, Madison, Gallatin and Johnson were organized, and Edwards at the session of 1814. At the session of 1816, White, Jackson, Monroe, Pope and Crawford were organized, and at the last session of the Territorial Legislature Franklin, Washington, Union, Bond and Wayne came into existence. At the first session of the Legislature after Illinois was admitted into the Union as a State, Jefferson County was formed, under the following act entitled an act for forming a separate county out of Edwards and White Counties, approved March 26, 1819:

Be it enacted by the people of the State of Illinois represented in the General Assembly, That all that tract of country within the following boundaries, to wit: Beginning where the line between Ranges 4 and 5 east intersects the base line; thence west with said line to the Third Principal Meridian; thence south twenty-four miles; thence east twenty-four miles; thence north to the place of beginning, shall constitute a separate county, to be called "Jefferson," and for the purpose of fixing the permanent seat of justice therein the following persons are appointed Commissioners: Ambrose Maulding, Lewis Barker, Robert Shipley, James A. Richardson and Richard Graham, which said Commissioners, or a majority of them, being duly sworn before some Judge or Justice of the Peace in this State to faithfully take into view the convenience of the people, the situation of the settlement, with an eye to future population, and the eligibility of the place, shall meet on the 2d Monday of May, at the house of William Casey, in said county, and proceed to examine and determine on the place for the permanent seat of justice and designate the same; *provided:* The proprietor or proprietors of the land shall give to the county for the purpose of erecting public buildings a quantity of land, not less than twenty acres, to be laid out in lots and sold for that purpose; but should the proprietor or proprietors refuse or neglect to make the donation aforesaid, then and in that case it shall be the duty of said Commissioners to fix on some other place for the seat of justice as convenient as may be to the inhabitants of said county, which place fixed and determined upon, the said Commissioners shall certify under their hands and seals and return the same to the next Commissioners' Court in the county aforesaid, which court shall cause an entry thereof to be made in their book of record, and until the public buildings be erected the courts shall be held at the house of William Casey, in the said county.

SEC. 2. *Be it further enacted*, That the Commissioners aforesaid shall receive a compensation of two dollars for each and every day they may be necessarily employed in fixing the aforesaid seat of

Marcus D. Bruce

justice, to be paid out of the county treasury by an order from the Commissioners' Court.

SEC. 3. *Be it further enacted,* That the citizens of Jefferson County are hereby declared entitled, in all respects, to the same rights and privileges as are allowed in general with the other counties in this State.

SEC. 4. *Be it further enacted,* That the county of Jefferson shall vote in conjunction with White County for Representatives to the General Assembly of the State, and it shall be the duty of the Clerks of said counties to meet at the court house in White County, within ten days after such elections, and make a certificate, signed by both Clerks, to the persons duly elected; and if the said Clerks shall fail to do the same they shall forfeit and pay the sum of one hundred dollars, for the use of said counties, to be recovered by action of debt in the county in which such delinquent Clerk may reside.

SEC. 5. *Be it further enacted,* That the county of Jefferson shall be and compose a part of the Second Judicial Circuit, and the courts shall be holden therein at such times as shall be specified by law.

This was followed by a supplemental act, entitled "An act supplemental to an act for laying off a new county out of the counties of Edwards and White," approved March 29, 1819, and is as follows:

Be it enacted by the people of the State of Illinois, represented in the General Assembly, That all that tract or part of country lying north of the county of Jefferson and west of the county of Wayne, and not included within the limits of the said counties of Jefferson and Wayne, established by the act to which this is a supplement, be and the same is hereby attached to and forms a part of the said county of Jefferson, and that the inhabitants thereof have and enjoy all the rights and privileges, as far as may be, that the inhabitants of the county of Jefferson have and enjoy.

SEC. 2. *Be it further enacted,* That the county of Jefferson be and the same is hereby attached to the Fourth Judicial Circuit of the State, etc., etc.

The county was named in honor of Thomas Jefferson, the third President of the United States, and who was inaugurated into office on the 4th of March, 1801. He was born at Shadwell, Albemarle Co., Va., April 2, 1743, and died at Monticello, his country seat, July 4, 1826, just half a century after the adoption of the Declaration of Independence, a document penned by his own hand, and which has rendered his name immortal, and dear to every liberty-loving citizen of the whole country. Jefferson's administration was very popular, and he was elected to a second term, receiving more than three-fourths of the votes in the electoral college. During his first term, the afterward notorious Aaron Burr was Vice President, and during the second, George Clinton was associated with him as Vice President.

On the 30th of March, 1819, two other acts were passed by the Legislature, pertaining wholly or in part to Jefferson County. The first authorized Lewis Watkins to administer the required oaths to all officers commissioned for the county; and the other ordered an election in Wayne, Jefferson, Clark and Alexander Counties, to be held on the fourth Monday of April, for County Commissioners, Sheriffs and Coroners. The Coroner then was an important officer, as, in the absence or inability of the Sheriff to serve, the Coroner acted in his stead until the Sheriff resumed his duties.

In pursuance of the last-mentioned act, an election was held at the house of William Casey, which stood where the brick building recently known as Taylor's Commercial Hotel now stands. Some thirty or forty votes were cast; and Zadok Casey, Joseph Jordan and Fleming Greenwood were elected Commissioners, and Lewis Watkins, Sheriff. The Commissioners met at William Casey's on Monday, June 7, for the purpose of organizing the county court. Their certificates of election were signed by Oliver Morris and Lewis Watkins, Justices of the Peace, and attested by Edward Maxey, acting Clerk of the Court; they were then duly sworn into office. Edward Maxey, the Clerk pro tempore, resigned, and the court appointed Joel Pace to the office of County Clerk. He gave bond in the sum of $1,000, with James Kelly and Isaac Casey as securities.

This completed the organization of the county, and it was now ready for business.

The Seat of Justice.—One of the first matters which engaged the attention of the court was the location of the seat of justice according to the provisions of the act for the formation of the county. As soon as the court convened, the Commissioners appointed for that purpose presented the following report:

According to an act of the General Assembly, approved March 26, 1819, appointing certain Commissioners to meet on the second Monday of May, at the house of William Casey, for the purpose of fixing a permanent seat of justice for and in Jefferson County, the following persons met, viz.: Lewis Barker, Ambrose Maulding and James A. Richardson, who, after being duly sworn, have proceeded, determined and fixed upon the southwest quarter of Section 29, Range 3, of Township 2, on the land owned by William Casey, the town to be laid off in the southwest corner of said quarter, to commence near the timber, on a point not far distant from Casey's house, and thence to the foot of the descent on a point on which Casey's house stands, or in such a manner as said County Commissioners shall designate. Given under our hands and seals this 12th day of May, 1819.

JAMES A. RICHARDSON,
AMBROSE MAULDING,
LEWIS BARKER.

This report was accompanied by the following paper, confirmatory of Casey having complied with the requirements of the twenty acre-clause of the legislative act:

Personally appeared before us the subscriber, William Casey, and made a donation of twenty acres of land, to be laid off in town lots and sold for the purpose of paying for public buildings in the county of Jefferson, which twenty acres of land shall be laid off by the County Commissioners on the land designated by the State Legislature for fixing the permanent seat of justice for said Jefferson County. Whereof the said William Casey has hereunto set his hand and seal this 12th day of May, in the year of our Lord one thousand eight hundred and nineteen.

WILLIAM CASEY.

N. B. Provided such Commissioners shall lay off said town so as not to include said Casey's house and farm.

[Attest] JAMES A. RICHARDSON, AMBROSE MAULDING, LEWIS BARKER.

The report of the Commissioners was received, and the selection made by them became the seat of justice of the new county, an honor which it has retained to the present day. There was, as is always the case, some little dissatisfaction at the selection thus made. Mr. Isaac Hicks wanted it near him, and offered a site known as "Post Oak Hill," which was a fraction nearer the geographical center of the county. Another "eligible location" was on the high grounds between Mrs. Samuel Casey's and Mrs. Dodds' residence. But Lewis Barker, one of the Commissioners, was the father-in-law of William Casey, and there were hints at the time that it was through his influence the present site was selected. Be that as it may, the location selected is a beautiful one for a town, and could scarcely be surpassed by any of the other sites offered. For their services in "fixing the permanent seat of justice," the court allowed Maulding $8, and Barker and Richardson $12 each. Maulding lived in Hog Prairie, a little this side of the present town of McLeansboro; Barker owned the ferry at Cave-in-Rock, and Richardson lived in the vicinity of Carmi. Of the laying-out of the seat of justice, and its growth and development as a town, the reader is referred to the chapters devoted to Mount Vernon.

The Courts.—Thus the county court was organized, the seat of justice established and the legal machinery of the newly created municipality put in motion. The first session of the court was taken up with the report of the Commissioners for locating the seat of justice, as already noticed; James Kelly and Jacob Barger applied for a writ to condemn a "mill seat;" license for retailing goods was fixed at $15, and the Clerk empowered to issue them when called on for the same; the laying off a town ordered, also the building of a court house, etc., etc. At the second session of the court, held June 25, 1819, James Kelly was appointed County Treasurer; a list of the taxable property was ordered; Lewis Watkins took out tavern license, for which he paid a fee of $4. At the third term of court, held September 6, among other business, the court house was received and the survey of the town ordered to be recorded. Also, W. Casey and J. Pace were ordered to "stake out" the town, and several roads ordered to be viewed and laid out. In this humble and unpretentious way, the county moved along quietly. The business coming before the county court was of a general character, as above given, and was dispatched without much debate or wrangling. The last session held by this (the first) board, tavern keepers' rates of charges were fixed as follows: A single meal, 37½ cents; lodging, 12½ cents; keeping horse all night, 50 cents; a single feed, 25 cents. The first term of the Circuit Court convened in the town of Mount Vernon (then comprising but four cabins) on Monday, October 28, 1819, Hon. William Wilson as Judge and F. A. Hubbard, State's Attorney. Joel Pace was sworn as Clerk, and gave bond in the sum of $2,000. Lewis Watkins was Sheriff, and gave bond in the sum of $10,000, with Zadok Casey, Joseph Jordan and John Wilkerson, securities. But thirteen men could be found, outside of the officers of the court, to serve as grand jurors. These were as follows: Edward Maxey, F. McBride, J. C. Casey, W. Jordan, L. Johnson, A. P. Casey, John Wilkerson, H. P. Maxey, Isaac Casey, James Johnson, S. Gaston, J. Lee and A. Harris. After receiving the usual charge from the court, they repaired to the jury room, which, in this case, was "God's first temples," and after an hour's deliberation returned into court, presented the indictments and were discharged. The next term of court was held on the 15th and 16th of May, 1820, Judge Wilson again presiding, and Henry Eddy acting as State's Attorney. But we will not follow the proceedings of the courts, as our readers would find them, doubtless, dry reading. The brief extracts have been made merely to show the commencement and organization of this important branch of the county's machinery.

Public Buildings.—At the first term of the County Commissioners' Court, it was resolved to build a court house. This building was unpretentious, but it served the purpose of those early days when we were not as proud as we are now. It was of hewed logs, and was 18x30 feet in dimensions. A stray pound was ordered, and at the February term, 1820, the court ordered a jail to be built. These early public buildings, however, will be noticed by Mr. Johnson, in his sketch of Mount Vernon, and all the facts pertaining to them and their successors will there be given. The part they bear in the organization of the county requires some reference to them in this connection, but this brief allusion must suffice.

Among the first acts of the court was laying off the county into civil divisions. At first it was divided into two districts, or townships, called respectively "Moore's Prairie" and "Casey's Prairie." At the June term of the court, in 1820, Walnut Hill Precinct or Township was formed. It included all of Jefferson and Marion Counties north of the line dividing Townships 1 and 2 south. The next change in the civil divisions, of which we find any account, is in June, 1832, when Grand Prairie Precinct was formed. It was in the northwest part of the county, and was eight miles square. The voting place was fixed at Poston's mill. In June, 1834, Horse Creek Precinct was laid off. It extended seven miles from the east line of the county, and was bounded north by the county line and south by the Fairfield road. The voting place was at Frank Haney's. Gun Prairie Precinct was formed in 1835. It began, the records say, where the "new hurricane" crossed the west line of the county, "ran with the hurricane to Morgan's mill, to A. Toney's, to W. Toney's, to the edge of Moore's Prairie, and on to the south line of the county." The voting place was to be at the house of William King. The next precinct was formed in 1845, and was called Long Prairie. It was bounded by the West and Middle Forks of Muddy River and the Grand Prairie road, with the voting place at the house of H. Hicks. In 1846, Elk Prairie Precinct was formed. Its bounds were from the mouth of Dodd's Creek to Mendenhall's quarry, west to Middle Fork, down it to the county line, then up the creek to the beginning. The voting place was fixed at J. Kelly's. At the same time, New Moore's Prairie Precinct was formed, including Township 4 and Range 4, with voting place at Wilbank's. With, perhaps, a few other changes in names and boundaries and geographical position, the county moved on for several decades, under the old precinct system.

The population of the county has increased regularly since its organization. At the census of 1820, the first taken after the county was formed, it had a population of 691; in 1830, 2,555; in 1840, 5,762; in 1850, 8,107; in 1860, 12,965; in 1870, 17,864; in 1880, 20,686. If it has not increased as rapidly as some other counties in population, its growth has been steady and good, and its class of citizens will compare favorably with those of any portion of the State.

County Officers.—As a matter of interest to our readers, we present herewith a very full and complete list of county officers, from the the formation of the county to the present time. It has cost considerable time and labor to prepare it, and it is believed to be substantially correct.

The County Commissioners come first, and are as follows: In 1819, they were Zadok Casey, Fleming Greenwood and Joseph Jordan; in 1820, William Casey, Joseph Jordan and Barton Atchison; in 1822, Samuel Gaston, William Hicks and Barton Atchison; in 1824, W. J. Tunstall, John Jordan and H. B. Maxey; in 1826, Edward Maxey, Arba Andrews and M. Ham; in 1828, Edward Maxey, Arba Andrews and M. Ham; in 1830, Edward Maxey, Arba Andrews and M. Ham; in 1832, Arba Andrews, Barton Atchison and Willoughby Adams; in 1834, Barton Atchison, George W. Watters and J. M. Scott; in 1835, Noah Johnston succeeded Watters; in 1836, Willoughby Adams, Barton Atchison and A. Bruce; in 1838, William Bullock, James Sursa and Barton Atchison; in 1840, James Sursa, B. Atchison and James Kirby; in 1841, Willoughby Adams succeeded Sursa; in 1842, Willoughby Adams, James Kirby and John Breeze; in 1844, James Kirby, F. S. Casey and A. D. Casey; in 1845, E D. Andrews was appointed to fill out Kirby's term; in 1846, A. D. Estes, E. D. Andrews and F. S. Casey; in 1847, W. Adams, John Troutt and F. S. Casey; in 1848, F. S. Casey, Dr. W. Adams and John Troutt; in 1849,* W. Dodds was elected

---

* The law was now changed, and the board was composed of a County or Probate Justice or Judge and two Associates.

Probate Justice or Judge, and Dr. W. Adams and F. S. Casey, Associates; in 1852, W. Dodds, Probate Judge, and F. S. Casey and Dr. W. Adams, Associates. Judge Dodds resigned, and J. R. Satterfield was elected to fill out his term.

Judge J. R. Satterfield, the successor of Judge Dodds, is one of the old landmarks of Jefferson County. He came here in the fall of 1818, a stripling of a lad. He is an old man now, and has grown gray in the service of the people. Indeed, so long has he been in the official harness, that he is almost looked upon as a pre-historic relic. His official integrity is above reproach, and his name is the synonym of fidelity and honesty. He was born in Pendleton County, Ky., and came to Illinois when but nine years old. Here he grew to manhood, and here he has spent an active life. He has been Sheriff, County Superintendent of Schools, County Judge or Probate Justice for over twenty years, County Recorder, Deputy Sheriff and Justice of the Peace for forty years. He and Mr. Bogan have been in office so long, that they could not survive in private life. They are what the sage has termed "the noblest works of God"—honest men.

In 1853, J. R. Satterfield, Judge, and F. S. Casey and A. D. Estes, Associates; in 1857. J. R. Satterfield, Judge, Dr. W. Adams and S. W. Carpenter, Associates; in 1861, J. R. Satterfield, Judge, and W. Adams and F. S. Casey, Associates; in 1865. A. M. Grant, Judge, and W. Adams and F. S. Casey, Associates; in 1866, J. R. Satterfield was elected to fill out Grant's term, he having resigned; in 1869, J. R. Satterfield, Judge, W. Adams and S W. Carpenter, Associates. After this date, township organization came into effect. Since the Board of Commissioners have been superseded by the Board of Supervisors, there have not been many changes in the office of County Judge. Jared Foster was elected County Judge in 1873, and in 1877 was succeeded by C. A. Keller, and he, in 1882, was succeeded by William B. Anderson, the present incumbent.

County and Circuit Clerks—Joel Pace was the first County and Circuit Clerk. He held both offices up to 1837, when Noah Johnston became County Clerk. He was succeeded by E. H. Ridgeway, in 1838, who held both offices until 1843, when J. F. Watson succeeded him; in 1857, W. Dodds came in; in 1865, C. H. Patton; in 1869, W. Dodds; in 1871, J. N. Satterfield; in 1873, W. H. Smith; in 1877, J. N. Satterfield; in 1880, Allen C. Tanner, the present incumbent. E. H. Ridgeway succeeded Joel Pace as Circuit Clerk in 1841, and in 1848 was succeeded by John Wilbanks. T. B. Tanner came in in 1852, and in 1854 was succeeded by J. S. Bogan, who is still in the office. It is a striking example of the "right man in the right place." He came very near being defeated once, that is, he lacked but three votes of carrying the county unanimously. This may have been fun for Bogan, but it was rough on his opponent. The people of Jefferson County show their good sense in retaining Mr. Bogan, for we have never been in a more neatly kept or admirably arranged office than his. He has a place for everything, and is particularly careful to keep everything in its place—even his deputies.

Sheriffs—Lewis Watkins was the first Sheriff, and was appointed in 1819; the next was W. L. Howell, who was appointed in 1821; in 1823, Howell was again appointed to the office; in 1824, Nicholas Wren came in; in 1828, James Bowman, who, it seems, filled the office to 1842, when W. J. Stephenson became Sheriff, and held the office until 1848, and was succeeded by Elijah Piper;

in 1850, J. R. Satterfield came in; in 1852, W. Dodds; in 1854, J. R. Allen; in 1856, James Westcott; in 1858, John Bagwell; in 1860, C. G. Vaughn; in 1862, J. B. Goodrich; in 1864, C. G. Vaughn; in 1866, William Dodds; in 1868, W. E. Coffey; in 1870, 1872, 1874, J. B. Goodrich; in 1876, 1878, 1880, George W. Yost; in 1882, Thomas M. Gray.

Treasurers—The first Treasurer of the county was James Kelly, who was appointed in 1819. He had but little trouble in taking care of the funds, and perhaps spent few sleepless nights through fear of "thieves breaking through and stealing" the funds of which the county had made him the custodian. In 1821, Edward Maxey came in; in 1826, John Wilbanks; in 1829, Joseph Pace; in 1833, S. Goddard, in 1835, J. Livingston; in 1837, G. P. Casey; in 1839, H. B. Newby; in 1843, A. B. Watson; in 1850, J. H. Watson; in 1851, Elijah Piper; in 1857, J. Q. A. Bay; in 1861, H. G. Goodrich; in 1863, W. M. Hicks; in 1867, S. W. Jones; in 1869, W. H. Smith; in 1871, S. W. Jones; in 1875, C. D. Ham; in 1877, G. L. Cummins; in 1879, C. W. Lindley.

School Commissioners—D. Baugh was the first School Commissioner of whom we have any account, and was appointed in 1836; J. R. Satterfield was the next, and was appointed in 1845; he was succeeded by J. H. Pace in 1847; in 1850, W. H. Lynch; in 1851, J. H. Pace; in 1859, J. R. P. Hicks; in 1861, J. M. Pace; in 1869, G. W. Johnson; in 1873, J. D. Williams, the present incumbent.

Miscellaneous—Of the early Surveyors we can learn but little. From 1850 to the present time, they have been as follows: L. F. Casey, 1850 to 1854; W. B. Anderson, 1854 to 1865; J. D. Williams, 1865 to 1871; B. C. Wells, 1871 to 1875; W. T. Williams, the present incumbent. The first Assessor was James Kelly, and the next Edward Maxey. Among the early Justices of the Peace were the following, in their order of appointment: O. Morris, Lewis Watkins and W. Maxwell, in 1819; William Maxey in 1820, and in 1822, J. Roberts, James Abbott, J. Pace, John Jordan, W. L. Howell, Barton Atchison and Samuel Gaston.

The votes cast at the November election, 1882, by townships, were as follows: Grand Prairie, 92; Casner, 115; Blissville, 139; Bald Hill, 98; Rome, 194; Shiloh, 213; McClellan, 166; Elk Prairie, 176; Field, 193; Mount Vernon, 731; Dodds', 182; Spring Garden, 250; Farrington, 105; Webber, 174; Pendleton, 304; Moore's Prairie, 180; total, 3,312.

The following is a partial vote of the county:

For Legislature—Varnell, Democrat, 2,775; Jennings, Democrat, 2,835½; Crews, Republican, 3,241; Judd, Greenbacker, 779.

County Judge—Anderson, Democrat, 1,972; Anglen, Greenbacker, 1,239; Anderson's majority, 733.

County Clerk—Tanner, Democrat, 2,010; Hobbs, Greenbacker, 1,262; Tanner's majority, 748.

Sheriff—Gray, Democrat, 2,036; Wall, Republican, 1,236; Gray's majority, 800.

County Treasurer — Carroll, Democrat, 1,931; Legge, Republican, 1,340; Carroll's majority, 591.

Township Organization.—The State constitution of 1847-48, contained the provision of township organization—a provision that was to be voted on by the people of each county, and leaving it optional with them to adopt or reject it in their respective counties. So, in accordance with the provisions of that constitution, the first township organization act was passed by the Legislature. But the law, in attempting to put it into practical operation, disclosed radical defects. It was revised and amended at the session of 1851, substantially as it existed until the recent revision in 1871. The adoption of township organization marks an era in many of the counties of the State. The northern part of the State adopted it first. The people who had settled there were mostly from the East, and were familiar with the township system and its practical workings. The people in the southern part of the State were much more slow to take hold of the new system.

Jefferson County adopted township organization in 1869 though township officers were not elected until the following year. At the time of the change, the election precincts of the county were Blissville, Elk Prairie, Gun Prairie, Grand Prairie, Horse Creek, Horse Prairie, Jackson, Jefferson, Jordan Prairie, Knob Prairie, Long Prairie, Moore's Prairie and Mount Vernon; total, thirteen. The new system involved a few changes, and the civil and Congressional townships were made to correspond, and the following are their names and the first Supervisors of each as elected: Mount Vernon Township, H. Warren, Supervisor; Field, John C. McConnell, Supervisor; Shiloh, John R. Moss, Supervisor; Casner, Eiljah B. Harvey, Supervisor; Pendleton, William A. Jones, Supervisor; Spring Garden, William S. Bumpus, Supervisor; Rome, Gilbert L. Cummings, Supervisor; Webber, S. V. Bruce, Supervisor; Blissville, Samuel Johnson, Supervisor; Elk Prairie, George W. Evans, Supervisor; Farrington, M. A. Morrison, Supervisor; Grand Prairie, Jacob Breeze, Supervisor; Moore's Prairie, J. A. Wilbanks, Supervisor; Bald Hill, John B. Ware, Supervisor; McClellan, William A. Davis, Supervisor; Dodds, Robert D. Roane, Supervisor. The following are the Supervisors at present: Thomas E. Westcott for Mount Vernon; Henry Breeze for Grand Prairie; William J. Bledsoe for Casner; J. B. Norris for Blissville; R. T. Wright for Bald Hill; Andrew Riley, Jr., for Rome; John C. Tyler for Shiloh; Elijah Collins for McClellan; S. H. Dolby for Elk Prairie; William J. Garrison for Fields; William S. Bumpus for Dodds; C. M. Brown for Spring Garden; Thomas F. Moore for Webber; L. E. Jones for Pendleton; G. W. Clark for Moore's Prairie; L. B. Gregory for Farrington.

The township system of Illinois is not closely modeled after the New England States. There, a representative is sent from each town to the Lower House of the Legislature. In New York, owing to her vast extent of territory, this was found to be impracticable, and a county assembly, denominated a Board of Supervisors, composed of a member from each township, was then established. This modified system has been copied almost exactly in this State.

CHAPTER V.*

SOME OF THE PIONEER FAMILIES OF THE COUNTY—THE CASEYS—THEIR EMIGRATION TO AMERICA—HOW THEY SERVED IN THE REVOLUTION—FACTS AND INCIDENTS OF THEIR RESIDENCE HERE—THE MAXEYS, ANOTHER OLD FAMILY—THEIR WELSH DESCENT—WHERE AND WHEN THEY SETTLED—THE JOHNSONS—THEY ARE AN OLD FAMILY, TOO—SOMETHING OF THEM AND THEIR DESCENDANTS—OTHER PIONEERS—INCIDENTS, ETC., ETC.

> "How wondrous are the changes
> Since sixty years ago,
> When girls wore woolen dresses,
> And boys wore pants of tow;
> When shoes were made of calf-skin,
> And socks of homespun wool,
> And children did a half-day's work
> Before the hour of school."
> —*Anonymous.*

THE early settlers of Jefferson County were mostly from the States south of the Ohio River. The great majority of them were poor in worldly wealth; they were what was termed "poor white trash" in the South, in old slave times, and when the first of them came here, Illinois was still a Territory, reposing under the famous ordinance of 1787. Since the late war between the States has forever blotted out slavery, it may be interesting to know what was the "compact" or "ordinance" of 1787, so often quoted, concerning the Northwestern Territory. It was as follows:

I. No person in peaceable demeanor was to be molested on account of his mode of worship or religious sentiments.

II. The inhabitants were guaranteed the benefit of the writ of habeas corpus and trial by jury, a proportionate representation to the Legislature and judicial proceedings according to the course of the common law. "All persons shall be bailable, unless for capital offenses, where the proof shall be evident or the presumption great. All fines shall be moderate, and no cruel or unusual punishment shall be inflicted; no man shall be deprived of his liberty or his property but by the judgment of his peers or the law of the land; and should the public exigencies make it necessary for the common preservation to take any person's property or to demand his particular services, full compensation shall be made for the same." No law ought ever to be made or have force in said territory that shall, in any manner, interfere with or affect private contracts or engagements made in good faith and without fraud.

III. Religion, morality and knowledge being necessary to good government and the happiness of mankind, schools and the means of education shall forever be encouraged. Good faith, justice and humanity toward the Indians was to be observed; their lands and property not to be taken without consent and peace and friendship to be cultivated.

IV. The territory and States to be formed therein were to remain forever a part of the United States, subject to her law, the inhabitants to pay a just proportion of the public debt, contracted or to be contracted, not to

---
*By W. H. Perrin.

tax the lands of the United States nor those of non-residents higher than those of residents; the navigable waters of the lakes to remain forever free to all citizens of the United States.

V. The Territory was not to be divided into less than three States, and, at its option, Congress might "form one or two (more) States in that part which lies north of an east and west line drawn through the southerly bend or extreme of Lake Michigan." With 60,000 free inhabitants, such States were to be admitted into the Union on an equal footing with the original States.

VI. "There shall be neither slavery nor involuntary servitude in the said territory, otherwise than in the punishment of crimes, whereof the party shall have been duly convicted." this section providing also for the reclamation of fugitives from labor.

Such was substantially the fundamental law of this vast territory, which has ever had a controlling influence upon the destiny of the States carved out of it, and saved some of them from the permanent blight of slavery. Many of the pioneers of Southern Illinois have left upon record the fact that they sought homes in this country because the land would not be blemished by Negro slavery, or that civil or social distinction would be yielded only to those who owned "niggers." A fat soil ready for the plow, "land flowing with milk and honey," and a temperate climate were not peculiar to Illinois or Jefferson County. But the pioneers thought not of this. Their grand aim was a home—a home free and untrammeled by arbitrary rules of social equality, and inspired by this noble purpose they plunged into the wilderness. They did not come in great rushing crowds, but alone or in meager squads, and they settled down to live where polite accomplishments were among the lost arts, and even where language was almost a superfluity. Rough they were, uncultivated, unrefined, but still noble in a rugged way and possessing the true qualities of heroism, courage and humility. They were men of action, and whetted their instincts in the struggle for existence against the wild game, the ferocious beasts and the murderous savage.

In a preceding chapter, we sketched the principal settlers and settlements, so far as we could obtain them, up to the organization of the county. In this chapter we propose to tell something of these pioneer families, also some of the later comers to the county, who they were, what they did, how they lived and what became of them. They found the soil when they came here unbroken by the hand of husbandry and the stillness of the forests undisturbed save by the noise of the hunter's tread and the crack of the Indian's rifle. But undismayed, they went to work with a will, and the result amply repaid them for the hardships and dangers they endured.

The Casey family was and is the most numerous, perhaps, as well as the most prominent, of all the pioneer families of Jefferson County. Abner Casey,* the progenitor of the family in America, was born in the County Tyrone, Ireland, and there, upon arriving at the years of maturity, married a Welsh lady, who, like himself, possessed great physical and mental powers. They emigrated to America somewhere about the middle of the eighteenth century and settled in Virginia, close neighbors to Edmund Randolph. Their children were all born while they lived on the Roanoke, and were Levi, Randolph and a daughter—Randolph being named for their illustrious neighbor. The family moved to South Carolina about the year 1760, lo-

---

*Compiled from Johnson's pioneer sketches.

cated near Spartansburg, where they lived until after the close of the Revolutionary war. They were stanch patriots and bore an active and honorable part in the war for liberty and independence. Levi was a Colonel of South Carolina troops during the Revolution; Moses was a Captain in the same service and Randolph was a Sergeant under Francis Marion—the "Swamp Fox of the Santee." He was present on the memorable occasion when Gen. Marion feasted the British officer on sweet potatoes, roasted in his camp fire. He was in many of the battles fought in the Carolinas and in Georgia during the war. His wife was Mary Jane Pennington, and their children were Levi, Randolph, Isaac, Abraham, Charity, Hiram, Samuel and Zadok. These were all born in South Carolina except Zadok, who was born in Georgia, whither the family had removed about the year 1795, and where they remained until about 1800, when they removed into Tennessee, locating in Smith County. Here the father, Randolph Casey, died.

Of Randolph Casey's children, all eventually came to Illinois to reside except Hiram. He was a minister of the Gospel and made a visit here once, and while in the county preached to the pioneers with marked effect. Samuel Casey was the last of the children to remove West, and came in 1832, locating in the edge of Grand Prairie, where he died in 1850, his wife dying only a few years ago. Zadok, the youngest, came in 1817. Of him we shall have more to say hereafter. Levi, the eldest son, came to Illinois in an early day, but never lived in Jefferson County. He settled in what is now Johnson County, where he died. Randolph, the second son, located on the Centralia road, about four miles from Mount Vernon. He afterward moved into Clinton County, and finally to Iowa and died there. Isaac Casey, the third son of Randolph Casey, came to Jefferson County, as noticed in a preceding chapter, in the spring of 1817. He was born in 1765, and in 1788 was married to Elizabeth Mackey. Soon after his marriage, he emigrated to Kentucky and settled in Barren County, from whence he came to Illinois in 1803, locating on the Ohio River a short distance above Cave-in-Rock. His wife died in 1834 and in the fall of 1836, he married Jemima Oard. She died in 1846, and he then made his home with his children until his death. He was a man of the strictest integrity, a true type of the old-time Christian. He helped the helpless, aided the weak, fed the hungry, was a friend of peace and always ready to work to promote the interests of the church. Honest in business, courteous and kind, he was a friend to all mankind as were all men who knew him a friend to him. His children were Rebecca, William, Polly, Abraham T., Thomas M., Brunetta Catherine and Miranda. Rebecca married Isaac Hicks; Polly married Clark Casey; Brunetta married Carter Wilkey; Catherine married Henry Tyler and Miranda married George Bullock.

William Casey, the eldest son of Isaac Casey, came to Jefferson County in 1817. About 1836 or 1837, he moved to the north part of the State, but in a year or two, came back to this county and resided here until his death in 1854. His wife was Amy Barker; their children were Blackford, Maletna, William "Buck," Abraham, Drury B., Thomas, Melissa and Zadok. Mr. Casey was a compound of noble and generous qualities, and passions dark and bitter when aroused. He was enterprising and industrious, and for a long time one of the richest men in the county. A story is told of him, that when he moved back from the north part of the State, where he had lived a short time, he had over a bushel of specie, and there are those who believe that he had large sums buried at the time of his death that will never be found, unless by accident. With all his faults, and who of us but has faults? he ever maintained the dignified bearing of a gentleman of the old school.

Abraham T. Casey, the next oldest brother of William, was a minister of the Gospel. He married Vylinda Maxey in 1819, and located on the Salem road, where he died in 1834. He was a faithful minister of the Cross, and preached through all the surrounding country. His children were Harriet, who married Dr. W. S. Van Cleve, of Centralia; Catherine, who married M. Morrow; Belveretta, who married J. R. Walker; Lafayette, an itinerant minister of the Methodist Episcopal Church; Sarah, who married John Sproule; Elizabeth, who married Marion Galbraith; and Martha, who married Dr. Shirley, of Xenia.

Thomas M. Casey, the third son of Isaac Casey, was born in 1801, while his father lived in Barren County, Ky., and hence was but sixteen when the family moved to this county. He married Harriet Maxey in October, 1819. Though but eighteens years of age, he was possessed with a spirit of independence, and early in the following January went out and selected a place on his own land to build a residence. He found a site, raked away the snow, put up a rail pen, put his roof on, using rails for "weight poles," moved in and set up housekeeping on his own account. This was near where the two-story dwelling stands in which his last years were spent. He was a very religious man and devoted Christian. He was licensed to exhort in 1831, and to preach in 1843; he was ordained a Deacon in the Methodist Episcopal Church by Bishop Morris, and an Elder by Bishop Janes. He arranged all of his business and said, "I am now ready whenever God sees fit to call me." His last words were, "Peace, all is peace." He had eleven children—Clinton M., Jane, William M., Cynthia, Caroline, Mary W., Barger, Rebecca, Nanny R., Abraham and Rhoda.

Abraham P. Casey, a son of Randolph, younger brother of Isaac Casey, settled in the county in 1818. In a few years, he moved out into Grand Prairie, where he built the first house in that part of the county. He did not remain there long, however, but came back to the neighborhood of his first settlement. He was a kind of migratory character, and moved around considerably, remaining but a short time in a place. True to the proverb that "a rolling stone gathers no moss," he did not accumulate as much property as some of the other pioneers of the county, though he was so fond of hard money as to obtain the sobriquet of "Old Silver." He despised a paper currency, and if he lived to-day he would be perhaps a tireless opponent of the Greenback party. He finally moved to Missouri and died there about 1841 or 1842; his wife died about 1866. Their children were John C., Green P., Franklin S., Martin S., Isaac and two daughters, Clarissa, who married Uriah Hamblin, and Elizabeth A., who married Burrell McConnell. John C. married Polly Casey, and finally moved to Missouri, but came back to Jefferson County, where, in 1862, he died. Green P. married Margaret Watkins, a daughter of Lewis Watkins, and died in 1858, at his home on the Carlyle road. Franklin S. married Rhoda Taylor. He was a man of industry and of business enterprise, and his wife was an excellent and faithful helpmeet. He was First Lieutenant in Capt. Bowman's company in the Black Hawk war; faithfully served his country during that short but vigorous campaign. He was for many terms one of the Judges of the county court, and in 1847 was a member of the Constitutional Convention. He died in 1871. Martin S. lived on the Richview road, near Grand Prairie, and died there.

Charity Casey was the only daughter of Randolph and Mary Jane Casey. She was born in South Carolina, and married William Depriest in Tennessee, whither her family had moved. They came to Illinois in 1819. She was a very large woman, weighing some 316 pounds when she came to this county. Illinois seemed to agree with her health, and she weighed before she died nearly 350 pounds. Her sons were Green and Isaac, who lived for awhile in the county, but afterward went to Missouri, and finally died there. Lucinda, a daughter of William and Charity Depriest, married Elijah Joliff, who was an early settler in the county.

This comprises a brief sketch of the Casey family and their settlement in Jefferson County, with the exception of Gov. Casey, whom we reserve for a subsequent chapter. The Caseys were a rather remarkable family, and produced some rather remarkable men and women. The old ones, the pioneers, are dead and gone, some of them many years ago, but this brief sketch will recall a type and character of that early day. The family was and is still a numerous one, as we have said, and numbers among its members some of the best and most distinguished citizens of the county.

The Maxey family comes next in historical importance in the early settlement of the county. Edward Maxey, the first of the name of whom we have any account, was a native of Wales. He emigrated to America long prior to the Revolutionary war, and settled in Virginia. Of him or his family but little is known, except that a son, Walter Maxey, was the father of Jesse, who was born and reared in Virginia, where he married, and afterward removed to Sumner County, Tenn. He was once attacked by the Indians, who tomahawked and scalped him and left him for dead. He recovered, however, and lived twenty years after the event. His children were William, Edward, Walter, John and Elizabeth. William Maxey, the eldest son was born in Virginia in 1770, and married Mary Emily Allen, a daughter of Rhoda Allen. In 1818, they removed to Illinois, and Maxey built a horse-mill in the fall of 1820, which proved a great blessing to the people of the county. He was one of the early Justices of the Peace, having been appointed in 1821, and filled that office for a number of years. Many jokes and anecdotes were told of his official life, of which the following will serve as a sample: Being naturally diffident, the marriage ceremony was a cause of great embarrassment, and its performance among the most difficult acts he was called on to execute. Cases of debt or assault and battery he could dispose of in short order, but when it came to tying the nuptial knot, he was, to quote a slang phrase of modern invention, "all broke up." His first attempt was in uniting in marriage Ransom Moss and Anna Johnson. Their marriage took place on the 6th of July, 1821, and he had carefully prepared for it. He thought he "knew his piece," but when the couple came before him he lost his cue and broke down completely. Some say he commenced to recite the Declaration of Independence, instead of the marriage ceremony, and discovering his mistake, went back and started over again, and this time drift 1 into the constitution of the United States. Gov. Casey used to accuse him of informing the happy couple by way of prelude that the Lord instituted matrimony in the days of man's ignorance instead of "innocence." Finally, with the aid of a Methodist book of discipline and Clark's Commentaries, he succeeded in getting through the ceremony and concluded with an invocation to the "Lord to have mercy on their souls." Mr. Maxey has now been dead for many years, but his influence for good was long felt in the community. His wife died in 1837 and he in 1838. They are described as an honest, industrious, pious old couple, full of kindness and simplicity of heart, and great lovers of children. Their whole lives were but the teaching of the sublime lesson about the cup of cold water to the little one, and their influence upon their immediate circle is not yet obliterated. They had eleven children—Clarissa, Henry B., Bennett N., Elihu, Harriet, Vylinda A., Charles H., Joshua C., Hostillina (who died in childhood), William M. A. and Jehu.

Henry B., or Burchett Maxey, was born in 1795, in an old block-house erected during the Indian troubles, soon after the Revolution. He came to Illinois and settled on what was called Maxey's Prairie. At the sale of lots in Mount Vernon in September, 1819, he bought one, on which he erected the first house built in the town. He was a man of considerable prominence, and held numerous offices; also built several houses at different times. Additional to his other accomplishments, he was a great hunter, and once killed eight bears in half a mile of his own house. He was shrewd, active, alert and rich in animal life and vigor, with many of his natural faculties cultivated almost to the perfection of the Siberian bloodhound. He once walked from Brownsville, a distance of seventy or eighty miles, through an unbroken wilderness full of wild animals. He slept at night in the woods, and when the sun was clouded he had only the moss on the trees to guide him in his course. He married Peggy Taylor, and their children were Eliza R., who married S. G. Hicks; William P., who died in 1818—the first death in the county; Thomas B., now living at Xenia; Elizabeth A., who married John Breeze; Elihu K., who died in Missouri; John H., who died in 1846, on his way from St. Louis; James C., who married Nancy J. Moss; Edward M. K., living in Missouri; Jehu J.; Henry B., who died in 1865; Franklin C., who moved West, and Harvey M.

Bennett N. Maxey was a soldier in the war of 1812, and was with Gen. Jackson at New Orleans. He was one of Col. Coffee's mounted men, and when those troops mistook an order and retreated, he alone of the entire command stood his ground until the men rallied and returned to their position. His comrades called him "Broadhorns," on account of his broad shoulders and prodigious strength. His wife, like many of the pioneer women, was about as "good a man" as he was himself, and did her full part in the battle of life. Their children were Emily, William H., James J., Charles H., Joshua C., Eliza and Thomas J. Their oldest daughter, Emily, married Andrew Ray and died in a few years. William and James were preachers; Charles was a Captain in the One Hundred and Tenth Regiment during the late war, and came home in 1863-64 and died; Joshua died of a wound in Louisville; Eliza married John N. White; Thomas served through the late war, and now lives near Ashley.

Elihu, the fourth son of William Maxey, married Eveline Taylor in 1819. He owned one of the early mills of the county, and hence was a benefactor of the early settlers. His first wife died, and he married Sarah

Guthrie. He met with death accidentally in October, 1853. He rode out into the woods one morning to "hunt the cows," but was absent so long his family became uneasy, and, his horse coming home without a rider, excited their serious apprehensions The neighbors were notified and search made. His body was found two or three miles from home, cold in death. It was supposed he had been kicked by his horse. He had ten children, five sons and five daughters: Talina married Mervil Smith; Perigan T. died on Puncheon Camp; Henry lives near Walnut Hill; Parmelia married Samuel Walker; William C. is dead; Elizabeth married a man named Penix; Margaret married Thomas Maddox, and Eliza married James Maddox; Thomas married Eliza Smith, and E. Phelps died at Nashville during the late war.

Charles H. Maxey married Sallie Bruce in 1824. He was the fifth son of William Maxey, and was a man of great physical power. His children who lived to maturity were Caroline, Mary, Martha, Susan and Drucilla. The first married S. F. Parker; Mary married Joseph Burke; Martha married C. Frost; Susan married George A. Collins and Drucilla married James Swift.

Joshua C. Maxey, the sixth son of William, was born in 1807, married Susan Criswell in 1831, and at present lives on the old Maxey homestead. He is a Methodist preacher, and several times has had charge of circuits by special appointment. He is a truly Christian man and an enthusiastic Sunday school worker. He raised but two children, two dying in childhood. William T. married Mary A. Cummins, and Martha married John C. Tyler.

Dr. William M. A. Maxey, the youngest son but one of William Maxey, married Edda Owens in 1830. He is a practicing physician and a local preacher. His children are Simeon W., who served in Stratton's company in the late war; Samuel T., a Methodist preacher, also served in the army; Harriet J., who married Frank Satterfield; William C., who married Gertrude Lane and served three years in the late war; Sarah C., married Sanford Hill; and Nelson, who married Miss Berger.

Jehu G. D. Maxey is the youngest son of William Maxey. He married Mary A. Bruce, and their only child, James H., died when he was but two years old. Mr. Maxey is an exhorter in the Methodist Episcopal Church, and an earnest worker in the Sunday school.

Edward Maxey, a brother to William Maxey, and the second son of Jesse Maxey, moved to Allen County, Ky., and from thence to Jefferson County, Ill. He married Elizabeth Pitner in Tennessee, but they never had any children. They raised several adopted children, among them Judge Satterfield. He was a man of high honor and integrity; was Justice of the Peace for twenty years, County Commissioner, a pioneer school teacher, a preacher and a man in whom there was no guile. He died about 1850, and his wife soon after.

John Maxey, the youngest son of Jesse Maxey, came to Illinois in 1823, in company with William and Jonathan Wells. He, too, was a Methodist preacher, and after living eight or ten years in the county, removed to Wayne County, where he died. He raised but one son, Stephen, who died many years ago, and three daughters. Theodosia married the Rev. Joseph Hellums: Elizabeth married Greenbury Wells, and Katie married Jesse Breeze, of Walnut Hill. Such, in brief, is the record of the pioneer Maxeys, who were among the early settlers of Jefferson County, and who contributed largely to its development and improvement. In other chapters will be found sketches of the younger generations of the name.

The Johnsons, perhaps, might next be mentioned in the catalogue of pioneer families. Like the Caseys and Maxeys, they are a numerous family, and have been a prominent one from the earliest settlement of the county.

Benjamin Johnson, the ancestor of the Johnsons living here, was a native of Maryland, but removed to Hanover County, Va., where he died. John Johnson, a son of his, was the father of the pioneer Johnsons who came to Jefferson County. He married Hannah Medlock, who died early, leaving three children. He afterward married Betsey Tyler, a widow, who had three children by her first husband. By this second marriage Mr. Johnson had four children—Lewis, James, Betsey and John. After his death (about 1803), his widow and her family moved to Sumner County, Tenn. The Tylers, Mrs. Johnson's children by her first husband, were also early pioneers in Illinois.

Lewis Johnson, the eldest son of John Johnson by his second marriage, was among the early settlers in Jefferson County. He married Mrs. Winn, formerly Miss Stone, by whom he had nine children—Milly, Anna, Lucy, James E., John T., Nicholas S., Elizabeth, Nancy and Susan. Mr. Johnson was licensed to preach in Tennessee in 1812; was ordained Deacon there by Bishop Roberts in 1816, and Elder by the same Bishop in Illinois in 1827. He was a pious man, and lived a purely Christian life. It is said that for a period of fifty years he held prayers in his family regularly three times a day. He died in January, 1857, at the age of eighty, and his wife in December following at the age of eighty-three years. Of his children, Milly married Asahel Bateman in Tennessee, but removed to Illinois in an early day. Anna married Ransom Moss in 1821 and has numerous descendants in the county. Lucy married Launcelot Foster. He died early from a peculiar disease brought on from exposure while hunting. Their house was burned a year or so after their marriage and their month-old infant burned to death in it. James E. was the oldest son of Lewis Johnson. He was converted in 1821 and soon after began to exhort. He went back to Tennessee, where he attended school during the winter and then returned to Illinois and commenced preaching. He preached throughout Southern Illinois, Missouri and Arkansas, as a minister of the Methodist Episcopal Church. His health gave way and he was forced to cease regular preaching. He came here and improved a farm where John T. Johnson now lives, or recently lived. He died at the age of seventy years. John T., the next oldest brother to James, was also licensed to preach, when but twenty-one years old. He joined the Illinois Conference (Methodist Episcopal Church) and for many years preached in this State and Indiana. In 1843, he located in this county on a farm, but still continued preaching. He has always been considered a lucid, interesting preacher, a successful farmer and a useful man. The next brother, Nicholas S., married Minerva Holliday. He lived in Grand Prairie some years, where he finally died. Elizabeth married T. B. Afflack and moved to Grand Prairie and then to Richview. Nancy married James Barnes and also lives in Richview. Susan married U. G. Witherspoon, of Kentucky. They finally removed back to Kentucky after living here for a time, and now reside in Crittenden County.

James Johnson, the second son of the pioneer, John Johnson, was born in Louisa

County, Va., about the year 1778. He married Clarissa Maxey in Tennessee, and in 1818 came to Illinois with five children. His wife died in 1847, and he afterward married Mrs. Livingston. He was a man of the most unswerving honesty, and was a respected and upright citizen. He died in 1860 at the age of eighty-two years. Sixteen children were born to him, one of whom died at the age of seventeen months, another at nine years, while the rest lived to maturity. His eldest son, John N. Johnson, marrie Sarah Hobbs in 1834. He was a stirring and enterprising man, and built several houses in Mount Vernon, among them the City Hotel, which was known as the Johnson House. He was a physician, and graduated in the healing art in Cincinnati, but did not follow the profession through life. He died in 1858, leaving a wife and five children. James D. and A. Curtis, his sons, are among the prominent citizens and business men of Mount Vernon. Others of James Johnson's children are mentioned elsewhere in this work.

John Johnson, the youngest brother of Lewis and James Johnson, came to Illinois in 1834, and hence can scarcely be reckoned among the pioneers of Jefferson County. He was a preacher in the Methodist Episcopal Church, and in discharge of his ministerial duties traveled over a large portion of Ohio, Kentucky, Illinois, Tennessee and Mississippi for a period of twenty-five years. He was a man of great power in debate and in the pulpit, and his fervent piety and patient endurance were unexcelled by any minister in the conference to which he belonged. He died in Mount Vernon in 1858, aged seventy-five years. His children were Dr. T. B. Johnson, who died in Kentucky in 1870; the wife of Blackford Casey; J. Fletcher, Washington S., G. Wesley, J. Benson, a girl and boy who died in childhood, and Adam C., the faithful historian of the pioneers of Jefferson County, and whose sketch of Mount Vernon forms several interesting chapters of this volume.

Among other pioneer families of the county who will receive adequate mention as we proceed with our work, we may note the following who came in a few years after the organization of the county: The Hickses, the Wilkersons, the Jordan family, Overton Harlow, the Baldridges, Fleming Greenwood, Thomas D. Minor, the Maxwells, Mathew Cunningham, and a number of others.

We have now given in this and in the chapter on the early settlement a record of some of the pioneer families. The sketches as they appear in this book are drawn by those who never saw the originals, and who can know of them only by much talking with those who did know them long and well, and while they were here and playing their part in life, and from the brief sketches that have hitherto been written of them. To pick out the representative people of all the different classes of a community and draw a true representation of them—so true that any reader can gather an actual personal acquaintance with those who were, perhaps, dead before he was born, is no easy task, yet one, if done well and truly, will give him a just and correct idea of those about whom he is studying history for the purpose of learning. For a certain quality of society will produce a certain kind of men or a certain kind of character—a leading character, with strong marks and signs, that arrests attention and fixes upon him the duty of furnishing posterity the key to the whole mass of his fellow-men who were his neighbors and cotemporaries.

The sketches, as we have said, are not drawn by those who personally knew the

original. This is best, for then there is less danger of prejudices, either for or against the subject that constitutes the picture, and false colors are not liable to slip in. There is less incentive (there should be none) to suppress here and overdraw there; in short, less of prejudice, and consequently more of truth. But men who write are affected by much the same prejudices of color of vision in viewing transactions of which they formed a part, as other men, and for this reason, history is written by strangers or the sons and daughters of strangers, who live in the long years and ages after the actors and their immediate descendants have passed away.

So far, we have attempted to give the names and settlement, as already stated, of the first actual settlers of the county, together with some of the old and prominent and numerous families who came here over half a century ago. These notices and sketches have been necessarily brief. Many of those already mentioned will receive further notice in connection with works upon which they were actively engaged, and with subjects wherein they bore important parts. In the chapters devoted to the history of the different townships, many other pioneers hitherto unnoticed will be written up and receive full justice according to their merits. That their works are confined to divisions so small as townships does not imply that they are of no moment or interest. Men, at most, are but as coral, feeble, insignificant, working out of sight, but they transmit some occult quality or power, upheave society until, from the moral and intellectual plateau, rises, as Saul above his fellows, a Shakespeare, a Phidias or a Hamilton, the royal interpreters of the finest sense in poetry, in art and statesmanship.

CHAPTER VI.*

THE BENCH AND BAR—SUPREME COURT—ITS LOCATION AT MOUNT VERNON—THE JUDGES OF THE SAME—BREEZE AND SCATES—OTHER LUMINARIES—THE APPELLATE COURT—SOME OF ITS GREAT LIGHTS—CIRCUIT COURT—JUDGE TANNER AND OTHERS—EARLY CASES TRIED IN THE COURTS—MARSHALL, BAUGH, ETC.—PRESENT MEMBERS OF THE BAR, ETC., ETC.

"The ethics of the bar comprehends the duties of each of its members to himself."

TO write a history of the bench and bar of this or any other place is to write the history of that department which absolutely guarantees the freedom and safety of our government. The perpetuity of our liberties depends more upon an honest and intelligent judiciary than upon anything else, and to accomplish the noble purposes for which it is created it must be supported by an honest and intelligent bar. It is by the courts of the land and the powers in them vested that criminals are apprehended and punished; it is through them that all wrongs are redressed; it is by them that the wrongly imprisoned are given their liberty; it is through them that the minister is permitted to occupy his pulpit. In fact, our government could

*By George M. Haynes, Esq.

not exist without its judiciary. It is the "jewel that from the cluster riven would leave all a dark and hopeless chaos." Localizing, we can say that Mount Vernon and Jefferson County may well be termed the seat of justice and the home of Judges. Since 1848, the Supreme Court has been located here, during which time the State has spent large sums of money in a building and its equipment. The library here is the largest and most valuable in the State. There is nothing written upon the law that has passed to the dignity of authority that may not be found here, and few finer collections can be found in the United States. Perhaps few towns of its size can boast of more Judges taken from its bar than can Mount Vernon. So marked has this been that it has almost became a proverb to say "Mount Vernon, the home of Judges." Although the county had been organized for fifteen years before we had a resident lawyer, the bar here has ever since stood high in line with the profession of the State. Since 1864, the Mount Vernon bar has been represented upon the bench. In that year, the Hon. James M. Pollock was elected from this county. He was succeeded by Tanner, and he by Casey, the present incumbent. Mount Vernon has, since the county's organization, furnished Baugh and Scates, in addition to those of later date already mentioned.

Supreme Court.—Under the Constitution of 1848, the State was divided into three grand divisions, the people in each division electing one Judge of the Supreme Court. The divisions were known as the First, Second and Third; this county was placed in the First, and after a strong and bitter struggle, Mount Vernon was selected as the seat of the court for the First Grand Division, which, through biennial fights, she has continued to retain until the present.

The first term of the court held in this place convened in December, 1848, with Samuel H. Treat, Chief Justice, and J. D. Caton and Lyman Trumbull, Associates; Finny D. Preston, Clerk. There were seventeen cases on the docket. The first case was Meridith Hawkins vs. Silas N. Berry, error to Franklin. Jefferson County furnished one case, William B. Thorn against Joel F. Watson, administrator of the estate of James Ham. Thorn had a claim against the estate which Watson thought had been filed too late, and consequently barred by the statutes. Watson defeated him in the lower courts, and Thorn took it up and was again beaten. The second term convened in November, 1849, with twenty-three cases, one from this county, Governor, etc., vs. E. H. Ridgway et al., Ridgway being successful. The court remained the same until November, 1853, when Trumbull resigned and Scates was made his successor.

In November, 1854, Preston resigned as Clerk and Maj. Noah Johnston was appointed by the court to succeed him. In 1855, Treat resigned and O. C. Skinner was elected in his stead, and Scates became Chief Justice.

In 1857, J. D. Caton became Chief Justice; Scates resigned and Sidney Breeze was elected, and as such he continued until his death.

In 1857, Skinner resigned and Pinkney H. Walker was elected, since which time he has been regularly re-elected, and is at present one of the Judges. In January, 1864, Caton resigned, and Corydon Beckwith was appointed and served until June of the same year, when Charles B. Lawrence was elected. By the constitution of 1870, the judicial department of the State was reconstructed, the three Grand Divisions retained, but the Court increased to seven Judges, instead of

HISTORY OF JEFFERSON COUNTY.

three. The State was divided into seven districts and one Judge elected from each district. After the election under this system, the court consisted of Lawrence, Walker, Breeze, Thornton, Scates, Sheldon and McAllister, and it is no reflection to say that at no time since the organization of the court was it ever stronger. Its opinions were cited and recognized during this period as of the first of American authorities. In 1873, Alfred M. Craig succeeded Judge Lawrence and John Schofield went on in the place of Thornton. In December, 1875, T. Lyle Dickey succeeded McAllister, who resigned.

June 28, 1878, Judge Breeze died and David J. Baker was appointed to succeed him by the Governor, and on the 2d of June, 1879, John H. Mulkey was elected to succeed Baker, since which time there has been no change, leaving the court now consisting of Sheldon, Schofield, Craig, Dickey, Walker, Scott and Mulkey. June 3, 1867, R. A. D. Wilbanks was elected Clerk, succeeding Maj. Johnston, and so continued until November, 1878, when he was in turn succeeded by J. O. Chance, the present incumbent. From 1848 until November, 1853, the court met in the old Odd Fellows Hall on Main street, paying an annual rent of $75. From November, 1853, until the court house was completed in about 1856, it met in the Masonic Hall, over Joel Pace's store, at the same rent paid the Odd Fellows.

In 1854, an appropriation was obtained from the Legislature of $6,000 for the building of a court house: T. B. Tanner, Maj. Johnston, Zadok Casey, William J. Stephens and Dr. John N. Johnson were appointed Commissioners to take charge of the building and superintend its construction. Plans were obtained, and it was found that the fund was insufficient, but finally parties in St. Louis were found who contracted to in-close it for the money, which was done, and in 1854, T. B. Tanner, who had been elected a member of the Legislature, obtained an additional appropriation of $10,000, with which the building was completed according to the original design. In 1874, an additional appropriation was obtained for the purpose of remodeling the building, and the north and south wings were added, and the building left in its present condition, an ornament to the county and a credit to the State.

Judge Sidney Breeze.—Illinois has produced some very great men—men whom all the world has been proud to honor—men who will go down in the national history, yes, in the history of the world, as truly great. In war, the Illinois' soldiers are said to be the greatest now living; in State-craft we sent Douglas and Lincoln—men prominent in statesmanship, men to whom the world's history must accord befitting space. But, great as they are, none have been greater in their particular line than has Judge Breeze in his—a jurist quoted in every civilized country, logical, analytical, just and blunt, severe, yet impartial. Judge Breeze was born in New York on the 15th day of July, 1800 —born at the beginning of the most brilliant century the world ever saw—born fitted and destined to bear a most prominent part in the many overshadowing achievements of the world's history. He received a classical education at Union College, New York, and at a very early age started with the star of empire westward. The year 1818 found Judge Breeze at Illinois' first capital, Kaskaskia, as Assistant Secretary of State to Elias Kent Kam—his old friend. During this employment, the State capital was removed to Vandalia. The responsibilty of removing the Secretary's office was left to Judge Breeze; he accomplished the task with a yoke of oxen and the old two-wheeled cart, and thus were the great State documents removed from the old to the new capital.

In 1822, he was appointed State's Attorney; in 1827, he was made United States District Attorney for Illinois by President John Q. Adams. In 1831, he published Breeze's Reports, to be found in every well-appointed law library, and the first book ever published in Illinois. In 1835, he first went upon the bench as Judge of the Second Judicial Circuit. In 1842, he was elected to the United State Senate and served as such for six years. His career in the Senate was not barren of results. Then Clay, Webster, Benton and Calhoun were there. In the forum or in the committee, Senator Breeze ranked with those giants.

While his mind, perhaps, was not employed in the more active and exciting elements of politics and State craft, yet he was never idle, his giant intellect reached out into the great unknown future; he read its hidden pages; he saw the future wants of this then young republic; he saw a few years in the distance the great chains of iron that were to bind this continent into indissoluble union; he saw the rapid strides of commerce; he realized its demands. He saw that in the great and rich valleys and prairies of the West was to spring the attributes of prosperity and wealth to this Government. He saw the great agricultural districts bending beneath the rich harvests, asking for transportation. 'Twas then his practical sagacity and comprehensive mind discovered and brought for the first time to the light of the nation the necessity of railroad connection between the Pacific and the Atlantic. He availed himself of his opportunity as Chairman of the Committee on Public Lands in the United States Senate in 1846, elaborated in detail and brought in the first report ever made, advocating and anticipating the construction of the Pacific Railroad twenty-three years in advance of its commencement. His friends were incredulous; his enemies thought, for the time, at least, that he had, by his own blunder, succeeded in throwing ridicule on himself. But no; he only lived as many great men before his time.

It has so happened that no man has left to his age or his country a more enduring monument by which he is to be known to posterity. This one act, had he done no other, would hand him down in history as long as the whistle of the engine and the rumbling of the cars are heard upon our great plains. But this was not all that Judge Breeze did in the Senate. He was a continual worker for the development of his adopted State and the resources of the nation, but to write of his activities and public services while in the Senate would of itself make a volume. The building of the Illinois Central Railroad was under consideration while he was in the Senate, and in Judge Breeze that enterprise found a strong and valuable champion.

He was defeated in 1848 for re-election to the Senate by the hero of Cerro Gordo, Gen. Shields, who had just returned from the Mexican war, covered all over with glory. The military sentiment ran riot, as it has many times before and since, and a great mind was forced to retire for the advancement of one who, while brilliant and brave on the field, yet had no qualification to represent the rising State of Illinois in the nation's councils. And again we have illustrated the senitment, "Put a man on a charger, call him a warrior, and the American people are ready to blindly follow him they know not whither, neither do they care; so long as the shouts of the 'General' ar heard they go." A few military gentlemen have been called to the White House from the same sentiment, and the experiment has in almost every instance shown the folly of such a selection. The better the soldier, the poorer the statesman. But we are digressing. After his retirement from the Senate, Judge Breeze remained in private life until 1850, when he was elected to the Seventh General Assembly, of which he was elected Speaker of the Lower House, defeating Gov. Z. Casey of this county. In June, 1855, he was again elected Judge of the Second Judicial Circuit, and from this time it may be said he began that course of life which has handed him down as the greatest jurist this State has ever produced, and the peer of any in the nation. This marked his final retirement from politics, not, perhaps, from his own inclination, for he early evinced a strong desire for political preferment, and for years cherished his political aspirations, but his defeat by Shields so mortified him that he never afterward pressed his claims or wishes. In 1857, he resigned the Circuit Judgeship to accept a seat upon the Supreme Bench, never more to leave it until the final summons, and it is as such that he achieved his highest honors. He was upon the Supreme Bench in 1841, when he was elected to the State Senate. He died June 28, 1878, a member of the court. We know of no more fitting words by which his judicial life may be reviewed than the remarks of Mr. Justice Scott, of the Supreme Court, at Ottawa, upon the presentation of resolutions announcing Judge Breeze's death. He says: "Judge Breeze was a man of great learning in the best and broadest sense of that term. To the studies prescribed by the college of which he was graduate, he added a life-time of study. Notwithstanding his constant employment in public life, he found time for the study of classic literature, both in Latin and in English. After the close of the labors of the day, extending to a late hour of the evening, I have often known him, in his private room, before retiring, to spend hours in reading standard works on literature or scientific subjects. It was his constant habit. It is a marvel the amount of intellectual labors he could endure. What relates to his personal history will soon fade from the recollections of the living and be forever forgotten. He will only be remembered by his public works.

"In two particulars Judge Breeze will stand out prominent in history. First, in his character as a statesman, and second as a jurist.

* * * * * * * * * *

"Few men have influenced in so large a measure the jurisprudence of this State or nation in which they lived as Judge Breeze. Every one, to some extent, creates the opportunities for success in life. The means he possessed were within the reach of others, had they possessed the ability to combine them. Genius makes opportunities as well as employs those at hand for successful achievements. We call men great only in comparison with others, and hence we are always looking to see what others have done in the same field of labor. When the real does not exist we may conceive the ideal, and institute comparisons. As no one appears anywhere in judicial history who conforms exactly to the ideal of the true Judge, it is no easy task to express the conception of such a character. Some few of the essential qualities readily suggest themselves. * * * While we may not expect to find in him whose character we are considering, nor in that of any other Judge of the present or past ages, all that we might conceive to belong to the ideal Judge, yet some of the grand essentials do appear in his character. Although making no parade of it, he possessed in a full measure that absolute incorruptibility that insures purity in the administration of the law—qualities which belong to the true Judge. His judgments were always distinctly marked with impartiality and even-handed justice. He believed in those fundamental principles embodied in our organic law—that every person ought 'to obtain by law right and justice freely and without being obliged to purchase it,' and that he ought to 'find a certain remedy in the laws for all injuries and wrongs which he may receive in his person, property or reputation.'

"He had not that degree of self-confidence possessed by many, yet he was free from that hesitancy that so embarrasses many Judges, as to destroy, in a marked degree, their efficiency. Although he wrote with unusual facility, yet so careful was he in preparing his opinions, I have known him when he deemed the case of importance, to write the same over as many as three or four times.

"His style was singularly perspicuous—as specimens of fine writing, it is my judgment that his opinions will suffer nothing in comparison with the best, the most distinguished jurists of this country and of England.

"In clearness of expression and splendor of diction, they are fashioned after the best models.

"Chief Justice Marshal was on the bench for a period of thirty-four years. His opinions, with the other members of the court, are comprised in thirty volumes, exclusive of his decisions on the circuit, many of which were written and published. Judge Breeze was a member of our Supreme Court not quite twenty-three years, and yet his opinions, with those of the other Justices, compose seventy volumes, including the opinions now in manuscript. Some idea of the magnitude of his labors may be obtained when it is stated as the truth, he did his full share of the work, and that for the greater portion of the time he was on the bench the court was composed of three Justices.

"If we except one of his associates still on the bench, he has, perhaps, written more opinions than any Judge who ever occupied the bench in any of the American States. The exception, if any, is Chancellor Kent, and it is, perhaps, quite correct to say that so many opinions do not appear to his name.

* * * * * * * * * *

"There is scarcely a question that concerns the public welfare or the jurisprudence of this great State upon which he has not written, and almost always with great clearness and accuracy.

"More enduring than a monument of solid granite are the official reports of the State to his learning and ability as a jurist. Including the opinions now in manuscript, in which he participated, we will have eighty more volumes of reports, with every one of which his name is connected, either as a reporter, counsel or as a Justice delivering the opinions.

"The questions discussed in the sixty years he was in some way connected with the court are of the utmost importance, and are such as would naturally be expected to arise in that formative period of a rapidly growing State, and especially in one that has so suddenly risen to the proportions of an empire in itself.

* * * * * * * * * *

"He rests from his labors, but how truly can it be said of him his works do follow him. His fame as a judicial writer will endure as long as the common law is administered anywhere among the nations of the earth; and the beneficent principles his learning and ability assisted to maintain will aid in establishing right and justice in behalf of the humblest as well as the most exalted of our race, so long as our civilization shall stand."

He was a jurist of clear and keen perceptions, surpassed by none and equaled by few. In politics, Judge Breeze in early life was a Whig. He was a bitter opponent of Andrew Jackson, and never lost an opportunity to strike. He afterward took a different view and became a zealous Democrat, and as such he died.

It is impossible for the writer hereof to paint with pen the true character of this man. He was too great for any but great men to write. He was at times cross and sensitive, at times kind and pleasant; when he felt like it, he was one of the most companionable men, well versed in literature, always entertaining in conversation. His knowledge of Illinois and the men and parties of the State was, perhaps, superior to that of any other man, and it is to be regretted that he did not find time from his labors to put his recollections in history. He made Hon. Melville W. Fuller his literary executor, and among his effects it is hoped that much valuable manuscript may be found.

He was extremely sensitive about his age, and seldom permitted an inquiry upon that subject. Upon one occasion a few years before his death, when asked by an old citizen of this county, who had known him for years and had grown old with him, how old he was, he replied by saying, "I may be fifty, sir, and I may be one hundred and fifty; it is none of your d—d business." I have heard of but one instance where he volunteered his age. In 1872, he was pressed by his friends for the Democratic nomination for Presidency, and had he been elected, he, no doubt, would have made an administration that would have been at once strong, honest, wise and popular. But, like Clay and Webster, he was too great to be President.

Shortly before his death, he was called upon by Maj. Johnston, who, in the course of the conversation asked the Judge if he would be a candidate for re-election. The Judge's reply was: "I want to die in the harness," and so he did die, working up to the very last, and thus died one of the three great men of Illinois.

Walter B. Scates.—The eminent character of this gentleman requires more than a passing notice; in fact a history of the State would be imperfect without an extended notice of him and his many public services. For more than fifty years, his life has been closely interwoven with the public affairs of the State, and we very much doubt if there is another man of Judge Scates' years that has rendered more public service than he.

Walter B. Scates was born January 18, 1808, at South Boston, Halifax Co., Va. He came from Revolutionary stock, his maternal grandfather, Walter Bennett, for whom he was named, being a Surgeon in the war of independence. In April, after his birth in January, his parents removed to Tennessee, and after a short residence in that State removed, and finally settled upon a farm near Hopkinsville, Ky., where Walter B. grew to manhood. The Indians had but recently been driven from that country, the car of civilization had scarcely entered, and the subject of this sketch was what now would be termed "brought up in the woods." The principal amusement of the young men of that day was in riding the old, gentle horse, with a "turn of corn," some miles to the old mill, and the associations found upon these occasions were, perhaps, about the extent of his mixing with the outside world until he left home. His parents being poor, and living on what would now be termed the "borders," he had not the opportunities of school, yet his mind dispelled the cloud, and looked beyond for more educational advantages than was afforded him at home. By continued effort, and that same energy which has marked his whole life, he acquired sufficient education to enable him to read, and from this time forward it may be said that his book was his constant companion. At the age of nineteen, he broke loose from the attachments of home, and without his family's permission or knowledge he went to Nashville, Tenn., and apprenticed himself to a Mr. Wilson, editor and publisher of a newspaper. Wilson had a good library, and young Scates had it stipulated in the articles of apprenticeship that he should have the use of the library. When he first went to Nashville, it was his intention to study medicine, but having no money and but little education, he was unable to make the necessary arrangements, hence his engagement with Wilson, the printer. He continued with Wilson for about three months when his father, ascertaining his whereabouts, went to him and proposed that, if he would return home, he would find some way to send him to school. This proposition was accepted, and Walter went with his father back to the home he had three months before left.

Upon his return, he attended the neighborhood school for about one year, the latter part of which he received some instructions in Latin and Greek from a Mr. Moore. It was the intention of himself and father that he should study medicine, and an arrangement was made with a Dr. Webber, of Hopkinsville, Ky., for Walter B. to enter his office as a student, but being unable to make satisfactory arrangements about board, the engagement with Dr. Webber was abandoned. In 1828, he entered the law office of Charles Morehead, afterward Governor of Kentucky, and became a student of Blackstone. In 1831, he was admitted to the bar, and in March of that year started on horseback to go to St. Louis to locate. On arriving at Old Frankfort, then the county seat of Franklin County, Ill., he found his money matters getting short, only having $12 in depreciated currency of the old Commonwealth Bank of Kentucky. Being thus depleted in his finances, he concluded he could not maintain himself in St. Louis, and at once settled in Old Frankfort. To this place he brought his clothes and books in his saddlebags. His father had obtained 160 acres of land near Belleville, this State, which he gave him. He went to Belleville, sold or traded the land for some old horses, shipped them to New Orleans, working as a deck hand to pay the freight. Judge Scates remained at Old Frankfort five years, in the practice of the law in Franklin and fourteen other counties —a territory 80 by 120 miles. During this period, he came in contact with many of the strongest men of the State, many of whom afterward attained distinction in their profession; among them were Breeze, Eddy, Gatwood, Hardin, David J. Baker (father of the present Judge Baker, of the Appellate Court)—in fact, the bar of that circuit was the strongest in the State. In 1835, Judge Scates was elected County Surveyor of Franklin County. He participated in the Black Hawk war; was at the battle of Kellogg's Grove. In 1835, he was also a candidate before the Legislature for the office of Judge of the Circuit Court of the Third Judicial District, but was defeated by Alexander Grant. In 1836, he was appointed Attorney General for the State and moved to Vandalia, then the capital. About this time, November 21, 1836, he was married to Miss Mary Ridgway, at Shawneetown, Ill. In about 1837, Scates was elected Judge of the Circuit Court by the Legislature, in place of Hardin, resigned, and removed to Mount Vernon. He held his first court in McLeansboro. In 1840, a law was passed, legislating all Circuit Judges out of office, and imposing circuit duties upon the Judges of the Supreme Court. The Supreme Bench was increased by the election of five new Judges. Under this law, Judges Douglas, Ford, Treat and Scates were elected. He occupied the Supreme Bench until 1847, when he resigned, and was elected a member of the Constitutional Convention from the counties of Hamilton, Jefferson and Marion. He was Chairman of the Judiciary Committee of that body. In the convention, he was active, industrious and able. He advocated the 2-mill tax, an elective judiciary, universal suffrage, prohibition of special legislation, prohibition of banking, limited sessions of the Legislature and strongly opposed the poll tax.

In 1853, Judge Lyman Trumbull, of the Supreme Bench, having resigned his seat for the purpose of accepting the office of United States Senator, Judge Scates was elected to the vacancy, and continued as such until 1857, when he resigned and removed to Chicago, and entered into the practice of the law with William K. McAllister, John N. Jewett and Francis B. Peabody.

In 1858, Mr. Peabody withdrew from the firm, leaving the firm of Scates, McAllister & Jewett—perhaps as strong a legal combination as then existed in the State. McAllister afterward became a member of the Supreme Bench, and is now on the Circuit bench in Chicago. The firm continued in a growing and lucrative practice until August, 1862, when Judge Scates, thinking his country needed his services in its hour of apparent darkness, retired from the law firm of which he was the head, and although beyond that age in life when such a sacrifice could be demanded, volunteered his services to the army, and was at once assigned to duty as Adjutant on Gen. McClernand's staff, and so continued, in camp and in field, doing brave and gallant service for the land of his birth until he was mustered out in January, 1866. He was brevetted Brigadier General for bravery and faithfulness in the line of duty. Of Gen. Scates, it is but just to history to say that he, in every post assigned him, was vigilant, active, faithful, brave and zealous. He was a true and tried soldier, prompt in the performance of every duty, undaunted in the hour of danger, and, although comparatively an old man, full of fire, courage and energy. Upon his return from the army, he re-entered the practice of his profession at Chicago, as the senior member of the firm of Scates, Bates & Towslee; but he was not permitted to remain long in the pursuit of his private business; he had proven himself so faithful a servant, and in the same year of his return from the army, President Johnson appointed him Collector of Customs at Chicago, vice Havan, deceased, and in this capacity he proved himself the same efficient and faithful officer that had characterized him throughout life. Of his integrity and ability in the administration of his duties, his regular reports to the department bear the strongest evidence, each showing an increase of receipts and a decrease of expenses. Judge Scates served his time as Collector of the Port with honor to himself and credit to the department, and it may well be said that with more men of the Judge's ability and integrity to superintend and handle the revenue there would not be heard so often the cry of fraud and embezzlement. After his retirement from public service, he again entered the law, and is still so engaged, although on account of his age (seventy-five years) and feebleness, he at present is not attempting the practice extensively, and is perhaps only engaged in some few matters in which he has a personal interest. He recently told the writer that he expected to visit Mount Vernon at the next session of the Supreme Court, in November, and there make an argument in an important case. Judge Scates was Chief Justice of the Supreme Court several terms, and it is, perhaps, as such that he shines brightest. He has written in many leading cases, and ably written. His opinions are recognized to-day by the courts and the bar as of the highest authority—the peer of any, and second to none; for clearness and analytical force, learned and soundness of law, his opinions are remarkable. To Judge Scates, together with Gov. Casey, Jefferson County and Mount Vernon to-day owe a debt of gratitude that they will, perhaps, never be able to pay. It was owing to their efforts, as members of the Constitutional Convention of 1848, that the Supreme Court was established there. All of the towns in this division were applicants, and pressed their claims with energy; but by the skill of Judge Scates, who had been a member of the Supreme Bench, and of Gov. Casey and Maj. F. S. Casey, Mount Vernon was selected, and has so far been able to retain it. Perhaps if Judge Scates was to be measured by the standard of greatness that is so prevalent to-day—so unjust, so short-sighted—he would not bear the test. We allude to the test of "means"—of "money." Judge Scates lived in a day when brains, not money-bags, constituted worth. He engaged in a few business ventures, but they were not successful, and to-day he is a poor man in money, but rich in mental results, which will remain an honorable monument to him long after a world of money has passed away. In fact, no higher compliment can be paid the public servant who has spent a lifetime in office than to truthfully say, "He closed his career a poor man." It is a sure record of honesty, and it might be added that, in the present day, it is a compliment too rarely deserved.

David J. Baker was Associate Justice of the Supreme Court, appointed by Gov. Cullum to the vacancy occasioned by the death of Judge Breeze.

Judge Baker was born in Kaskaskia, on the 20th of November, 1834, and was the third son of the late Judge D. J. Baker, of Alton. He graduated at Shurtleff College in 1854, carrying off the prize of the Latin oration. He read law with his father, and was admitted in 1856. In the same year, he cast his first vote, for John C. Fremont for President, and from that day to the present there has been no perceptible change in his politics. Yet it is safe to say that the bummers and corruptionists that have so nearly wrecked the Republican party find no sympathy in Judge Baker. In 1864, he was elected Mayor of Cairo, and in 1869 was elected Judge of the Nineteenth Judicial Circuit.

In July, 1864, he was married to Miss Elizabeth White, daughter of John C. White, of Cairo. He was re-elected Judge in 1873; resigned, to accept the appointment of Judge of the Supreme Court, in 1878; was again re-elected to the Circuit Bench in 1879, and was, by the Supreme Court, assigned to Appellate Court duty—which position he now holds.

As a Judge, he is logical, discriminating and just; in private life, he is social, kind and genial.

Judge John H. Mulkey, who now occupies the Supreme Bench from this division, is a man who has long been known to the bar of Southern Illinois.

He was born about 1823, in Kentucky, and with his father's family came to Illinois and settled in Franklin County. The family, with the exception of the Judge, were farmers. He soon discovered that he was not specially adapted to farm life. He obtained a fair education, and by persistent reading soon stored his mind with a fund of general information.

At twenty-five years of age, he entered the commercial world, and opened a cross-roads store in Franklin County, but he did not continue long in this business. The "dogs of war" were beginning to growl, and the military spirit was pervading the country with irresistible force, and Judge Mulkey did not escape its attack. He volunteered as a private of Company K, Second Illinois Regiment, and took up the line of march for the land of the "Montezumas." He was afterward promoted to Second Lieutenant of his company. Upon his return from war, he taught school and began the study of the law, reading, as some of his friends have said, in "the brush." He afterward read some at Benton, Franklin County, after which he tried farming, but was not a success, and again became a merchant for a short time. His career in this direction was brought to a sudden close, however, by an unfortunate adventure; he invested largely in lumber (hoop poles), loaded them on a flat-boat and started for the market, but danger was ahead of him. His craft struck a snag, and down into the waters of the Mississippi went boat, hoop poles, and about all of the Judge's earthly effects, and left him in a seriously damaged condition; in fact, he was a "busted merchant." He then, with ax and hoe, undertook to subdue the wild forest and make him a home; but again he failed.

In 1857, he removed to Perry County, and was admitted to the bar. It was not long until he and his friends discovered that he at last had drifted to his element. He soon attained a high rank in his profession—"rode the circuit," as was the custom in those days.

It is, perhaps, not out of place to say that his father, a prominent minister in the Christian Church, long cherished the hope that his son should follow his footsteps and likewise enter the ministry, and made some effort to prepare the Judge for clerical duties. And no doubt the son made strong effort to comply with his father's wishes in this particular, and while he was noted for his early and exemplary piety, this enterprise was no more successful than his farming and merchandising. He was plain, unassuming and fun-loving in his young manhood, and yet he must have been a close, hard-working student in order to carve out the bright and honorable career that lay before him. In 1860, he located at Cairo, and formed a partnership with the present Judge D. J. Baker, and from this time we may date his rapid rise to the head of the bar in Southern Illinois.

April 2, 1864, he was commissioned Circuit Judge of the Third Circuit; but previous to this he was, for opinion's sake, made one of the victims of arbitrary arrest, and at the suggestion of the authorities, for a time took up his residence at the old capitol in Washington—a hotel conducted exclusively by the Government—and while the accommodations were not altogether of a desirable nature, yet they were regular, and all the bills paid by the Government. On June 2, 1879, he was elected to the Supreme Bench, vice Baker, and is at present filling the high position.

Judge Mulkey owes nothing to fortunate circumstances or surroundings. He has not been favored with the aid of strong and influential friends; but alone, and by his own inherent strength of mental power, he has achieved, apparently without effort, the prize for which so many ambitious men have toiled and struggled.

Appellate Court.—The Constitution of 1870 provided for the creation of Appellate

Courts, after the year 1874, of uniform organization and jurisdiction in districts created for that purpose, to which such appeals and writs of error as the General Assembly may provide may be prosecuted from Circuit and other courts, and from which appeals and writs of error may lie to the Supreme Court in all criminal cases and cases in which a franchise or freehold or validity of a statute is involved, and in such other cases as may be provided by law. Such Appellate Courts to be held by such number of Judges of the Circuit Courts, and at such times and places and in such manner as might be provided by law; but no Judge shall sit in review upon cases decided by him, nor shall said Judges receive any additional compensation for such services. Under this provision of the constitution, the Legislature, in 1877, created four Appellate Courts in the State; the first to consist of Cook County, the second to include all of the counties of the Northern Grand Division of the Supreme Court except Cook, the third to include all of the Central Grand Division, and the fourth to include all of the Southern Grand Division. The Judges of these Appellate Courts to be assigned by the Supreme Court from the Circuit Courts of the State, and each court to consist of three Judges thus assigned. Two terms each are held every year.

On the organization of the court in this, the Fourth District, Judges Tazewell B. Tanner, James C. Allen and George W. Wall were assigned by the Supreme Court to Appellate Court duty. Judge Tanner became the first Presiding Justice of the court, and R. A. D. Wilbanks was its first Clerk, by virtue of his offices as Clerk of the Supreme Court.

In June, 1879, Judges Wall, David J. Baker and Thomas S. Casey were assigned to the Appellate Court, and now constitute that court. While this branch of the new judicial machinery of the State has only been in practical operation since 1877, yet it is in good favor by the bar of the State. Its effect has been to greatly relieve the Supreme Court in the then rapidly accumulating business. It insures more promptness and greater dispatch in the law than could have possibly been obtained without it or some other relief measure.

Judge Tazewell B. Tanner.--Perhaps no member of the bar of this county became so thoroughly identified with every material interest as did the subject of this sketch.

He was born in Henry County, Va., and died at his residence in this place on the 25th day of March, 1880. He came to this county in 1846 or 1847, and took charge of the public schools, after which he became connected with the *Jeffersonian*, a Democratic newspaper then published here. In 1848 or 1849, he was taken with the gold fever, and crossed the plains in search of wealth. He met with some success, returned in 1850 or 1851, was elected Clerk of Circuit Court, served two years and resigned. He had taught school in Belleville before he came here, and while there read law with Gov. Matteson. While Clerk of the Circuit Court, he continued the study, and upon his resignation he was admitted to the bar, and at once entered upon the practice with the now Judge Thomas S. Casey. In 1854, he was elected to the Legislature, and while there secured an appropriation for the building, at this place, of the Supreme Court House, and was made one of the Commissioners to superintend its construction. In 1862, he was elected a member of the Constitutional Convention. He early attained a high standing in the profession as a lawyer, and 'hile "riding the circuits" always had his share of the business. In 1867, he was a candidate for Judge of this circuit, but was defeated by the Hon. James M. Pollock. In 1873, he was again a candidate, and was elected over Judge Pollock and Col. John M Crebbs, of White County. In 1877, upon the organization of the Appellate Court, he was, by the Supreme Court, assigned to the Appellate Bench, and became its first presiding officer. In June, 1879, he was, for a time, a candidate for Judge of the Supreme Court, but withdrew before the election. Upon his retirement from the bench, he again engaged in the active practice, and so continued until stricken down by the disease which terminated his life. It is not our purpose to give an extended sketch of Judge Tanner in this chapter—his full biographical sketch will be found elsewhere—but a history of the bar would not be complete without something of him. He was a kind, social gentleman, full of interesting anecdotes, and always fond of relating them. There are many good stories told of him, one of which the writer hereof well remembers: He was defending a man charged with shooting at some negroes. The prosecuting witness was a colored gentleman known here as George or Capt. Scott. The Captain had sworn very positively to the shooting, and had made a rather strong case against the Judge's client; but the cross-examination came, and Tanner took the Captain in hand to break the force of his evidence, if possible. He commenced by asking him if he was in the house at the time the shooting occurred.

Scott answered, "No."

"Were you out doors?" asked Tanner.

"No, sah."

"Were you under the bed?"

"No, sah."

"Were you in the loft?"

"No, sah."

"Were you under the floor?"

"No, sah."

"Were you in the chimney?"

"No, sah."

Tanner, now thinking he had him fast: "Well, sir, if you were not in the house, out doors, under the bed, in the loft, under the floor nor in the chimney, where were you, sir? Now, answer me that, sir;" and he drew down his eyebrows and closed his eyes, as was his custom when he thought he had his man fast, and paused for the answer.

The answer came with promptness: "I was a-standing in the door, sah; that's whar I was, sah."

It is needless to say that the examination proceeded no further.

Judge Tanner was a profound lawyer; well read in all the books. In practice, as well as on the bench, he went to the bottom of every case presented. He brought to his aid an intelligent industry, that made him a better lawyer at the end of each year than he was at the beginning. To young men just entering the profession, he was most kind; he always had words of encouragement for them. It was the good fortune of the writer to study law with the Judge, and no man was ever kinder to a student; he always had a good word. To his client he was honest and just. If the client did not have a case, the Judge did not hesitate to tell him so; and frequently has he lost clients because he did not advise success; but his principle and theory was that if the client did not have a case, to frankly tell him so.

On the bench he was most painstaking. He sifted every case and brought to the front the equities. Of unimpeachable integrity, a purer man never sat in judgment.

"A judge—a man so learned
So full of equity, so noble, so notable;
In the process of life so innocent;
In the management of his office so incorrupt;

In the passages of rights so wise; in
Affection of his country so religious;
In all his services to the State so
Fortunate and exploring, as envy
Itself cannot accuse, or malice vitiate."

Judge G. W. Wall, at present member of the Appellate Court and its presiding officer, was born in Chillicothe, Ohio, April 22, 1839; came with his family to Illinois in the latter part of 1839 and located in Perry County, where he grew to manhood. For a time was a student at McKendree College, but graduated at the Michigan University in 1858. He read law with C. I. Simons, in Cairo, and afterward graduated at the Cincinnati Law School in 1859, and was at once admitted to the bar. In 1866, he was a member of the law firm of Mulkey, Wall & Wheeler, of Cairo, which continued for many years, and until he was elected Judge of the Circuit Court. He was attorney for the Illinois Central Railroad, and while thus acting a good story is told of him. He was called upon to attend a case at Effingham for the railroad, which had been sued by a citizen for the value of stock killed by defendants' train. The venerable and ever ready O. B. Ficklin was prosecuting the company, together with some other attorney whose name is not now remembered. The evidence was heard, and counsel went to the jury. The plaintiff's case was opened by Ficklin's associate, who indulged in considerable bunkum and bombast about giant corporations, etc. After he closed, Wall replied for the defense, and during the course of his remarks compared the gentleman who had preceded him to Dickens' famous character of "Sergeant Buzfuz," and, as he thought, completely annihilated the gentleman, and left nothing to be done but for the jury to return a verdict for the defendant, and thus closed his case.

It was now time for Ficklin to make the closing argument for the plaintiff, and after speaking to the testimony and the law, he concluded in the following vein of pathetic and injured innocence:

"And now, gentlemen of the jury, it becomes my painful duty to reply to the malignant and uncalled-for attack upon one of the best men this country ever produced; a man who has long since slept with his fathers, and upon whose character no man, until today, has dared to cast the shadow of suspicion. I allude, gentlemen of the jury, to the attack of my young friend Wall upon the memory of that good and kind man, Sergeant Buzfuz. Gentlemen, it was not, perhaps, your privilege, as it was mine, to have known him personally. I remember him well, in the early and trying times of this country. He first assisted to cut out the roads through this county. He was the early pioneer; who was ever ready and willing, with honest heart and active hand, to aid a friend or brother in distress. In fact, gentlemen of the jury, there are few men, living or dead, that this country owes more to than it does to my old friend Sergeant Buzfuz. It is true, gentlemen, that he was somewhat uncouth and blunt in his way, but his every action, I assure you, was prompted by a noble and honest motive. He was not blessed with the brilliant and accomplished education of my young friend. He, gentlemen of the jury, wore no starched shirt, or fine neckties; he was humble and retired. In his leather leggins and hunting shirt he went about the country, not as a representative of a rich railroad monopoly, but as an humble citizen doing good to his fellow-man. His bones have long since moldered into dust; the sod grows green over his grave; his work is done, and he is gone from among us to return no more forever; and I was surprised to hear his just and amiable character attacked in the manner it has been upon this occasion; and it is impossible for me, his last remaining friend, to permit it to go by unnoticed. And to you, sir [turning to Wall, who was by this time completely dumb-founded], I say, no better man ever lived than he whom you have so unjustly abused. Youth, sir, should have more respect for the men who have made life pleasant for those who come after them, than to assail their character in the manner you have done;" and thus he continued until his close, with great earnestness and the utmost apparent sincerity. At its close, the jury could hardly wait until they could write their verdict for the full amount of damages claimed by the plaintiff, and, it is said, so worked up were they that Wall had difficulty in escaping personal violence.

In 1862, Judge Wall was elected a member of the Constitutional Convention; in 1864, he was State's Attorney for the Third Judicial Circuit, and in 1870 was again a member of the Constitutional Convention.

In August, 1877, he was elected Judge of the Third Judicial Circuit, which position he still holds. In September, 1877, he was assigned to the Appellate Court for the Fourth District, and has so remained to the present time. As a Judge, he is clear, concise and sound, of unimpeachable integrity; and for ability and legal learning he takes front rank in the State's judiciary. Yet, it is said, he has never referred in a disparaging manner to any of the early settlers since he made the acquaintance of Judge Ficklin.

Hon. Thomas S. Casey, one of the Circuit Judges of this judicial district, and also one of the Appellate Judges, was born in Jefferson County, Ill., April 6, 1832, and is a son of Gov. Zadok Casey. He was educated at McKendree College, Lebanon, Ill., and after completing his allotted course of studies and securing the degree of Master of Arts, he applied himself to the study of law under the preceptorship of Hugh B. Montgomery, with whom he remained as a student for three years. At the expiration of that time, he was (in 1854) admitted to the bar. In 1860, he was elected State's Attorney for the Twelfth Judicial District, having, up to this time, been engaged in the practice of his profession. In 1864, he was re-elected to the same position. In 1862, he entered the army of the United States as Colonel of the One Hundred and Tenth Regiment of Illinois Volunteer Infantry, and served during the succeeding eleven months. He participated in the battle of Stone River, and took part, also, in many other minor engagements. On his return from the field, he resumed his professional labors, and until 1868 filled the position of States Attorney. In 1870, he was elected to the Lower House of the Legislature, and while a member of that body delivered a powerful free-trade speech, which is noted as being the first speech of its kind ever delivered in the Legislature of Illinois. In 1872, he was elected to the State Senate, and served for four years. In 1879, he was elected one of the Judges of the Second Judicial Circuit Court, and immediately thereafter was, by the Supreme Court, assigned to duty as one of the Judges of the Appellate Court of the Fourth District; which positions he still holds. In politics, he has always been an "Ironside Democrat." He was married, in October, 1861, to Matilda S. Moran, of Springfield, Ill.

Judge Edwin Beecher, one of the Judges of this circuit, was born in Herkimer County, N. Y., September 11, 1819. He received a collegiate education, and, in September, 1837, removed to Licking County, Ohio; and at Lancaster, Ohio, he read law with the Hon. Henry Stansbury. In 1844, he settled in Fairfield, Wayne Co., Ill., and entered at once upon the duties of his profession. At that time, there was but one lawyer, a Mr. Ward, in the county, and he died the spring after Judge Beecher's arrival. Judge Beecher at once took a front rank in the profession, and in 1846 was elected Probate Justice of Wayne County. He was elected Judge of the Circuit Court for this circuit in 1855, and held the office for six years. In 1860, he edited the second edition of Breeze's Reports, and made the volume more valuable by additional notes and citations. He was appointed Paymaster in the United States Army in November, 1862, and continued as such until 1869.

Judge Beecher has always been regarded as a profound lawyer and a wise counselor; he made an excellent Judge—and in whatever position he has been called, he has discharged the duties required of him faithfully and honestly. He is still residing at Fairfield, where he first settled, and although he is now in his sixty-fourth year, he is hale and vigorous, and enjoying a lucrative practice.

Circuit Court.—The first term of Circuit Court held in this county was convened on the 8th day of October, A. D. 1819, with William Wilson as Judge; Joel Pace, Clerk; Lewis Watkins, Sheriff, and Frederick Adolphus Hubbard, Prosecuting Attorney.

The grand jury, after a laborious session of about two hours in the woods north of the public square, about where the livery stable of Walker & Pattison now stands, returned two indictments, one against William Casey and one against Lewis Watkins, Sheriff, both for assault and battery. Watkins confessed the soft impeachment, and a fine of $2 and costs was imposed.

May term, 1820, Wilson presided and Henry Eddy was appointed Prosecuting Attorney for the term. Two civil cases appeared on the docket, both dismissed by plaintiff, six indictments for assault and battery and five for selling liquors without a license, from which we gather that the early settlers came here with the impression that a good knock-down was a luxury to be sought after by those who would have distinction linger around their names. This sentiment, accompanied with a bit of the "elixir of life," or "corn juice," as it may have then been called, was well calculated to make things interesting and not a few sore heads.

At the October term, 1820, Hon. Thomas C. Brown presided. At this term an indictment was returned against Ferdinand Herrin for counterfeiting, and for the first time the county found itself in need of a jail; but none was at hand, and the prisoner was taken to the White County Jail, from whence he proceeded to make his escape, but after a while he was recaptured and lodged in jail at Old Covington, Washington County, where he remained until the June term of the court, 1821, Judge Joseph Phillips presiding. On the 19th day of June, 1821, Herrin was placed on trial, and as it was the most important criminal trial that had been called, considerable interest was manifested, and after due legal forms, a jury was called and testimony heard. After due and careful consideration, the jury returned a verdict of guilty, and the court immediately proceeded to pronounce the following sentence: " It is therefore considered by the court that the defendant pay a fine to the people of the county aforesaid in the sum of $20 and costs of this prosecution, and that he be whipped thirty-nine stripes on his bare back, which the Sheriff of the county is ordered to inflict at half past 6 o'clock this evening, and it is further ordered that he be committed until fine and sts are paid." Speedy justice, indeed! It was the first time an opportunity had presented itself to give

to the citizens a practical illustration of the "terrors of the law," and it could not be lost. The whipping part was executed at the appointed hour, and considering the number of inhabitants in the county at that time, no larger number of the fair daughters and stalwart sons of Jefferson County were ever gathered together. He was committed under the order of the court, but wages being low and payments poor in jail, he did not accumulate very rapidly, and after awhile he was released and the fine and costs are still unpaid. A little management in the way of gate fees might have paid it, but it was a free show.

At the November term, 1822, Hon. Thomas Reynolds presided and William Wood sued John M. Pace for false imprisonment. Parties not being ready, the cause was continued until the May term, 1823, at which term the Hon. John Reynolds presided. The case of Woods against Pace was called and tried by jury, and the following verdict returned: "We the jury find damages in favor of plaintiff $38.37½ in paper of this State." Judgment was accordingly rendered.

October term, 1823, Thomas Reynolds presided and for the first and only time in the history of the county, the Grand Jury adjourned without finding any indictments. Peace and good will seems to have reigned throughout the entire county.

At the May and October terms, 1824, Thomas Reynolds presided. In April, 1825, James Hall was upon the bench; October, 1825, James Wattles wore the title and James Hall was here again in April and October, 1826.

March, 1827, court opened with Thomas Brown on the bench. The grand jury at this time in hunting for violators of the law, discovered that Joel Pace, the Clerk of the court, had been a little pugnacious, and they returned a bill against him for assault and battery. Defendant first thought the indictment was bad and entered his motion to quash. The court, however, was inclined to be satisfied, and overruled the motion. Defendant by this time came to the conclusion that he was not guilty, and so entered his plea and called for a jury. A jury came, and after full investigation of the case, came to the conclusion that the defendant was again mistaken in his plea, and returned a verdict of guilty as charged, whereupon defendant was required to contribute the sum of $1 to the school fund and also to pay the costs of the prosecution.

Judge Brown continued to hold the courts until the March term, 1835.

In March, 1835, Alex F. Grant came to the bench.

March and August terms, 1836, Jeptha Hardin presided. About this time Judge Hardin's brother-in-law killed a man, and the Judge resigned his seat to prosecute him, and in doing so said he would rather be the owner of a tub mill in Kentucky than a Circuit Judge in Illinois.

After Hardin came Scates, who held court from 1837 to 1846.

At the August term, 1838, Downing Baugh was indicted for retailing clocks without having first obtained a license therefor. Defendant entered his plea of not guilty, as inferred from the following order entered in the case: "Now on this day came the people by Marshall, State's Attorney, and the defendant in his own proper person, and the said defendant for plea says he is not guilty and for trial puts himself upon the country and State's Attorney does the like, whereupon let a jury come, and thereupon a jury came, to wit: James Montgomery, Samuel Cummins, John R. Allen, Joseph Dorrel, Granville Jones, James Bennett, John Dodson, William R. Little and Uriah Witherspoon, who being elected, tried and sworn, well and truly to try the issues joined, upon their oaths do say, we, the jury, find the defendant guilty. It is considered by the court that the plaintiff recover of the defendant the sum of $5 and costs of this proceedings."

We conclude that the proceedings had in this case did not materially affect the defendant's popularity, because he was afterward made Judge of the Circuit Court.

With this one exception, nothing of special interest seems to have come before the court until the April term, 1841, when the first indictment for murder was returned into court against Rollin Bradley, charging him with killing and murdering one Elijah P. King. Nothing was done at this term in the case except to recognize the witnesses and continue. The witnesses were Robert A. D. Wilbanks, father of the present Clerk of the Appellate Court; William H. Short, John Browning, James W. Garrison, Nathan Kirk, A. D. W. Williams, Elijah Piper, George Black, Bershall Black and James A. Hamilton.

At the special November term, 1841, the case was called and the trial entered upon. But in order that the case may be fully understood, we will give the circumstances of the killing as we have gathered them from a history of the county by Dr. A. Clark Johnson, published in the *Free Press* a few years ago:

Elijah P. King, the victim, lived near the east side of Elk Prairie. Bradley lived on the west side, was an industrious man, kept a barrel of whisky, and was gaining property as rapidly as was common in that day. He was, however, always a determined and dangerous man.

King came to Bradley's for some whisky; before he left a quarrel arose, and King, being a large, stout man, and rather anxious for a fight, took a chair, knocked Bradley down, and gave him a very severe beating, and, leaving him, got on his horse and went home. Wesley Hicks came in a few minutes afterward, and finding Bradley insensible and the floor all bespattered with blood, pronounced him a murdered man. But by the help of Hicks' dressing and good attention, he was able to be up next day and swore he would kill King on sight.

The next morning King concluded he would go to Bradley's and make friends with him and get some more whisky. When he rode up, Bradley met him with his gun. King said, "Bradley, you are not going to shoot me, are you?" Bradley replied, "Yes, by —, I am." King dismounted on the opposite side of his horse, exclaiming, "For God's sake don't shoot me." Bradley stepped around the horse, placed the gun to King's side, fired, and King died in a few minutes. Bradley then fled. He was, however, captured, indicted, and trial set for the special November term, 1841. Scates was on the bench; Willis Allen was Prosecuting Attorney; Henry Eddy, W. J. Gatewood, S. G. Hicks and E. Jones represented the defense. After an examination of about fifty men, a jury was impaneled, consisting of Coleman Smith, W. M. Fuller, J. H. Watson, S. B. Shelton, B. McConnell, Jesse Phillips, D. Baugh, John Holt, D. McLaughlin, Joel Smith, Edward Owens and W. Gibberson. The examination of witnesses began on November 30, and December 7, the argument opened, continuing until December 8, when the case went to the jury. In a short time, however, the jury returned a verdict of guilty.

Motion for new trial and arrest of judgment being overruled, the court pronounced sentence of death on Bradley and fixed the 3d day of January, 1842, between the hours of 12 and 2 o'clock, for his execution. Judge Scates is said to have evinced considerable feeling, but Bradley listened with much indifference and at the conclusion, got up and took a drink of water as if nothing had happened.

A gallows was erected somewhere near where the machine shop now stands, and every arrangement made for the execution; but Bradley had friends, and they were not idle. A petition was at once circulated, asking for his pardon. Bluford Hayes took it to Springfield, obtained the pardon and returned just in time to disappoint one of the largest crowds that ever assembled in the county, many of them leaving mad and hot at their disappointment.

Thus we give the history of the first murder ever committed in this county, and the only one where the sentence of death was passed.

Judge Scates was on the bench from 1837 until 1846, when the Hon. William A. Denning was elected, and continued to hold court until the election of Judge Marshall in 1851, when he resigned, and Downing Baugh was appointed to fill the vacancy. Edwin Beecher followed Baugh in 1855, and in 1861 Marshall came back, remained until February, 1865, when he again resigned to accept a seat in Congress, and James M. Pollock was elected and served until 1872, when he was succeded by T. B. Tanner, and in 1878 he gave way to Thomas S. Casey, the present incumbent. Thus have we given a brief sketch of the Circuit Court.

William Wilson was born in Loudoun County, Va., in 1795. At eighteen, he studied law with Hon. John Cook, a lawyer of much prominence at the Virginia bar and who was afterward Minister to the court of France. In 1817, young Wilson came West in search of fame and success. He settled near Carmi, White County. In 1818, he was a candidate for Judge of the Supreme Court before the Legislature, but was defeated by six votes; but within less than one year he was appointed to a vacancy and served as Justice, when he was made Chief Justice, then in his twenty-ninth year. He was not a politician in any sense of the word; he did that which he conceived to be his duty regardless of consequences, and this trait, together with some considerable legal knowledge and ability, kept him on the Supreme Bench for thirty years. His composition was clear, distinct and to the point. He possessed an analytical mind; his judgment as a lawyer was discriminating and sound, and upon the bench his learning and impartiality commanded respect, while his own dignified deportment inspired decorum in others. He was greatly esteemed by the members of the bar.

In politics, Judge Wilson was a Whig. He was an amiable and accomplished gentleman in his private life, with manners engaging and friendship strong. His hospitality was of the "Old Virginia" order, and during his summer vacations he almost always had many friends and men of distinction visit him at his home on the banks of the Little Wabash near Carmi.

With the re-organization of the judicial system of the State in 1848, Judge Wilson retired to private life. He died April 29, 1857, at his home near Carmi, in his sixty-third year, one-half of his life having been spent upon the bench of the highest court of his State.

Samuel S. Marshall, a native of Illinois, has spent his whole life in this State. He was born in Gallatin County, near Shawneetown, on the 12th day of March, 1821, and there grew to manhood, during which time he obtained a fair education. He entered the law office of Henry Eddy, of Shawneetown, one of the then prominent lawyers of the State. In 1844, Judge Marshall was admitted to the bar, and shortly after located at McLeansboro, where he still resides, and began the practice of his profession. He was not long permitted to remain in private life. He already began to develop traits of character and ability which pronounced a leader, and in 1846 he was elected to the Legislature, where he at once took a front rank in the councils of the State. During his term as a member of the Legislature, he was elected by that body Prosecuting Attorney of this judicial circuit, then comprising the counties of Jefferson, Marion, Hamilton, Franklin, Williamson, Jackson, Union, Alexander, Pulaski, Massac, Pope, Hardin, Gallatin and Saline, fourteen in all, extending from what is now the Ohio & Mississippi Railroad to the southern boundary of the State at Cairo; and from the Ohio River on the east to the Mississippi on the west. In those days, it will be remembered that no railroads were in this county, and the traveling accommodations were not as good as at present. The court and bar "rode the circuit" from county to county, sometimes in a stage, sometimes in a wagon, then on horseback and again on foot, with a rail on their shoulder to pry the stage out of the next mud hole. Those were trying times on the bar, and yet many pleasures were had that are not to-day enjoyed; telling stories and cracking jokes was the pastime on the way. At court, four or five would be stowed away in a small room at the best hotel, which was nothing to speak of. But whisky was cheap, and the trials were bravely endured. For two years Judge Marshall "rode the circuit" in this manner as Prosecuting Attorney, on a salary of $250 per year, and really though he was on the road to prosperity. To-day, each county has a prosecutor, at an average salary of $1,000 per year, amounting in the aggregate to $14,000, for the same territory in which Judge Marshall received $250. At the time the Judge was elected Prosecutor, he had been in court but little, but by a persistence which is characteristic of him, he soon learned the harness and taught the violators of the law that their acts would receive due and ample consideration. At the expiration of his term of office, he declined a re-election and returned to the practice, but in 1851 he was again called to public life, and elected Judge of this judicial circuit over the Hon. Charles H. Constable, then of Wabash County. He continued upon the bench until 1854, when he was elected to Congress as the Democratic candidate from this district. He was re-elected in 1856, and declined to be a candidate in 1858, and was succeeded by John A. Logan.

In March, 1861, Judge Marshall was again elected to the bench and served as Judge of the Circuit Court until 1864, when he was again called by his party to bear its standard for Congress, and was regularly re-elected in 1866, 1868, 1870 and 1872; was a candidate in 1874, and was defeated by Hon. W. B. Anderson, of this county, who had become the leader in this district of that short-lived tidal wave, the farmers' club movement. Judge Marshall had, during his entire life, adhered strictly to the Jeffersonian Democracy, and refused to pander to the caprices of the occasion for the sake of present political preferment. Time has only proved the wisdom of his course, for the mushroom hallucination which placed Gen. Anderson and many others for a time to the front was scarcely born ere it began to die, and has long since been numbered with things that were, "a schoolboy's tale, the wonder of an hour," and, in its receding, has left many of its followers stranded upon the shores of the uncertain and dangerous sea of politics.

Since Judge Marshall's retirement from Congress, he has not been in public service. As a prosecutor, he was faithful, fearless and unflinching; as a Judge, he was upright, just and able; as a legislator in both State and nation, he was strong, forcible and convincing, and in every conflict he was found watching and battling faithfully and honestly for the people whom he represented. Judge Marshall has ever enjoyed the full confidence of his party; at one time he received the vote of the Democrats in Congress for Speaker of the House.

Space will not permit us to enter his Congressional life; it would be a history within itself. Suffice to say that he was the peer of any member, recognized as a man of strong ability and great industry. As before stated, from his youth he has been an unalterable, uncompromising Democrat of the Jefferson school, ever believing that within the Democratic principles are found the elements of the most good to the most people, and in every conflict to which our State and nation is subject Judge Marshall may be heard where the battle is hottest advocating the political questions in an able manner from a Democratic standpoint. In his official life, he was always found at the post of duty, and it is remarked of him that although in poor health, he was never absent from the court room when by law it was his duty to be there. Talented and cultured, of unimpeachable integrity, has been the life of Samuel S. Marshall, a man known to the State and nation and one who has not lived in vain.

Downing Baugh was born April 22, 1798; is still living, hale and hearty. He is a native of Barren County, Ky., from which State many of Illinois' early great men came. He moved to this State in about 1820, lived a short time in Bond County, and finally settled in Mount Vernon. He married Milly Pace, the youngest child of Joel Pace, senior sister of the late Joel and Joseph Pace, of this county. Judge Baugh's father was a man of some education, and was a school teacher in the early days. The Judge acquired some education, and when a young man also taught school. In those days the scholar who could study the loudest was considered the best; quite a contrast with the present system. Could we step into one of the Judge's old-time schools to-day, we would hear every student studying his lesson "out loud," if he studied at all. After teaching school awhile, he went to merchandising, in which business he was not successful. He was Postmaster here for many years. At the age of forty-seven, he began the study of law, which he finally completed, and for some years pursued the practice with success. In 1854, he was appointed Judge of the Circuit Court by Gov. Joel A. Matteson, to fill the unexpired term of Judge Marshall, who had been elected to Congress. Judge Baugh presided as Circuit Judge for the nine remaining months. He was honest and upright and performed his duties without reproach to the judiciary or to himself.

In 1840 and 1841, he was Enrolling and Engrossing Clerk of the Twelfth General Assembly. He was Probate Justice of this county for a time, and many years a Justice of the Peace. In 1857, he removed to McGregor, Iowa, where he has since resided. Shortly after his removal to Iowa, he was elected Judge of the City Court, and so acted until the Supreme Court declared the law creating the City Courts unconstitutional.

He has for many years been an enthusiastic Mason; is now Grand Chaplain of the

Grand Chapter of Iowa and Grand Prelate of the Grand Commandery. He has lived a consistent Christian life, and always commanded the respect of those among whom he has lived.

For years, Judge Baugh has been entirely blind. He is now in his eighty-sixth year, yet his mind is as clear and vigorous as ever. He may be termed one of those pioneers who helped to form and mold the early sentiment of this country and get it started off on the right foot.

He has two children living in Mount Vernon—J. W. Baugh and Mrs. Elizabeth Fly.

William H. Green is among those once members of the bar of this county, who have attained distinction in their profession and in politics. None, prehaps, stand more prominent in the profession than Judge Green. He was born in Danville, Boyle Co., Ky., December 8, 1830, and was the son of Dr. Duff Green and Lucy Green (née Kenton).

His ancestors were among the earliest settlers of Virginia and extensive land-owners in the Shenandoah Valley. They came originally from the province of Leinster, Ireland, about the year 1730. His mother was a niece of Simon Kenton, the celebrated pioneer and Indian fighter of Kentucky, and was of Scotch parentage.

Judge Green was educated at Center College, Danville, Ky., and without graduating became a fair classical scholar, and has all his life been an extensive reader of history and belles-letters, and kept pace with the modern investigations of scientists. His range of thought and study has been upon the higher plane.

In 1846, he came, with his father's family, to Mount Vernon, where, after teaching school for a time, he entered upon the study of the law under the direction of Judge Walter B. Scates, was admitted to the bar in 1852, and for one year pursued the practice of his profession in Mount Vernon. Then he moved to Metropolis, where he remained in active practice for ten years and then removed to Cairo, where he has since resided. He has served two terms in the lower branch of the State Legislature, 1858 to 1862, and one in the Senate. In 1865, he was elected Judge of the Circuit Court for the district in which he lived, and since 1861 he has been the attorney for the Illinois Central Railroad except during the times his official positions made it inconsistent for him to be so.

He attended the four National Democratic Conventions as a delegate, at Charleston, Chicago, New York and Cincinnati; has for years been a member of the State Democratic Central Committee, and for twenty-two years has been a member of the State Board of Education, the only Democrat upon it.

Judge Green is now in the prime of intellectual life, and already has he filled the measure of a just ambition, not so much by the eminence of the political or judicial positions he has filled, as by the unalloyed respect and confidence he has inspired in all men by his able and upright bearing to all.

Lewis F. Casey was born on the 23d day of April, 1821, in this county. By perseverance and industry, he acquired a fair education and was elected County Surveyor in 1841. In 1843–44, he read law together with Robert F. Wingate in the law office of Judge Scates. He was admitted to the bar in 1845. In 1846, he was a member of the Legislature and voted for Stephen A. Douglas for the United States Senate. In about 1848, he formed a law partnership with Judge Breeze, which c⋅tinued for two years. In 1852, he removed to Texas, and in eighteen months after his arrival was elected Prosecuting Attorney for the district in which he lived, and was also made the financial agent of the State.

In 1861, Mr. Casey was elected to the State Senate of Texas for four years. He was a member of the Senate at the time the State passed its ordinance of secession, voted for Lewis T. Wigfall for member of the Senate of the Confederate Government, and of course voted for Jefferson Davis for President of the Confederate States. He returned to the State of Illinois in 1866, and located in Centralia, where he has since practiced law. As a lawyer, he is able and ready; in argument he is forcible and always has the attention of the court he addresses. He, in connection with Capt. S. L. Dwight, enjoys a large practice in Marion, Clinton, Washington and Jefferson Counties. He is a nephew of the late Gov. Casey, and possesses much of the ability, energy and other characteristics which so marked the Governor.

Richard S. Nelson. Among the members of the bar of early days no man figured more conspicuously than did Richard S. Nelson. He was born June 12, 1815, in the city of Douglas, on the Isle of Man. His father was an eminent divine in the Established Church of England, and it was his desire that the subject of this sketch should follow in his footsteps and take the pulpit, but as he grew to manhood the young man's tastes differed from his father's, and he chose that other profession that is next of kin to the clergy—the law. He completed his studies and at once turned his face to America, and at twenty years of age he landed in New Orleans and began the practice of his profession. He, however, did not remain there long, but soon removed, coming directly to Southern Illinois. He landed at Shawneetown and opened an office, but not meeting with the success he desired, he removed to Old Frankfort, Franklin County, and from thence to Mount Vernon. After a few years' residence at this place, he removed to Metropolis, Massac County, and there remained for eight years. During his residence there, he passed through, perhaps, the most exciting scenes of his life.

It was during this period that the Regulators and Flatheads inaugurated what has passed into history as the "Massac war." Mr. Nelson was strongly identified with the law and order party, who were known as the "Flatheads." Exciting and active demonstrations were had by both sides, until at last the opposing factions met in battle line, and on the 7th day of December, 1846, in front of Mr. Nelson's house, proceeded to fight it out. The Regulators finally won the day and the Flatheads were put to flight. Mr. Nelson made his escape by flat-boat to Cairo and thence to St. Louis, and then to Springfield. The Regulators after their victory held control of things for some months, and until, at the earnest entreaties of Mr. Nelson, Gov. French sent between 400 and 500 militia to the scene of the troubles. Mr. Nelson returned with them and did all in his power to sustain the soldiers. In two weeks his table furnished 316 meals, and he fed and stabled 200 horses, for which not 1 cent was ever paid to him or his family. This should receive the early attention of our State authorities, and restore to this family the long delayed justice. Mr. Nelson never resumed the practice in Metropolis, but left his desolated home, which had been reduced to ashes, and moved again to Mount Vernon, where he at once entered upon a large and remunerative practice. He soon reached a high standard in his profession. In 1862, amid the demoralizing influences of the late war, he removed to Centralia, where he remained until his death, on the 19th day of August, 1865. He was attending court at this city when he was attacked by apoplexy, and soon died.

Mr. Nelson was a man of more than ordinary intellect. He applied himself with much assiduity to his profession, and soon became widely and favorably known throughout the southern part of the State. He was what might be termed a self-made man, and rose to prominence in his profession by his own exertions. He occupied such a position only as his own talents and moral worth commanded. He rose to distinction not only without the patronage of influential friends, but in opposition to a degree of prejudice which is encountered by every foreigner. His success was due to native talent and to the energy with which he devoted himself to his profession. His native energy of intellect, his legal erudition and his unbending integrity commanded respect and confidence wherever he was known.

Hon. S. F. Crews was born in 1845, in Wayne County, Ill., and came to Jefferson County in 1872 and formed a law partnership with George M. Haynes. In 1876, he was elected State's Attorney, and in 1882 was elected to the Legislature. Upon the adjournment of the Legislature, Mr. Crews removed to Chicago, where he is at present enjoying a reasonably good practice.

Of the present members of the Mount Vernon bar, we shall but briefly speak, leaving the histories of their triumphs and their glories, to the writers who shall come after us, saying, however, in a general way that the bar of Jefferson County will compare favorably with that of any county in the southern part of the State.

Robert H. Carpenter was born September 30, 1837, studied law and was admitted in 1871.

A. M. Green was born in 1846, studied law in Mount Vernon, attended at Ann Arbor, Mich., and was admitted in 1870. In 1872, he was elected State's Attorney and served four years. In 1877, he was elected to the Legislature.

W. N. Green, born in ———, 1858, read law and was admitted in 1878. In 1877, he was appointed Master in Chancery and served two years.

C. A. Keller was born November 24, 1851; read law, and was admitted in 1873. In 1877, he was elected County Judge, serving acceptably as such for four years. A more extended sketch of his career will be found in the biographical department of this volume.

George B. Leonard was born December 16, 1849, and was admitted in 1876.

Norman N. Moss was born March 25, 1856, and admitted May 5, 1882.

C. H. Patton was born May 9, 1834, came to Illinois in 185-, taught school, was elected County Clerk and admitted to the bar on March 21, 1862. For further particulars the reader is referred to our biographical department.

Hon. James M. Pollock was born in ———; came to Mount Vernon in 185-; in 1864, was elected Judge of the Circuit Court and re-elected in 1866. His life and history will also be found in the biographical department.

W. C. Pollock was born July 12, 1853, and admitted in June, 1877.

James L. Pollock was born March 1, 1859, and admitted February —, 1881.

James M. Pace was born in Mount Vernon on the 29th day of November, 1826, and is said to have been the first white male child born in the city. For a number of years he was County School Superintendent, and upon the organization of the city government was elected the first Mayor. He was admitted in 1870.

W. T. Pace was born December 22, 1853, and was admitted June 6, 1878.

Norman A. Pearcy was born January 4, 1856, and admitted in 1882.

E. V. Satterfield was born January, 1836, and admitted ———— ——.

W. N. White was born October 17, 1856; was admitted in 1879, and elected State's Attorney in 1880, which position he still holds.

Albert Watson was born April 15, 1857, and was admitted in September, 1880.

George M. Haynes was born August 27, 1847, and was admitted in 1870.

Robert A. D. Wilbanks, born in 1846, was admitted in 1867; for twelve years was Clerk of the Supreme Court of this grand division; is now Clerk of the Appellate Court.

There were and have been many other members of the bar of this county, among them Gen. R. F. Wingate, F. D. Preston, and others, of whom we have been unable to obtain sufficient data from which to write them. Also Col. S. G. Hicks, whose history and life is fully given elsewhere in this volume.

CHAPTER VII.[*]

POLITICAL HISTORY—BIRTH OF THE WHIG AND DEMOCRAT ORGANIZATIONS—PARTY STRIFE AND SCRAMBLE FOR OFFICE—JOEL PACE, FIRST CLERK OF THE COUNTY—POLITICIANS OF THE TIMES—ZADOK CASEY—HIS LIFE AND OFFICIAL SERVICES—GOV. ANDERSON—SKETCH OF HIS PUBLIC CAREER—NOAH JOHNSTON AND OTHER DISTINGUISHED CHARACTERS—SENATORS AND REPRESENTATIVES, ETC.

"The greatest friend of Truth is Time;
Her greatest enemy is Prejudice."

IN the early history of Jefferson County, there was but little, if, indeed, any, party strife. The exciting events of the war of 1812, which had closed a few years prior to the organization of the county, had wiped out the old Federal party—a party that had bitterly opposed President Jefferson and his official acts. The war measures of President Madison, and the dominant party in Congress were very generally, and even earnestly, supported by the people throughout the country. The Presidential election of 1824, the second after the formation of Jefferson County, was attended with unusual excitement, probably with more than any election that had ever taken place in the Republic, with the exception of the Presidential election of 1800, which resulted in the success of Mr. Jefferson over the elder Adams. At this election (1824), the candidates were Gen. Jackson, with the laurels of New Orleans still blooming upon his brow; Henry Clay, the sage of Kentucky; John Quincy Adams, a born statesman, and William H. Crawford, of Georgia, all intellectual giants, truly. Each of these distinguished gentlemen had his friends, who supported their favorite candidate from personal preference and not from party predilection. None of them, however, had a majority of the votes in the electoral college, and under the Constitutional rule, upon the House of Representatives, for the first and the last time in the history of the country,[*]

[*]By W. H. Perrin.

[*]Originally, it was the law for the candidate receiving the highest number of votes in the Electoral College to be declared President, and the one receiving the next highest to be declared Vice President. In 1800, Thomas Jefferson and Aaron Burr received the same number of votes, and the question went to the House of Representatives for its decision, where it was hotly contested by Burr but finally decided in favor of Jefferson. The law was afterward changed, and candidates nominated for President and Vice President, which rule is still followed, and the election of 1824 is the only one in which the House of Representatives had to decide between the Presidential candidates alone, and make a President.

devolved the duty of making choice of President, each State, by its delegation in Congress, casting one vote. Gen. Jackson led Mr. Adams, in the Electoral College, by a small plurality; Mr. Crawford was the third on the list of candidates, and Mr. Clay, who was the hindmost man, was dropped from the canvass. Mr. Adams was chosen President by the casting vote of the State of Kentucky. Mr. Clay was a member of the National House of Representatives, and its Speaker, and it was at once claimed by many of his political enemies, that it was through the great influence of Ohio, which State, as well as his own, Mr. Clay had carried in the Presidential contest, that the delegation from Kentucky was induced to cast the vote of that State for Mr. Adams, an Eastern man, in preference to Gen. Jackson, a Western and Southern man. By that *coup d'etat*, Mr. Clay was instrumental in organizing political parties that survived the generation of people to which he belonged, and ruled in turn the destinies of the Republic for more than a quarter of a century.

In the new Cabinet, Mr. Clay was placed at the head of the State Department by Mr. Adams, which gave rise to the charge of "bargain and sale" between the President and his chief Secretary, that threw the country into a blaze of excitement from one end to the other. At this time, when Henry Clay has been dead for more than thirty years, and his faults and errors have been enveloped in the mantle of charity, no one will presume or dare to question his patriotism or honesty; but the charge was persistently made by the partisans of Gen. Jackson, it greatly injured Mr. Clay in the public estimation, and contributed largely to the General's success in the Presidential race of 1828, and forever sealed Mr. Clay's own doom, so far as regarded the Presidency. At the Presidential election of 1828, party lines were closely drawn between Gen. Jackson and Mr. Adams, and the result of a hot and bitter contest was the triumphant election of the hero of New Orleans, both by the electoral and popular vote. At this time parties were known throughout the country as the Jackson and Anti-Jackson parties.

The gubernatorial election in Illinois, following this contest, presented a curious phase of the politics of the times. There were two tickets in the field for Governor and Lieutenant Governor, all professing strong Jacksonism, but really were what to-day would be termed, perhaps, Stalwarts and Half-breeds. Mr. Kinney was the stalwart candidate for Governor, or as he was called then, the "out and outer" Jackson candidate, while Zadok Casey was the candidate for Lieutenant Governor on the same ticket. John Reynolds was the "Half-breed" candidate for Governor, but claimed to be as good a Jackson man as Kinney; and associated with him as a candidate for Lieutenant Governor was Rigdon B. Slocumb, of Wayne County. The peculiar feature of the election was, that Reynolds and Casey were elected, representing the two different wings of the Jackson party. And as an illustration of the great power and influence Casey ever wielded over his constituency, is the fact that he was the only stalwart candidate elected in the State in that contest. With but few changes in their platform of principles, the Jackson and Anti-Jackson eventually became the Whig and Democrat parties.

The scramble for the "loaves and fishes" of office in the early period of the county's existence, compared with later years, was almost nothing. But few offices were sought for their emoluments, and much oftener then than now the office sought the man. The most lucrative offices were filled by appointment, and not by popular vote, as they are now. It was not for years after the formation of the county that local offices were made elective, and it is even now a question for discussion, whether the latter is the best policy. In most cases, the offices were filled by faithful and competent men. The appointing power conferred by the Legislature upon the Commissioners and the courts, although anti-Republican in principle, seems to be, judging from the experience of the past, the best calculated to secure efficiency and competency in office. Experience has shown pretty conclusively that the less frequently changes are made the better it is for the public service, notwithstanding the present political war-cry of "turn the rascals out." Chancellor Kent has said that the great danger to this country is "the too frequent recurrence to popular election." The early records of the county show, under the appointing power, but few changes. From the organization of the county in 1819 to 1837, the duties of both County and Circuit Clerk were faithfully performed by Joel Pace, an excellent and competent man. It is not inappropriate in this connection to devote a few words to the county's first Clerk.

Joel Pace was born in Virginia, and his father, Joel Pace, Sr., emigrated to Kentucky, locating in Woodford County. On reaching manhood, young Joel went to Frankfort, Ky., where he engaged to work for one Thomas Long. The latter gentleman had a brother-in-law—Owen Riley—who was a merchant in Vincennes, Ind., and once when on his way to Philadelphia for goods, Riley stopped at Frankfort and asked Long to refer him to a trusty young man who would do for a salesman. He recommended Joel Pace, and Riley employed him, and sent him with a stock of goods to Vincennes. Here he remained for a year or two, when Riley had a stock of goods damaged by the sinking of a boat, and sent Pace to sell them out as best he could at Shawneetown. But Riley soon abandoned himself to drink, and Joel left him, and was employed by Peoples & Kirkpatrick. Judge Brown was then living at Shawneetown, and he gave Joel Pace the appointment of Circuit Clerk for Jefferson County, and procured for him also the offices of Recorder and Notary Public. So he had three offices when he came to the county in the spring of 1819, and was soon appointed to a fourth. Yet there was so little business that he found time to attend to them all, and besides to teach a school—the first ever taught in the county. Such was the man who held one, or rather several, of the most important offices of the county, and for almost twenty years faithfully discharged his official duties. The early officers of the county were faithful and efficient, but none of them wore the official harness so long without rest as did Mr. Pace. This, however, is not intended as a reflection upon those who have held office under the elective system; for truly Jefferson has been favored in the official integrity of its public servants in late years, as well as in the early period of its existence, as that pattern of old fidelity, Mr. Bogan, so eminently proves, with its many other true and faithful officers.

It was during the memorable campaign of 1840 that the "Liberty party" was organized and a ticket for President and Vice President was nominated. For several years previous to this, the anti-slavery agitation had been making slowly, but unmistakingly, its deep impressions upon the public mind, and more especially the minds of the religious portion of the people North and East, but it was not until about this period that the friends of the cause of emancipation proposed political action. James G. Birney, a former slave-holder of Kentucky, but then a resident of Michigan, was placed at the head of the ticket, and Thomas Morris, of Ohio, was placed second. This ticket had but little popularity so far west as Illinois, and was scarcely heard of in the southern part of the State. The small vote polled for the ticket throughout the country was taken principally from the Whig party. Four years later, the vote of the party was largely increased. This organization was believed by many of its friends, and doubtless was, premature and misguided, but no party was ever actuated by loftier or purer motives. The anti-slavery movement, at that time, was not larger than the cloud the Hebrew prophet saw, that so rapidly spread over the whole heavens and filled the earth with refreshing showers. At that time, no one expected to live to see the institution of negro slavery in America abolished, but in less than the period allotted by Providence to a generation of men, by an amendment to the Federal Constitution, slavery, and involuntary servitude of every species, in all the States and Territories belonging to the American Union, was forever abolished.

But notwithstanding the drafts the anti-slavery party, the temperance party, and other parties from time to time made upon the Whigs, they continued to be one of the ruling parties until the repeal of the Missouri Compromise in 1854, which led to the organization of the Republican party, and the absorption of the Whig, as well as the Liberty, or Abolition, party, For a quarter of a century the Republican has been the dominant party in Illinois, but has never attained to a majority in Jefferson County.

That other political organization—the Democratic party—which sprang into existence or, assumed distinctive form during the administration of Gen. Jackson, is still one of the great political parties of the country. For fifty years it has maintained its organization without change of name or principles, and to-day the indications for its success were never more flattering. It has always been the ruling party in this county. Indeed, the county has been and is still a stronghold of Democracy. Many of the early settlers fought under Gen. Jackson in the Indian wars of the the South, and were with him at New Orleans, and it is not strange, nor was it inconsistent with their duty or honor that they should look upon the old hero in the light of their political patron saint. And when he had passed away to his reward, they reverently placed his mantle upon the worthy shoulders of Stephen A. Douglas, and accepted him as their leader. With unbounded faith in the wisdom of their choice, they transferred their political allegiance to the "Little Giant," and in all party fights they rallied around him as solidly as the Old Guard around Napoleon at Waterloo, or the Stonewall brigade, of Confederate fame, around its idolized leader. When his sun went down forever in the dark political storms of 1860, they, so to speak, "hung their harps upon the willow," and mourned as those without hope and without faith. But eventually they aroused anew for the fight, and now they present to their political enemies a solid and unbroken front.

Other political parties have sprung up in the county, and in the country at large, and under the name of "Greenbackers," "Prohibitionists," "Independents," "Grangers," etc., have flourished for a period to a greater or less extent, and succeeded sometimes in electing their candidates to office, but only in a very few instances. It is not probable that any of them will rise into formidable opponents of the two great ruling parties. The county is and doubtless will continue largely Democratic for years to come.

Zadok Casey.—It is eminently appropriate in the political history of the county to notice at length some of those active spirits who participated in the early politics, and bore a prominent part in the scenes and the times of which we are writing. Indeed, the political history would be incomplete without sketches of those men who contributed so largely in molding the political life and affairs of the county. Foremost of the list, as well as first in chronological order, is the Hon. Zadok Casey, who for a long period of his life devoted his time and his talents to the service, in one capacity or another, of his country and his fellow-men.

Zadok Casey was born in the State of Georgia March 17, 1796, and was the youngest child of Randolph and Mary Jane (Pennington) Casey. He was married, when scarcely twenty years of age, to Rachel King, a daughter of Samuel King. From the pioneer sketches of Mr. Johnson, and from other sources at our command, we gather some of the facts of Mr. Casey's early life, and his removal to this county. Soon after his marriage. he began to preach, and kept it up through life, even when most thoroughly engaged in politics. He was very poor, and after his father's death the care of his mother devolved on him, as well as that of his own family. When he came to Jefferson County in 1817, he brought her with him, and the worldly goods of them all comprised but a very small number of necessary articles for housekeeping. In a few days after his arrival here, he had selected a location, and beside a large log erected a camp to shelter them until he could build a house. He soon put up a cabin of small logs because there were not men enough in reach to raise a house of large logs. The floor was rough puncheons, the door of clapboards, beds of board scaffolds, a shovel, a skillet; this was their early home in Illinois. But he was young, strong, and a good worker, and soon there was a sign of improvement and thrift about his place. He was a man of strong character and a powerful native intellect. When he came here he was entirely uneducated; indeed, it is said that he learned his A B C's partly with the aid of his wife after he was married. But his natural thirst for knowledge led him to improve every moment, and he eventually became an excellent scholar. As we have said, he was a minister of the Gospel, and continued to preach at intervals during his whole life. But it is principally of his political career we shall speak in this connection.

Mr. Casey's active public life commenced almost with his settlement in the county. He took a prominent part in securing the formation of the county, and was one of the Commissioners composing the first County Court. In 1820, he made his first race for the Legislature against Dr. McLean, of White County, and was defeated, but at the next election (1822) he was elected over his former competitor, and was again elected in 1824. In 1826, he was elected to the State Senate for four years, and, in 1830, to the office of Lieutenant Governor, John Reynolds, as already stated, being elected Governor. So great and so universal was his popularity that in his race for the Legislature in 1824, he received every vote cast in the county but one. Before his term as Lieutenant Governor had expired, he was elected to Congress over Mr. Allen, of Clark County. He was re-elected in 1834 over W. H. Davidson, and, in 1836, over Nat Harmerson; was elected again in 1838, and elected in 1840 over Stinson H. Anderson. But at this session he voted for a national bank, for a bankrupt law and against the independent treasury. This, to a great extent, injured his popularity in the district, and, in 1842, he was defeated by John A. McClernand. This left Gov. Casey for a time to the obscurity of private life, and for several years he was engaged in local and domestic enterprises. He was elected in 1847, together with Judge Walter B. Scates and F. S. Casey, to the Constitutional Convention, and to him and Judge Scates, more than to any other influence, is Jefferson County and the city of Mount Vernon indebted for the location here of the Supreme Court House. He was elected to the Legislature in 1852, and was a member of the State Senate at the time of his death, September 4, 1862. He was employed by the Ohio & Mississippi Railroad to secure the right of way through Illinois but when the company failed he lost heavily by not being paid for his services.

Gov. Casey was a Democrat in politics, though not as strongly partisan as many of his associates in public life. There are those who knew him well, that even intimate that his politics were "shaky," and that he was disposed to be just a little hypocritical. His great popularity, however, with the mass of the people, refutes all such charges. He was an excellent financier. Though he commenced life poor and penniless, he accumulated considerable property, and in after life, whatever he took in hand seemed sure to prosper. His children were Mahala, Mary Jane, Samuel K., Hiram R., Alice, Newton R., a physician of Mound City, Ill.; Thomas S., of Mount Vernon, one of the Judges of this judicial circuit; and John R., a practicing physician at Joliet, Ill.

We have now given in detail the record dates of the birth, removal to Illinois, and the different important official positions filled by Gov. Casey during life, and it only remains now to fill up the strong outlines of this sketch by a just delineation of those physical, moral and mental characteristics of the man that stand out like the bold promontories that divide the troubled waters and embrace those harbors of safety for the ships upon life's sea. We have sketched his life from his birth in 1796, in the humble pioneer home of his parents in Georgia, his early marriage and removal to Illinois in the spring of 1817, where, beholding the territory in all its natural beauties of woodland grove, green prairie sward, decked and covered with rich foliage and lovely flowers, that, becoming enamored with so much natural wealth and beauty of country, he determined to make it his permanent home. With his wife and child, he came to what is now Jefferson County, and built his rude log cabin upon the spot made historic by his acts, and which will be known to remote history as the old Casey homestead. He was barely twenty-one years of age when he landed in the territory with his little family. They came here, the wife riding the only horse he was able to possess, and carrying the child and their all of earthly goods, particularly the "skillet," being strapped to the saddle, and in front of this caravan walked the young husband and father, leading the way with his rifle upon his shoulder. When, upon the first night of his arrival, he had built his camp fire by the side of a large log, and his wife had set about preparing the first frugal meal, he wandered off a short distance, looking about him, and finally stopped and leaned in wrapt contemplation against a large oak tree, and there, with the silent stars looking down upon him as witnesses, he knelt in prayer and earnest supplication to the great God of the universe, and asked that his enterprise might meet the favor of heaven, that his family might be given happiness, health and security, and that he might be only a Christian, sincere man, and an upright, honorable and good citizen. That honest petition to heaven was granted as soon as it was asked, as his great and pure life has so abundantly testified to all the world. Here was the humble beginning of a pioneer life, that was only given for the short space of forty-five years to his family, to his neighbors, to the county, the State and the nation, and yet its impress is everywhere, and its good effects will be known and deeply respected by the millions who may come after him, and are now and will continue to reap what he has sown. He came to Illinois a poor and wholly illiterate young man, a wife and child and pony being his chief and nearly the whole of his possessions, and looking much like an awkward, overgrown boy, to whom the alphabet was an unexplored mystery. He only knew how to work, and soon a floorless cabin had gathered beneath its clapboard roof his household goods, and his first years were only marked by hard work and humble Christian piety. There was nothing self-asserting in his nature, and he lived and worked and struggled the true hero, and in front of his fire of an evening, he would lie upon his back, while his wife was singing the song of the spinning-wheel, and aiding him in the mastery of the alphabet, that he might more acceptably advance the cause of Christianity. Before he came to Illinois, he had been regularly licensed by his church—the Methodist Episcopal—to preach the Word of God, and this holy work he continued until the day of his death. He had soon grown into physical and mental strength and symmetry. He was nearly six feet and two inches in height, of perfect proportions, lithe, active and graceful in his movements, and courtly of manners, his presence in any crowd would arrest the attention and command deference and respect at all times and in all places. Soon he was drawn into political life and into public office, and here he was even a greater man, and wielded a wider influence upon the stump than he had in the pulpit, although in his most active political life, when a leading politician and office holder in the State, he never relaxed his ministerial duties, but mentally expanded, and grew with all his multifarious work, until, in the very threshold of his life, he lived and moved a great, commanding and central figure. With his own strong hand, he was first a great farmer and an eminent financier, calling about him numerous dependents, to whom he was as a kind father and indulgent friend, giving good advice, employment, subsistence, and in the fullness of a heart that was big enough to take in all the world, he attached all to him in bands of steel, and at the same time his busy brain thought out schemes of industry, that built up his county and his State beyond any other man of his day or age.

When it is remembered that in the times when Gov. Casey lived his most active young life, when his destiny was shaping itself, the surroundings were such as we know little or nothing of now except by traditions. The pioneer people were rough, rude, simple, sincere, honest, warm-hearted and hospitable, and the men of mark were mostly brilliant, erratic, often irreverent and dissipated. Their lives were fevered and delirious, and upon the rostrum or in the forum, where they would gleam and flash like blazing meteors, they would easily descend to the revel or orgie, and their flashing lights would be quenched in gloom and darkness. In the society of the young State were the two extremes, the rude simplicity and the gifted, brilliant children of erratic genius, and amid these surroundings Gov. Casey trod alone his pathway of life, the sincere preacher, the pure and spotless politician and statesman, the great, the grand man of his time.

It was the inherent force of a great mind alone that enabled him to enter upon a long and exciting political campaign, and from the stump to discuss with wonderful power the absorbing and often exasperating questions of the day, and when Sunday came he could gather about him even those who had waged hot political controversy with him all the week, and all thoughts and all stirred up passions were laid aside in a moment, and as the minister of God he would lead the entire flock to the fold of the Great Shepherd—to that fountain of life for all mankind and for the ages. In religion, he was not a fanatic; as a teacher of the truths of Holy Writ, there was not a trace of dogmatism, and hence in his intercourse with men or in the pulpit, he was as natural, pure and commanding, as the simple and sublime truths that his life and preaching exemplified.

As a politician, he was equally pre-eminent, whether in the hustings, the Legislature, the State Senate, or the Congress of the United States; he was respected whether as the humblest new member of these bodies, or as the presiding officer, the master spirit of the important committee, or the orator and speaker upon the floor. Here as elsewhere, he was the born leader among men, and his well-poised mind was never at fault—never brought in question the justness of his leadership. His fellow-members in Congress soon learned that he made no mistakes, and it was an almost every-day occurrence in the State Legislature while he was a member, and the Speaker was called on to unravel by his rulings some difficult parliamentary question, to announce to the House that the chair "desired to take the opinion of the member from Jefferson County," and the business or discussion would suspend until Gov. Casey could be consulted, and the tangled questions be made plain and settled to the complete satisfaction of all.

A grand old man, whose pure and exalted life is one of the most important chapters in the history of the Northwest for the study and contemplation of the youths of our country. His death, in the meridian of his intellectual manhood, was a National grief and calamity, for which a grateful posterity can only now have the consoling compensation that may come from the pen of the biographer, whom, we trust, may gather the hint from this brief sketch, and make an immortal book, entitled the "Life and Times of Gov. Casey."

Stinson H. Anderson.—Carlyle said, "great men, taken up in any way, are profitable company." This is very true, like all the aphorisms that fell from the pen of the great author and essayist. We cannot look, however imperfectly, upon a great man without gaining something by him. He is the living light, fountain of native, original insight of manhood and heroic nobleness, which it is good and pleasant to be near. No great man lives in vain. And happy is the country, and happy the commonwealth, if it produce but one, whether it be a soldier, the foremost of the age, or a statesman who administered the affairs of a nation.

It is the naturally great men—men of strong intellects and force of character—that come to the front when important work is to be done. Such a man was Stinson H. Anderson. He came here at a time when he was most needed, and his finger-marks are still to be seen—telling the story of his handiwork, and writing his epitaph in the hearts not only of his descendants, but of the thousands who are reaping and who will in the future enjoy the fruits of his labors. He came here, no doubt, impelled by the Napoleonic impulse of destiny. A new county was still in its first decade of "successful experiment," and while he did not, at once, rush into the vortex of political and official life, yet he soon became a recognized leader. He drew men to him as the magnet draws the steel. Even his opponents and political enemies acknowledged his merits and admitted his power and great intellectual strength.

Gov. Anderson was born in Sumner County, Tenn., in 1800, and while still a young man came to Jefferson County. He engaged in agricultural pursuits, and soon became one of the most successful and enterprising farmers of the county. He devoted considerable attention to fine stock, especially to horses, of which he was extremely fond. He loved the fleet-footed coursers, and the sports of the turf were his greatest pleasure and pastime.

In illustration of his love of the turf, the following incident is related of him: He had a little race mare called Polly Ann, that he cherished next to his wife and children. He believed that she could outrun any animal (her distance) that stood on four legs in the State of Illinois, and was willing to stake his all on such an issue. Dr. Logan, father of Gen. John A. Logan, the "swarthy Senator from Illinois," had a very fine race horse —a stallion called Walnut Cracker—of which he entertained much the same opinion as the Governor did of Polly Ann. Logan lived in Jackson County, and after considerable bantering between the owners of the rival nags, a race was finally made—distance 1,000 yards. To such a pitch of excitement were the principals wrought up, and so confident was each in the speed of his animal, that they staked, not only all their ready cash, but all the property they possessed in the world. The race was run upon Logan's own track at Murphysboro, and Gen. Ander-

son, of Mount Vernon, a son of the Governor, then but a lad, and Gen. John A. Logan, were the riders. When they appeared upon the race track, Walnut Cracker, the Logan horse, came with his head up and nostrils distended, like the war-horse of old, as though he scented the battle from afar, while little Polly Ann stood with her head down and her ears flopped over her eyes, seemingly almost without life. Young Anderson was somewhat awed by the appearance of the Logan horse, and with a sort of whimper, told his father he believed Polly Ann would be beaten. "William," said the Governor, "she's got to beat; if you don't make her win, I'll whip you sir, as a boy was never whipped before, by —— sir!" Such fiery eloquence had its effect on William, and in the race, which followed a few minutes later, Polly Ann passed under the wire several lengths ahead of Walnut Cracker, thus carrying to the ownership of the Governor all the cattle, horses, hogs, sheep, etc., of Dr. Logan.

But the talents of Gov. Anderson were not destined to be hidden under a bushel, nor his abilities

"To rust unburnished, not to shine in use,"
and duty to his country called him from his plow, Cincinnatus-like, to take his place in her councils. He was elected Representative of Jefferson County in the legislative session of 1832, and re-elected in 1834. He naturally became a leader, as one born to command, and by his rare judgment of men and things, convinced his fellow-members that he committed few errors. In 1838, he was elected Lieutenant Governor on the ticket with Thomas Carlin, and for the succeeding four years was the presiding officer, by virtue of his position, of the Senate. Hon. Noah Johnston, who served in the Senate during those four years, describes him as an able, courteous and dignified presiding officer, and one whose knowledge of parliamentary law and usage enabled him to avoid all mistakes. While President of the Senate, says Mr. Johnston, but one of Gov. Anderson's decisions was appealed from, and in that case he was sustained in his ruling. After the close of his term as Lieutenant Governor, he entered the United States Army, and was appointed Captain of dragoons, and served in the Florida or Seminole war—a war which continued with varying results for twenty years before the Indians were finally subjugated. He was Warden of the penitentiary at Alton for four years, and upon the accession of Mr. Polk to the Presidency, was appointed United States Marshal for the State of Illinois, which position he held until the close of President Polk's term.

Gov. Anderson's political life commenced just at a time when the two great parties assumed distinctive names. That of the National Administration took the name of Democrat, and the opposition that of Whig. Gov. Anderson cast his fortunes with the Democrats, and was ever after a faithful, active and energetic worker for his party. During his Presidency of the State Senate, party strife ran high and the bitterest political vituperation was indulged in by the Whigs and Democrats, but such was his tact and power in the management of men that throughout the stormy sessions of his official term he maintained the profound respect of the opposition as well as of his own party.

In all the official positions held by Gov. Anderson, he discharged his duties with unswerving fidelity. A man of the most exalted integrity—the very soul of honor—he scorned a mean or dishonorable act as he scorned the dirt beneath his feet. He was free and open in his speech, and would readily say before a man's face what he thought behind his back, but was just and generous, and willfully wronged no man. In his family, he was a devoted husband, a kind and indulgent father, and liberal in the education of his children. Although of no religious belief particularly, yet he contributed freely of his means to the support of the churches and the Gospel, and his heart was tender, yielding in sympathy and relief to distress wherever he found it.

Gov. Anderson died in September, 1857, deeply regretted and mourned alike by the country which he had so faithfully served, and the people who knew him so well.

The political history of Jefferson County for years was embellished with the finger marks of the two statesmen whose sketches we have above given. Although of the same political faith—good Democrats—yet, to say that at all times they were in full party harmony, would be in direct conflict with the true political history of the county. Not infrequently was it the case, that in exciting and important campaigns there were found to be two Richmonds in the field, and who always proved foemen worthy of each other's steel. For years it has been another "war of the roses," and without the bloodshed and carnage which charactarized the political differences of the houses of York and Lancaster, it yet crops out occasionally between the descendants of the two great leaders. It is not material to the subject of this chapter that we enter into the details of this political feud—the party *brouillerie*, which had for its prime cause the fact that the county was too small for these two master spirits, a fact that led them to often cross swords upon the points of political power and aggrandizement. It never culminated in open rupture or party dismemberment, but has been more good-natured than otherwise. It only shows in local contests, wherein more than one aspirant for official position can charge his defeat to a member of the rival faction. These little local differences, however, cut no figure upon national questions or in national contests. In these, all stand shoulder to shoulder, and pour in their fire where it is most needed, and where it will do the most good. And, indeed, this is but another peculiarity of the political history of the county. It matters not how much wrangling there may be upon local issues, or how much scramble for local offices, when it comes to a general fight with the common enemy all petty differences are forgotten, all county squabbles are laid aside, and a larger majority than ever piled up for Gen. Jackson. For proof of the truth of this portion of political history the reader is referred to Gen. Anderson, George Haynes, Judge Casey, Bob Wilbanks, and other young politicians of the day, now in the zenith of their glory, and whose "lives and times" will be more fully written up in the next centennial history of Jefferson County.

Noah Johnston. Another of the representative men of the county and who has contributed largely to its high rank, politically, is Maj. Johnston. The following excellent sketch of him was furnished us by Mr. George M. Haynes:

For more than fifty years Maj. Noah Johnston has lived in this county. He has become, as it were, one of the fixtures, one of the land-marks known by every person, and knowing as many of the old settlers and the men who first cut out the roads through this part of the State as perhaps any one now living. He is in his eighty-fourth year, and as he passes along our streets we and he well know that in the order of things he must soon "cross the river;" that but a few years at most, and his familiar face will no longer be seen. But will he die? No; such men rarely die; they continue to live long after their bodies have mouldered into dust. For generations, at least, after his flesh and bones have returned to the earth from whence they came, he will live in history and in memory. And as we see him day by day, we can but be impressed with the thought that he is of that class that leads us back to other days. His life has been long and eventful; it began just two days before the close of the last century, and along the line of march he has not been idle: he has gathered and stored knowledge. Possessed of an active and intelligent mind, he has suffered few things of importance to escape him, and one cannot converse with him for any length of time without feeling that he has learned something from him of the men and manners of former times that he did not before know. He stands forth, as it were, a friendly guide-board, ready to point out to the traveler the rocks and snares on the road of life—a gentleman of the old school in every sense of the word, made so by nature.

Maj. Johnston was born on the 29th of December, 1799, in Hardy County, Va., on the waters of the South Branch of the Potomac, the oldest but one of ten as healthy children as could then be found in the "Old Dominion." His father, George Johnston, moved from Hardy County to Woodford County, Ky., in 1812, and settled near old Lexington. The summer after, his family were taken with bilious fever, a disease in that day not understood by the physicians, and before its ravages ceased four of the same healthy children of the year before were buried and one crippled for life. His father, George Johnston, died in Adams County, this State, in his eighty-fourth year. The Major is now the only surviving member of that family, who in the early days of the republic started West to secure to themselves the homes which were not so accessible in the older States.

In 1824, the family removed to Clark County, Ind., and after a few years' residence removed to Parke County, same State, where Maj. Johnston's mother died and was buried. The Major continued to live at home and work on the farm with his father until he was thirty years of age, when he left his family in Parke County and returned to Clark and married a Miss Mary Bullock, his present wife, who has since been the sharer of his triumphs and of his reverses; together have they trod life's journey, sometimes in rain, sometimes in sunshine. Through life there are many dark sides and many bright sides, but they have been met and almost passed by this venerable couple, he in his eighty-fourth, she in her eightieth year. They are going—and soon; their work is almost done; their trials and tribulations about over, and right well are they prepared for this earthly ending.

Soon after his marriage, Maj. Johnston moved to this county and began farming. He was a man of more than an average education for that day, although he never attended school more than three or four months, yet his father was a good English scholar and devoted a good deal of his personal attention to the education of his children. After farming for a short time in this county, the Major engaged in mercantile pursuits, which, with some surety investment, did not succeed, and he soon found himself heavily in debt and forced out of business with no property or means to pay with, and thus [his little craft went down beneath the financial crash. After his failure, and, in fact, awhile before, he began to give some attention to politics, and was soon elected one of the County Commissioners, and afterward was elected County Clerk.

But perhaps it would not be out of place to here relate a little incident of his family. A brother of his father left home in Virginia and went to Mississippi and located near

Natchez. He never married and accumulated considerable property, consisting largely of negroes and lands. While the Major's father lived in Kentucky, this brother died, and another brother, the only remaining one, came from Virginia to Kentucky, and the two brothers went on horseback to Mississippi to look after the estate. While they were not abolitionists, they were opposed to slavery and were followers of Henry Clay's doctrine of gradual emancipation. On their arrival at Mississippi, they simply took what money there was, and being unable to give a bond for the good behavior of the negroes, as the law then required, they were unable to free them, and they returned home and left the slaves and lands there and never afterward returned.

In 1838, Maj. Johnston was elected to the State Senate from this and Hamilton County, serving four years. During his term of office, there were two regular and two special sessions; in fact, it was a period of much legislative interest. The first session of 1838 was the last held at Vandalia, and there was considerable excitement over the proposition to remove the capital to Springfield. The Sangamon County delegation, with Abraham Lincoln as its leader, consisted of A. G. Herndon, E. D. Baker (afterward killed at Ball's Bluff, Va.), John Calhoun, John Dawson, Ninian W. Edwards, William F. Elkins, Andrew McCormick and Thomas J. Nance. In the excitement of the occasion, the delegation was termed by some gentlemen of the opposition as the "Long Nine." Lincoln in reply said, "Yes, we are the 'long nine' and I am the longest of the nine," and as such they have passed into history. They succeeded and the capital was removed to Springfield, where it has since been retained. In this session was to be found many who afterward gained renown and became a part of the permanent history of the State. One gained the Presidency, many seats in Congress, and some renown upon the battle-field. Marshall was there and Baker, and Ficklin, and DuBois, and Logan, father of the present Senator, and many others. For some years after the capital was removed, the Legislature met in a church in Springfield.

At the first session after the removal the Bank of Illinois suspended payment and the suspension was legalized by the Legislature until the end of the next session. In November, 1840, following, the Legislature met in special session; the time for the regular session by law was December 7, 1840. There was considerable agitation over the bank suspension. The Democrats were determined that the bank should resume and the Whigs that they should not before the end of the regular session, and to carry their point attempted to run the special session into the regular session, and thereby prevent an adjournment. The time was drawing near when the matter had to be settled one way or the other. The Democrats being in the majority, the Whigs resorted to every means known to parliamentary rules to delay and prevent a vote upon the question of adjournment. For days the battle was waged; the "Long Nine" were there, with Lincoln at their head. At last, when all their tactics had been exhausted and it was evident the Democrats would carry the adjournment unless something was done, Lincoln asked that the roll be called; it was called and found that there was one less than a quorum. The Speaker at once ordered the doors closed and instructed the doorkeeper to go out and bring in another member. Lincoln, seeing that his chances were getting no better, quietly raised the window and jumped outside and left, which left the House two members short. But when the doorkeeper returned he had two members instead of one. The vote on adjournment was then put and carried, and the Legislature adjourned on the 5th of December, just two days before the regular session convened. On the same evening of the adjournment the officers of the bank called a meeting of the Directors, and at once resumed specie payment.

In 1852, Maj. Johnston, together with Abraham Lincoln and Judge Dickey, of Chicago (not the present Judge of the Supreme Court), were appointed a commission to take and report the evidence on claims filed against the State on account of the construction of the Illinois Canal. The Commissioners opened an office in Ottawa, Chicago and Springfield. In 1845, he was Enrolling and Engrossing Clerk of the Senate, and under his inspection passed the entire revision of 1845, which is claimed by many prominent lawyers to be the best the State has ever had. In 1846, he was elected as a "floater" to the Fifteenth General Assembly from the counties of Hamilton, Franklin and Jefferson. During this session the proposition to issue State bonds for the payment of the State indebtedness was presented and carried. The Major was presented by his friends as a candidate for Speaker, and but for the action of the Cook County delegation, which then, as now, had an ax or two to grind, would have been elected. They sent for the Major to meet them, which he did at the old American House. When he arrived the Chairman of the delegation informed him that they had decided to vote for him, provided he would make certain promises in reference to the appointment of the committee on canals, which then, as now, was an important question to Cook County. The Major replied that there were certain fixed rules which had been observed in the formation of the committees of the House which he thought fair and just, and that if elected Speaker he could not and would not depart from them. This answer was not satisfactory, and they supported Mr. Newton Cloud, the member from Morgan County, who was elected by a very small majority, and it is not improper to here say that he was a good man and made an excellent presiding officer.

Shortly after Maj. Johnston's return home in March, 1847, he received the appointment of Paymaster in the United States Army, with the rank of Major of dragoons, and ordered to report at St. Louis for duty. Gov. Anderson, then United States Marshal, brought him the news of his appointment one night after he had retired. At that time the Major was running a small "sueing shop" as Justice of the Peace, and had an office on the west side of the public square, about where the Thorn building now stands. He took the appointment, together with the bond sent out for execution, which was for $20,000, to his office, and after due consideration became satisfied he could never fill it, and prepared a letter to the President, Mr. Polk, declining the appointment, had it all ready to mail, when some of his friends came in and asked him when he was going to the war to pay the boys off. He informed them that he had decided to decline the honor, and had just so written the President, giving as his reason that he could not fill the required bond. It will be understood that up to this time he had not asked a single person to sign the bond with him. His friends who had called prevailed on him to sign the bond, which he reluctantly did, and it was at once taken out by his friend, who in a short time had it all complete and ready with ample sureties to present to the department. The Major then destroyed the letter he had written declining the appointment, at once proceeded with his preparations to leave, and soon was on his way to Alton to present the bond for approval, which was done by the proper officer on presentation, and he at once reported at St. Louis for duty. He continued to receive and disburse the money of the Government to its soldiers until the war closed, receiving and taking charge at times of as much as $200,000 in specie. On one occasion he went to Fort Leavenworth with $200,000 to pay Gen. Price's men, but upon his arrival he found Maj. Bryant a ranking officer already there, and the Major transferred his money to Bryant and returned to St. Louis. In the spring of 1848, he crossed the plains with $100,000. He traveled between 25,000 and 30,000 miles, received and paid out over $2,000,000 and never lost a five-cent piece. When Congress called upon the Paymaster General for an account of losses to the revenue through his thirty-six different Paymasters, his reply was "not one dime." The handling of so much money on $20,000 bonds would not be productive of such results at this day.

While Paymaster, the Major, by economy and prudence, saved enough from his salary to enable him to relieve himself from his financial embarrassments, which had continued to abide with him since his failure before mentioned.

In November, 1854, Finny D. Preston, then Clerk of the Supreme Court, for the First Grand Division, resigned, and Maj. Johnson was appointed to succeed him by the Supreme Court. In June, 1855, he was elected as his own successor, and was re-elected in June, 1861, serving altogether, by appointment and election, about thirteen years. In November, 1866, he was again elected as Representative to the Legislature from this and Franklin Counties; this was the last public office held by him. In about 1853 or 1854, the Legislature made an appropriation of $6,000 for the purpose of building a Supreme Court House at this place. The Governor appointed as Commissioners to superintend the construction of the building Zadok Casey, T. B. Tanner, Dr. J. N. Johnson, W. J. Stephenson, and Noah Johnston. Upon the organization of the Commission, Maj. Johnston was made the General Superintendent and thus, under his immediate supervision, the building was constructed.

During his residence in this county he has held the office of Justice of the Peace for twelve years, and for many years was Postmaster, although he permitted Daniel Kinney to attend to the office and receive all the emoluments. He was Deputy United States Marshal for four years under Gov. Anderson. It will be noticed that for more than two-thirds of his life in this county he has occupied important public positions in one capacity or another, in all of which he has proven himself faithful and capable. The Major was never an orator, and although the greater part of his life has been spent in politics, yet to unflinching integrity and competency, rather than to oratory, does he owe his success. In no place, in no position, public or private, can, nor has there, lodged the least stain upon his character; straightforward, plain, frank and honest has been his conduct, and as such he is to-day.

He is in some respects a remarkable man; he has lived to see this now great State of Illinois develop from the beginning as it were to its present grandeur. He has, in fact, done his part in the progression that has been so marked. A man of no surplus words, a wise and honest counselor, he enjoyed the most friendly and personal relations of many men of distinction, among whom were Lincoln, Douglas and Breeze, the three really great men produced by this State, and of whom we shall never cease to be justly proud. There are few men now living so rich in personal reminiscences of the men of the earlier days of the State. The vitality and clearness of his mind is indeed wonderful; although near the close of his eighty-fourth year, he converses readily and with much more freshness than many much younger men. He has witnessed every material improvement and advancement made both by county and State, and in many has contributed largely. He is now the President of the Mount Vernon National Bank, giving it his daily personal attention.

He has always been a partisan Democrat, never, we believe, departing one single time from that faith. Born just at the close of power by the old Federal party, the early enemy of Democracy, and just as Jefferson was establishing so firmly his more liberal and democratic ideas, the Major early became a student of that political school which had Jefferson for its founder, and "the most liberty for the most people" its beacon light. Although earnest and zealous in his politics, yet he always enjoyed the confidence of his political enemies.

In religion, he has belonged to no church, although a constant and attentive attendant and a firm believer in the Christian religion. His faith has been, to judge from his life, "to do right in all things, be just and honest to all men," and a just God will make all things well.

A more appropriate conclusion to this chapter on the county's political history could not be given than a list of the faithful who have served the people—many of them faithfully and well. The list of Senators and Representatives, and others, which follow will recall names of men who were once well known, but some of whom are now almost forgotten by the mass of the people.

State Senators.—The following are the State Senators representing Jefferson County since its organization: 1822–24, Thomas Sloo, Jr.; 1824–26, Thomas Sloo, Jr.; 1826–28, Zadok Casey; 1828–30, Zadok Casey; 1830–32, Ennis Maulding; 1832–34, Ennis Maulding; 1834–36, Levin Lane; 1836–38, Levin Lane; 1838–40, Noah Johnston; 1840–42, Noah Johnston; 1842–44, Robert A. D. Wilbanks; 1844–46, Robert A. D. Wilbanks; 1846–48, William J. Stephenson; 1848–50, J. B. Hardy *; 1850–52, J. B. Hardy; 1852–54, Silas L. Bryan; 1854–56, Silas L. Bryan †; 1856–58, Silas L. Bryan; 1858–60, Silas L. Bryan; 1860–62, Zadok Casey; 1862–64, Israel Blanchard ‡; 1864–66, Daniel Reilly; 1866–68, Daniel Reilly; 1868–70, Samuel K. Casey; 1870–72, Samuel K. Casey §; 1872–74, Thomas S. Casey ¶; 1874–76, Thomas S. Casey; 1876–78, Charles E. McDowell ‖; 1878–80, Charles E. McDowell; 1880–82, John C. Edwards **; 1882–84, Thomas M. Merritt.

The Representatives in the Lower House of the Legislature are as follows: 1822–24, Zadok Casey; 1824–26, Zadok Casey; 1826–28, Nicholas Wren; 1828–30, Israel Jennings; 1830–32, William Marshall; 1832–34, Stinson H. Anderson; 1834–36, Stinson H. Anderson; 1836–38, Harvey T. Pace; 1838–40, Harvey T. Pace; 1840–42, Stephen G. Hicks; 1842–44, Stephen G. Hicks; 1844–46, Stephen G. Hicks; 1846–48, Lewis F. Casey; 1848–50, Zadok Casey (the county is now in the Sixth District); 1850–52, Zadok Casey; 1852–54, John Wilbanks; 1854–56, T. B. Tanner (Jefferson is now in the Eighth District); 1856–58, William B. Anderson; 1858–60, William B.

---
* of Hamilton County, and Jefferson is in the Third District.
† of Marion County, and Jefferson is in the Twentieth District.
‡ of Jackson County, and Jefferson is in the Third District.
§ Casey died, and William B. Anderson was elected to fill out his unexpired term.
¶ Jefferson is now a part of the Forty-sixth District.
‖ of White County.
** of Hamilton County.

Anderson; 1860-62, ———; 1862-64, Henry M. Williams (the county is now in the Fifth District); 1864-66, John Ward; 1866-68, Noah Johnston; 1868-70, C. C. M. V. B. Payne; (whose name is Christopher Columbus Martin Van Buren Payne) 1870-72, Thomas S. Casey (Jefferson is now in the Eighteenth District); 1872-74, ——— 1874-76, Amos B. Barrett (the county is now in the Forty-sixth District); 1876-78, Thomas J. Williams; 1878-80, Alfred M. Green and John R. Moss; 1880-82, R. A. D. Wilbanks; 1882-84, George H. Varnell.

Additional to the Representatives in the General Assembly of the State, the county has furnished two Lieutenant Governors, viz., Zadok Casey and Stinson H. Anderson; one Attorney General, Walter B. Scates; and two Congressmen, viz., Zadok Casey and William B. Anderson.

CHAPTER VIII.*

SOMETHING MORE ABOUT THE PIONEERS—THOSE WHO CAME IN LATER—THEIR SETTLEMENT— GAME AND WILD ANIMALS—PIONEER INCIDENTS—MRS. ROBINSON AND THE PANTHER— SOME RATTLING SNAKE STORIES—FEMALE FASHION AND DRESS—WOMAN'S LIFE IN THE WILDERNESS—HARD TIMES, FINANCIAL DIFFICULTIES, ETC.

"The cry of the beast from his unknown den
They haunted the lonesome wood
Only to deepen its solitude."

THE pioneers, the men who skirt the outer confines of civilization on this continent, have entirely changed in their characteristics since the memorable days of '49, when the discovery of gold on the Pacific slope set all the world in a blaze of excitement. They are now, perhaps, the most cosmopolitan people in the world, and we incline to the belief that the old Californians were and are the best practically educated people, for they were suddenly gathered togther in large numbers, representing every civilized people of the globe, many of the half civilized, and even some of the totally barbarous. This heterogenous gathering of such varieties of people resulted in the world's wonder of a public school. It rapidly educated men as they never had before been taught. It was not perfect in its moral symmetry, but it was wholly powerful in its rough strength, vigor and swiftness. It taught not of books but of the mental and physical laws—of commerce, of cunning craft; it was iron to the nerves and a sleepless energy to the resolution. This was its field of labor, its free university. Here every people, every national prejudice, all the marked characteristics of men, met its opposite where there was no law to restrain or govern either, except that public judgment that was crystallized into a resistless force in this witches' caldron. This wonderful alembic, where were fused normal and abnormal humanities, thoughts, false education, prejudicies and pagan follies, into a molten stream that glowed and scorched ignorance along its way, as the volcanic eruption does the debris in its pathway. It was the untrammeled school of attrition of every variety of mind with mind, the rough diamond that gleams and dazzles with beauty only when rubbed with diamond dust. The best school in the world for a

*By W. H. Perrin.

thorough practical education—we mean real education and not "learned ignorance," as Locke has aptly called it. Such an education is the grand leveler of the human mind. It is like the struggle for life, where only "the fittest survive" and the unfit perish.

But the pioneer's school life was spent in a wholly different one from that just described. The surroundings of the Illinois pioneers differed radically from that of the old California "forty-niners." They did not come here in rushing crowds as men sought the gold fields of California, nor did they represent all the civilized nations of the earth. They came, as we have already stated, mostly from the Southern States, and they settled down in the wilderness to live, where unremitting toil was required to maintain life. In a former chapter we have noticed the advent of the first pioneers, that forlorn hope of civilization in Jefferson County, and the erection of their rude cabins which formed the germ of a large and prosperous settlement. Further on we gave sketches of some of the prominent pioneer families, who came a few years later and might be termed the "second crusade." In this chapter we shall notice the arrival of those who came in at a still later period, and also some of the hardships and difficulties endured by the people in the pioneer period.

The Jordan family, Felix McBride, Nicholas Wren, John Sanders, John Lee, Samuel Bradford, Elijah Joliff, and several other families, additional to any mentioned, settled in the county about the year 1819. The Jordan family were early settlers in Franklin County, where they had built a kind of fort or block-house, but afterward moved into Jefferson. Nicholas Wren was a son-in-law of William Jordan; McBride lived in Mount Vernon, but finally went to Galena; John Sanders helped to build the first court house, and Bradford settled near the present town of Belle Rive, but afterward moved into Wayne County; Joliff married Lucinda Deprist in Tennessee, and came here and entered land in Section 1 of Township 2 and Range 2, in October, 1819. He was accidentally shot, and died in the house where he settled.

In the year 1820, still further accessions to the population were made in the arrival of Joseph Pace, Reuben Jackson, Joseph Reed, W. L. Howell, Thomas Hopper, Benjamin Vermilion, Rhoda Allen, James Chaffin, Ebenezer Daggett, Nathaniel S. Andrews, Henry Watkins, James Phipps, Samuel Hirons, Mrs. Hays, Nathaniel Wilson, Butler Arnold, Ransom Moss, Gessom Moss, Herbert Avent, etc., etc. The Paces are a numerous family in the county still. Reuben Jackson settled in Grand Prairie. He remained but a short time and moved North; Howell was the second Sheriff of the county, and in a few years returned to Tennessee; Hopper came from Tennessee and settled west of Moore's Prairie; Vermilion was an early tavern-keeper in Mount Vernon; Rhoda Allen died in 1820—the first man who died in the county—and his widow afterward married James Douglas; Chaffin moved away to the north part of the State; Andrews died soon after he came to the county; Watkins lived in Grand Prairie; Hirons was the builder of the first brick court house; Nilson was one of the very first settlers in Grand Prairie; Arnold was from Butler County, Tenn.; the Mosses and Avent came together. Ransom and Gessom Moss were brothers, and Mrs. Avent was their sister. They were from Virginia, and Avent was once very wealthy, but poor when he came here; he was a fine pattern of a Virginia gentleman.

Additions were made to the settlements in 1821, as follows: Other members of the Pace family, Israel Smith, Burrell and Alfred McConnell, John Blackburn, Aquilla Alexander, John Gibson, Emery P. Moore, Joel Hargrave, the Tunstalls, etc. In 1822, came William Porter, William Rearden, Jacob Norton, the Chandlers, Absalom and Joseph Estes, William Hicks, Robert Snodgrass, George Webb, Young Lemore, William Southwood; and in 1823, Rhodam Allen, William Drummond, Jarvice Pierce, Sr., Thomas Kell, Azariah Bruce, Parson Upshaw, the Wellses; and in 1824, James Dickens, Simon McCenden, Blalock and Lyon, William Crabtree, Taurus Rife, Wallace Caldwell, Elisha Plummer, Robert Stockton, John Summers, Drs. Adams and Glover, Downing Baugh, Blagdon East, Samuel Foster, Josiah League, Henry Lewis, George May, Jesse Lee, etc. From this time up to 1830, we may mention the following additional settlers: David Hobbs and Aaron Yearwood came in 1826; Robert Breeze, in 1827; Joseph McMeens settled in Jordan's Prairie in 1826–27; northwest of town, Howe, John Cash, and others settled; Enoch Holtsclaw about 1826–27; and Samuel Cummins and John Watters soon after; the Bullocks came about 1828 or 1830; Billington Taylor in 1828; Caleb Barr and Elisha Myers the same year; Peter Owen, soon after; William Finch, a few years earlier; Julius Scott and Thomas A. Nicholas about 1829; and quite a number of others we cannot now name.

We can only make the briefest mention of these early settlers in this portion of our work, as they necessarily figure in the different townships, and will there receive further notice. Their names are merely given here to show the increase of population and the growth of settlement.

Wild Game.—Although we have alluded to the hard life of the pioneers already, yet, doubtless, we cannot interest our aged readers more than by giving further details of the early trials, hardships, manners, customs, game, etc., of the early settlers. Again drawing upon the sketches of Mr. Johnson, he says that when the first settlers came, there was no elk here or comparatively none. That those animals had once been plenty in this region was evinced by the fact that the settlers found bones and horns in great profusion in certain portions of the county, notably in Elk Prairie, and which name they gave that prairie in consequence. That seemed to have been their great resort, as their bones were numerous there—or perhaps it was their cemetery. Sinbad, the sailor, tells of the elephants having cemeteries or "boneyards" in their own "country," where their dead was deposited. Tunstall, we are told, took away a couple of tame elk with him when he moved from the county. The last one was seen, it is said, by William and James Hicks while out on a hunt, but it escaped them. Bears were quite plenty, especially along the water-courses and in the heavy timber. The pioneers used their flesh for meat and their hides for clothing. If they made them into clothing, like Tom Bolin's breeches—"with the fleshy side out and the woolly side in"—we dare to say they were warm and comfortable. But in a few years after the organization of the county, they had (the bears) almost wholly disappeared. Mr. Johnson relates the following "bear incident," as among bruin's "last appearances" in the county: "When Abraham Buffington went to Horse Creek, he found bears. With a courage equal to Putnam's when he followed the wolf into her den, Buffington followed an old she bear into her den, and by the aid of her gleaming eyes shot her in the darkness of the cave." But of all the four-footed game, perhaps deer were the most abundant. It was not uncommon to see 50 to 100 in a gang on the prairies or on the barrens at "one look." Nobody that could shoot—and all pioneers could do that, it was a part of their education—was ever out of meat long at a time. If a man on rising from his couch in the morning was informed by his spouse that there was no meat in the larder, he coolly said, "Well, wife, just wait a little," and often in less than half an hour his game was lying at the door, and meat, for the time, was plenty. Sometimes a man could stand in his own door and shoot deer as they grazed within easy range. A great deal of clothing was made of deerskin, before the raising of cotton and flax. The first efforts to tan the hides were almost a failure. A new method, however, was introduced which was much better. This was, after removing the hair, the skins were thoroughly rubbed and dressed with brains. They were then stretched on stakes driven into the ground, around a large hole, and the hole filled with light and rotten wood, which was set on fire. The warmth caused the brains and oil to permeate the skins and the smoke gave them a beautiful color. Tanned in this way, they are said to have been very soft and pliant, and were handsome. One girl is mentioned by some of the old settlers as having a buckskin petti—ahem! of which she was very proud. Her word, however, had to be taken as to its beauty, for that garment was worn, in the pioneer days, invisible to the naked eye.

Wolves were almost as abundant as deer. Wolf Prairie received its name from the great numbers found in that section, and for at least twenty years after the formation of the county there were many wolves in the unsettled portions. They did not often become dangerous, never unless provoked or nearly famished by hunger. Thompson Atchison once had a severe fight with two or three wolves that had attacked his dogs. Dr. Wilkey was once pursued by a small pack, but paid little attention to them for some time. Finally, when they had become a little too impudent, he turned and shot one, when the others scampered away. Mrs. Robinson—Aunt Rhoda, as she was called—once killed a wolf that came prowling around her cabin at night. Her husband had brought home a deer in the afternoon, which he had shot, and the wolf had scented the slaughtered game and followed to the cabin, when it was attacked by the dogs. In those early days, the dog was a respected member of the family. Any man would fight for his dog. Literally it was "love me, love my dog," or take the consequences. Every man knew every dog in the neighborhood by his bark, just as he knew a man's voice when he heard him speak. When the wolf was attacked by the dogs, Mrs. Robinson ran out to help the latter, and as she ran caught up a "chink" that had fallen from a crack of the cabin. Arriving upon the scene, she gave the wolf a blow with the billet that laid him dead at her feet. She was once pursued by a panther as she wended her way, alone, and on foot, through the forest. A less brave and resolute woman would have been paralyzed with fear, and to say that she was not frightened would, perhaps, be a violation of the truth; but the pioneer women had to fight their own battles, as it were, side by side with their husbands. Mrs. Robinson was going to a neighbor's several miles distant, with no company but her dog and the babe she carried in her arms, when a large panther appeared upon her trail in close pursuit. Her dog ran to her and crouched at her feet for protection. As the panther came too near to be pleasant, she threw down her bonnet as she ran. This stopped the panther a few moments, for he tore it into fragments, and then started again in pursuit. As he came near, she threw down her shawl, and again he stopped long enough to tear it in pieces; and when she was almost ready to drop from exhaustion, and the hungry beast was near enough for her to distinctly hear his teeth snap, she fortunately met a man who shot and killed it, and thus relieved her of further danger.

To young hogs and sheep were wolves, wildcats and panthers particularly destructive. Vast numbers of them were killed. Even young calves were not secure against them. A wolf one day ran a calf up to William Casey's very gate. The women folks hurried out, opened the gate for the calf, and thus saved its life. Indeed, for years it was almost impossible to raise hogs and sheep; but the persistent vengeance with which the pests were hunted by the settlers finally cleared them out, until at present there are none to be found in the county, not even in the wildest regions. The panthers and wild cats were found here in quite as great numbers as wolves, and they were even more dangerous when "met by moonlight alone." Such small game as foxes, raccoons, turkeys, and other feathered denizens of forest and prairie were too numerous to mention.

Snakes.—According to the early history of the county, snakes were as plenty here as they were in Ireland prior to the days of St. Patrick. It may be that the patron saint of the "gem of the say" drove them to this country when he cleared them out of "ould" Ireland. Says Mr. Johnson: "Snakes were fully represented here when the settlers came. It was in 1820 that the first little log schoolhouse was built at old Shiloh.

Soon after the man, James Douglas, made his appearance in the neighborhood, and though addicted to drink, he got up a reputation for scholarship, and then got up a school at Shiloh. A few weeks after a school began, the scholars found so many snakes about the hill that all concluded there must be a den of them in the vicinity. The report of a snake den produced great excitement, and the settlers, fond of sport and apprehensive of danger to their children, turned out in a body, armed with hoes, axes, spades, clubs and guns, and still not prepared fully for such a task as awaited them. It really seemed as if the immediate vicinity was literally alive with the descendants of the first apple vender. Every tuft of grass concealed a snake; every rock covered one; every hole and crevice contained one; every imaginable nook was full of them. Frequently, on turning a moderately sized rock out of its bed, eight or ten snakes, all coiled together, were found underneath it. Rattlesnakes, copperheads, vipers, adders, moccasins, all seemed to have made peace and taken up their abode together. The rattler was largely in the majority, nearly 300 being killed, laid out and counted; the whole number killed and counted was largely over 500. If every man had had an attack of the jim-jams, he probably could not have seen more snakes. It will readily be allowed that those who were particularly afraid of snakes felt nervous when out in tall grass for some time after this onslaught on the reptile population of the community."

Shiloh, however, did not contain all the snakes, but, on the contrary, they seem to have been numerous most everywhere. Johnson thus continues his dissertation on snakes: "Henry Tyler settled at what is now known as the Brown place in March, 1823, some seven miles north of town. Aunt Katy found a rattlesnake one morning coiled on one of the bars when she went to let the cow in to milk her. Some time after, Elihu Maxey, went up to spend the day with Tyler, and the snakes spread themselves. One crawled out of the jam, another out of a crack in the hearth, another sprawled himself on the door step. In the course of the day, seven snakes were killed in the house. This was pretty good, but it got better. Tom Casey went up to see his sister (Mrs. Tyler), and he and Tyler went out to take a little hunt, expecting to kill a deer in a thicket that had escaped the autumnal fires. One took each side of the thicket to go around it. Tyler saw an otter in the branch, stopped to watch it until Casey came round, and in a few minutes saw seven snakes crawl down to the branch. Thinking like the Irishman, that 'where there's two snakes there's sure to be one,' they hunted about awhile and killed and laid out 170. Next day they raised a little help and dug out and killed 217." It seems that this aroused a suspicion in the mind of Tyler that that whole hill had "snakes in its boots," and he lost no time in moving away. In addition to all these, a den was found on Joliff's sugar camp branch, and some two or three hundred were killed there. Many of the snakes were exceedingly venomous. Wallace Caldwell was riding along the road one day, and a snake bit his horse on the leg. With all these stories, it was not considered strange when Mr. Edwards settled where Capt. Henderson lives, and had been there a short time, his wife, who was quite a nervous woman, became so alarmed over snake stories she could not stay, but had her husband pull up stakes and return to Kentucky, whence they had come.

This cleaning out of snake dens and the great slaughter of the reptiles soon had the effect of visibly diminishing their numbers. It became more safe and pleasant for the timorous to perambulate through the tall grass, and when a cow or horse started or a hen "chuckled" in alarm, it was no longer considered a "snake sure." But it was many years before they were generally gone; even now one may occasionally be seen. Northeast of Rome there was a stream named Snake Den Branch in memory of the venomous reptiles.

Thus the dangers and annoyances of the early settlers were such as none but brave hearts would dare to encounter. Nothing but the hopeful inspiration of manifest destiny urged them to persevere in bringing under the dominion of civilized man what was before then a howling wilderness. They were exceptions, in a great degree, of the accepted rule, that "immigrants in settling in a new country usually travel on the same parallel as that of the home they left." Coming from the South as they did, where most of them were poor, and regarded as no better than the black slaves by the haughty aristocracy, they launched out sovereign citizens, independent, free and equal, and acknowledging themselves in the presence of no superior being, except when kneeling alone in prayer to the King of Kings. It was a wise conclusion that prompted them to come here, where they were far more useful in church and State than they ever could have been in the regions they left behind, where others held the places of influence.

The fashions in the primitive days of the county were few and simple, compared with the gaudy and costly paraphernalia of the present time. Comfort and freedom were always consulted in preference to personal appearance, and the dude was then unknown. The principal articles for clothing were of home manufacture, such as linsey-woolsey, jeans, tow linen, etc. The world was not laid under tribute, as now, to furnish the thousand and one mysteries of a lady's toilet. Powders and lotions and dangerous cosmetics, by which the modern belle borrows the transient beauty of the present, and repays with premature homeliness, were unknown to her frontier ancestors, whose cheeks were rosy with the ruddy glow of health, painted by wholesome exercise and labor. The beauty and symmetry of the female form was not distorted or misshapen by tight lacing, The brave women of those days knew nothing of ruffles, curls, switches or bustles. Instead of the organ or piano, before which sits the modern miss, torturing selections from the majestic operas (!) they had to do their part of the work.

"The girls took music lessons
Upon the spinning wheel,
And practiced late and early
On spindle swift and reel."

and were contented with their linsey clothing, their rough-made shoes, and a sun-bonnet of coarse linen The women believed it their highest duty—as it was their noblest aim—to contribute their part in the great work of life. The "hired girl" had not then become a class. In cases of illness—and there was plenty of it in the early times— some young woman would leave home for a few days to care for the afflicted household, but her services were not rendered for the pay she received. The discharge of the sacred duty to care for the sick was the motive, and it was never neglected. The accepted life of a woman was, to marry, bear and rear children, prepare the household food, spin, weave and make the garments for the family. Her whole life was the grand, simple poem of rugged, toilsome duty, bravely and uncomplainingly done. She lived history and her descendants write and read it with a proud thrill, such as visits the pilgrim when at Arlington, he stands at the base of the monument which covers the bones of 4,000 nameless men who gave their blood to preserve their country. Her work lives, but her name is only whispered in a few homes. Holy in death, it is too sacred for open speech.

Hard Times.—The financial pressure in the early days was very heavy. Quite a gale of prosperity swept over Illinois just after the close of the war of 1812, and a large flow of immigration followed that event. People were seized with a spirit of speculation and much land was bought. Land sold at $2 per acre—$80 down on a quarter section, the balance to be paid in five years. Everybody bought all the land on which they could make the advance payment, with the expectation of selling enough to emigrants to make the other payments. Wild-cat banks were established and flooded the country with their worthless bills, and then—"bust." The emigrants so confidently expected did not come, and hence there was little or no sale for real estate. The flood of bank notes had driven out specie, and when the banks failed there was no money of any kind, and pelts, tallow, beeswax, wolf-scalps, etc., became the circulating medium of the country. Under a State law, wolf scalps were made a legal tender for taxes. These, together with fox, coon and opossum skins, passed current for tobacco, whisky and other *necessaries* of life. Indeed, it is said that a man would enter a "grocery—" there were no saloons, they were all groceries—for a glass of whisky, present a coon skin, receive his glass of whisky and a "possum" skin in change. Under these depressing circumstances, the country improved and settled very slowly for a number of years. These were some of the trials and difficulties and dangers the pioneers of Jefferson County had to contend with. They would appear almost insurmountable to us of the present day.

CHAPTER IX.*

INTERNAL IMPROVEMENTS—EARLY ROADS AND TRAILS—SALINE AND WALNUT HILL ROAD—THE VANDALIA ROAD—OTHER HIGHWAYS AND BRIDGES—RAILROADS—HOW THEY GREW OUT OF THE OLD IMPROVEMENT SYSTEM—JEFFERSON COUNTY'S EFFORTS FOR RAILROADS—ST. LOUIS & SOUTHEASTERN—THE AIR LINE—PROJECTED ROADS, SOME OF WHICH WILL BE BUILT, ETC., ETC.

"And fast, and fast, and faster still,
As though some superhuman will
The Iron Horse did guide."

AMONG the internal improvements of a country, none are of more importance than its roads and public highways. It has been said that a stranger may judge of the civilization to which a community has attained by its system of public roads. In this chapter we propose to treat of the public roads and railroads of the county, taking them from their first inception to their present perfected system. First, we shall consider the wagon roads in their order, and then direct our attention to the railroads.

The Saline and Walnut Hill Road.—The reader will pardon us for giving most space to this first road, and the one hardest to get of all our roads. At the beginning, the Goshen road was the only one, and it crossed the present Fairfield road four miles east of town, just beyond Samuel Bruce's. It was necessary to have one through the county seat. There were a few trails, but not even a trail led to Mount Vernon. It was said that all roads led to Rome, but it was just the reverse in regard to Mount Vernon—all roads led somewhere else. On the third day of the first term of the County Court, June, 1819, the subject of roads came before the Commissioners, and it was "ordered that William Goings, Thomas Jordan, James Abbott, James Johnson and John Abbott, or any three of them, do view and make a road the nearest and best way from Mount Vernon to where the old road leaves the county." It was "further ordered that John Jordan, Nicholas Wren, John C. Casey, Joseph Reed and Robert Cook, or any three of them, do view and make a road from Mount Vernon to where the Prairie road crosses the east boundary line of the county, near Hodge's"—both boards of Viewers to report in September. These intended roads were what is now within this county of the McLeansboro and Centralia roads.

But when September came it brought no report from Viewers, and a new board was appointed for the whole road. It was "ordered that William Casey, William Jordan, Sr., and Samuel Bradford, or any two of them, do view a road, beginning at or near the southeast corner of this county, on the nearest and best way to Mount Vernon; from thence, on the nearest and best way, to the lower end of Thomas Jordan's Prairie, taking into consideration a road hereafter to be cut out on a direction to Vandalia, and from Jordan's Prairie, on the best and nearest way, to where the old road crosses the northern boundary line of this county, and report," etc.

It was found easier, however, to make

*By Dr. A. Clark Johnson.

orders than to induce men to do what they were not compelled to do, and indeed, hardly knew how to do. On the same day with the last order—September 7, 1819—Curtis Caldwell, John Jordan and Robert Mitchell were appointed to view a road from the ford of the creek near Jordan's—now Garrison's—to where the new road from Maulding's intersected the county line. This last was a road that Maulding had just cut out from his house in Hog Prairie, a few miles this side of where McLeansboro now stands, to Hodge's—late Abe Irvin's—crossing the east line of the county near the southeast corner. These men in due time made a report: "We, John Jordan and Curtis Caldwell, having been appointed, etc., do hereby certify that we have examined and believe that the nearest and best way is on a straight line from where Maulding's road intersects the county to Joseph Jordan's; thence along the old road to the ford of the creek, interfering with no person's farm, by the Overseers making some small amendments if necessary." This report was approved, and John Jordan made Overseer. The "Old Road" here was a trail from Jordan's to where Lew Beal lives. The "Old Road" in the previous orders was the Goshen road. William Casey, James Johnson and William Goings were now—October 4—ordered to view the road toward Carlyle. But still some were dissatisfied with the Viewers' report just received, and John C. Casey, Samuel Bradford and Oliver Morris were ordered to view the route over again.

Incredible as it may now appear, all those orders and views and reports failed to accomplish anything; and this arose from the fact, we suppose, that, as is now the case when a railroad is talked of, almost every man thought he lived exactly where the road ought to be made, and a man was unwilling to offend so many of his neighbors as did not live on the route he might recommend.

But at length a bold and working board was found. January 4, 1820, William Jordan, James Abbott and Reuben Jackson were ordered to view and mark the road, and James Kelly was requested to procure the services of William Hosick as surveyor. A month or more elapsed and Hosick came not. It was then ordered, February 10, 1820, that the order authorizing Kelly to employ Hosick be rescinded, and Joseph Pace be appointed in his stead. Let this report speak for itself:

"We, James Abbott, William Jordan and Reuben Jackson, appointed, etc., met at Mount Vernon on Thursday, the 24th day of February, and viewed to the creek (Muddy) and adjourned until the next day; 25th, met at the creek below the ford at a suitable place for a bridge, viewed on thence, crossing the little prairie at the upper end; thence on to the Little or Jordan's Creek, which we crossed, about a quarter of a mile above Hood's Ford; thence on to an arm of Moores' Prairie, at the Bushy Ridge; thence on to Watkins', and, it being night, adjourned; 26th, met and ran on a straight line to Crenshaw's; thence, with the general direction of the old road to where the new road cut by Thomson and Crenshaw intersects the said old road; thence down said new road to the county line. We met on Monday, the 28th, agreeably to appointment, at Mount Vernon, viewed to the right of Henry Wilkinson's, thence on a line through a corner of Harlow's field, thence on by Elisha Perkins', thence on to a small creek, and, it being night, adjourned till morning. Tuesday, the 29th, we met agreeably to appointment, and continued our course on through an arm of Jordan's Prairie, running within a quarter of a mile of Wren's place; thence on to Gaston's, thence on to the old

William J. Garrison

road where it comes to the base line. We do hereby certify that we believe the above to be the nearest and best way for a road through the county, and as near to the prayer of your petitioners as one can be got."

This report was dated March 10, 1820; the road was ordered to be made on the route surveyed; it was to be opened eighteen feet wide, and for their services Abbott, Jackson and Jordan, the Viewers, and A. P. and G. P. Casey, the chain carriers, were ordered $12 each, and Joseph Pace $24 as surveyor. Daniel Crenshaw was appointed Overseer from the county line to the ninth mile tree; Joseph Reed, from the ninth mile tree to Muddy; A. P. Casey from Muddy to the fifth mile tree, northwest of town; and Samuel Gaston the rest. Just one incident: Two of the Viewers, Jordan and Abbott, were very fond of drink, and when they started out of town the second time they took a bottle of whisky along. When they got near Harlow's, as mentioned in their report, they began to drink, and after drinking freely themselves, they gave Uncle Joe Pace the bottle and he turned away and emptied it on the ground. But he was too late. Jordan already had more than he could carry, so he sat down to rest while the others went on. We believe the rest all put up at Perkins' that night; at any rate, no Jordan appeared till some time next day. When he had rested sufficiently to travel, he had lost his way and spent the night in the woods.

The road crossed no stream requiring a bridge but Casey's fork of Muddy. Here the first bridge in the county was built by Ben Hood and Carter Wilkey. From the settlement at the March term, 1821, it seems that the structure cost $44.15. Hood and Wilkey sawed the lumber by hand. As soon as the bridge was done, old Mr. Harris came along and was anxious to be the first man to ride over. The workmen considered it unsafe, as the old man had taken some "tea;" but they compromised, the old man dismounted and led his horse, and so got safely over. The road still runs very nearly where it was originally located throughout its entire length.

The Vandalia Road.—Before the opening of the Vandalia road, there was a trail to Peddling Billy Hicks', where old Mr. Bruce afterward lived, and a trail from the Carlyle road by Fleming Greenwood's to the Whitesides settlement, near where Flowns lived more recently, in Jordan's Prairie. These were the avenues leading north. But October 5, 1821, Abraham Casey, James Young and William Maxwell were ordered to "view the ground from Mount Vernon to Lee & Hicks' mill and report the nearest and best route for a road from Mount Vernon to said mill." Emboldened by this beginning, the court also "ordered that the said reviewers continue the review of said road from the said mill on the nearest and best direction toward Vandalia to the county line of Jefferson County."

On the 3d of December, the report came in: "By order of the County Commissioners of Jefferson County, to us, the undersigned, to view the ground from Mount Vernon to Lee & Hicks' mill, and from said mill to the north boundary line of Jefferson County, on the direction of Vandalia, and report whether there is ground fit to make a road, and we having received a plat of the Clerk of the Court, have viewed and marked one as straight as we possibly could, and report that we think we have gone as straight as can be without surveying, and think that the ground will answer. Signed by us, Abraham Casey, William Maxwell, James Young." The report meeting with no opposition, was received and the said road was "established a public highway."

For the purpose of opening this road, it was next day ordered that Elihu Maxey be Supervisor of that part "that lies between Mount Vernon and the north line of Section No. 25, Range 2, Township 1;" to William Maxwell was assigned the portion "lying between the north line of Section No. 25 and the north line of Section 23, Range 2, Township 1 north, with all the hands east of the county or Carlyle road;" to James Young fell the part "lying between the north line of Section No. 23 and the northern line of the attached part of this county, with all the hands north of the line where he commences." "The said road to be opened eighteen feet wide and made passable for carriages; to be opened smooth," and to be completed by June.

But the road was not opened very smooth, and, indeed, was not used a great deal, so that it was really in danger of growing up. Hence it became necessary, September 1, 1823, to order "that the Sheriff inform Thomas D. Minor and William Maxwell, Supervisors on the Vandalia road, to proceed to cut out said road twelve feet wide and keep the same in repair." This imperative demand had the desired effect, and the road became a permanent highway.

The Frankfort or Golconda Road.—The idea of this road seems to have originated in 1822, from the people of Franklin County having opened one leading from Frankfort to our county line. The friendly challenge from Franklin was accepted by our Commissioners, and at their March term—March 5, 1822—it was ordered "that Barton Atchison, Esq., James Dawson and Nicholas Wren view the ground for a road from where the Frankfort road intersects the county line to where the said road will intersect (the Sa-line) road at or near the bridge." In due time the report came in:

"Agreeably to an order of the court, we, the undersigned viewers, have viewed and marked the intended road, beginning one-half mile east of the middle line dividing Range 3, where the Frankfort road intersects our county, thence a little northwest, until we come to the Gun Prairie; continuing the same course through said prairie until we struck the above line; thence on and near the said line to the Saline road near the bridge. We, the viewers, think this to be the nearest and best ground for said road, allowing the Supervisor to vary as he may think necessary." Dated April 12, 1822.

To open this road, James Dawson was appointed Supervisor, with all the hands hitherto belonging to Moses Ham on the Saline road, where Ham had succeeded Crenshaw, except Young Lenore, Ignatius Atchison, William Southwood, Joseph Jordan, Daniel Crenshaw and John Crenshaw; "and further ordered that the said road be opened twelve feet wide and it be done by the December term of this court."

Notwithstanding these orders, it was not "done by the December term," and at that time it was found necessary to order that Amos Chandler be " Supervisor on that part of said road between the bridge across Muddy and Rollins' Creeks, with all the hands north of the creek on which Mr. B. Atchison lives, except the hands formerly allotted to Mr Ham," and that Absalom Estis supervise the portion south of Rollins' Creek, with all the hands south of Atchison's branch, except those formerly allotted to Mr. Ham. This move secured the opening of the road. In 1838, William Redman built the first bridge over Gun Prairie Creek for $175.

The Covington or Richview Road.—Covington, as many of our readers are aware, was originally the county seat of Washington, and stood on the Okaw, near the mouth of Crooked Creek, about fourteen miles north of Nashville. Indeed, it still stands there, but in considerably reduced proportions. When Clinton was formed out of the northern part of Washington, Covington was no longer central, and for a short time before Nashville arose, Georgetown, almost a village, a few miles west of Nashville, was the county seat. Clinton County was formed in 1825.

Well, the Grand Prairie people, who had only a winding trail by which to come to town, and the town people who wished to build up, asked for a road to Covington, June 4, 1822, the court ordered that Jacob Norton, Isaac Hicks and James E. Davis view and mark the route as far as the county line, and report in September. This certainly was sufficient time, but September brought no report, and it was necessary to issue a new order: "Agreeable to an order agreeable to a petition handed into this court at the June term, on which Viewers were appointed, but have failed to act, therefore ordered that Curtis Caldwell, Thomas Jordan, Jr., and William Casey be appointed to act as Viewers, to be viewed on the straightest and best way on a direction to Covington, as far as the Washington County line, and make return at the December term."

This order was slightly mixed, but "agreeable" and easy to be understood; yet it was entirely without effect. Nor was a "view" obtained till after March 4, 1823, when Thomas T. Tunstall, Felix McBride and William Deprist were appointed for the purpose. June 10, they reported that they had marked the road on the nearest and best way, to the best of their knowledge, and that the "course generally runs west of northwest." This road ran not far from where the Richview road now runs.

Still the road was not opened till December. Then, December 1, 1823, "for the purpose of opening said road," it was "ordered that William Deprist be and he is hereby appointed Supervisor on that part of said road between Mount Vernon and the Middle Fork of Muddy, with the hands as follows, to wit: Isaac Deprist, Jordan Tyler, Lewis Johnson, John T. Johnson, Nicholas Johnson, James E. Davis, Nicholas Stull, Overbay and his son-in-law, Rhodam Allen, William Maxey, Charles H. Maxey, Joshua C. Maxey, Edward Maxey, Zadok Casey, Samuel Hirons, Jarvis Pierce, William Wilkerson, Joel Wilkerson, Samuel Reed and Asahel Batemen." A. P. Casey was Supervisor on the rest of the road, "with all the hands west of Foster's Creek, including the Long Prairie settlement," "said road to be opened by the March term of this court wide enough for carriages to pass." In 1828, this road was vacated, but in a few years it was restored as the Grand Prairie, afterward the Richview, road, a change being made at the west, and under Jacob Breeze, Joe Baldridge and John Switzer, and at the east end under L. F. Casey, H. D. Hinman and J. C. Maxey, all in 1844. The present western terminus was at last located in 1846 by Duncan Cameron, Esq., Isaac Casey, Jr., and Samuel Watkins.

The Georgetown or Nashville Road.—At the June Court, 1828, at the same time the last road was vacated, a new one to Georgetown was called for. It was to "cross the Middle Fork of Muddy near Shiloh Meeting House and the West Fork near Hamlin's." Most of our readers will no doubt recollect Noah Bullock's and Bill Maby's "meeting house" better than this Shiloh that stood about the same place. William Casey, Robert Holt and A. Buffington were the viewers, and on their report the Covington road was vacated and the Georgetown road established. Green, Dysnish and Jim Johnson of Long Prairie were chosen to open the road. It issued from town at the west end of Main street, and ran nearly southwest by west to W. Casey's house on the hill.

The Fairfield Road.—In 1824, John Summers bought A. P. Casey's improvement east of town; and June 5, 1826, he and others petitioned for a road toward Fairfield. Accordingly, he and Joe Jordan and Isaac Casey were appointed to view the route. September 4, they made their report:

"Pursuant to an order of the County Commissioners' Court at their June term, 1826, we, John Summers and Joseph Jordan, have viewed and marked for a road from Mount Vernon to the county line to Fairfield, commencing at the court house; thence to John Summers'; thence to William Jordan's; thence intersected the road from Fairfield at the county line." John Summers was appointed to open the road, together with Bridges Hynes, Edmund Hines, Jesse Green, Thomas Hopper, John Vance and Hiram Hodge. The next spring court gave him the hands in Adam's Prairie also. The road as then established, ran near where it now does, except that it struck out nearly due east from the court house ran by a cabin that stood where Dr. Green lives, ran nearly a hundred yards south of the Shields House, then wound around to the ford below where the old bridge was. In 1838, Coleman Smith built the first bridge over Seven Mile for $25.87¼. In 1839, James Ross, John Johnson and E. H. Ridgway, in accordance with an act of the Legislature, relocated the road from town to the creek, throwing it into Main street, and so on, nearly where it is at present.

The Brownsville and Pinkneyville Roads.—The roads toward Brownsville and Pinkneyville attracted a good deal of attention, considering how little business we ever had at either of the places. The Brownsville road began in 1834. September 27, "the Viewers appointed to view and mark a road from Mount Vernon to intersect a cart way in Horse Prairie and on a direction to Brownsville, do make the following report: That we have viewed the same to run from Mount Vernon, the present leading road to John Hays' at Elk Prairie; thence angling down said prairie near the east side of John Black's farm; thence down a little arm of said prairie to the lower end of the same; thence crossing Muddy below the hurricane; thence to the county line above the head of Honey Point." Signed by Samuel Boswell and John Hays.

In 1835, Isaac Casey, A. Buffington and Jesse Green were sent to view a road toward Pinkneyville, and failing to do it the job was next year assigned to John Dodds, I. T. Davenport and William Hicks. They located it by John Dodd's house from the Nashville road, by Rhodam Allen's field across the prairie, and so on to the Brownsville road. Thus it remained till 1839, when A. Milcher, P. Osborn and J. A. Dees were sent out to see if it were not useless. For anybody but Dodds and Rhodam Allen, it certainly was, so there it died. Then an Elk Prairie road sprang up, 1837, running between Joseph Pace's and Dr. Greethan's, to Bodinis, to Reed's ford, across Muddy, and to the old road at the county line. After changing routes frequently, the Pinkneyville road was located not far from where it now runs, in March, 1845, by Sam Boswell, Sid Place and Jesse A. Dees, the route having been suggested by J. R. Allen and Eli Gilbert in 1844.

Other Roads.—We have given details of the first old roads, not only to show when and where they were located, but to give an idea how we got them; and the recital also gives an idea that the best evidence as to where they run, is the fact that they run there, the record evidence of exact location being slim. At length, however, roads became literally too numerous to mention. We note the principal ones: In 1838, a road from Nashville to Equality, across the southwest corner of the county, was laid out under the direction of George W. Lee, Thomas Thompson and George McCary. The same year, a road was opened from Salem to Chester, across the northwest corner of the county, and Allen Dolson was the first Supervisor. It was also in the same year that the Maysville road was located. Isaac Casey, Azariah Bruce and Lloyd Buffington were the Viewers, and it was described as running with the Fairfield road to a point near the Goshen road; thence to Wright Bullard's, thence to the bridge over Shiloh Fork above Slocum's mill. In 1839, the new State road from McLeansboro to Mount Vernon was located, Ben Hood, Ophey Cook and Wm. Sturman being the Viewers. It was described as coming through John Lowry's field, through Willis Holder's and to a post of Atchison's mill and to the old road between Atchison's and Osborn's. In 1848, a road was opened from the Academy by Short's mill on the creek and by Samuel Atchison's to the county line at or near the Spurlock place. The Farmington road was located in October, 1849, by Jonathan Gregory, Joe Buffington and Lafayette Casey. In the same year, the Richview & Fairfield—now the Richview & Farmington—road was located by G. P. Casey, N. S. Johnson and P. T. Maxey. The east Long Prairie road from Seven-Mile bridge was laid out in March, 1850, Abram Marlow, Alexander Moore and Peter Bruce being Viewers. The same year, the Frog Island road began, A. D. Estes, J. Y. Shelton and Andy Elkins locating it from the Frizzell bridge to A. D. Estes', and southeast to Shelton's mill. The route from Ashley to Willbanks' was completed by S. S. Mannen and S. K. Allen in September, 1852. A road from Rome to John Foutts' on the Carlyle road was viewed in 1853 by Owen Breeze, John Foutts and Arch Maxwell. The toll road began in June, 1854, and a road was opened from Rome to Kuneville by E. Wimberly and others in 1854. Isaac Garrison, Thomas Moore and Rolla M. Williams located the Mount Vernon & Lynchburg road in July, 1855. B. T. Wood, W. A. Dale and D. B. Davis located one from Council Bluffs to Lynchburg in July, 1857. The Spring Garden and Tamaroa road began the same year, viewed by J. B. Ward, James Kirk and Henry Williams, and in the same year a way was opened from Lynchburg to Ham's Grove by J. Taylor, W. D. Daily and A. D. Estes, and the next year one from Ham's Grove south by G. H. Puchett, Joshua Hopper and Morgan Harris.

And now roads get to be so numerous it makes our head swim to try to follow the story any further. Indeed, there are so many that a stranger can hardly get anywhere. And the changes have been so many! Some have kept wriggling like a snake. For instance, the Brownsville road. If every move had made a move forward, too, like a snake's, it probably would now be in the middle of Arkansas. We might add that, under township organization, we have very expensive roads and hardly any good ones.

The Railroads.—We desired to give a complete history of the struggles made by our people to secure railroads, but the story looms up before us now so long and wide that we submit in despair and consent to give a mere outline.

The struggle began long ago. Illinois

had a large amount of Saline lands in Gallatin County, about four townships that had long been withheld from sale and leased out by the United States, but at length donated to the State. It was about the year 1831 (L. 1831, p.15), it was determined to sell 20,000 acres and distribute the proceeds among the counties. Jefferson's share was $200, but we never got it. In 1836 (Laws, p. 129), the Illinois Central road was chartered and our people made an effort to get it, but got only about 400 yards of it across the northwest corner of the county. The older citizens all remember the crazy fit that the Legislature had in 1836-37 and 1838. It was attempted to supply the whole State with railroads at once. One was to be built from Galena to Cairo, one from Alton to Shawneetown, one from Alton to Mount Carmel, one from Alton to Terre Haute, one from Quincy, by Springfield, to the Wabash, one from Bloomington to Pekin and one from Peoria to Warsaw—over 1,300 miles. All this was undertaken just as the State had begun to recover from a general financial depression and had got out of debt. The result was a debt of $14,000,000 and about 100 miles of railroad from Springfield to the Illinois River, that was never worth over $100,000. Our Representative, H. T. Pace, strongly opposed these measures, and this was one cause of our getting none of the railroads. But in 1839 (L., p. 252), by the efforts of Noah Johnston in the Senate and H. T. Pace in the House, an act was passed which gave us (?), in addition to the $200, an interest in $200,000 that was appropriated to counties that failed to get any railroad. Yet if a future survey should put Mount Vernon on the road, our interest in the fund was to "determine." So we missed getting a railroad that time; so did the rest; so did we miss getting the money—except $100 at one time and $50 at another, secured by the persistent efforts of H. T. Pace.

Illinois bonds, credit, railroads, and everything else were "dead as a mackerel" until 1850-51, when the new Illinois Central Railroad Company was chartered, and the road now bearing that name was begun. This moved hope and enterprise, and other roads were projected. The Sangamon & Massac road was chartered (L., 1853, p. 177), and February 15, 1855, gave birth to two or three charters that promised roads for us (L., p. 249. 296). One was the Belleville & Fairfield with J. L. D. Morrison, et al., of St. Clair; A. D. Hay, et al., of Washington; J. M. Johnson, T. M. Casey, Z. Casey and H. T. Pace, of Jefferson; and D. Turney, et al., of Wayne, composing the company, capital unlimited and six years to begin it. The other was the Mount Vernon Railroad, capital $500,000; election of officers at Mount Vernon, when $1,000 per mile should be subscribed; to run from Mount Vernon to the Central or the Chicago branch, and Jefferson allowed to give her swamp lands if the people so voted. The charter members were J. N. Johnson, Z. Casey, H. T. Pace, S. H. Anderson, Q. A. Willbanks, J. R. Allen, S. K. Allen, S. W. Carpenter, B. T. Wood, J. H. McCord, Uriah Mills and G. W. Pace. The Bloomington & Toledo road was changed to or united with the St. Louis & Louisville. February, 1857, a consolidation was perfected and this was confirmed by the Legislature February 22, 1861.

Before recurring to the Mount Vernon Railroad, we must notice the swamp lands, as these have been the basis of all our efforts. Congress passed a law September 28, 1850, entitled "An act to enable the State of Arkansas and other States to reclaim the swamp lands within their limits," which gave to the States named in the act all the swamp and overflowed lands within their limits for drainage, education or internal improvements. Our Legislature, in the winter of 1851-52, accepted, and gave the land to the several counties wherein it lay. September 6, 1852, our County Court appointed Elijah Piper Drainage Commissioner, with power to sell first-class lands at $1, second at 75 cents, and third at 50 cents per acre. But Piper gave no bond till December, when the order was made for a sale at public outcry. February 28, 1853, for cash or work on the drains. From some cause, perhaps finding an injunction staring him in the face, Piper didn't sell, and all was quiet for awhile. In December, 1854, the Clerk was ordered to notify magistrates to watch for trespassers, and all was quiet again.

As soon, however, as the Mount Vernon Railroad Company would organize, they, by Scates, asked the County Court for a vote at the judicial election, first Monday in June, 1855, on a proposition to donate the swamp lands to aid in the construction of the road. On the eve of the election, it was postponed until the November election. The donation was conditional, on the road being done in three years, and the land to be sold for not over $2.50 per acre in one year, or $5 after one year. The proposition carried.

In the meantime it was found that the Illinois Central had taken 7,000 acres of swamp lands in this county, and W. B. Anderson was appointed, August 17, to select other lands instead. On the 28th, he reported nearly 1,000 acres, and notices were sent to the land offices and to Springfield, but we believe that Mr. T. A. Hendricks replied that the resolution was void. A list of our swamp lands was received from T. H. Campbell, Auditor, August 20, footing up nearly 19,000 acres.

Soon after the election, a Mr. Alton, from Wisconsin, came with proposals to build the road, but was incontinently snubbed. Gov. Casey founded a company under the style of Vanduzer, Smith & Co., and to these the work was awarded. For Gov. Casey was President, and A. M. Grant Secretary of the old company. Vanduzer was from Ohio, Smith from Troy, N. Y., Vooris from Ohio and Gortschius from New York, but at that time from Peoria, Ill. They came; books for subscription were opened at Anderson & Mills' store, and about $40,000 subscribed and several thousands paid in. All went lively. The track was cleared from Ashley to Fairfield and the road-bed nearly finished. Joel Pace, June 2, 1856, was appointed Trustee of the swamp lands, and June 11 filed his bond in the sum of $8,000. Vanduzer, Smith & Co. were everybody's pets. Newby took them out in his buggy or carried out luscious dinners to them on the road. They located a station at John Wilkerson's and went for his beef and spotted horse. They went in debt to everybody. Ties were piled along the line. They borrowed $6,000 from Shackelford and Givens and got our Trustee to give them a deed to 4,500 acres of our land. Dr. Green and others found themselves guarantors for them to the tune of about $10,000. One of them married one of our handsomest ladies, Vanduzer, accompanied by Casey and Grant, took $500,000 in bonds to New York to sell and we believe his report is not in yet. Things began to drag, slow, slower, slowest, then a full stop —one gasp and all is over—the company is "smashed." The aforesaid guarantors attach what little there is to attach, and are further idemnified by the county with a somewhat dead claim on Warren, and by another party with a somewhat dead note on Vanduzer, Smith & Co. for $3,000. The note died entirely when suit was brought upon it, and the indorsers proved that it was only "a goak." Smith—not Gen. but Dr.—went back to Troy and his wife got rich; Vooris went to Memphis and got shot; Gortschius went to Paducah and got a fatal fall, and Vanduzer went to Michigan and got into the penitentiary. Dr. Green didn't get the depot on his land as promised; Capt. Newby didn't get it on his, as promised; and Gov. Casey didn't get it on his, as promised; most of us got " skun " for larger or smaller amounts, and none of us got any railroad.

Of course, by their failure, Vanduzer, Smith & Co. forfeited everything. The original company brought suit for recovery of franchise, etc., by Scates's advice the road bed was suffered to go to sale, and they sent Tom Hobbs to Springfield with $1,000 and he bought it. A new charter, however, was procured for the Ashley & Mount Vernon Railroad, February 21, 1861, with all the privileges of the Central, Z. Casey, H. T. Pace, J. R. Allen, W. D. Green, T. B. Tanner, C. T. Pace and Noah Johnston, being the company. (This was to cover contingencies.) Then came Maurice H. Baron, of New York, and June 28, 1860, contracted to build the road—a four-cornered contract—Baron, one County Court, two; J. Pace, three; several other men, four. Baron was to build the road and run it ninety-nine years for the road-bed and swamp lands, and to pay the other parties $30,500 by October 1. The "several other men" were to make the swamp lands up to 19,000 acres. All went smoothly, especially Baron, and he went to London to sell bonds and never came back again. The enterprise was now considered as dead and buried. And so it was, for it didn't exhibit a sign of life for five or six years.

In September, 1866, came in petitions for a vote on the $100,000 proposition again, and the result, November 6, was, for, 691; against, 1,188. Nothing daunted, the friends of the project held a public meeting the next spring, and May 3, 1867, court was again petitioned to have a vote on it at the June election. The petition was granted, the county was " stumped " and the proposition carried. The stock-holders of the road met in Mount Vernon, November 8, 1867, and chose as Directors W. D. Green, S. T. Stratton, S. K. Casey, H. B. Newby, G. H. Varnell, T. H. Hobbs and T. S. Casey. Dr. Green was chosen President and T. S. Casey Secretary. April 23, 1868, it became necessary to increase the capital stock $200,000, and Varnell, Stratton, Newby, Green and Hobbs went in $40,000 each. Next day a contract was made with Crawford & Doane. John H. Crawford was from Buffalo, N. Y., where he had been engaged in lake commerce; and Isaac S. Doane was from Meadville, Penn., and was a regular railroad man. The same day Joel Pace resigned and Thomas H. Hobbs was appointed Trustee in his stead. Crawford & Doane agreed to build the road for the swamp lands, the right of way, depot grounds and $100,000, to begin work July 1, 1868, and finish by May 1, 1869. If work was not progressing by September 1, all was to be null and void. Mr. Crawford was elected Vice President and fiscal agent for the company July 3. A move was made toward organizing an Ashley & St. Louis Company, and our company, August 18, approved it and resolved to get a through line. They therefore extended the time for work to begin to October 1.

It was difficult at that time to raise money, and Crawford & Doane could not begin according to contract, though backed by Beldon with the promise of help to the amount of $6,000,000. During the pause that ensued, March 10, 1869, a new company got a charter for a road from St. Louis to Shawneetown and took the name of St. Louis & Southeastern Railroad Company. The company was O. Poole, James H. Wilson, J. J. Castles, S. S. Marshall, A. G. Cloud, R. W. Townsend, S. K. Casey, W. D. Green, T. H. Hobbs and E. F. Winslow. All these were old residents except Gen. James H. Wilson, who was Grant's chief of staff during the war, and Gen. Winslow, who was from Maine, had been a merchant in Iowa, broke, went to the war, was in a dry goods house in Cincinnati, built the Brough road by Vandalia etc., sold out for $100,000 profit and became a railroad man.

At a meeting of the Mount Vernon Railroad Company, in Mount Vernon, March 26, 1869, Dr. Green was directed to go to Chicago to confer with Crawford, who now resided there, and renew the contract with him or form one with Mr. Winslow, or otherwise, as he might think best. He here met with Douglas, who was then President of the Illinois Central Railroad Company, and Douglas said, "build your road yourself; we will indorse your bonds and lease your road." But Green knew that nothing but a through road would satisfy his company and reluctantly declined the generous offer. He found Crawford with good vouchers, but no through charter, and Winslow just the reverse. As our company had been repeatedly twitted about wanting a "bob-tailed road," for the benefit of Mount Vernon, Dr. Green inclined to prefer Winslow. Another fact confirmed this inclination; he found on a slip of paper that Crawford had accidentally left in a record book, a list of distances, etc., which indicated that it was Crawford's design to make the railroad junction in Moore's Prairie and build up a large town there at the expense of Mount Vernon. So he gave the contract to Winslow, saying,

"You shall have it on one condition, that you build the depot south of town, opposite the court house." "I will do it," said Winslow.

Dr. Green, knowing there had been irregularities enough in the elections and legal proceedings in regard to the Mount Vernon Railroad to vitiate everything, if contested and pushed to investigation, went to Springfield, and by help of W. H. Green, lobby member from Cairo, put a bill through by which everything hitherto done in the business was legalized, and the title of the Mount Vernon Railroad Company to the road, franchises, etc., confirmed, March 31, 1869. April 8, the contract with Crawford & Doane was rescinded, and next day the contract was let to Winslow & Wilson. It was a four-cornered contract: St. Louis & Southeastern, one; Mount Vernon Company, two; Court, three; and Hobbs four, thus:

It was first agreed to begin May 24, and finish by January 1. Iron, forty-five pounds to yard and fish-scale joint; guage and grade of Illinois Central; ties, eight feet long, six inches thick, six-inch face, 2640 to the mile; bridges, workmanlike; three stations, at Ashley, Mount Vernon and between.

Second, agreed to give $100,000 county bonds, 14,700 acres of swamp lands, three acres in 600 yards of court house for a depot and right of way from Ashley to Mount Vernon.

Third, agreed to issue the bonds on order of President of Mount Vernon Railroad and completion of road to Ashley, bonds bearing 8 per cent, principal due in twenty years, payable after five years, and to cause swamp lands to be conveyed—the bonds to be a subscription to the capital stock of the railroad.

Fourth, agreed to convey the swamp lands, etc. This was signed by E. F. Winslow, W. D. Green, T. S. Casey, J. R. Satterfield, W.

Adams, F. S. Casey and T. H. Hobbs. The claim of the county against the United States for lands entered after donated by the swamp land act, which sums from the County Court record B, page 632 to have been part of the proposition to aid the Mount Vernon Company, is entirely omitted in this contract. These proceedings secured the road.

Perhaps we ought not to go back to say that in 1855 a Marion and Jefferson County Railroad was chartered, but limited to two years to begin, so it didn't begin. In 1865, a Shawneetown branch of the Illinois Central was chartered, which was expected to give us a road from Tonti through Mount Vernon. This lay pretty still until 1869, when April 1, the St. Louis, Mount Carmel & New Albany Company was chartered. So at the April meeting, 1870, the Supervisors received plenty of petitions, some asking a vote on giving $500,000 to the St. Louis & Southeastern when the road extended to the east county line; some the same for a road toward Benton; some the same for the St. Louis, Mount Carmel & New Albany Company; some the same for almost anybody. The only tangible result was the extension of our road to the southeast, which was completed in 1871. Then those splendid machine shops were built which were burnt, as we shall notice hereafter.

The Air Line.—We have already noticed that under the internal improvement scheme by the State during the mania of 1835 to 1838, a road was undertaken from Alton to Mount Carmel. The $4,000,000 borrowed to build all these roads was exhausted before any railroads were built. Gen. William Pickering was specially interested in this Albany & Mount Carmel road, and when the whole scheme fell through, the road was seized by its creditors, and thus passed into the hands of Pickering. He undertook to finish it, and spent his fortune upon it, but only got a road from Princeton, Ind., to Albion, Ill. He had arrangements made with Eastern capitalists for money, but when Elijah P. Lovejoy was killed at Alton and his press thrown into the river, they became alarmed, considering it an unsafe country for the investment of money, and withdrew their support. Gen. Pickering could go no further, but he held on to what he had till about the time he was appointed Governor of Washington Territory, when he sold out to Blueford, Wilson and others. He got none of the money, but after his death his heirs got about $14,000. To cover contingencies, a charter was obtained, April 1, 1869, for the St. Louis, Mount Carmel & New Albany Railroad, and perhaps another under the name of the Louisville, New Albany & St. Louis Air Line Railway Company. Under the latter name, the company, by Augustus Bradley, President, and George Lyman, Secretary, executed a mortgage to Calhoun & Opdyke, of New York, for $4,525,000, due in 1902, but we don't think they ever got any money.

Not much was done then till 1881. May 20, the stockholders met at the office of Bell & Green, in Mount Carmel, and resolved to issue $3,000,000 first mortgage bonds and $3,000,000 four per cent, fifty year cumulative income bonds and $1,000,000 second mortgage bonds. Robert Bell was then President, holding two shares, while Goldthwaite, Burr & Wilson held 3,806. The same day it was resolved to increase the capital from $3,000,000 to $5,000,000. In November of the same year, the name was changed to Louisville, Evansville & St. Louis Railway Company. But in June 1881, the company had executed a mortgage to the Mercantile Trust Company and Noble C. Butler, in which the route is described as being from New

Albany, by Huntingburg, Ingleton, Oakland City, Princeton, Mount Carmel, Albion and Fairfield, to Mount Vernon, about 192 miles, forty-five miles being already finished from Ingleton to Albion. The change of name was made necessary by a consolidation with roads from Evansville to Jasper, Ind, and from Rockport to Gentryville, Ind., making now a total of 260 miles. March 1, 1882. the road was completed from Mount Vernon to Huntingburg, in all 202 miles, and by a mortgage $1,000,000 was raised to finish it to New Albany. Jonas H. French succeeded Mr. Bell as President, and he was succeeded in turn by John Goldthwaite, the present incumbent. Thus it will be seen that the Air Line was built without costing our people any great effort or expense. Most of the money was really furnished by Ballou, of Boston. After it was completed, the road was much damaged by high waters, and lay quite awhile before trains ran regularly, but the result was a settling of the earth which made it the best new road-bed in the State. Its business has grown rapidly, and it is already a paying road. The Salisbury Company do its repair work at present, but we expect other shops and a depot at no distant day. The Air Line is using the Louisville & Nashville track to St. Louis, but expect to build a line of their own, when a connection with the Chesapeake & Ohio will give us the most direct route from St. Louis to the Atlantic. The road is noted for the courtesy of its officials.

Coming Roads.—The Kaskaskia, St. Elmo & Southern Railroad Company was incorporated in September, 1882, but by a delay in the notice of a meeting of the stockholders last spring, it was apprehended that damage might result, and a new incorporation was perfected July 30, 1883. B. F. Johnson, B. C. Smith, L. R. Stocker, I. H. Johnson, W. H. Smith, A. M. Johnson, Joseph Micksch and J. B. Leash, all of St. Elmo, are the incorporators; capital, $10,000; shares, $50 each; route, Altamont by Mount Vernon, etc., to the Ohio, opposite Puducah. From Altamont there is a line of roads to Chicago already, 200 miles. The estimated cost of the road is $3,500,000, of which $500,000, to be raised on stock and $3,000,000 on bonds. A meeting is to be held in October to issue the bonds. Timothy Genay and G. M. Haynes are the financial agents. They have secured the indorsement of Gov. Hamilton, ex-Gov. Cullom, the Chicago Board of Trade, Mayor Harrison, Farwell & Co., the Missouri Pacific and the Chesapeake & Ohio Railroad Companies, and many others, and have every assurance of being able to place the bonds at once when issued. The right of way has been secured for nearly the entire route.

The Mount Vernon & Tamaroa Railroad comes in place of the Tamaroa, Mount Vernon & Vincennes Railroad, of two years ago. The latter lapsed by the two-years clause. Its length will be twenty-six miles; estimated cost, $450,000, of which $50,000 are to be raised on stock and $400,000 on first mortgage bonds. It is to connect with the Wabash, Chester & Western, whose eastern terminus is Tamaroa, with the Air line, and beyond the Mississippi with the Chester & Iron Mountain. This road has been consolidated with the Kankakee, St. Elmo & Southern, Col. Evans, of the Mount Vernon & Tamaroa, becoming Treasurer of the consolidated company, and R. A. D. Willbanks one of the Directors. All the right of way has been secured except a short distance near Mount Vernon.

The Toledo, Texas & Rio Grande Railroad Company began June 7, 1882, incorporated for fifty years. The route is from Charleston, Coles County, by Martinsville, in Clark County, to Cairo. Capital, $2,500,000. The incorporators are J. C. Allen, of Olney, John Mason, of Newton; J. G. Rupert, of Decatur; E. Pratt Buell, of Warsaw; O. B. Ficklin, of Charleston; F. A. Vongassy, of Effingham; William Lindsay, of Martinsville; Robert Hannah, of Fairfield; John H. Halley, of Newton. Judge J. C. Allen is President, J. G. Rupert, Secretary. The great advantage of this road is that it has its outlet to the northeast, striking the lake commerce 600 miles nearer to the seaboard than Chicago, parallel with scarcely any other road, crossing them all, and running through an excellent but chiefly undeveloped or very imperfectly developed country. The right of way has been obtained, the timber cut off, and a great deal of the grading done. It runs across the southeast corner of the county, through the flourishing town of Belle Rive.

Besides these roads, the Jacksonville, Northwestern & Southeast Railroad Company was chartered in 1867, and is gradually moving down upon us from the northwest.

CHAPTER X.*

EDUCATIONAL—EARLY EFFORTS AT FREE SCHOOLS—THE DUNCAN LAW—EDUCATION AT PRESENT—STATISTICS—THE PRESS—EDITOR JOHN S. BOGAN—FIRST NEWSPAPERS—MOUNT VERNON A NEWSPAPER GRAVEYARD—THE PRESS OF TO-DAY—RELIGIOUS HISTORY—OLD-TIME CHRISTIANITY—PIONEER MINISTERS—CHURCHES ORGANIZED—REV. JOHN JOHNSON, ETC.

THE subject of education should interest every reader of this work, more, perhaps, than any other mentioned in the general history of Jefferson County. For we are told that it "is education forms the common mind," and our forefathers appreciated this fact when they declared, in their famous ordinance of 1787, that "knowledge, with religion and morality, are necessary to the good government of mankind." In that little clause they struck the very keynote of American liberty. The governing power in every country upon the face of the globe is an educated power. The Czar of the Russias, ignorant of international law, of domestic relations, of finance, commerce and the organization of armies and navies, could never hold, under the sway of his scepter, 70,000,000 of subjects. An autocrat must be virtuous and intelligent, or only waste and wretchedness and wreck can wait upon his reign. England, with scrupulous care, fosters her great universities for the training of the sons of her nobility, for their places in the House of Lords, in the army, navy and church. What, then, ought to be the character of citizenship in a country where every man is born a king, and sovereign heir to all the franchises and trusts of the State and Republic? An ignorant people can be governed, but only an intelligent and educated people can govern themselves.

When the survey of the Northwest Territory was ordered by Congress, it was decreed that every sixteenth section of land should

* By W. H. Perrin.

be reserved for the maintenance of public schools within each township. The ordinance of 1787 proclaimed that "schools and the means of education should forever be encouraged." By the act of Congress passed April 18, 1818, enabling the people of Illinois to form a State Constitution, the "Section numbered 16 in every township, and when such section had been sold or otherwise disposed of, other lands equivalent thereto and as contiguous as may be, should be granted to the State for the use of the inhabitants of such township for the support of schools." The act further stipulates "That 5 per cent of the net proceeds of the lands lying within said State, and which shall be sold by Congress from and after the 1st day of January, 1819, after deducting all expenses incident to the same, shall be reserved for the purposes following: Two-fifths to be disbursed, under the direction of Congress, in making roads leading to the State; the residue to be appropriated by the Legislature of the State for the encouragement of learning, of which one-sixth part shall be exclusively bestowed on a college or university." In other words, Congress donated to the State a full township, six miles square, for seminary purposes, and the thirty-sixth part of all the residue of public lands in the State and 3 per cent of the net proceeds of the sales of the remainder, to support common schools and promote education in the then infant State. Truly a most magnificent and princely donation and provision for education. The sixteenth section, so donated, amounted in the State to nearly a million acres; in Jefferson County to over ten thousand acres.

Laws were first passed, directing Commissioners' Courts to appoint three Trustees for the school land in each township, where the inhabitants of such townships numbered twenty white persons. These Trustees had power to lease the school lands at public outcry, after twenty days' notice, to the highest bidder, for any period not exceeding ten years, the rents to be paid in improvements, or in shares of the products raised. The laws were crude, and fell far short of their intended object. The school lands, under the lessee or rental arrangement, yielded little or no revenue; many of the renters, having no title to nor common interest in the land, only opened and cultivated enough for a bare support, and of course produced nothing to divide. Then squatters took possession of a considerable portion, and wasted the timber, and in many ways depreciated the value of the lands. As a result, the cause of education languished, and was at a standstill for years. There were a great many influences and obstacles in the way of a general diffusion of knowledge. The settlements were sparse, and money or other means of remunerating teachers were scarce; and teachers, competent to impart even the common rudiments of an English education were few and far between.

This state of affairs continued until 1825, when Joseph Duncan, then a member of the State Senate, introduced a bill for the support of common schools by a public tax. The preamble to the act was as follows: "To enjoy our rights and liberties, we must understand them; their security and protection ought to be the first object of a free people; and it is a well-established fact that no nation has ever continued long in the enjoyment of civil and political freedom which was not both virtuous and enlightened; and believing that the advancement of literature always has been and ever will be the means of developing more fully the rights of man; that the mind of every citizen in a republic is the common property of society and constitutes the basis of its strength and happiness; it is, therefore, considered the peculiar duty of a free government, like ours, to encourage and extend the improvement and cultivation of the intellectual energies of the whole." The text of this admirable law may be divined from the preamble. It gave education a powerful impetus, and common schools flourished in almost every settlement. But notwithstanding all this, the law was in advance of the civilization of the times. The early settlers had left the older States— the Southern States, where common school education never has flourished as it should— and plunged into the wilderness, braving countless dangers and privations in order to better their individual fortunes and to escape the burdens of taxation, which advanced refinement and culture in any people invariably impose. Hence, the law was the subject of much bitter opposition. The very idea of a tax was so hateful, that even the poorest preferred to pay all that was necessary for the tuition of their children, or keep them in ignorance—which was generally the case— rather than submit to the mere name of tax.

This law—the Duncan law, as it was called—is the foundation upon which rests the superstructure of the present common school system of Illinois. The law provided for the division of townships into school districts, in each of which were elected three School Trustees, corresponding to Directors of the present day, one Clerk, one Treasurer, one Assessor and one Collector. The Trustees of each district had supreme control and management of the school within the same, and the employment of teachers and fixing their remuneration. They were required to make an annual report to the County Commissioners' Court, of the number of children living within the bounds of such district, between the ages of five and twenty-one years, and what number of them were actually sent to school, with a certificate of the time a school was kept up, with the expenses of the same. Persons over the age of twenty-one years were permitted to attend school upon the order of the Trustees; and the history of education in Illinois discloses the fact that it was no uncommon thing for men beyond the meridian of life to be seen at school with their children. The law required teachers, at the close of their schools, to prepare schedules giving alphabetically the names of attending pupils, with their ages, the total number of days each pupil attended, the aggregate number of days attended, the average daily attendance, and the standing of each scholar. This schedule was submitted to the Trustees for their approval, as no teacher was paid any remuneration except on presentation to the Treasurer of his schedule, signed by a majority of the Trustees. The law further provided, that all common schools should be maintained and supported by a direct public tax. School taxes were payable either in money or in produce, and teachers would take the produce at market price, or if there was no current value, the price was fixed by arbitration. Fancy the schoolma'am of the present day, taking her hard-earned salary as a teacher in potatoes, turnips or coon skins! We have heard it related of a teacher in one of the counties bordering the Wabash River, that he was paid in coon skins for a ten weeks' school; and after his school was out, he footed it to Vincennes, with his pelts upon his back, a distance of over thirty miles, and there disposed of them.

When this wise and wholesome law was repealed by the Legislature, Gen. Duncan wrote, as if gifted with prophecy, " 'That coming generations would see the wisdom of his law, and would engraft its principles on their statute-books; that changes in the condition of society might render different applications of the same necessary, but that the principle was eternal, and the essence of free and enlightened government; and legislators who voted against the measure will yet live to see the day when all the children of the State will be educated through the medium of common schools, supported and maintained by direct tax upon the people, the burden falling upon the rich and poor in proportion to their worldly possessions." These predictions, yellow with the years of a half-century and over, have been faithfully fulfilled and verified.

The Duncan school law remained in force only a little over two years, when it was repealed. The great objection, as we have said, to the law, was the tax clause. This was, substantially, that the legal voters of any school district had power, at any of their meetings, to cause either the whole or one-half of the sum necessary to maintain and conduct a school in said district, to be raised by taxation. And if the voters decided that only one-half of such required amount was to be so raised, the remainder was to be paid by the parents, masters and guardians, in proportion to the number of pupils which each of them might send to such school. No person, however, could be taxed for the support of any free school unless by his or her consent first obtained in writing, though all persons refusing to be taxed were precluded from sending pupils to such school. In almost every district there were those who had no children to educate, and then there was an uncivilized element of frontier life, who believed education was a useless and unnecessary accomplishment, and only needful to divines and lawyers; that bone and muscle and the ability to labor were the only requirements necessary to fit their daughters and sons for the practical duties of life. A proverb then current was (in many localities), "The more book-learning the more rascals." To quote a localism of the day, "Gals didn't need to know nothin' about books, and all that boys orter know was how to grub, maul rails and hunt." That senseless prejudice, born of the crude civilization of the early period of the country, has descended, in a slight degree, to the present, and yet tinges the complexion of society in many different localities.

After the repeal of the Duncan law, education, for nearly a generation, was in anything but a flourishing condition, either in this county or in the State. Like the stagnant waters of a Southern lagoon, it was difficult to tell whether the current flowed backward or forward. For many years the schoolhouses, school books, school teachers and the manner of instruction were of the most primitive character throughout the whole of Southern Illinois. The houses were the proverbial log cabin, so often described in the early annals. A few of these humble schoolhouses, unused and almost rotted down, may still be occasionally seen, eloquent of an age forever past. The early books were as primitive as the cabin schoolhouses, and the early teacher was, perhaps, the most primitive of all. The old-time pedagogue was a marked and distinctive character of the early history—one of the vital forces of the earlier growth. He considered the matter of imparting the limited knowledge he possessed a mere question of effort, in which the physical element predominated. If he couldn't talk or read it into a pupil, he took a stick and mauled it into him.

The schoolmaster usually, by common consent, was a personage of distinction and importance. He was of higher authority, even in the law, than the Justice of the Peace, and ranked him in social position. He was considered the intellectual center of the neighborhood and was consulted upon all subjects, public and private. Most generally he was a hard-shell Baptist in religion, a Democrat in politics and worshiped Gen. Jackson as his political savior. But the old-time pedagogue—the pioneer of American letters—is a thing of the past, and we shall never see his like again. He is ever in the van of advancing civilization, and fled before the whistle of the locomotive or the click of the telegraph was heard. He cannot live within the pale of progress. His race became extinct here more than a quarter of a century ago, when the common school system began to take firm hold and become a fixed institution among the people. The older citizens remember him, but to the young of to-day he is a myth, and only lives in tradition.

The school laws, after the repeal of the Duncan law, were often changed—they were revised and changed again before they attained to the perfection we at present have in them. Even now, they are susceptible of improvement, though they are superior to those of many other States. A peculiarity in the different State constitutions is that pertaining to education. The constitution of 1818, while indorsing education in a general way, is silent upon the subject of educating the masses through the medium of the common schools. The framers of the constitution of 1848 went a little further; they said that the General Assembly *might* provide a system of free schools. It was not, however, till after half a century of existence as a State, that her delegates, in convention assembled, engrafted upon the pages of her organic law a mandatory section, declaring "that the General Assembly *shall* provide a thorough and efficient system of free schools, whereby *all* children of this State may receive a good common school education;" and the last General Assembly (1882–83), among the few redeeming acts of its long, turbulent session, was one compelling all parents, guardians, etc., to educate the children intrusted to them.

The first school ever taught in Jefferson County was in 1820, by Joel Pace, whom we have mentioned elsewhere as the first County and Circuit Clerk. It was taught in a floorless cabin, without ceiling or window—perhaps without a shutter to the door. The pupils comprised the children of William Maxey, probably, and John and Henry Wilkerson's, one or two of Isaac Casey's and a few of James and Lewis Johnson's. The next school was taught by James Douglas, at Old Shiloh. Douglas was a man of education, and, it is said, understood several different languages. He boarded at Zadok Casey's much of the time, and from him Mr. Casey received the rudiments of an English education. The Shiloh house in which Douglas taught was burned down the next fall, and hence his was the only school taught in it. Another was afterward built, near the same site. Emory P. Moore taught, perhaps, the third school in the county at Union, in 1820–21. In 1822, W. L. Howell taught in the same house. About 1821–22, an Irishman named Freeman taught a school on Mulberry Hill, in a cabin that had been built by Clark Casey and afterward abandoned. Referring to the early schools of the county, Mr. Johnson says: "The schools were not large nor learned. The Testament, spelling-book and arithmetic, with writing. constituted the course of study; and it didn't 'run smooth,' for nearly all the schools were loud—just as loud as the children's lungs could make them, every one studying at the top of his voice; yet the teachers were more rigorous in discipline than is common at present."

ELI GILBERT.
(DECEASED.)

The following statistics will show something of the present status of education in the county:

Number of children in the county under twenty-one years......................	11,041
Number of children between six and twenty-one years........................	7,414
Number of graded schools in county....	2
Number of schoolhouses, brick, 4; frame, 90; log, 15; total.....................	109
Number of males attending school, 2,942; females, 2,787; total..................	5,729
Number of male teachers employed, 89; female, 52; total......................	141
Fund for school purposes from all sources,	$38,139.37
Total expenditures for schools, etc.......	32,191.23
Balance on hand June 30, 1883.........	$ 5,948.14

The Press.—A history of the county which did not give a full and complete history of the press would be incomplete, to say the least. Jefferson County, like many other portions of the State—and many portions, even, of the whole country—has been a great newspaper graveyard. For a history of the many enterprises—living and dead, past and present—in the "art preservative of all arts," we are indebted to Dr. A. Clark Johnson, who knows more of the press history, as well as the entire history of Jefferson County, than any other man living. His sketch of the press is as follows:

It ought not to be difficult to prepare a full and connected account of our newspaper enterprises, but it is so; and chiefly, we suppose, because our papers changed owners so often, and so many of our editors and publishers have left us. We trust, however, that the reader will find nearly all the leading actors and events in this line in the following sketch:

The Jeffersonian.—Our present Circuit Clerk, John S. Bogan, was the principal one "to be, to do and to suffer" in this, our first attempt. A few words of him are not out of place here. The son of a printer, Mr. Bogan had learned the art in the *Congressional Globe* office at Washington City in early boyhood, and followed types till 1840. He then located a few miles out of town, near the line of Montgomery and Prince George Counties, in Maryland. He was born in Shenandoah County, Va., in 1820. His father, Benjamin Bogan, was also a Virginian, and a fine type of that old Virginia gentleman now fast passing away. For many years he edited and published a newspaper in both Virginia and Ohio, and then located in Washington City. Our old editor, John S., has been with us so long that we all know him. He is a part of us—a very large part, for his heart is large enough and warm enough to take in the whole human race. He came here young, and buoyant with hope and life, and now he is growing old and is fast descending the shady side of life. For forty years he has gone in and out among us, and his long and active life is without spot or blemish. Although he long ago retired from the editorial chair, he has always been in public life, until the county machinery would hardly run without his aid.

He came to our county in 1846, at the suggestion of Gov. Casey, who was ever trying to bring the better class of immigration hither, and bought the old Sam Casey place in Grand Prairie. He was quite a successful farmer, and remained here till 1851. T. B. Tanner, having learned from Gov. Casey that Bogan was a printer, rode out to his farm and remained a day or two with him, discussing the project of starting a paper in Mount Vernon. The result was that the paper was determined upon, and a subscription by the citizens footed up $150. A pause ensued. H. T. Pace inquired how much more was wanted, and finding it was $200 offered to loan that sum, taking notes due in one and two years.

Bogan found a partner in the person of Augustus A. Stickney, then at Centralia. Stickney, we believe, was originally from St. Clair County, and was related to the O'Malvenys. He was a man of brain and vim, but not much physical strength. An old Rammage press was secured at Belleville. It had formerly done service at Alton. It was inked with balls instead of a roller. Its mahogany frame would indicate that it had once been a fine one, but it required four tremendous pulls to print a paper. This was too much for Stickney, who got to spitting blood when he went to strike off the paper; so in a few weeks he retired, went to Fairfield and started a paper there. Let us finish him: From Fairfield he went South, and at length brought up in San Francisco, where he published, and perhaps still publishes, the Alaska *Herald*. We have a copy of his paper, Vol. VI., No. 140, a good deal English, some Russian, and in his terms he agrees to take greenbacks at par.

The first number of the *Jeffersonian* was issued in August, 1851. It was a modest sheet, of six column size, with some advertisements, and enjoyed a circulation of about six hundred copies. The Hamilton County printing was done here, but beyond this the job work did not amount to much. Probably, in the way of Eastern exchanges, the *Jeffersonian* excelled any other paper we ever had. The Alton *Telegraph* and the *State Register*, both dailies, were also on the exchange list, besides the few papers then published in Southern Illinois, as the Cairo *Argus*, Benton *Standard*, Shawneetown *Advocate*, Belleville *Advocate*, Salem *Advocate* and the rest of the Advocates, whether so-called or not. It was not, however, a financial success, resembling, in this respect, Grossman's Benton *Standard*, and most of the papers of that day in Southern Illinois.

After Stickney left, Bogan had helps— Wallace; Matchett, the universal tramper, who could scare all the boys by his fearful recitations of Shakespeare; Frank Manly, who married and went to Mount Carmel and died; John A. Wall for a short time, T. T. Wilson, E. V. Satterfield, *et al.* This office produced the first roller ever used in the county. Bogan was the building committee, and Ed Satterfield the master mechanic. Ed Noble made a tin mold; the materials were mixed and cooked in an old iron pot, and the whole performance took place in the middle of Main street, in front of the office. Thus the modern improvements were introduced. Yet the enterprise failed to pay, and in three years was hopelessly in arrears—as papers are apt to be when their subscribers are. Pace sued on his notes, and finally Bogan, his paper and his farm all "went under" together.

Tanner, at this time, was Circuit Clerk, having been elected in 1852, and he reproached himself as the cause of Mr. Bogan's misfortune. Downing Baugh was now Judge, filling the unexpired term of S. S. Marshall. So Tanner, having first obtained a promise of Judge Baugh, resigned his office and Bogan was appointed to succeed him. Thus began Bogan's somewhat protracted term as Clerk of the Circuit Court, dating from September, 1854.

In August of that year, however, in winding up his affairs, he had sold his old press to Bowman & Robinson for $325 in gold. These gentlemen were from St. Louis; the former a son of wealthy parents, the latter fresh from California; both nice young men —too nice to be satisfied with so rough a press. Before they had run it long, they offered to sell Mr. Bogan the whole concern for about $200. Robinson soon quit, and Bowman persevered for about six months when he sold out to Dodds, Johnson & Co. The origin of this company was peculiar. The county had recently come in possession of about 19,000 acres of swamp lands. One party was in favor of selling these lands immediately, and talked of a great system of drainage and numerous new schoolhouses as the result. Dodds favored selling, partly, it may be—and very naturally—because he was County Clerk, and would receive $1.50 for every deed made by the county. A caucus of those opposed to selling and in favor of holding the lands as a means of some day securing a railroad, was held— Casey, Scates, Johnson and Tanner, perhaps, forming the caucus. They resolved to form a company and buy the *Jeffersonian*, and run it in the interests of their railroad project, fighting the proposed sale of the lands. Of course this design was not even whispered to Dodds. The company was soon formed, composed of W. Dodds, John N. Johnson, Z. Casey, W. B Scates, T. B. Tanner, Anderson & Mills, J. Pace & Son. This was in April, 1855.

Tanner, fresh from the Legislature, became the editor. A Mr. Smith—not John, but Lute B., from Evansville—an inferior printer but not easy to get rid of, was foreman, aided by any boys he could pick up, especially, and for most of the time, by John A. Wall. Tanner went to St. Louis and secured a number of advertisements. The people were talked to, and the subscription list ran up to eleven or twelve hundred. A new press was bought from Frank Manly, and Daniel Anderson took a wagon to Grayville and hauled it home. In short, the enterprise was quite a success. After Dodds, Johnson & Co. had run the concern one year, and had accomplished their design—the selling of the lands had been voted down by the people—but still wishing to have a county

paper, they fell into the generous course of giving the use of the press to anybody that would take it and publish a paper.

The Sentinel.—This was the next paper that made its appearance. Tanner and Tom Casey were practicing law together and William Anderson was studying. Casey and Anderson were ambitious, and wished to try their hands at the newspaper awhile, and Tanner consented to the use of his name. So Tanner, Casey & Anderson it was. They took the office for one year. The paper was styled the *Sentinel*, and Anderson was the ostensible editor. John A. Wall and Joel V. Baugh were the typos. John had been "devil" a good deal, but we believe Joe just went in with scarcely any initiation. It was before Casey had learned to write—we mean like he does on the Judge's docket—so the boys could read nearly all his articles. Tanner wrote the long articles—so long, the boys did not have time to correct the proofs carefully; and Anderson not being a born writing master, it went hard with the editorials. Tanner said that sometimes when the paper came out, and he looked at the "leader," he could hardly remember whether he had ever written anything like it or not. The *Sentinel* did not prove very profitable, in fact, it began at the wrong time—just after the Presidential election in 1856, when everybody was cooling off—so, when the year was out, Tanner, Casey & Anderson went out. And Baugh went out.

The Egyptian Torchlight.—Dodds, Johnson & Co. now sold their press and fixtures to William R. Hollingsworth and John A. Wall. They christened their paper the *Egyptian Torchlight*, and published under the firm style of Hollingsworth & Wall, Ed Satterfield and Sam Bird assisting. In the fall, 1857, Wall withdrew and went to Murfreesboro, Tenn., and Hollingsworth went on alone, but not long. The *Torchlight* did not shine so long as the *Sentinel* did—not much over six months—say from spring till late in 1857. Hollingsworth then surrendered the office, not having yet paid for it, and went to Missouri or Arkansas. He came from Iowa. After Hollingsworth & Wall had both gone, Ed Satterfield issued the paper for a few weeks, making no notable change in it except the adoption of a motto that some were wicked enough to say was ambiguous: "Egyptian darkness and Jackson Democracy —one and inseparable.". The paper then again changed hands and name

The Advocate.—This was the name of the new paper. S. Turner Brown was the new proprietor and Ed Satterfield and Frank Dowler were his forces. This enterprise lasted from "late in 1857," *vide supra,* until very late in 1857—that is, for about three weeks. Dr. Brown was from Alabama by way of Metropolis, and his tall, slender figure, his very tall, slender coat, his nervous locomotion, his fray with Mr. Thorn, his real estate speculations, his marriage to Miss Jennie Lewellyn and his departure will be well remembered by many. The lady mentioned was a niece to H. D. Hinman, was out on a visit from West Virginia, was quite handsome and accomplished and was with the Doctor when they were heard from—what was long the last time; they were then at Memphis, he a surgeon in McCullough's army, which was moving into Arkansas. Recently we learn that the Doctor now lives near Little Rock, and is succeeding well. After the Doctor left, Ed Satterfield again came in as the forlorn hope, and kept the paper going till after the publication of the delinquent tax list in the spring of 1858.

The Mount Vernon Star.—Up to January, 1858, the press was still owned by Dodds, Johnson & Co., and occupied the room over Joel F. Watson's store, east of the present Phœnix Block. J. R. Satterfield now bought the office for about $250, and kept it till after the sale of delinquent tax lands, as above-mentioned, when he sold it to Curtis & Lane for $800, and, we suppose, "was happy." The new men, S B. Curtis and James S. Lane, were both from Ypsilanti, Mich., both were school teachers and Curtis had studied law. Wall was in Centralia, and Curtis & Lane sent for him to take charge of the type and press work, as they were not printers, and Wall felt "passing rich" on a promise of $450 a year. Todd Wilson was his only "devil." We now find the office over James M. Pace's store, in the Johnson House, and the paper comes forth as the Mount Vernon *Star*, with a Latin motto, something like *Non nobis solum, sed toto mundo nati.* The proprietors were strongly anti-slavery—perhaps Abolitionists would not be too strong a word; but they tried to make the paper neutral and failed, as usual. People found them out, and did not support them well. So, in 1859, at the end of one year, they retired, giving Wall a lease for another year. We believe they both returned to Michigan. Lane went into the army and was killed, and Curtis is practicing law.

Wall soon after moved the office into the basement of the old Odd Fellows Hall. Todd Wilson and Ham Watson—now Dr. Watson, of Woodlawn—were his helpers. At the end of nine months, Curtis & Lane, and Wall and all of them failed to finish paying for the press;] Wall's lease succumbed to a prior claim, and Judge Satterfield closed up the business by taking possession. But the *Star* was not extinguished. The Satterfield boys, Ed and John, moved into a room up-stairs in the court house, where it remained until they sold out to Hayes in the fall of 1865. In the meantime it was still changing hands. We had Satterfield Bros., or Satterfield & Bro., till 1861. Ned went to the war, and John ran it till the close of the year, then he went South, and Judge Satterfield and Wm. Davisson ran it till the next spring. Ned came back and ran it till fall, then both ran it till Hayes bought it.

The Mount Vernon Guardian.—In April, 1860, the *Guardian* appeared. It was published by Russell & Wall. Alex Russell was from Minnesota, and was son-in-law to Mr. Erwin, who had bought and located on the hill where L. N. Beal lives. Russell & Wall bought their press from Judge O'Malveny, of Centralia; it was the same that had been used by the somewhat noted J. G. D. Pettyjohn, when he was publishing his *Modern Pharos*. It was located up-stairs in the building now occupied by W. E. Jackson, south side of the public square. This was our first Republican paper; indeed, it rather claimed to be a War Democrat. Thus it went on for one year, when Wall joined the army, and was succeeded by William Durlinger, another son-in-law of Mr. Erwin. In a few months, Russell sold his interest to Durlinger, and went to Belleville, and started the Bellville *Democrat*. Durlinger held up manfully for some time, but at last gave way, and retired to a farm near Tamaroa. Not liking that, he changed again, went to Belleville, and is still there with Russell, publishing the *Democrat*. We believe it was in March, 1863, that the *Guardian* went down.

The Unconditional Unionist.—By this time—1863—Wall came home from the army, crippled, and some of his friends aided him to purchase the *Guardian* office. He moved to the room formerly occupied by Jack Fly as a furniture shop, near the old stand of D. Baltzell, and gave his paper the name of *Unconditional Unionist*. Of course it was unquestionably Republican. After publishing this paper for three years, Wall pulled out and went to Salem. Then A. B. Barrett and others formed a stock company, that we might not be left without a Republican paper, and soon found a man—A. J. Alden —to publish it. Jack kept it going, aided, of course, by Barrett and others, until the summer of 1867. He then went to McLeansboro, and started the *Hamilton Sucker*, and was succeeded by George W. Moray. But Moray did not seem to succeed any further, for in five weeks he subsided and went to Princeton, Ky., and started a paper there.

The Statesman.—This paper followed the *Unionist*. Henry Hitchcock, from Indianapolis, bought the press and fixtures, put Theodore Tromley in as chief "type tosser," and issued his first paper September 3, 1867. Hitchcock was a nice, pleasant gentleman, and his paper did well until domestic afflictions compelled him to relinquish the business. He sold out in 1873.

The Free Press.—C. L. Hayes, as before noticed, bought the *Star* office from Satterfield in November, 1865, and on the 6th day of December issued his first paper, with the name of the Mount Vernon *Free Press*. From the court house he moved to the room over Tom Goodrich's store, where it was burned in the great fire of March 16, 1869. His friends promptly rallied to his aid, and in about a month after the fire he had a new press, and resumed the publication of his paper. Hayes, with all that bitterness which sometimes injured him, must ever be ranked very high as an editor and newspaper manager. He was a good hand to gather news, judicious in the use of the scissors, and much above the average in his editorials. He published the first history of Jefferson County, and expended $100 in assisting the writer in gathering up materials and preparing the sketches that appeared from week to week in his columns. In March, 1872, he sold to R. A. D. Wilbanks and G. M. Haynes, under whose management it continued till the next October, John Wightman being chief printer. This last purchase may have been made for a political purpose—we can't say.

The press was still nearly new; it was one that Wilbanks & Haynes had traded the old *Star* press for in Chicago, paying the difference. These gentlemen, now having no special object to accomplish, let the office to W. H. Mantz. He continued till the spring of 1876, when he assumed a hostile attitude toward Wilbanks & Anderson, whereupon they "elected that his lease should terminate," and he went out, and became correspondent of the Missouri *Republican*. He was succeeded in the *Press* office by Don Davisson. Don was a Greenbacker now, and so was the *Free Press*, and the editorials presented a rare combination of softness and roughness. It will be remembered that the Greenbackers that year—1877—elected two of their candidates—John N. Satterfield, County Clerk, and John D. Williams, Superintendent of Schools.

But it soon became necessary to do something more; so, in April, 1879, the *Jefferson County Greenback* Printing Company was organized. William B. Anderson, Seth F. Crews and William H. Smith were the Commissioners to obtain license, etc., from the State. The object, as stated in their application, was to print and publish a weekly newspaper and to do a general printing, publishing and book-binding business, with power to change the weekly to a semi-weekly, tri-weekly or daily. Their capital was $2,000, in 200 shares of $10 each, and their corporation was to run for ninety-nine years. The principal stockholders were W. B. Anderson, W. H. Smith and S. F. Crews, fifteen shares each; G. W. Evans, G. L. Varnell, John Wilbanks, Ananias Knowles and Jesse H. Smith, ten shares each; the rest running from nine shares down to one. November 8, 1879, they elected as Directors, for three years, T. Anglen, L. B. Gregory, J. B. Pearcy, Ananias Knowles, Alonzo Jones and G. W. Evans. Thus backed—and greenbacked—the thing looked fearfully strong; but the high colors soon began to fade, and in February, 1880, they sold out to H. H. Simmons, of the *News*. During the brief existence of the *Free Press*, in its last days, Anderson was the editor, and the vigor and earnestness—not to say acrimony,—with which he threw hot shot into the defunct old parties are too fresh in mind to be referred to here.

The News.—September 2, 1871, is the date of the first issue of the Mount Vernon *News*. It was published by Lawrence F. Tromly, the auxiliary side being furnished by Kimball & Taylor, of Belleville, and the style of the concern being L. F. Tromley & Co. Theodore Tromley, who had handled some types for Satterfield, and had graduated under Jack Alden, on the *Hamilton Sucker*, joined Lawrence and they bought the office. Under the style of Tromly Bros., they then changed the paper to a quarto of eight pages, and moved from Varnell's Block to the Phœnix Block. L. F. Tromly began his experience with Durlinger & Russell, in 1861, and now publishes the *Shawnee News*.

In the spring of 1876, the Tromly brothers sold out to C. L. Hayes, and Hayes to C. A. Keller in January, 1877, Hayes retaining possession till April 1. November 28, Keller sold to H. H. Simmons. Simmons was an Eastern man, who came West in 1849. After exploring the West, from Dubuque to New Orleans, he went into the Alton *Democrat* office with John Fitch, and remained there two years. He then went to Greene County, and published the Carrollton *Democrat* for one year, and then the *Logan County Democrat* for one year, and through the Presidential campaign, fighting Fremont. He was then correspondent for the *Herald* for a time, after which he traveled several years in the East, in the interest of the North Missouri and the Atlantic & Great Western Railroad. In 1867, he started the Lebanon *Journal*, as an independent and local newspaper, and continued it for several years, when he sold out to Eckert and went back to Washington County, Ohio. He there bought a half interest in the Democratic paper and remained one year, when his wife died and he went to Cleveland, where his sister lived. Thence, he came here in April, 1877, and ran the *News* for C. A. Keller till November 28, when he bought it, as before stated.

In February, 1880, Mr. Simmons bought the *Free Press*, and his paper is now the Mount Vernon *News and Free Press*. He paid what was, perhaps, a good price for the *Free Press*—$1,100; but he has shown himself what most printers are not—a good financier, and has the whole outfit of both papers paid for. The *News* is the first paper in the county that proved a financial success. By this, and by a dignified course, with a good deal of editorial ability, the *News* has attained a high rank among the local papers of the State.

The Sucker State.—In May, 1873, C. L. Hayes and R. M. Morrison bought Henry Hitchcock's *Statesman* office, and began the publication of the *Sucker State*. In changing hands, the *News* changed politics — from Republican to Democratic—without change of name; but in case of the *Statesman* the change of name was as conspicuous as that of its political complexion. Morrison retired from the *Sucker State* December 27, 1873, and January 17, 1874, Hayes dropped the co-operative outside, after which he claimed to have "the only paper printed in Jefferson County." But this county is too small a stream to float large or heavily-laden craft, so he finally ran aground and went to pieces.

The Weekly Exponent.—In our biographical department will be found a sketch of Mr. Edward Hitchcock, the editor and proprietor of the *Exponent*. This supersedes the necessity to notice here his previous labors as a journalist. In November, 1878, when solicited by Republicans of Jefferson County to publish a paper here, he was, and had been for two years, publishing a paper at Casey, in Clark County, bearing the name of the *Exponent*. At that date—November, 1878—the Republicans of Jefferson County invited Mr. Hitchcock to locate at Mount Vernon, and to bring hither his press and printing material. He did so; and on the 5th day of December, 1878, the first number of Vol. III of the *Exponent* was issued in Mount Vernon. Since that date, and up to the present, during a period of nearly five years, the paper has regularly appeared, notwithstanding difficulties and trials that can scarcely be appreciated by those who never tried to stem the tide of adverse political sentiment and contend with a majority such as uniformly sweeps all before it at election in Jefferson County. The paper is now well established, with a good circulation and liberal patronage in the way of job work and advertising. The office has been recently moved from the northwest corner of the same block to rooms in the Crews building, corner of Bunyan and Washington streets. It will not, perhaps, detract from Mr. Hitchcock's reputation to attribute his success, in part, to the amiable character of his family, as well as to his own ability as a journalist.

Church History.—The state of society fifty

or sixty years ago here was rough and rude. But for all this, that curse of humanity, intemperance, was no more prevalent, in proportion to population, than now—perhaps not as much. Scarcely was the nucleus of a settlement formed ere a distillery was started; for where there was such profusion of snakes there must be whisky to cure their bites! The settlers endured privations and hunger, and their children cried for bread for want of mills, they groped in ignorance for want of schools and churches, but the still house was reared in their midst, where the farmer exchanged his bag of corn for the pioneer beverage of the border. This is but the history of Illinois, and particularly of the southern part of the State. In every family the jug of bitters was to be found, and was regularly partaken of by every member of the household, especially during the chill season. The visit of a neighbor was signalized by producing the bottle or demijohn. At all rustic gatherings, liquor was considered an indispensable article, and was freely used. Everybody drank whisky. Even ministers sometimes took a little as an—ague preventive, or for the stomach's sake. There were some rough neighborhoods in which the people resisted all advancement and progress. In these, liquor was used to great excess, and then, as now, was an active promoter of broils, disturbances and fights. In these affrays—to their credit be it said—fists and feet were alone used, and were called "rough and tumble." The knife, the pistol and the bludgeon were then unknown, and are the products of a much later and more advanced civilization. These sections were known as "hard neighborhoods," and were shunned by all respectable emigrants seeking homes, who were so fortunate as to find out their reputation.

Into this rude state of society came the pioneer preacher, as "one crying in the wilderness." These old-time ministers were characters, in their way. They were possessed of an individuality peculiarly their own, and as different from the high-bred clergymen of the present day as possible. As a class, they were uneducated, rough and resolute, and exactly suited to the day and civilization in which they lived. They encountered and overcame obstacles that would appall their effeminate representatives of a later period. They were exactly suited, we repeat, to the civilization in which they lived, and seem to have been chosen vessels to fulfill a certain mission. These humble pioneers of frontier Christianity proclaimed the glad tidings to the early settlers, at a time when the country was so poor that no other kind of ministers could have been maintained. They spread the Gospel of Christ where educated preachers with salaries could not have been supported. They preached the doctrine of free salvation, without money and without price, toiling hard in the interim of their labors to provide themselves with a scanty subsistance. They traversed the wilderness through sunshine and storm; slept in the open air, with the green earth for a couch and the blue sky for a covering; swam swollen streams, suffered cold, hunger and fatigue with a noble heroism, and all for the sake of doing their Master's will and of saving precious souls from perdition.

Many of these old-time preachers sprang from and were of the people, and were without ministerial training, except in religious exercises and the study of the Scriptures. In those days it was not thought necessary that a minister should be a scholar, but that he might be from the common people, just as some of the disciples were from the lowly fishermen of Gallilee, and that it was sufficient for him to preach from a knowledge of the Bible alone; to make appeals warm from the heart; to paint the joys of heaven and the miseries of hell to the imagination of the sinner; to terrify him with the one and exhort him, by a life of righteousness, to attain the other. Many of these added to their Scriptural knowledge a diligent perusal of Young's Night Thoughts, Milton's Paradise Lost, Jenkins on Atonement and other kindred works, which gave more compass to their thoughts and brighter imagery to their fancy. In profuse and flowery language, and with glowing enthusiasm and streaming eyes, they told the story of the crown of thorns, of Golgotha and Calvary.

Their sermons sometimes turned upon matters of controversy—unlearned arguments on the subjects of free grace, baptism, freewill, election, faith, jusitfication and the final perseverance of the saints. But that in which they excelled was the earnestness of their words and manner, the vividness of the pictures they drew of the ineffable bliss of the redeemed and the awful and eternal torments of the unrepentant They painted the lake of fire and brimstone and the torments of hell so plain, that the startled sinner, in his excited imagination, could hear the ponderous iron doors open and their rusty hinges creak. But, above all, they inculcated the great principles of justice and sound morality, and were largely instrumental in promoting the growth of intellectual ideas, in bearing the condition and in elevating the morals of the people; and to them are we indebted for the first establishment of Christian institutions throughout the county.

The first religious sect represented in the county was the Methodists, and of course they organized the first church society. This was different from most of Southern Illinois, for in many other portions, in fact in a majority of the counties, the Baptists—the hard shells—were the pioneers of religion. But here the Methodists got the start. We have said elsewhere that Jefferson County was a stronghold of Democracy; it was also a stronghold of Methodism. Several of the very earliest settlers were not only Methodists, but were Methodist preachers. Among these were Zadok Casey, Edward Maxey and Lewis Johnson. John Johnson, another pioneer preacher, came in later. As pioneers, these men are noticed in other chapters. They were the old-time ministers we have already described, plain and unvarnished, and preached the Word of God, not for "the world's dross," but from a sincere conviction of right and a desire to benefit their fellow-men. Next to the Methodists, the Baptists were the strongest in numbers and earliest in settlement. Elder Harris was one of their early preachers. The first sermon preached in the county is said to have been delivered by Zadok Casey. It was preached in the fall of 1817, in a house that had been just erected by Isaac Hicks, and we have the authority of Johnson, the historian, for stating that every man, woman and child then within the present limits of Jefferson County was present. The first house used for church purposes was the one already mentioned as the one in which Joel Pace taught the first school. It was used until the fall of 1820, when it was destroyed by fire.

In the spring of 1819, or thereabouts, the first religious organization in the county was effected. It was at a meeting held at Edward Maxey's cabin, and the society thus formed comprised Edward Maxey and wife, William Maxey and wife, Burchett Maxey and wife, Fleming Greenwood and wife, James Davis and wife and Zadok Casey. In the fall of 1820, a house was built at Union, and in the fall of 1821, that at Shiloh. These were used both for school and church purposes.

We cannot, however, go into details of organization of the different churches in this chapter, but in the history of the towsnhips shall devote considerable space to each of them.

Rev. John Johnson.—A more fitting conclusion, perhaps, could not be given to this chapter than to append a sketch of the Rev. John Johnson. No minister of his day stood higher in Southern Illinois. Rev. G. W. Robbins, who preached his funeral sermon, only spoke the unanimous verdict of all who knew him best, when he said "John Johnson was no ordinary man." He was born in Louisa County, Va., January 7, 1783. Born in poverty, he was left an orphan when less than two months old, and sank to the extremes of poverty more trying still. When her sons had grown to manhood and had gained sufficient wealth to own a cart and yoke of cattle, the mother moved to Sumner County, Tenn. There Mr. Johnson, slender and feeble in his youth, lived to the age of twenty-eight, developing a strength of frame that would be deemed almost gigantic at the present day. With increasing strength, there came a desire for improvement. By the help of a slave, he learned the alphabet, and by the help of a piece of an old song book, containing songs he knew by heart, he learned to read. He was converted, and felt himself called to preach before he could yet read so as to be understood. By the light of pine-knots, he studied at night, after his hard day's work was over, and on Sundays, at some little cabin on the hillside, he would proclaim the Gospel, with little of man's learning but with a pathos and a power that always carried the hearts of his rustic hearers by storm. He applied for admission into the old Western Conference, but even that primitive body, looking at his uncouth garb and listening to his stammering effort to read, rejected his application and kindly advised him to abandon his design of trying to preach. He was not humbled by this—he was as humble as man could be before. He returned to his home, his studies and his toil. The next year, the Conference admitted him on trial, but seemed curious to see how much hardship he could bear. They sent him to the Sandy River, where climbing mountains and swimming unbridged streams was his daily work. Two hundred times he had to swim in the course of the year. He then traveled two years in different parts of Ohio —then the frontier—and was next sent to Natchez, in Mississippi, a point it required 1,500 miles' travel by the zigzag routes to reach, most of this distance being by-paths and trails, 600 miles of it through the "Indian nations."

We have not space to follow Mr. Johnson through his various experiences of trial and toil. August 10, 1814, he married Miss Susannah Brooks, who showed herself a worthy helper for such a man, and who still lives, one of the most aged and venerable of the few survivors of her generation in Jefferson County. Without a trace of ambition or a suspicion of self-seeking, but by the overpowering weight of mind and character alone, Mr. Johnson rapidly made his way to the very front. In the palmiest days of the Kentucky Conference, when it contained many such men as Peter Cartwright, Peter Akers, Thomas A. Morris, Jonathan Stamper and Henry B. Bascom, it was asserted by a writer of that day that "Bro. Johnson was the most popular and effective preacher in the State." An evidence of his standing is found in the fact that, in 1822, when the conference sat at Bells' Camp Ground, near Lexington, Mr. Johnson was unanimously chosen to preach the funeral of that great and saintly man, Valentine Cook, to one of the largest and most august assemblies that had ever met in Kentucky. After filling nearly all the most important positions, having been stationed at Nashville, Maysville, Louisville, Hopkinsville and other points, and Presiding Elder for several years on the Hopkinsville District, Gum River District, etc., he located and came to Mount Vernon in 1834, and here, on the 8th day of April, 1858, he passed away.

In person, Mr. Johnson was of medium height—about five feet eleven inches—his weight 170 to 180 pounds, complexion dark, hair black as the raven. His movements seemed slow; but he pushed forward what ever work he had to do with an energy that never tired. In his labors, whether on the circuit or the farm,' he seemed incapable of fatigue and had physical strength sufficient for all demands. But with all his rugged vigor he had a heart as tender as a woman's, and a sympathy that extended even to the insect under his feet. He had a voice of most unusual power. Even when speaking in tones so loud that he could be heard two miles away, he seemed to speak with ease, and his voice never lost that peculiar quality that melted the hearts of all who heard. His profound learning and his masterly intellect commanded the respect of all; but it was more, perhaps, by the tenderness and intensity of his emotions that he swayed the multitudes. Yet his discourses were short, seldom over twenty or thirty minutes. A camp meeting was once held near his home; he returned from a business trip on Saturday evening; the meeting was dragging on, heavy and cold; he preached on Sunday, at 11 o'clock, and it was as if a cyclone had struck the congregation, carrying saint and sinner alike before it. The uproar after he closed lasted longer than the sermon. One evening in Hopkinsville, the sexton was absent with the church key, and Mr. Johnson talked a few moments to the group that was shut out, and when he closed, all were in tears, and they went shouting along down the streets in every direction. Perhaps there never was a man who could open a shorter way to the heart. At a love-feast at old Union, he once spoke not more than half-a-dozen words, but everybody's cup seemed to run over at once, for a general shout was the result. He was not fond of debate, but when it was forced upon him showed himself a David ready for any Goliath he might meet. While stationed at Nashville, Tenn., the Methodist Episcopal Church was assailed, and defiance thrown out by a Mr. Vardiman, distinguished alike for polished manners, learning and skill as a debater. Mr. Johnson accepted his challenge. When the appointed day came, Johnson walked humbly in, alone, and soon Vardiman strode in, with Felix Grundy on one arm and Andrew Jackson on the other. The contest was to last three days. On the second morning Vardiman failed to appear, and he never was seen in Nashville again. It may be that there was what some ministers term a divine power about his ministry; for he was one of the most fully consecrated of men, and there was a solemn gravity about the man such as is very rarely seen. It may have been this that made a certain man declare that it "made the cold chills run over him to see Mr. Johnson walk down the aisle to the pulpit." It is, no doubt, largely owing to his influence that the Methodist Church has grown from D. Baugh and wife, the only members at the time he came, to 400 members now. His remains, with those of his youngest son, who died in 1853, repose in Salem Cemetery.

CHAPTER XI.*

AGRICULTURE—ITS RANK AMONG THE SCIENCES—HOW TO KEEP THE BOYS UPON THE FARM—EDUCATE THEM TO IT—PROGRESS OF AGRICULTURE IN THE COUNTY—SOME STATISTICAL INFORMATION—COUNTY FAIRS AND ASSOCIATIONS—OFFICIALS OF THE SAME—HORTICULTURE—VALUE OF FRUIT GROWING—STATISTICS—THE FORESTS, ETC.

"Oft did the harvest to their sickle yield,
   Their furrow oft the stubborn glebe has broke;
How jocund did they drive their team afield!
   How bowed the woods beneath their sturdy
      stroke."—*Gray.*

THE advantages of science, a superior soil and the use of machinery will always render agriculture the most attractive, manly and profitable branch of industry in which the people can engage, contributing, more than any other pursuit to individual comfort, and proportionally adding to the prosperity of the country. The cultivation of the soil, in all ages, has furnished employment for the largest and best portion of mankind; yet the honor to which they are entitled has never been fully acknowledged. Though their occupation is the basis of national prosperity, and upon its progress, more than any other branch of industry, depends the march of civilization, yet its history remains, to a great extent, unwritten. Historians duly chronicle the feats of the warrior who ravages the earth and beggars its inhabitants, but leaves unnoticed the labors of him who causes the desolated country to bloom again, and heals, with the balm of plenty, the miseries of war. When due worth is recognized, instead of the mad ambition which subjugates nations to acquire power, the heroism which subdues the soil and feeds the world will be the theme of the poet's song and the orator's eloquence.

The people of Southern Illinois generally have not fully comprehended the natural advantages of their soil, and its agricultural advantages. Hence, they have worked in the dark, so to speak, for many years, and the development of the country, as a consequence, has fallen behind what was its just due. The farmer will take his place among the best and noblest of the earth, only when he forces his way there by the superior intelligence, culture and elegance, with which such a mode of life is capable of surrounding itself. Each branch of the science of properly cultivating the earth is dignified and ennobling, if the farmer himself will exert his abilities to make it so. It is worthy of the devotion of the greatest intellects, and offers a field for the finest powers of the best endowed of mankind. A great need of the times is to make rural life so attractive, and pecuniary profit in it so possible, as to hold the boys and young men on the farm, that, not by mistaken ideas of gentility, of ease of life and opportunities for winning fame, so large a percentage of them may be drawn into the so-called learned professions or into trade. With proper surroundings, education and administration of the economies of the farm, with a sufficient understanding of the opportunities for a high order of intellectual and social accomplishment in the rural life of the country, this need not and would not be so. A bright,

* By W. H. Perrin.

high-spirited boy is not afraid of labor, but he despises drudgery. He will work hard to accomplish a fine end, when the mind and heart both work together with the muscles; but he will escape from dull, plodding toil. Let the boys learn that rural life is drudgery only when the mind is dull; that the spade and the plow are the apparatus with which he manipulates the wonderful forces of the earth and sky, and the boy will begin to rank himself with the professor in the laboratory or the master at the easel. The farmer should be educated to feel that there is no occupation in life that leads the educated man to more fruitful fields of contemplation and inquiry. The scientific mind finds every day, in the fields and orchards, new material to work upon, and the cultivated taste endless opportunities for its exercise.

Agriculture, then, should rank first among the sciences, for without it life itself would soon cease. All important interests, all thriving industries and all trades and professions receive their means of support, either directly or indirectly, from it, and, therefore, are but secondary to it in actual importance.

It is too often the case that farmers do not pay the attention to their lands necessary to keep them in a highly productive state, but through excessive cultivation exhaust their vitality while yet they should only be in their prime. Johnston, in his "Chemistry of Common Life," gives the following description of the system of farming commonly adopted by the first settlers on this continent, and the truths uttered apply with as much force to a single county or community as to the country at large. He says:

"Man exercises an influence on the soil which is worthy of attentive study. He lands in a new country, and fertility everywhere surrounds him. The herbage waves thick and high, and the massive trees sway their proud stems loftily toward the sky. He clears a farm in the wilderness, and ample returns of corn repay him for his simple labor. He plows, he sows, he reaps, and the seemingly exhaustless bosom of the earth gives back abundant harvests. But at length a change appears, creeping slowly over and gradually dimming the smiling landscape. The corn is first less beautiful, then less abundant, and at last it appears to die altogether beneath the scourge of an unknown insect or a parasitic fungus. He forsakes, therefore, his long-cultivated farm, and hews out another from the native forest. But the same early plenty is followed by the same vexatious disasters. His neighbors partake of the same experience. They advance, like a devouring tide, against the verdant woods; they trample them beneath their advancing culture; the ax levels its yearly prey, and generation after generation proceeds in the same direction—a wall of green forest on the horizon before them, a half desert and naked region behind them. Such is the history of colonial culture in our own epoch; such is the history of the march of European cultivation over the entire continent of America. No matter what the geological origin of the soil may be, or what the chemical composition; no matter how warmth and moisture may favor it, or what the staple crop it has partially yielded from year to year; the some inevitable fate overtakes it. The influence of long-continued human action overcomes the tendencies of all natural causes. But the influences of man upon the productions of the soil are exhibited in other and more satisfactory results. The improver takes the place of the exhauster and follows his footsteps on these same altered lands. Over the sandy and forsaken tracts of Virginia and the Carolinas he spreads large applications of shaly marl, and the herbage soon covers it again with profitable crops; or he strews on it a thinner sowing of gypsum, and, as if by magic, the yield of previous years is doubled and quadrupled; or he gathers the droppings of his cattle, and the fermented produce of his farmyard, and lays it upon his fields, when lo! the wheat comes up luxuriantly again, and the midge, and the rust and the yellows all disappear from his wheat, his cotton and his peach trees. But the renovator marches much slower than the exhauster. His materials are collected at the expense of both time and money, and barrenness ensues from the early labors of the one far more rapidly than green herbage can be made to cover it again by the most skillful, zealous and assiduous labors of the other."

There is a great deal of truth in the above extract, and we see it illustrated in every portion of the country. The farmer, as long as his land produces at all plentifully, seems indifferent to any effort to improve its failing qualities. And hence, the land, like one who has wasted his life and exhausted his energies by early dissipation, becomes prematurely old and worn out; when, by proper care and timely improvement, it might have retained its rich, productive qualities thrice the period.

The agricultural history of Jefferson County is but little more than a repetition of the history of almost every county in Southern Illinois. The area of the county is 576 square miles, and the greater portion of it is susceptible of cultivation. But little of this is prairie—perhaps about one-fifth. These prairies occupy the more or less elevated lands between the creeks and water-courses, and are generally very productive. The white under-clay, which is such an unwelcome feature of some of the prairies farther north, hardly anywhere extends into Jefferson County. The land outside of the prairies, is mostly well adapted to the cultivation of grain and all sorts of fruit.

For the first twenty to forty years of settlement in the county, there could be little incentive to grow crops there was no market for. Each settler raised corn and potatoes and "garden sass" enough for his own use and no more. The implements of agriculture consisted of a small bull-tongue plow, an old "Cary" plow and a hoe made by the blacksmith. The main point in farming, in those days, was to have a herd of wild hogs in the woods, corn enough for bread and to feed the pony—when the settler was so fortunate as to have one—and a few ears to toll the hogs home to mark them.

When spring came, the crop time was rather a hard life to live. About all the revenue that could be counted on was hens' eggs—after these domestic fowls had been introduced—to buy the small luxuries, such as coffee, sugar, salt or anything in that line; and if the hens failed to come to time on the "lay," the old man and the children would strike out to the woods to dig "ginseng." This was after game began to get a little scarce. A large sack of the then staple article of ginseng could be dug in a few days, and, when dried, would bring $3 or $4 —a sum that would help out the family finances in good shape. There was but little provision made for the cattle, as they could almost live through the winter in the woods. But very little wheat was grown here then, as there were no mills to grind it, and no market for the surplus. Indeed, the early settlers were at great inconvenience to get their corn ground; there were but few mills, mostly run by horse power. But all this is changed now. The coming of railroads has produced a wonderful revolution in the mode of farming. Saw mills have cut the timber off, to a great extent, and much of the land has been brought under cultivation. From the sickle and old-fashioned scythe and cradle, the wheat is now mostly harvested with self-binders. The hay crops are of great value. Timothy, red-top and clover flourish as finely here as in any part of the State

In the early history of the county, the pioneers were favored by the mildness of the climate, the abundance of wild game and the fertility of the land when brought into cultivation. Step by step, the hardy settlers made their inroads into the heavy forests, enlarged their farms and increased their flocks and herds until they found a surplus beyond their own wants and the wants of their families. There was then but little outlet for the products of the farms, and far less of the spirit of speculation than at the present day. The result was that after a few years the farmers had plenty at home; they handled less money, it is true, but they lived easier. They did not recklessly plunge into debt; they lived more at home with their families, and were far happier. There was, too, much more sociability, neighborly feeling and good cheer generally among them. There was not such a rush after great wealth, and hence fewer failures among farmers. The accumulated wealth of farm products directed attention to the question of markets, which had hitherto been confined to a kind of neighborhood traffic among the farmers themselves. Until the opening of railroads, markets were mostly reached by hauling on wagons to St. Louis, Vincennes, Shawneetown and Cairo. Much of the surplus produce was hauled to Shawneetown and Cairo, and shipped from those places to New Orleans. But the opening of railroads changed all this, and the best markets of the country are now easily accessible.

The following statistics, compiled from the last report of the State Board of Agriculture, show something of the products of Jefferson County, and will, doubtless, be of interest to many of our readers:

No. of acres of corn cultivated	37,221
No. of bushels produced	577,016
No. of acres of wheat	63,456
No. of bushels produced	678,683
No. of acres of oats	8,852
No. of bushels produced	123,244
No. of acres of Timothy	8,601
No. of tons produced	7,852
No. of acres of clover	245
No. of tons produced	161
No. of acres of prairie	1,534
No. of tons produced	1,292
No. of acres of Hungarian and millet	114
No. of tons produced	123
No. of acres of sorghum	109
No. of gallons of sirup	8,677
No. of acres of pastures	18,075
No. of acres of woodland	92,825
No. of acres of uncultivated	12,341
No. of acres of city and town real estate	388
No. of acres not included elsewhere	10,278
Total number of acres reported for the county	258,574
No. of fat sheep sold	1,766
Gross weight of same—pounds	159,140
No. of sheep killed by dogs*	490
Value of same	$1,170
No. of pounds of wool shorn	32,736
No. of fat cattle sold	1,718
Gross weight of same—pounds	1,418,364
No. of cows kept	3,661
No. of pounds of butter sold	58,589
No. of pounds of cheese sold	200
No. of gallons cream sold	100
No. of gallons milk sold	870
No. of fat hogs sold	6,985
Gross weight of same—pounds	1,320,165

In 1860, an agricultural association was organized, which, with some changes, is still in existence. Its first officers were J R. Allen, President; Jeremiah Taylor, Vice President; J. S. Bogan, Recording Secretary; Dr. E. E. Welborn, Corresponding Secretary, and Joel Pace, Treasurer. Direc-

*From these statistics, it will be seen that one-fourth as many sheep were killed by dogs as were sold, and yet farmers still persist in keeping worthless dogs.

tors, F. S. Casey, William Woods, Jesse A. Dees, John Dodds, James J. Fitzgerell, John Wilbanks, Dr. W. Adams, Benjamin T. Wood, S. W. Carpenter, Joseph Baldridge, Charles McClure and S. K. Allen. Forty acres of land, the site of the present fair grounds, were bought on a credit from A. M. Grant. The sum agreed on was $800, with 10 per cent interest until paid. On motion of Judge Tanner, a Committee to solicit subscriptions for the association was selected, as follows:

Jordan's Prairie Precinct—Samuel Cummins, J. F. Caldwell and Hiram Williams.

Grand Prairie Precinct—J. C. Baldridge, Lemon Fouts and Henry Breeze.

Blissville Precinct—H. Creet, Thomas Bagby and Andrew Welch.

West Long Prairie Precinct—James Smith, J. Q. A. Bay and Isaac Hicks.

Knob Prairie Precinct—John Hagel, Sidney Place and Joseph Laur.

Horse Prairie Precinct—William Clampitt, J. B. Wood and Joseph Hartley.

Elk Prairie Precinct.—William Wells, Elisha Wilson and W. B. Anderson.

Gun Prairie Precinct—C. G. Vaughn, Henry W. Williams and Solomon Goddard.

Jackson Precinct—F. Hicks, John Ham and H. W. Goodrich.

Moore's Prairie Precinct—David Kiffin, David Rotramel and John Lowry, Sr.

Lynchburg Precinct—Curran Jones, S. V. Bruce and Jesse Laird.

Horse Creek Precinct—B. E. Wells, Robert French and E. H. Flowers.

Mount Vernon Precinct—Capt. H. B. Newby, John Bagwell and D. Baltzell.

The foregoing Committee was selected by a committee consisting of Dr. Green, Samuel Schenck and William Dodds, which had been appointed on the motion of Prof. B. C. Hillman. The following committee:

Dr. Green, W. B. Anderson, J. R. Allen and J. S. Bogan, was appointed and drafted a constitution and by laws.

The first fair was held on the 23d, 24th and 25th of October, 1860, and was well attended and proved successful. The old officers were re-elected, except Charles T. Pace was elected Treasurer in place of Joel Pace. In 1862, no fair was held, on account of the excitement of the civil war then in progress. The Directors elected this year were F. S. Casey, Jesse A. Dees, William Wood, J. J. Fitzgerrell, John Wilbanks, Joseph Baldridge, P. T. Maxey, John Arnold, C. G. Vaughn, S. Place, S. Cummins, T. G. Holland and A. Kiffin.

For 1863, the following officers were elected: J. R. Allen, President; S. V. Bruce, Vice President; Charles T. Pace, Treasurer; J. S. Bogan, Recording Secretary, and E. J. Winton, Corresponding Secretary. Directors—S. Cummins, Joseph Baldridge, E. B. Harvey, William Wood, J. A. Dees, Isaac Place, J. J. Fitzgerrell, John Wilbanks, C. G. Vaughn, J. H. Smith, John Arnold, J. C. Jones, R. S. Young and F. S. Casey.

For 1864—J. C. McConnell, President; John Wilbanks, Vice President, Charles T. Pace, Treasurer; T. H. Hobbs, Assistant Treasurer; Dr. Welborn, Corresponding Secretary; J. S. Bogan, Recording Secretary. Directors—F. S. Casey, John Arnold, W. Knowles, J. H. Smith, Curran Jones, S. Cummins, J. C. Baldridge, Sr., E. B. Harvey, William Wood, J. A. Dees, John Dodds, J. J. Fitzgerrell, James Bodine and Mark Hails.

For 1866*—G. H. Varnell, President; J. C. Jones, Vice President; A. F. Taylor, Treasurer; W. D. Watson, Assistant Treasurer; J. S. Bogan, Recording Secretary; J. W. Baugh and A. M. Green, Assistant

---
*No election of officers for 1865.

John W. Hails

Secretaries. Directors—F. S. Casey, William Wood, John Arnold, T. J. Williams, Q. A. Wilbanks, J. Foster, B. E. Wells, J. C. McConnell, Jacob Breeze, E. B. Harvey, J. A. Dees, J. Q. A. Bay, J. J. Fitzgerrell and John Wilbanks.

For 1867—G. H. Varnell, President; J. C. Jones, Vice President; A. F. Taylor, Treasurer; Dr. Welborn, Corresponding Secretary; J. S. Bogan, Recording Secretary; J. W. Baugh and T. J. Casey, Assistant Secretaries. Directors—F. S. Casey, M. Fitzgerrell, J. K. Jones, J. C. McConnell, E. B. Harvey, J. A. Dees, J. J Fitzgerrell, J. Arnold, C. H. Judd, B. E. Wells, Jacob Breeze, William Wood, John Dodds and Col. W. B. Anderson. The same officers were re-elected in 1868, with one or two changes in the directory. Mr. Varnell, during the year, resigned as President, and J. C. McConnell was elected, August 13, to fill the vacancy. The same officers served through 1869.

For 1870—Jesse A. Dees, President; J. M. Galbraith, Vice President; A. F. Taylor, Treasurer; J. S. Bogan, Recording Secretary; R. F. Pace and G. W. Johnson, Assistant Secretaries; C. H. Patten, Corresponding Secretary. Directors—F. S. Casey, J. M. Scott, John Gibson, G. L. Cummings, E. B. Harvey, H. Moore, J. R. Knowles, J. Arnold, J. Watters, B. E. Wells, Jacob Breeze, William Wood, A. J. Norris and John Wilbanks.

For 1871—S. W. Jones, President; S. H. Allen, Vice President; W. E. Collins, Treasurer; J. F. Baltzell, Assistant Treasurer; A. F. Taylor, Corresponding Secretary; J. S. Bogan, Recording Secretary; Capt. J. R. Moss, General Superintendent. Directors—J. C. McConnell, G. L. Cummins, J. W. Johnson, S. V. Bruce, S. K. Casey, B. W. Towner, E. B. Harvey, J. A. Dees, John Wilbanks, John Arnold, J. C. Jones, C. H. Judd, C. M. Brown, D. C. Jones, S. S. Mannen and Jacob Breeze. In 1872, there seems to have been no election.

For 1873—Capt. J. R. Moss, President; Edgar Jones, Vice President; A. F. Taylor, Treasurer; C. D. Ham, Corresponding Secretary; J. S. Bogan, Recording Secretary; J. C. McConnell, General Superintendent. Directors—John Hawkins, H. N. Maxey, G. S. Cummins, R. Howell, Dr. W. D. Green, T. C. Moss, T. B. Lacy, J. A. Dees, G. W. Evans, John Frizell, J. Foster, M. McPhersen, C. M. Brown, J. C. Gwinn, J. Willis and H. Breeze.

For 1876*—J. S. Bogan, President; T. B. Lacy, Vice President; J. W. Baugh, Recording Secretary; G. M. Haynes, Corresponding Secretary; A. F. Taylor, Treasurer and James A. White, General Superintendent. Directors—J. C. McConnell, J. C. Maxey, J. M. Gaston, A. Marlow, W. A. McConnell, J. C. Johnson, W. R. Champ, T. H. Mannen, W. Dodds, G. D. Jones, G. W. Clark, J. A. Glazebrook, G. W. Bodine, Dr. T. F. White and Jacob Breeze.

For 1878—S. Gibson, President; J. R. Moss, Vice President; A. F. Taylor, Treasurer and J. S. Bogan, Secretary. Directors —S. Moffitt, J. C. Gwinn, J. A. White, J. E. Goodrich, E. Jones, J. C. McConnell, J. S. Bogan, John Wilbanks, W. A. McConnell, J. A. Dees and A. F. Taylor.

For some time, efforts had been made to change the association into a joint-stock company. This was accomplished during the year 1879, when, on the 10th day of May, an agreement was "signed, sealed and delivered" to the Jefferson County Fair Association. The first officers under the new regime were as follows:

For 1879—Jesse A. Dees, President; John Wilbanks, Vice President; A. F. Taylor, Re-

---

* This year (1876) seems to have been the next election of officers.

cording Secretary; J. S. Bogan, Corresponding Secretary; G. W. Evans, Treasurer, and J. C. McConnell, General Superintendent.

For 1880—J. A. Dees, President; John Wilbank, Vice President; J. S. Bogan, Recording Secretary; A. F. Taylor, Corresponding Secretary; C. D. Ham, Treasurer, and J. C. McConnell, General Superintendent.

For 1881—J. G. Gee, President; Dr. H. F. White, Vice President; G. W. Evans, Treasurer; J. S. Bogan, Secretary, and J. A. Dees, Marshal.

For 1882—J. G. Gee, President; A. Gilbert, Vice President; J. S. Bogan, Secretary; G. W. Evans, Treasurer, and Dr. H. F. White, General Superintendent.

For 1883—John Wilbanks, President; A. Gilbert, Vice President; J. S. Bogan, Secretary; G. W. Evans, Treasurer, and S. H. Watson, General Superintendent. Directors —S. H. Watson, J. Wilbanks, A. Gilbert, C. D. Ham and E. A. Jones.

Horticulture.—Gardening, or horticulture in its restricted sense, cannot be regarded as a very prominent or important feature in the history of Crawford County. If, however, we take a broad view of the subject, and include orchards, small fruit culture and kindred branches, outside of agriculture, we should find something of more interest and value. The flourishing trade the writer has witnessed in apples alone in the city of Mount Vernon, since he commenced his work of writing this history, is the most convincing proof that horticulture and fruit-growing is a valuable industry, to which the county is well adapted. The following statistics, we think, will bear us out in the assertion:

Number of acres in apple orchards	3,801
Number of bushels produced	139,487
Number of acres in peach orchards	65
Number of bushels produced	2,116
Number of acres in pear orchards	2
Number of bushels produced	40
Number of acres in vineyard	6
Number of bushels produced	240
Number of acres in fruits not included in orchards	2
Value of same	$150
Number of pounds of grapes produced	11,979

There can be little doubt but that, if the farmers were to devote more of the attention that is given to wheat—a crop that has, of late years, proven to be very uncertain in this latitude—to fruit growing, the experiment would pay, and pay well. The climate of this portion of the State is better adapted to fruit culture than further north, though, as a fruit-growing section, it is, perhaps, not to be compared to some portions of our country.

The apple is the hardiest and most reliable of all the fruits for this region, and there are more acres in apple orchards than in all fruits combined in the county. The first fruit trees were brought here by the pioneers, and were sprouts taken from varieties around the old home, about to be forsaken for a new one hundreds of miles away. Lewis Johnson, Sr., brought the first fruit trees here that ever flourished in the county, except the wild fruits found here by the early settlers. Apples are now raised in the county in great quantities, also peaches somewhat, while small fruits are receiving more and more attention every year. Many citizens, too, are engaging, to a greater or less extent, in grape culture.

That the cultivation of fruit is a union of the useful and beautiful is a fact not to be denied. Trees covered in spring with soft foliage, blended with fragrant flowers of white and crimson and gold, that are succeeded by fruit, blushing with bloom and down, rich, melting and grateful through all the fervid heat of summer, is indeed a tempting prospect to every land holder. A people so richly endowed by nature as the people of

Southern Illinois should give more attention than they do to an art that supplies so many of the amenities of life, and around which cluster so many memories that appeal to the finer instincts of our nature. With a soil so well adapted to fruits as that of Jefferson County, horticulture should be held in that high esteem which becomes so important a factor in human welfare.

The Forests.—Our rapidly disappearing forests have awakened apprehensions in the minds of many close observers, and is calling out much discussion of the subject. A late writer has remarked: "The disappearance of our old forests threatens to fulfill the prediction of Frederick Gerstaecker, who prophesied that the progress of our reckless civilization would soon make the United States as barren as Western Asia. But before the end of this century, protective legislation would not come too late. Our mountain ranges at least, have still forests enough to preserve the agricultural regions from anything like an Asiatic drought." Forest culture has already attracted the attention of the Legislatures of many of the older States, and steps are even now being taken to not only protect the forests, but for planting forests in the less timbered regions of the country. Indeed, the only measure of relief thus far suggested, with any definite prospect of success, is the planting of new forests. Much has been said, and many plans proposed, for the preservation of those that remain, but the words seem meaningless in view of the fact that private property is beyond the control of the Government, and Congress declines even to grant means to prevent the destruction of that which still pertains to the public domain.

No one now living, it is true, can reasonably expect to see our forests entirely destroyed, yet that they are disappearing more rapidly than new forests, of spontaneous growth, attain maturity, it naturally follows that, unless some means are adopted to protect them, sooner or later Frederick Gerstaecker's prediction will be fulfilled. No doubt the time will come, and that soon, when the protection and improvement of our forests will receive the attention they unquestionably merit.

CHAPTER XII.*

WAR HISTORY—THE REVOLUTION AND THE WAR OF 1812—WHAT WE GAINED BY THEM—THE MEXICAN WAR—JEFFERSON COUNTY'S PART IN IT—HER OFFICERS AND SOLDIERS—THE LATE CIVIL WAR—SKETCHES OF THE REGIMENTS IN WHICH THE COUNTY WAS REPRESENTED—GEN. ANDERSON, COL. HICKS AND OTHER VETERANS—INCIDENTS, ETC., ETC.

"Rash fruitless war, from wanton glory waged,
Is only splendid murder."—*Thomson.*

AS a nation, we have had but few wars aside from our troubles with the Indians. While still colonies we took part in the old French and Indian war, which, for a time, settled the question as to the ownership of the vast Northwest Territory. The war of the Revolution transferred this magnificent domain to us, and the war of 1812 settled its ownership perhaps for ages to come. The result of these several wars was the securing to the puny Republic of the thirteen American Colo-

*By W. H. Perrin.

246   HISTORY OF JEFFERSON COUNTY.

nies, an empire greater than that over which the Roman eagles soared in gilded triumph. A grand result truly, and one that has made the American Republic, or contributed very largely to making it, the foremost nation on the globe.

It is not known that any of the early settlers of Jefferson County participated in the Revolutionary war, but it is altogether probable that they did. Many of the early settlers in Southern Illinois were Revolutionary soldiers, and hence, some of the pioneers of Jefferson County may have been; but if so, we have not learned their names. Quite a number of them, however, took part in the war of 1812. But as both of these wars occurred before there were any settlements made in the county, they are of no special interest to this work, except as a kind of introduction to the general war history of the county, and to show the advantages we as a people received from them.

The Mexican War.—The Black Hawk war—a war which personally effected the people here—has been noticed in a preceding chapter. Next in order comes the Mexican war. Early in 1846, war was declared against Mexico, and Illinois was required to furnish three regiments. Later she was allowed to furnish another regiment, making four altogether. Jefferson County contributed two companies, one under the first call and one under the second call for troops. The first was enrolled in June, 1846, as Company H, of the Third Regiment, Col. Ferris Foreman, of Vandalia, commanding. The roster of Company H is as follows: Stephen G. Hicks, Captain; Lewis F. Casey, First Lieutenant (resigned November 1, 1846, at Matamoras, Mexico); William A. Thomas, promoted from Second to First Lieutenant November 1, 1846; Thomas S. Livingston, Second Lieutenant. Sergeants—John Bagwell, Gazaway Elkins, Jacob Casey and Marcus D. Bruce. Corporals—Joseph F. Thomasson, John Q. A. Bay, William Summers and John McConnell. Privates—Thomas J. Atchison, Peter Bean, James R. Brown, Thomas H. Ballard, Eli Blalock, John Brady, Samuel Bullock, John Butler, James C. Bateman, Benjamin Buckout, Loring R. Beal, James F. Caldwell, James A. Donohoo, William H. Dorris, Jesse J. Fly, Abraham W. Fields, Nicholas Gray, J. J. Garrison, James M. Galbraith, James Hull, Thomas Harlow, John Hawkins, Jesse Hawkins, Marcus Hailes, William Hicks, Albert Hailes, Johnson Hatfield, George Knox, James Kelley, John B. Lynch, John T. Lisenby, James W. Lewty, James Murphy, John Nielburn, Alexander Moore, James McCarver, Pleasant McFarland, Andrew McGivin, Edward McAtee, James C. Overbay, Benjamin Patterson, John M. Poston, James Scott, H. H. Wilkerson, Quincy A. Wilbanks, James Westcott and David H. Warren. Discharged—Sergt. William B. Braden, and Privates Joseph T. Atchison, Samuel W. Avant, William Foster, Alexander M. Hill, E. B. Harvey, Benj. Ivey, William J. Crisel, L. C. Moss, William R. McClenden, S. R. Owens, John E. Newby, Robert B. Rankin, Charles W. Stearns, James E. Summers, William J. Stephenson, Daniel Smith, P. T. Thurman, James Teeters, Benjamin Veasy, J. A. Wallace, V. P. Williamson, Harrison Wilkey, John Yearwood, John Williams, all on surgeon's certificate of disability. Died—Corporals James Bruce, January 16, 1847, en route to Tampico, Mexico, and James Wimberly (killed) April 30, 1847, near Jalapa, Mexico. Privates Jonathan H. Breeze, died December 6, 1846, in general hospital at Matamoras; Moses Harlow, died October 26, 1846, in hospital at Matamoras; Joseph Harvey, May 13, 1847, fell overboard on the way to New Orleans; James C. Newby, died August 13, 1846, at Brazos Santiago, Texas.

The company left Mount Vernon on the 18th of June, and marched to Alton, the place of rendezvous, where the regiments, after they were organized and equipped, embarked for Mexico. They saw hard service during their term, and were at Vera Cruz, Cerro Gordo, and in other battles and skirmishes. At Matamoras, the company was divided, a part of it under Lieut. Casey going to Comargo in charge of a wagon train, the main part, under Capt. Hicks, remaining on guard duty at Matamoras. Lieut. Casey's squad, after remaining a month at Comargo, was ordered back to Matamoras to report to Gen. Taylor. Lieut. Casey, from failing health resigned here and returned home. In January, Gen. Taylor marched for Buena Vista, but Gen. Shield's command, to which the Mount Vernon troops belonged, was ordered to report to Gen. Scott at Vera Cruz. After the surrender of Vera Cruz, the next move was on Cerro Gordo. In the operations here, they were actively engaged, and acquitted themselves with honor and distinction. Their courage at Cerro Gordo elicited from Gen. Twiggs the well-merited compliment: "Well, I never saw such fellows as you Illinois men are in my life! Here the regulars are broke down and the horses are all given out, and you darned ragged rascals pitching around like squirrels, or something that never get tired and hungry."

After the capture of Jalapa, they remained in camp on the Puebla road until their term of service had expired, when they returned home and were discharged.

The second company was enrolled at Mount Vernon June 3, 1847, under the President's second call for troops. The rank and file were as follows: James Bowman, Captain; he died at Jalapa December 28, 1847, and L. H. Powell became Captain; Eli D. Anderson was First Lieutenant; he died at Vera Cruz September 11, 1847, of yellow fever, and Willis B. Holder was promoted to First Lieutenant; he died at Jalapa January 2, 1848, and James B. Hinde became First Lieutenant; H. B. Newby, Jr., Second Lieutenant; he died at National Bridge September 16, 1847, of yellow fever, and J. J. Anderson became Second Lieutenant. A. H. Cox and Jacob Keller were also promoted to Second Lieutenants. Sergeants— Jonathan Wells, Gilford D. Connolly, John P. Newell and Jonathan S. Cook. Corporals— Edward Bond, Robert R. Ingram, Elias M. Holmes and William Bullock. Privates—John Ames, R. C. Anderson, Calvin M. Brown, William Cassidy, James Cummins, Richard Childers, Martin Clark, Thomas D. Crey, Julian Elee, John B. Green, Caleb Godfrey, Newton A. Gastin, R. S. Hillhouse, Lewis Johnson Henderson Kimball, Peter Kaltenbach, A. J. Kinman, Damon C. Kennedy, Josiah McCormick, Preston McCulloch, William McCassilin, Thomas Mullen, Aaron Messecher, Martin McRorgh, James McDonald, Job A. Orton, James L. Osborne, Welcome Root, John Rose, Andrew Stephens, Alonzo Soule, Oliver Safford, Laurence Stull, Jacob Sanders, William A Thornton, Thomas J. Vance, Isaac Wilson John D. Watts, Thomas Weymon, Bennett M. Weldon, Sherman D. Wood and Henry Wentworth. Died—Sergeant James Mathewson, in hospital at Vera Cruz October 28, 1847; Sergeant Benjamin F. Bogan, in hospital at Jalapa, Mexico, January 11, 1848; Corporal William C. Cook, in hospital at Jalapa December 2, 1847; Corporal Jonathan Reilly, in General Hospital at New Orleans September 14, 1847. Privates, died—John Bodine, November 13, 1847, General Hospital at New Orleans; Matthew Ballard, November 22, 1847, General Hospital at Vera Cruz; Hiram Bruce, May 17, 1847, at Puebla; William Cummins, December 18, 1847, in Regimental Hospital, Jalapa; John Crooms, February 1, 1848, at Jalapa; Dillard B. Caster, January 15, 1848, at Jalapa; William Clark, December 14, 1847, at Jalapa; Isaac Dawson, January 2, 1848, at Jalapa; Joseph Dorrell, September 10, 1847, in General Hospital at Vera Cruz; George W. Dornell, August 17, 1847, at Jalapa; James F. Griffith, December 16, 1847, at Jalapa; Robert Goodrich, August 28, 1847, in General Hospital at New Orleans; John Gilbert, May 4, 1848, in General Hospital at Puebla; John A. Jenkins, September 17, 1847, in General Hospital at Vera Cruz; William Knox, April 21, 1848, at Puebla; John Keller, January 11, 1848, at Jalapa; John Mylett, December 16, 1847, at Jalapa; Hiram Leonard, December 2, 1847, at Jalapa; Thomas A. Long, November 24, 1847, at Vera Cruz; Henry Lawson, December 1, 1847, at New Orleans; Reuben Light, December 2, 1847, at Jalapa; Zedick Marlow, December 1, 1847, at Jalapa; William R. Maynor, June 30, 1847, at Carrolton, La., James McConnell, September 12, 1847, at Camp Bergara, Mexico; William N. Moss, August 16, 1847, at Alton, Ill.; John McLaughlin, April 2, 1848, at Puebla; Henry Piper, December 5, 1847, at Jalapa; William Pierce, October 12, 1847, at Vera Cruz; John Redmon, December 29, 1847, at Jalapa; William Reynolds, March 5, 1848, at Jalapa; William G. Stewart, January 23, 1848, at Jalapa; John H. Stull, December 20, 1847, at Camp Bergara; Wright Taylor, May 6, 1848, at New Orleans; William G. Worley, September 10, 1847, at Vera Cruz; Charles Weston, September 2, 1847, at Camp Bergara; Thomas A. White, February 1, 1848, at Jalapa, and Daniel Wallace, February 15, 1848, at Jalapa. Discharged—Sergeant Jeremiah Morgan, disability; Privates William Baker, William C. Brooks, Clinton Brown, Robert Ballard, Oliver Forward, George W. Green, S. A. Honey, Arthur Leach, Robert Osborne and John Vickey for disability. The company was A of the Second Regiment, commanded by James Collins, Colonel, Stephen G. Hicks, of Mount Vernon, Lieutenant Colonel, and Thomas S. Livingston, Major.

The company proceeded to Alton, and there on the 26th of June, 1847, was mustered into the United States service. Maj. Noah Johnston, of Mount Vernon, was Paymaster of the army during the last years of the war, and a more faithful officer in that important line of duty never wore the livery of Uncle Sam. The troops did not leave Alton until the 13th of August, and on the last day of the month they arrived at Vera Cruz. They were on active duty until after the close of the war, though they were engaged in no hard fighting. On the 2d of June, they were ordered home, and arrived at Alton July 7, where they were in due time paid off and discharged.

The Rebellion.—After the close of the Mexican war, for a little more than a decade, we remained in peace and tranquillity, save an occasional skirmish with the Indians. But war clouds were gathering, and our political atmosphere foreboded the coming storm. No outside foe or foreign enemy, however, now opposed us. Internal dissensions were shaking the country from center to circumference, and it bade fair to become a "house divided against itself." In 1860, the storm grew dark and angry, and at the election of Abraham Lincoln to the Presidency, and his inauguration in 1861, it burst in all its fury. It involved us in a civil war, the magnitude of which the world had never before seen. When the stars and stripes were hauled down from the battlements of Sumter, and the palmetto of the so-called Confederacy raised in its stead, it set the country in a blaze of excitement. Old soldiers who had fought in the Black Hawk and Mexican wars came to the front, and scarcely had the President made his first call for troops ere the quota was filled, and many left out who were clamoring to enlist. Jefferson County was no laggard in the path of duty, and her patriotism was equal to any of her sister counties. She was not into the fray quite as soon as many other counties, but when once in she stuck to it until the old flag waved in triumph again over every State and Territory.

The Fortieth Infantry is the first regiment in which we find the county represented, and only in this by a very few men and officers.

The regiment was made up principally in Marion, Wayne, Hamilton and Franklin Counties, with a few representatives, as we have said, from this county. It was commanded by that brave old warrior-hero of the Black Hawk and Mexican wars—Stephen G. Hicks. John W. Baugh was Adjutant, and Albion F. Taylor, Quartermaster, both honorable citizens of Mount Vernon, and perhaps others, of whom sketches will be found in the biographical department of this volume.

Stephen G. Hicks, a Sergeant in the Black Hawk war, a Captain, and afterward Lieutenant Colonel in the Mexican war, and Colonel of this (the Fortieth) regiment, was born for a soldier. He was the son of a soldier, possessed all the elements for a good soldier, and was one than whom none braver ever wore the uniform, nor followed the flag of the Union. He was born February 22 (the anniversary of Washington's birthday), 1809, in Jackson County, Ga., and was the son of John Hicks, one of the seven men killed in the battle of New Orleans, January 8, 1815. Hence, he was left an orphan at the age of six years, with few advantages for education or mental culture. But he was an energetic lad, had a vigorous body and an active mind, that could not be content in idleness. After his father's death, his mother married Jacob Weldon, by whom young Stephen considered he was cruelly treated, and long before arriving at manhood he left the parental roof, and hired to a man living near Springfield. He worked during the summer, and went to school in winter, thus picking up a moderate education, and finally he found his way to the lead mines at Galena. Returning a few years later, he worked at the carpenter's trade with his uncle, Carter Wilkey. When the Black Hawk war broke out in 1832 he was among the first to enlist, and was appointed First Sergeant of Capt. Bowman's Company, in which position he faithfully served during the war. He was married, in October, 1829, to Miss Eliza R. Maxey, a daughter of Burchett Maxey, who still survives him, and is a resident of Mount Vernon. Mr. Hicks represented Jefferson County in the Lower House of the State Legislature from 1842 to 1848, and as a legislator proved himself worthy and efficient, receiving the highest commendations of his constituents. He studied law, was admitted to the bar, and practiced law for a number of years.

At the breaking-out of the Mexican war, Col. Hicks recruited Company H, of the Third Regiment (Col. Foreman), and when his term of service had expired, he re-enlisted as a private, but was promoted Lieutenant Colonel of the Second Regiment as re-organized, before it left Alton, the place of rendezvous. His record throughout the Mexican war was that of an excellent and efficient officer, and a brave soldier. The following incident is illustrative of the man, and of his courage and bravery: A bad feeling was engendered during the first year of the war between Maj. Marshall and himself, and in their difference Col. Hicks proposed to go down on the river bank and fight it out. Maj. Marshall accepted the proposition, and, armed with pistols, they were about to test each other's courage, when the Lieutenant Colonel of their regiment found it out, and put a stop to it. He and Lieut. Bagwell had a little "spat" also during the first year in Mexico, in which Bagwell questioned Hicks' bravery. In the battle of Cerro Gordo, when bullets were flying as thick as hail, Hicks held his hand aloft, and cried out, "Lieut. Bagwell, show your hand, and we will see who is the bravest." Both men were brave even to rashness. Bagwell was at one time Sheriff of Jefferson County. He recruited a company during the late war, and joined the confederate army, and was killed in the battle of Shiloh, gallantly fighting at the head of his men. Hicks became Colonel, as we have seen, of the Fortieth Infantry, in the late rebellion, and served his Government faithfully to the close of the war. He was severely wounded in the battle of Shiloh, while leading his regiment in the thickest of the fight. Waving his sword in the direction of the enemy, and turning in his saddle to cheer his men, a ball struck him in the back or shoulder, and he fell from his horse. His men swept on to avenge his fall, and Col. Hicks crawled a half a mile to water, and washed the blood from the wound with his own hand. During his service in the late war, he had four horses shot under him. After he recovered from his wounds, Gen. Sherman, struck with the bravery of Col. Hicks, and in consideration of the wounds he had received, offered him the command of any post between Cairo and New Orleans. Col. Hicks had been stationed for awhile at Paducah in the early part of the war, and, liking the place, told Gen. Sherman he would accept the command of Paducah, which Sherman readily granted. Hicks also asked that Capt. Taylor, his Regimental Quartermaster, and who was his son-in-law, might be detached, and go with him as Post Adjutant. This Gen. Sherman also granted. Col. Hicks remained in command of Paducah from October, 1863, for about one and one-half years, and then went to Columbus, where he remained in command until after the close of the war. While in command at Paducah, the place was attacked by the confederate Gen. Forrest, who sent in a demand to Col. Hicks for its unconditional surrender, otherwise no quarter would be shown if it was captured by force. Hicks sent him word that his Government had placed him there to protect its property, and he would prove a traitor if he surrendered it, and wound up by telling Forrest he would have to come and take it. Gen. Thompson, of Mayfield, Ky., who commanded a brigade, had asked the favor of Forrest to let him take the fort where Hicks commanded in person, and was granted the request. He attacked it with great fury, but was struck by a cannon ball and literally torn in pieces, his bowels being scattered over the ground, and a portion of his spinal column being thrown several rods from where he fell. The battle was terrible while it lasted, the rebels losing 1,200 men in killed and wounded. The Union forces, who were protected by a fort, lost but seventeen killed and a number wounded.

Col. Hicks remained in the service until the establishment of peace. His defense of Paducah was one of the most brilliant achievements of the war, and won for him unqualified praise, but did not bring the promotion he merited. After his return from the war, he made his home in Salem, Marion County, where he had some time lived. He died there December 14, 1869, and his widow now lives in Mount Vernon, a highly respected elderly lady.

The Forty-fourth Infantry was a regiment in which Jefferson County was well represented. Company F contained some fifteen or twenty men from this county, together with its first and Second Lieutenants, William Hicks and George W. Allen. Hicks resigned April 5, 1862, and Allen was promoted from Second to First Lieutenant, and resigned January 1, 1865. The other commissioned officers of the company were from Ashley and Richview.

Company I was almost wholly from this county, and was enrolled with the following commissioned officers: Jasper Partridge, Captain; Russell Brown, First Lieutenant; and Jesse C. Bliss, Second Lieutenant. Capt. Partridge and First Lieut. Brown were mustered out at the end of three years, and Lieut. Charles M. Lyon was promoted to Captain of the veteran company, and T. J. Abbott became First Lieutenant. Second Lieut. Bliss was mustered out at the end of his term, and Andrew J. Young appointed Second Lieutenant under reorganization. The non-commissioned officers were Cyrus A. Barrett, John A. Wall and Morris H. Taylor, Sergeants; an... Learner B. Allen, Franklin S. Parker, Henry P. Daniel, Isaac

Price, Edwin R. Bliss, Andrew J. Watson, William H. Pavey and John C. Crawford, Corporals. Wall was discharged April 8, 1862, on account of wounds; Taylor re-enlisted as a veteran; Daniel was discharged April 8, 1862, from disability; Price was killed at Stone River, December 31, 1862; Watson was discharged from disability May 29, 1862, and Pavey died at home, February 1, 1862. The others were mustered out with the regiment.

The Forty-fourth Infantry was organized in August, 1861, at Camp Ellsworth, Chicago. It was mustered into the United States service on the 13th of September, and the next day proceeded under orders to St. Louis, Mo., and took up its quarters in Benton Barracks. It was supplied with arms from the St. Louis arsenal, and on the 22d embarked on a steamer for Jefferson City, which was threatened at that time by the rebel Gen. Price, jubilant over his recent victory at Lexington. It remained here until the 29th, when it was ordered to Sedalia, where it was assigned to Gen. Sigel's division. Here it was engaged in drilling, camp duty, scouting, foraging, etc., until the 13th of October, when the army took up its line of march toward Springfield, Mo., arriving at that place a little too late to participate in the bloody charge led by Maj. Zagonia (of Gen. Fremont's body guard) against the rebel cavalry stationed there. With much marching and countermarching, and in daily expectation of meeting the enemy, the fall and winter wore away, and on the 2d of February, 1862, Gen. Curtis having assumed command of the army, it marched from Rolla, where it had been for some time, back toward Springfield, where Gen. Price was concentrating his forces, with the intention of offering fight should he be attacked. But he "retired in good order," and the Union forces took possession of the town on the 13th without serious opposition. Then began an exciting chase, which many of Company I doubtless still remember, as the Forty-fourth was continually in advance until the army reached Camp Halleck, Benton County, Ark. The pursuit was abandoned on the 20th of February, and the troops were allowed a few days' rest after their arduous service. They had marched four consecutive days, during the most inclement weather (there being six inches of snow a part of the time on the ground) and skirmishing almost continually during the last week's march. The troops remained here until the 5th of March, when news was received that the combined forces of Van Dorn, Price and McCullough were advancing to attack them, when they moved toward Sugar Creek Valley, and in the afternoon of the sixth the rear guard was attacked by the enemy and repulsed. This was the opening of the terrible battle of Pea Ridge, which resulted so disastrously to the rebels. The Forty-fourth took a prominent part in it, and after the enemy had been routed was one of the regiments selected to follow up the retreat. For three days they pursued the fleeing rebels, capturing one stand of colors, and taking many hundred prisoners, and several pieces of artillery. They remained in this vicinity until the 5th of May, when they moved toward Forsythe, Mo., but was ordered back to Batesville, Ark. Here the army was re-organized, and the Forty-fourth became a part of the brigade commanded by Gen. Osterhaus. On the 8th, the army was put in motion, and started for Little Rock, but orders were received ordering it to Cape Girardeau, Mo., where, upon its arrival, it embarked for Pittsburg Landing, to re-enforce the troops then besieging Corinth, Miss. The troops arrived at Pittsburg Landing on the 26th, and the next day marched up within supporting distance of the main body of the army, arriving two days before the evacuation of Corinth. After the evacuation, the brigade to which the forty-fourth belonged was attached to Gen. Pope's army, and sent in pursuit of the retreating rebels, but owing to bad roads the pursuit was soon abandoned. The troops returned to Rienzi, Miss., and went into camp, where they remained until the 26th of August, when they were ordered to Covington, Ky., to protect that place and Cincinnati, Ohio, against threatened attacks of the enemy. They arrived there about the 1st of September, and were on duty there until the 17th, when they crossed to Cincinnati and proceeded to Louisville, then threatened by Gen. Bragg.

The command remained in Louisville until the 1st of October, and during the time, it was again re-organized, the Forty-fourth being assigned to the Thirty-fifth Brigade, Eleventh Division, Army of the Ohio. October 1, the command (including the Forty-fourth) started on the memorable campaign through Kentucky in pursuit of Gen. Bragg, and participated in the battle of Perryville on the 8th, being at the time in the division commanded by Gen. Phil Sheridan. They followed in pursuit of the enemy to Crab Orchard, and on the 20th of October marched toward Bowling Green, arriving there on the 1st of November. Here Gen. Rosecrans assumed command, and on the 4th the army took up the line of march toward Nashville, where it arrived on the 7th, relieving the garrison at that place and re-opening communication with Louisville. On the 26th of December, the army moved against the enemy at Murfreesboro. The Forty-fourth was now attached to the Second Brigade, Third Division, Twentieth Army Corps, Col. Schaffer commanding the brigade, Gen. Sheridan the division, and Gen. McCook the corps. The Forty-fourth took an active part in the bloody battle of Stone River, losing more than half its members, killed and wounded, Capt. Hosmer of Ashley, being among the killed. It remained with the army at Murfreesboro, until the 26th of June, 1863, when it again marched to the front and crossed swords with the enemy at Hoover's Gap, Shelbyville and Tullahoma. In the early part of July, it proceeded to Stephenson, Ala., where it remained until the 21st of August, when the movement began against Chattanooga. The Twentieth Corps moved down toward Rome, Ga., when the balance of the army was attacked near Chickamauga by Bragg and Longstreet. The Forty-fourth was ordered to return at once and join the main army, and after three days and nights of forced marches, it arrived on the field in time to take part in the desperate conflict of September 19th and 20th. Falling back to Chattanooga, it remained there until the latter part of November, when it again advanced, and on the 25th was one of the foremost regiments in the bloody charge on Mission Ridge, Gen. Sheridan bestowing unmeasured praise upon it for having placed one of the first flags on the enemy's works. Following the enemy next day, it captured many prisoners and several pieces of artillery. On the 27th, it was ordered back to Chattanooga, to prepare for a forced march to Knoxville, 150 miles distant, to relieve the forces then besieged by Gen. Longstreet, but arrived three days after the siege had been raised by Gen. Burnside. The Twentieth and Twenty-first Corps were consolidated at Chattanooga, and the Forty-fourth was assigned to the First Brigade, Second Division, Fourth Army Corps, Col. W. T. Sherman commanding the brigade, Gen. Sheridan the division, and Gen. Granger the corps. After considerable maneuvering, the troops went into camp at Blain's Cross Roads, where they were several times on the point of starvation, having, for days at a time, nothing but corn in the ear, and but a limited supply of that. Said a writer upon the subject : " Nothing could more fully prove the patriotism of the men than the fact that here, on the point of starvation, exposed to the most inclement weather (it being so cold that the ink would freeze to the pen as the men signed their names), over three-fourths of the regiment voluntarily consented to serve three years more, for that Government for which they had suffered so much during the past two and a half years."

The regiment remained at Blain's Cross Roads until the 12th of January, 1864, and then marched to Dandridge, Tenn. On the 16th and 17th an attack was made by the enemy in full force, and the Union forces fell back to Knoxville, and from there marched to Kingston, where they remained until the 30th, when the Forty-fourth was ordered to Chattanooga to receive veteran furlough. It arrived there on the 3d of February, and drew full rations for the first time in four months, and started home on the 18th, arriving at Chicago on the 1st of March. On the 4th the men were furloughed and started for their homes. From the time the regiment left its rendezvous in September, 1861, to the time of its re-enlistment, it had marched over five thousand miles.

The Forty-fourth reached Nashville April 14, 1864, on its way back to the field, and two days later marched toward Chattanooga, where it arrived on the 30th, moving from there to Cleveland, Tenn., where it was immediately ordered to the front with the main army, then moving toward Atlanta. It passed through nearly all the battles and skirmishes of the Atlanta campaign, among which were Buzzard Roost, Rocky Faced Ridge, Resaca, Adairsville, Dallas, New Hope Church, Kenesaw Mountain, Culp's Farm, Chattahoochie River, Peach Tree Creek, Jonesboro and Atlanta. From the 28th of September it was on active duty, engaged nearly every day in scouting, skirmishing or fighting until the 30th of November, when it took part in the battle of Franklin, Tenn. This was one of the most desperate battles, while it lasted, in which the regiment was engaged during the war. The honor of winning the battle and saving the army, in a general order, was given to the brigade of which the Forty-fourth was a part. The next day the army reached Nashville, and the Forty-fourth took part in the battle of Nashville, December 15 and 16, and followed the broken columns of the rebel army to the Tennessee River. The army went into camp at Huntsville, Ala., on the 5th of January, 1865, where the battered old Forty-fourth enjoyed a few weeks' rest. Its fighting was now about over. The confederacy fell soon after, and with the tableau at Appomattox, the curtain went down on the bloody drama. But the war-worn veterans of the Forty-fourth were not yet permitted to lay aside the trappings of war. On the 15th of June, it started, under orders, for New Orleans, arriving on the 22d, and after remaining there until the 16th of July, it was ordered into Texas. It remained on duty in Texas until September 25, 1865, when it was ordered home, arriving at Springfield on the 15th of October, and was paid off and discharged.

The Forty-ninth Infantry is the next body in which we find Jefferson County represented. Company K was from this county, and its commissioned officers were as follows: Benjamin F. Wood, Captain; Joseph Laur, First Lieutenant, and James G. Gilbert, Second Lieutenant. Capt. Wood resigned June 10, 1862; Lieut. Laur was promoted to Captain in his stead, and mustered out with the regiment September 9, 1865. Upon the promotion of Lieut. Laur, Second Lieut. James Lemmon became First Lieutenant. His term expired January 9, 1865, and Second Lieut. Jonathan Foster was promoted in his stead. Lieut. Gilbert resigned March 5, 1862, and James Lemmon was promoted to the vacancy, and afterward to First Lieutenant. Edward Barbee became Second Lieutenant upon the promotion of Lieut. Lemmon; he resigned July 5, 1865, and Jonathan Foster was promoted to fill the vacancy. Foster was promoted to First Lieutenant, when John S. Brooks became Second Lieutenant, and as such was mustered out with the regiment.

The Forty-ninth Infantry, Col. William R.

Morrison commanding, was organized at Camp Butler December 31, 1861, and mustered into the United States service. On the 3d of February, 1862, it was ordered to Cairo, Ill., and on the 8th it moved to Fort Henry, where it was assigned to the Third Brigade of McClernand's division. It moved to Fort Donelson on the 11th, and participated in that battle, losing fourteen men killed and thirty-seven wounded. Among the wounded was Col. Morrison, who commanded the brigade to which the Forty-ninth belonged. The regiment remained at Fort Donelson until the 4th of March, when the army was put in motion, and on the 6th the Forty-ninth, with other troops, embarked for Pittsburg Landing. It bore an active part in the battle of Shiloh April 6 and 7, and lost in the two engagements seventeen killed and ninety-nine wounded. Among the wounded in this engagement were Lieut. Col. Pease, commanding the regiment, and Maj. Bishop. It was engaged in the siege of Corinth, and on the 4th of June it moved to Bethel, where it was assigned to the division of Gen. John A. Logan, district of Jackson, Maj. Gen. McClernand commanding. On the th of March, 1863, the regiment moved from Bethel to Grand Junction, and from thence to Germantown, and on the 12th to White Station, where it was assigned to the Fourth Brigade, First Division, Sixteenth Army Corps, Col. Sanford commanding the brigade, Gen. Smith the division, and Gen. Hurlbut the corps. It was ordered to Helena, Ark., August 21 to join Gen. Steele's expedition against Little Rock. September 2, it joined the main army at Brownsville, Ark., and on the 10th participated in the capture of Little Rock. From here it proceeded to Duval's Bluff, and from thence it returned to Memphis, where it arrived on the 21st of November.

On the 15th of January, 1864, about three-fourths of the regiment re-enlisted, and were mustered as veterans, and were assigned to the Third Brigade, Col. Wolf commanding, Third Division, Gen. Smith, and the Sixteenth Army Corps. It remained on active duty, was with Gen. Sherman on the Meridian campaign, was assigned to the Red River expedition and served in Louisiana until June 24, when it was ordered home on veteran furlough. The non-veterans remained in the field, commanded by Capt. Logan, and participated in the battle of Tupelo July 14 and 15 while their comrades were at home enjoying themselves. At the expiration of their furlough, the veterans rendezvoused at Centralia, and proceeded to Cairo, and from thence to Memphis and Holly Springs, where they joined the command. August 12, they participated in the Oxford expedition, and on the 30th of September embarked for Jefferson Barracks, Mo., and proceeded to Franklin. They drove the enemy from that place, and with the main army went in pursuit of Gen. Price, after which the Forty-ninth returned to St. Louis on the 18th of November. From St. Louis they were ordered to Nashville, Tenn., where they arrived December 1, and took part in that bloody battle on the 15th and 16th. It was ordered to Paducah, Ky., on the 24th of December, where the non-veterans were mustered out of the service, their term of enlistment having expired. The veterans remained on garrison duty at Paducah until September 9, 1865, when they were ordered to Camp Butler, Ill., and on the 15th were paid off and discharged.

The Sixtieth Infantry contained more Jefferson County men, perhaps, than any other regiment of the war. Its second Colonel, William B. Anderson, is a native of the county, has always lived here, and is known to nearly every man, woman and child; the last Colonel of the regiment, George W. Evans, is now a prominent citizen of Mount Vernon; the last Quartermaster, James H. Rogers was also from the county; while Jefferson contributed to nearly every company, and very largely to C, D and

G, furnishing more than half the men in those companies.

William B. Anderson, who, upon the death of Col. Toler—the First Colonel of the Sixtieth—succeeded to the command of the regiment, was born in Mount Vernon April 2, 1830, and is a son of Gov. Stinson H. and Candace (Chickering) Anderson. He was educated in the common schools of Jefferson County, and at McKendree College, Lebanon, Ill., and at the age of twenty-one years began the study of the law under Judge Scates, then on the Supreme bench. Mr. Anderson was admitted to the bar in 1857, but owing to failing health resulting from a too close application to study, he gave up a profession in which he was eminently fitted to shine as an ornament, and betook himself to the more humble life of a farmer. Thus was lost to the legal profession a man who, had he remained at the bar, would no doubt have become one of the leading lawyers of Southern Illinois.

Mr. Anderson soon displayed an interest in the political affairs of the county, and in 1856 was elected Representative in the Lower House of the State Legislature, and re-elected in 1858. He took an active part in both sessions, which were rather stormy, as political controversy, consequent upon the recent organization of the Republican party, ran high. Such were the strength and solidity of his abilities that he won the most honorable position among the members of those bodies. He introduced a resolution in the session of 1856 to prohibit special legislation, and to make all legislation general, as special legislation had been carried to such excess as to become a nuisance, and greatly retard business. He fought it all the way to the end, but was overpowered at last. But he could not give it up, and in the Constitutional Convention, some fifteen years later, he again brought it up, and succeeded in having it engrafted in the new constitution. It was a sore stroke to Chicago, and still rankles in her people. The only way that Chicago can now secure special legislation is through a general act "applying to counties of 100,000 inhabitants and upward."

But it is as a soldier, perhaps, that Mr. Anderson is best fitted for a noble and brilliant career. It has been said "that the poet is born, not made," and to the soldier does the saying apply with equal truth, as proven by many of our citizen soldiers during the late civil war. Scores of officers could be enumerated who never saw West Point, and who retired from the army at the close of the rebellion, the equal in military talent and ability of any graduate of West Point that ever wore sword. It is the natural talent for a trade or profession that qualifies a man to adorn that trade or profession, and, while education may the better fit him for them, yet education alone will not make a mechanic, a lawyer, or a soldier.

In February, 1862, Mr. Anderson enlisted as a private soldier in Company B, of the Sixtieth Illinois Volunteer Infantry. But upon the organization of the regiment, which took place on the 17th, at Camp DuBois, Illinois, he was made its Lieutenant Colonel, Silas C. Toler, of Jonesboro, being Colonel. Col. Toler died March 2, 1863, and Lieut. Col. Anderson was promoted Colonel in his place. March 13, 1865, he was promoted to Brigadier General for brave and meritorious service, a promotion more than merited, though long deferred. Unfortunately for Gen. Anderson's military preferment, he was of the wrong political faith, and unlike some of his brother officers from Southern Illinois, he refused to change his politics for the sake of official advancement. He adhered to the principle that "the leopard cannot change his spots, nor the Ethiopian his skin" (consistently, at least), and saw frequent examples of men selling their political opinions for military rank. Loyal to the core, and brave as a Roman warrior, he was doomed to the humiliation of witnessing promotion upon promotion over his head wholly for political reasons. And, when, in view of his long and faithful service, promotion could no longer be withheld, it came somewhat grudgingly, or indifferently rather, much as we might throw a bone to a dog. The war then, was, in a measure, over, and the hard fighting about through with, and Gen. Anderson, soon after his promotion as Brigadier General, resigned, and returned to his home in Jefferson County.

Gen. Anderson was a brave and efficient soldier, and seemed born for military service. That he did not receive his just deserts, is a shame and a reproach upon the Government he faithfully served through four long and terrible years. As a Major General, he would have won a name and a fame equaled by few and surpassed by none of Illinois' citizen soldiers. But his political principles, to which was no doubt added a jealousy of his growing reputation, conceived by other officers, whose ambition led them to covet his hard-earned laurels, kept him in the background, while those less worthy and less qualified rose to prominence. The language of the late George D. Prentice seems eminently appropriate here:

"The flame
Had fallen, and its high and fitful gleams
Perchance had faded, but the living fires
Still glowed beneath the ashes."

After his return from the army, Gen. Anderson again entered upon farm life, but in 1869 he was elected to the Constitutional Convention, and in 1871, upon the death of Hon. S. K. Casey, he was elected to fill out his unexpired term in the State Senate. In 1874, he was elected upon the Independent Greenback ticket to the National Congress, and in 1876 came within two votes of being elected to the United States Senate, instead of Hon. David Davis, and but for a little private jealousy perhaps would have been chosen to that honorable position. In 1882, he was elected County Judge, which position he now occupies.

Col. George W. Evans, who was mustered out as the commanding officer of the Sixtieth Infantry, was a citizen of Johnson County, Ill., at the breaking-out of the war. He there recruited Company E, of the Sixtieth, of which he was made Captain. He was promoted Major of the regiment March 2, 1863, and on the 21st of May following, was promoted Lieutenant Colonel, in place of Col. Hess, who had resigned. Upon the resignation of Gen. Anderson, Col. Evans succeeded to the command of the regiment, and was promoted to Colonel May 11, 1865, but never mustered as such. He was mustered out with the regiment, July 31, 1865, as Lieutenant Colonel.

Col. Evans was a brave, gallant and faithful soldier. During his whole term of service, he never missed a march or a battle in which his regiment participated. He was in all the principal battles from Nashville to the sea, and was at the surrender of Gen. Joe Johnston, and with his gallant old regiment went to Washington via Richmond, participated in the grand review at Washington, and was finally mustered out with it at Louisville, Ky. He then returned to Illinois, and has since been a citizen of Jefferson County.

Company C, of the Sixtieth, in which Jefferson County was largely represented, was enrolled with the following commissioned officers: John R. Moss, Captain; Thomas J. Rhodes, First Lieutenant, and Mark Hailes, Second Lieutenant. Capt. Moss resigned December 19, 1862, and Simeon Walker was promoted to the vacancy. His term expired March 14, 1865, and John R. Allen was promoted Captain, but declined the commission, and resigned as First Lieutenant, April 5, 1865, when Francis L. Ferguson was promoted Captain, and as such was mustered out with the regiment, July 31, 1865. First Lieut. Rhodes was promoted to Captain of Company A, and Mark Hailes became First Lieutenant. December 20, 1862, John R. Allen succeeded him as First Lieutenant, and upon his resignation Francis L. Ferguson becames First and was promoted Captain, when James H. Guthrie was promoted First Lieutenant, and was mustered out with the regiment. Second Lieut. Mark Hailes was promoted, and Simeon Walker became Second; he also was promoted and was succeeded as Second by John Tweedy, who resigned January 25, 1864, and Edward A. Patterson was promoted to Second Lieutenant, but mustered out with the regiment as Sergeant.

Company D, which contained some forty odd men from this county, went into the service with the following commissioned officers: Alfred Davis, of McLeansboro, Captain; Edmund D. Choisser, of Mooresville, First Lieutenant, and James Stull, Second Lieutenant. Capt. Davis resigned, and was succeeded by Capt. L. S. Wilbanks, who also resigned, and was succeeded by John B. Coleman. Capt. Coleman was killed July 26, 1864, during the Atlanta campaign. Green S. Stuart then became Captain, resigned, and William H. Thorp was promoted Captain and mustered out with the regiment. First Lieut. Choisser resigned, and was succeeded by Lieut. Coleman, who, upon promotion, was succeeded by Anozi Kuiffen. Lieut Kniffen was killed May 12, 1864, and Green W. Stewart became First Lieutenant, who was promoted, and succeeded as First by William H. Thorpe; he was also promoted and Eli Webb became First Lieutenant. Second Lieut. Stull resigned and Anozi Kniffen was promoted in his stead, and upon his own promotion was succeeded by Alfred Kniffin, who resigned January 9, 1864, and was succeeded by M. W. Smith, who was mustered out with the regiment.

Company G also contained a number of Jefferson County men, and the following commissioned officers from the county: Jehu J. Maxey, the First Lieutenant and the second Captain of the company; Cornelius N. Breeze, the second First Lieutenant, and E. H. Redburn the third Second Lieutenant of the company; while Company I also contained men from the county, and the following commissioned officers: John Frizell, the first Captain, Asa Hawkins, the second Second and the second First Lieutenant, and John W. Moses, the third and John A. Johnson the fourth Second Lieutenants of the company.

The Sixtieth Infantry was organized at Camp Du Bois February 17, 1862, and mustered into the United States service. On the 22d, it was ordered to Cairo, and March 14 it moved to Island No. 10. After the surrender of that place, it returned to Columbus, Ky., and afterward to Cairo. It was ordered to the Tennessee River on the 7th of May, and on the 12th arrived at Hamburg Landing, where it was assigned to the Second Brigade, First Division, Army of the Mississippi, Col. Charles M. Lynn of Michigan commanding the brigade. The Sixtieth was engaged in the siege of Corinth, and was a part of the force that pursued the enemy beyond Booneville, Miss. July 21, it was ordered to Tuscumbia, Ala., thence to Nashville, where it arrived September 12, and where it remained during the siege. On the 7th of November it was engaged in repelling an attack on Edgefield, made by Gen. Morgan. December 12, it was transferred to the Second Brigade, Third Division, Fourth

Army Corps, and on the 5th of January, 1863, it had a skirmish with Wheeler's cavalry, between Nashville and Murfreesboro, in which the latter were repulsed. After the battle of Murfreesboro, the Sixtieth returned to Nashville, and on the 2d of March Col. Toler died, and Lieut. Col. Anderson succeeded to the command. July 20, the regiment moved to Murfreesboro, and August 26 it proceeded via Columbia, Athens, Huntsville and Stevenson, to Dallas, Tex., where it arrived the 12th of November. Here the Sixtieth was assigned to the First Brigade, Second Division and Fourteenth Army Corps, and participated in the battle of Chattanooga and took part in the memorable march to Knoxville. Ragged and footsore, the tattered regiment returned to Chattanooga, arriving December 24, and going into winter quarters at Rossville. February 22, 1864, about three-fourths of the regiment re-enlisted, and on the 26th took part in the reconnoissance toward Dalton, Ga., which resulted in the battle of Buzzard Roost. In this battle the Sixtieth suffered severely, forty-two being killed and wounded. On the 6th of March, the regiment, or the veterans of it, was sent home to Illinois on furlough. When its veteran furlough had expired, the regiment returned to the field via Louisville, Nashville and Chattanooga to Rossville. The Atlanta campaign commenced on the 2d of May, and the Sixtieth bore an honorable part in those stirring times. It participated in the battles of Ringgold, Dalton, Resaca, Rome, Dallas, New Hope Church, Kenesaw Mountain, Nickajack, Peach Tree Creek, Atlanta and Jonesboro. For its brave and gallant conduct at Jonesboro, September 1, the regiment received the highest praise, of both the division and corps commanders. It remained in camp at Atlanta until September 29, when it moved to Florence, and October 10 it proceeded to Chattanooga. On the 18th it marched from La Fayette, Ga., to Gatesville, and from thence to Atlanta. It took part in the famous march to the sea, and was in many of the battles and skirmishes of that hard campaign, that at Bentonville, March 19, 1865, being as severe as any in which the regiment was engaged during its long service. At one time, it was surrounded on all sides, but behaved gallantly, and finally extricated itself and escaped capture. April 10, it moved to Raleigh, N. C., and remained there until after the surrender of Gen. Joe Johnston, when it proceeded to Richmond, the quondam confederate capitol, and from thence to Washington, where, on the 14th of May, it participated in the grand review.

The war was now ended, and the boys were eager to exchange the sword for the plow. On the 12th of June the regiment was ordered to Louisville, Ky., where it performed provost guard duty until July 21, when it was mustered out of the United States service. It then proceded to Camp Butler, Ill., where it received final payment and discharge.

The Eightieth Infantry is the next regiment in which the county was represented. Company E was a Jefferson County company, while Company H contained some Jefferson County men. Company E was enrolled with the following commissioned officers: Stephen T. Stratton, Captain; Newton C. Pace, First Lieutenant; and Charles W. Pavey, Second Lieutenant. Capt. Stratton resigned December 22, 1862, and was succeeded by Lieutenant Pace, who was honorably discharged May 15, 1865. Lieutenant Pavey was promoted to Captain, but was absent on detached duty at the muster out of the regiment. He is now Collector of Internal Revenue for this district. William Randall was

promoted to First Lieutenant January 1, 1863, but was not mustered as such; William C. Maxey was promoted to Second Lieutenant May 15, 1865, but was mustered out as Sergeant June 10, 1865, with his regiment. Of Company H, John R. Cunningham, of Rome, was made Second Lieutenant August 25, 1862, First Lieutenant March 8, 1864, and Captain May 15, 1865, and mustered out with the regiment; and Robert H. Milburn was promoted to Second Lieutenant May 15, 1865, and mustered out with the regiment June 10, 1865, as Sergeant. Rev. John W. Lane, of Mount Vernon, was Chaplain of the regiment.

The Eightieth was organized at Centralia, and mustered into the United States service August 25, 1862; and, on the 4th of September, was ordered to Louisville, Ky. Here it was assigned to the Thirty-third Brigade, Tenth Division, Army of the Ohio, Gen. Terrell commanding the brigade, Gen. Jackson commanding the division, and Gen. McCook commanding the corps. It formed a part of Gen. Buell's army in pursuit of Bragg from Louisville, and took part in the battle of Perryville, October 8, losing heavily, having fourteen men killed and fifty-eight wounded. Lieut. VanKendal, of Company D, was killed; Lieut. Andrews, of Company H, mortally wounded, and died on the 26th of November; Lieut. Col. Rogers, and Lieut. Pace, of Company E, severely wounded; while Gen. Terrell, the brigade commander, and Gen. Jackson, the division commander, were both killed. After the battle of Perryville, it maneuvered in Kentucky until the close of the year, at one time pursuing the rebel Gen. John H. Morgan for several days. On the 2d of January, 1863, it started for Nashville, Tenn., where it arrived on the 8th, and two days later moved to Murfreesboro, where it was assigned to the Fourteenth Army Corps, and Gen. Reynolds' division. On the 20th of March, the brigade to which the Eightieth belonged had a skirmish with Gen. Morgan, in which the latter was repulsed. It moved to Nashville April 7, and was brigaded with the Fifty-first and Seventy-third Indiana, Third Ohio, and two companies of Tennessee Cavalry, with two mountain howitzers, and embarked for Eastport, Miss., arriving there on the 19th. It next moved to Tuscumbia, Ala., where the regiment was mounted, and on the 26th, while on a scout, were attacked at Dug's Gap, and again, on the 29th, at Sand Mountain. The Eightieth in these two engagements lost two men killed and sixteen wounded Capt. Jones, of Company F, being killed, Adjt. J. C. Jones mortally wounded, and Lieut. Pavey, of Company E, severely wounded.

On the 3d of May, the regiment was captured by a largely superior force under Gen. Forest. They were taken to Rome, and the officers sent to Libby Prison, and the men paroled. On the 23d of June, the enlisted men were declared exchanged, and proceeded to St. Louis, and from thence to Nashville, Lieut. Steinecke, of Company C, taking command of the regiment. September 8, it moved to Stevenson, Ala., where Capt. Cunningham, of Company H, took command; on the 23d, it marched to Bridgeport, and reported to Gen. Howard, commanding the Eleventh Army Corps, and was assigned to the Third Brigade, Col. Hecker, Third Division, Gen. Carl Schurz. On the 16th of October, it moved to Battle Creek; on the 27th, up Lookout Valley, and participated in the battle of Wauhatchie; and on the 24th and 25th took part in the battle of Mission Ridge. It started to Knoxville on the 29th, but Longstreet having retreated it returned, reaching Lookout Valley on the 17th of December, suffering severely from want of clothing and shoes. January 27, 1864, it broke camp and moved to Blue Springs, via Chattanooga, Cleveland and Charleston. It was engaged in the Atlanta campaign, and participated in the battles of Dalton, Resaca, Adairsville, Cassville, Dallas, Pine Mountain, Kenesaw Mountain, Marietta, Peach Tree Creek, Atlanta, Jonesboro and Lovejoy Station. During this stirring campaign, the Sixtieth lost twenty-five killed, and sixty wounded. It pursued Hood in his long retreat, and December 15 and 16 took part in the battle of Nashville, where it behaved with great gallantry. On the 5th of January, 1865, it arrived at Huntsville, Ala., where Maj. Bates, who had returned from captivity, assumed command of the regiment. The remainder of its service was in marching and skirmishing, and June 10, 1865, its term of service having expired, it was mustered out of service, and sent home to Camp Butler for final discharge. During its term of service, the Sixtieth traveled over 6,000 miles, and took part in more than twenty battles. Only four of the captured officers ever returned to the regiment.

The One Hundred and Tenth Infantry also contained a company from Jefferson County, together with its first Colonel, Thomas S. Casey; its Quartermaster, Thomas H. Hobbs; and its First Assistant Surgeon, Hiram S. Plummer. Sketches of Col. Casey and Dr. Plummer will be found in other chapters of this work. Company B, the company from this county, had for its commissioned officers the following: Charles H. Maxey, Captain; Samuel T. Maxey, First Lieutenant; and John H. Dukes, Second Lieutenant. Capt. Maxey resigned March 22, 1863, and was succeeded by Lieut. Maxey, who was mustered out under the consolidation of the regiment. Lieut. Dukes was promoted to First Lieutenant, and transferred to Company A, under the consolidation, and promoted to Captain, and as such mustered out with the regiment at the close of its term of service. Thomas J. Maxey was promoted to Second Lieutenant March 22, 1863, and transferred to Company A, under the consolidation.

On the 8th of May, the One Hundred and Tenth was consolidated, by reducing the regiment to a battalion of four companies, under the following special field order: "Maj. Gen. Palmer, commanding Second Division, Twenty-first Army Corps, will cause the consolidation of the One Hundred and Tenth Regiment Illinois Volunteers, under the instructions contained in General Order No. 86, War Department, current series. The officers to be retained in the service to be selected by him. The Assistant Commissary of Musters, Second Division, Twenty-first Army Corps, will muster out of service all officers rendered supernumerary by the consolidation. By command of Maj. Gen. Rosecrans." Under the consolidation, Col. Casey, Quartermaster Hobbs and Surgeon Plummer were mustered out of service, and the battalion given in command of Lieut. Col. Crawford, who afterward resigned. E. B. Topping, of Springfield, was promoted Lieutenant Colonel, and remained in command of the battalion until the close of its term of service.

So far as we have been able to obtain information, this completes the sketch of those regiments in which the county was represented by commissioned officers or an organized body of men. Many men, however, from Jefferson County served in the late war, besides those belonging to the regiments we have described. In nearly every regiment recruited in Southern Illinois, Jefferson County was represented with more or less of enlisted men, while they were even found scattered through more than one Indiana. Missouri and Kentucky regiment. A close perusal of the history of the Black Hawk and Mexican wars, and the rebellion, will tell the story of Jefferson County, and of Illinois soldiers generally. A hundred battle-fields attest their bravery in the late civil war, and their depleted ranks, as the broken regiments struggled homeward, disclosed the sad evidence that they had met foes as brave as themselves. Many who went out came not back, but sleep in peace—now that their battles are ended—in the unknown graves where they fell. *Requiescat in pace!*

A few words of tribute, in conclusion of this chapter, are due to the noble women whose zeal and patriotism were as pure and as strong as those who bore the brunt of the battle. They could not shoulder their guns and march in the ranks, but they were no idle spectators of the struggle. How often was the soldier's heart encouraged; how often his right arm made stronger to strike for his country by the cheering words of patriotic, hopeful women! And how often the poor lad upon whom disease had fastened, was made to thank devoted women for their ceaseless and untiring exertions in collecting and sending stores for the comfort of the sick and wounded. A war correspondent paid them the following merited tribute: "While soldiers of every grade and color are receiving the eulogies and encomiums of a grateful people, patient, forbearing WOMAN is forgotten. The scar-worn veteran is welcomed with honor to home. The recruit, the colored soldier, and even the hundred days' men receive the plaudits of the nation. But not one word is said of that patriotic widowed mother, who sent, with a mother's blessing on his head, her only son, the staff and support of her declining years, to battle for his country. The press says not one word of the patriotism, of the sacrifices of the wife, sister or daughter, who, with streaming eyes and almost broken heart, said to husbands, brothers, fathers, 'Much as we love you, we cannot bid you stay with us when our country needs you,' and with Spartan heroism they bade them go and wipe out the insult offered to the star-spangled banner, and to preserve unsullied this union of States."

Brave, noble, generous women! your deeds deserve to be written in letters of shining gold. Your gentle ministrations to the unfortunate, and your loving kindness to the poor, war-worn soldiers will never be forgotten while one soldier lives; and your noble self-sacrificing devotion to your country will live, bright and imperishable as Austerlitz's sun.

CHAPTER XIII.*

ODDS AND ENDS—DE OMNIBUS REBUS ET QUIBUSDAM ALIIS—A BRIEF RETROSPECTION—MILLERS AND MILLS—BLACKSMITHS AND OTHER MECHANICS—BIRTHS, MARRIAGES, DEATHS—A BATCH OF INCIDENTS—BUCK CASEY PLAYING BULL CALF—DONNYBROOK FIGHTS—FOREST FIRES—A RUNAWAY NEGRO—COUNTERFEITING—THE POOR FARM, ETC., ETC., ETC.

"It is not now as it hath been of yore."
—*Wordsworth.*

WE have followed the history of Jefferson County from the period of its occupation by the aboriginal tribes down to the present, and may now take time to look back and to stop and breathe. When the county was formed—nearly sixty-five years ago—it was a wild waste, with only here and there meager settlements of hardy pioneers, but few of whom are now living to tell over the strange story of their early lives in the wilderness. They have passed away in their day and generation, and the very few who have come down to us from a former era have forgotten and forgiven the early hardships that encompassed them, and remember only the wild freedom and joys of their eager childhood. We look back over the departed years and see a wilderness, uninhabited by white people, its solitudes unbroken by a sound of civilization. We look around us to-day and what do we see? The red man is gone, and has left nothing behind him but fading traditions. The verdant wastes of Jefferson County have disappeared, and where erst was heard the dismal howling of the wolf, or the far-off screech of the hungry panther, are now productive fields, covered with flocks and herds and with growing grain. Rapid as have been the changes in this section, Jefferson is only well upon her course. The energies which have made the present will not falter, for

"Lo! our land is like an eagle, whose young gaze
Feeds on the noontide beam, whose golden plumes
Float moveless on the storm, and, in the blaze
Of sunrise, gleams when earth is wrapped in gloom."

In our sketch of the county, we have touched upon most of the principal facts connected with it of a historical character. By way of conclusion of the general history, we design, in this chapter (composed of the odds and ends) to gather up the scattered threads and weave them into a kind of valedictory to the first part of the volume. A few items and incidents have been overlooked and omitted in the preceding pages, and these we shall group together in this chapter.

The rifle and the fish hook antedated the grater and the stump mills among the very earliest settlers in supplying food. The first famines that occurred among the people were caused by the lack of salt, notwithstanding the close proximity of the Saline, as they could make bread of meat by using their lean meat for bread and the fat for meat when driven to it. Mr. Johnson says that bear meat was used for bread and the venison for meat. The question of bread

*By W. H. Perrin.

after the first coming of a family until they could clear a little truck patch to raise their family supply was often a serious one indeed. Then, too, even after the first corn was raised, there were no mills accessible to grind it. Corn was the staple production. Wheat was not raised for several years. Nearly all the bread used until the fall of 1818 was brought from the Wabash or from Kentucky. The first mode of procuring meal by the settlers of Jefferson County were by the mortar and pestle, the mortar being a hollow stump, and the pestle a billet of wood swung to a sweep or made with a handle and used by hand. It was a dozen or more years before these were laid aside. Of this mortar-made meal, the finest was made into bread, and the coarser into hominy. Families were sometimes without even this kind of bread for weeks at a time.

One of the first mills known to Jefferson County was kept by old Billy Goings, as early as 1817, but it is said that as he also kept a tavern, a grocery (what we would call a saloon now), and a great many other things, including bad company, his mill was only resorted to by the better class of people in cases of extreme emergency. In the fall of 1818, Dempsey Hood put up a mill, of his own manufacture, except the buhrs, which he had bought from Goings. It was of the simplest mechanical construction, and was operated by horse power. Many good stories are told of these early mills. One man used to say he always took his corn to mill in the ear, as he could shell it faster than the mill could grind it, and then he had the cobs to throw at the rats to keep them from eating all the corn as it ran down from the hopper. Another story was told on Hood's mill, that if a grain of corn got in "endways" it stopped the mill until the obstruction was removed. Still another story is told on the first water mill erected. The miller put the grist in the hopper, turned on the water, and about the time the mill got under good headway he heard a turkey "gobble" in the woods near by, so he caught up his gun and started out after the turkey. While he was gone, a blue jay alighted on the hoop around the buhrs, and as fast as a grain of corn would shake down from the hopper, he would eat it. When the miller returned, the jay had eaten all the corn and the mill stones were worn out.

William Maxey built a mill near where Cameron Maxey now lives, in the fall of 1820, and for a number of years contributed largely to the supply of bread for the settlers. About the same time or soon after, Carter Wilkey put up a "stump" mill, and in the fall of 1823 Thomas Tunstall put up a tread-mill, the first of the kind in the county. A short time after, Arba Andrews built a wind mill. By the year 1825, the country was pretty well supplied with mills, such as they were. They were much superior, however, to no mill at all, and whether hand, stump, wind, tread or horse mill, they all had one family resemblance, and that was in speed. A blue jay might have eaten the corn from any of them faster than they could grind it. This is all changed now, though, and the county is supplied with mills that are without superiors in quality. But it is hard to realize that only fifty or sixty years ago, there were no mills, but such as we have described, in the county. What a gradual but wonderful development is there in the slow growth of the splendid perfected roller patent process mills from the pioneer hand-mill and mortar!

Elisha Plummer is the first blacksmith we have any account of, and came to Mount Vernon in 1820. If his "smithy" was not under a spreading "chestnut tree," it was probably because there was no chestnut tree, for houses of all kinds were scarce. John Cooper, another blacksmith, came in 1824. A man named Lane was the first gunsmith, and this was a very important business then. He was in the county as early as 1822-23. Buffington was also an early gunsmith; Rhoda Allen's sons were the first cabinet-makers, etc., etc. Thus the trades became represented in the county as business and population demanded.

The first birth, marriage and death are always matters of considerable interest in a new country, and usually are preserved on record. The first birth we have failed to learn definitely, but it is believed to have been a son of Isaac Hicks, born in 1817. But that there has been a first one, followed by many others, the present population of the county is indisputable evidence. The first marriage was a daughter of Joseph Jordan, to Garrison Greenwood, a son of Fleming Greenwood, but the date is not remembered. Apropos of weddings, the following is related of Green Depriest, who is represented as a kind of devil-may-care fellow, as fond of fun and a good time as a monkey of a basket of apples. He started out one day for Walnut Prairie to have a little spree. On his way, he stopped at the Widow Allen's to inquire the way. While talking with Mrs. Allen, a young woman, her daughter, came out of the house to speak with her. Depriest was impressed favorably with the young woman's appearance, and, according to his abrupt way of doing things, told her who he was and that he would like to marry her if she had no objections. She replied that "Barkis was willin'." So he said he would go to the field and see the boys about it, while she could talk it over with her mother. The result was he married her, took her up behind him on his horse and went home, to the great surprise of his friends and family. Thus he had his spree after all, but altogether a different one from that he had started out to enjoy.

The next wedding was three—a kind of wholesale or job lot. On the 5th of October, 1819, Harriet Maxey was married to Thomas M. Casey, Vylinda Maxey to Abraham T. Casey, and Bennett N. Maxey to Sally Overbay, all at the same time and place. This was overdoing the poet, for instead of "two souls with but a single thought," it was six, four more than the poet bargained for. It was the largest wedding of the period in the style put on and the numbers present, as well as in the profusion of brides and grooms. Every family was invited, and every man, woman and child, who possibly could, attended, and the good cheer was the best the country afforded. Ransom Moss and Ann Johnson were married July 6, 1821, and thus the good work went on.

The death of Rhoda Allen, who was a man, notwithstanding the peculiar name, was the first death of a grown person. He passed to his reward in August, 1820, and was buried at Union—the first person buried there. A child of one of the Maxeys died a short time before Allen, and is supposed to have been the first death in the county. Death has not been idle since then, as the many graveyards in the different portions of the county show.

An incident occurred in 1826 that cast a gloom over the whole settlement and excited the sympathy for the afflicted family. Joseph McMeens had recently settled in Jordan's Prairie and had a family of several children. In the fall and winter of 1826, his boys devoted considerable attention to trapping. One day they left the house to visit their traps as usual, when a little sister, only four years old, started unknown to them, to follow. Her parents supposed she was with her brothers until their return and reported that they had seen nothing of her. An alarm was at once spread and search made and kept up until in the night without any success. It was renewed the next day and continued for many days, but the child was never found. The strangest part of it was not the slightest trace of her, not a shred of her clothing or a footprint was ever discovered to tell the story of her fate, or suggest a theory as to her strange disappearance, and to-day, after a lapse of nearly sixty years, when the circumstance is forgotten by all except a few old people, the mystery is as deep and impenetrable as when it first occurred. The most plausible theory was that she had been picked up and carried away by some prowling band of Indians, though no trace of Indians were discovered in the vicinity. It was one of those mysteries that will probably never be cleared up until that great day of final settlement.

A fight with a wild cat is related by James Dawson, in which he triumphed over his feline antagonist in a summary manner. Dawson was a son-in-law of Fleming Greenwood, and a man who is represented as not being afraid of the devil himself. Such a thing as raising domestic fowls was impossible in the early times, without a stanch house to keep them in at night. Even then the "varmints" were as sure to find them sooner or later as the colored American citizen is to find the hen roost of the present day. One night Dawson heard a racket in his chicken house, that denoted the presence of some unwelcome intruder, and he ran out with a light to investigate the trouble. Upon looking into the chicken house, he discovered a huge wild cat in possession. Sticking his torch in a crack of the building, he gave the monster battle, and in a few minutes succeeded in making a flank movement, seized it by the hind legs and knocked its brains out against the side of the house.

Quite an amusing story is told of a man named Dickens—James Dickens. He was a rather early settler, and for some time had charge of Tunstall's mill. The story goes that one day, while in charge of the mill, some ladies came to him who had become considerably bothered and perplexed in their calculations about a piece of cloth, and asked him if he knew figures. Now there was a tailor living in Mount Vernon named Figgers, and supposing the ladies referred to the little tailor, Dickens exclaimed in his off-hand style, "Know Figgers? Wy, yes; dod-ding if I didn't make him out of rags— all but his head." The result of the joke was a dickens of a fight, for the little tailor, like little men generally, was inclined to be a little "fierce," and he took mortal offense at Dickens for the remark, and a fist-fight followed.

The state of society on the frontier fifty to seventy-five years ago was not perfect in its moral symmetry by any means. Every community had its rough characters, and it is not improbable that the rough element sometimes predominated. Public days, such as muster and election days, where cheap whisky got the upper hand of the less free-willed, free fights were often inaugurated which would have done credit to a Donnybrook Fair. Jefferson County was no exception to the rule, and had its little episodes that would now be considered quite disgraceful. Mr. Johnson alludes to a general fight that occurred in 1820, in which nearly the whole population of the county took part. He says: "It was said that some of the Maxeys had said that the Maxeys and Caseys were going to rule the country. John Abbott determined to refute the idea by whipping the first one of them he might meet. This was noised abroad and it fell upon Elihu Maxey to measure strength with Abbott. They met in town one day when nearly everybody else was there, and at it they went, like a couple of modern pugilists. Everybody got excited, even Uncle Jimmy Johnson laid aside his usual gravity, threw his old straw hat as far as he could send it, and requested any other man that wanted to fight to come to him, while Jim Abbott danced around and said, 'anybody that whips John Abbott will have to whip Jim', but Billy Casey picked up Jim and ran clear off with him. But it was all over in five minutes or less time. It was roughly estimated that every man in town had his hat, coat or vest off, calling for somebody to fight him." This was no isolated case, but of common occurrence in the early history of the county, when

"Frontier life was rough and rude,"

and to be considered the "best man" in the neighborhood was an honor greatly coveted and highly cherished by him who was so fortunate as to possess the enviable (?) notoriety. But with the progress of Christianity and the refining influences of education, society improved, gradually at first, but then more rapidly, until, at the present time, we find the county equal in civilization and refinement to any portion of the State, and as to Mount Vernon, it may very appropriately be termed the Athens of Southern Illinois.

The best incident illustrative of the pioneer period is told at the expense of "Buck" Casey, or rather, he tells it at his own expense. Although the incident has traveled over the State and has been located in a score or more of different places, yet it is vouched for as having originally occurred in this county and of Buck Casey having been the actual hero of it. In early times, when the settlements here were in their infancy, teams were very scarce and the means of hauling and plowing were restricted to the narrowest limits. To such straits were the settlers sometimes reduced, and so sorely taxed was their ingenuity to rig out a team, that means would often be resorted to that in this day of inventive perfection would appear ludicrous in the extreme. It was not uncommon for a settler to yoke up a pair of bull calves when so young and small that only dire necessity—which we are told is the mother of invention—would suggest their ability to be of much service, even in "snaking" up firewood. One year, so meager was the supply of bull calves in the neighborhood, that Buck Casey conceived the happy idea of yoking himself with the only one his family possessed, for the purpose of hauling wood from the adjacent forest. The yoke was adjusted, and with his younger brother, Abram, to drive, the team was ready for work. It is a tradition, however, that Buck made such an "onery" looking bull calf that his mate refused to pull or budge a step in the right direction, but whirling his business end to leeward, turned the yoke. Buck had heard of tying the tails of young cattle together to prevent such catastrophes when breaking them to the yoke, so he gathered up the big end of a corn-cob in the slack of his leather breeches, and to this he securely tied the calf-tail, then told Abe to give 'em the gad. The calf made a bound, found his tail fast, became frightened and then plunged forward at the top of its speed, helter-skelter, pell mell, over stumps, logs and brush at a rate that bade fair to break the necks of both. Buck became worse frightened than the calf, and as they approached the house, he yelled out at the top of his voice: "Here we come, head us off, pap, dar'n our fool souls, we are running away." It was Buck's "last appearance" in the role of a bull calf.

One or the great dangers the early settlers were subject to were prairie and forest fires. It is true, the danger is not so great here as farther north, where miles and miles of prairie grew rank with grasses, ten or fifteen feet high, and without a tree or shrub in sight to break the endless monotony, but still there was danger. When the grass dried up in autumn and the leaves fell from the trees and they, too, became dry, the whole presented one immense tinder box, that, once ignited, no power could resist or control. The roaring flames would sweep over the prairies, and, reaching the woods, where the leaves lay thick, diminished but little in volume, but crackled, roared and swept on, scorching the trees, sometimes, forty feet from the ground. We have heard of no loss of human life in this county, but stock often perished, and houses, stacks of grain and other property were destroyed. In many portions of the State much loss of life has resulted from these autumnal fires.

Crime has never prevailed in Jefferson County to that extent it has in some portions of the State, though, of course, the county has not been wholly free from it, and from lawless characters. Among the first settlers, there were a few whose morals would not bear too close a scrutiny. Goings, who has already been mentioned as having one of the first mills in the county, was accused of being a counterfeiter. Goings always had a lot of men around him of bad repute, and it was generally believed that his house was a regular rendezvous or headquarters for horse-thieves, negro stealers and all sorts of low, vicious characters. He left the county in 1821, impelled, no doubt, by the urgent wish (!) of his neighbors. John Breeze, who afterward occupied Goings' house, found a quantity of unfinished counterfeit money, that he had been obliged to hide when he suddenly left the neighborhood. A man named Herron also became involved in counterfeiting. He was arrested, and was tried at the June term of court, 1821, and was fined $20 and costs and sentenced to be whipped. The sentence was carried out, the prisoner receiving thirty-nine lashes upon his bare back. This seems to us a rather barbarous sentence now, but fifty or seventy-five years ago it was common, not only in Illinois but in many, if not all, of the older States. Another case, we noticed in running over the old records, of whipping, that occurred here in 1830. It was that of James Vance, who was tried and convicted as a horse-thief. He was fined $22 and costs and sentenced to ten days in jail and to receive twenty lashes upon his bare back, which penalty was duly executed. A number of other criminals, more or less vicious, might be noticed, but such history is better forgotten than perpetuated.

A case that caused the most intense excitement was that of a "runaway negro," who made his appearance in the county in 1843. Runaway negroes, in old slave times, were a common occurrence, and there are still many people living who well remember the line of underground railway through Illinois on which negroes, fleeing from slavery in the Southern States, traveled on free passes to the land of freedom. There were not many people in this portion of this State, perhaps, who would actually help the negroes to escape from their masters, but there were many who would not help the masters to re-capture the negroes, and a little further north there were many warm friends of the slave. Runaway negroes, as we have said, were common, and were much feared by the women and children. A fretful child could nearly always be quieted with the threat that "a runaway nigger would get it." But it was in the spring of 1843 that the runaway negro

Frederick first appeared in the county. He was seen northwest of Mount Vernon, near Jefferson City, where he attacked an old lady named Campbell, but he became alarmed and fled. The neighbors were aroused, and soon there were several hundred men scouring the woods in search of him. He was again heard of in the the eastern part of the county, where he had abused a Mrs. Sursa. Next, he was heard of in Wayne County, where his pursuers soon followed him, but he had fled into Clay County. Finally, he was captured near the town of Maysville, Clay County, and was brought to Mount Vernon, where the excitement went up to fever heat. Some wanted to burn him, others to hang him, and it was only by the utmost exertions of the more law-abiding citizens that he was not lynched. Judge Scates, as soon as he found a chance to be heard, made a speech to the excited people, setting forth the sufficiency of the law, the consequences of mob-law in general and the penalties to which they laid themselves liable, individually, by persisting in it. Concluding his speech, Judge Scates remarked to Sheriff Stephenson: "I wish you to watch this proceeding, and report to me the very first man that you see doing what is contrary to law; I will issue a writ, and have him arrested, if there is force enough in the State to do it." Law and order at length prevailed, and the excited people withdrew. The negro was indicted at the August term of the court, 1843, for rape and attempt to commit rape. Upon these he was tried, found guilty on both counts and sentenced to the penitentiary, on the first charge, "for the full term of his natural life," and on the other for "fourteen years" longer. As there was no Gov. Blackburn to pardon him out, the negro was still serving his sentence the last known of him.

The care of the poor is a duty we owe to that unfortunate class, who have found the thorny path of life "rough, adverse and forlorn," and crave our assistance. "The poor ye have with ye alway," said the Master, and we, who have been more fortunate than they, should not fail to contribute of our earthly goods, when we can, to smooth the path of some poor unfortunate.

"A little word in kindness spoken,
  A motion or a tear;
Often heals the heart that's broken,
  And makes a friend sincere."

Kindness costs but little, and to the child of misfortune it sometimes goes almost as far as dollars and cents. None of us know how soon we may go "over the hill to the poor house" ourselves. We recently visited one of these institutions, and were pointed out an inmate who once could ride ten miles, we were told, in a straight line upon his own land. But a multitude of misfortunes brought him to the poor-house. Then, be kind to the poor, for in so doing you may entertain angels unawares.

As early as 1830, we find allusions to county paupers. They were then usually kept by some person who was paid for it by the county. In 1843, the pauper list is referred to by Mr. Johnson in his sketches, as being a Mrs. Henly, H. M. E. Herron, William Tuck, a man named Beasley and a woman named Shoulders. These were all kept by individual citizens, at the expense of the county. A few years later, they had increased to some twelve or fifteen, who were maintained in the same manner.

In 1859, the first steps were taken for the establishment of a regular poor-house. Two and a half acres of land were purchased, situated in the northeast quarter of the southwest quarter of Section 2½, Township 2 and Range 3 east. March 19, 1859, 120 acres were purchased in Section 27 of the same Township and Range, by the County Board, composed of J. R. Satterfield, W. Adams and S. W. Carpenter, for the sum of $1,150, upon which the requisite buildings were erected. This is still used for a county farm and poor-house, and is the home of all the county's poor who are maintained at the public expense.

This chapter closes the history of the county at large, and the succeeding pages will be devoted to individual towns and townships respectively. The foregoing, though a sketch, and admitting of anecdote, excursive digressions and a flexible texture of narrative, yet, for the most part, it is essentially historical. We have endeavored to narrate some of the physical and moral features of the county; its formation, settlement, local divisions and progress; the habits and customs of the early pioneers, interspersed with individual incident. These we have recorded as best we could, and now submit them for the verdict of the general reader.

PART III.

HISTORY OF THE TOWNSHIPS.

PART III.

HISTORY OF THE TOWNSHIPS.

CHAPTER I.*

MOUNT VERNON TOWNSHIP—DESCRIPTION, TOPOGRAPHY, ETC.—EARLY SETTLEMENT—OLD SURVEYS AND LAND ENTRIES—A CLOSER ACQUAINTANCE WITH THE PIONEERS—WHO THEY WERE AND WHERE THEY LOCATED—THEIR GOOD TRAITS AND PECULIARITIES—THE SELECTING OF A SITE FOR A TOWN—MOUNT VERNON CHOSEN AS THE COUNTY SEAT, ETC.

"The hunt, the shot, the glorious chase,
 The captured elk or deer;
The camp, the big, bright fire, and then
 The rich and wholesome cheer."
—GALLAGHER.

THE public lands of Jefferson County were surveyed in 1814 and 1815. The field notes of the exterior lines of Town 2 south, Range 3 east, are signed by Charles Lockhart, Deputy Surveyor, and dated "December 18, 1814;" those of the interior lines, by Joseph Meacham, Deputy Surveyor, "April 19, 1815." The surveys seem to have been very accurate, as the aggregate—23,022 acres—falls only eighteen acres short of an exact township; but there was carelessness somewhere, as this note on the records will show:

ST. LOUIS, MO., February 17, 1817.
There are no notes of the east boundary of this township on file in this office. D. DUNKLIN,
Surveyor General.

And the deficiency has never been supplied.

In looking over those old field notes, we are surprised at another feature—the frequent occurrence of "White Oak" among the bearing trees. It may have been that the surveyors sought this as the most enduring variety of oak; possibly it may sometimes mean water oak; yet the proportion seems very large. Of about 200 bearing trees, there were twenty-five hickory, fifty-seven "Black Oak," five "Pin Oak," nine elm, three sassafras, two ash, one each of gum, locust, mulberry and walnut, and ninety-six "White Oak."

At the time when our sketch begins, the natural features of the country differed from anything we have seen here for a generation or more. The prairies, valleys, hills and water-courses were where they are to-day, of course, but all were dressed in quite another garb. The annual autumnal fires, sweeping over all, burned out and kept down the undergrowth; and the woods were so open, the trees so lofty, the branches so high, and the ground so bare of anything like a bush, that game could be descried in any direction at almost any reasonable distance. A deer could be seen a quarter of a mile in the woods, and a man on horseback nearly a mile, at any point where there were no intervening

*By Dr. A. Clark Johnson.

hills to stop the view. The eastern part of this township consisted of open barrens, as if a few trees had been scattered over a somewhat broken or rolling prairie. These facts explain what would seem very odd in the old field notes above referred to, that the section corner between four and five on the township line had to be marked by a "post in mound;" that the half mile corner on the north side of Section 29 is marked "no trees," and the same note is made of the corner between Sections 11, 12, 13 and 14.

The prairies generally ran into the woods without any border of small trees or thickets; and the grass was generally higher than a man's head, frequently high enough to hide a man on horseback at the distance of a hundred yards. They appeared much more nearly level than now. This was partly because the grass was ranker on the lower ground, and partly because, before the grass was eaten and tramped down so closely, the water filtered away or stood in the valleys, whereas it now washes a channel that carries away the soil.

There was this peculiarity, too, in both prairie and timber, that wherever the ground was level or low, it was wet and marshy throughout the year. Being trampled but little and very porous, besides being shaded by the luxuriant grass, the earth held water so that it hardly ever became thoroughly dry. Bottom lands were extremely wet, and their soil a heavy clay, utterly unlike the loam that has since been carried down from the adjacent uplands.

With these facts all in view, and knowing that the township is somewhat hilly on the west, rolling off to the creek two miles to the east, rising gently into hills beyond, with a little prairie of about 1,000 acres on its south side, the reader can form a pretty good idea of what the present Mount Vernon Township was at the beginning. There was no trace of man, except the surveyor's marks upon the trees, and the Goshen road. This famous road led from Goshen, a settlement four or five miles this side of Edwardsville, to the salt-works on the Saline; and was made by parties going to the Saline for salt. It struck this county just south of where the town of Walnut Hill now stands, and passed out near the southeast corner. It entered this township about Section 5, and running west of the old Short camp-ground, passed out east of where John Waite lives. So noted was this old trail, that it is referred to over fifty times in the Government surveys of the county, and eight or ten times in the field notes of this township. In numberless places it may still be seen. Yet it was only a narrow trail, almost buried under the rich growth of summer, coming out in wonderful distinctness after the autumnal fires.

About the year 1815, a man by the name of Black came up from Pope County on a hunting expedition. On his return, he gave a glowing account of the country, and especially of a beautiful prairie he had visited. Among others, he told his story to the Caseys, near Cave-in-Rock. They soon set out in search of Black's Prairie, and this was the occasion of their first visit to this part of the country. They never knew whether they found Black's Prairie or not. But in the autumn of 1815, Isaac Casey and his two sons—William, a married man, and Thomas M., a large boy—came out to look at the country. They came by Crenshaw's; and he glad of new-comers, as all pioneers are, accompanied them in their search for locations. A circumstance occurred on their way up, which afforded them much amusement. As they took a northwesterly course across the prairie, a deer (a very large buck) started up at a little distance from them, and the men

all blazed away at it at once. It ran a little way, and fell. They ran up, each one shouting, "I killed it! I killed it! It's my deer, I killed it!" when lo! only one bullet-hole was to be found in all its tawny hide. The animal was opened and the bullet found, when it proved to be from the gun of Crenshaw, the oldest man, indeed the only old man in the company. This party went a few miles beyond the present site of Mount Vernon, and returned.

In the spring of 1816, Isaac Casey, William, his son, Brunetta, his daughter, and Isaac Hicks, his son-in-law, all came out and built a camp at the northern edge of the prairie, just east of where the Supreme Court building now stands. They broke and cultivated a little field, without any fence of course, extending to where the Methodist Church stands. In after years, when the old camp had been left and had rotted down, a locust tree sprang up on the old chimney pile —the same tree that now stands in the street east of the Supreme Court House. In the fall of this year, 1816, these all went back to the Ohio River where they came from, and brought out their families and the rest of their stock. William Casey, with wife and child, came into the cabin just referred to. Isaac erected a cabin near where L. N. Beal lives, Section 31, while Isaac Hicks located near the place at which he died.

While these pioneers were raising this year's crop, they had no trouble about meat or "sass," as game was abundant and honey more abundant still, but bread was a serious matter. William Casey brought their first supplies of meal from Kentucky, and corn in the following year. Isaac Casey and one or other of his daughters, several times went to the Wabash bottoms, ten miles beyond Carmi, to lay in a supply of meal. "Uncle" Isaac rode a horse and led one, but a single horse and "turn" of meal was found enough for a girl. One of them, Mrs. Katy Tyler, tells how that, on their return from one of those trips, she chanced to slip off the horse near where the fair grounds are located; and there was not a stump, rock, hillock, log or anything else, from which she could remount "in all that part of the country;" so she had to walk home.

Of the pioneers of 1817 and 1818, most located in Moore's Prairie and Shiloh. Henry Wilkerson, about this time, settled on the hill just south of the Jake Stitch—now Bates —house; and William Jordan settled on Seven Mile Creek, where Coleman Smith afterward lived so long, and Thomas Jordan southwest of him. Thomas D. Minor, located a little southwest of where Thomas Johnson lives. Very little as to progress of settlement can be learned from the land entries. The first entries were made in 1817. In that year William Casey entered land in Section 30, Isaac Casey in 31, and Gorum A. Worth in 32. In 1818, Elihu Maxey entered land in Section 6, William Casey in 29 and 30, and Thomas Sloo, Jr., in 31. In 1819, Jeptha Hardin entered in Section 20, Abraham P. Casey and Henry Bechtle in 28, Joel Pace and Dorris and Maxey in 30, Gray and Grant and John Johnson in 32. Then there was not an acre of land entered in the township for seven years! So we find hardly half a dozen families in the township at the time Mount Vernon began; and before proceeding further, we must stop and become better acquainted with the persons already mentioned.

Isaac Casey used to say that his father and uncle came over the ocean and settled at Goldsboro, N. C., whence they passed by successive removals to South Carolina and Georgia. There is another account—that Abner Casey, reared in the North of Ireland, married a Welsh lady and came to Virginia, on the Roanoke; their children were Levi, Moses, Randolph and a daughter; all went to South Carolina about 1760; Randolph married Mary Jane Pennington, and Levi, Randolph, Isaac, Abraham P., Charity, Hiram, Samuel and Zadok were their children. This family went to Georgia in 1795, thence to Smith County, Tenn., a few years later. Isaac Casey was born in South Carolina in 1765, married Elizabeth Mackey in 1788, and went to Barren County, Ky. He was Sheriff of that county about six years. In 1803, he came to Illinois, and located on the Ohio River, a mile or two above the Cave-in-Rock. A double murder occurred there some years after. A Mr. Ballinger killed a Mr. Billingsly, and then one Fisher killed Ballinger. Fisher was related to the first victim, and also to Casey; and Casey was almost the only witness against Fisher. Isaac Casey did not want a man hung on his testimony alone, so he went up into the hills along the Saline, and spent months there; he then went to Arkansas Post and was gone a year, and probably it was really a similar motive that brought him to this section. After living where L. N. Beal does for seven or eight years, he sold out to Abe Buffington in 1825; made a little improvement near where Lewis Johnson lives; went to merchandising with Joel Pace at town in 1828; but soon retired, and spent most of his remaining days in the country. He was a man of great energy and activity, a dignified Christian gentleman, though he had been dissipated in his younger days. Isaac Casey was the father of Isaac Hicks' wife, Rebecca; Clark Casey's wife, Polly; Dr. Wilkey's wife, Brunetta; Henry Tyler's wife, Catharine; George Bullock's wife, Miranda. His sons were William, Abram T. and Thomas M. The old man died at Thomas M. Casey's, in 1848, at the age of eighty-four years.

William Case.—or "Billy," as more commonly called—was the oldest son and the second child of Isaac Casey; was born in Barren County, Ky., in 1794 or 1795. His wife was Amy Barker, daughter of Lewis Barker, who owned the ferry at Cave-in-Rock so long; and they brought one child, Blackford, with them to this county. After living awhile in the cabin before mentioned, he built a pretty decent house of hewn logs where the Commercial Hotel now stands, saying jocosely when it was up, "Boys, here is the first house in town." When the town was laid off, however, this house was just outside the limits. He then cleared a field reaching nearly to where the Presbyterian Church stands. A few years later he built on the hill where Samuel Casey last lived; he sold that place to Joseph Slater in 1836, and moved to a place on Puncheon Camp Creek, and thence soon after to the northern part of the State. In a year or two he came back, lived at the Harlow place two miles from town, thence going to Puncheon Camp, thence to Moore's Prairie. His wife died in 1846, and in 1850 he married Miss M. J. Shelton; lived at the Prairie two or three years; moved back to the Harlow place, and died there in 1854.

The name of William Casey was one that suggested a strong mind, a very strong and active body, and passions deep and terrible when once aroused. He worked and traded with excellent judgment, and received some assistance from his father-in-law; so that he was for some time the wealthiest man in the county. He and Isaac Hicks were all the men who brought surplus money with them, and much of the land entered by the settlers in that day was entered with money borrowed from them. He never sought office, but was once, in 1820, elected as one of the County Commissioners. At all times he walked with a kingly dignity that made our boyish eyes look for the ground to shake under him. Mrs. Casey was a good woman. Their children were Blackford, Maletna (Mrs. A. D. Estes), William B. (or Buck), Abraham, Drury B., Thomas, Melissa (Mrs. Grubbs and afterward Mrs. Lester) and Zadok. Newton, recently deceased, was a son of the second wife.

Henry Wilkerson had a brother John, and Phebe, wife of Rhodam Allen, was his sister. They were Virginians by way of Tennessee. Henry lived for many years on the place he first settled, in a round-pole cabin, for he was fond of drink and never accumulated much; he was long subject to fits of insanity, in one of which he would set out and walk hundreds of miles; he made three or four trips thus from Tennessee to Virginia, and one from Tennessee to Illinois; he at length became entirely deranged, and remained so till his death, sometimes being furious, at other times nearly rational; but he never was so rational as not to run, when he saw a storm coming, and throw his hat, shoe, sock, or whatever came to hand, into the fire, to stop the wind from blowing. By trade he was a cooper. He lived at Robert's for fourteen years, in a small house in the yard, and died in 1846, aged nearly eighty-four years. His wife, from whom he had long lived separate, survived him, and lived to the age of ninety-nine years. Their sons were William, who went to Louisiana; Edward, who died in Union County, and Robert. Few descendants of these remain. Mrs. Stockird, of Mount Vernon, is a daughter of Edward, and Rosa Wilson a grand-daughter of Robert—a short list. Of Henry Wilkerson's daughters, Sally married Jarvis Pierce; Phebe married Spencer Pace; Rachel, George Crosno; and Rebecca, J. Wesley Hicks. Many descendants of these are with us.

William Jordan was the son of William Jordan, Sr., and the nephew of Thomas Jordan, who settled near him. The older set were William, Joseph, Thomas and Francis —the last remaining in Franklin County. Thomas lived a few years near where David H. Warren lives, then moved to where Elias Howard lives, and gave name to Jordon's Prairie. His wife was a Whitesides. William Jordan, Jr., had a sister married to Moses Ham and one married to Nicholas Wren, and a brother named Aaron, who married a Crooms. Most of the Jordans remained here till 1830 and 1832, then some went North and some to Texas. A man of the name of Parker from Vincennes got a donation of a league of land in Texas, and took off quite a colony of Jordans, Greenwoods and others. Joe Jordan, William, Jr., Thomas, Jr., Oliver Morris, etc., all went to Texas.

The act of the General Assembly, forming Jefferson County, approved March 26, 1819, as set forth in a preceding chapter, contained this clause: "And for the purpose of fixing the permanent seat of justice therein the following persons are appointed Commissioners: Ambrose Maulding, Lewis Barker, Robert Shipley, James A. Richardson and Richard Graham; which said Commissioners or a majority of them, being duly sworn before some Judge or Justice of the Peace of this State to faithfully take into view the convenience of the people, the situation of the settlement with an eye to future population and the eligibility of the place, shall meet on the second Monday of May, at the house of William Casey, in said county, and proceed to examine and determine on the place for the permanent seat of justice and designate the same; *provided*, that the proprietor or proprietors of the land shall give to the county for the purpose of erecting public buildings a quantity of land, not less than twenty acres, to be laid out in lots and sold for that purpose; but should the proprietor or proprietors refuse or neglect to make the donation aforesaid, then and in that case it shall be the duty of the Commissioners to fix on some other place for the seat of justice, as convenient as may be to the inhabitants of said county; which place fixed and determined upon, the said Commissioners shall certify under their hands and seals, and shall return the same to the next Commissioners' Court in the county aforesaid."

When the first County Board met in June, 1819, the location of the county seat was one of the first matters that demanded its attention. The Commissioners appointed by the Legislature presented the following report:

"According to an act of the General Assembly, passed the 10th day of March, 1819, appointing certain Commissioners to meet on the second Monday of May at the house of William Casey, for the purpose of fixing a permanent seat of justice for and in Jefferson County, the following persons met, viz.: Lewis Barker, Ambrose Maulding and James A. Richardson, who, after being duly sworn, have provided, determined and fixed upon the southwest quarter of Section 29, Range 3, Town 2, on the land owned by William Casey, the town to be laid off in the southwest corner of said quarter, to commence near the timber, on a point not far distant from said Casey's house, and thence to the foot of the descent, on a point on which said Casey's house stands, or in such manner as said County Commissioners shall designate.

"Given under our hands and seals this 12th day of May, 1819.

"It is unanimously agreed that the name of the town shall be Mount Pleasant.

"JAMES A. RICHARDSON,
"AMBROSE MAULDING,
"LEWIS BARKER."

This settled the question of locating the county seat. Isaac Hicks had been expecting to have it near him, as "Post Oak Hill," his place, was very near the geographical center of the county, and the land lay well for the purpose. An effort had also been made to locate it on the high grounds between the Casey place and the Dodds place, west of the present site; but the influence of William Casey with Lewis Barker, his father-in-law, predominated, and it was put as close to him as it could be without including his house and improvements.

Of the men just named, we may here add: Lewis Barker, as just stated, was the father of Mrs. Casey, and the owner of the ferry at Cave-in-Rock, and was a member the first four sessions of the State Senate from Pope County. Ambrose Maulding lived near his brother Ennis, in Hog Prairie, a few miles this side of where McLeansboro is now. Ennis, it will be remembered, went to the State Senate; he also built a famous mill on Skillet Fork. James A. Richardson lived about Carmi. We don't know what became of Shipley and Graham. A year or two later, the county allowed Maulding $8 and Barker and Richardson $12 each for their services.

CHAPTER II.*

CITY OF MOUNT VERNON—THE LAYING-OUT AND BEGINNING OF THE TOWN—SALE OF LOTS—ERECTION OF PUBLIC BUILDINGS—THE FIRST COURT HOUSE—STRAY POUND, GAOL AND CLERK'S OFFICE—STICK CHIMNEYS, COURT HOUSE LOCK, ETC.—THE PIONEERS AND FIRST SETTLERS IN THE TOWN—THEIR GENEALOGICAL TREES, ETC.

"———— the waving fields
Bow to the reaper, where I wildly roamed;
Cities now rise where I pursued the deer;
And dust offends me, where in happier years
I breathed in vigor from untainted gales."
— *The Aged Pioneer.*

ON the 9th of June, the court proceeded to consider the expediency of laying off the town, so as to enable them to sell the lots and place them in a situation to erect public buildings, wherefore it was ordered: "That Joel Pace be, and he is, hereby appointed and empowered to contract with a surveyor to lay off the said town in such manner as will be most advantageous to the county, or in such manner as the County Commissioners may direct; and it is further ordered that the sale of said lots shall commence on the third Monday of September next; and further ordered, that an advertisement to that effect be inserted in the *Illinois Emigrant* for three weeks previous to the commencement of said sale, and that fifty copies of said advertisement be printed on handbills, to be sent to the different parts of the country, for the information of those who may want to attend the sale, for which service the editor of the aforesaid paper shall be paid out of any money that may be in the treasury, not otherwise appropriated. And it is further ordered that the town be called Mount Vernon." The payments were to be made in four equal installments, six, twelve, eighteen and twenty-four months. Mount Pleasant was the name first proposed, and almost became the name of the town; but the popular love for Washington was yet warm, and Mount Vernon, his ancestral home, prevailed.

In a few weeks, the services of William Hosick were engaged; the town was surveyed and platted, and the notes and plat ready for record by July 10. This man, Hosick, was the son of a little Scotchman, who lived in Livingston County, Ky., about nine miles from Golconda, Alick Hosick. William was a one-armed man, and lived at Shawneetown. The new town, of course, included but twenty acres. It extended from Harrison street north of the jail, on the north, to Jordan street on the south, and from Casey street east of the Commercial Hotel on the west, to Johnson Alley, west of Westbrook & Co.'s Mill, on the east. The lots were numbered from the northwest corner, where Crebs lives, and ended with Lot 48 in the southeast corner, where Kline's boarding house stands. They lay in eight squares, three each way, and one to the county, but nothing was said about blocks in the survey. Here, then, the business lay till September, when, the time of sale drawing nigh, it is "ordered that William Casey and Joel Pace be, and they are, hereby employed to set four mulberry stakes around the public square, *i. e.*, one at each corner, to drive all the stakes in the

* By Dr. A. Clark Johnson.

town, and also to number the lots, for which they are to be paid by the county the sum of $5."

The day of sale arrived. About a hundred persons assembled, many of them strangers, and they sallied forth into the town. It was a little nook on a gentle swell at the north side of the prairie. The edge of the timber ran from near where the academy afteward stood, northwest, past Fletcher Johnson's, by the New York Store, by the jail, by Joel Watson's, west a hundred yards or more, then southwest, past William Casey's field, and so on down to where the woolen factory stands; while clumps of sturdy white oaks stood west of the square, and at Porter's corner, and near where D. C. Warren lives. The prairie was not so smooth as it had been a few years before, but here and there was a little hazel or brier patch, or a bunch of sumach or elder bushes. But the lines had been hacked or staked out, and the lots could be found. When well out into the open space, James E. Davis, a Cumberland Presbyterian preacher, raised the cry, "O yes, gentlemen! I am now going to sell you some lots in the beautiful town of Mount Vernon, all covered now with a beautiful coat of green, but destined soon to be covered with magnificent buildings.' Lot No. 1, Crebs's, was struck off to Bennett Maxey for $41; No. 2, to Barton Atchisson; Burchett Maxey bought No. 4, south of Herdman's, where he soon after built a large double log house; Lewis Watkins took the corner lot, the Joel Pace lot, at $162.50; Nelson Ferguson, the corner east of that, now bank corner, for $165; Edward Maxey, the Thorn lot, for $60; Clark Casey, the corner west of Nieman's, at $160; Thomas Jordan, the lot where J. D. Johnson's store is, at $153; William Maxey, the lot now Porter's corner, for $95; Dr. McLean, afterward of McLeansboro, bought the H. T. Pace corner at $136; Isaac Casey was his security, McL. failed on it, Isaac took it, and passed it over to Burchett Maxey. But more of these matters hereafter.

Watkins had already made some preparations to build on his lot, though he never paid for it, and Thomas Jordan took it off his hands; and Burchett Maxey, as before stated, at once put up a house on his. These buildings were scarcely under headway, when Clark Casey moved his walnut-log house from near where Joseph Pace lately lived up to his lot, and the town was fairly begun.

Of course, one of the first subjects that occupied the attention of the County Court was the erection of public buildings for the use of the county. Indeed, the court house was already built, and standing there in all its glory at the time the sale of lots above described took place. The first sitting of the County Commissioners began, as before stated, June 7, 1819; and on the 9th they determined to build a court house:

"As it is inconvenient to hold court in a private house for several reasons,

"Ordered, That the building of a court house be let to the lowest bidder on Friday the 24th inst., to be eighteen by twenty feet, thirteen feet high; to be built of hewed logs that will face from ten to twelve inches, closely notched down; to have a good roof made of boards; also a good under floor made of plank, rough, and closely laid; and joist-plates, with holes cut for joists; the house to have one door and one window, cut and faced, and to them good shutters hung, made of rough plank; the house and all the work about it done in workman-like manner, completed and delivered to the County Commissioners' Court at their next September term, subject to the inspection of the County Commissioners, said house to be built in the public square, or on the spot the said Commissioners shall designate. The timber to be furnished by Isaac Casey, William Casey and Joseph Jordan. The building of said house to be paid for out of any moneys that may be in the treasury not otherwise appropriated."

Accordingly, on Friday, June 25, the court again met at the house of William Casey; and, "in pursuance of an order of the last court, the building of a court house was this day let to the lowest bidder, the building of which John Sanders undertook for the sum of $85, and entered into bond with James Kelly, his security, conditioned for the faithful performance of his contract." Isaac Casey, William Casey and Joseph Jordan furnished the timber, and many others found employment in cutting and hewing the logs, sawing the plank, "riving" the boards, hauling, etc. It must not be understood, however, that the gentlemen named furnished the timber from their own lands. There was good timber on the United States lands on the ridge a mile or two northwest of town, from where Judge Keller lives to old Union, and there all the materials for this house were "got out." Henry Tyler hewed nearly every log in the building. We can readily imagine how much the public attention was excited by so important an enterprise. Notwithstanding the whole was to be done in the sultry months of July and August, the work went bravely on, and when the court met in September, Monday, 6th, they found the building nicely finished and ready for use. "According to an order of the last court, for letting the building of a court house, it was let to John Sanders, who completed and delivered the same to the court at their present term; wherefore ordered, that the Clerk grant him a certificate for the same."

It stood about the center of the public square, its only door fronting to the south, its only window in the west side, and the bushes around were so broken down that its bright logs and roof were plainly visible from all the business part of town. But the best of earthly things are imperfect. As winter came on, it became too evident that, large and commodious as the court house was, it was not a comfortable place for a winter session. Hence, when the court met in December, 6th, it was ordered that the finishing of the building should be let to the lowest bidder on the following day. And this was to be the manner of it: "To be completed as follows, to wit: A chimney place to be cut out, and a good chimney, back and hearth to be built, after the form of the chimney to the house in which Lewis Watkins now lives, and to be as good as said chimney was when it was first finished; also a set of good hewed or sawed joists put in, and an upper floor of sawed plank to be closely laid, the plank to be one and a fourth inches thick; also the cracks to be closely chinked inside, and well daubed outside with well wrought mortar. There is a platform to be constructed in the west end of the house, to be of proper height, four feet wide, of good hewed puncheons or thick plank, to lack but three feet of reaching from one side of the house to the other; at the end of said platform are to be steps composed of blocks or planks, and a hand-rail in front of the aforesaid platform of a proper height, and a seat in the rear of the platform of the same length of the platform, and two seats in front of the platform of the same length on the floor, all the seats to be made of good hewed puncheons or plank, to be made in such a manner as to be steady, and movable at pleasure. The platform is to be supported by good substantial posts, pillars or blocks. All of which is to be completed by the first Monday in March next, and to be done in a workmanlike manner." All of this Oliver Morris undertook to do for the sum of $80. But he signally failed, the Commissioners, on an examination of the work, finding it so imperfect that they determined to deduct $5 from the amount he was to have received. He accepted the $75. The building now, though not indeed everything that a court house ought to be, had cost the county $160.

The next demand was a Stray Pound—not because there were more cattle than criminals running at large, nor because they were more likely to be taken up, but because the law imperatively required it. And this again was because, from the scarcity of inclosures, stock was very liable to go astray. By an act approved March 23, 1819, the County Court in all new counties was required, within three months after locating court house, etc., to cause a Pound to be made near the same place, under penalty of $20 for every term of the court after the three months till it should be built. In this Pound all stray horses, mules, etc., over two years old, taken up within twenty miles, were to be kept from 12 till 4 o'clock on the first day of the County Court for three terms next after the taking up, to enable the owner to find and prove his property. Strays under two years old were advertised nearly as at present. If over twenty miles away, the stray was to be put in pound on the first day of the second term after the taking up. The keeper was to keep and tend the pound on court days, under penalty of $8 fine.

On the second day of this December term, therefore, the court "Ordered that the building of a Stray Pound be let to the lowest bidder, of the following form, to wit: Forty feet square, five panels on each side of equal length, to be made of posts and rails, the posts to be made of white or post oak, neatly hewed, four by seven inches; the rails to be sufficiently strong; the cracks from two feet downward not to be more than four inches, and from that upward not more than six inches; a good strong gate, and fixed to it a good lock and key, to be affixed to one side of said pound; the posts of said fence to be set in the ground not less than thirty inches, to be in all respects strong and firm; said pound to be completed and delivered to this court at the next March term."

John C. Casey took the contract for building the pound for $33.87½, but he does not seem to have been in haste about it, for at the February term, February 10, 1820, the court ordered that the pound be built on Lot No. 31. Garrison Greenwood having bought that lot, and failed to execute the required notes, it of course went back to the county. The Pound was ordered upon that lot, and "six feet from the southeast corner." And there it was located in due time, being received March 6, and the architect appointed to keep it. This lot, No. 31, is that on which the county jail now stands.

The Jail. Before the Stray Pound was finished (February 10, 1820), it was determined to build a jail on the same lot as follows: "Ordered, that the building of a gaol be let to the lowest bidder on the second day of next March term, to be built as follows, to wit: The first floor to be composed of two layers of timbers squared to twelve inches laid crosswise, and the whole to be covered with two-inch plank closely laid and spiked down, the floor to be sunk within six inches of the surface of the earth; the wall to be composed of timber squared to twelve inches, of which two walls are to be built thirteen inches apart, the vacancy between which is to be filled with timbers not less than twelve inches square to stand perpendicularly; the walls to be built in the way above described ten feet high, the timbers to be laid as close as possible; on which a second floor is to be made of twelve-inch square timber closely laid and covered with two-inch plank, closely laid and spiked down, the spikes to be not less than four inches long; the room above described is for a dungeon. On the second floor there is a debtor's room to be built by continuing the outside wall of timber as before described, eight feet high from the second floor; then there is to be a third floor composed of timbers twelve inches square, closely laid, reaching from the outside of each wall, the house to be well covered with shingles. The lower room to be ten feet square in the clear, the walls and floors to be composed of good, sound oak timber. There is to be a door cut in one side of the upper or debtor's room, to which a good shutter is to be made and hung sufficiently strong, to be made of two lay of two-inch plank spiked together with spikes to go through and clinch; there is to be two windows to each room, twelve inches square, with eight bars of iron two feet long and an inch and a half square to each window put crosswise; about the middle of the second floor there is to be a hole cut two feet square, and to it there is to be hung sufficiently strong a trap-door to fit the hole made in the same manner that the other door is to be made; there is to be made to reach up on the outside of the gaol to the door, a good and substantial pair of steps, and also a platform made at the top of the steps four feet square, and a railing three feet high from the platform around the same and also on one side of the steps; the whole to be completed and delivered in a workmanlike manner to the County Commissioners' Court at their next December term."

Burchett Maxey took the contract for building the jail at $320. It cost more than the court house—twice as much—and rightly, for while there were but fifty or sixty logs in the court house, there were largely over 200 in the jail. No sooner did Burchett Maxey secure the job than Zadok Casey, who was an extra hand with an ax, either in chopping or hewing, was taken in as a partner. Lewis and James Johnson and others assisted in getting out the timbers, but John Wilkerson hauled nearly every log in the building. It was "erected on the southwest corner of Lot No. 31, eight feet from the line." And on the 5th day of December, "Henry B. Maxey, who undertook the building of the jail, delivered the same to the court, which being completed agreeably to the order, was received by the court." The platform required by the contract was formed by putting in four logs four feet longer than the rest, the projecting ends forming the platform and needing no support, while the steps were literally "a pair," being formed of two large timbers twelve or fourteen inches square, in which the steps were cut. We see economy in all the transactions of the court. In settling for the jail, the Treasurer was ordered to pay Z. Casey $114, and H. B. Maxey $96, and Zadok pledged himself to take his own paper for the rest, the court authorizing the Treasurer to receive it.

At the October term of the county court— October 20, 1820—it was "Ordered, that the building of a Clerk's office be let to the lowest bidder on the third Monday in October, inst., to be built as follows, to wit: The house to be built of hewed logs, fourteen feet square, the logs to face from ten to twelve inches, the wall to be nine feet high, to have a good, strong and tight clapboard roof, the ribs and weight poles the bark shaved off, the wall well chinked on the inside and well daubed on the outside; the house to have a good floor of good and well-seasoned plank, jointed and well laid, to have a door place cut, and to it hung with good, strong iron hinges a good batten door, made of well-seasoned plank, one window cut and faced the proper size for a nine-light sash, the sash and glass the undertaker to put in, also to have a chimney built after the same manner that the chimney to the court house is built, with good back wall, hearth and jamb-stones, the corners neatly sawed down, and a good batten shutter hung to the window with strong iron hinges; the house to be built of any kind of oak except Spanish oak. The whole to be finished in a workmanlike manner and delivered to the County Commissioners' Court at their next December term."

This building was undertaken by John Wilkerson, but at the next court his time was extended until March. Accordingly, March 5, 1821, "the court proceeded to examine the Clerk's office, the workmanship of which being done in a satisfactory manner, was received, and in discharge for building the same, ordered the County Treasurer to pay to William Casey $41, to William Jordan $2.25, to Henry B. Maxey $4, and to John Wilkerson $12.37½, all which amounts to $59.62½." Three months later the court ordered W. L. Howell $1 for a lock for the Clerk's office, and it was complete. It stood about midway on the north side of the public square, the door fronting south, the window north, and the chimney east like that of the court house. And we may add, it is not expressly stated in the record, but it was expressly done—both chimneys were built wholly of wood except the "back, hearth and jamb-stones." They were genuine mud and stick chimneys, albeit they were very neat ones. And speaking of the lock for this office reminds us that in September after the court house was finished—six months—they had to pay Lewis Watkins for a lock and chain for that building. The lock, you will at once understand, was a padlock, and the door was secured by putting the chain through a little chink between the logs and through an auger hole in the door, and locking the end links together. You will notice, too, as the rib poles were shaved, that it was not intended that the Clerk's office should ever have a ceiling.

So much for the public buildings. They constituted about half of the town. It was in the court house that Burchett Maxey lived while finishing his own house on Lot No. 4, and it was in the Clerk's office that Joel Pace spent the last years of his single and first months of his married life. It was here that he lived with his family when Harvey T. Pace came out from Kentucky in the vigor of youth, and split 3,000 rails for him at 50 cents per hundred in State paper, equal to 25 cents in specie. Harvey boarded with his uncle, and fourteen feet square seems to have been room enough for them and their goods, and also the office.

It is proper, perhaps, that we now tell who those men were that we have sometimes mentioned in connection with these first buildings in Mount Vernon.

James E. Davis, who cried the sale of town lots, was one of a little colony of Maxeys, Johnsons and others, that came in from Sumner County, Tenn., in 1818. He lived near where Robert Edwards lives. His wife was a sister to Burchett and Elihu Maxey's wives, and to James Bowman's and John Afflack's, all being daughters of Perry Taylor, of Wilson County, Tenn. Davis remained here till he had one daughter grown and married to John Tade. John was a son of David Tade, and David Tade was the father also of Mrs. W. Finch. They lived about where Elijah Knox lives, but in a year or two Mr. Davis, old Mr. Tade, and all their families, went to Tazewell County, and thence to Iowa.

Of those who bought lots: Bennett N. Maxey was the second son of William Maxey and brother to Joshua C. and Jehu G. D., who are still here; was the father of William H., James J., Charles H., Joshua C., Jr., and Thomas J.; also of Mrs. Emily Ray and Mrs. Eliza White; and died at the place he first settled, a mile east of Pleasant Grove, in 1846, aged fifty-one, his widow, Sally, *nee* Overbay, dying at Rome seven years later. William and Edward Maxey were brothers, sons of Jesse Maxey, of Virginia. William married Rhodam Allen's sister Emily, in 1798, and came to Illinois in 1818, and was the father of Henry Burchett, Bennett Nelson, Elihu, Charles Hardy, Joshua Cannon, William McKendree Adney and Jehu; also of Mrs. Clarissa Johnson, Mrs. Harriet and Mrs. Vylinda A. Casey, and Hostillina, who died in 1818; and William himself died in 1838, his wife having died in 1837. Edward married Elizabeth Pitner, went to Allen County, Ky., and came thence to Illinois in 1819; was a Methodist preacher, held office many years, raised no son or daughter, but raised Judge Satterfield and others, and died at Gov. Casey's about thirty-five years ago, his wife soon following. Barton Atchisson was from Georgia, by way of Tennessee; married a Hill, sister to old Mrs. Wilkey and Mrs. Dempsey Hood; came to this county in 1815–16, was much in public life, and died in November, 1847, leaving sons, William, Ignatius, Samuel and George W., and daughters Winney Myers, Martha Chaffin, and one the wife of Theophilus Cook, Jr. Nelson Ferguson came to this county in 1819, and lived one year on James Johnson's land, and went back to Tennessee, to Station Camp Creek, six miles north of Gallatin; his wife was a Tyler, sister to Jordan Tyler, now among us. Clark Casey—John C.—was a son of Abraham P., and son-in-law of Isaac Casey; came to this county in 1818, and raised the first cabin on Mulberry Hill, where Capt. Wolff lives, moved several times, lost his wife, married a Bingaman, went to Missouri, and at last came back and died here in 1862. Lewis Watkins was prominent in the history of Jefferson County for several years, living first in Moore's Prairie, then in Mount Vernon, and at last went back to Tennessee, leaving one child here—Margaret, wife of Green P. Casey, and mother of Lewis F. Casey, of Centralia.

Of those concerned in the public buildings: John Sanders was from Franklin County, his first wife, Nancy, a sister to Abraham and Joseph Estes. He was the first Constable, his appointment dating in June, 1819; next year he married a Miss Cox, soon after got license to keep tavern—somewhere in the south part of the county, and then we lose all trace of him. Henry Tyler, was the son of John Tyler, and John was a half-brother to James and Lewis Johnson. John Tyler and Lewis Johnson came from Sumner County, Tenn., in 1819. Henry married Catharine, daughter of Isaac Casey, lived awhile at the Brown place on the Salem road, and awhile where the eastern part of Mount Vernon is. He built a cabin east of where Thomas Hobbs lives; discovered the springs, but despised them because the water tasted "brackish," concluded his land would never be worth anything, and sold his pre-emption on the eighty acres to Thomas Tunstall for $92. He lived many years on the Centralia road, and died there in 1877. John C. and Isaac, of this county, are his sons; Mrs. Pat Ingram, of Richview, his daughter. He never had the headache in his life, but died of something like apoplexy. Oliver Morris, was son-in-law to Joseph Jordan. He was a man of some means, living in Moore's Prairie, where he built a brick house in 1823. He and Lewis Watkins were appointed Justices of the Peace before the county was organized; and Morris "swore in" the first officers. He went to Texas about 1831; there his only child married Crockett Glenn, a nephew to Davy Crockett. They all came back about seven years later, fearfully reduced in fortune Morris located on the high point east of the Benton road, about five miles south of Mount Vernon, where he died in August, 1839 John Wilkerson was brother to Henry as before stated. He first married Dicey Keelin, in Virginia, then a Mrs. Thomas, sister to Rhodam Allen and William Maxey's wife. Allen, father of H. H. W. Wilkerson, was a son of the first wife. Mrs. Thomas by her first husband had five children—Mrs. Thad Moss's grandfather, "Aunt Polly" Parker, and Edward Wilkerson's wife were of these. John's last set of children were Mastin, John, Ransom, Betsey Webber, Sallie Daniel, Jane Hill, Emily Hill and Patsy Lynch. So his descendants are all over the country. Zadok Casey, who occupied such a place in our history, is extensively noticed elsewhere in this volume.

CHAPTER III.*

CITY OF MOUNT VERNON—MORE ABOUT ITS EARLY CITIZENS—SOME PEN PHOTOGRAPHS—THE SECOND COURT HOUSE—MOUNT VERNON FROM 1824 TO 1830—A FEW OF THE OLD HOUSES—RELICS OF A BY-GONE PERIOD—MORE TOWNSHIP ITEMS, AND A TRIPLE WEDDING—LATER SETTLERS—COUNTY ROADS—THE FIRST CHURCHES OUTSIDE OF TOWN, ETC., ETC.

"All that I prized have passed away like clouds
Which float a moment on the twilight sky
And fade in night."—*Shreve.*

WE now go back to the fall of 1819. The only buildings in the town at this time are the court house, Burchett Maxey's, Lewis Watkins' and Clark Casey's. The place was overgrown with rank weeds and grass; and not a road led into it or out, except trails and foot-paths. William Casey's house, where the Commercial Hotel stands, was quite out of town. He now built out on the hill west of town, and Lewis Watkins left his half-finished shanty on the corner and moved into Casey's house. W. L. Howell came to town in 1820, and located in Watkins' house till he could put up some kind of a house on Lot 41, east of the court house. This man, William Lasater Howell, was the son of a wealthy farmer in Tennessee. The old gentleman lived in a large brick house on the turnpike, not many miles from Gallatin. We think no relatives of his came to this county except Mrs. Alexander, and she was not much honor to him. She said herself she had had eleven husbands, had no children to bind her to any of them, and was going to have another man or more if she saw any she liked. Howell taught a school at Union in 1822. He was Sheriff after Watkins. He was a nice man, but a bad manager; and was kept in office till he could not give security or file the necessary bond.

* By Dr. A. Clark Johnson.

He lived awhile in Jordan's Prairie, at the Whitesides place. While living here, his little boy of four years (Erasmus) was lost. Mrs. Howell started to the branch for water, and the little fellow undertook to follow. There were only paths—one to the branch, some to the neighbors, some cow-paths, etc.— and Erasmus took the wrong path. On her return, the mother missed him. She soon raised the alarm, but it was so near night that little could be done. Howell was at town with his horse and wagon; and he was so excited, on hearing the news, that he drove the horse home at full speed, and did not notice a large tree that had fallen across the road—horse and wagon jumping it together. For two nights and a day, the search was kept up. Green Casey then lived at the Maj. Frank Casey place; he went out to feed in the dusk of evening, and heard a child crying and calling in the woods, but fearing it might be a panther, he would not go near. Next morning, taking his gun, he went out, and there on the ground sat the child, quite exhausted and in despair. He looked as if he had given up and sat down to die. He was soon restored to his parents, and great was the joy among the friends. Howell, not long after, went back to Tennessee, then to Arkansas, and died in Scott County.

The same year, 1820, in the spring, Felix McBride came, took Clark Casey's lot—now the corner west of Nieman's—off his hands, and set up a grocery. We think McBride came with the Whitesides. He married Nellie Hensley, a sister to John and Leftridge Hensley, near Walnut Hill. She was the second woman buried at Union, "Aunt Milly" Tyler being the first. Her grave is close beside "Roaring Billy" Woods', and was covered with a brick arch of pretty neat workmanship. Their only child was soon after buried in the same grave. McBride enlarged the Clark Casey house to a double log building, with open passage, and nearly two stories high. On the death of his wife, he left here and married again, went to Galena, and was at length killed by a miner.

The next man was Elisha Plummer. Watkins returned to Tennessee, vacating the William Casey house; Plummer moved into it, and put up a rough blacksmith shop, just east of where the Methodist Episcopal Church stands. He did not stay long. His wife was a daughter of James Tally, and he and Tally went to the American bottom. At last accounts, Tally was keeping a boarding house in St. Louis. Next, Thomas Tunstall came, in 1821, and bought the "Kirby Tavern," as it was afterward called, and put up a log storehouse, where Herdman lives. Thomas came first, then the old people and his brothers. William Tunstall, the father, had his second wife, the first having died childless. They were familiarly called "the old Colonel" and "Aunt Sally." Aunt Sally was a Mrs. Whorl, of the Todd family; and, as we are told, was an aunt to Mrs. Lincoln. Tom's name was Thomas Todd. They were all Kentuckians. The old lady died in 1825, and the old Colonel went back to Kentucky, where he died a few years later. The Colonel drank, and was found dead in bed one morning. Their children were Thomas T., Edmund, George and Jane Webb. Thomas kept tavern and sold goods and groceries. He bought and sent South a great deal of stock. He could buy a good yearling for a set of plates, or a set of knives and forks, or a pair of shoes. While here he sent off no less than 1,500 head of cattle, and a good many horses. He gave Nolin forty cows and calves for a race-horse called Moneymolder. He had the treadmill erected, which stood just north of where Judge Pollock lives, bringing John Summers up from Shawneetown to superintend it. Not long after this, he went to Vicksburg, then to Little Rock, and among other adventures, won a steamboat at the card table. He bought a large body of land on White River, and laid out the town of Jacksonport. James and William were his oldest sons; one of his daughters was married to John Boyer, one to McHenry, etc. He died at Memphis during the war. Edmund married Miss Baugh at Vandalia, came to Mount Vernon in 1823, lived a while at the Howell House, east of the court house, and succeeded Burchett Maxey as tavern keeper at the H. T. Pace corner in 1824. He next went South, and died, and John Baugh went down—spring of 1828—and brought his widow back. She had two sons, Edmund and James. About thirty years ago, the boys went South; James became Captain of a steamboat on White River, fell overboard at Buffalo Shoals, and was never found. Mrs. Tunstall married a Hart. George, son of the old Colonel, went South, and Jane W. was married in 1824 to Dr. W. Adams. William Rearden came about this time, and put up two cabins on Lot No. 16, south and west of where Urry lives. He was a cabinet-maker, perhaps the first in the county, and his wife was a sister to Jarvis Pierce. His house was not only out of town, but entirely out of sight of town. He did not remain long. The preacher, better known as Col. Rearden, was his son.

This brings us up to the fall of 1823, with Plummer at the Casey house, Burchett Maxey at the H. T. Pace corner, Thomas Tunstall at the Kirby tavern, Edmund Tunstall east of the court house, McBride at the corner west of Nieman's, and Rearden away out in the brush southwest of town. All the rest of the town was in the brush, and these lots are only partly fenced, and that with crooked rail fences. The Clerk's office, too, on the north side of the public square, and Joel Pace living in it from the spring of 1822 to 1823, ought not to be forgotten.

But Joel Pace built a cabin about a hundred yards east of where Gen. Pavey lives; a new court house was built, and the old Clerk's office was left tenantless. This new court house was first determined on at the December term, 1821, William Casey, then one of the County Commissioners, being the ambitious man who ventured to propose it, and this was to be the fashion of it: "The wall to be built of brick, twenty-four by thirty feet, two stories high; the first story nine feet, the second seven and a half, two sets of joists to be put in, nine sixteen-light window-frames the lights eight by ten below, and eight twelve-light window-frames, lights same size above, two door-frames to be put in, four fire-places above, the house to have a good, firm, brick floor; the house to be well covered with good oak shingles without sap, the brick and timber to be of the best quality; the house completed * * * by next December term." McBride undertook the job, and handed it over the next summer to Thomas Jordan. McBride got $300, Jordan $202, and Edward Tunstall $110, when it was paid for. But it was not finished till the summer of 1823—nor even then. For, in 1829, an order was made for finishing the house—laying the upper floor, enlarging the hearth-boxes, putting stairs in the southeast corner, dividing the upper part into four rooms with dressed gum planks, ceiling the room with good shaved oak boards (four-foot boards split by hand, of course), putting in bricks that had fallen out, and painting the outside with three good coats of Spanish brown. John Wilkerson bid off the job of inside work at $89, which was done by Cannon Maxey and

Stephen Hicks, and the painting at $79.93¾, this part of the work being mostly done by Jarvis Pierce. The same year, 1829, the jail was moved to a place just east of the court house, and about fifteen feet from it, by Green Depriest.

Mount Vernon from 1824 to 1830.—In 1824, William Casey sold ninety rods off the west side of the southwest quarter of Section 29, to James Gray for $1,000. The conveyance ignores the existence of Mount Vernon right in the heart of the tract. This is what was laid out and added to the town in 1840, the whole forming "Storm's Survey." About the same tme, 1824, John Cooper, another blacksmith, came, and moved into one of Rearden's houses. He afterward went to the Henry Wilkerson place—of late, Jacob Stitch's—where Jonathan Wells had lived awhile and had built a shop. Another noted arrival about this time was a medical firm—Drs. Adams & Glover. They boarded awhile at Edward Tunstall's, the H. T. Pace corner, and when Tunstall left they bought the property. They soon after sold to Pace. Glover went to McLeansboro—then a bran new town—married a Miss Locke, and went to Missouri. Dr. Adams was from Alabama. When Glover left, or sooner, he married Jane Tunstall, October, 1824, and lived many years about town, part of the time two or three miles west of town; then went to the place in an arm of Moore's Prairie, where he died in January, 1873. Downing Baugh was also here, remained a year or two, married Milly Pace, went to Vandalia, and thence to Collinsville; then concluded to locate in Mount Vernon. He sold goods, and was for several years a Justice of the Peace. He built a store about where Seimer & Klinker now keep, in 1832; and he built the two-story frame on the north side of the square, that was burned before the Phœnix Block arose. He has ever been a zealous Methodist. He was appointed Judge of the Circuit Court, Twelfth Circuit, August 11, 1854, *vice* S. S. Marshall, resigned, and held the office till the election of Edwin Beecher, in 1855. He was pronounced one of the best judges of statute law in the State. He now lives in McGregor, Iowa, at the age of eighty-four years. His wife died here in May, 1846, and he married a Miss Sophronia Davis. His daughters were Mrs. H. H. Wilkerson, Mrs. J. J. Fly, Mrs. W. W. Thurston; his sons, Thomas J., John W. and Joel V. T. J. and Mrs. W. are dead. Jack and Moses Baugh were brothers to the Judge; Mrs. Edmund Tunstall, two Mrs. Foleys, of Galena, and Mrs. Buck Pace, of Salem, his sisters.

In the spring of 1825, William Flint built on Lot No. 19, and set up another grocery. The house is still standing, the first residence south of the Crews building. Perhaps Flint sold to D. Baugh. Baugh owned the place when H. T. Pace lived there. It was also in 1825 that Simon McClenden built a small frame house west of the court house. McClenden first settled in Moore's Prairie, then moved up to the Samuel Bullock place west of town, then to town. One of his daughters, Jane, married a Gilbert, and Polly Ann Billardy was the name of the other. Riley married a Quinn, then a Daniels, and is in Texas. Joseph Wilbanks came to town this season, and in the fall he went into the Thomas Tunstall or Kirby tavern, and kept it for about a year. The Wilbankses began to come in 1824, as will be seen in other chapters. Joseph Wilbanks bought Lot No. 9, the Thorn lot, from Pace, who transferred title bond from Edward Maxey, for $40, moved the Rearden house up here for a residence, and bought McClenden's house for a store room. He soon after went to South Carolina on business, and died there, leaving John, Luke, Quincy and Margaret, his children. Dr. Adams followed Joseph Wilbanks at the Tunstall House. But before Wilbanks bought McClenden's house, he, in partnership with a Mr. Hancock, sold goods at the corner—now east of Porter & Bond's drug store.

We will now finish the story of some of those first houses of the olden time. The log court house was sold to some man—perhaps William Hamblin,—who moved and rebuilt east of Hansackers. Capt. Newby bought the lot, and moved the logs down to his residence (now Capt. Gibson's), where, after various uses, they went into a "shuck" pen, a few remains of which were to be found there only a few years back. We don't know what became of the old Clerk's office; some tell us it was burned—catching fire from the burning prairie; and some that it was moved down to the lot where Wlecke's Hotel stands. A log house stood for years on that lot. Harvey Pace worked in it the first year that he lived in town. Dr. Adams lived there for a while. Mrs. Keller was born there, and it was in this house, or one erected on the corner north of it, that Daniel Anderson kept his first grocery. Of Thomas Tunstall's old tavern stand, perhaps enough has been said. After Wilbanks & Adams, E. D. Anderson kept there, 1830 to 1836, and James Kirby came in and bought it, and occupied it from 1836 till his death in 1844. The house that Watkins built at N. C. Pace & Co.'s corner, was used as a stable by John M. Pace—Jack Pace, as he was generally called, who kept a blooded animal there one spring and summer. It was then occupied as a stable by a Mr. Black. This man (James Black), had married Joseph Wilbanks' sister, and was carrying the mail from Shawneetown to St. Louis on horseback. Black was killed in the Black Hawk war; his widow married Compton, and died, and Compton married Miss Sarah Hawkins; then at Compton's death his widow married a Combs, father of Samuel. In 1828, this old house was moved to the corner where Porter & Bond's drug store stands, the first house on that corner, but was still used as a stable. No trace of it remains. Joel Pace bought the lot of James Gray in 1829, for $45, and built on it in 1831. The log house that Burchett Maxey built on the H. T. Pace corner, stood there till after H. T. Pace bought the lot. Indeed, Burchett had reared a two-story house just south of it, about 15x30 feet, longest from east to west, and had it inclosed and floored, a stairway up, etc.; and he sold the whole, houses and lot, to Pace, for $250, in 1827. Pace then, in 1830, built a store room in front, east of the log house, doing nearly all the work himself; rented it awhile to D. Baugh, then to E. H. Ridgeway, and began business in it himself in 1832. The log house was occupied for a time by W. W. Pace in 1829. From that he went to the Tunstall tavern, where he lived one year; then he went to the Wilbanks house west of the square, then to the Howell house east of the square, and then to Salem in 1834. But the old log house, after he left it, was bought by John Scott, and moved to the country. This last location was about south of the William Baugh house, where Cherry lives. Scott sold out to James Bowman, and Bowman was burned out in 1835. He had commenced a house in town in 1834, east of the square, and before it was nearly finished, sold to John Johnson, the writer's father, and now having no house instead of two. He rebuilt out east, and this second house stood within the memory of many of us. Wesley Johnson now lives in the house Bowman started east of the square. Joseph Wilbanks, as stated, bought the Rearden

J. G. Holland

house, and moved it up to the lot where Mrs. Thorn lives—Lot No. 9. Then in 1826, Harvey Pace built an addition for Wilbanks south of the old house, and Stinson Anderson in 1831; after he married Mrs. Wilbanks, built the part Thorn used for a shop. Thorn added the upper stories to these about 1855. The old Rearden house was moved back long before that for a kitchen, and is now "gone back" entirely. At Wilbanks' death, 1829, one-third of his north lot was sold to pay debts, and was used for a residence by various persons. In 1828, Uncle Isaac Casey and Joel Pace went into business in the Wilbanks storehouse, and continued there till Joel built at his corner lot in 1831. W. W. Pace bought part of the Wilbanks lot, including the residence; sold it to W. D. Isbell in 1832, for $125. Dr. Simmons lived there one summer; Dr. Moore got it, Lewis Moore got it, and at last Harvey Pace got it, bought the rest of the lot from Abner Melcher a few years later; and in the fall of 1844 moved the store to where it now stands, performing the office of milliner's shop, late dining-room. The old original William Casey house stood many years. After Plummer, Samuel Hirons occupied it, and many others succeeded him. Old Cesar lived there in 1834, and we know not how long before or after; and finally, L. C. Moss bought it, and moved it out to a place he had bought this side of where Mr. Tankersly lived. The Clark Casey house, west of Nieman's, was considerably enlarged by Felix McBride; but in 1824 Mrs. McBride died, and he left. He was followed by William Thacker, he by old Mr. Davenport, he by Samuel McConnell; he by old Mr. Boswell, father of Felix; he by Noah Johnston, and he by William Hickman, from Kentucky. Hickman came in 1836, built the large frame now occupied by W. E. Jackson, and sold to Witherspoon & Barker in 1837. W.

B. Scates moved it to where it now stands. Thomas Cunningham bought the old houses and rebuilt them where Charles J. Pool lives. Witherspoon staid a few years, married Lewis Johnson's youngest daughter, Susan, and went back to Kentucky. Barker, Wesley Barker, was a brother to William Casey's wife, and his wife was a sister to Robert Wingate. Wesley went to Louisville. We just now referred to W. W. Pace's having bought the Howell house; he built an additional room, and sold to Dr. Moore in 1835. Moore did not tarry long; went to Carlyle, then to Franklin or Columbus in Tennessee, then to St. Louis, where he became eminent. The Doctor sold out to John M. Pace late in 1835. Next year Pace went back to his farm, then came to the Joseph Wilbanks houses; returned to his farm, rented the old Howell house for awhile to Bowman, and finally, in 1836, sold it to Eli D. Anderson. Eli was succeeded by William Gibberson, a tailor, after whom a great number lived there, until Strattan demolished the house to "build greater," in 1859. We have dwelt on these details, because, if the record is not preserved here and now, the whole story is gone forever.

In 1819, October 5, the third wedding in the county occurred at William Maxey's, in Shiloh Township, and three couples were married at once. And two of the couples, Abraham T. Casey and wife and Bennett N. Maxey and wife, with Elihu Maxey and his wife, newly married, and just back from Tennessee, all settled in Sections 6 and 7 of Mount Vernon Township. A. T. Casey's wife was Vylinda Maxey. Bennett Maxey's wife was Sally Overbay, raised by Edward Maxey, but a daughter of James Overbay, and sister to Carroll Overbay; Coleman Smith's wife, Joel Harlow's, Fountain Jarrell's, Garland H. Jarrell's, James McIntire's,

Green Duncan's, Thomas Blaloch's, and—we believe that's all. Elihu Maxey's wife was Evaline Taylor. Well, A. T. Casey settled just north of where Windsor Pettit lives, and remained there till his death in 1834, and his family remained till old Mr. Lane bought the place. Elihu Maxey settled north of Casey, and south of where George Smith lives, and lived there till he was killed in October, 1853. Bennett Maxey settled a mile east of Pleasant Grove, and lived there till 1846, when he died. These young people, and Thomas Casey, just married to Harriet Maxey, and settled over the Shiloh line, made a good start in the world. They had cabins, some had floors in their cabins, some had pole bedsteads, and some slept on board pens, filled with leaves, on the floor; but all had plenty, and were happy. Deer, turkeys, bears, wolves and wild cats were always handy; and if there was no meat for breakfast, the man would bid his wife wait a few minutes, take down his gun, and directly bring in the game.

Dr. John W. Watson came to Illinois in 1821, arriving November 21. He lived on the Mulberry Hill until the next spring, when he, or rather John and Asa, built a large crib on the place a mile north of town, where he afterward lived. The crib had two or three apartments, one for grain, one for a toolhouse, etc., and into one of these they came and lived till a hickory log house could be raised, the same that Thomas Hunt tore down about twelve years ago. This year (1822), the Doctor rented ground from John Wilkerson near Union, and by the next he had opened land of his own. He was the first physician that was located in the county, and in that day he paid well for his drugs. An ounce of quinine that he got of Atwood, in St. Louis, cost him $10.50, and an ounce of veratrum that he got from Philadelphia, $40. He was County Assessor in 1822 and 1823, when his fees amounted to $17, and the whole revenue to $70. The home-dressed fawn-skin cover that he or his boys made for his Assessor's book is still preserved in the Clerk's office. Mrs. Watson died March 3, and the Doctor June 3, 1845. His children were John, who died in Virginia in 1803; Virginia, who was married to John Summers in 1824; John H., who married Betsy Rankin in 1827; William B., who married Margaret and afterward Sarah Leonard; Asa B., who married Diana Harr in 1833; Joel F., who is among us and well known; Amelia, who died single, and Horry M., who married Minerva Cummins. Joel Pace located on his farm adjoining Dr. Watson's in 1823, as before stated, and there reared a large family, lost his venerable companion in 1877, and himself died, in 1879, at the age of eighty-eight years.

In 1822, William Hix—as he spelt it, and Hicks as nearly everybody else spelt it—located and made an improvement four miles north of town. A man by the name of Lee came about the same time, and they had a little mill. Hix was related to Mrs. William Casey; what relation we cannot say, but she called him "Cousin Billy." He and William Casey and Joseph Jordan composed the second Board of County Commissioners. He sold his improvement to Azariah Bruce in the fall of 1823, and went to the "Western District" in Tennessee. About the same time (1823), Jarvis Pierce, Sr., formerly of New York, came up from White County, and moved into a cabin that stood south of the Hinman or Strattan place, a mile west of town. He was the father of Jarvis, Joseph and Henry, Mrs. Rearden, Mrs. Tolle, Mrs. Charles Mills; Mrs. Hick, afterward Mrs. John Storms; Mrs. Summers and Mrs. Martin Gillett. He did not stay long. Azariah

Bruce came in 1823, and succeeded William Hix on the Salem road, four miles north of town. He was a native of Halifax County, Va. He went to Tennessee, and married a Keelin in Wilson County. He served two terms as County Commissioner, lost his wife in July, 1853, and died himself in March, 1854. Of his children, Sally was married to Hardy Maxey; Nancy, to Harvey Pace; Polly, to Jehu Maxey; Betsy, to John Baugh now in Texas; Armstead W. lives in Wayne County; Marquis, north of Rome, in this county; John, in Gallatin; Leonard W., in Webber, and Savanner in this township; Melissa died in youth; Harmon died in Wayne County in 1868. Next year, 1824, John Summers, the Englishman whom Tunstall had brought from Shawneetown to superintend his mill, and who had just married Virginia Watson, bought Abram Casey out, and moved to the place two miles east of town, where he lived so long. Here he built a tread mill, and continued to improve it till at last he had a very good steam mill. He went to Texas, and died there. Of his descendants, only William's family and Jackson's family are here now. William and Jackson are dead, and Jackson's widow is the wife of James Brown, of Field.

Aaron Yearwood came in December, 1826. He was accompanied by his mother, with her two sons, Joseph and Robert, and by his brother William. With William came his wife's sister Betsy, now Mrs. Watson. The father of these ladies, Robert Rankin, Sr., came a year or so later, and after a short stay, went to Shelby County, but left here his son Robert and Mrs. Robert Yearwood. Old Mrs. Yearwood's husband's name was Frederic; she herself died in 1847. The next fall after Aaron's arrival, 1827, James Sursa, whose wife was sister to his wife and to Ward Webber, came out with his brother Jack Sursa. These men and one daughter were the children of Richard Sursa, who died in the war of 1812. Benjamin Webber came with the Yearwoods, married a Wilkerson, and settled at the Jordan or Coley Smith place on Seven Mile Creek. Ward Webber and John came three years later, 1829, the latter settling in the edge of Wayne County, while Ward located where Daniel Barfield afterward lived. Daniel was step son to James Sursa. About the same time, 1829, William Byers came to the place still known as the "Old Byers place." Mrs. Byers— "Aunt Nancy"—was sister to old Mr. Yearwood. Byers had a daughter already married to Joseph Brown. Pete Bruce, or Armstead W. and Moses Baugh, took one each, and the last girl (we suppose, not finding a B. to suit her) was married to Fountain Garrison. He and James Garrison came in 1827, and James died of small-pox a few years ago. James married a Wimberley; in two or three years after coming out, F. died.

CHAPTER IV.*

CITY OF MOUNT VERNON—THE DECADE FROM 1830 TO 1840—GROWTH OF THE TOWN—NEW BUILDINGS AND NEW BUSINESS—A LOOK BEYOND THE TOWN—BRIEF RETROSPECT—ANOTHER COURT HOUSE—SOME OF THE BUSINESS MEN AND WHAT THEY DID—STILL ANOTHER COURT HOUSE—THE JAIL—ORGANIZATION OF MOUNT VERNON TOWNSHIP—OFFICIALS, ETC.

"What is the city but the people?
True, the people are the city."—*Shakespeare.*

AS early as any of these, perhaps in 1825, Jacob Ford settled in a little cabin now better known as the Tommy Short place, north of the Coley Smith place, on Seven Mile, and here he was soon joined by Joab Peterson, a Swede; they had married sisters—cousins to old Mrs. Malone, by the way—and lived together for three or four years. The Garrisons, cousins to Isaac, etc., lived on the Herdman place. We may add that Aaron Yearwood ran the still-house on the creek for a year or more, Allen and John Wilkerson being the original owners. Aaron had no scruples about it till Abram Casey (A. T.) came in and mildly said, "Don't you think you are doing wrong?" Aaron reflected; conscience was not satisfied, he resolved to quit it, and did. Jack Sursa afterward operated there. James Sursa built a mill, which was extensively useful in its day; he was also County Commissioner for several terms. He died December 27, 1852, and Jack had been dead ten years the past August.

The Roads.—We have referred to the Goshen road and the trails and bridle paths that traversed the country. No road whatever touched Mount Vernon for a year or two after it was laid out. Even the new road or trail from Crenshaw's crossed the prairie nearly half a mile south of town, and went to Isaac Casey's house on the hill, where Beal lives. The history of our roads is given elsewhere, but we may here say that on the third day of the first term of the County Court, the subject of roads came before the Commissioners. Orders were made at that time, and in September and October, 1819, but without result; at length in February, 1820, a Board of Viewers, with Joseph Pace as Surveyor, located the road running diagonally across the county, near where it has ever since been, now running from McLeansboro to Centralia. In the spring of 1822, the Vandalia road was opened to the north line of Marion County, which was then an attached part of Jefferson, Elihu Maxey opening the first section, and William Maxwell the next. But the road was not used much, and was not fairly open until the fall of 1823, when Thomas Minor and Maxwell were ordered to cut it out twelve feet wide and keep it in repair. The next road was the Covington road, opened, after two or three fruitless orders, in the spring of 1824, not far from where the Richview road now runs. In 1826, by the influence of John Summers, the Fairfield road was opened, Summers being one of the Viewers and the first Supervisor. It ran nearly where it does now, except that it started out nearly due

*By Dr. A. Clark Johnson.

east from the court house. In 1828, the Covington road was vacated, and the Georgetown road was opened, now much better known as the Ashley or Nashville road.

The early religious settlers of the county, a majority of them, at least, were Methodists, several of them ministers. The next strongest denomination was the Baptist. Zadok Casey, Edward Maxey and Lewis Johnson were Methodist preachers; James E. Davis, a Cumberland Presbyterian, and Archibald Harris, a Baptist, but all, these, all the preachers in the county, lived in a mile of where Thomas Moss lives. The first religious society in Mount Vernon Township was the Baptist. It was organized in the old log court house in 1820. Chester Carpenter was holding a meeting at this time. The official members were Jacob Norton, Joseph Jordan, Oliver Morris and Overton Harlow. Not long after, a little log church was raised between where Isaac Garrison lives and the creek, this location being considered nearer the center of the population than the court house. Joseph Reid at the time lived in a small cabin near where Joseph Jordan and Frizell subsequently lived. This place of worship was not used as such more than a year or two, when the frequent floods in winter and spring proved that the site was not well chosen. The meeting was then, perhaps in 1823 or 1824, moved to William Hicks', two miles west of town, and continued there for five or six years. But in the spring of 1829, a very nice and spacious house, for that day, was built near the creek, the site now being inside the Fair Ground. Thomas Pace and others in town, who kept horses, had opened a road to the creek for the purpose of watering their horses. This road left the Shawneetown road not far from the Wyatt Parrish house, ran southeast near where Newby afterward built a horse-mill,

then nearly a due east course to the creek at a pretty deep hole called the horse hole. The road diverging from this one a quarter of a mile or less from the creek, and crossing at a ford below was of more recent date. On a rise north of the road near that horse hole this church was built. In the fall of the same year, an association met at this house, puncheon seats were provided and public services were held in the woods. Carpenter was pastor of the society first organized, and continued in the same situation, wherever the meetings were held, for ten or fifteen years. But perhaps we may as well finish this last house before we leave it. It was used regularly as a meeting place till 1835 –36, and the puncheons being preserved, services were held in the grove when the weather allowed. A season of foot-washing was occasionally appointed here and conscientiously observed. After societies were organized in other places and this house no longer met the demands of the church, it was sold; Capt. Newby bought it and converted it into a shop. He already had a small shop west of the road and nearly opposite his dwelling, and he put the second shop east of the road north of his dwelling, put up two forges in it and used it for years. It was in this house that George Starner worked for Newby, and here Jefferson Stephenson, afterward County Judge of Washington County, hammered iron for a long time after he came to Mount Vernon. Many of our readers will remember the church, and still more the shop.

The second Baptist Church in the county was erected near what was called the soap ford on the creek, less than half a mile north of the Fairfield road. It was reached from town by a trail that went by where Hobbs & Sons' mill now stands, by where Charley Patton lives, and so on to the creek, a trail frequently used by Capt. Sursa and others in the upper part of that settlement, coming to town. This church consisted of four large shanties standing about ten feet apart, forming an oblong square, with two halls crossing at right angles. The hall running north and south was closed at both ends. Of course it was the design to hold camp-meetings here, and several were actually held, one room or shanty being used for worship and the others used as camps. Meetings were held here regularly for years. This curious structure was built about 1833, and stood and was used for six years or more. Traces of it may still be seen there.

We left the various buildings and improvements in Mount Vernon about 1830, closing up the history of the first houses. In the meantime, other houses were coming on. George Pace married, lived awhile in the north room of the Kirby House, then built a chimney to Tunstall's old store room, on the lot where Herdman lives, and lived there a year; built a house on Bennett Maxey's lot, No. 1, now Crebs', and finally bought Lot No. 37, where the Prince House stands, built and moved there. The house he built on Lot No. 1 was occupied by many after he left it, but perhaps as much by a negro called Old Nick, as anybody else. Nick died there, and it was not used as a dwelling house afterward. Yet some have said that this house was the old Clerk's office, moved up there by Dr. Adams, and the same that Mrs. Crosnoe got torn down in 1841. George Pace sold his lot, now the Prince House, to John Van Cleve and went to Salem, as before noticed, in 1836. In the spring of 1829, Buck Pace, or W. W. Pace, by consent of John Tyler, who was agent for Nelson Ferguson and brother-in-law to both men, built a cabin on Lot No. 28, where the National Bank stands. Here Buck kept grocery. He or some one else subsequently built another cabin just east of this. Both were quite small, built of small logs and "skelped down." After Pace left, S. G. Hicks lived for a time in the corner house. By this time, however, Edward H. Ridgway had built a huge, hip-roofed house, in 1832, west of the square, where Hudspeth & Taylor keep. It was furnished with a store room, and here Hicks sold goods in 1834, 1835 and 1836, when he built a large frame north of the square, where Varnell's meat shop stands, Lot No. 25. Some years later, Hicks built a house near where the Methodist Episcopal Church stands. Benjamin Miller bought it in 1854 and moved it to his lot; Coffee enlarged it, and Maj. Summers now lives in it. (You see, we took up Hicks and ran clear away with him.) After he left the cabin on the Ferguson lot, Isaac Casey lived there, and in 1837, when Stinson Anderson came back from Alton, where he had been Warden of the penitentiary, he lived there long enough to build a cabin a little west of where Dr. Green lives. And there Anderson remained, out east of town, till he traded the farm to Edward Ridgeway for land in Elk Prairie. It was not long after Anderson left the Ferguson lot before John Rahm married Ellen Kirby, about 1837, and came to town about 1840, setting up business at the old house on the corner, which Kirby had already used for a grocery, but making great additions to it. After Rahm, John Bostwick went in with a grocery, and kept what some called a very disorderly house. As John is alive and we do not know how stout he is, we will not say much about it, but folks said that three or four old ladies went to his grocery one night, about 1849, took out his chattels to the middle of the street and tore the old house into a thousand pieces. It was never ascertained what ladies, if any, did it, but John left in disgust, went to Rome and had the first house built that Rome ever contained, Asa Watson being the boss carpenter.

In 1830, Dr. Adams built a house on Lot No. 26, where Goodale keeps. William Baldridge had bid off this lot at the first sale for $70, but lots declined. He sold it to H. T. Pace in 1825 for $20; he to Burchett Maxey in 1827, for $25; and he to Oliver Morris for $35. Dr. Adams built a house on it, but Downing Baugh soon after bought it, and Adams prepared to move to an improvement he had traded for west of town. But Thomas Minor had a claim against him, and put Stephen Hicks, who was Constable, after him with an attachment. Adams showed signs of resistance, and Hicks struck him on the throat with a rock, a blow that came near proving fatal. Adams now went to the cabin where Wlecke's hotel stands, then went—perhaps took the house with him--to the place where Old Nick died. Noah Johnston and William Bullock put up a two-story house, now owned by Russell Dewey and occupied by Hughes. Adams bought this frame and lived in it till he left town in 1835-36. Baugh built a store north of the square, about where Shepherd's drug store is, in 1832, and he built a two-story frame house a little east of it; but he sold these, rented Van Cleve's house, and a Dr. Allen came into the old house, built a porch to it, inclosed the porch, putting in a glass front, and the house then went by the name of the glass house. As we have mentioned Noah Johnston and William Bullock, we may add that they came to Bullock's Prairie in 1831, and that Johnston came to town in 1833, sold goods some time where the Crews building stands, some time in 1834-35, at the next corner west, Lot No. 21, lived awhile at the Ridgway building, where Hudspeth & Taylor's store also stands, and finally bought and located where he now lives. William Bullock first lived in a cabin that he built near this end of the Spiese farm, some sign of his shop being still discoverable in the road there. He then came to town and had his blacksmith shop almost in the middle of the block south of the square, on the "big road." The south part of town was all open, and the road came directly toward the court house. His dwelling house was located where Bob Wilbanks lives, but he died at Noah Johnston's.

Somewhere back in the olden time, Green Daniel built a cabin on John Johnson's (the writer's father), Lot No. 18, corner of Jordan and Washington streets, and lived there for several years. Samuel Goodrich afterward lived there for some time. It was still later, perhaps, that Mr. Goodrich built a small house south of where Westbrook's mill was burned, near the northwest corner of Curtis Johnson's lots, and not far from the same time that Allen Stanton, a shoe-maker, built near the southwest corner of the same lots. These houses were all pretty good forty to forty-five years ago. As old as Green Daniel's cabin, was a shop that John Williams built northeast of the court house. John built this house about 1830-31, used it for a time, made a visit to Tennessee and never came back. He was brother to Mastin Wilkerson's wife. So the shop stood there until Bowman built a frame house in front of it, and sold the lot, or let Rhodam Allen sell it to John Johnson. The writer's father bought it in 1834, finished the house, used the old shop awhile for a kitchen, built or had Wm. Yearwood to build a new kitchen, that still stands there, and we believe moved the shop on to some of his lots. About the time that we came, perhaps in the spring of 1834, James Ross, a hatter, moved in, lived a year in the old house north of Herdman's, then got Lot No. 44, the south lot under Strattan & Johnson's block, built the log house that Mr. Schanck took away twelve years ago, and after awhile succeeded in trading for Daniel Anderson's grocery that stood on the corner, where he erected a large frame building for a shop. In this period also comes the grocery built by A. D Estes at the Crews corner. Joseph Estes, Absalom's father, had long owned the next lot west, and when Absalom married he built a small house there, where Morgan & Reid's shop stands, and painted it red, and it was universally known as the red house. Absalom also set up the grocery at the corner. Edward Wells kept a grocery there for a time. This house on the corner remained *in statu quo* till Robert Castles got it in 1840, built a room west, a dwelling in the rear, etc. And thus it stood till Crews got it. It was also in 1834-35 that W. B. Thorn bought the lot second from the corner south of Hobbs' mill. He got it from the writer's father for $100. He then erected a large blacksmith shop in front, one that he had brought from beyond Jordan's Prairie, and a very neat hewed-log house back for a dwelling. In 1837, John Johnson built a hewed-log house where Taylor's Hotel stands, and Thomas B. Johnson and Dr. Greetham used it for a year or two for an office and drug store; then Thomas went to Kentucky and Mr. Thorn put up a harness and saddle shop in the house. Thorn had converted the former blacksmith shop into a dwelling. In 1841, he sold it to William Edwards and moved to the house that still stands just west of Merrill's livery stable. We remember but two other houses of this period, the Poteet house and the Lamar house. Alfred Poteet, in 1835-36, built where E. M. Walker lives and lived there while he remained in Mount Vernon, but the house afterward fell into the hands of Josiah Melcher, and he moved it up and made a stable of it on the west end of what is now known as the Thorn lot, and it still stands there. The Widow Lamar had two sons, Shelby and James. The boys built a cabin on John Johnson's lot south of the jail; it was occupied by them, Mrs. Foley, Blackhawk Williams, Sullins, Decoursey and many others, and only twelve or fifteen years ago passed away.

A little later and on up to 1840, houses began to be numerous. Dr. Greetham built the house where Urry lives and went into it from where Mrs. Thorn lives, in 1839. W. A. Thomas built just north of Greetham's, now Hitchcock's, in 1840. The same year, or the next, the Rev. A. E. Phelps built the house Conger lived in till lately, on the south end of Casey street, and Henry Pierce the house across the street east of Urry's, and Ridgway put up the four houses where J. R. Palmer, Peter Brown, etc., live, long known as the Ridgway Row. Jarvis Pierce erected the tavern that stood opposite the present site of the Methodist Episcopal Church, sold to Eli Anderson and he built a two-story house north of Phelps'; Anderson improved his tavern and Grant added rooms to the east end of it at a later date by moving a schoolhouse in from the woods near Noah Johnston's. Little, a tailor, put up Joel Watson's house in 1839; Daniel Baltzell the house just across Union street west of Joel's; and Rufus Melcher the house recently torn down by Mrs. Baltzell. The old Methodist Church went up from 1836 to 1840, to which the parsonage north of it was added under the regime of J. H. Dickens; the third court house was built, etc. D. Baugh built the house that stood where Heiserman's new brick is going up, Thomas Cunningham the house that stood where Charley Pool lives, M. Tromley the old house north of Latham's,

Isaac Faulkenberry the old house that stood on the east end of Latham's lots, and John Livingston the one that stood where George Ward lives. The Cesar and Guyler cabins went up near where is now the Baptist Church. W. Prigmore built the house now better known as the Klinker House, north of the Prince house, and Johnny Smith the old house that stood on the corner of Walsh's lots. Thomas Pace put a house on the lot west of the old Odd Fellows Hall, now Mrs. Pace's, McAtee got it *et al.*, and it formed part of the old Bogan houses near the Supreme Court House. Hiram McLaughlin put one on the east side of Casey street, opposite George Haynes', Gray got it, Nelson got it, and it now forms part of the residence of Jeremiah Taylor. From all this it appears that this was an era of unusual prosperity in Mount Vernon, and this will be in part explained by taking another look at what has been going on outside of the town.

We have already stated that not an acre of land was entered in the township for seven years after the county was organized and the town laid out. This was caused by the pressure referred to elsewhere, growing out of the re-action that followed the inflation at the outset. The first entry was then made by Isaac Casey, 1826, in Section 18, now part of Lewis Johnson's farm. A. T. Casey in Section 7, was the next man, 1829; Azariah Bruce, 1830, entered in the same section, and Thomas D. Minor, the same year, in Section 19. Still it went slow; land was plenty and a man settled wherever he pleased, stayed as long as he pleased, and ejectment was unheard of. In 1831, Bennett N. Maxey entered in Section 7; in 1833, James Susca and William B. Watson in 21; Isaac Hicks in 31, and E. D. Anderson in 32, and Dr. Adams in 29, in 1835. Then everything went with a rush. In 1836,

Overton Harlow entered in Section 2, Elihu Maxey in Section 6, T. M. Casey, M. Bruce and C. H. Maxey in 7; Benjamin Webber in 14; Brewneaty Wilkey and Lewis Johnson, Jr., in 18; John Livingston, David Hobbs and Z. Casey in 19; Z. Casey in 20; Coleman Smith in 22; John Summers in 23; Calton Summers and John, in 27; W. B. Watson in 28; H. T. Pace, D. Baugh and S. H. Anderson in 29; William Bullock and Isaac Casey in 30; Thomas E. Pace in 31; and J. Johnson in 33, etc. In 1837, Harlow entered more land in Section 2; Elihu Maxey and W. F. Johnson entered in 5; John Dodds in 10; Henry D. Allen in 11; James M. Bridges in 13; Matilda Massey and William Byers in 18; Thomas Cunningham and Priscilla Meek in 19; Virginia Summers in 22; T. Cunningham in 27; W. B. Watson, John Summers and S. H. Anderson in 28; Asa B. Watson, E. H. Ridgway, Thomas E. Pace, John Johnson and Cephas A. Park in 29; T. Cunningham in 31; and H. B. Newby and E. H. Ridgway in 33. In 1838, James Newby entered in 14; A. M. Grant in 15; William Byers in 18; Joel Pace in 20, and D. Baugh in 28. But 1839 was as fast as 1838 had been slow. Simeon Walker entered in Section 1; Hiram Duncan in 2; O. Harlow in 10; H. Duncan and Mary Ann Summers in 11; M. A. Summers in 12; D. Summers and Meredith Strickling in 13; D. Summers and J. Newby in 14; John Hart, Martha Grant, Freeman Burnet and David Stewart in 15; Abraham Buffington in 18; Armstead W. Bruce, James Sursa, Daniel Barfield, Aaron Yearwood and Robert B. Rankin in 21; Moses Kirby in 22; John W. Summers in 23; Benton Y. Little in 26; William Marlow and George W. Summers in 27, etc.

The above is for reference, and not to be committed to memory. It shows, too, that up to 1840 no land was entered in Sections 3, 4, 8, 9, 16, 17, 24, 25, 34, 35 or 36. Many of these were already settled upon their entries, and some had been occupying them for many years.

We have now reached a period when individual arrivals and buildings did not amount to so much. But before bidding adieu to the past, we present a brief *resume*, in different form, of the last ten years' business. Joel Pace, merchant, licensed March, 1831, remained till 1837, when he sold out to Randle & Grant; then I believe Grant bought Randle out in 1838; D. Baugh, licensed March, 1831, still in business, 1840; Henry Isbell, of Belleville, or his sons, 1831, kept a few months at the corner west of Nieman's; E. H. Ridgway, licensed 1831 and again 1833, was in partnership with Eli Anderson in 1837, opposite the present site of the Continental. In 1832, W. W. Pace and Harvey T. were licensed as merchants; in 1833, H. B. Newby came in when Isbell went out, and in 1837 he had merchant's license. In 1834, Noah Johnston was licensed; next year it was Thompson & Johnston; in 1836, Thompson and Johnston were again separate, after which both disappeared from the record as merchants. Johnston first kept at the Crews corner, then Thompson & Johnston at the Hudspeth & Taylor corner. Dr. Adams held forth on the west side, renewing his license in 1836. Sanderson & Estes, 1834, kept at the National Bank corner; then Estes alone at the Crews corner. In 1835, John M. Pace comes in, but soon goes back to his farm; W. W. Pace comes in for a year, and switches off; B. Wells and A. D. Estes take out a merchant's license each, mostly selling—not dry goods, but to dry customers. In 1836, the licensed men of the town were Hickman & Witherspoon, L. C. Moss, A. B. Watson and James Kirby. In 1837, Bowman takes license; so does Mr. England, Cunningham & Shields followed Adams; S. G. Hicks followed Thompson; Barker followed Hickman, and Davis & Dodds went in on the west side. In 1838, W. S. Van Cleve followed Davis & Dodds, and William Dishon opened up at the Crews corner. In 1839, Van Cleve was succeeded by Addison, Daniel & Co. And we may as well add here that for the last ten or fifteen years, we mean prior to 1840, peltry was the chief staple of the country. Sometimes it seemed to be the only thing anybody had to sell or to buy goods with. Merchants sent deer hides to St. Louis by the hundred, some shaved, some with hair on. The shaving was done fast and cheap. A man hung a hide up by the neck, took a knife and scraped upward, and literally "made the fur fly;" and scraping a deer's hide was considered to be worth from 3 to 5 cents.

In 1840, the principal event was the building of the new court house. The old one never was really finished till now. It had long been considered unsafe, but the county court would not undertake a new one. But one bright, still morning in 1839, after "a calm, still night," it was found that the house had partly fallen down. There was a hole in one side big enough for a wagon to drive through. Nobody seemed to know how it had happened, but there was no doubt now; it had to come down. So everybody in town got out with ropes, which they ran in at one window and out at another; everybody pulled and halloed, and soon it was only a pile of rubbish. The town was full of dust and noise and fun. The county court thereupon, March 7, 1836, made the following order:

"Ordered the Clerk advertise in the *Western Voice* at Shawneetown and the *State Register* at Vandalia that this court will at the next June term receive sealed proposals for the building of the brick court house on the public square in Mount Vernon, and that Noah Johnston, John W. Greetham, Downing Baugh and A. M. Grant, who in connection with the Clerk of this court, shall constitute a committee whose duties shall be to superintend the advertising, planning and building of said house, subject at all times to the direction of the court and liable to be removed by said court."

Still the Commissioners, Barton Atchisson, James Sursa and William Bullock, did not fully surrender their authority to "said committee." They all mounted horses and rode to Carmi, examined the court house there, thought it good enough, and in spite of the earnest protest of the committee, determined to take it as a pattern. So that, June 5, 1836, it was "Ordered by the court that the Clerk shall advertise in the Shawneetown newspaper that they will let on the 20th of July the building of a court house in Mount Vernon on the plan of the court house at Carmi, Ill., and of the same size and finish." William Edwards got the contract at $5,500. He was an Englishman, married Sarah Hyde in London, came to Washington, there got acquainted with Gov. Casey, bought land of him in Grand Prairie and moved out just in time to get this contract. He was a Methodist preacher; of his family let us further say, that Francis H., his oldest son, finished his education here, became a physician, married Miss M. E. Hicks and died recently at Sandoval. Joseph, the youngest son, also a physician, married Miss Higgins and lives at Mendota; and the daughters married William Kidd, William McLaughlin and William Gibberson. The court house was finished in 1840. But the county was hard run to pay for it. Orders were issued for small sums, but these were not quite satisfactory. In December, 1840, the Legislature was petitioned for authority to borrow money, and in May, 1841, the Clerk, E. H. Ridgway, was authorized to make a loan of $2,200 at the Bank of Illinois at Shawneetown. But not till October 14, 1841, was the final settlement made. It then appears that Edwards had drawn in orders $3,061.61; he took notes on different parties to the amount of $474.86, and four bonds due June 8, 1846, for the remainder. This settlement did not settle. In September, 1842, Edwards returned the orders and bonds and took five $500 bonds, bearing 12 per cent, due June 8, 1848, 1849, 1850, 1851, 1852. This court house was forty feet square, square roof, cupola supported by pillars and surrounded by railing, court room below, Judge's seat on north side, stairways in southwest and southeast corners, floor, half brick outside bar, bar cut off by railing with gates, four rooms for offices above, front door south, plain doors east and west. Cattle and sheep used the old house all through vacations, but by the efforts of Dr. W. S. VanCleve, the public square was now fenced for the first time, and the bushes and weeds cut. So it looked well.

About the time of the court house excitement, the Methodist Church was finished, the old Academy was built and the town was incorporated, but these will come up under the heads of churches, schools and city government. It was in the time of this prosperity, all in five or six years, that Jonas Eddy, Castles, Baltzell, Phelps, Dr. Short, Schanck, Hinman, Thomas, Clement, Dick Nelson, Haynes, Robert Wingate, Shaffner, Scates, Dr. Caldwell, Dr. Roe, Dr. Gray, Rahm, Stephenson, Palmer, Barrett, Tromley, Alexander Barnes, and many others located in Mount Vernon. Then followed nearly ten years with much of the slow and heavy movement of the olden times. The pulse quickened a little when the Central Railroad Company was chartered, but became irregular again as soon as it was located. Among the accessions to our population worthy of note were Dr. Green, Tanner, Mills, Thatcher, Preston, McAtee, Bogan and Condit.

There is not much to add respecting the general history of Mount Vernon. Most of what remains to be told is included in the various sub-headings that follow, or is sufficiently set forth in the biographical and other departments of this work. A general outline reaching up to the present may be given in few words. The most conspicuous improvments in 1854 were the Johnson House and the Methodist Episcopal Church. John N. Johnson came to town a few years before, with little means, practiced medicine a while, got a small stock of goods, managed with eminent judgement, won everybody's confidence, built up rapidly, and by a very large purchase of hogs in the fall of 1853, made about $5,000. With part of this money he built the hotel that bore his name for several years, but has been most recently known as the Commercial Hotel. He died the next winter, and the business, the church, the lodge, the town, the whole country, felt the loss. In 1857, Strattan and Pavey came out from Ohio, bought the farm of John Johnson, the writer's father, southeast of town, traded it to Thorn for a very large stock of goods, and from that time to the present, Strattan & Pavey, in conjunction with Fergerson, Allen, Taylor, Westbrook, and other associates, have occupied a very large space in our little business world and contributed largely to the growth of the town and the development of the country. Strattan & Fergerson built the store now occupied by J. D. Johnson in 1859, and Strattan & Johnson the three-story block south-east of the public square in 1872, both the Johnsons just named being sons of John N. Johnson above mentioned, and the last named, Alva C., being Strattan's son-in-law. Pavey & Allen built the store now occupied by Hudspeth, Taylor & Company, in 1875, and Strattan his residence in 1873. George H. Varnell was the next important accession to the ranks of business—proving indeed an accession to the town and the entire vicinity. He is brother-in-law to John S. Bogan, who has been so intimately connected with our history for thirty years, and came from Washington City in October, 1861. In the winter of 1862–63, Joseph J. Hollomon came from near Humboldt in Tennessee. He had bought of Mr. Elder, of Gibson County, Tenn., thirteen tracts of land in Franklin, Jefferson and Washington Counties, containing about 1,300 acres, for something over $13,000. He erected a tobacco warehouse east of town, now inside the city limits, and did a lively business here until it was burnt down in 1864. He and Varnell built the "New York Store," northeast of the public square, in 1863, and the mill now owned and run by Hobbs & Son in the same year. Hollomon sold out to Varnell in 1865 and returned to Tennessee. Varnell pushed along. He built the Continental Hotel in 1877 to 1880, and the block north of the Episcopal Church in 1872. Henry W. Seimer came earlier than some of those just mentioned, built up a fortune gradually, and has contributed much to the improvement of the town and the activity of its business. A tailor by trade, he has shown himself fitted for other kinds of business, and has succeeded in all. In March, 1869, the old court house was burnt, and the officers found rooms in the Phœnix Block, and the court a room in the Presbyterian Church. At the September term, 1870, the Board of Supervisors ordered an election on the question of building a new court house to cost not over $30,000; and in April, 1871, a contract was made with W. E. Gray, of Alton, at $29,315. The Building Committee were G. W. Evans, Q. A. Wilbanks, Samuel Johnson, D. H. Warren, John C. McConnell and Henry Breeze, and the house was to be finished by March 1, 1872. The rest of its story is well known. The new jail was erected in 1872-73. The town received a wonderful impetus from the railroad as long as it was a terminus, over seventy houses being built in as many weeks.

The township was known in land descriptions, but had no political existence for many years. In August, 1841, James Sursa, Aaron Yearwood and Armstead W. Bruce were appointed Trustees of school lands in the township, like Trustees being appointed at the same time for all the townships.

The growth of townships as political divisions was very gradual. For twenty years at all general elections, everybody voted at Mount Vernon. But it was necessary to have districts for magistrates and constables, and for these officers to be elected within the districts. In a preceding chapter, these different divisions are given from the formation of the county down to the time of township organization.

September 10, 1869, S. F. Grimes presented to the county court a petition for township organization, as stated in the chapter on organization of the county, and an election was ordered for November. The result was 1,330 for, and 633 against, out of a total vote of 2,182. D. C. Jones, William Kirk and G. L. Cummins were appointed Commissioners to lay off townships. At the March term, 1870, they reported Grand Prairie, Rome, Field, Farrington, Casner, Shiloh, Webber, Blissville, Allen, Bald Hill, Anderson, Spring Garden, Moore's Prairie, each including an exact township; Mount Vernon, including Township 2, Range 3, and all of Township 3, Range 3, west of Muddy; and Pendleton, Township 4, Range 3, and all of Township 3, Range 3, east of Muddy. At the next June term, Anderson was changed to Elk Prairie and Allen to McClellan; and at the September term, Dodds was formed of Township 3, Range 3. The first Board of Supervisors were Jacob Breeze, S. V. Bruce, W. S. Bumpus, G. L. Cummins, W. A. Davis, G. W. Evans, E. B. Harvey, Samuel Johnson, W. A. Jones, John C. McConnell, J. R. Moss, M. A. Morrison, J. B. Ward, D. H. Warren, Q. A. Wilbanks, and after Dodds was formed, R. D. Roane.

The Supervisors of Mount Vernon have been, 1870-71, D. H. Warren; 1872-73, 1876 and 1877, J. D. Johnson; 1874, G. H. Varnell; 1875, T. H. Hobbs and J. D. Robinson; 1878, John Klein; 1879, John Gibson; 1880, 1881 and 1882, W. H. Herdman; 1883, T. E. Westcott.

CHAPTER V.*

MOUNT VERNON—ITS RELIGIOUS HISTORY—THE METHODISTS, THE PIONEERS OF CHRISTIANITY IN THE COUNTY—A LIST OF MINISTERS—THE FIRST CHURCH—PRESBYTERIAN CHURCH—BAPTISTS—CATHOLICS AND OTHER DENOMINATIONS—CHURCHES OF THE TOWNSHIP—SCHOOLS IN AND OUT OF THE CITY, ETC., ETC.

"God attributes to place
No sanctity, if none be thither brought
By men who there frequent."—*Milton.*

AT the conference of the Methodist Episcopal Church which met in the fall of 1819, David Sharp was sent as Presiding Elder, with five circuits in this State—Illinois, Okaw, Cache River, Wabash and Mount Carmel. On the Wabash was Thomas Davis, and he included the church at Old Union in his work. The next year, fall of 1820, two circuits were added to the Illinois District—Sangamaugh and Shoal Creek. Davis went to Cape Girardeau, and Hachaliah Vreedenburg and Thomas Rice came to Wabash. In the general minutes for 1822, Mount Vernon first appears upon the record: Illinois District, Samuel H. Thompson; "Wabash and Mount Vernon, Josiah Pattison and William Smith." These were followed by Smith and Ruddle in 1823; these by William Moore in 1824; he by Orceneth Fisher in 1825 for part of the year, Philip Cole a few months and John T. Johnson for the remainder of the year. In 1826, Thomas Files was sent to the Mount Vernon Circuit, Charles Holiday being Presiding Elder of the Wabash District. For several years we were in the Wabash District, then for several in the Kaskaskia District, before a Mount Vernon District existed.

The following is a very nearly correct and complete list of the Methodist preachers here from 1825 to the time Mount Vernon Station was formed in 1854; the date given being that in which the conference year began, in autumn: 1826–27, Thomas Files; 1828–29, John Fox; 1830–31, John H. Benson; 1832, Simeon Walker; 1833, James Walker; 1834, Warren L. Jenkins; 1835, —— Collins, one round, or month, and Joshua Barnes for the rest of the year; 1836, William Mitchell; 1837, David Coulson; 1838, James M. Massey; 1839, John Shepherd; 1840, William T. Williams; 1841, James M. Massey; 1842, James H. Dickens; 1843, James I. Richardson; 1844, Allison McCord; 1845, Reuben H. Moffitt; 1846–47, Arthur Bradshaw; 1848, David Blackwell and John Thatcher; 1849, I. C. Kimber; 1850, John Thatcher; 1851, James A. Robinson; 1852, John H. Hill; 1853, Thomas W. Jones; 1854, Norman Allyn.

For many years the Methodists had no house of worship in Mount Vernon. The ministers preached at Old Union, and the people walked out from town. Sometimes services were held in the court house, sometimes in private houses. In 1834, I think my father's and Downing Baugh's were the only Methodist families in town; but very soon re-enforced by James Ross. They determined to build. September 8, 1835, James Gray conveyed what is now Lot No. 1 in Block 19 —the Episcopal Church lot—to John Johnson, Thomas M. Casey, Joel Pace, David

* By Dr. A. Clark Johnson.

Hobbs, Downing Baugh, Joseph Pace and James Ross, as Trustees, etc. Here they built a small, plain house, with no pretense of a steeple or bell, and with very plain benches to sit on. It had one coat of plaster and a small box of a pulpit. But preaching was had here monthly, the Sunday school and prayer meeting sometimes, and occasionally some other kind of meeting. We had no Sexton, so the house was not very well kept, and the first one to come, on preaching days, generally swept the house and made a fire. One very cold winter morning we found the door standing open—and it may have been open a week, for it was out of town and nobody passed that way—and the first act in the drama was to drag a dead calf out. It had taken refuge from the storm within the open door, and died there, perhaps several days before. The roof was of boards, and soon warped, so as to let in some rain and a good deal of snow. This made it bad on us, especially in winter. John Van Cleve once came to hold quarterly meeting. It had snowed. Judge Baugh had a big dog. McKay was a tall, lank, sickly, weak-minded fellow, dressed in rags; and Baugh's dog had a mortal hatred for McKay. That morning both were at church. As the room got warm, the snow overhead melted, and chunks of plaster fell. Baugh's dog thought it was McKay, so he bristled up and growled. Other chunks fell, and the dog got up, looked daggers at McKay and growled. At the third racket, the dog jumped up, barked furiously and made for McKay in a way that made him stretch his long legs over the benches with a very unusual show of activity. It almost broke up the meeting, as the people all smiled very loud.

In 1840, funds were raised to fix up this church, adding ten or twelve feet to the east end, putting a belfry on it, a new roof, etc.

Before it was done, Circuit Court came on, and as the old court house had fallen down, court was held in the still unfinished church—the only room in town big enough. While the court was in session, Abraham Lincoln and John A. McClernand, Presidential Electors, Whig and Democratic, came to address the people. McClernand occupied the noon hour or two intermission, but when Lincoln's turn came, politics were summarily put out, and court began. Scates, the Judge, and Bowman, the Sheriff, were Democrats; perhaps this was why. But Mr. Kirby said he was "for fair play, even in a dog fight;" so he invited Lincoln and everybody to the shade in front of his hotel, got a huge goods box, Lincoln mounted it, and the crowd listened and laughed and swore at him for another hour or two. Court over, the house was finished, having, besides the improvements named, a much larger pulpit, and here a large variety of meetings were held, besides the regular services.

At length, a desire sprang up for better quarters. The church resolved to build. July 18, 1853, a deed was obtained from Ambrose C. Hankinson, of Peoria, to the Trustees—Downing Baugh, Darius C. Warren, William J. Stephenson, Lucilius C. Moss, John N. Johnson, Joel F. Watson and Charles T. Pace—conveying Lots No. 65, 66, 71, 72, the present site of the Methodist Episcopal Church. The church was erected in 1854, at a cost of over $4,000. So it remained, with minor improvements from time to time, till they put an end to it—in fact, put two ends to it and a new steeple in 1881-82, at a cost of over $4,000 more.

In September, 1854, the Southern Illinois Conference met at Mount Vernon, and at this session the society at Mount Vernon became a station, with eighty-four members and eleven probationers. John H. Hill was Presiding Elder of the district, and James Leaton was appointed to the station. This man Leaton was an Englishman; a thorough scholar; had been a hard case in youth; had later been Professor in McKendree College, and was the most lucid speaker and the most perfect pronouncer we ever heard. He still preaches up North. The official members were John Johnson, L. E.; Zadok Casey, L. D.; John H. Watson, H. Davisson and Samuel Schanck, Class Leaders; and the Stewards first elected were Zadok Casey, Joel F. Watson, John N. Johnson, Charles T. Pace and Downing Baugh. At the first quarterly conference, the Sunday school report showed seventy-five scholars, ten teachers. The allowance for the Presiding Elder was $41.40; for the preacher in charge, as salary, $272; table expenses, $150; traveling expenses, $50. In August, 1858, the quarterly conference discussed the subject of a return to the circuit, but action was postponed. The question came up again at the fourth quarterly conference, 1861, and the church here again become a part of Mount Vernon Circuit. So it remained till the annual conference of 1865, when it again became a separate station, and continues.

The stationed preachers here have been—coming about September each year—1854, James Leaton; 1855, Norman Allyn; 1856, Ephraim Joy; 1857, James Leaton; 1858, Thomas A. Eaton; 1859-60, R. H. Manier; 1861, M. House; 1862, G. W. Hughey, who left early in the spring because the place was, politically, too hot for him, and was succeeded by John Ellis; 1863-64, John H. Hill; 1865, D. Chipman, whose health failed in six months, and Thomas H. Herdman took his place; 1866-67, B. R. Pierce; 1868, John Leeper; 1869-70-71, Joseph Harris; 1872-73, D. W. Phillips; 1874, N. Hawley; 1875-76-77, C. E. Cline; 1878-79-80, C. Nash; 1881-82-83, John W. Locke. The Presiding Elders, most of whom removed to Mount Vernon, have been John H. Hill, George W. Robins, James A. Robinson, J. P. Davis, Z. S. Clifford, B. R. Pierce, L. C. English, J. Leeper, B. R. Pierce again, C. E. Cline, C. Nash. The most prosperous period in the history of this church was when C. E. Cline was pastor. The former parsonage, on Lots No. 24 and 21—east half of 21—was transferred to the circuit September 19, 1855, and the site of the present one, Lots No. 64 and 73, Block 11, was bought of Dr. Dixon March 23, 1867. The present parsonage was built in 1877; cost, $1,100. The church now has about four hundred members enrolled, two hundred scholars and nineteen teachers in the Sunday school; pays its pastor $1,000, and expends about $1,000 on other religious and benevolent objects; pays $100 on the Presiding Elder's salary.

The Presbyterian Church.—The growth of the Presbyterian Church in Illinois has been more gradual—perhaps, also, more solid—than that of some others. Up to 1829, the Presbyterians were included in the Missouri and Wabash Presbyteries, each of which lay mostly beyond the State lines. October 28, 1828, the organization of Central Presbytery was authorized, and it was organized in January, 1829. It was central because it lay between the Missouri and Wabash. In September, 1831, the Synod of Illinois was formed, with Presbyteries of Illinois, Sangamon, Kaskaskia and Missouri, Kaskaskia Presbytery, to which this part of the country belonged, having been formed in 1830. In 1838, the division of the Presbyterian Church into Old and New School took place, Mount Vernon Presbyterians, the few that were here, being of the Old School. B. F. Spillman organized a church here in 1841, with ten members and two Elders. This church

was served, more or less regularly, by Mr. Spillman, Alexander Ewing, Blackburn Leffler, and others, Leffler residing for several years in Mount Vernon. The Kaskaskia Presbytery held its spring session here in 1846; Judge Scates and Jonas Eddy were the principal members. But the church never became strong; and in April, 1852, upon the request of the members, the Presbytery—of Kaskaskia—dissolved the church, and the members transferred their membership to the Church of Gilead, at Rome. Thus ended the Old School organization at Mount Vernon.

Alton Presbytery, New School, now gave us some attention, and February 21, 1854, Robert Stewart effected an organization. The first list of members included Warner and Eliza White, John S. and Louisa M. Bogan, George and Hannah Mills, John C. and Juliana Gray, Sarah A. Tanner and William D. Johnston. The Elders were Miles White and Bogan. Other Elders: T. Condit, April 29, 1855, died April, 1861; James F. Fitch; Samuel Gibson and W. B. White, January 2, 1870; S. B. Kelso, December, 1874; James M. Pollock, July 25, 1876. The pastors have been Samuel R. H. Wylie, a native of Logan County, Ky., who took charge July 13, 1854, and died August 11, 1854, aged forty-three; in 1855, William H. Bird, also a native of Kentucky, and brother-in-law to Wylie, died 1877; 1856, Hillery Patrick, a native of Virginia; 1858, Charles Kenmore, an Irishman, who went South, and died in 1871; 1858, after K.'s brief stay, John Gibson, also an Irishman, who died 1869; 1869-70, R. G. Williams; 1870-73, Gideon C. Clark; 1873-74, Solomon Cook; 1874-76, Adam C. Johnson; 1876, for three months, M. M. Cooper; 1876-78, George B. McComb; 1878, J. J. Graham, employed in June, installed August 16. In the interval between 1858 and 1869, the church was without a settled pastor, but the Presbytery's missionary, Joseph Gordon, made many visits, and other ministers came occasionally. In the meantime, the members worked, the Sunday school and prayer meeting went on. The church was organized at Dr. Gray's house. The public services were in the basement of the old Odd Fellows Hall. Rev. Eben Muse has been pastor since December, 1882.

The Odd Fellows, with their usual generosity, gave the church the use of their hall gratis; but the members desired to be independent, and at once prepared to build. The first design was a one-story house; but Judge Scates and Mr. Condit, especially Scates, wanted it two stories, and promised to see the extra $2,000 raised to have it so. The plan was changed, and they saw the money raised—but saw Mills and Bogan and Dr. Gray raise it. The house was finished, almost, at a cost of $4,000, and August 6, 1856, Zadok Casey conveyed Lots No. 7 and 8, in Casey's Addition, to George Mills, John C. Gray and John S. Bogan, Trustees. To finish paying for the house, the Trustees now got a loan of $500 from the Church Erection Fund, which was not finally settled till 1871. The church now numbers 100 members, pays its pastor $700, and has a Sunday school of 130 members and twelve teachers.

The Baptist Church.—We have already noticed the earlier Baptist Churches. We always had Baptists in Mount Vernon, but no permanent church before the present. "The First Baptist Church of Mount Vernon" was organized August 6, 1868; Rev. J. W. Brooks, Moderator, Daniel Sturgis, Clerk of the meeting. R. A. Grant, D. Sturgis, G. J. Mayhew and G. W. Morgan were chosen to carry letter to Salem Association, asking for recognition as a church. September

21, 1868, J. W. Brooks was elected Pastor, and G. J. Mahew and R. A. Grant, Deacons. After being some time without a pastor, the church called I. S. Mahan, for a quarter of his time; but for some reason he rejected the call, June, 1871. The following July, D. W. Morgan was called, and served as pastor for one year. July 31, 1872, J. F. James was called, and remained till after the first Sabbath in January, 1873. In May, Mr. Wilson, then Principal of our public school, consented to preach for this church while he remained here. W. Sanford Gee was the next regular pastor, from March 4, 1874, to June, 1876. Then Mr. Crawford was employed for three months, and in October Crawford and Calvin Allen were invited to preach on alternate Sabbaths. In April, 1879, Allen resigned, and Charles Davis was elected. W. W. Hay was employed February 1, 1880, and W. B. Vassar in February, 1881. After an interval, the present pastor, Mr. Medkiff, was employed, February, 1883.

From the first, the building of a house of worship was discussed. Various changes were made in the Board of Trustees, and various plans were proposed and rejected. April 17, 1871, a deed was made by Pollock Wilson, conveying Lots No. 9, 10 and 12, in Block 3, to the following Trustees: James M. Pollock, R. P. Rider, Daniel Sturgis and James M. Ferguson. To perfect their title, they afterward obtained a deed from Peter Hayden, of New York, November 28, 1873. The building, begun in 1871, was finished, and dedicated by Rev. Mr. Ford, of St. Louis, the second Sabbath in August, 1872. In 1875, the Southern Methodists were granted the use of the house one Sabbath in each month, paying for lights and fuel; but this did not last long. Perhaps the most memorable service in this church was the ordination of Mr. Vassar, April 5, 1881. There were present Rev. I. N. Hobart, D. D., Superintendent of Missions for the State of Illinois, as Moderator; Rev. Gilbert Frederick, of Centralia, as Clerk; Rev. D. Sechman, of Ashley; Rev. William Lowry, of Moore's Prairie; Rev. W. H. Carner, of McLeansboro; Rev. W. W. Hay, of Zion's Grove; Rev. John Washburn, of Ewing, and Rev. J. Barry, of North Star Church, Chicago.

This church was first connected with Salem Association; then with Vandalia, and is now connected with the Association of Centralia.

It was much embarrassed for several years, the cost of the church building having run up to about $4,000; but it is now in a comparatively easy financial condition. The membership is about sixty; average attendance at Sabbath school, sixty-five, with seven teachers.

The Catholic Church.—For many years there was scarcely a Catholic in Mount Vernon. Then a few came in—Mrs. T. S. Casey, Mr. Maloney and others; and these were visited occasionally by their priests, and the rites of the church performed. Their meetings were held at the private houses of the members, seldom in more public places. The first step toward an organization was taken by Rt. Rev. Peter Joseph Baltes, Bishop of Alton, and Very Rev. John Jansen, Vicar General of the same diocese. January 20, 1871, they appointed Rev. John F. Mohr, priest of the church at Alton, and William O'Connell and Lorenz Fahrig, laymen, as Trustees of the diocese. May 20, 1872, Bishop Baltes and Vicar General Jansen, with Rev. John Neuhaus, who had been appointed pastor of "St. Philip Neri's Roman Catholic Church and Congregation of Mount Vernon, Illinois," appointed Michael Ward and Phillip Russell to act with themselves as Trustees for the church in Mount Vernon.

For several years the services were still held in private houses, and at irregular intervals. At length, under the leadership, in this undertaking, of Mrs. T. S. Casey—without whom, it is safe to say, it would not have been done for years—means were raised to purchase ground; and May 21, 1880, James Bell, of Cobden, in Union County, for $1,500, conveyed to the Trustees of this church the block—four lots with the vacated alley—north of the Supreme Court House, Lots No. 1, 2, 3, 4, etc., Casey's Second Addition. Father Hissen, of Belleville, now took charge of the church, and under his supervision the present very neat church edifice was erected in 1881. It cost about $2,000, mostly raised by the untiring efforts of Mrs. Casey. And we are requested by some of their own people to say that without the generous aid of Protestants and "outsiders," the means to secure the completion of the house could not possibly have been secured, as the members were comparatively few in number, and a large proportion of them poor. Father Becker succeeded Father Hissen, and after remaining about a year went to Kaskaskia. Just at present, the church is without a settled pastor, but is under the oversight of Father Spaeth, of Carmi.

The Episcopal Church.—For some years Bishop Seymour, Episcopal Bishop of Illinois, now of the diocese of Springfield, residing at Springfield, has been hunting up his scattered sheep in Southern Illinois, and seeking to gather and crystallize whatever strength could be found in this section, by sending out missionaries and organizing churches. Rev. Martin Moody was appointed to labor in this part of the field, giving special attention to Ashley, Mount Vernon, McLeansboro and Carmi. These were, and we believe still are, called mission stations. On the 15th day of March, 1878, a church was organized in Mount Vernon by Mr. Moody, when William Pilcher and H. W. Preston were elected Wardens, and H. H. Simmons, T. T. Wilson and J. J. Beecher, Vestrymen, and the name adopted was "Trinity Episcopal Church." Still under the pastoral charge of Mr. Moody, the church services were held first at a private house; then at a room in the Supreme Court building; then at Strattan's Hall. After the death of Mr. Moody, Rev. I. N. W. Irvine was appointed as his successor. Mr. Irvine was a man of remarkable zeal and energy, and, to the admiration of every one, succeeded in securing handsome church edifices both at McLeansboro and Mount Vernon.

It will be remembered that the Methodists went into their present church in 1854. They had already sold the old church to Harvey T. Pace November 3, 1853, for $345. Pace at once improved it in every part, even supplying cushions for the seats, so that its old acquaintances could hardly recognize it. It was then used as a church by the "Christian order," or Campbellites, all at Pace's expense, until his death, August 13, 1876. As he grew old, however, services were less regular, he being Sexton and everything else but preacher. After his death, his heirs divided his estate by deeds, and this lot fell to W. H. Pace, a grandson of H. T., and the only child of George T. Pace. W. H. P. now rented it out to anybody that wanted it, and for almost any purpose. It was once rumored that a saloon and billiard tables were going into it; but instead of this, Ferguson went in with his carpenter shop, the steeple was cut off, and a huge sign put up on top, so its old acquaintance could hardly recognize it again. Pace at length sold out to Mrs. Cramer, and after a few turns, "the Trustees and Rector of the Protestant Episcopal Church of the city of Mount Vernon" got a deed to the property from Mrs. Annie Pace, wife of W. H., February 25, 1881, and a deed from Gottsworth and Minnie Eilenstine April 27, 1881. The lot is forty-one feet north and south by sixty-six feet east and west, at the southeast corner of Block 19. This was accomplished chiefly by the efforts of Mr. Irvine, who also had the whole building renovated within and without. After Mr. Irvine's term expired, the Bishop appointed as pastor the present incumbent, Mr. R. B. Hoyt. Last April's parochial report shows 27 families, 39 communicants, 7 baptisms, 6 teachers and 35 scholars in Sunday school, and a total of contributions of $467.79, parochial and diocesan.

The Second Baptist Church.—This is a church of colored people. For many years there were very few of these in Mount Vernon. Cesar Hodge and Maria his wife, their daughter Amanda Guyler, and Sam, her husband, Guyler's two boys, William and another, and Old Nick, were all. But about 1850, others came in, and in three or four years they became quite a colony. They had meetings in the old academy, and Overton and Loggins and others preached for them. They settled in between the creeks east of town, till that section became well known under the name of Africa. They had Sunday school and a church organization, and so moved on for a few years, till about 1857, when some evil-disposed persons played Ku-Klux on them, and they soon scattered; Africa was depopulated, and scarcely a colored family was left in the county. After the war, their numbers increased very slowly for a time, then more rapidly, until they found themselves in force sufficient to again organize a church. This was done in the spring of 1879, Willis W. and Rosa Wilson, Marshall and Margaret Campbell, Margaret Scott, Henry Bradford and William H. Jones were the members. Wilson was their preacher, and, May 27, Bradford, Campbell and Jones were elected Trustees. They had Sunday school awhile in the house south of Hobbs' mill; then they rented the Pace church of Mrs. Cramer, tried to buy it, failed, and at length bought of Mr. Strattan their present house of worship, west of the Episcopal Church, for $300. Wilson was pastor two years; then Henry Jackson, of Richview, two years; the pastor last employed is named Williams, of Carmi. There are seventeen members; all attend Sunday school, in which are two regular teachers.

The Colored Methodist Church.—Perhaps our readers know that, after the war, the Southern Methodist Church encouraged its colored members to form a separate organization; and by easy steps they at length, in 1875, reached the point of absolute independence, under the name of "The Colored Methodist Episcopal Church in America." A section of this was called the "Missouri and Kansas Conference." A member of this conference, formerly from Kentucky, W. C. Davis, visited the colored people in Mount Vernon in May, 1881, and organized a church of ten members—G. W. Persons, S. P. Tandy, Charles Steager, and their wives, D. B. Bell and his two sisters and Thomas Slaughter. G. W. Persons was appointed pastor, and has continued. Their meetings have been held sometimes in private houses; for a time they used the Colored Baptist Church, and now hold meetings up-stairs north of Wlecke's Hotel. They have secured a lot, and are preparing to build a church.

The Camp Ground, or Pleasant Hill.—The first house erected here was for the Cumberland Presbyterians. David Summers moved down from the Samson Allen place, south of Rome, to the place in this township, where he lived so long, in 1838. It was not long before Rev. Mr. Finley, of the Cumberland Presbyterian Church, found him, and began to preach at his house. There being neither church nor schoolhouse on that side of Seven Mile, the neighbors agreed to build a church. The host included David and Caltin Summers and their boys, Coleman Smith, Nathaniel Parker and his boys—"only that and nothing more." But they built a small house of logs. It was used for several years as a place of worship. But Mr. Finley was sent to labor in other fields, and Arthur Bradshaw, preacher on Mount Vernon Circuit, formed a Methodist Society here, 1846–47. A camp ground was prepared, and for five or six years camp meetings were held here every fall. August 8, 1848, George Leonard, son-in-law to Mr. Parker, conveyed a lot beginning at the northeast corner of the southwest quarter of the northeast quarter of Section 23, Township 2, Range 3, thence running south twelve rods, east twelve rods, north twelve rods to beginning, to Bennett Short, Thomas Short, William Brookman, Benjamin Webber, Nathaniel Parker, Aaron Yearwood and W. H. Lynch, Trustees of Pleasant Hill Meeing-House. The description of the lot was imperfect, but every one knew where it was. The camp meetings were now less regular, and finally ceased; but it was a regular preaching place, services being held in the house in cold, and under the "shed" in warm, weather. October 10, 1853, James T. Parker conveyed an additional lot, beginning at the northwest corner of the southeast quarter of the northeast quarter of Section 23, Township 2, Range 3, south twelve rods, east six and two-thirds rods, north twelve rods, and west to beginning, to the Trustees; the board then being Coleman Smith, R. A. Grant, Aaron Yearwood, George Grant, Thomas Short, Jr., Littleton Daniel, Samuel Musgrove and James Kelly. But deaths and removals made sad inroads on the society; churches sprang up in adjoining neighborhoods; other denominations came in, and after the war there was little of the old society left. I suppose it would be impossible to tell just at what point the organization went down. The house went into a heap, and was finally hauled away.

As Pleasant Hill began to decline, W. F. Johnson and other born Methodists, some four miles northwest, could not be satisfied without a church. John Thatcher was the circuit preacher. The neighbors agreed to build, and met to select a site, but failed to agree. Some wanted it east of where Mont Morrow lives, some west. They compromised by leaving it to Tommy Casey and Jick Maxey. Mr. Thatcher would not interfere; he sat on the ground, leaning against a tree, and read Peter Parley. At length, the "Commissioners" drove down the stakes just east of where the present handsome church stands, and there the house of logs was built. It was several years before they got a deed of the ground. At length, July 15, 1854, James A. Donoho conveyed the lot, beginning at the northwest corner of the northeast quarter of the northwest quarter of Section 4, Township 2, Range 3, running south eleven chains, east eighteen rods, south seventeen and three-fourths rods, west eighteen rods, north seventeen and three-fourths rods to beginning, to James J. Maxey, Mont Morrow, W. H. Chastain, S. D. Misenheimer, W. F. Johnson, John Sproul, James Dodson, Matthew Humphrey and William H. Maxey, Trustees. This log house stood for about fifteen years, when it was sold to Dr. Cam Frost, who moved it home and uses it for an office. In 1869, it was determined to build a better house; but they were in danger of being shut out from the public roads, so they got an outlet by two deeds, one from John McLaughlin, for twenty feet off the west side of the northeast quarter of the northwest quarter of Section 4, Township 2, Range 3, and one from Ed R. Collins, beginning three rods west of the southeast corner of the southwest quarter of southwest quarter of Section 33, Township 1, Range 3, north eighty rods, west one rod, south eighty rods, east one rod to beginning; the latter dated November 7, 1870, the former dated August 19, 1867, and made to J. Sproul, M. Morrow, G. A. Collins, F. M. Bates, W. F. Johnson, Jehu J. Maxey, M. Wilson, A. S. Way and E. R. Collins. The new building is one of our best country churches, and the society there honor themselves and their profession by uprightness of life and zeal in maintaining the institutions of their church. Their Sunday school is of the evergreen variety.

The Methodist society at Liberty was organized by Rev. J. Thatcher or J. A. Robinson, in 1851. It included Anthony and John Waite, James Hails, Ransom Wilkerson and a few others. They built a log church in the usual way, every man working at whatever he could do till it was done; and it was a preaching place as long as it stood, the society experiencing the vicissitudes of decline and revival common to country churches. The house stood on James Hails' land, and he was always willing to make a deed, but never ready. So it went on till 1874, when H. began to talk of selling out, when, February 4, a Board of Trustees was elected to receive the deed. It was composed of George Stitch, James Hails, John Waite, Elijah Thickston, John W. Coates, James D. Askew, Alonzo Paine, Patrick Presslar and Joseph Howard. But even this effort failed. Mr. H. sold his land to the present owner, Daniel Hershey, conveyed to him without reserve, and Mr. Hershey took the house down and moved it away. The meetings are now held in the schoolhouse. The society is growing in numbers and in activity, maintains a good Sunday school and has regular services.

The Baptist Church at Salem was organized in 1856, by James A. Keele. Some of the earliest members were Bird Warren, Johnson Mofield, Zebulon Sledge, R. Hawkins, R. A. Grant, Robert Harlow, G. W. Luster, William Stroud, Jesse Clark and William Hutchinson and their wives.

Their meetings were held for several years in the Seven Mile Schoolhouse. They procured a lot from Bluford Harlow, March 13, 1860, beginning at the northwest corner of the southwest quarter of the southwest quarter of Section 11, Township 2, Range 3, run east twenty-three rods, south eight rods for beginning corner, then south sixteen rods, east twenty-three rods, north sixteen rods and west to beginning. The Trustees were Richard V. Hawkins, William Hutchison, William C. Beal, George W. Lester and Zebulon Sledge. Here was erected a substantial house of hewn logs, and afterward a large shed in front to accommodate the overflow on special occasions. Thus it remained till last year, when a new house was begun on a lot bought from Hiram Duncan, November 1, 1882. It was finished this spring. This lot begins 12.57 chains east of the southwest corner of the northwest quarter of the northwest quarter of Section 11, Township 1, Range 3, runs north 6.20 chains, west 2.75 chains, south $12\frac{1}{2}°$ west 1.85 chains to road, south $57°$ west 3.06 chains, south 2.68 chains, east 5.72 chains to beginning, being just half a mile north of the old one. The pastors of this church, since its organization, have been James A. Keele, George W. Grant, Thomas J. Burton, W. P. Proffitt (for a short time), F. W. Overstreet, J. T. Tenison, B. D. Esmon and S. W. Derrickson.

Southern Methodist Church.—The career of this denomination in Mount Vernon has been rather inglorious. After all its struggles, the writer remains almost its sole representative, and has to confess that he feels like a tall rag-weed in the middle of a frost-bitten turnip patch, " whose lights are fled," etc. Soon after the war closed, and largely through the efforts of Rev.—or Hon., perhaps both—John W. Westcott, the Methodist Episcopal Church South was planted in Mount Vernon—planted a little too deep, and the ground was heavy, so it didn't come up well. They got the use of the Presbyterian Church, and Rev. Dr. Reed had services there for some time in 1867-68. A preacher by the name of Frost organized a church at the Summers Schoolhouse; and this church being planted while the Frost was on the ground, the soil was mellow, and under good cultivation the crop turned out well—about sixty bushels; that is, about sixty members. Davis, Halsey, Jones and others preached for us, but we still grew "small by degrees and beautifully less." Then, for a year or two, we had no preacher. Afterward, about 1872, a little man by the name of Ward—a sickly young man, with a Bible and hymn-book and two shirts in one end of his saddle-bags, and about five bottles and three pill-boxes in the other—came to preach for us. He was irritable, of course. We got the use of the Baptist Church awhile, and he preached and flew around like whiz; but the bottom of his tender fell out, and he blew the crown sheet off his boiler and quit. The writer then switched off, and ran on the Presbyterian track awhile, but his drive-wheel slipped on the rails so badly that he went back to the Southern Methodists. In the meantime, 1877-78, we tried to build a church in East Mount Vernon, for the joint use of the Presbyterians and Southern Methodists. We met at Hinman's saloon and elected the writer, John Yearwood and George Haynes, Trustees, and got about $100 subscribed in a week or two. We bought Lots 8 and 9, Dewy's Addition, and gave notes and trust deed. We took a deed, and while one thought another had it recorded, it got lost—we have no idea what became of it. Rev. Mr. Prine almost wore all the nap off his plug hat trying to get up a Southern Methodist Church, but failed and abandoned the field. The writer had to pay off the notes and assume the debts; so he was out about $200, and in for about $100 more. He got a deed from the Trustees and one from Hobbs & Guthrie, and a resolution of a called meeting confirming the action of the Trustees and accepting their resignation. The church was "busted;" so was the writer. He tried to sell to some church, or somebody for a church, or anybody for anything, at almost any price, but no—not any. Yet the building was a church, or stood for one, about four years. And now, as far as Mount Vernon is concerned, the Southern Methodist Church is no more -- indeed, not near so much.

Schools—In Town.—The people of Mount Vernon, for several years, patronized schools in Shiloh Township. In 1830-31, a log schoolhouse was erected on the point, now in the northwestern part of city, north of the Tolle property, or nearly south of Gen. Pavey's. But in 1831 it was out of sight of town—purposely so, that the children might study with less disturbance, and that the neighbors north and west might be accommodated. Scholars came from the west as far as Bullock's Prairie. Here Mr. Tally taught our first schools, in 1831-32. In the winter of 1833-34, John Baugh, Sr., taught here; the next winter, Abner Melcher, and his daughter Priscilla the following summer; and both father and daughter the next winter. In 1836-37, John Downer, who is still living among us, taught; after which I think the house fell into disuse. Miss Rand, one of the teachers sent West by an association in the East, taught in a room over Dr. Parks's dwelling—the south end of the reconstructed dwelling in which Mrs. Thorn lives, west of the square. To all these schools scholars came from a circle six or eight miles in diameter. We believe Joshua Grant, brother of A. M., taught the next school, in the Methodist parsonage, a small frame building on the northeast corner of Block 19, where Varnell's three little brick houses stand, 1838-39. Here Miss Elizabeth Bullock also had a summer school. It was in the edge of the woods, and we remember seeing the school thrown into excitement by the appearance of snakes in the room.

At length the people of the town became ambitious to do something better; it was determined to have an academy, and the site was chosen. In February, 1839, the Legislature passed the act of incorporation, and the names of the Trustees augured well for the result. They were Zadok Casey, Stinson H. Anderson, Joel Pace, W. S. Van Cleve, H. B. Newby, E. H. Ridgway, D. Baugh, Thomas Cunningham, J. W. Greetham, Angus M. Grant. On the 5th of July, 1839, they received from S. H. Anderson a deed to a lot 180 feet square. It was in a very pretty grove, just out of town, on the southeast. A Building Committee had been appointed, Tom King, et al., and the building, furnishing materials, etc., was let to John H. Watson for $350. Of course, at this price, the house was not long in being completed; John and Asa Watson and John Leonard doing the work. There were large schoolrooms—one below and one above—a hall and stairway on the north below, and over these a room for apparatus, etc. A fine little apparatus, with chemicals, was furnished, chiefly, we believe, by Gov. Casey's liberality, at a cost of about $100.

The first sessions were taught by Lewis Dwight, "a down-easter," a graduate, perhaps, of Yale College, and a minister of the Methodist Episcopal Church. His assistant, the first term, was a Miss Evans, the next term Joel F. Watson. Dwight began in the fall of 1839, and taught two terms. In the meantime, he married Mahala, oldest daughter of Gov. Casey, who died the following year, leaving an infant son—now Samuel L. Dwight, Esq., of Centralia. People were pretty well pleased with Dwight, as Principal, except Bowman, Sheriff, father of two extra bad boys—Frank and Jim—one of whom Dwight ventured to correct. Bowman tried to raise an altercation with Dwight on the street, and threw a brick bat at Dwight's head, inflicting a very severe wound. Bowman was fined $1 for this cowardly assault.

The writer feels some pride in having been a pupil in the academy, though he received of Mr. Dwight the only blow he ever received in school. Many of the pupils have since risen to some degree of eminence. Among them may be mentioned Dr. Newton R. Casey, of Mound City, Mayor, and member of the Legislature; Thomas S. Casey, now Judge of this judicial circuit and also of the Appellate Court; Robert F. Wingate, of St. Louis, ex-Attorney General of Missouri; Tom B. Lester and Ab F. Haynie, of Salem, both distinguished in medicine, the latter also a poet and scholar, the former Professor in Kansas City Medical College; Isham N. Haynie, Adjutant General of Illinois; James M. Pace, first Mayor of Mount Vernon; G. W. Johnson, Superintendent of Schools; Lewis F. Casey, of Centralia; Charles T. Pace, long a leading man here in business and in his church; Dr. W. C. Pace and E.

C. Pace, bankers, of Ashley; Moses Shepherd, a minister of the Methodist Episcopal Church; Robert Yost, a lawyer of Thebes; John H. Pace, many years in various offices here; Thomas H. Hobbs, Alderman, and yet more prominent in other positions; Joel F. Watson, for sixteen years County Clerk, and others.

J. F. Watson taught a summer school after Dwight's second term closed; then came Johnson Pierson, who married a Miss Howard, wrote an epic poem, the "Judaid," and went to Burlington, Iowa. After Pierson, Dr. Beech and lady—the Miss Bullock before-mentioned, W. W. Bennett, T. B. Tanner, Mr. Walbridge with his sister, and the notorious Robert G. Ingersoll, were successively Principals of the institution.

But all this while the academy was gradually slipping away from the Trustees. The later teachers taught on their own hook. The financial career of the academy was inglorious. The tangle began early. The first schedule, from some cause, missed fire; and February 24, 1843, an act of the Legislature was passed, authorizing and requiring the School Commissioner to receive the schedule of a school taught in 1840, and apportion thereon its share of the funds of 1842, provided all other schedules in the county were paid in the same manner—rather an odd act. Then there was a balance due Watson and Leonard on the building; John B. Leonard obtained a judgment against the house for $40.53; the claim changed hands a few times, not being considered worth much litigation. Asa Watson found a purchaser in the Ragan family; execution had issued in November, 1852; Watson transferred the claim, and Sheriff Dodds, in 1854, conveyed the property to Richard and Barzilla Ragan. After the death of these old people, on partition of the estate, the lot was sold to C. R. Poole, who transferred it to Mrs. M. G. Rohrer. She had the old building taken down in 1882, and a neat brick cottage erected in its stead.

After the fall of the old academy, we had schools at various places, as happened to be convenient. When Mr. Leffler, Presbyterian minister, was here, he undertook a private enterprise, and put up a schoolhouse west of Noah Johnston's a short distance. But his school broke down on the start, or soon after, and Judge Grant bought the house, moved it into town, and annexed it to the east end of his hotel. There it stood till the old hotel was torn down several years ago. A more successful effort was made by H. T. Pace in 1851-52. He had bought a lot with a beautiful grove on it, just north of where Dr. Plummer lives, on Union street, and here he erected and furnished a very neat schoolhouse at his own expense, employed a teacher and kept up a school. Miss Willard, afterward married to Rev. John Ingersoll, taught in this house; then Miss Chamberlain, Mrs. Hogue, A. M. Green and others. Some schools were taught in the old Methodist Church—notably those of the Misses Martha and Sarah Green, both now residing at Normal, where the former, now Mrs. Haynie, is a Professor; the latter is the widow of the late Dr. Gray.

When the Methodist Episcopal Church was built, it was understood that the three rooms below were for school purposes; and here Prof. J. Leaton, the first stationed preacher, opened a school in the fall of 1854. February 6, 1855, a charter was granted by the Legislature to Zadok Casey, James Leaton, John N. Jonson, John H. Watson, Joel F. Watson, Charles T. Pace and Walter B. Scates, who, with three others, to be named by the Southern Illinois Conference, were to be Trustees of "The Mount Vernon Academy." Prof. Leaton was chosen Principal, of course, and continued for three years. He succeeded well, being a finished scholar and thoroughly systematic. After he left, Prof. A. C. Hillman, now of Carbondale, John H. Pace, Charles E. Robinson and others conducted the school. But there was a steady decline of enthusiasm, till the academy degenerated into a common school—sometimes very common.

After the war, however, interest revived, and the Board of Trustees was re-organized. It then, 1865, consisted of S. T. Strattan, Joel F. Watson, C. T. Pace, J. S. Bogan, W. H. Herdman, Dr. W. D. Green, D. C. Warren, James Lyon, C. D. Morrison and Thomas H. Hobbs. The services of Rev. Thomas H. Herdman, of Greenfield, Ohio, were secured as Principal, with Mrs. Carrie Smith, of Mattoon, as assistant. The school numbered sixty to seventy-five pupils. At the end of the first year, Mrs. Smith returned to Mattoon, and Miss Sadie K. Sellars, who had formerly taught with Prof. Herdman, in Ohio, was chosen to take her place. Miss S. remained two years, and was succeeded by Miss Anna Waggoner, now Mrs. A. M. Strattan. Thus Prof. Herdman remained four years, giving entire satisfaction to his patrons, and winning, in an unusual degree, the love and respect of his pupils.

In 1866, the subject of building a schoolhouse was warmly discussed—indeed, it was hot. Several sites were proposed, but it required an effort of the board to get the people to say they wanted any. The effort cost Bogan, Satterfield and others their positions. But a site was chosen—Lots No. 1, 2, 3, 4, 5, 6, Block 4, Green's Addition, and a deed was obtained of W. H. Herdman November 6, 1866. After so long a time, a large, two-story brick building was erected, costing about $12,000, and having two large rooms above and two below. A Mr. Barbour was employed to teach, but got cut by Duff Green, one of his pupils, and quit before his time was out. E. V. Satterfield finished his term. Then followed G. W. Johnson in 1869, then Ryder, Forbes, Wilson, Woodward, Courtney, Frohock and Barnhart, the present Principal. It was made a graded school under Mr. Ryder.

When the schoolhouse was finished, the classes that had been in the Methodist Episcopal Church went into it. Those in the Presbyterian Church remained till 1878. The contract made with the Presbyterian Church August 3, 1859, by N. Johnston, C. T. Pace and I. G. Carpenter, Directors, was for the use of the room ninety-nine years, for females only; the Directors were to finish the house and keep it continually in good repair, and to keep account of all expenses, and the church could annul the contract by refunding the sum expended. In 1878, the church asked for a settlement. The Directors presented a bill of about $555. The Trustees of the church thought this too much, as nothing had been done but lathing and plastering the room, running a partition and putting up two cheap privies and fencing the lots. They specially kicked at $50 or $60 for the privies. They also claimed to have kept up the repairs. They also wanted something for the seats that were in the room at first, but now gone. A hot war was brewing, but was finally compromised by the Trustees allowing the Directors to use the rooms for one more term and paying $50. Thenceforward, the school was consolidated. In 1881, an addition eighty feet long was erected, and now our six or seven hundred pupils are pretty well accommodated.

Country Schools.—The first school in the township, outside of Mount Vernon, was taught by the late William H. Chastain. He came in 1838, and located near the spring, near where Johnson Hutchison lives, about three miles northeast of town. Finding out that he was a teacher, the neighbors combined and put up a log house on the rise— now the eastern part of Joseph Dawson's farm. Here Chastain, Holt, Leech, Stockton and others taught for a number of years. The patrons of these schools were O. Harlow, Mr. Lisenby (Chastain's father-in-law), Burrell Warren, James Carroll (who lived near where George Stitch lives), A. D. Estes (near the mouth of Two Mile), Freeman Burnett, Mr. Marlow, the Summerses, the Yearwoods, etc.

As the country became more populous, a division became necessary, and a school was taught in the Cumberland Church at the Camp Ground, by a Mr. Wineburger. I think the next school there was taught by Miss Hamline, now Mrs. William B. Casey, Miss Tempe Short following in the summer, and William H. Summers the next winter. These schools were about 1848 to 1851. The writer taught three schools there in 1853, 1854, 1855. July 12, 1856, John Wright conveyed to J. R. Satterfield, W. M. A. Maxey and R. A. Grant, Township Trustees, a lot beginning at the southeast corner of Pleasant Hill Church lot, running north 208 feet, east 208 feet, south 208 feet and west to beginning.

About the time the Chastain or hickory log house fell into disuse, and the division above spoken of ensued, the northern neighborhood erected a house of split logs near Hiram Duncan's. This was known as the Split Log, the Seven Mile, or the Duncan Schoolhouse. After doing service for five or six years, this house was burnt down, and in 1853 the hewed log house was erected near the same place, where most of the people in that part of the township received their education.

After the Hutchisons and some others came into the border neighborhood, between Mount Vernon and the Camp Ground, still another schoolhouse was demanded, and a site was secured from John W. Summers April 7, 1856. It is described as beginning at the northwest corner of the southwest quarter of the southwest quarter of Section 22, Township 2, Range 3, running south ten rods, east eight rods, north ten rods, and west to beginning. A house was built here, and so continues, except the addition of ten or twelve feet to the north end.

Later school buildings are of such recent date as to require but brief notice. The Collins Schoolhouse was built on a lot bought from Joshua C. Maxey May 3, 1863. It is in the southeast corner of the southwest quarter of Section 4, and is eight rods wide from north to south, and twenty from east to west. The Block Schoolhouse was built in a district organized chiefly by the efforts of C. G. Vaughn, and is built on a square half-acre bought of Garner McWalker October 9, 1876. It is in the southeast corner of the southwest quarter of the southeast quarter of Section 16. The Waite Schoolhouse was built on a lot bought of Mrs. Jane C. Webber December 6, 1880. The boundary of the lot begins 24.89 chains west of quarter-section corner on the east side of Section 35, Township 2, Range 3, runs east 4.47 chains, south 2.23 chains, west 4.47 chains, north 2.23 chains to beginning. The schools in these houses are well sustained, and the people aim to employ better teachers and have better schools with each succeeding year.

CHAPTER VI.*

MOUNT VERNON—TOWN SURVEYS AND ADDITIONS—"MORE THAN ANY MAN CAN NUMBER"—CASEY'S ADDITION—GREEN'S, STRATTAN'S AND SEVERAL OTHERS—THE NUMBER OF ACRES COVERED BY THE CITY—MUNICIPAL GOVERNMENT—CITY OFFICIALS, ETC., ETC.

WE have already noticed the survey of the original town of Mount Vernon. It is dated July 10, 1819, and signed by William Hosick. The question is often asked why our corners are not right angles. A sufficient answer is found in "Will's" statement of his beginning and first line: "The public square beginning at the northwest corner at a mulberry stake, running thence thirteen degrees east, agreeably to the magnetical direction run by a compass made by Thomas Whitney, of Pihladelphia, No. 419, thirteen poles to another stake of the same description," etc. This was the west line. The survey and plat are acknowledged by Henry B. Maxey, John Jordan and William J. Tunstall, before Oliver Morris, Justice of the Peace. The fact that William Casey sold ninety rods off the west side of the quarter section on which the town stood to James Gray has been referred to. Gray sold a lot to the Methodist Church September 8, 1835. September 12, 1835, he also sold to John Johnson all the ground he owned east of the town and north of Bunyan street, now Blocks 14 and 15. August 25, 1837, he sold a square acre in the northwest corner of his tract to Rhodam Allen, now Block 31; October 5, 1837, he sold to James Ross, Dr. Adams and John Stanford all the ground he owned west of the town and south of Bunyan street, now Block 6; October 7, 1839, he sold to W. S. Van Cleve a strip including the ground where Merrill's livery stable stands, running as far west as Mrs. Baltzell's and back to the alley. Downing Baugh bought all the ground Gray owned south of the town and east of Union street, now Blocks 3 and 4.

Some of these were at once laid out in lots. Adams, Ross & Stanford's Addition, of six lots with a twenty-one foot alley—"North west Alley"—on the west, was surveyed by Daniel P. Wilbanks, Deputy Surveyor, November 27, 1837. Baugh's Addition of thirty-two lots in two blocks was laid out by the same surveyor, April 20, 1838, comprising the ground above named; the blocks were not numbered. The lots were numbered retroversely; acknowledgement taken by Noah Johnston. The title to the lots in this addition was pretty badly tangled for some time, but finally came out pretty straight in most cases.

By this time Gray had sold out most of his land around the town that was available for building lots. Very naturally the Village Trustees wished to see the town grow and branch out in good shape; so they, and not Jimmy Gray, as some suppose, but no doubt, at Gray's suggestion, employed John Storm, County Surveyor of White County, to come up and survey the town. Storm's survey was to include all the tracts just mentioned and what Gray had left and the original town. Fortunately, there was not a block in the whole menagerie, so he was free to num-

---
*By Dr. A. Clark Johnson.

ber his blocks any way; but wherever lots were numbered the numbers could not be changed. This explains the numbers running so irregularly in some parts of the town. The ninety rods off the west side of the quarter section made about ninety-four acres. The plat is dated September 18, 1840. The key corner stone was set at the southwest corner of Section 29, and the variation maintained 6 degrees. The blocks ran from 1 in the southwest corner to 35 in the northeast. Block 24 and several others in the north and east were not lotted; they were so far from town and so badly in the woods, Storm states in his certificate, that the survey was "made pursuant to the request of the Trustees of said town." The survey and field notes fill thirty pages of the record, Book C, and J. R. Satterfield, Recorder, certifies that they were recorded from the 1st to the 27th of September, 1845.

But of all the parties interested, not a man but Jimmy Gray acknowledged the "act and deed." This raised grave doubts as to the legality of it. Hence an act of the Legislature was procured and approved February 21, 1843, declaring "That the survey of the town of Mount Vernon in Jefferson County, made by John Storms in the year 1840, and the plats and profiles made by him of said survey, are hereby legalized and shall be taken and received in all courts as *prima facia* evidence of the facts therein contained and set forth, and the beginnings, endings, boundaries and abuttals thereby established are hereby legalized and confirmed." Thus perfected, Storms' survey has remained almost unchanged. In February, 1865, by act of the Legislature, six feet were taken off the east side of Washington street from Main to Harrison, and added to the several lots, but in March, 1869, this was repealed. Block 24 was laid off into thirteen lots for J. F. Watson by B. R. Cunningham, April 27, 1880. And Varnell opened an alley in Block 19, and S. H. Watson and others an alley through Block 26. Lots 7 and 8, Block 12, have been cut up by H. T. Pace's heirs, but no record made of it. It may be added that Storms' chain may have been just slightly too long, as many of his lines overrun a little. I may also add, as I am better at addition than multiplication, that Judge Pollock, April 14, 1881, carved four lots out of the parts of Blocks 28, 29, 30 and 31, lying west of the Salem road. He opened a street and an alley, but failed to give them names, and A. Curt. Johnson has divided Block 5 into lots.

Casey's Addition soon followed Storms' survey. November 14, 1840, Zadok Casey had E. M. Grant, Deputy Surveyor, to lay out some lots on a triangular piece of ground just west of town, from the Nashville road to the Carlyle road. It had been a field. He moved his east fences back to a line west of where Judge Casey lives, and the town looked expansive. He built two cottages and a store, now on Main street, and invited improvement. But Jarvis Pierce had an idea that the improvement would take the opposite direction, and center about the academy; so he bought a strip ten rods wide, and about fifty rods from north to south, in the northwest corner of the east half of the northwest quarter of Section 32, from James Gray, and laid out sixteen lots, with Seminary street twenty feet wide on the west side, and South street fifty feet wide on the south. This was done by A. M. Grant, Deputy Surveyor, May 18, 1841; and Pierce's Addition stretched from where Mr. Bruning lives toward the Sunny South. But Jarvis failed to pay for the ground; failed to sell lots, failed all over, and it all "went under." He and Albert Towle and Almon N.

Towle, his nephews, held Gray's bond for a deed, but it did no good. In September of the same year, the same three men, with Joel Pace, laid out South street, hoping this would help Pierce's Addition out. It ran from Union street east 639 feet, and was sixty-six feet wide. There was nothing but open prairie south of it—nothing to hinder its being 639 feet wide. It was not surveyed, but it was recorded twice. The first time they had it south of Blocks 3, 4 and 5 of Baugh's Addition. But they found there were but two blocks in the addition, and they next got it south of Baugh's and Ross, Stanford & Adams' Additions. This was no better, but they let it go so—and I don't know that it ever came back. Our blood did not call for any more additions until after the Supreme Court came. Casey's Second Addition was the result. Gov. Casey moved his fences in again, and May 5, 1854, W. B. Anderson surveyed one tier of lots south of Bunyan street two blocks north of them, a huge block for the Supreme Court, and three blocks north of that. The lots ran from 1 to 25. On the plat of the huge block aforesaid was written "Block 1, donated to the State of Illinois." This was all the "Block" in it, and this is all the deed the State ever had for that. Fourth street, which ran north and south from the middle of the court house lot, was soon after vacated. The court house and the Presbyterian 'Church soon brought this addition into notice.

Green's Addition came next. The tidal wave had moved west—it now turns back to the east. Billy Casey had sold the east seventy acres of this quarter section to Stins. Anderson, March 1, 1836. Anderson had sold it to Edward Ridgway, April 4, 1850, and at length, October 20, 1856. Ridgway had sold it to Dr. W. Duff Green. When Storm made his survey, everything east and north of where Fletcher Johnson now lives was in the woods, except an awfully small and more awfully stumpy field on the hill north of the Fairfield road, and a field not quite so small and stumpy south of it. But now those fields had grown vastly, and merely a few clumps of the black jack woods were left. So Dr. Green, October 29, 1859, had Mr. L. J. Germain, Deputy Surveyor, under Mr. Grant, lay out the entire seventy acres into blocks and lots. This added seventeen blocks to the town, in three tiers running north and south, with Breckinridge and Spring streets between, and Green street separating all from the old town. Jesse J. Fly owned Block 7; H. D. Hinman most of Block 17; Block 9 was owned by Dr. Brown; Dr. Green reserved Block 12 for his home, and 15 and 16 included the springs, so that these blocks, as well as two and three, were not lotted. The street between 15 and 16 was soon after vacated. Fly had Block 7 divided into lots by a Mr. William S. Morgan. Deputy Surveyor, April 9, 1861, making eleven lots, except a strip at the northeast corner that he did not own. Indeed, he did not own near all the rest, Frank Parker coming in on the west and Benjamin Miller on the east, etc. Block 9 was subdivided by B. R. Cunningham, February 26, 1880, or rather he surveyed and platted its seven lots, for it was already divided among as many owners. The rest of this addition remains about as it was. Improvement progressed slowly until the railroad was built, when it swept over the whole addition like another tidal wave. Newby's Addition, surveyed by Germain June 20, 1860, also improved slowly for several years and experienced a like revival when the railroad was first built. Perhaps a sufficient clew to the location of this addition is furnished by the record, for it seems to have one corner at the intersection of

Breckinridge street and the Shawneetown road, its northeast corner. The record don't say where it is.

As soon as the railroad was an assured thing, several more additions were made. Samuel K. Casey came, bought out the Gov. Casey heirs, and October 9, 1867, had a large square tract on the southeast quarter of the southeast quarter of Section 30 laid out into twenty-one lots. The southeast corner, or key corner, is north 68 degrees west 3.90 chains from the key corner of Storm's survey, vernier set at zero. This throws it 150 feet west of First street or the Brownsville road; Mills and Elm are its principal streets. Gov. Casey had sold a lot at the corner of First and Bunyan to Dr. Short, and lots fronting on First to various persons from time to time, south of the Short lot and running back the same distance. After Samuel Casey had platted his square, as he called it, it was hard for the Assessor to properly describe the lots between it and First street, as they hardly seemed to be still "parts of the southeast quarter of the southeast quarter of Section 30, Town 2 Range 3." So Samuel W. Jones, then Treasurer and Assessor, had the County Surveyor make a plat of those lots. Joel Pace owned one at the corner; N. C. Pace one west of that, and south of it were lots owned by Samuel Hawkins, T. H. Herdman, J. J. Garrison's heirs, J. J. Fly, J. F. Johnson and J. & J. Slevin, a bad place for jays. The surveyor's plat of these lots has no name on the record, but is generally known as the Williams Survey. It was made May 21, 1868. Then in the same year, August 3, S. K. Casey's Second Addition was surveyed. It lies entirely west and north of the Supreme Court lot, beginning sixty feet west and sixty feet north of the northwest corner of it. It consists of two tiers of large lots, its lots being numbered from 1 to 9. The town now reached as far west as the depot south of the railroad, and as far as the west line of Bell's and Goodale's lots, etc., north of the railroad.

The pendulum of improvement now swings to the east, and A. M. Strattan opens up Strattan's Addition, May 7, 1869. This is on the same tract with Green's Second, that is, the southwest quarter of the southeast quarter of Section 29, Town 2, Range 3. The Yearwoods owned eighteen rods off the east side, and Strattan had bought a strip west of theirs, 5.235 chains wide, and sold an acre off the south end to Fitch; on the rest he laid out his addition. But it is described as beginning at a point fifteen feet south and 176 feet west of the northeast corner of the southwest quarter of the southeast quarter of Section 29, thus lapping over on to the Yearwoods 121 feet. A recent deed from Dr. Green, however, corrects this error. This addition contains four lots. Rynd L. Strattan put a good house and barn on No. 1, now owned by Dawson, and the rest are unimproved. In fact, the Strattans have sold two strips, fifty and twenty feet, off the east side of Lot No. 4, and what is left is two feet eight inches wide by 630 feet long.

Then the pendulum swings back to the west, and S. K. Casey's Third Addition is thrown open. It was surveyed by John A. Garber, civil engineer, January 25, 1870. It includes seven blocks, on both sides of the railroad, north of Bunyan street or the Ashley road, and lies just within the western limits of the city, extending to Bogan street. It is there, and seems to be well fastened down with stakes and things, but it's hard to tell how it got there, for Garber located it on the northwest quarter of the southwest quarter of Section 30, Town 2, Range 3, about where the big pond is. Then it swung back to the east—the pendulum—and Varnell's First Addition was the result. Varnell owned the south half of the northwest quarter of the southeast quarter of Section 29, and November 24, 1870, he laid out about half of it along the Fairfield road—or Main street—into lots, in three blocks. It is ninety feet seven inches, widest at the east end.

The improvement now swings round to the south. First, Green's Second Addition, January 4, 1871, took in or let out all he had left of the southwest quarter of the southeast quarter of Section 29. The Doctor seldom did things by littles—don't think he ever gave a quit-claim deed, but always a warranty.) There are nine blocks, only the first four being laid out in lots; all the rest fronted on the Fair Ground road. But the demand for lots was such that September 18, 1871, he divided Block 5 and the south part of Block 6 into lots. This is Green's Division, etc. He had sold 300 feet off the north end of Block 6 to the Lowrys. This Second Addition is bounded on the east by Lee avenue and the east line of the tract, on the west by Park avenue, and divided in the middle by Lee avenue. Next, August 16, 1871, George S. Winslow throws over seventy-five acres of lots into the market in Winslow's Addition. It occupied the northwest quarter of the northeast quarter and all of the northeast quarter of the northwest quarter, except four and one-half acres off the south side of Section 32. Its avenues ran east and west, Casey, Opdyke, Castleton, Walnut and Newby; its streets, Temple, Water and Summer, north and south. It had 224 lots and no blocks. Lot No. 222, including the machine shop grounds. But afterward, December 22, 1877, Lots 1 to 166 were vacated, except Lot No. 128, being all of the northwest quarter of the northeast quarter of Section 32, except one lot. Still swinging around, we next see Newby's Second Addition, August 29, 1871.

It is more definitely located than his first, beginning at the northwest corner of the southeast quarter of the northwest quarter of Section 32, running north 140 feet, east 714 feet, south 492 feet, west 714 feet, and north 322 feet. All lies south of the shops, at the extreme south end of town. Then, November 14, 1871, John Liebundgut lays out an addition, west of Winslow's, on ten acres north of the railroad, bought of Joel Pace. This addition lies on both sides of the south end of Washington street. It was part of the northwest quarter of the northwest quarter of Section 32, extending south 407 feet and west 633 feet, from the northeast corner.

But there is still a demand for lots in the east; so, August 8, 1872, Dewy's Addition begins. John Yearwood had, February 18, 1865, sold thirty-one rods eight links off the south end of his five acres, eighteen rods wide, to Joe; the next October Joe sold it to Bob, and in June, 1868, Bob sold the west half of it to Russel Dewy. Dewy, then, April 20, 1870, bought fifty feet off the east side of Lot 4, Strattan's Addition, to give him an outlet to Main street. He then laid out his addition, as above stated. This addition, according to the recorded survey, has these impossible boundaries: Beginning 255 feet south and nine rods west of the northeast corner of the southwest quarter of the southeast quarter of Section 29, Town 2, Range 3, running south 361 feet, west 198½ feet, north 595 feet, east fifty feet, south 234 feet, east 188½ feet, to beginning. There are nine lots, 1 and 2 reaching for Main street, the rest lying east and west. Then, April 22, 1873, Varnell lays out his Second Addition, covering the rest of his twenty-acre tract. There is one tier of lots in three blocks, reaching across the north-

west quarter of the southeast quarter of Section 29. This and Dewey's were surveyed by B. C. Wells. With these additions the disposition to go east seems to have been exhausted, and the movement has since been in the opposite direction.

May 14, 1874, Fry's Addition of twenty-two lots is surveyed, with First street on the east and Franklin street on the west. This street, of course, was named in honor of Franklin S. Casey, Z. A. Fry's father-in-law. This addition occupies the east part of the south half of the northeast quarter of the northeast quarter of Section 31. April 26, 1875, John J. Casey's Addition was surveyed by S. C. Polk. John had inherited six acres west of S. K. Casey's First Addition and of Fifth street, extending from the Ashley road south to the south line of Section 30, and about six and one-third chains in width. This he laid out into five lots, one west of Edgewood street and four east of it. In a few years, Buck Casey bought the four east lots, and February 25, 1878, had them cut up into twenty-six lots, under the name of William B. Casey's Subdivision. December 1, 1876, Noah Johnston's Addition was surveyed. It differs from all other additions. It has no streets, no alleys, and each lot is totally unlike the rest in both shape and dimensions. It is an irregular triangle, bounded by the section line between Sections 29 and 30 on the east and the Carlyle road on the southwest. There are four lots; No. 1 is a small wedge, while No. 4 has 600 feet front on the road and the same on its north or northwest line, and over 700 on the east. No. 4 is the Major's home, and his "cabin" has been there fifty years. William T. Pace's Addition, January 20, 1877, is the last. "Harvey Pace's meadow," in the northwest quarter of the northwest quarter of Section 32, was a well-known field for many a long year. When its owner died, his heirs, in making a division of his estate, found it convenient to convey this tract to William T. Pace, a grandson, and have him cut it up into lots and re-convey to each as might be agreeable. It contains six blocks, three on each side of Casey street, with two east and west avenues—the northern Pace avenue; the southern, Virginia.

As a result of all these surveys, Mount Vernon has about 500 acres now laid out into 875 lots, of which about 490 are improved and 385 unimproved.

Municipal Government.—The effort to incorporate Mount Vernon was made in 1837. At that time the statute required a population of 150 to entitle towns to be incorporated, so an act was passed to enable Mount Vernon, Mount Salem and Carlyle to incorporate without the requisite population under the general law. But the records of the town are now lost and few of its officers remain. The government continued for nearly ten years before it faded out and had to be renewed. Then it ran on for nearly twenty years longer before it had to be sent to the renovator again. See below. It generally appeared in feeble health, but in 1853, when Capt. Newby tried the experiment of starting a saloon on South Union street without its authority, he found it was still alive. At the end of six months, he had to move out. John Johnson, William Edwards, A. Melcher and D. Baugh were members of the old board for years; we understand there were not many third termers in the later board.

May 2, 1864, a meeting of the citizens was held to decide whether or not they would be incorporated under the general law. R. W. Lyon was President and A. N. Pace Secretary of the meeting. A vote was taken and was unanimously in favor of the proposition —82 to 0. On the 17th of the same month, an election for Trustees was held, and among nearly twenty candidates, the five who received the highest votes were T. B. Tanner, 83; Thomas H. Hobbs, 64; Harvey T. Pace, 64; J. J. Holloman, 62; J. R. Satterfield, 61. John H. Pace received 60 votes for Police Magistrate, D. C. Warren, with 24, being the next highest man. The Trustees were sworn in by J. S. Bogan June 13, 1864, and the board was ready for business. Most of this, however, was routine business, and not much to note, except the annual struggle on the license question, which we may consider under the head of temperance movements.

In 1872, Mount Vernon became a city under the general law respecting cities and villages. The last Board of Trustees was Walter E. Carlin, President; John N. Satterfield, Clerk; and James D. Johnson, Russell Dewy, Newton C. Pace and William E. Jackson, Trustees. The following is a list of the Mayors and Aldermen under the city government:

1872—J. M. Pace, Mayor; T. Hansacker, T. H. Hobbs, A. Smart, J. J. Bambrook, Aldermen. W. D. Watson succeeded Smart in the fall. Four wards and four Aldermen.

1873—N. C. Pace, Mayor; H. W. Seimer, R. Dewey, C. A. Loomis, J. R. Allen, S. S. Porter and J. J. Bambrook, Aldermen. Three wards and six Aldermen.

1874—N. C. Pace, Mayor; James Guthrie, H. W. Seimer, J. Taylor, C. A. Loomis, Silas Downer and H. Davisson, Aldermen. J. Bambrook succeeded Downer, moved out of city.

1875—G. H. Varnell, Mayor; J. Taylor, James Guthrie, C. A. Loomis, J. A. Clinton, J. J. Bambrook and H. A. Baker, Aldermen.

1876—G. H. Varnell, Mayor; H. A. Baker, J. J. Bambrook, J. A. Clinton, D. B. Goodrich, C. A. Loomis and N. C. Pace, Aldermen. In September, R. L. Strattan appeared as successor to Baker.

1877—G. H. Varnell, Mayor; J. J. Bambrook, J. A. Clinton, J. B. Crowder, D. B. Goodrich, N. C. Pace and R. L. Strattan, Aldermen.

1878—G. H. Varnell, Mayor; J. J. Bambrook, J. A. Clinton, J. B. Crowder, D. B. Goodrich, Alexander Smart and R. L. Strattan, Aldermen.

1879—G. H. Varnell, Mayor; D. B. Goodrich, J. D. Johnson, J. A. Clinton, A. Smart, H. W. Preston, G. W. Yost, Aldermen. Johnson soon moved out of his ward and was succeeded by M. M. Goodale; then Goodrich moved out and was succeeded by C. D. Ham.

1880—G. H. Varnell, Mayor; M. M. Goodale, C. D. Ham, W. A. Keller, H. W. Preston, S. T. Strattan and G. W. Yost, Aldermen.

1881—G. H. Varnell, Mayor; J. R. Allen, R. Dewy, C. D. Ham, John Gibson, S. T. Strattan and W. Barg Casey, Aldermen.

1882—G. H. Varnell, Mayor; J. R. Allen, R. Dewey, John Gibson, M. M. Goodale, A. W. Plummer and A. M. Strattan, Aldermen.

1883—H. S. Plummer, Mayor; M. M. Goodale, W. T. Goodrich, R. Dewy, A. W. Plummer, A. M. Strattan and G. F. M. Ward, Aldermen.

Peter Brown has been City Clerk ever since 1873.

The City Marshals were E. J. Watson in 1872; S. D. Cooper in 1873; J. R. Guthrie, 1877; I. F. Hamlin, 1878; F. W. Fry, 1878; T. J. Casey, 1879; R. A. Smith, 1880; and C. C. Satterfield, 1882.

The Police Magistrates were John H. Pace, 1872; James M. Pace, 1874; J. W. Baugh, 1876; Wesley Yost, 1880.

The City Attorneys were T. T. Wilson, 1872; E. V. Satterfield, 1875; T. T. Wilson, 1877; S. Laird, 1879; Albert Watson, 1881; and W. H. Green, 1881.

The Street Commissioners were W. D. Edgington in 1874; John Maloney, in 1878; and in 1882, G. W. Johnson.

CHAPTER VII.*

MOUNT VERNON—TEMPERANCE MOVEMENTS—THEIR GOOD WORK IN THE COMMUNITY—VILLAGE OF EAST MOUNT VERNON—MYSTIC ORDERS—MASONS, ODD FELLOWS, ETC.—MISCELLANEOUS—WHICH COMPRISES FIRES, FIRE DEPARTMENT AND MANY OTHER LOCAL ITEMS—BIRTHS, DEATHS, ETC., ETC.

"Finis coronat opus."—*Shakespeare.*

AS the temperance movement has been one of the most important factors in our public life, it will not be amiss to give it considerable space in these pages.

The first temperance organization in the county was the "Mount Vernon Temperance Society," organized in March, 1832. The basis of their action was this preliminary resolution:

"*Resolved,* That the meeting proceed to form a temperance society, provided they can form a constitution that shall be free from all sectarian taint and shall be liberal in all its provisions."

The pledge was couched in Article II of the Constitution, as follows: "The members of this society mutually agree to abstain from the use of ardent spirits only in cases of necessity, and they further agree to use their influence in every mild and prudent way with others for the same purpose." It will be seen that this language is very ambiguous, but everybody understood that signing the pledge meant temperance.

Their annual meetings were to be held in September, with other meetings at the call of the President or two Managers. As they were all akin to us, I have a mind to give the whole outfit: John Baugh was President; Samuel E. Goodrich, Vice President; Joel Pace, Secretary; Joseph Pace, Abraham T. Casey, Samuel Cummins and William Criswell, Managers. The members gathered from the whole country during the year were Zadok Casey, Joel Pace, Abraham M. Knapp, Lewis Johnson, John Baugh, Joseph Pace, William Criswell, Samuel Cummins, Edward Maxey, John Maxey, John Milburn, James Overbay, Abraham Buffington, Spencer Pace, Isaac Casey, James G. Bruce, Edward King, Abraham T. Casey, Bennett N. Maxey, Charles H. Maxey, Thomas M. Casey, Samuel E. Goodrich, Abel Overbay, Harvey T. Pace, Nathan Goodrich, James Tally, David Little, Polly Baugh, John Parker, Margaret Buffington, Jane Buffington, Susan Buffington, Jonathan Wells, Rhodam Allen, James A. Brown, John Hudlow, John C. Casey, James Dodds, H. J. Scott, Nathaniel Parker, Philip Buffington, Ann Anderson, Margaret Anderson, Martha Anderson, Caroline Anderson, Pamela Pace, Asahel Bateman, Sofronia Scott, Jerusha Wells, Keziah Scott, Sarah Scott, Scynthia Scott, Mary Knapp, Rebecca Wilkerson, Littleman Wells, Phebe Pace, Mary Wilkerson, Mary Atwood, Patsy Goodrich, Calendar Goodrich, Robert Goodrich, Maranda Goodrich, Elgelina Goodrich, Armilda Goodrich, Henry Goodrich, Mary Goodrich, Jehu Scott, Downing Baugh, Milly Baugh, Mary Pace, Elihu Maxey, Loyd Buffington,

---

* By Dr. A. Clark Johnson.

William Maxey, Wallace Caldwell, Samuel W. Carpenter, George Johnston, Goodman Elkins, Ananias Elkins, Henry B. Maxey, Jehu G. D. Maxey, Robert Maxwell, William M. A. Maxey, Henry Tyler, James Johnson, Lewis Johnson, Jr., John N. Johnson, William F. Johnson, Matthew M. Taylor, William Wells, Reuben S. Crosno, Green B. Wells, John Tyler, Russell Tyler, Benjamin Patterson, Azariah Bruce, John Baugh, Jr., Allen Hunt, Marcus Bruce, John Bruce. Sarah Maxwell, Sarah Tyler, Rhoda Casey, Hannah Taylor, Elizabeth Taylor, Nancy Roland, Delia Hunt, Polly A. Maxey, Vylinda Casey, Milla Carpenter, Elizabeth Bruce, Eddy Maxey, Theodore Maxey, Harriet Casey, Rhoda Overbay, Elizabeth Casey, Catharine Tyler, Clarissa Johnson, Patsy Johnson, Emily Johnson, Elizabeth Johnson, Susan Maxey, Catherine Maxey, Lucinda Allen, Polly Crosno, Rachel Crosno, Sally Crosno, Mary Maxey, Elizabeth Wells, Lucinda Overbay, Patsy Bruce, Elizabeth Baugh, Emily Baugh, Sarah Maxey, Jarvis Pierce, Peter Bingaman, John M. Pace, Joab Peterson, Nancy Pace, E. H. Ridgway, Sarah Maxey, Nancy Johnson, Ransom Moss, Susannah Johnson, H. Bingaman, William Bingaman, John E. McBryan, Margaret E. Black, Joel Harlow, James Carroll, Green Depriest, Robert Elkins, Daniel G. Anderson, John M. Lane, William Hicks, Solomon Goddard, Gazaway Elkins and Robert Yearwood.

At the first meetings of this society Gov. Casey was the chief speaker. Dr. J. S. Moore came in the fall of 1833 and took a very active hand, as did Rev. John Johnson, who came in from Kentucky in the fall of 1834. The impulse was sustained by the arrival of Rev. John Van Cleve as Presiding Elder the next year. But it was such a sweeping revival that a lull followed; yet a new constitution was drawn up, and under the name of the Jefferson County Temperance Society, met on the 4th of July, and sometimes oftener. Among the Presidents were John Baugh, Sr., Edward Maxey, Joseph Pace, Downing Baugh, Arba Andrews and John Johnson. The record of this society, preserved in the archives of the Pioneer Association, extends to 1840.

Another record in the same archives begins the story of a new society, January 25, 1842, under the old name, Jefferson County Temperance Society. Judge Scates was one of the leading spirits. James Kirby was Chairman and H. T. Pace Secretary of the first meeting. The pledge was simply an agreement not to use intoxicating liquors as a beverage, nor traffic in them, nor provide them for others, etc. The record runs over four years, to June, 1846, and contains over 300 names of persons subscribing the pledge. During this period, the Presidents were James Kirby, John Johnson, W. J. Stephenson and Joel F. Watson; the Secretaries were H. T. Pace and J. R. Satterfield. During the existence of the society, it brought out some good speakers, as Johnson Pierson, Samuel D. Marshall, John Moore (afterward Governor), Rev. R. H. Moffit, Dr. J. C. Gray and S. S. Hayes—all in 1842; Edward Jones, W. B. Scates, R. F. Wingate, Mr. Kittinger, of Alton, Dr. Roe, of Shawneetown, in 1843; John Dougherty in 1844. In 1843, the speakers at their 4th of July meeting, all selected from the academy, were James M. Pace, Wesley Johnson, Charles T. Pace and Thomas S. Casey. I have half a mind to give the names of a few of those who appear as signers on the later lists—up to 1846; but perhaps it would only make some of us ashamed of ourselves—of ourselves in contrast with our fathers and mothers, or of ourselves now in contrast with what we were then, so we forbear.

For several years after 1846, the temperance societies were short-lived, and temperance meetings were held at irregular intervals. But about the year 1855, and largely through the influence of Judge Scates and Prof. Leaton, a division of the Sons of Temperance was organized and a section of the Cadets. These flourished a few years with the usual routine of initiations and expulsions, installations, public meetings and processions, till the novelty wore off and interest began to fail; then the whole machine went to pieces. But it soon revived again under a different form—the Good Templars—and in this form subsisted till after the war. The war which destroyed slavery and at the same time nearly everything of any value in our social fabric, sowed the seeds of destruction in the Good Templars' organization. It was agreed that every member should be "good on the books" as long as he was in the army, whether he paid dues or not. After the war, some complained of not having been treated properly, a division arose, and a part of the lodge seceded. It culminated thus in the winter of 1868–69. McClure and Williamson, with Hill—a new man, but for temperance all over—started the Sons of Temperance again in that modified form which admitted both sexes, and the Good Templars, having lost this distinguishing advantage, went under—no, come to think, most that went anywhere, went over to the new organization. This went on till some of the most zealous got married, when it began to wane, and finally went out.

But still the friends of temperance were moderately active. Many of them were business men, and afraid of offending good customers; some were hoping one day to get office, and, of course, had to be cautious; and some were weak-kneed on general principles. Yet every winter, or just before the city election in spring, at the latest, they got lecturers from a distance and got up more or less rousement. G. W. Hughey, Col. Campbell and Miss Frances E. Willard were chief among them. In the winter of 1878–79, Col. Campbell carried the town away, and the blue ribbons met the eye everywhere. Everybody wore them, whether they quit drinking or not; in one ward, a new convert beat the most staid old temperance man in town for Alderman. But all that goes up has to come down, and in due time down came the blue ribbon.

Soon after the spring election, however, Miss Willard and Mrs. Anderson came and began work in a different way. Miss Willard lectured and left the same night; but Mrs. Anderson remained to organize a branch of the Ladies Christian Temperance Union. This was done May 22, 1879. The original officers were: President, Mrs. Sarah A. Gray; Vice Presidents, Mrs. Sue A. Pace and Mrs. Louisa Bogan; Recording Secretary, Mrs. (G. W.) Morgan; Corresponding Secretary, Mrs. Mary S. Pace; Treasurer, Mrs. Margaret A. Johnson. This organization proved to have the requisite amount of vitality, and is still vigorously at work. They circulate temperance documents, sometimes hold jubilee meetings, and every week have something sound and sensible to say in their own special column in each one of our county papers.

To other temperance societies, reference is made elsewhere. We must not omit to mention, however, the time when the city fathers agreed to license saloons for $1,000 each, if a majority of all persons of twenty-one years said so. The women voted, and about 530 said no, while only about sixty said yes. By such and various efforts, Mount Vernon was made for ten years a temperance town. But last spring, by the help of St.

Louis, Belleville and East Mount Vernon, the whisky element prevailed and elected a Mayor and a majority of the Aldermen. It is but due to the reputation of our town, as well as to the truth of history, to say that only about ten per cent of the whisky party were permanent residents, owning their homes and interested in the real welfare of the town. Nine-tenths of the solid men of the town were opposed to saloons, and seeing the amount of drunkenness increased twofold by the saloons has made them more so.

The Village of East Mount Vernon.—This settlement or village grew out of the whisky contest. In 1859, as before stated, Dr. Green sold five acres, being a strip eighteen rods wide and about forty-four rods long, off the east side of the southwest quarter of the southeast quarter of Section 29, to John Yearwood. John started a grocery on his purchase and sold lots to Joe and others, and thus sprang up what was called Yearwood Town. John sold his grocery to some one else and started a gunshop, and this added to its importance. At length, tired of getting along without any saloons in town, as above stated, it occurred to some admirers of the institution that if they had a village organization, they might have a saloon there, even though it were within the interdicted distance of the city. Of course, many went into the project with no thought but of the advantages of a separate government in the way of internal improvements.

At the May term, 1877, May 24, "the petition of Robert A. Yearwood, John Liebundgut and Samuel Laird for the organization," etc., came into the County Court in due form. The village was to be eighty rods wide along the east line of the city limits, one mile north and south, including part of the west half of the northeast quarter, part of the west half of the southeast quarter, part of the east half of the northeast quarter, and part of the east half of the southeast quarter of Section 29, and part of the west half of the northeast quarter, and part of the east half of the northeast quarter of Section 32, 160 acres. The petition was signed by thirty-three persons. An election was ordered for June 12, 1877; W. H. Newcum, Robert A. Yearwood and William Hall were appointed Judges, and G. B. Leonard and Thomas H. Goodwin Clerks. The result was twenty-six for village organization, one against. From the returns it appears that the Judges who actually held the election were James Webber, George Beagle and John Yearwood, and the Clerks W. H. Hinman and Peter Brown—not exactly the Board that Judge Foster appointed. At the June term of the County Court, the case was docketed "No. 11," but the whole page is blank. At the July term, it is again docketed "No. 17," and the case stated as "canvass of election return," and all is blank again—no order or semblance of one—not one word. But an election for officers was held July 10, 1877, when T. H. Goodwin was elected Police Magistrate, and J. William Leonard, William Randall, William Hall, William B. Wright, William H. Newcum and John Yearwood, Trustees; and William Goodwin, Clerk. July 17, the Williams—we mean the Trustees—met, organized and adopted thirty-three ordinances. Everything went nicely for awhile, the best elements controlling the business; a street was opened east of Strattan's Addition, walks were built and all seemed orderly and in good shape.

But the saloons produced their legitimate fruit. Hinman & Hutchison kept as good a house as can be of the kind, honestly trying to keep from violating the law; but those on the south side seemed to go on from bad to worse, till at length, in 1880, Mr. Thomas Caborn concluded that he would endure them no longer. So, at the May term of the Circuit Court, Keller & Carpenter commenced a suit—People *ex rel.* Caborn *vs.* Satterfield, County Clerk and the Village of East Mount Vernon—in an action of certiorari. This suit was dismissed at the cost of the petitioner. Before court adjourned, however, the suit was revived as an action quo warranto, a change of venue asked and cause continued till it could be tried before a Judge not objected to—Judge Jones. At the December term, a trial was had and judgment of ouster obtained, Conger, Presiding Judge, and an appeal granted. In the Appellate Court, the defendants got a continuance, and at next term dismissed their appeal. It then came up in the Circuit Court under "Motion to Amend and Correct Record of Judgment," before Judge Jones. At this time the court declared they had assumed to act and had acted as Trustees without legal authorization, and ordered a writ of ouster against the defendants and their successors. An appeal was again allowed and bond filed; but it went no further, the village had money enough to pay its lawyers, did this, and quit. So people often do in divorce suits—pay nobody but their lawyer. It may be well to state that the grounds for ouster were that the village never had 300 inhabitants, that some of the petitioners were non-residents, that one was a woman, that the first election was illegal; and that the record showed no canvass of the vote.

The fall of East Mount Vernon brought all the whisky forces into the city election last spring and helped to carry the whisky ticket through.

Mystic Orders.—Marion Lodge, No. 13, I. O. O. F., was organized April 30, 1845. The charter members were John W. Greetham, James B. Tolle, Thomas Metsler, Henry Wood and William White. Besides other accessions, Dr. W. D. Green came in the following year and contributed much to give the order character, vim and success. Never was a better worker than Mr. Tolle, but he was less eminent than the Doctor, who rapidly rose to the position of presiding officer of the Grand Lodge of the State. Daniel Baltzell was another important accession, a man of rugged mold, but kind and generous, one of nature's noblemen. But we cannot now mention other names in our limited space. In 1849, May 21, Gov. Casey donated a lot—No. 28 of his addition—for a hall, conveying it to Daniel Baltzell, Lewis F. Casey, John N. Johnson, Hezekiah B. Newby and William B. Thorn, Trustees, and their successors in office. Here the lodge at once proceeded to erect a building, now known as the "old Odd Fellows Hall." Here they celebrated their mystic rites and devised their works of charity for nearly thirty years without accumulating much wealth in their treasury. But at length, ——, they bought a lot off the south end of Lot 28, Block 17, and proceeded to erect their present splendid hall, at a cost of over $6,000. It proved a good investment, as the building is already paid for, the lodge is out of debt and has about $500 in the treasury, with about 100 members.

Jefferson Encampment, No. 91, was organized October 13, 1868. The charter members were J. K. Albright, R. L. Strattan, J. S. Bogan, G. E. Welborn, T. H. McBride, J. B. Tolle, W. D. Green, J. G. Rease, G. C. Vaughn and J. F. Carroll.

Lodge No. 104, Independent Order of Mutual Aid, was instituted December 14, and chartered December 27, 1880. Its charter members were H. S. Plummer, J. H. Mitchell, R. W. Lyon, Julian L. Frohock, G. F. M. Ward, J. F. Baltzell, F. S. Burnett, R. E. Ryan, G. H. Bittrolf, W. A. Jewell, J. S. Gowenlock, V. G. Haag, T. H. Goodwin, J. T. Daily, H. Burger, J. H. Rainey, F. W. Herman, J. W. Cochran, J. J. Stern and V. Lippert. Of course, the two last named organizations met in Odd Fellows Hall.

Iron Hall, No. 68, was organized a few years ago. This also meets in the Odd Fellows Hall. Its charter members were J. S. Bogan, W. B. Anderson, W. M. White, N. Staats, W. V. B. Bogan, E. Iddinge, W. J. Levall, M. O'Connor, A. L. Hobbs, Joseph Boswell, S. Rupert, J. W. Morgan, A. A. Hamilton, J. M. Davis, F. D. Boswell, W. S. Davis, V. G. Haag, W. D. Rogers, W. H. Herdman, R. Dewy, J. H. Mitchell, W. A. Jones, Peter Brown, N. H. Moss, Joseph Hudson, W. H. Smith, J. T. Daily, T. H. Goodwin, N. C. Malone, R. P. Moyer, T. H. Hobbs, B. C. Strattan, C. W. Lindley and William Blythe.

Mount Vernon Lodge, No. 186, A. O. U. W., began June 14, 1881, and meets in the Odd Fellows Hall. Its first officers were William J. Ellis, P. M. W.; C. A. Keller, M. W.; W. C. Pollock, G. F.; William A. Goodwin, O.; N. Staats, Recorder; George W. Reid, F. & R.; Van Wilbanks, G.; J. T. S. Brattin, I. W.; and William B. Hawkins, O. W.

Mount Vernon Council, No. 7, R. T. of T., was instituted January 17, and chartered January 23, 1880. Its first officers were, C. A. Keller, S. C.; S. C. Polk, V. C.; W. N. White, P. C.; Adam C. Johnson, Chaplain; C. W. Lindley, Recording Secretary; A. Ransom Merrill, Financial Secretary; John C. Bray, Treasurer; James Hitchcock, Her'd; Mrs. Annie E. Hitchcock, Deputy Her'd; John A. Greenhoe, G.; William D. Rogers, Sentry; Dr. W. Watson, Medical Examiner. There were forty-two charter members. The council meets in the old Odd Fellows Hall. This society has demonstrated that the average toper will drink if he knows the drink will cost his needy family $2,000.

Coleman Post, G. A. R., of the Department of Illinois, was organized by Department Commander H. Hilliard, of Springfield, July 26, 1876, with about forty members. Its officers were Frederick D. Boswell, Post Commander; William Randall, Senior Vice Com.; J. A Phillips, Junior Vice Com.; T. H. Goodwin, Adjutant; John B. Crowder, Quartermaster; H. S. Plummer, Surgeon; C. E. Cline, Chaplain; D. K. Goodale, Officer of the Day; A. J. Williamson, Officer of the Guard; C. C. McBryant, Sergeant Major; J. W. Phillips, Quartermaster Sergeant. Its meetings were held in the old Odd Fellows Hall. A year or so since, the attendance became so small that the burden of expense fell heavily on a few, and they paid up the rents and suspended their meetings. In the meantime, the higher powers have changed the work, and the post is not prepared to take it up; but recently it has received a permit to get the new work and go on, and it is now waiting till a sufficient number can be got together to take it up.

K. of H. Lodge, No. 683, was organized September 3, 1878. The charter members were S. F. Crews, W. H. Smith, L. B. Salisbury, D. Sturgis, C. W. Lindley, S. C. Polk, R. L. Strattan, C. Zierjacks, J. G. Brunner, James Owen, C. H. Patton, J. C. Dawson, E. E. Hazzard, James Hitchcock, T. H. Goodwin, William Hill, Frank Smith, John Stumpp and Jacob Smith.

Jefferson Division, No. 154, Brotherhood of Locomotive Engineers, was chartered August 19, 1882.

Evening Star Lodge, No. 112, Brotherhood of Locomotive Firemen, was chartered July 2, 1882. The charter members were A. J. Randall, W. N. Hansacker, P. C. Johnson, J. Murphy, R. L. Bracy, B. W. Vawter, C. Joyce, J. G. Boswell, T. Lancey, T. F. Thixton, J. C. Branham, F. C. Wyard, A. D. Isom, Daniel Messitt, James W. Burns, I. T. Carr, William Stephenson, A. Vogt, F. P. Nance, T. H. Buckley, J. Melton, T. E. Peck, R. W. Lindley, Harry Laswell, J. M. Covington, C. O. Simms and Bruce Rawson. The last three orders meet in the Masonic Hall.

Mount Vernon Lodge, No. 31, A. F. & A. M., is nearly as old as Marion Lodge I. O. O. F. The charter is signed by W. F. Walker, G. M., and is dated at Jacksonville, October 9, 1845. It is granted to William W. Bennett, M.; W. A. Thomas, S. W.; and W. H. Short, J. W. It goes without saying that this ancient order has grown more gradually than the others. At first they met, like everybody else in those days, where they could. Their first hall, entitled to the name, was in the room over the store of J. Pace & Son, corner of Main and Union streets. This they occupied till the Strattan & Johnson building was erected, at the corner of Washington and Bunyan, when they secured the upper story with its ample accommodations. They meet on the first and third Monday evenings in each month, although for thirty years they had met by the moon.

H. W. Hubbard Chapter, No. 160, R. A. M., dates back to October 31, 1873, and the charter is signed by Asa W. Blakesley, G. H. P., at Chicago. The list of charter members shows that its start in the world was eminently respectable. They were C. H. Patton, R. A. D. Wilbanks, S. S. Porter, H. S. Stephenson, Frederick Merrill, Z. C. Pace, A. F. Taylor, N. C. Pace, J. W. Baugh, J. C. McConnell, H. S. Plummer, J. J. Bambrook, A. W. Plummer, T. T. Wilson, T. Gowenlock, Joel Dubois and George Pickett. The principal officers were C. H. Patton, H. P.; R. A. D. Wilbanks, K.; S. S. Porter, S. Their meetings are held on the first Friday of each month.

United Brothers of Friendship Lodge, No. 11, was organized in December, 1881. The first officers were Charles Bisch, Master; Henry Bradford, Deputy Master; W. H. Jones, Secretary; J. K. Kearney, Treasurer; Henry Jackson, Senior Marshal; Samuel Martin, Junior Marshal; Thomas Tinsley, Chaplain; Jesse Redman, Outside Sentinel; Prince Neal, Inside Sentinel; Nelson Gorman, R. H. Supporter; George Scott, L. H. Supporter. It is a colored institution and meets at the old Odd Fellows Hall.

The first fire in the town occurred in February, 1842. It burned a large two-story building erected by T. B. Afflack, but then occupied by W. J. Kirby, that stood where Merrill's livery stable now stands, on the corner of Main and Casey streets. It was entirely destroyed. Bowman's house burned near where D. K. Goodale lives, was not in town. The next fire of any magnitude destroyed the tobacco warehouse of Varnell & Holloman, near East Main street, in the spring of 1863. The next swept nearly the entire block north of the public square, about the 9th of March, 1868. This fire was charged to a tailor, a new man here, who worked in a little shop near where Seimer & Klinker now keep. He had been arrested and fined for brutal treatment of a bound-boy he had, and he disappeared about the time the fire broke out. It is supposed he fired his shop to get revenge of the people for their having him prosecuted. The buildings were of combustible material, all wooden, and the mud was about four inches deep in the street, so it was found impossible to save the buildings and very difficult to save any of the goods. In the frenzy that always possesses some crazy fools at fires, thousands of dollars worth of goods were thrown down in the street and trampled in the mud. A brick wall saved the building on the southwest corner of the block. After the fire, C. H. Patton, J. S. Klinker and J. C. Dawson combined their forces and put up the Phœnix Block, which still stands, an ornament to our city. Nearly exactly twelve months after this, March 16, 1869, the old court house took fire in the night and burned to the ground. It was generally believed to have originated in some late bacchanalian revels of W. E. Coffey, the Sheriff, and was supposed by many to have been contrived by him to cover up some of his financial crookedness. All the books and nearly all the papers belonging to the offices were saved. The fire was discovered by the Circuit Clerk, J. S. Bogan, who, in answer to an extraordinary call, was making his way to the office at the dead hours of night to issue papers. The next grand attack of the fire fiend was upon the beautiful machine shops of the St. Louis & Southeastern Railroad Company. Just before night on the 27th of May, 1874, when the men had had but just time to get home from their day's work, a prolonged sound of the whistle was heard, and the citizens soon gathered, but only to see the flames sweeping like a tornado over the combustible roofing of the magnificent shops. Little of the machinery was saved and the building was a total loss. Before the year closed, the city was visited by another calamity. December 20, 1874, the woolen factory and mills of J. B. Tolle and others were burned. The fire started early in the night, but the oil, etc., rendered all so inflammable that it was impossible to save it. The loss fell heavily on all parties, but was ruinous on Mr.

Tolle. Two fires involving larger losses have occurred this year—S. W. Westbrook's mill, on the night of July 2, and Bell's lumber yard a week later. The latter is believed to have been fired by tramps, or by some of our own night-hawks. The former may have been from spontaneous combustion or from some part of the machinery, or from some juvenile tramps seen hanging about the previous day. The loss by the lumber yard was about $4,000; by the mill, over $10,000. Besides these, Henry M. Williams lost a fine dwelling a mile north of town some fifteen years ago. In 1874, Strattan & Johnson procured a force pump and some hose, and provided temporary trucks. After this had been borrowed for every fire alarm for a year or so and began to need repairs, they proposed to the City Council to donate what they had to the city if the latter would buy another pump with hose and furnish the trucks. This offer was accepted, and a fire company organized which has proven very efficient.

Speaking of the factory reminds us that our first woolen factory, which was really only a carding machine, was built about forty-five years ago on the same lot where Westbrook & Co.'s mill was burned. Jarvis Pierce got up the enterprise, and the machine was run by a pair of oxen on a huge inclined wheel. After a few years, Abner Melcher got up a similar machine on Lot No. 16, south of where James Urry now lives. A corn mill was attached, and for many years they did excellent service. Tolle's mill followed, a mile northeast of town, and was run for twenty years or more before it was burned out there and came to town. Not far from the time that Tolle started up on the creek, Dr. Short built a mill at the present northeast corner of the fair ground, where he made a large amount of meal and lumber.

It was here that Sager got an arm fearfully mangled with a saw, as many of our citizens remember. John Summers made very good flour at his steam mill, two miles east of town already mentioned, but it was not till Varnell & Holloman put up the mill now owned by Hobbs & Sons that we began to have a better class of mills. The Jefferson Mills and the Mount Vernon Milling Company, now furnishing the best of everything, are recent enterprises.

The First National Bank of Mount Vernon was chartered June 10, 1872, and opened up and commenced business August 14. The stockholders were J. J. Fitzgerald, A. M. Grant, C. D. Ham, T. G. Holland, Noah Johnston, S. S. Marshall, J. Taylor and B. Temple. The banking house of Evans, Wilbanks & Co., composed of G. W. Evans, John Wilbanks and Van Wilbanks, began operations in June, 1873. Both are institutions of the highest repute.

Our first resident lawyer was Clement, in 1838-39, soon followed by Henry Eddy for a few months in 1840, and R. S. Nelson and R. F. Wingate soon after, for much longer periods. These, with D. Baugh and S. G. Hicks of our own men, and E. H. Gatewood, J. A. McClernand and A. C. Caldwell, of Shawneetown, Edward Jones, of Elizabethtown, H. Boyakin, of Belleville, and others, constituted our bar from 1840 to 1850. But our lawyers are noticed elsewhere. Dr. Watson was our first physician (1821); then Adams & Glover, 1823; then Dr. Simonds; then Dr. J. S. Moore, in 1833; Dr. Parks, Dr. Greetham, Dr. Allen, Dr. Gray, Dr. T. S. Roe, Dr. Green, Dr. Edwards, etc. The names of the high contracting parties to the earliest weddings cannot now be given. The first death, perhaps, was a child out east of Pleasant Grove neighborhood a little later. Our first tombstone cutter was Washington Dale, about 1842. Our first brickyard was west of town, Mr. Hirons', 1823; the next was made by Hirons and W. B. Hayes, north of the Fairfield road and west of the creek, in what is now Ragan's field. Our earliest tailors were G. W. Duckworth, William Gibberson and Sethman, before and up to 1840, and A. H. Barnes, now of Lampasas, Tex., and Wallace Campbell, a few years later. Our first and only pump-maker was J. J. Fly, about 1845. Our first shingle-cutter was William Campbell, with his brother-in-law, Shipley, followed by R. C. Jarrell and others. Our first tinner was Jacob Shaffner, of Ohio, brother-in-law to Edward and Richard Noble, in 1840. Our first and only hatmakers were James Ross and Wylie Prigmore. Our first jeweler was Michael Tromly, about 1841. Our first tanner was Nathaniel Parker, just south of the Short camp-ground. Abraham Buffington was our first gun-maker. In other branches of business, or most of them, there was no exclusiveness, almost every one working at them, in more or less clumsy style. *Quantum sufficit.*

CHAPTER VIII.

SHILOH TOWNSHIP—GENERAL DESCRIPTION—TOPOGRAPHY AND BOUNDARIES—EARLY SETTLEMENT—PIONEER HARDSHIPS AND PRIVATIONS—MILLS, ETC—AN INCIDENT—BIRTHS, DEATHS AND MARRIAGES—ROADS AND BRIDGES—STOCK-RAISING—SCHOOLS AND CHURCHES—WOODLAWN VILLAGE, ETC., ETC.

"Youth smiled and all was heavenly fair—
Age came and laid his finger there,
And where are they?"—*Old Spanish Poem.*

NEXT to Moore's Prairie and the immediate settlements around Mount Vernon, this division of the county dates back in its history beyond any other township. More than sixty years have dissolved in the great ocean of the past since the first of our race located in what is now Shiloh Township. And what a story, what a history is enveloped in those threescore years. They have witnessed empires shaken to their centers by the throes of popular revolutions; they have seen the hand of oblivion passed over principalities and powers, and their places upon the maps blotted out forever. They have looked upon the old man full of years and honor, gathered to his fathers, and watched the young bride stricken down at the very altar.

Each of these sixty years has been the very reflex and symbol of human life. The young babe is shadowed in the opening leaves and buds and flowers. The strong and lusty youth appears in all his manly strength and beauty in the vigorous spring; the man of mature years and approved wisdom, and stands erect in the fullness and flush of the summer; the descent of life is seen in the fading glories of autumn, and the nigh approach unto the end is too well foreshadowed in the hoary and infirm winter. Life is one long day of ceaseless and weary labor, and much truer did the pioneers find this to be so fifty or sixty years ago than do we in this age of civilization and refinement, when education and wealth surround us on every hand. The years that have elapsed since the first settlement in Shiloh have made the frontier of Illinois almost the very center of civilization. A State that then contained but a few thousand people, now has almost as many as the Republic had when it won its independence; and a county that had but a score or two of souls has a population now of over 20,000, so rapidly has the country so rapidly the great West—grown and developed in the last half or three-quarters of a century.

Shiloh Township lies west of Mount Vernon, south of Rome, east of Casner and north of McClellan Townships, and is designated in the Congressional Survey as Township 2 south, and Range 3 east. It is one of the finest agricultural regions in the county, except Moore's Prairie, and many fine farms are to be found within its limits. The surface is rolling, and even broken in some portions of the township, and originally was mostly timbered land, on which grew in great abundance several kinds of oak, hickory, elm, ash, locust (black and honey), sweet gum, sassafras, papaw, etc., etc. It is watered and drained by the West

*By W. H. Perrin.

Fork of Big Muddy, formerly called Casey's Fork, Hooper's Creek, Cole's Creek, and several smaller streams. An excellent stone quarry has been opened, and is owned by Thomas Knott. It is pretty extensively worked, and affords a good building stone. The principal crops are wheat, corn, oats, hay, potatoes and beans. Considerable attention is paid to fruit, particularly apples. The St. Louis Division of the Louisville & Nashville Railroad passes through Shiloh nearly from east to west, with Woodlawn Station on its west line, a village of considerable business enterprise. The railroad has been of great value to the township, increasing the price of lands and affording excellent shipping facilities. The township received its name from old Shiloh Church.

The first white settler in what is now Shiloh Township is said to have been Zadok Casey, who is so often mentioned and so extensively noticed in other chapters of this volume, that nothing additional can be said here without repetition. He served his country in the field as a soldier in the Black Hawk war, in the General Assembly of the State, in the halls of Congress and as Lieutenant Governor, and better than all, he served his fellow-men as a minister of the Cross of Christ. For almost half a century, he served the people of Jefferson County, and at last laid down his life with the harness on, for he was a member of the State Senate at the time of his death. But it was the death of all deaths he would have chosen to die—that at the post of duty. Calmly he sleeps amid the scenes where his active life was spent. He sleeps, and his mantle is folded about him with but little probability of its ever being disturbed by his successors. He sleeps, and the billows of faction, which heave like the waves of a stormy ocean, break not his deep repose more than the hail, the lightning, and the thunder that fall around his tomb.

Gov. Casey, as elsewhere stated, came here in 1817, and made his first settlement in what is now Shiloh Township. He was poor, and brought his earthly all, which consisted of his wife, one child and a few articles of household use, upon a single horse, himself walking most of the way. He built a cabin, cleared a piece of ground, raised a small crop, and thus began life, where he was destined to live long and serve his people faithfully. The history of his life-work is told in preceding chapters, and to them the reader is referred.

William Maxey was another of the early settlers of this township, and like Gov. Casey has been extensively written up in the preceding chapters. He came from Sumner County, Tenn., but was a native of Virigina. He settled here in 1818, and raised a large family of children, most of whom were born and some of them married before he came to Illinois. His son Henry B. was married while they lived in Tennessee and had one child—an infant—when they came here. It died soon after their arrival, and is said to have been the first death and burial of a white person in the county.

The Maxeys were a prolific family of people. William Maxey's children were Clarissa, Henry B., Bennett N., Elihu, Harriet, Vylinda A., Charles H., Joshua C., Hostillina, William M. A. and Jehu G. D. Of these Henry had twelve children; Clarissa seventeen, Bennett thirteen, Elihu twelve (he was killed by a kick from his horse), Harriet twelve, Vylinda seven, Charles thirteen, Joshua four, William ten and Jehu one. William Maxey, the pioneer, had 101 grandchildren, forty-four of whom are now living. He died in 1838; his wife, the year previous; and in their death the county lost two good citizens and most exemplary Christians. As they moved about in their daily walks, doing good to all, myriad spirits hovered over them uttering the tones they had learned in heaven, and as the good old couple drifted down the somber and mysterious pathway that leads to the door of the tomb, all were fain to acknowledge that the world was better for their having lived in it. A lasting monument to their Christian piety is the fact that they left every one of their ten living children professing the same Christian faith, and zealous members of the Church of God. Their sons have been prominent citizens of the county, some of them preachers, some physicians, some of them civil officers, and all farmers to a greater or less extent. Joshua C., or "Canon Maxey," as more commonly called, is living on the old homestead, a place settled originally in 1818, and which has never been out of the possession of the Maxey family. Canon Maxey is a preacher of the Methodist Church, and for nearly forty years he has been pointing the unregenerate to that "far country" beyond the "River," where those who have gone before are waiting to welcome them home.

William Depriest was an early settler in this township, and came in about 1821. He settled where Joseph Philips now lives, and is long since dead. His wife was a sister of Gov. Casey, and a remarkably large woman, weighing over 300 pounds. She died a short time before her husband, and both sleep side by side at old Shiloh Church. They had two sons—Isaac and Green, both of whom went to Missouri, and, we believe, died there. Lewis Johnson came here in 1819, and settled on Section 22. He had a large family, many of whom and their descendants are still living in the county. A. Bateman, a son-in-law of Lewis Johnson, came to the neighborhood with him. Archibald Harris also came about the same time, and was from Kentucky. He had been a Baptist preacher, but had backslidden—if the Baptists ever do such things—and became a drunkard, and, as we have been informed, died intoxicated. The Holtsclaws were early settlers, as will be seen by sketches elsewhere. William Woods came here early (about 1819) and raised a large family, of whom some are still living here. James E. Davis was also an early settler in this township, and came from Wilson County, Tenn. He did not remain long, but moved away. Lewis Green, the step-father of Jesse A. Dees, was an early settler in this township, but the people were now moving in so fast it was impossible to keep trace of them.

There were plenty of Indians here when the first settlers came. The Maxeys remember to have seen Indians passing their cabin in early times. A hundred of the "red sons of the forest" passed there once in a body and camped within a hundred yards of their house. They were friendly, and made no trouble nor interrupted any one further than to call at the house and beg some salt and meal. On the Gov. Casey farm (where Capt. Moss now lives) the Indians used to camp in numbers when hunting on Camp Branch, a tributary having its source on this farm and emptying into Hooper's Creek. For seven years after Gov. Casey came here, the Indians camped upon this branch during their fall hunts. The woods at that time were full of game, and the savages frequently came into the neighborhood to hunt, but so far as we can learn never committed any depredations after the murder of Moore in Moore's Prairie, and even that has never been definitely settled; it has only been supposed that he was murdered by Indians. As we have said, there was plenty of game here then, and some of the Maxey boys, notably Bennett and Jehu were great hunters. Hundreds of deer could be seen sometimes at a "single look," feeding on the prairie, as cattle can now be seen; and as to wild turkeys, "the woods were full of them," and the settlers had but little trouble in supplying their larders with meat. Indeed, it was great fun for the most of them to lay in their winter's supply of meat, but the procuring of bread was an altogether different thing. The first meal was brought with the settlers from the older States, and afterward gotten at the little horse mills put up in the new settlements, which were very rude in their construction and very poor at best, but better than none at all. The first mill in this township was built by William Maxey. It was a horse-mill of the usual primitive kind, but was of great benefit to the community, and for many years was their chief source of supply of breadstuff. A distillery was kept by Abner Hill in a very early day, in the northwest part of the township, but it is a landmark that has long since passed away. The old wooden mold-board plows were the kind most in use by the early settlers. J. C. Maxey used to stock these old-style plows, making the mold-boards himself, and hence, next to the blacksmith who made the plows, was a man in great demand among the farming population.

Joseph McMeens, one of the pioneers of this section, met with a sad bereavement soon after his settlement. A child, a little girl only four years old, was lost in the woods and was never found, nor was her fate ever clearly established. Whether she was devoured by wild beasts or carried off by prowling savages will probably never be known.

Births, deaths and marriages are matters of great interest in new countries, particularly among the female portion of the inhabitants. The first birth in Shiloh Township cannot be recalled, but knowledge of the first death is more easily attainable. All things earthly are fleeting and transitory, even to the human beings who occupy this planet of ours. We look around us at the landscape clothed with beauty, ornamented with flowers of the fairest hue and rich with verdure. But yet a little while and winter invades the beautiful fields and hills and valleys, and with a relentless hand shrouds in gloom the gorgeous scenery. We behold the sky drawn above us as a magnificent canopy, dyed in azure and beautiful with pictures of floating silver; but as we gaze upon the beautiful scenery, the world, awhile radiant with beauty, is mantled in darkness. Man looks upon these changes in nature, and seems unconscious of the fact that he, too, is as perishable as they, and is heedless of the warning voice that tells him " Dust thou art, and unto dust shalt thou return." Journeying to the tomb, he wastes his price less time, until finally death knocks at his door and finds him unprepared.

"And years may go,
But our tears shall flow
O'er the dead who have died." etc., etc.

Death entered the settlement through the Maxey family, and an infant of Henry B. Maxey was the victim. It was brought here an infant in arms, and survived the change of climate but a short time. It was the first death in the township, and believed also to have been the first in the county. The well populated graveyards in the township and surrounding country show how well death has done his work and how busy he has been among the " children of men."

The third wedding to occur in the county took place in Shiloh Township, and was a kind of wholesale wedding. Three couples were married at the same time and place, viz., Thomas M. Casey and Harriet Maxe

Abraham T. Casey and Vylinda Maxey and Bennett N. Maxey and Sally Overbey. The ceremony was performed October 5, 1819, and the affair was a grand one for those early days. To use a backwoods expression, "the big pot was put in the little one," the fatted calf (deer) was slain, a great feast prepared, and everybody within reach invited. This triple wedding was long remembered as an event worthy of note.

Shiloh Township is as well supplied with roads and bridges as any portion of Jefferson County. Good wagon roads traverse it in every direction, and substantial bridges span the streams wherever needed.

Previous to 1869, the county was divided into election precincts, but in that year, it, under a law of the State, adopted township organization. Since the change, the following is a list of the township officers:

Supervisors—John R. Moss, 1870-71; J. C. Tyler, 1872; J. M. Galbraith, 1873-74; W. C. Webb, 1875; V. G. Osborne, 1876; A. D. Dollins, 1877; G. L. Moss, 1878; J. J. Willis, 1879; N. L. Frost, 1880; J. C. Tyler, 1881; Thomas C. Allen, 1882; J. C. Tyler, 1883, the present incumbent.

Town Clerks—John T. Johnson, 1872; Sanford Hill, 1873; W. Greer, 1874; J. D. McMeen, 1875; E. S. Dillon, 1876-77; N. H. Moss, 1878; W. A. Piercy, 1879 to 1881; L. Bond, 1882; W. A. Piercy, 1883, now in office.

Assessors—J. M. Galbraith, 1872; J. D. McMeen, 1873; W. T. Webb, 1874; O. A. Dickerman, 1875; J. N. Bond, 1876; J. H. Payne, 1877; J. A. Reed, 1878; W. T. Maxey, 1879-80; J. A. Reed, 1881-82; S. B. Gilbert, 1883, now in office.

Collectors—W. C. Webb, 1872-73; J. C. Payne, 1874; Sanford Hill, 1875; W. C. Webb, 1876; J. A. Reed, 1877; J. J. Willis, 1878; T. C. Allen, 1879-80; Henry B. Walker, 1881 to 1883.

School Treasurers—J. Payne, Sr., J. C. Maxey, T. C. Johnson, J. Henderson, T. C. Allen, J. C. Tyler, C. C. Mayfield, J. T. Payne and R. H. Hubbard, the present incumbents.

Highway Commissioners—R. H. Hubbard, C. B. Harper, W. B. Casey, J. M. Beckham. C. B. Harper, T. W. Beal, George Hill, J. M. Beckham, J. E. Ward, J. B. Pearcy, J. R. Driver and J. E. Ward.

Justices of the Peace—C. B. Harper, J. Q. A. Berry, J. R. Driver, C. M. Casey, J R. Driver, J. DuBois, C. M. Casey, J. DuBois, L. H. House and C. M. Casey.

Constables—Sanford Hill, L. C. Johnson, A. J. Smith, L. C. Johnson, J. M. Galbraith and S. B. Gilbert.

Considerable attention is paid to stock-raising in this township, and that there is not more than there is the more's the pity. When the farmers of this section of the State devote more time and attention to stock and fruit and less to wheat—a crop that has proved so thoroughly to be an uncertain one —it will be far better for them and a good revenue will result. Capt. J. R. Moss and A. J. Moss are among the largest stock-raisers in this immediate section. They raised horses, Durham and Jersey cattle, Berkshire hogs and Cotswold sheep—the latter were originally imported from Canada. Capt. Moss was the first man who brought Cotswold sheep to the township and has done more, perhaps, to improve the stock interests than any other man. Others have more recently embarked in stock-raising, until at the present time it is getting to be the leading pursuit of the farmers of this region.

The people took a deep interest in educational matters, and schools were organized very early. Among the early teachers were Joel Pace, Edward Maxey, a man named Douglas, E. Knapp, Anderson Booth and

others. The old "Jefferson Academy" was one of the first schoolhouses in the township. Shiloh has never let its interest flag in the cause of education, and to-day it has nine comfortable schoolhouses within its limits, all of which support good schools. Christianity occupied the minds of the people as early as the cause of education. Some of the earliest settlers were ministers of the Gospel---notably Zadok Casey, of whom much has already been said. Abraham T. Casey and Lewis Johnson were also preachers, as well as some of the Maxeys. These were all ministers of the Methodist Church, and several societies of this denomination were formed very early. Old Union Church in Mount Vernon Township, was the first. Pleasant Grove Methodist Episcopal Church was organized in 1839 in the schoolhouse, and the first preacher was the Rev. W. T. Williams. Among the early members were Thomas M. Casey and family, Abraham T. Casey and family, Bennett N. Maxey and Elihu Maxey and their families and others. The present church building was put up some twenty-five years ago, and is of brick, 30x40 feet in size, costing about $2,000. It has some eighty members. There is at present a Baptist Church in the northwest corner of the township called New Hope Church. Old Shiloh Methodist Episcopal Church was one of the first churches organized in the township. Among the early members were Lewis Johnson, Zadok Casey, William and Edward Maxey, Mr. Depriest and their families. Their early meetings were held in a house put up for church and school purposes in 1821, and was given the name of Old Shiloh. For years it was used both for church and school purposes, but has long since passed away. The New Shiloh Church was an early organization. The present church building was put up in 1858; the membership is about seventy-five; the present minister Rev. L. S. Walker. The church maintains a Sunday school with some seventy-five pupils and five teachers. Little Grove Church was organized in 1833, near James Westcott's, who gave the land upon which it stood. Salem Church was also an early organization, and its origin was due principally to Rhodam Allen, who was a zealous Christian, and took great interest in religious affairs.

Woodlawn Village was laid out by John D. Williams for S. K. Casey and W. D. Green, and the plat recorded October 1, 1869. It is located on the range line in Section 25, and is on the Louisville & Nashville Railroad, west of Mount Vernon, and has about 300 inhabitants. The first house was built by Hiram Ferguson. Among the first merchants of the place were Benton. Masters, J. Q. A. Bay and Dubois. James Farmer put up a fine mill in 1872, and Hicks put up a drug store. The post office was established in 1870, and Dr. Masters was appointed Postmaster; the present Postmaster is G. B. Welborn. An excellent school building is in the town. It is a frame, 24x36 feet, and the school attendance is about sixty. A lodge of Odd Fellows was organized in 1874. The present officers are J. T. Slade, N. G.; J. F. Brooks, V. G.; L. H. Hawes, Treasurer; and G. W. Fyke, Secretary. In 1878, James Dillon put up an oil factory in a part of Farmer's Mill, and for several years carried on the business. It was said at the time to be the biggest thing of the kind in the whole country. Pennyroyal and sassafras came in by the hundreds of wagon-loads and was made into oil.

The following is the business outlook: Payne & Sharp, Smith & Capp, general stores; George B. Welborn, drug store; John A. Lelfield, groceries; Mrs. E. P. Reynolds, millinery; R. Richie, blacksmith, etc. The village was incorporated under the State law in 1880, with the following officers: Dr. Watson, President; Emery Wood, James Trout, Harvey Reynolds, J. W. Beckham, J. H. Hicks; and W. P. Willis, Clerk. The present officers are J. H. Hicks, President; J. H. Clayborne, J. P. Morgan, W. H. Breeze, Andrew Ferguson and L. A. Stevens.

The Methodist Church was organized in the township in the Hicks Schoolhouse, and among the original members were Isaac Hicks and wife, Benjamin McKinney and wife, Peter Shaffer and wife, George Knox and his mother, John Lemmon and wife, and others. The church was built in the village in 1879, and cost about $1,200. The society has some forty members and a good Sunday school is kept up all the year.

CHAPTER IX.

PENDLETON AND MOORE'S PRAIRIE TOWNSHIPS—GENERAL DESCRIPTION AND TOPOGRAPHY—THE FIRST SETTLERS—MOORE'S PRAIRIE A HISTORICAL SPOT—PIONEER HARDSHIPS AND DIFFICULTIES—EARLY INDUSTRIES AND CUSTOMS—TOWNSHIP OFFICERS —CHURCHES AND SCHOOLS—LYNCHBURG—BELLE RIVE AND OPDYKE—THEIR GROWTH, BUSINESS, ETC., ETC.

"Of 'a the trades that I do ken
Commend me to the ploughman."
—*Burns.*

THERE is no truer saying than that of the philosopher that our lives are what we make them. In the city, the village or on the farm is this true, but it is pre-eminently true of the farm. If farming is only given over to ignorant and unkempt boors, it will to that extent be forbidding to the growing young men. If the rural population inform themselves and pursue their business in the most ennobling way, their every movement guided by a type of intelligence that brings the best adaptation to the natural means surrounding them, it will become the most inviting pursuit for the best men and women. There is no foolish notion that more urgently needs to be exploded than the prevalent one which makes a country life below the ambition of a young man of education and spirit, and which regards towns and cities as the only places in which men rise to distinction and usefulness. Farming is called a tame and monotonous vocation, but can anything better be claimed for the plodding, exacting and exhaustive pursuits which nine-tenths of those who live in cities are compelled to follow? It is a great mistake to suppose that the population of a city is made up of great capitalists, proprietors, manufacturers and eminent lawyers and surgeons, and that it is an easy thing for a young man endowed with the quality of "smartness" to achieve wealth and distinction, or even independence, in the fierce, pitiless whirl of city life. The wrecks to be encountered in city streets every day disprove it. Comparatively few persons amass fortunes in cities, and fewer still retain them. It has been estimated that where one man becomes independently rich in a city, a hundred never get beyond moderate livers, and five hundred are but little better than beggars. That riches in cities take wings and fly away is proven by the fact that in at least five cases out of ten of a wealthy business man in middle life, he will die penniless.

Farming is not subject to these rapid and ruinous chances. In this pursuit industry, economy and good management, aided by the increase which time itself brings, will insure a competence in fifteen or twenty years; and it is a property of substance accumulated in farming, that, unlike fortunes acquired in mercantile pursuits, generally lasts through life. Few thrifty, industrious farmers die poor; few prosperous merchants who continue in business die rich. The farmer's profits come in slow and small, it is true, and often he does not find himself in comfortable circumstances until middle age. But it is in the middle of old age he most needs the comforts of independence, and if he is wise enough to keep out of debt, the moderate competency which he has managed to accumulate through his better years will come unscathed through the storms and convulsions that sweep away towering fortunes in the business world. These reflections are suggested in consequence of writing of townships that are devoted almost wholly to agricultural pursuits, and it is our wish to impress upon the young men of the country their own power to make their lives just what they would have them to be. There is no better pursuit or no more ennobling one than that of a farmer, if we choose to so make it.

The history of this township and the one immediately south of it is so interwoven that it is hard to separate them, and we shall therefore incorporate them in one chapter. The history of Moore's Prairie is really the history of both townships, and outside of Mount Vernon is the most historical spot of the county. It dates back almost three-quarters of a century, to the period of the first actual white settlement.

Pendleton Township lies in the east tier of townships, and Moore's Prairie Township forms the southeast corner of the county. They have for their boundaries Hamilton County on the east, Franklin County on the south, Spring Garden and Dodds Townships on the west, and Webber Township north of Pendleton. The latter is Township 3 south, Range 4 east, and Moore's Prairie is Township 4 south and Range 4 east, under the Congressional survey. The fine scope of country known as Moore's Prairie, which forms the larger part of one of these townships, and extending far into the other, is probably the finest body of farming land in all the surrounding country. Beautiful rolling prairies, sufficiently undulating to drain well, it is specially adapted for grain and is a wheat-growing region almost unsurpassed. Some of the finest and most valuable farms in Jefferson County are to be found in this extensive prairie. The timbered portions of the townships produce oak, hickory and a few other kinds common in this section. There are no water-courses, except a few small and nameless streams that go dry in the summer season.

The first settlement in the county was made in Moore's Prairie by one Andrew Moore, for whom the prairie was named. He settled here in 1810, and the event and his unknown, but supposed tragic, death by the Indians is detailed in a preceding chapter, and need not be repeated. He was the pioneer of all the pioneers of Jefferson County. After Moore's untimely death, no further effort was made at a settlement here until in the spring of 1816, when Carter Wilkey and Daniel Crenshaw came. The latter moved into Moore's cabin and cultivated his patch of ground, while Wilkey raised a crop in the prairie. Robert Cook came soon after Wilkey and Crenshaw, and settled in the lower end of the prairie. In the fall of the same year, Barton Atchison came. He bought Wilkey's crop and settled near Cook. Mrs. Wilkey, Carter Wilkey's mother, and Maxey Wilkey, an older brother of Carter's, and his family came in October, and during the winter the two last-mentioned families occupied one room of Crenshaw's cabin. But, like the settlement of Moore, these settlements are written up in another chapter, and nothing additional can be said here.

The next settler, perhaps, was Dempsey Hood, who came in 1817, with four stalwart sons, one of whom was a carpenter, and together with Carter Wilkey, also a carpenter, built many of the first houses in the country. In the following winter Theophilus Cook, the widow Hicks, mother of Col. Stephen G. Hicks, and several other families came in and settled in Moore's Prairie. Uncle "Ophy" Cook, as everybody called him, settled near Sloo's Point. He was a most excellent man, and all who knew him were his friends. He was a pure and upright Christian man in his character, was without blemish so far as man may judge, and as friend and neighbor he lived above reproach. The Cooks, Wilkeys, Mrs. Hicks, Atchisons and Hoods were originally from Georgia. Mrs. Hood and Mrs. Atchison were sisters, and their maiden name Hill. Mrs. Hicks was the widow of John Hicks, who, as stated in a previous chapter, was killed in the battle of New Orleans. Soon after the settlement thus mentioned, a man, Hodge, came in, and a little later Mrs. Robinson came; also about the same time a man named Fipps, Bales, Fannin and Mrs. Moore, widow of Andrew Moore, moved in and made settlements, which have been noticed elsewhere. Cren-shaw, whose settlement has already been mentioned, sold out in 1822 to Tunstall, and moved to St. Clair County. In 1824, Daniel Wilbanks bought out Tunstall and settled in Moore's Prairie, and since that date the name of Wilbanks has been a prominent one in Jefferson County and closely connected with its history. Daniel Wilbanks was originally from North Carolina, but emigrated to South Carolina, and from the latter State came to Illinois about the year 1820. He settled in St. Clair County in a place called Turkey-foot Hill and was engaged in the survey of the lands in that county. But the malaria fastened on him, and to escape its effects he came here in 1824, and, as we have stated, purchased the Crenshaw place in Moore's Prairie. His sons were Joseph, Robert A. D., William, Daniel, Davis, and several daughters. One of his sons, Robert A. D. Wilbanks, once carried the mail—when Uncle Sam traveled mostly on horseback—from Belleville to Metropolis, a fact, perhaps, that many of the old citizens still remember. He was a prominent man of his time, and held many offices and positions of trust, and had also represented his district in the State Senate. The family is still a numerous one, and the male members are to be found among the leading business men of the county, of whom sketches will be found in the biographical department of this work. Robert Wilbanks, the accomplished and accommodating Clerk of the Appellate Court, is a grandson and an able representative of the old pioneer, Daniel Wilbanks.

Other early settlers embraced the following families: The Hineses, William Jourdan, Isaac Fortenberry, Aaron Jourdan, Samuel Atchison, Lewis Watkins, etc., etc. Hines came very early and left early. There were bad stories concerning him; he kept a tavern on the Goshen road, and there were dark deeds hinted at—travelers stopping at this tavern who were never seen to leave. How true were these stories, we do not pretend to know. The time has been so long ago they are becoming dim traditions. William Jourdan settled here in 1818. He was the father of a large family, and a number of grandchildren are living in this and adjoining counties. The old house he built is now used by George Walters as a barn. Isaac Fortenberry came soon after Jourdan and settled on Section 18, but afterward sold out and moved to Missouri. C. and Aaron Jourdan settled in 1825, on Sections 9 and 10. Descendants are still living. Samuel Atchison came in early. Watkins had a store and sold the first goods in the precinct. Samuel Bradford settled near where Belle Rive now stands, but some years later moved to Wayne County. James Vance settled south of Bradford about 1820. He was from Tennessee. Others came in, including James Bellow, Willis Harderick, Isaac Smith and John Lowrey, and Moore's Prairie was rapidly settled up, as well as the timbered land adjacent to it.

There has been so much said in previous chapters of this work upon the early settlement of Moore's Prairie, that really but little additional can be said here without repetition. Moore's Prairie is a historic section, and deserves considerable space, and we deem no excuse necessary for the prominent place we have accorded to it.

The beauty of the country pleased the eye of these pioneers when they first came here, and the abundance of wild animals gratified their passion for hunting. They were surrounded by an enemy subtle and wary, but they flinched not from the contest. Even their women and children often performed deeds of heroism from which the iron nerves of manhood might well have shrunk in fear.

They had no opportunities for the cultivation of the arts and elegances of life—of refined life. In their seclusion, amid danger and peril, there arose a peculiar condition of society, elsewhere almost unknown. The little Indian meal brought with them was often expended too soon, and sometimes for weeks and months they lived without bread. The lean venison and the breast of wild turkey they taught themselves to call bread, while the fatter venison and the flesh of the bear was denominated meat. This was a wretched "makeshift," and resulted in disease and sickness when necessity compelled them to indulge in it too long, preceded by weakness and a feeling constantly of an empty stomach, and they would pass the dull hours in watching the potato tops, pumpkins and squash vines, hoping from day to day to get something to answer the place of bread. What a delight and joy was the first young potato! What a jubilee when at last the young corn could be pulled for roasting ears, only to be still intensified when it had attained sufficient hardness to be made into a johnny-cake by the aid of a tin grater. These were harbingers from heaven that brought health, vigor and content with the surroundings, poor as they were, and were only still further surpassed when mills were built and put in operation.

This was the manner in which the people lived, for the first years of their settlement here, and is a very brief and feeble sketch of some of their trials and hardships. The difficulties they encountered were very great, and would have utterly discouraged men and women less brave and resolute. They were in a wilderness, far removed from any cultivated region, and ammunition, food, clothing and implements of industry were almost unattainable.

The townships of Pendleton and Moore's

Prairie are devoted principally to grain, and as we have before stated, is the finest wheat-growing section of the county. It is too exclusively devoted to wheat for the good of the farmers. If they would divide their attention between grain, stock and fruit, they would soon find a great improvement financially in the results of their farms. Then when wheat or fruit failed they would have the other, together with their surplus stock, to fall back on.

The early churches and schools of these townships were on a par with other portions of the county. The schoolhouses were of the primitive log-cabin style, often described in this work, and the first religious meetings were held in the cabins of the people, or in summer beneath the spreading trees. The first schoolhouse of which we can learn anything was a log cabin on Section 7 of Pendleton Township, and the first teacher was a man named Gibbs. The township of Pendleton now has nine schoolhouses, and Moore's Prairie has six. These are all comfortable buildings—palaces, when compared to those the first settlers built and in which their children obtained their meager learning. The first church was organized in the northwest part of Pendleton Township, and the Estes family were among the original members. Of this organization, however, we obtained very little information.

Pendleton and Moore's Prairie Townships are closely connected historically, as previously stated, and not easy to separate the sketch of them. Originally they comprised Moore's Prairie Precinct. Upon the adoption of township organization by the county in 1869, they were divided and the south end retained the old name of Moore's Prairie, while the north half was called Pendleton, as we have been informed, for George H. Pendleton, the able Democratic statesman of Ohio, who was the Vice Presidential candidate on the ticket with Gen. McClellan in 1864. Since the adoption of township organization, the township officials of Pendleton have been as follows:

Supervisors—W. A. Jones, 1870; Solomon Patterson, 1871; R. Brown, 1872-73; T. J. Holland, 1874; A. Kniffen, 1875; John Gibson, 1876; T. J. Holland, 1877; R. Brown, 1878-79; W. S. Alexander, 1880-81; J. A. Wilbanks, 1882; L. E. Jones, 1883.

Township Clerks.—H. Patterson, 1872; L. W. Cremens, 1873; W. W. Watters, 1874 to 1876; J. S. Brooks, 1877; R. W. Shelton, 1878; J. W. Gilpin, 1879; C. M. Jackson, 1880-81; S. C. Gilbert, 1882-83.

Assessors.—J. Guthrie, 1872 to 1874; H. Patterson, 1875-76; O. P. Nesmith, 1877; J. Guthrie, 1878; E. Price, 1879-80; D. D. Smith, 1881; W. H. Estes, 1882-83.

Collectors.—J. A. Creel, 1872; T. Cornelius, 1873; J. Maulding, 1874-75; A. Kniffen, 1876 to 1878; O. M. D. Ham, 1879; L. E. Jones, 1880; R. G. Wall, 1881; J. Guthrie, 1882; O. M. D. Ham, 1883.

Highway Commissioners.—W. B. Goodner, W. C. Henry, J. N. Miller, E. Jones, G. A. Creel, E. Moore, J. W. Miller, E. Jones, William Barbee, J. Smith, P. Williamson, J. B. Jones and R. G. Wall.

Justices of the Peace.—William Carpenter and G. W. Bliss, 1870; Alfred Moore and G. W. Bliss, 1871-72; O. M. Tennison; 1873 to 1876; G. D. Jones and E. Price, 1877-80; J. R. Williams and A. C. Jones, the present incumbents.

Constables.—S. Tennison, W. H. Estes, S. L. Holder, J. E. Miller, J. Boswell, G. H. Edwards, S. L. Holder, L. McCann, W. Carpenter, E. B. Jacobson and William Price.

The following are the township officers of Moore's Prairie since the date of township organization:

Supervisors.—Q. A. Wilbanks, 1870; W. Oram, 1871-72; R. W. Burshead, 1873-74; C. H. Judd, 1875; W. G. Casey, 1876; C. H. Judd, 1877-78; J. H. Smith, 1879; A. J. Lionberger, 1880; J. D. Kniffen, 1881; A. J. Lionberger, 1882; G W. Clark, 1883.

Town Clerks —C. C. Allen, 1872 to 1874; J. McPherson, 1875-76; J. H. Zahn, 1877-78; W. H. Cofield, 1879; T. N. Woodruff, 1880 to 1882; J. W. Nooner, 1883.

Assessors.—W. G. Casey, 1872 to 1874; J. H. Smith, 1875; R. F. Heck, 1876; W. H. Hunter, 1877-78; A. Kniffen, 1879; R. S. Compton, 1880; J. H. Price, 1881; W. H. Cofield, 1882; O. H. Birkhead, 1883.

Collectors.—J. A. Irvin, 1872; J. D. Kniffen, 1873-74; H. C. Allen, 1875; E. F. Burchead, 1876; A. Kniffen, 1877; W. H. Cofield, 1878; J. D. Kniffen, 1879-80; George Shipley, 1881; G. N. Allen, 1882-83.

School Treasurers.—H. C. Allen, 1875; C. H. Judd, 1876; W. G. Clark, 1877-78; D. S. Hunter, 1879; C. H. Judd, 1880; J. T. Watters, 1881; C. H. Birkhead, 1882; E. N. Karn, 1883.

Highway Commissioners.—J. Lionberger, Henry Bonnett, J. T. Watters, W. F. Wiley, J. S. Brooks, J. Hopkins, W. J. Finley, Joseph Shirley, William Cofield, J. H. Zahn and J. A. Smith.

Justices of the Peace.—Edward Price, D. Boyles, R. S. Compton and H. L. N. Mills.

Constables.—J. J. Fannin, F. Hicks, J. S. Cook, T. G. Barnett, T. Shipley, William Pearson, T. Shipley, G. Keons and J. W. Heck, Jr.

These townships, particularly Pendleton, are well supplied with villages. Lynchburg was laid out in 1852-53, by W. H. Lynch, who immortalized himself by giving it his name. It is located in Sections 5 and 8 of Pendleton Township, and originally comprised four blocks of eight lots each. Mr. Johnson gives the following introduction to the history of Lynchburg:

At the time Lynchburg was laid out, Jonathan Belieu lived at Mount Vernon, making himself conspicuous as an exhorter, in a protracted meeting. Lynch moved a small log house to the southwest corner of his town, and into this moved Belieu. The latter built a frame addition to the end of the house, for goods, but by this time he had no means left. To replenish his treasury, he resorted to measures not becoming a good Christian and an exhorter. He took one horse from Mr. Smith in Mount Vernon and one from a negro near town. These he took to Fairfield, sold Smith's horse and was returning home on the other, intending to turn him loose on Black-oak Ridge and walk home. But he missed his calculations by about half a mile. Just before he came to his place to change cars, he was met by Capt. Newby, who at once recognized him and the horse, and marched him on to town. Into jail he went. He was visited by his poor, afflicted wife, who brought him an auger, with which he bored the door in twain and made his escape. Dr. Gray found him, brought him back to town, and again he was incarcerated, this time in the dungeon. Then he tore his blanket into strips, and by its aid got through the scuttle hole up stairs, and when Mr. Thorn went to pass his breakfast down to him, he slipped out in his sock feet and again made his escape. This was the last heard of him and his family soon followed. This was quite a blow to the town, but Barnet Lynch moved into the deserted house and built a small shop east of it. Then W. H. Lynch and Stephen G. Hicks built a storehouse and opened out a stock of goods. Lynch bought out Hicks, and in 1854 sold to Russell Brown. D. E. Lynch came about this time and built a blacksmith shop east of Barnet's shop. Soon after selling out to Brown, Lynch died and Brown undertook to make an addition to the town, when the fact was developed that there was no town on record to add to. So he waited till the Legislature assembled, when he got Gen. Anderson, then in the Legislature, to put a bill through, by which the original survey of Lynchburg was legalized and the title of purchasers established. This act is dated February 17, 1857, but Brown's Addition bears date July 31, 1854. A little later a post office was established. T. O. Brown joined his brother, Russell, in the store, but a year or two afterward they sold out to Dr. Short. He (Short) was a leading and active spirit until his death, which occurred in 1859. He built a house just north of town, and also a mill, and practiced his profession. Charles Rahm traded his farm for Anderson & Mills' stock of goods at Mount Vernon, and moved it to this place, where he flourished for a brief season.

At one time Lynchburg had a fair, even flattering, prospect for a railroad, and it appeared accordingly. Houses were built, stores opened and business flourished. Benjamin Brewer built a house; Davenport also improved; Richard Lyon, from Mount Vernon, opened a stock of goods and built one or two houses, thus making times pretty lively. Frank Parker built a two-story house and Dr. Stonemets came to where Major Estes lives. Brown made a second addition to the town and Romine also made an addition. Dr. Gray for several years had a business house. About the year 1862, a schoolhouse was built, with a hall above. But the poet of Bonny Doon tells us that the likes of "men and mice gang aft aglee," so it was with Lynchburg. When the St. Louis & Southeastern Railroad was built it passed Lynchburg " by on the other side." With the railroad came Opdyke and Belle Rive, and Lynchburg went. Montgomery and Stonemets went to Opdyke; Davenport went to Belle Rive, and so the town scattered. There is but little left of it now but a store and a shop or two, with a few dwelling houses.

"A place for idle eyes and ears,
 A cobwebbed nook of dreams;
Left by the stream whose waves are years
 The stranded village seems."

Belle Rive was laid out April 1, 1871, on Section 27 of Pendleton Township. It was surveyed by Mr. Williams for Moses Waters, William Canfield and Jesse Laird, the owners of the land upon which it is located. The original plat was sixty-seven blocks; Waters afterward four blocks and Laird eight blocks, and like all new railroad towns, it improved rapidly. It drew inhabitants from the other hamlets in the county until they were left almost depopulated. Lynchburg and Spring Garden particularly suffered in this respect. A number of men came from the latter place; Barbee moved in from the prairie and put up a mill. Drs. Hughey and Eaton, from Harris Grove, moved in, and Mr. Wall came from Farrington; Boudinot came from St. Louis and opened a store, and Howard opened a lumber yard; other mills were built. A schoolhouse was built, and soon every branch of business is represented in the live little town. At present the business of the place is about as follows: R. J. Eaton, W. S. Chaney, J. W. Wright, S. T. Grimes, general stores; S. C. Guthrie, drugs; J Guthrie & Son, dry goods and post office; R. M. Seeley, M. D. Guthrie, J. Parks, J. Griffin, grocery stores; T. L. Boswell, hardware; G. P. Yeakley, tinware; Hunter & Davenport, lumber and farming implements; John Garner, harness and saddlery; J. W. Miller, furniture; J. H.

Gilpen, restaurant and family grocery; Belle Rive Hotel, by Jesse Laird; Miller Hotel, by John Miller; Buchanan & Co., lumber yard; physicians, W. R. Ross, W. A. Hughey, E. M. Miller and R. J. Eaton; J. W. Piper, Police Magistrate; Rudd & Maulding, blacksmiths; E. E. Fancher and Smith, wagon and blacksmith shops; L. D. Davenport, blacksmith; L. C. Waters, attorney; F. M. Goodwin, tailor, and Miss Leake, millinery.

A Christian Church was organized about 1873-74; a good frame edifice has been built. Elder B. R. Gilbert is present pastor.

A Masonic lodge was organized in 1871, with C. S. Todd Worshipful Master. They meet in a hall over Dr. R. J. Eaton's store. The membership is about forty-five, with C. S. Todd, Master; Edward Miller, Senior Warden; E. N. Karn, Junior Warden; R. M. Seeley, Secretary. In 1878, this lodge was consolidated with the lodge of Middleton, Wayne County.

Belle Rive was incorporated under the general law in 1872, and the present are the Board of Trustees: B. R. Gilbert, Jesse Laird, Scott Cook, C. A. Baker, H. A. Shields and W. A. Hunter. Of this board, B. R. Gilbert is President and J. W. Piper, Clerk.

Opdkye was laid out April 14, 1871, and like Belle Rive, its neighbor, was the result of building the railroad. It is located in Section 17 of Pendleton Township, and had almost as many proprietors as blocks in its plat. Among them were George D. Edgar, James K., Jonathan, Jefferson H. and Alonzo Jones and D. T. Philips. It covered originally about 160 acres of ground and embraced some sixty-four blocks. The first residences in the new town were built by Dr. Stonemets and another by Dr. Montgomery. Dr. Stonemets built a house which was for some time used as a store room. Joshua Allen then put up a store house; W. S. Alexander also built a house; also Carpenter; James K. Jones and John Keller put up a mill. The town, like Belle Rive, improved rapidly, and became quite a lively place. Its business still continues, and is even growing constantly, as the country increases in wealth.

There are now two mills in the town—Barbee & Co., who own the one built by Jones & Keller, and the Atlas Mills, by Montgomery & Co. William Poole, Rentchler & Smith, William A. Jones, Jesse D. Jones, general stores; Henry Philips, drugs; A. C. Jones, harness; Estes Brothers, hardware; John Adams and G. Hale, blacksmiths; W. W. Teltz, cooper shop; physicians, Drs. Stonemets and Montgomery.

A Methodist Episcopal Church was organized in 1872. At present it has about fifty members, under the pastorate of Rev. Mr. Franklin. A good Sunday school is maintained.

The school is an excellent one, with two departments, and an average attendance of about sixty children.

A Masonic lodge, which was originally organized at Lynchburg, was moved to this place about 1876. They meet in the room with the Odd Fellows. The officers are M. V. B. Montgomery, Master; John Adams, Senior Warden; W. W. Feltz, Junior Warden; and William Young, Secretary.

The Odd Fellows lodge was also organized in Lynchburg and removed to Opdyke. The present officers are George C. Hutson, N. G.; J. J. Jones, V. G.; Alonzo Gibson, Recording Secretary; and J. W. Estes, Permanent Secretary.

A post office was established in 1872, and W. S. Alexander was the first Postmaster.

The present Postmaster is J. C. Tucker. The village contains about 200 inhabitants, and is an enterprising, stirring little town.

The railroad has been of great benefit to Pendleton Township, and has increased the value of property greatly since it was built. So far, Moore's Prairie Township is without railroads; but as there are several projected roads, and which when built may give it railroad facilities, so the people live in hope. There are no villages in Moore's Prairie Township, nor manufacturing industries. It is an agricultural region entirely, and as such is not surpassed in the county.

CHAPTER X.*

ROME TOWNSHIP—TOPOGRAPHICAL AND PHYSICAL FEATURES—OCCUPATION BY WHITE PEOPLE—WHO THE PIONEERS WERE—THE MAXWELLS AND OTHERS—HARDSHIPS AND TRIALS—MILLS AND OTHER IMPROVEMENTS—TOWNSHIP OFFICERS—SCHOOLS AND CHURCHES—VILLAGE OF ROME—GROWTH, IMPROVEMENT, ETC.

> "Another land more bright than this,
>   To our dim sight appears,
> And on our way to it we'll soon
>   Again be pioneers."
> —*William Ross Wallace.*

NIGH upon sixty years have been gathered into the Great Cemetery of the ages, since the first pioneers came to this division of the county. Thirty years are a generation's lifetime, and thus the period alloted to two generations have passed. A few of the "old guard" remain, but they are fast hastening to the solemn valley where "Death sits robed in his all-sweeping shadow." The life of man upon the earth is short. Even his "threescore and ten years" are but a swing of the pendulum of the clock of Time. Were it not for the duty which, acted upon, becomes a part of our moral nature, it would be hardly worth while to undertake any great labors, to harbor any wearing anxieties. We would be as children building play-houses of sand upon the shore, and little caring how we build, for the driving wave, pulsating to the heart throbs of old ocean, would soon erase all results of our task and toil. But while life is short, society is long. "Men may come and men may go," but society remains forever—an edifice whose foundations were laid when it was found "not good for man to be alone." Each generation adds a story, solid and beautiful, polished in the similitude of a palace; or, unsteady and shapeless, daubed with untempered mortar.

The advent of the pioneers is now but a dream of the past—it is a book, the pages of which are turned. Few now remember when the first cabin was erected in Rome Township, and when the first man came to its territory. Rome, it is said, was not built in a day, neither was Rome Township settled in a day. Its occupation by white people extends over a period of several years, from the time the first adventurous pioneer wandered into the section now embraced in Rome until the land was all taken up. The first comers were people who sought homes here because land was cheap and game plenty. Many of them were hunters, and spent much time in their favorite pastime.

Rome Township lies in the north tier of townships in the county, northwest of Mount Vernon, and is bounded north by Marion

* By W. H. Perrin.

County, east by Field Township, south by Shiloh, west by Grand Prairie, and is known and designated in the Congressional survey as Township 1 south, and Range 2 east. The surface is generally level, or slightly undulating, and divided between prairie and woodland, the latter predominating, and covered originally with oak, hickory, walnut, sassafras, wild cherry, etc. The principal stream is a branch of Big Muddy, which has its source in the north part of the township. No railroads intersect it, but the country is thoroughly a farming one, and is occupied by a set of thrifty and industrious farmers. Corn, wheat, oats, hay, etc., are the principal crops. But little attention is paid to stock-raising, except horses.

The first settlers in what is now Rome Township are supposed to have been the Maxwells. Mr. Johnson says there were three brothers, viz., Robert, William and Archibald Maxwell. Another authority, however, says that Robert and Archibald were the sons of William Maxwell, and that the latter came about 1816-17, locating on Section 7. He was from Bourbon County, Ky., and sold out and left here about 1824. He is described as a man somewhat wild, dissipated and reckless, and when under the influence of whisky, a little dangerous. His boys would have choked him to death on one occasion, for some of his devilment, but for the interference of the neighbors. He was a good kind of man when sober, but, like hundreds of others, even at the present day, he let whisky steal his senses and then he was almost ungovernable. His sons, Robert and Archibald Maxwell, came soon after him, and Robert Maxwell entered the first tract of land in Jefferson County, and paid the full price in cash for it. He lived in Section 11, northwest of where Mr. Bruce now lives. Archibald Maxwell died in the county, and had quite a large family; Robert had no family but a wife. He left his property with M. D. Bruce, and went back to Kentucky about 1848-50, where both he and his wife died. Mr. Bruce settled up his estate by order of the court, and after paying Maxwell's debts, turned over the residue to the County Treasury.

William Goins was an early settler here, and kept a tavern, one of the first kept in the county. He had a bad reputation, and was accused of being connected with horse-thieves, counterfeiters, and all sorts of lawless characters. He finally left, for the good of the community, as detailed in a preceding chapter. His tavern was the head-quarters of a band who committed, as was supposed, many dark deeds. Even murders were attributed to them. But as the country settled up, a better class of people came in, and the lawless band who frequented Goins' tavern were cleaned out, and, like their king-bee, Goins, were forced to leave for the good of the country.

Davis and Philip Whitesides, brothers-in-law of Thomas Jordan, settled in Jordan's Prairie very early. They were noted fighters, and considered the bullies of the neighborhood. Billington Taylor, originally from South Carolina, was also an early settler in this township, as well as his son-in-law, Nelson. The latter, however, finally went to Salt Lake and joined the Mormons. A Mr. McDaniel settled in the South end of Jordan's Prairie, and died there. Mr. M. D. Bruce came in 1838, with his father, and were from Tennessee. The elder Bruce was known as one of the best farmers in the county. James Lewty settled early, but sold out and went to Texas. He afterward returned to this county and died. Arba Andrews located in this township, and built the first horse mill in this part of the county.

Thus the township was settled, and the wilderness reclaimed from its wild and natural state, and converted into a fine agricultural region. But the labor required to do this was great, and required many years to accomplish. When we consider the rude simplicity of the times, and the few and inferior implements the people had to work with, we find ourselves wondering that they succeeded in their great work. Their mill facilities were meager, and as rude as the implements they had to work their farms with. The latter consisted of bull-tongue and shovel-plows, and the old "Cary," with the wooden mold-board These were made by Arba Andrews, who was the first blacksmith, as well as the proprietor of the first horse mill. He is said to have been quite a "mechanical genius." He made plows and stocked them for the farmers. He built a horse mill, the first mill in the township, an institution largely patronized for miles around, and a great accommodation to the people. He also made all sorts of agricultural implements, such as plows and harrows, and even essayed horse-power threshing-machines. He put up the first steam mill in the township, but previously operated a horse-power circular saw mill, and earlier had a wind-power mill for grinding corn, and earlier still, a common horse mill. This steam mill stood a little south of Rome Village, and Squire Carpenter now has the original engine in his mill. Several other horse mills were put up in the township in early times, but the history of one is the history of all.

The educational history of Rome is similar to that of other portions of the county. So much has already been said upon the subject, that but little can be added here. The first schoolhouse in the township was a log cabin, 18x18 feet, on the land of M. D. Bruce, and is still standing. The first school in it was taught by Mahulda Martin, who came here with her parents from Kentucky. Other early teachers were William Dill, S. Andrews, now a merchant in Centralia, and C. Andrews. The township now has eight good, substantial schoolhouses, and supports good schools.

The township is well supplied with churches, and if the people are not religious it is their own fault. Among the churches are Pleasant Hill Baptist Church, Ebenezer Methodist Episcopal Church South, and the Methodist Episcopal Church at Rome Village. Pleasant Hill Baptist Church was organized about 1850-52, and among the original members were Freemen and Mary Walker, B. B. Harvey and wife, James Ward and wife, Levi Williams and wife, and R. Whitlock and wife, It was formed in a log cabin, and the first preacher was Elder James Keel, now dead. The present church was built in 1867, is a frame 34x40 feet, and cost $1,375. It has 122 members, under the pastorate of Elder W. W. Hay, of Mount Vernon. It has a good Sunday school, with an attendance of eighty to ninety, of which Andrew Riley is Superintendent.

The Methodist Episcopal Church South was organized in 1863. Among the first members were Elijah Wimberly and wife, S. W. Carpenter and family. The present membership is about ninety, under the pastorate of Rev. C. M. Whitson. A Sunday school is kept up, under the present superintendence of J. M. McCormick. The church is an excellent brick edifice, built about 1865-66, and is 34x50 feet in dimension.

The Methodist Episcopal Church in Rome Village was built about 1867, is 36x40 feet, and cost about $3,000. It has some fifty members, and Rev. Mr. Boyer is pastor. A

Sunday school is maintained, of which William Ayers is Superintendent.

Originally, this portion of the county was embraced in Grand Prairie Precinct, but when the county, in 1869, adopted township organization, it became Rome Township, and received the name from the village. Since township organization, the following is a complete list of township officers:

Supervisors.—G. L. Cummings, 1870; William Wood, 1871-72; W. A. Boggs, 1873; G. L. Cummings, 1874; Robert White, 1875; Robert White, 1876; G. L. Cummings, 1877; J. V. Bruce, 1878; Matthew Tilford, 1879; Matthew Tilford, 1880; Matthew Tilford, 1881; W. Snow, 1882; A. J. Riley, 1883.

Town Clerks.—J. D. R. Brown, 1870-73; J. M. Thompson, 1874; A. J. Riley, 1875; A. J. Riley, 1876; J. M. Thompson, 1877; A. J. Riley, 1878; W. Cobb, 1879; J. H. Rupe, 1880; J. H. Rupe, 1881; G. W. Lee, 1882; G. W. Lee, 1883.

Assessors.—J. V. Bruce, 1870-73; T. W. Self, 1874; T. W. Self, 1875; R. Casey, 1876; J. H. Clayburn, 1877; Matthew Tilford, 1878; B. J. Hawkins, 1879; W. Cobb, 1880; J. M. Thompson, 1881; R. White, 1882; M. Jennings, 1883.

Collectors.—R. White, 1872; R. F. Casey, 1873; J. D. Bruce, 1874; Matthew Tilford, 1875; J. D. Bruce, 1876; J. D. Bruce, 1877; J. M. Kellogg, 1878; J. N. Brown, 1879; J. N. Brown, 1880; M. Jennings, 1881; W. Talbott, 1882; F. W. Purcell, 1883.

School Treasurers.—W. S. Hodges, 1872-73; B. P. Maxfield, 1874; W. P. Fizer, 1875; W. P. Fizer, 1876; W. P. Fizer, 1877; Edwin Puffer, 1878; J. M. McCormick, 1879; B. P. Maxfield, 1880; B. P. Maxfield, 1881; J. T. McConnell, 1882; B. P. Maxfield, 1883.

Highway Commissioners.—W. P. Fizer, J. R. Ward, J. Saunders, H. Milburn, William Snow, E. D. Puffer, Hiram Williams, R. Tate, M. D. Bruce, R. Baltzell, T. Patton, R. White.

Justices of the Peace.—R. M. Breeze, J. M. B. Gaston, William Snow, John Tilford, W. S. Rupe, J. M. B. Gaston, J. H. Ward, J. M. B. Gaston, J. Roberts.

Constables.—F. M. Purcell, D. Copple, J. F. Caldwell, S. T. Caldwell, J. N. Hawkins, S. N. Dakes, J. N. Hawkins.

Politically, the township is pretty evenly divided between Democrats and Republicans, while the Greenbackers hold the balance of power. In old times, this section was largely Democratic. The first voting place was at James Bates' house, but was afterward moved to Rome; the vote polled was small—from 130 to 140—and the precinct was a good deal larger in extent than Rome Township now is. The township has always been patriotic, and turned out soldiers in the Black Hawk, Mexican and late civil war. M. D. Bruce and S. W. Carpenter are old Black Hawk soldiers. Indians were plenty in this section when the first whites came, and there are those living who still remember the noble red men, and saw them often as they hunted the wild game of the woods, without the benefit of soap and breeches. Mr. Bruce well remembers the noted chief Whitefeather. He was a rather intelligent Indian, and spoke very good English.

Village of Rome.—Rome, not the mistress of the world, seated upon her seven hills, but the little, unpretentious village in this township, was laid out March 14, 1849, by Arba Andrews, and the survey made by L. F. Casey. It is situated on the east part of the southwest quarter of the northwest quarter of Section 13; and comprised four blocks of five lots each. Andrews afterward made an addition (December 15, 1857) on the west, nearly equal in extent to the original town. The first house was put up by or for John

Bostwick for a grocery, as saloons were then called. He occupied it about three years, and then went to Mount Vernon, and while absent from Rome John Caldwell sold goods in his house. He afterward returned and occupied it again himself. Since his day, Dr. Hart, Lakin & Branson, Swain, Thomas Pace, Harlow and others have used it as a business house, but it is now the reception parlor of a stable. The next house erected was a hotel, built by Andrew Harmon, and the third was put up by J. R. Brown, a mechanic. William Parker was the village blacksmith. Hiram Milburn built a storehouse in 1853, and the next year built a hotel. It is related of this house, or the frame of it, that it blew down with two men on the joists, and fell all in a pile, but nobody was hurt. Milburn and West bought Lewty's Mill, which stood about a mile from Rome, and moved it into the town. Isaac Pierson added a carding machine to it. James Sursa opened a grocery store, and in 1854-55, Henry Blalock built a house at the south end of town, and opened a stock of goods, but in a few years later sold out to Dr. Jones. A schoolhouse was built in 1854, and some years later (during the war) a church, and in 1869 the brick church was built, and thus the village became quite a moral little place. The Doctors of Rome have been Jones, Booth, Murphy, Darter & Burns, Burns & Ayres, Ayres & Darter, Skillings, Young, Nichols, Mabry, Clark, Bradford, et al.

The town was named for Rome, N. Y., and not for the capital of the Roman Empire. Mr. Andrews, the father of the place, came from near Rome, N. Y., and named it in honor of that place. When the post office was established at Andrews' house in 1830, it was called Jordan's Prairie Post Office. But when Rome was laid out, it was moved to town, and it was then found that there was oanther Rome in the State, and some other name must be selected. Dr. Jones, who believed in "shooting on the spot" any man who would "haul down the American flag," named the post office for Gen. Dix, the author of that patriotic injunction, and Dix Post Office it has since remained. Rome became the voting place of Jordan's Prairie in 1852, and when the township was formed in 1869, it remained the polling place.

Rome was incorporated in 1866, and S. W. Carpenter, Hiram Milburn, —— Hayworth, J. J. Maxey and Dr. Nichols were the Trustees. An Odd Fellows Lodge was instituted June 12, 1869, and the following were the first officers: James Robinson, N. G.; L. Leffingwell, V. G.; J. N. Maxey, Secretary, and C. Douchet, Treasurer. The membership at present is twenty-three, and the officers are George Watson, N. G.; S. Davis, V. G.; —— Hays, Secretary, and J. D. McMeens, Treasurer.

A Masonic lodge was organized October 4, 1874, and the first officers were John F. Robb, W. M.; Robert F. Casey, S. W.; G. L. Cummings, J. W.; John C. McConnell, Treasurer; Thomas W. McNeeley, Secretary. The present roll of officers are as follows: R. F. Casey, Master; F. M. Purcell, Senior Warden; S. B. Bogan, Junior Warden; H. H. Hutchison, Treasurer; G. W. Lee, Secretary, and the records show thirty-six members.

The present business of Rome is: R. F. Casey, dry goods; Dr. W. E. Bradford, drugs and dry goods; H. Williams, groceries; S. W. Carpenter & Son, grist mill; David Thompson, wood-shop; Miller & Shinning, blacksmith shop; Rachel Bruce and daughter, millinery store; William Kyser, furniture store; James Fields, boot and shoe shop; one schoolhouse, in which two teachers are employed; two churches, and Drs. Tucker, Bogan and Bradford, physicians. The town, though old in years, has never grown to very large proportions, and never will, but it is quite a business little place.

CHAPTER XI.*

SPRING GARDEN TOWNSHIP—GENERAL DESCRIPTION AND TOPOGRAPHY—SETTLEMENT OF THE WHITES—THEIR EARLY TRIALS AND TRIBULATIONS—ROADS, MILLS, ETC.—SCHOOLS AND CHURCHES—TOWNSHIP OFFICIALS—SPRING GARDEN VILLAGE— ITS GROWTH, DEVELOPMENT, ETC., ETC.

> "This cannot last;
> For I am of the mould that loathes to breathe
> The air of multitudes."—*Daniel Boone.*

NO age fully understands itself or the place it occupies in the great secular movement of human history. If we would catch the "increasing purposes" which run through the ages, we must learn to look at them in the widely separated epochs which mark the decline and fall, the rise and growth of political empire. Though to-day be a yesterday and though the morrow shall be as to-day, it still remains to be seen that the subtle elements of historical change and development are constantly at work with a transforming power which is the more or less efficient in its results because it is invisible in its operation. If we would clearly discern the fact of human progress in knowledge and virtue, we must look at the file leaders of humanity not as they mark time in the pauses and breathing spells of the daily march, but as they set up the trophies which signalize the turning points of human destiny, whether it be some decisive battle which saves Europe from the domination of the Persian civilization, as at Marathon, or a transfer of the world's scepter from Pagan to Christian hands, as typified by the conversion of Constantine. And in like manner, if we would clearly perceive the progress that has been made by the separate nations of the world now competing with each other for the prizes of place and power, we must contemplate their history in its periodic times and not in its daily revolutions.

At this distance of time from the feeble beginning of the progress and development of this county, a point has been reached from which a survey may be made of the steps that have so far been taken. Although we may look back with pride at the progress we have made, yet our retrospection must necessarily be tempered with some grief for the loss of those who bore an honorable part in the great work of subduing the wilderness and transforming it into the "spring garden" of loveliness. They made history, little recking who might come after them to write and read it. The greatest honor that we can pay them is to perpetuate their names upon the pages of the history they themselves made.

Spring Garden Township is situated in the south tier of townships in the county, and takes in quite a little corner of Moore's Prairie, as fine a body of land as lies out of doors. Many excellent farms are seen in this section, and corn, oats and wheat are the principal crops. Some fruit is raised and if more attention was paid to it than there is, it would be much better for the farming community. It has been very satisfactorily

---

* By W. H. Perrin.

demonstrated in late years that wheat in Southern Illinois is an uncertain crop, and the farmers sooner or later must see the advantage of stock-raising and fruit-growing in this region. Spring Garden is bounded on the north by Dodds Township, on the east by Moore's Prairie Township, on the south by Franklin County, on the west by Elk Prairie Township, and is designated in the Government survey as Township 4 south, Range 3 east, of the Third Principal Meridian. In the woodland portion the timber is that similar to other portions of the county. The streams are Casey's Fork of Big Muddy, Atchison's Creek, Gun Creek, Poplar Branch, etc. Casey's Fork runs south and touches the west side of the township; Atchison's Creek flows west through the west part and empties into Casey's Fork, while Gun Creek and Poplar Branch have their source in the northeast and east portions of the township and pass out through Section 33 on the south line.

The settlement of Spring Garden Township dates back sixty-five years or more. Among the early settlers we may mention the Smiths, some of the Atchisons, James Pritchett, Thomas Hopper, John D. Vaughn, Wiley Prigmore, Uriah Compton, John Hull, Nathaniel Wyatt, E. Crane, James McCann, Nathaniel Morgan, Thomas Softly, ——— Armstrong, Matthew Kirk, William Harmon, Richard and Reuben Sweeton, Daniel Parrett, etc., etc.

The Smiths and Hopper are supposed to have settled here as early as 1816, but they were probably not here quite so early as that. Of the Smiths there was Isaac Smith and one or two sons, one of whom was named Abram. Hopper was the father of Abram Smith's wife, and they were all from Tennessee. He settled on Section 1 and died there. Abram Smith had a large family of children, some of whom are still living. His father, Isaac Smith, was an Old-School Baptist preacher. He organized a church of that faith very early in a log cabin on Benjamin Smith's farm. Solomon Goddard and Noble Anderson were also preachers. The latter was quite an eccentric character.

Uriah Compton settled at the old springs called the Compton Springs, and from which the township finally received its name. He was a very early settler and improved the springs, making them quite a resort. Wiley Prigmore was an early hatter, when hats were manufactured at home instead of being bought at the stores. Pritchett settled on Section 1 and was from Tennessee. He was a carpenter, and has a son, George Pritchett, still living here. Two of Barton Atchison's sons were among the early settlers. Wyatt settled near the Compton Springs, and is represented as a very excellent man. Morgan was a good farmer and died in the township. Hull settled near Crane's mill and acted in the capacity of miller for Crane, who owned a horse mill. Hull was a large man and an Irishman, and, like the majority of his race, was extremely fond of a "dhrap of the craythur," and when a little "tight," was quite as fond of a fight. McCann was from Tennessee, and came first to Montgomery County, and from there went to Madison County; then came here and settled in this township. Softly came early. He was a plain but successful farmer; was a candidate once for the Legislature, but an unsuccessful one. He was as strong as Sampson, somewhat addicted to drink, and when under the influence of liquor was quarrelsome and always ready for a fight. Alexander was a very early settler; he was a cripple and went on crutches. Finally he moved into Franklin County. Kirk had a large family, and many of them are still living.

The Sweetons and Harmon were early settlers, but of them we know little beyond the fact of their settlement. Parrett settled about one mile from Spring Garden. He was a strict, close, but honest man, and a member of the old "Hardshell" Baptist Church. William Davis and William Braden were early ministers of the Baptist Church, as well as early settlers of the township.

Of a little later date came a number of settlers, among whom we may mention John D. Vaughn, who came about 1830 or 1832. He came from Madison County here, but was originally from Tennessee, and settled on Section 22. He died eventually in Dodds Township, and is buried at the Arnold Graveyard in that township. He had twelve children, and ten of them grew up and raised families of their own. Many descendants are still living here. Mr. Vaughn was a a liberal-spirited man, full of energy and enterprise, and did much to better the condition of the neighborhood in which he lived.

He engaged in a general mercantile business, and would exchange goods for pelts and venison hams. These he would haul to St. Louis by wagon, bringing back goods in return. He was also a carpenter, and built many houses in the township. But finally he was unfortunate in becoming surety for friends, through which means he lost heavily and died a comparatively poor man. He was ever ready to take hold of anything to make money. On one occasion he and his son Christopher G. hired to some cattle dealers to drive cattle from this section up into Michigan, a distance of about 600 miles, for which he received 75 cents per day and his son 50 cents per day. Returning home, they walked the entire distance, often walking forty miles a day.

The struggles, the hard times and dangers to which the pioneers were exposed in the early history of this division of the county is but the same as noticed in other chapters of this volume. One of the most trying difficulties was the procuring of bread, which sometimes could not be obtained at all. The mortar and pestle was the usual resort until horse mills made their appearance. One of the first horse mills in this section was Crane's, which was liberally patronized by the people. But, as the country settled up, other and better mills were built, and this trouble passed away, as did all the difficulties of the early settlers.

Who taught the first school in what is now Spring Garden Township we cannot say, nor can we give the exact location of the first schoolhouse in the township. The early schools and schoolhouses were of the usual primitive kind. The township now has six comfortable schoolhouses, situated in Sections 11, 16, 21, 29, 31, and at Spring Garden Village, in which good schools are taught each year.

The church history of the township is somewhat limited, at least so far as church edifices go. But religious meetings were held early, and a number of the early settlers were ministers of the Old-School Baptist Church. Among these were William Davis, William Braden, Solomon Goddard, Isaac Smith and Noble Anderson. Of these, the latter, perhaps, was the leader. He preached the Gospel to the simple pioneers pure and unadulterated as he understood it, not for pelf, but solely for the good of mankind, and because, as some of his neighbors used to say, he was too lazy to do anything else. There was within him the smoldering fires of a rough eloquence, that, when once in his pulpit and warmed to his work, were soon fanned into fierce flames, as he drew frightful pictures of an angry God or the horrors of a literal hell of fire and brimstone. A favorite expression of his was, "my brethering and sistering, the world is as round as a horse's head and ten times rounder." What meaning he intended to convey by the phrase no one seems to know—or care. Such was Elder Anderson, and such as he was, he never seemed to tire of proclaiming to the world that he was not "ashamed to own his Lord and Master." Whether this compliment was returned or not is wholly immaterial to this narrative. Elder Anderson was no band-box preacher. He was not a Beecher, a Talmage, a monkey, nor a fool. He was a humble, sincere, great pioneer preacher, with fists like a maul and a voice like the roar of a Numidian lion, and thus arrayed and equipped with the two-edged sword of faith, he went forth upon his mission and waked the echoes of the primeval forests as he proclaimed in his rude, wild eloquence the promises of the Gospel.

Elder Smith organized a church of the Hardshell Baptist persuasion in the neighborhood, and among its early members were many of the pioneer families of Spring Garden Township. Church buildings are scarce in the township, but religious meetings are held in many of the schoolhouses and the morals of the community are looked after by the ministers of the neighboring churches.

Spring Garden Township is untouched by railroads, but its citizens live in hope that some of the projected roads will strike them. The wagon roads of the township are equal in quality and quantity to other portions of the county, and bridges span the streams where many of the more important roads cross them.

Originally this township was included in Elk Prairie and Moore's Prairie Election Precincts, but when the county adopted township organization, some fifteen years ago, this became Spring Garden Township. Since then the following is a complete list of township officers:

Supervisors.—W. S. Bunessus, 1870; C. M. Brown, 1871–72; J. F. Carroll, 1873 to 1875; T. Anglen, 1876–77; Benjamin Smith, 1878; J. F. Carroll, 1879–80; C. M. Brown, 1881; J. W. Peavler, 1882; C. M. Brown, 1883, the present incumbent.

Town Clerks.—T. S. Vaughn, 1872; T. S. Vaughn, 1873; G. M. Kirk, 1874; G. M. Kirk, 1875; R. J. Prince, 1876; R. J. Prince, 1877; R. J. Prince, 1878; W. P. Davis, 1879; W. P. Davis, 1880; W. P. Davis, 1881; E. P. Bevis, 1882; E. P. Bevis, 1883, the present incumbent.

Assessors.—T. Anglen, 1872 to 1875; W. A. Clark, 1876; T. W. Davis, 1877; A. Pasley, 1878 to 1880; T. Anglen, 1881; A. Pasley, 1883; W. A. Clark, 1883, now in office.

Collectors.—J. W. Peavler, 1872; J. W. Peavler, 1873; F. M. Carroll, 1874; J. W. Marshall, 1875; F. M. Carroll, 1876; T. J. Bevis, 1877; F. M. Carroll, 1878; J. W. Peavler, 1879; R. N. Prigmore, 1880; J. W. Peavler, 1881; L. E. Lloyd, 1882; F. M. Carroll, 1883, now in office.

School Treasurers.—Anderson Clark, 1874; Anderson Clark, 1875; J. W. Marshall, 1876; J. W. Marshall, 1877; T. H. Bernard, 1878; Joseph Jones, 1879; Joseph Jones, 1880 to 1882; T. H. Bernard, 1883, present incumbent.

Highway Commissioners.—G. Peavler, J. M. Duncan, S. L. Dunbar, Benjamin Smith, T. A. Stringer, C. H. Howard, J. E. Hopper, T. A. Stringer, C. H. Howard, S. L. Dunbar, Benjamin Smith, G. W. Page, etc.

Justices of the Peace.—J. W. Marshall, R. G. Cook, J. M. McKinney, Charles Howard, J. M. McKinney, J. Johnson, J. M. McKinney, J. Johnson and A. P. Clark.

Constables.—Silas J. Arlow, W. A. Clark,

HISTORY OF JEFFERSON COUNTY.

J. W. Clinton, R. N. Prigmore, C. A. McCullough, L. Harmon, C. A. McCullough and L. Harmon.

The village of Spring Garden is one of the old towns of Jefferson County. It was surveyed and laid out by L. F. Casey for James F. Duncan and John S. Lucas, October 24, 1848, and is situated about twelve miles nearly south of Mount Vernon, on Section 22 of this township. W. W. Creek put up a house on the site of the town and commenced business the year before the place was laid out. Creek was a brother-in-law to Michael Fitzgerrell and bought land from him. In the winter of 1850-51, James E. Cox put up a house in which he kept groceries and furniture. About this time Duncan sold out and left, and John H. Wyatt went in with Lucas in the mercantile business. He remained with him a while; was then with Hawkins, then with Prigmore, and then—died. The first hotel was built by James M. Williams. He owned a farm in the neighborhood, which he traded to Creek for his interest in the village, put up a house and succeeded well. He built the brick hotel in 1859-60. Joseph Williams built a house in 1853, and the next year his brother Henry went into business with him.

In 1854, W. B. Anderson laid out an addition to the town, comprising six blocks of two lots each, and two of four lots each. The first mill in the place was built by Driver & Pollock, and was a steam mill. This was a great curiosity here in those early days to the people, who had been used mostly to horse mills. Many came miles to see this modern wonder. The following incident is related of this mill: One night soon after its completion, when quite a number of people had come in to see it, the proprietors, somewhat elated at their success in the mill business, and to celebrate their growing propserity, drank deeply, and the miller, who was a green hand, crowded on steam until the speed was so great that the mill stones burst into fragments, scaring the proprietors, spectators and employes half to death and making a grand "scatterment" of all present. James R. Combs came to the town in 1854, and finally got an interest in the mill. He was an enterprising man; married Mrs. Compton, engaged in merchandising and finally died. Wiley Prigmore moved into the town in 1856. One Joshua Kilabrew opened a store, and some time later was succeeded by Thomas Williams, and he by John Clinton. Driver & Pollock's mill finally went down and Harvey Williams built one some distance from town. Among the physicians of the place are Drs. Bernard, Reed, Cox and Hughey. The two latter left in a few years. Drs. Bernard and Reed were both from Tennessee. An excellent schoolhouse was built in 1857, which is still doing duty. Carroll and Scott have carried on blacksmithing here for many years, sometimes in partnership and sometimes each for himself.

Upon the building of the St. Louis & Southeastern Railroad (now the Louisville & Nashville Railroad), and the springing up of the towns of Opdyke and Belle Rive, they have drawn heavily on Spring Garden. Several of the stanch citizens and business men of Spring Garden moving to those places on account of the railroad facilities. Spring Garden, perhaps, has passed the zenith of its glory and prosperity, and is now on the down grade to desolation and obscurity, unless some of the railroads now in contemplation pass it. Then its properous days may return.

CHAPTER XII.*

WEBBER TOWNSHIP—INTRODUCTION AND DESCRIPTION—BOUNDARIES, TOPOGRAPHY, ETC.—EARLY SETTLEMENT—PIONEER LIFE AND TRIALS—PIGEON POST OFFICE—A LAW SUIT—TOWNSHIP OFFICIALS—SCHOOLS AND CHURCHES—MARLOW, BLUFORD, ETC., ETC.

"And he shakes his feeble head,
That it seems as if he said—
'They are gone.'"—*Holmes*.

THAT impulse which forces each generation to do something, however small, to make the world wiser, better and happier than they found it, the struggles and sorrows through which each generation passes in the accomplishment of the self-imposed yet imperative task, are the sublimest tragedies of history. Upon this theme Carlyle has said. "Generation after generation takes to itself the form of a body and, issuing forth from the Cimmerian night, appears Heaven's mission. What force and fire is in each he expends. One grinding in the mill of industry, one, hunter-like, climbing the Alpine heights of science, one madly dashed to pieces on the rocks of strife, warring with his fellow—and then the heaven-sent is re-called; his earthly vesture falls away, and soon, even to sense, becomes a shadow. Thus, like a God-created, fire-breathing spirit, we emerge from the Inane. Earth's mountains are leveled, her seas are filled up in our passage. Can the earth, which is but dead and a vision, resist spirits, which are reality and are alive? On the hardest adamant some footprint of us is stamped in. The last rear of the host will read traces of the earliest van. But whence? Oh Heaven, whither? Sense knows not; faith knows not; only that it is through mystery into mystery, from God to God." When we remember how uncertain is life at best, and that its average duration is not more than forty years, nearly half of which is spent in preparing to live, the wonder is that man is not content to stay where he finds himself, " to let well enough alone," and do as little for posterity as possible. But spurred up and on by the divine impulse, he can neither explain nor resist, he labors as if life were to last a thousand years; as if his eyes were to see the harvest from the seed he plants, his soul rejoices at the onward and upward march he aids.

Webber comprises one of the east tier of townships of the county and lies east of Mount Vernon. It is bounded north by Farrington Township, east by Wayne County, south by Pendleton Township, west by Mount Vernon Township, and according to the Congressional survey is Township 2 south, Range 4 east, of the Third Principal Meridian. The surface of the township is somewhat rough and broken, and is mostly timbered land, but takes in a small portion of Long Prairie. The timber growth is several kinds of oak, black hickory, wild cherry, sassafras, hazel, etc. The streams are Puncheon Camp Creek, which received its peculiar name from the puncheon camps erected along its banks by the early hunters; Bear Creek, Four Mile Creek and Two Mile Creek. Puncheon Camp Creek rises northeast of Mount Vernon and empties into Horse Creek; Bear Creek has its source in a sulphur spring on Pope's farm and runs east

*By W. H. Perrin.

and north into the Puncheon Camp Creek. Four Mile Creek empties into the Skillet Fork of the Little Wabash. Black Oak Ridge, running nearly through the center of the township, forms a water-shed, the waters on the east side flowing into the Skillet Fork, finally reach the Ohio River, while those on the west side flow into Big Muddy, and thence through it to the Mississippi. The products of the township are grain, stock and fruit. The latter of late years is receiving considerable attention, apples being mostly grown, and to which the township seems well adapted.

To particularize each settlement in the county and tell just where each family settled as they came in is not a task easily accomplished. A list of the early settlers of the county has been given in different chapters, but it has been impossible to locate them all. Among the pioneers of Webber Township we may mention the following: Jacob Norton, Isaac Casey, Daniel Scott, Word Webber, H. Wade, William Dale, Peter Bruce, James Archie, Alexander Moore, James Bridges, W. Willett, William Green, David and Elijah Davis, Joseph Childers, James Hunt, Joseph Brown, etc., etc. Jacob Norton was a brother-in-law to Gov. Casey, and settled here about 1822. He remained but a few years and then went back to Tennessee and died there. Isaac Casey, one of the early settlers of the county, and who first located in Mount Vernon Township, came into this about 1838, and lived here a few years. But after the death of his wife in 1846, he broke up housekeeping and went to live with his children. Daniel Scott settled in the township in 1838. Webber came in 1840 and settled on the Fairfield road, but about the time of the war moved into Pendleton Township and located near Lynchburg. He was quite a prominent man, and has the honor of giving his name to the township. Wade settled in the south part of the township, and was a plain, hardworking farmer. Dale came in early and carried on a tan yard—the first in the township. The farm on which he settled is now owned by Levi Harris. Peter Bruce was originally from Virginia, came to Illinois and settled in this township in 1840. He made what was called the "Ridge road," a prominent thoroughfare in early times, but of which there is now no trace. It extended from the old Joseph Brown place to East Long Prairie, and was much traveled by the pioneers. James Archie was a "squatter," and "squatted" on the Ridge road. He stayed quite awhile, but left a short time before the war. Alexander Moore lived in the southeast corner of the township, and was a large stock-raiser for the time. Bridges settled on the place now owned by Leonard W. Bruce. Willett settled where Mrs. Carter now lives and opened a small farm. Green was among the first settlers in the township; the place on which he located is now owned by Mrs. Lancaster Green. It belonged awhile to Dr. Wood, a practicing physician here. He took the flux and died, and his wife went back to Indiana. The Davises were from North Carolina and came here about 1839-40. David settled where he now lives, near the Black Oak Ridge Schoolhouse; Elijah died on the place where he settled. Joseph Childers settled in the same neighborhood. He kept a large pack of hounds and was quite a hunter. Hunt settled on Two Mile Creek near its source. Joseph Brown was a very early settler on what is known as Spring Hill farm, so named from a fine spring that breaks from the side of a hill on the farm. Doubtless there were others entitled to mention as early settlers of the township, but we failed to learn their names.

A great change has taken place in this section in the last half a century. Where the first pioneers crossed the border there are now no deer to pay the sportsman for trudging through the forests and over the hills. Could the old hunters who used to enjoy their broiled venison and roasted coon around the evening camp fire come back here and see the wonderful changes that have taken place, they would doubtless turn away in supreme disgust at the signs of civilization that would everywhere meet their gaze. Aye, could they revisit these scenes of their youth, and behold their degenerate successors with no hunting grounds, no moccasins, no leather breeches, no flint-lock guns, broiled venison nor roasted coons, they would no doubt gather their mantles about them (their buckskin hunting-shirts) and lie down and die. Would not their big hearts burst asunder upon seeing the men of this day in plug hats and store clothes, riding in carriages and sleeping cars and chasing no other game than the metaphorical tiger up stairs behind closed blinds and under bright gas lights! Wonderful, wonderful the change the years have wrought!

Among the pioneer improvements were mills, roads, bridges, tan yards, etc., etc. Willett & Fagan built a mill about 1848. It was of very poor mechanical construction, but did good service for a number of years. James Hunt erected a mill on Two Mile Creek, which received its power from that stream. It was short-lived, however (the mill, not the stream, for it is there yet), and soon passed away. W. B. and Lewis Logan built a saw mill about the year 1867, the first ever in the township. William Dale had a tannery as early as 1841-42. All the shoes then that were worn at all were made at home, and not bought at the store as now, and hence a tan yard was an important pioneer industry—next, perhaps, to the mill. A free-stone quarry in the township was operated in an early day, from which material was obtained for building chimneys throughout the neighborhood.

The first road through the township was the road leading from Mount Vernon to Fairfield, and was known as the "Fairfield road." The Black Oak Ridge road was also an old road, and was made by Peter Bruce. Mr. Marlow, who settled here just after the Mexican war, was instrumental in getting a road entitled the "East Long Prairie road," diverging from the Fairfield road at the seven mile bridge and running to Long Prairie. The township is now well supplied with roads, and where the more important roads cross the streams they are spanned by substantial bridges.

Previous to the township system coming into vogue, the county was divided into election precincts, but in 1869 the county adopted township organization, when the whole system of government was changed and each township became a separate and distinct municipality. It may be a matter of some interest to some of our readers to give the township officers, the first of whom were elected in 1870. They are as follows:

Supervisors.—S. V. Bruce, 1870-71; J. Harlow, 1872-73; A. Marlow, 1874 to 1876; J. H. Newton, 1877-78; John Hopper, 1879; W. B. Esman, 1880; D. S. Etlington, 1881; B. D. Esman, 1882; T. F. Moore, 1883.

Township Clerk.—G. T. Bruce, 1872; H. M. Maxey, 1873; J. H. Dulaney, 1874; J. H. Newton, 1875-76; B. Bruce, 1877-78; H. Benton, 1879; H. J. Benton, 1880; G. M. Davis, 1881-82; G. M. Davis, 1883.

Assessor.—W. H. Morris, Jr., 1872-73; J. H. Newton, 1874; J. B. Young, 1875; G. L. Bruce, 1876-77; B. D. Esman, 1878; W. B. Dulaney, 1879; W. S. Maxey, 1880;

William Dulaney, 1881; R. Young, 1882; R. S. Young, 1883.

Collector.—T. F. Moore, 1872; G. M. Watts, 1873; R. J. Scott, 1874; J. T. Howell, 1875; B. D. Esman, 1876; B. G. Ward, 1877; J. T. Howell, 1878-79; R. C. Wood, 1880-81; E. W. Wallace, 1882; G. W. Rosenberger, 1883.

School Treasurers.—J. W. Gregory, 1872-73; Wiley Green, 1874; J. H. Dulaney, 1875 to 1878; J. C. Maxey, 1879; L. Harris, 1880; E. M. Green, 1881; T. D. Fry, 1882; L. R. Laird, 1883.

Highway Commissioners.—W. H. Morris, Sr., H. M. Richards, C. Gowler, E. Gentle, J. W. Gregory, E. Gentle, R. A. Allsbrook, L. W. Bruce, C. Gowler, L. W. Bruce, William Stone, W. F. Adams, A. Cook, T. Green, and W. T. Adams.

Justices of the Peace.—W. S. Davis and R. S. Young, 1870-73; O. J. Byard and R. S. Young, 1874 to 1876; Wiley Green and A. Marlow, 1877; B. G. Wood and A. Marlow, 1878; Wiley Green and A. Marlow, 1879-80; W. S. Dodds and B. G. Wood, 1881; W. A. Watson and B. G. Wood, 1882-83.

Constables.—J. M. Bruce, 1874 to 1876; O. J. Byard, 1877; J. T. Feltz, 1878-79; O. J. Byard, 1880; J. T. Feltz, 1881; and G. Keele, 1883.

Some years ago, during Squire Marlow's term as Justice of the Peace, a suit was being tried before him, to which M. Waters and Fayette Osborne were the parties, and the nature of which was "squatterism," or the right to a certain improvement. While the trial was going on a large rat caught a chicken in the midst of the court room, when some one with great gravity made a motion that the rat be fined for contempt of court. Fact!

A post office was established in 1875 in the north part of the township called Pigeon Post Office, of which Mr. Partridge was Postmaster. It received its name from the great flocks of pigeons that used to roost in the low trees in the vicinity. It is said that millions of these birds might be seen there at one time. The early settlers used to kill great numbers of them.

Schools were taught in the township as soon as there were children to support them and money to pay teachers. One of the first schoolhouses was a log cabin erected on Section 28, on Black Oak Ridge. Among the early wielders of the birch within this primitive temple of learning, were Jehu Hodges, Joel Hawkins, John Vick, Brown and Davis. Another schoolhouse was built in the north part of the township, which was known as the Young Schoolhouse. Before this house was built, a school was taught in the old Council Bluff Church. The Barren Schoolhouse was, perhaps, the next one built. It received the name on account of the barren country around it. About the year 1850, the precinct was divided into four school districts. The township now contains six districts, in all of which are good, comfortable schoolhouses. The first School Trustees in the township (prior to township organization) were D. B. Davis and C. M. Casey.

The pioneers of Webber Township looked early to their spiritual welfare as well as their temporal. Meetings were held at private houses. Congregations assembled regularly in the old Ridge Schoolhouse, and preaching was held whenever a preacher came along. The first religious society formed in the township, perhaps, was the old Council Bluff Church. Among the early members were the Caseys, Maxeys and Johnsons, and Thomas Casey, A. Maxey and Simeon Walker were among the preachers.

The Black Oak Ridge Methodist Church

was organized about 1855. Among the original members were John Fagan and family, D. B. Davis and family, and Abraham Marlow and wife; the first class-leader was D. B. Davis. A flourishing Sunday school with about thirty pupils is maintained.

Hickory Hill United Baptist Church was organized in 1868, and the Dales and Davises were among the first members. Elder C. Richardson is the present pastor.

The Universalists and Adventists hold meetings occasionally. The Adventists have an organization, but no church building.

The Louisville, Evansville & St. Louis Railroad, commonly called the "Air Line," passes through Webber Township from east to west. There are two stations in Webber, viz., Marlow and Bluford. The latter was laid out about the time the road was opened for travel, and consists of but a few houses. It is located on the land of Evans and Crews, citizens of Mount Vernon. The place contains two stores—Thomas Moore & Co. and B. D. Esman—a grocery and saloon, a saw mill, a shop or two and a few residences.

Marlow Station is situated on Section 30, on John Scott's land. Like Bluford, it is a small place and has sprung up since the building of the railroad. W. & H. Morris carry on a general store. A grain house was put up by Mr. Marlow, with wagon scales attached; he also owns a dwelling house here. A saw mill was started here and run one year by Dallas & Burk. It was portable, and hence has left the town. A post office was established in 1882, and Mr. Marlow appointed Postmaster. He resigned in April, 1883, and Mr. Morris was appointed in his stead. Drs. Newton and Hillard are the practicing physicians of the township, and care for the physical ailments of the people.

CHAPTER XIII.*

ELK PRAIRIE TOWNSHIP—TOPOGRAPHY AND PHYSICAL FEATURES—COMING OF THE PALE FACES
—INCIDENTS OF THEIR SETTLEMENT—HARD TIMES, ETC.—ROADS, MILLS AND BRIDGES—
SCHOOLS AND SCHOOLHOUSES—CHURCHES, ETC.—TOWNSHIP OFFICIALS—VILLAGES, ETC.

"Should you ask me whence these stories,
Whence these legends and traditions
With the odors of the forest—
I repeat them as I heard them."
—*Song of Hiawatha.*

TO illustrate the life the people lived in the pioneer days of Southern Illinois, we give an extract from the diary of an early citizen of this portion of the State, and which was written in 1824. It is true of the times in which it occurred, and is as follows: "I well recollect the first time I ever saw a tea-cup and saucer, and tasted coffee. My mother died when I was six years old. My father then sent me to Maryland, to school. At Bedford, everything was changed. The tavern at which I stopped was a stone house, and, to make the change still more complete, it was plastered on the inside, both as to the walls and ceiling. On going into the dining-room, I was struck with astonishment at the appearance of the house. I had no idea there was a house in the world not built of logs; but here I looked around the house and could see no logs, and above I could see no joists. Whether such a thing had been made so by

* By W. H. Perrin.

the hands of man, or had grown so of itself I could not conjecture. I had not the courage to inquire anything about it. I watched attentively to see what the big folks would do with their little cups and spoons. I imitated them, and found the taste of the coffee nauseous beyond anything I had ever tasted in my life. I continued to drink, as the rest of the company did, with tears streaming from my eyes; but when it was to end, I was at a loss to know, as the little cups were filled immediately after being emptied. This circumstance distressed me very much, and I durst not say I had enough. Looking attentively at the grand persons I saw one person turn his cup bottom upward and put his little spoon across it. I observed after this his cup was not filled again. I followed his example, and to my great satisfaction the result, as to my cup, was the same." This is the experience of a rough, backwoods boy, who had been raised in Southern Illinois when the country was but a wilderness. There are, however, many old people to be found who can give episodes in their own lives of equally as rude a character.

Elk Prairie Township lies in the south tier of townships in Jefferson County, and contains considerable fine farming lands, though it is rather rough and broken along the streams. The township is bounded on the north by McClellan Township, on the east by Spring Garden, on the south by Franklin County, on the west by Bald Hill Township, and by Government Survey is Township No. 4, south of the base line, and is in Range 2 east of the Third Principal Meridian. Big Muddy Creek flows south nearly through the middle of the township, receiving numerous small streams in its course. Casey's Fork touches the east portion, flowing in a southerly direction between this township and Spring Garden. Along these streams was originally heavy timber, and there is still considerable of it left, principally oak, hickory and walnut. The land is rather hilly and rough along the streams, but back from them some distance it becomes of a more even surface, and has some small prairies. Elk Prairie, from which the township derives its name, is an excellent body of land, though of rather small extent. It takes its name from the number of bones and horns of elk found here by the early settlers. Some very excellent farms may be seen in this township.

Of the early experiences of Elk Prairie, there is little to be said. There was nothing out of the usual, every-day pioneer life to individualize the community. It settled up much as other portions of the county did, and as other settlements were made. As to the name of the first settler in this division of the county, where he came from and the spot whereon he settled, we can say little. for we failed to learn anything definitely. Among the early settlers we can mention the Stephensons, William King, the Whitmans, Ezra Lanier, James and Martin Teeters, John D. M. Cockram, Willis Holder, the Picketts and some of the Wilbankses, and others whose names are not now remembered. The Stephensons—John, Edward and Isham —came from Tennessee, and settled here in an early day. William King first settled in Gun Prairie, but afterward came here. He was not very strict in his moral characteristics, and followed Solomon's lead in a plurality of wives. He finally sold out to Uriah Compton, took his brother-in-law's wife, leaving two or three of his own behind, and left the country. Cockram first settled here, but afterward moved into Spring Garden and settled near the village of that name. Teeters first settled in Moore's Prairie. Martin Teeters was James' father, and they came form Alabama originally. The old man did not come here until some fifteen years after James Teeters had settled here. But we can not follow the settlement of the township further. So much has already been said in preceding chapters of this work, of the coming, the settlement and life of the pioneers, that anything further can be little else than repetition.

The experiences of the people here were similar to other pioneer settlements, as we have said. They lived in log cabins, wore home-made clothing, subsisted upon game and the products of the soil, and indulged in the recreations common to the rest of the county. With all the growth and activity, which assumes larger proportions in the recital than in actual experience, the community which gathered in what is now Elk Prairie Township, was essentially on the frontier at that time, and the people experienced all the hardships and discomforts incident to frontier settlements. For the first few years, supplies were brought from a distance; mills were built rather early, but owing to a lack of power or adequate machinery, most of the meal and flour were obtained only by going long distances and enduring tedious delays. The general settlement was of slow growth, but sure; here and there the smoke curled upward in the air from the scattered log cabins, as the busy pioneer protracted the clearing-up of his farm long into the night.

Deer were shot in large numbers, while wolves and panthers, "Congress hogs," a few bears and the whole class of small game found in this section, and afforded wholesome meals or rare hunting sport. The distance from any market was long felt among the farming community, and did much to retard growth and prosperity. But these inconveniences were lived over, and as civilization increased, comforts and luxuries increased also.

Elk Prairie Township suffered from the same inconveniences in the lack of roads and mill facilities. The first settlers used the mortar and pestle to pound their corn, the finest of which was used for meal and the coarser for hominy. A few years later, horse mills were built. These were a great improvement on the mortar and hand mills, but we of to-day would think it a poor way to obtain bread. Some of the pioneers, doubtless, still remember the bustle and preparation for "going to mill." The shelling of the corn the day before, the rising long before day in order to make the trip in one day if possible, the careful wrapping up in cold weather, the cautions about the creek or branch crossings, and the anxiety felt at home if "the boys" were gone much longer than was expected. But as settlements became more numerous, mills were built at shorter intervals, and the inconveniences in this respect passed away. The first roads were only trails through the township from one neighbor's to another's, or to the horse mill. But these also were improved and increased with the demand for them, and the settlements were soon well supplied with good roads. Bridges of substantial build now span the streams where all the important highways cross them, thus rendering travel comparatively safe and pleasant.

The early educational history of Elk Prairie Township is involved in considerable obscurity, and it is not definitely known now when or by whom the first school was taught, nor where the first pioneer schoolhouse was erected. At the present day the township devotes as much attention to educational interests as any portion of Jefferson County. There are eight good, comfortable schoolhouses, all well and commodiously furnished in the most approved style. These schoolhouses are located respectively on Sections 6, 10, 11, 13, 15, 20, 27 and 32, and in them good schools are annually taught for the usual terms by competent teachers.

Christianity in the township dates back to its first settlement by white people. Many of the pioneers had been active members of different churches in the States from whence they came, and this soon led to the organization of religious societies here. Meetings were held in private houses, and in the summer time in the groves until the building of schoolhouses, when they were utilized for religious worship as well as for school purposes. Thus churches were organized by these simple pioneers in an early day. There are now two church buildings in the township. A Methodist Church near Mr. Dare's, which is a neat and substantial frame edifice. East of it is a Campbellite or Christian Church. The building was originally put up for a schoolhouse, but a few years ago the township built a new schoolhouse in the district, and sold the old one to the Christians. They repaired it, and have made quite as neat and tasty church building of it. It has a good membership for a country church.

This township was originally Elk Prairie Election Precinct. In 1869, the county adopted township organization, when this became what it is now—Elk Prairie Township. Since then, the following is a complete list of township officials:

Supervisors.—G. W. Evans, 1870-72; J. R. Knowles, 1873-74; G. W. Evans, 1875; J. H. Crosno, 1876; G. W. Evans, 1877; J. R. Knowles, 1878-80; L. M. Cole, 1881-82; S. H. Dolby, 1883, the present incumbent.

Township Clerks—J. G. Gee, 1872-74; William P. Hamilton, 1875; B. S. Bowenmaster, 1876-77; J. H. Wheeler, 1878; L. B. Kelso, 1879; T. R. Fox, 1880; J. B. Boswell, 1881-83, now holding the position.

Assessors—Lewis M. Cole, 1872; G. G. Dolby, 1873; L. M. Cole, 1874-75; H. H. Hartly, 1876; William Dodds, 1877-78; L. M. Cole, 1879; William Dodds, 1880; H. H. Hartly, 1881; J. D. Dodds, 1882; S. Kirk, 1883, now in office.

Collectors—J. R. Knowles, 1870-72; A. J. Sweaton, 1873; C. C. Brown, 1874; William Graham, 1875; J. R. Knowles, 1876-77; G. G. Dolby, 1878-79; J. Stansberry, 1880; J. D. Dodds, 1881; S. P. Sheaton, 1882; J. B. Dougherty, 1883, the present incumbent.

School Treasurers—Eli Gilbert, 1874; S. A. Block, 1875-77; Isaas Ward, 1878; J. W. Wells, 1879; S. A. Block, 1880-81; H. Wells, 1882; J. Loman, 1883, now in office.

Justices of the Peace—A. J. Sweaton, Eli Gilbert, W. Hampton, A. J. Sweaton, Eli Gilbert, H. R. Dare, A. J. Kelly, L. T. Coffman, H. R. Dare.

Constables—W. T. Dare, L. T. Coffman, S. P. Shelton, J. Sulcer, J. H. Hestley, D. G. Peterson.

Highway Commissioners—J. J. Fitzgerrell, John Dodds, J. Wilbanks, J. G. Gee, John Doyle, J. Wilbanks, J. G. Gee, S. P. Shelton, S. H. Dolby, S. Hirons, J. Rowe, W. T. Peterson.

The village of Winfield was laid out by A. M. Grant for J. J. Fitzgerrell, the owner of the land. It is situated in Horse Prairie, in the northwest quarter of the northwest quarter of Section 32 of Elk Prairie Township, and the plat is dated March 26, 1860. The original survey (which is all there is of the town) consisted of four blocks of four lots each. The first store in the village was opened by Isaac Boswell. Some years later the Wards opened a store. A Mr. Graham also opened a store. A mill was built by Isaac Clampet. It afterward passed into the possession of John Knowles, who operated it several years, and finally it became the property of the Wards. They greatly improved it, and made it an excellent mill. Dr. Gee came to the place in 1867, and afterward married Mr. Fitzgerrell's daughter. Dr. White was also a citizen for some years, and then moved to his farm. A good schoolhouse with a hall above was built some years ago. Also a church building has been erected. The town is not as large as Chicago—perhaps it never will be—perhaps it has already attained its full growth. It is in the midst of a good farming region, however, and ought to be quite a prosperous place.

This comprises a brief history of Elk Prairie Township, from its settlement by the pale-faced pioneers to the present time. It is one of the fine agricultural townships of the county, and its citizens are an intelligent, industrious and prosperous class of farmers. No more need be said of them.

CHAPTER XIV.*

FARRINGTON TOWNSHIP—GENERAL TOPOGRAPHY, BOUNDARIES, ETC.—SETTLEMENT OF WHITE PEOPLE—EARLY INDUSTRIES—SCHOOLS AND CHURCHES—TOWNSHIP OFFICERS—VILLAGES—STOCK-RAISING, ETC.

"He bent his way where twilight reigns sublime,
O'er forests silent since the birth of time."

IN the early history of Jefferson County, people were not farmers, but hunters. They would "squat" on a piece of land, put up a rough cabin, and some of them cleared a little "truck patch," which was mostly cultivated by their wives and children. But in a few years the real farmers began to come in, and then hunters began to get ready to pull up stakes and "move on"—go West, where the crowding civilization and settlements would not trouble them or disturb the game they were wont to chase. Of the hunter class were those whose necessity, in the chase and in protecting their pigs and chickens from the hungry wolves and other wild beasts, required the services of the dog, and hence always a goodly portion of many families were made up of "mongrel, puppy, whelp and hound, and cur of low degree." But most unfortunately, with the disappearance of the simple trappers and hunters, the dogs "did not go," but remained in unlimited numbers for many years after their usefulness had ceased, and even now they may be seen plentifully in some places. They are one of the relics of barbarism that linger "alone, all alone." And just here we may add—for it is a fact beyond dispute—that one of the greatest misfortunes to Southern Illinois has been its large number of worthless, sheep-killing dogs. These perpetual pests have cost every county thousands of dollars for every 5 cent piece they have saved them. If there never had been a dog here there would now be large flocks of sheep raised where there is not one to be seen. And yet the farmers will persist in keeping a lot of mangy dogs, and for what purpose? None under heaven, but because it is the custom to have dogs to, to—— to prey on their neighbors' sheep. Verily, I say unto you, one sheep is of more value than ninety and nine worthless dogs. Selah!

Farrington Township, to which this chapter is devoted, comprises the northeast corner of the township. Marion County lies on the north, Wayne County on the east, Web-

---
* By W. H. Perrin.

ber Township on the south and Field Township on the west. Farrington, according to the Government survey, is Township 1 south of the base line, and in Range 4 east, of the Third Principal Meridian. It is divided between prairie and woodland, and is of very good surface, unless it be along the little streams, when it becomes somewhat hilly in places. The principal water-course is Adams Fork, which flows in a southeast direction, then leaving the township through Section 36. Adam's Fork, with a few nameless branches, comprises the natural drainage system of Farrington. The timber is that mentioned as growing in other portions of the county. The inhabitants are an industrious and intelligent class of people, and are devoted mostly to farming and stock-raising.

Following close in the wake of the hunters and trappers came the regular settlers. Their privations, though settlements here were not made as early as in other sections of the county, were such as only brave hearts could endure. Nothing but the hopeful inspiration of manifest destiny urged them to persevere in bringing under the dominion of civilized man what was before them—a wild and tangled wilderness. Just who was the first settler in what is now Farrington Township we cannot say, as settlements were made in many adjoining neighborhoods before this, and it is not easy to say just when the first man stepped over into Farrington and pitched his tent. But among the first settlers were the Wellses, the Gregorys, Haynies, Abraham Buffington, William B. Johnson, Joseph Norman and others. Berryman and Barney Wells were, perhaps, the first of these; at least, they were here when the Gregorys came. They were from Tennessee, and Berryman Wells settled on Section 14, Barney on Section 8; they have long been dead, but have descendants living in the county. Of the Gregorys, there were Jonathan and Benjamin, who came here about 1828–30, and Absalom Gregory, a brother, came some two years later. They were all Kentuckians, and settled, Jonathan on Section 23, Benjamin on Section 24 and Absalom on Section 26. They are dead, but still have descendants living, among whom is Dr. L. B. Gregory, the Postmaster General of Logansville, and the model farmer of the township, whose barn is a pattern for all to follow after. The Doctor is quite a stock-raiser, and the extreme docility of his stock, particularly his domestic animals, show the great care and attention they receive from their owner. We have been there, and witnessed that whereof we speak. Dr. Gregory owns some 1,400 or 1,500 acres of as good land as may be found in Farrington Township. He is one of the self-made men of the country, and deserves great credit for what he is. He began life, as he informed us, without a dime, and what he is he is indebted to no one for but himself. His own energy and indomitable will has wrought for him a fortune, which speaks well for the Doctor, and we may add, for no one else. His mind is well stored with incidents of the early history of the county, many of which he regaled us with. He came here but a lad, and his busy life has extended through all the hard times, the trials and hardships to which the early settlers were subjected. He delights to tell of the time when he collected nearly the entire revenue of the county in coon skins and deer skins, which were a legal tender. John Allen was then Sheriff; the season had been a hard one; people had but small crops; but few had made enough to live on, and as to money, that was an unknown quantity. In this state of affairs, Sheriff Allen employed Dr. Gregory to collect the county taxes. Gregory says every farmer in those days, who could raise $8 or $10, would buy a barrel of whisky to sell again (license to sell whisky did not then cost as much as now), and as there was no money they would take coon skins for whisky. Hence, nearly every man had a large number of coon skins on hand and these were nearly all these whisky sellers who were able to pay their taxes. So he collected the biggest part of the taxes in coon skins and deer skins.

Francis, William and James Haynie came about the same time the Gregorys came. Francis Haynie settled on Section 26, James on Section 24, and William on Section 23. They, too, came from Tennessee, and are dead. Francis was an old Revolutionary soldier. Mr. Johnson says: "Mr. Haynie never had any permanent home after the death of his wife. He came to his relatives here; staid sometimes for months; but it was said that he came and went with the wild geese. Many of our people remember him as he passed among us many years ago, with the same old hat, the same long hunting shirt closely belted around him, and the same walking stick, at least five feet long, grasped a foot or so from the end. The old man's last visit here was in 1838. He spent most of the last years of his life at his son's, north of here." William Haynie moved West and died somewhere out there. Joseph Norman came here from Tennessee, and settled in the same neighborhood as the Haynies. Abram Buffington settled near Farrington. He was a noted hunter, and used to kill a great deal of game. William B. Johnson was also an early settler in this part of the township. He has a son, John W. Johnson, living just west of Farrington, one of the prosperous farmers of the county, and withal an enterprising citizen. William Casey also lived in this township for some years in the early times, and may be reckoned among the pioneers.

Such were some of the leading men who gathered here. It is difficult in most cases to distinguish marks of individuality in the smaller settlements of a county, especially where all are derived from the same general section. But in the early community of Farrington, there was less of this difficulty in the way. A majority, in fact nearly all of the early settlers here were from Tennessee and Kentucky, and came here for the purpose of making permanent homes. They were men possessing little literary taste. The rugged experience of frontier life and the isolation from the closer restraints of older civilization has a tendency to unduly elevate the importance of brawn and muscle in the general consideration, and brawling and carousing are tolerated to a much greater extent than where there are gentler influences to counteract such tendencies. This rough element predominated in many portions of the county among the early settlers. It was no worse in Farrington than elsewhere—perhaps it was no better. The prevailing custom of the nation had educated the church of the early day to see no harm in the general use of whisky, and it may not be said that the members were free from intoxication. As year by year the inevitable result of the practice was foreshadowed, they had not the moral courage to reject it. Brawling disputes were common, and the general sentiment was not very favorable to intellectual progress. But all this has changed now, and Farrington Township is noted throughout the county at the present day for its intelligence, civilization and refinement. The usual pioneer improvements of Farrington consisted of the rude mills of the early settlers, and the making of roads. The first road through the township was the Mount Vernon

& Maysville road, and the next the road leading from Mount Vernon to Xenia. The township now is blest with as good roads as any other portion of the county, and good, substantial bridges span the streams where the principal roads cross them.

As to the educational and religious facilities, not as much can be said as in some other localities. Church edifices are not plentiful, and most of the schoolhouses are a little dilapidated, though there are some new ones and some that are used for church as well as school purposes.

Dr. Gregory says the first teacher he went to school to was a Mr. Joseph Price, and he thinks it was the first school in the township. The Doctor's description of that school and schoolhouse and his attendance at it is quite humorous. The house, he says, was a pole cabin about sixteen feet square, slab seats and without any floor except the ground. The fire was built in the middle of the room, and around this "council fire" the pioneer boys and girls attained the wisdom and inspiration to fit them for after life. Dr. Gregory says he wore buckskin breeches and buckskin hunting-shirt, and on his way to school of a morning through the rain and snow, his breeches, which were not very well tanned, would get wet and stretch out until they would be down under his feet. But, sitting around that log-heap fire in that old schoolhouse, they would get dry and draw up until they were nearly to his knees, thus displaying his "shapely shins," which had stood exposure to the elements until they were about like young scaley-barked hickories.

The next school teacher after Price was probably Absalom Gregory, an uncle of the present Dr. Gregory, alluded to above. He was followed by Elder R. T. Camp, a Baptist preacher, who, notwithstanding his holy calling, was as illiterate and unlearned as the fishermen of Gallilee. William Johnson was also an early teacher. Another of the early schoolhouses was built on Horse Creek. It was also a rude log cabin. The next schoolhouse in this portion of the township was built at Farrington. There are now six schoolhouses in the township; some of them good, substantial buildings and some of them badly needed to be replaced with new and better ones. Farrington Township is Democratic in politics. It is not as great a Democratic stronghold as it used to be, mainly through the influence of that old Republican wheel-horse, Dr. Gregory, who says he intends to make it Republican yet, if he lives long enough. According to the late Ohio election, he has an army contract on hand. In 1869, Farrington was made a township. Since then, the following is a list of the township officials:

Supervisors—M. A. Morrison, 1870-72; L. B. Gregory, 1873; L. B. Donohoo, 1874; L. B. Gregory, 1875; W. L. Young, 1876-78; L. B. Gregory, 1879; J. W. Johnson, 1880; L. B. Gregory, 1881; J. W. Johnson, 1882; L. B. Gregory, 1883.

Township Clerks—J.W. Johnson, 1872; John Pierce, 1873; M. A. Morrison, 1874; John Pierce, 1875-80; J. Burke, 1881; J. Young, 1882; Charles Burke, 1883.

Assessors—W. L. Young, 1872-74; F. M. Harvey, 1875; M. A. Morrison, 1876-77; William Summers, 1878; W. L. Young, 1879; S. C. Clark, 1880; W. L. Young, 1881; W. L. Young, 1882; J. B. Young, 1883.

Collectors—L. B. Gregory, 1872; J. P. Clark, 1873-74; W. L. Young, 1875; J. D. Alton, 1876; G. W. French, 1877; Charles Burke, 1878; C. S. Burke, 1879-80; J. Williams, 1881-83.

School Treasurers—M. A. Morrison, 1874; W. L. Young, 1875; S. Brookman, 1876-77; W. L. Young, 1878; W. E. Wilson, 1879;

W. L. Young, 1880; W. D. Morrison, 1881; R. French, 1882; J. McCormaughty, 1883.

Highway Commissioners—L. Buffington, J. Bradly, Pinckney Green, J. Bradly, S. Greenwalt, S. M. Burns, James Norman, B. Sledge, J. Cooper, J. Sumner, William T. Fry and W. Wilson.

Justices of the Peace—J. W. Johnson, Isaac Dodds, Pinckney Green and J. Bradly.

Constables—Robert French, F. M. Haynie, W. R. Donohoo, John R. Webb, M. Redburn, J. R. Cameron, J. Norman and C. Donohoo.

The village of Farrington was laid out June 2, 1856, and was surveyed by A. M. Grant for Jehu J. Maxey. It comprised six acres of ground adjoining Mr. Johnson's place, and there were two blocks of five lots each and two of eight lots each. Maxey & Johnson built a store-house, the first house erected after the town was laid out. George Lear came next and then Abram Casey, and after him Kirk & Underwood. The next comer to the new town was, perhaps, Dr. Bradford; Dr. Johnson also built a house in the town. When the latter left the place, Munsell came; then Bradford and Ingalls. John Bagwell had a shop some distance from Farrington, but afterward put up one in town, and he and Perry Maxey worked in it. About the beginning of the war, King Maxey put up a mill just south of town. He sold it to a Mr. Powers in 1862, and after the close of the war William Summers came home from the army and bought an interest in it; some four years later it was sold to a man named Snow, and moved to Walnut Hill. W. A. Dale came soon after the town was laid out, and started a tanyard, which was carried on a number of years. April 15, 1857, an addition to Farrington was laid off by Johnson & Collins, which was surveyed by Ambrose Meador. A schoolhouse was built and a few years later an excellent church was put up, which was blown down in a storm a few years afterward. Farrington is in a beautiful place for a town, but it seems to have reached the zenith of its glory, and now to be on the downward road to the "vale of obscurity." A town of 2,000 or 3,000 inhabitants could be built here upon as pretty a location as ever a town stood on.

Logansville, a little northeast of Farrington, consists of the post office of that name and a small store kept by Dr. Gregory. He commenced selling goods here some fifteen or twenty years ago, and about the same time, through the influence of Gen. John A. Logan, then in the United States Senate, he got a post office, and honored the "swarthy Senator" by giving it his name. Although rejoicing under the high-sounding name of Logansville, there is no town, nor has there been a town laid out here.

At the present time there is no church building standing in the township; Mount Zion Baptist Church was burned a few years ago and has never been rebuilt. A church was erected in the northeast part of the township, but was never finished, and, as already stated, the church in Farrington was blown down in a storm a few years ago. So now the township is dependent upon the schoolhouses in order to hold religious service.

Farrington Township is an excellent farming region. Corn, oats, rye and wheat are produced in large quantities, and also fruits and vegetables. Many farmers, too, have gone into stock-raising. Dr. Gregory and Mr Bradford are, perhaps, the most extensive raisers and dealers in the township. But others are beginning to pay more or less attention to the business, and doubtless, in a few years Farrington will become quite a stock-producing community.

CHAPTER XV.*

GRAND PRAIRIE TOWNSHIP—BOUNDARIES AND TOPOGRAPHY—EARLY SETTLEMENT—HARDSHIPS OF THE PEOPLE, ETC.—FIRST MILLS AND ROADS—BIRTH, DEATH AND MARRIAGE—AN INCIDENT—FIRST VOTING PLACE—TOWNSHIP OFFICIALS, ETC.—SCHOOLS AND SCHOOLHOUSES—CHURCHES, ETC., ETC.

"——ramble for our delight,
For the world's all free, and we may choose," etc.
—*Hood.*

FOR some years after the trappers, fishers and pioneers began to skirt with sparse cabins the Ohio River, Fort Massac was the only point within reach where these people could resort for the little trading in those essential supplies of ammunition, etc., that they were compelled to have. For a long time, too, this place was a landing-point for all those pioneers from the Southern States that came down or crossed the Ohio River on their way to the Illinois settlements. At first this was a route for nearly all the immigration into Southern Illinois, much of which came down the Ohio River on batteaus, pirogues, canoes and skiffs, while some crossed the river at Shawneetown, but the larger number (in the earlier years of immigration) at Fort Massac. But by the time settlements had begun in Jefferson County and the country immediately contiguous thereto, Shawneetown was the gateway into the territory. Nearly seventy years have passed since the first settlement by white people in what is now Jefferson County. There is a tradition, however, not well authenticated, that several years prior to this a man had settled in Moore's Prairie, the facts of which have been given in preceding chapters of this work.

*By W. H. Perrin.

Few people of Southern Illinois know the history of its possession by their own race. In the early part of the eighteenth century there were white men passing up and down the Ohio River, and the governments that at different times had possessions, had erected Forts Massac, Wilkinson and Jefferson, and at these forts were stationed soldiers. These, however, were merely guard-posts of armed men for the purpose of keeping the possession and retaining the ownership of the country. Often the Indians would gather in great force and besiege the place, and bloody battles would ensue, and then for years the place would be untenanted. The tenure of these places was frail and uncertain, as they were often the prizes of unprincipled white men as well as of the native savages. But much of this preliminary history is given in other chapters of this work. In this chapter our attention and that of the reader is directed to a single division of the county.

Grand Prairie Township is situated in the extreme northwest corner of Jefferson County. It has Washington County on the west, Marion County on the north, Rome Township on the east, Casner Township on the south and in the Government survey it is known as Township 1 south, and Range 1 east of the Third Principal Meridian. Perhaps as much of this township is prairie as any one township in the county. It takes its name from the preponderance of prairie land in it. The surface is generally level or slightly rolling and undulating, and drains well without artificial means. The timber is the same as in other portions of the county. The principal streams are a branch of the Big Muddy and Rayse Creek, with a few smaller brooks and branches, which drain the land well and afford an abundance of stock water. Grand Prairie is a fine farming and stock-raising region, and can boast of some of the best farms and some of the most prosperous farmers in the county.

Among the early settlers of what is now Grand Prairie Township were Abram Casey, James Ray, the Baldridges, William Fulton, the Breezes, Stephen Cameron, James French, John Roberts, J. A. Taylor, Green Depriest, Peter Bingaman, Alfred Woods, Isaac Reilley, John C. Poston, Clark Casey and others. Abram Casey is considered the first white settler in this township, which, however, was not settled up as early as some other portions of the county. Casey settled, previous to coming here, near Mount Vernon. He was a brother of Gov. Casey, and moved about a great deal, finally moving to Missouri, where he died in 1841–42. James Ray bought him out in the township. On Christmas morning, 1828, Mr. Ray accidentallly shot and killed his uncle, Elijah Joliff, near Mount Vernon. The circumstance is related in another chapter of this work, and need not be repeated here. The Baldridges were from North Carolina and came previous to 1827. Daniel and William came with their families and still have descendants living here. Fulton came from the East somewhere about 1826, and settled in the north part of the township. The Breezes came from Orange County, Ind., but the family was originally from Pennsylvania. Robert Breeze used to boat down the river. He once went down the Lower Mississippi with a boat, and when he sold out he came back to St. Louis and walked from Kaskaskia across the State to Vincennes, where there was not a house on the trail lying between the two places. He and John Breeze came here about 1826 or 1827, and their descendants are still numerous in the county. Cameron was also from Orange County, Ind., and has descendants still living. French and Roberts came from the same neighborhood. Roberts was French's son-in-law, and they both had large families when they came to the country. Taylor settled in the southeast portion of the township.

Green Depriest, who settled originally in the vicinity of Mount Vernon, came here about 1832. He finally went to Missouri. In 1828, Peter Bingaman settled where Richard Breeze now lives. Alfred Woods settled here in 1829 on Section 22. He engaged in making sugar, and also devoted much time to hunting bee trees. He once cut down a bee tree, and in its fall a limb struck him, killing him instantly. Isaac Reilly settled afterward on the place occupied by Woods. Poston came about 1831, and had an early mill. Clark Casey also settled in the township about 1830, on Section 28. The people were now coming in rapidly, and the fine country of Grand Prairie was soon all occupied.

The pole cabins, the homely fare of wild game and hominy and ash cake of grated or pounded meal, the old wooden mold-board plows, and other rude pioneer tools, implements and hardships were common here, as in other newly settled portions of the State. The people lived hard; their comforts were few and their luxuries fewer still. They had to struggle hard to keep the wolf from the door, both figuratively and literally. The wolves were plenty in the forests and prairies, and the wolf hunger, often stalked abroad by day as well as by night. But we are told that "time, patience and perseverance will accomplish all things;" so they did in this, and with the passing years came peace and plenty.

The mortar and pestle as a means of procuring meal finally gave way to an ox tread-mill, put up by D. Baldridge, on the place now owned by his son, James Baldridge. Joseph Baldridge afterward bought it and moved it to another locality, but continued the ox tread-wheel power as the means of running it. John C. Poston put up a horse-mill soon after he came in 1831, near where Richard Breeze lives. Jacob and Owen Breeze operated a circular saw mill near Big Muddy, which was run by horse-power, but it proved a poor investment, and they retired from the business some time before the war.

The first road that ever passed through Grand Prairie Township was the old Vincennes and Kaskaskia trace, which touched the north part of the township. It was improved, as the country settled up, and made a road. In 1827, this was the only road except the Mount Vernon road. The township has as good roads now and as many of them as any portion of the county. The first death which occurred in this section, or the first one recalled, was Joseph Baldridge, Sr., but the date is not now remembered. One of the first marriages was Clark Casey to Polly Bingaman, and the ceremony was performed by Gov. Casey. The first birth is lost among the multitude of events that have transpired.

For the first few years after settlements were made here, the people voted in Mount Vernon, but afterward a precinct was formed including Grand Prairie, and the voting place was at Poston's mill. Since the adoption of township organization, the following is a complete list of township officers:

Supervisors.—Jacob Breeze, 1870; Henry Breeze, 1871; Henry Breeze, 1872; Jacob Breeze, 1873; John W. Hails, 1874; John W. Hails, 1875; Henry Breeze, 1876; T. L. Ratts, 1877; Henry Breeze, 1878; W. L. Fisher, 1879; Henry Breeze; 1880; I. G. Carpenter, 1881; I. G. Carpenter, 1882; Henry Breeze, 1883, the present incumbent.

Town Clerks.—Samuel Copple, 1872; Samuel Copple, 1873; J. M. Gresamore, 1874; A. J. Hartly, 1875; W. A. Hartly, who took a mortgage on the place, and has held fast to it from 1876 to the present (1883) writing.

Assessors.—H. M. Bogan, 1872; W. Gaston, 1873; A. J. Hartly, 1874; E. S. Noleman, 1875-76; L. H. Breeze, 1877; E. S. Noleman, 1878; J. H. Fisher, 1879; E. S. Noleman, 1880; A. J. Hartly, 1881; J. W. Fisher, 1882; and T. L. Ratts, 1883, now in office.

Collectors.—J. W. Fisher, 1872; E. S. Noleman, 1873; W. T. Fisher, 1874; Samuel Copple, 1875; T. Beadles, 1876; W. D. Baldridge, 1877; A. J. Hartly, 1878; G. P. Baldridge, 1879; R. W. Gaston, 1880; W. E. Beadles, 1881; W. E. Beadles, 1882; E. S. Noleman, 1883, at present in the office.

School Treasurers.—Jacob Breeze, E. Copple, J. Baldridge, Charles Mills, T. B. Moore, Sr., H. W. Beal, J. W. Hails, T. B. Moore, Sr., T. L. Ratts and J. W. Hails, the present incumbent.

Highway Commissioners.—W. M. Galbraith, Essex Payne, T. L. Ratts, I. G. Carpenter, W. C. Pitchford, Thomas Baldridge, Ira G. Carpenter, W. C. Pitchford, Thomas Baldridge, William Galbraith, J. W. Hails and Thomas Baldridge.

Justices of the Peace.—Franklin Cruzen,

Henry Breeze, T. B. Moore, Sr., H. Breeze and T. B. Moore, Sr.

Constables.—N. Rogers, J. W. Due, W. C. Pitchford, O. P. Moore, S. J. Shaw, J. H. Dickinson, W. C. Pitchford and J. Sprouse.

Grand Prairie Township, as we have said, is a fine section of country, and has many fine farms. In addition to raising large quantities of corn, wheat, oats, grass, etc., etc., much attention is paid to stock-raising. Here we may see in all their glory and beauty some of the finest specimens of the Norman horse. Jacob Breeze and Eli Copple imported three of these animals, the first ever brought to this township. Much attention is now given to the breeding of these magnificent draft horses. Considerable fruit is also raised in the township. In the north part, Mr. Galbraith and Ira G. Carpenter make a specialty of strawberries, and raise and ship large quantities annually. Richard and Jacob Breeze have a very fine sugar camp, which is worked every year. There are several other "camps" in the township, and hence a good deal of maple sugar and molasses are made; sugar cane is also raised to some extent. This diversity of crops and farming is seen in the thrift and prosperity of the farmers over those in sections where an entire neighborhood is devoted to a single crop, as wheat, for instance, which every year is becoming more and more uncertain in this latitude.

The following incident was related to us, which we give as we heard it, and without any comment. Somewhere about 1840, one John Switzer came here and settled the farm now owned by R. Breeze. Here he lived until some time during the war, perhaps about 1863. One night three masked men came to his house and claimed to be looking for refugees. There was a man named Timmons at his house who was a deserter, or supposed to be, from the Confederate army. This man the maskers took away with them, but soon two of them came back and robbed Switzer of all the money he had about the house or all that the rogues could find. So far as we could learn, no clew to the perpetrators was ever unearthed. Switzer soon after sold out and left the neighborhood.

The first school, or one of the first, was taught by a man owning the uncommon name of Smith. He boarded with R. Breeze, but ran away before his school was finished without even remunerating Mr. Breeze for his board. The first schoolhouse built was on the Poston farm, and was a log cabin sixteen feet square, with slab seats, a puncheon floor and stick chimney. The township now has six good, comfortable schoolhouses, located in Sections 2, 7, 9, 13, 26 and 29, in which first-class schools are taught each year.

The first religious meetings were held at the people's houses, and were attended by everybody in reach. The organization of the first church society was at the Widow Gaston's. Rev. Samuel Walker, a pioneer Methodist minister, was the organizer of it, and among the first members were the Gaston family, Clark Casey and family, and others of the early settlers of the neighborhood. The first church was built as a schoolhouse on the farm now owned by Mr. Hails, and was a log cabin. It was used both for school and church purposes. Mrs. Gaston's house was finally burned, and as the church had been organized at her house, this old church and schoolhouse was now given her as a residence. The first building put up for a church exclusively was a Methodist Church called Pisgah. It was a frame edifice, and was built about 1852. It is still standing, but has been purchased by the township and converted into a schoolhouse.

Gilead Methodist Episcopal Church on Section 5, in the north part of the township, is the only church building, but several of the schoolhouses are used more or less as places of worship. A good Sunday school is kept up in the township, at the voting place near the center, under the superintendence of Mr. E. S. Noleman.

There is not a railroad nor a town or village in Grand Prairie Township. It is decidedly an agricultural region. The people, however, do not need towns, as they have a number in close proximity on the Illinois Central Railroad, which passes near them. Richview and Irvington are near by, and even Centralia is but a few miles' distant, and thus they have town facilities without the expense of them in their own midst. At these neighboring towns they do their trading, shipping, and even get their mail at them, as there is not even a post office within the limits of the township.

CHAPTER XVI.*

McCLELLAN TOWNSHIP—INTRODUCTION AND DESCRIPTION—TOPOGRAPHY—EARLY SETTLEMENT—TRIALS, HARDSHIPS AND GOOD TIMES—PIONEER IMPROVEMENTS—ROADS, BRIDGES AND MILLS—EDUCATION, SCHOOLHOUSES AND TEACHERS—EARLY CHURCHES—TOWNSHIP OFFICIALS, ETC., ETC.

"Everything has changed so much
Since sixty years ago."
—*The Pioneer.*

IN our systems of agriculture, we are exhausting our soils, regardless of the lessons which the history of by-gone peoples teach us, and with no thought of the perils which the present system of robbing the soil will inflict upon future generations, when barren fields shall fail to yield the necessary food for the teeming population which our vast resources of fertile land is so rapidly calling into existence. The exhaustion of soil in this country is being accomplished much more rapidly than was the case with older nations centuries ago. We are living in a faster age, in a time when the means of transportation are so much superior to those of former times, as not to admit of comparison. The markets of the whole world are open to the products of our fields, and we are taxing our soil to its utmost capacity in order to meet the demand, without making judicious use of the means at hand to replace what this continual drain is taking from the land. The almost inexhaustible fertility of the soil, especially the soil of Illinois, which has been spoken of much and praised so highly, is already being shown to be something of an idle boast. The prairie land as a general thing looks much richer than it really is, and most of the cultivated fields at the present time would respond gratefully to a liberal application of barn yard litter. This is an agricultural section; this township is devoted wholly to farming, and the above remarks are applicable and should be heeded by the farmers. All the manure and refuse matter about the barns should be carefully preserved and spread upon the fields. Because land is still fresh

* By W. H. Perrin.

and productive is no reason why it should not be manured and improved. There is nothing like beginning in time to improve the quality of the land and of restoring its exhausted strength. McClellan Township lies southwest of Mount Vernon, and is bounded north by Shiloh Township; east by Dodds; south by Elk Prairie; west by Blissville; and is designated as Township 3 south, Range 2 east. It is diversified between woodland and prairie, and somewhat rough and broken along the streams. The prairies are all small, and are Town Prairie, named for the county seat; Wolf Prairie in the southwest part, together with a portion of Elk Prairie which extends into it. The timber is mostly hickory, oak, ash, wild cherry, walnut, etc. Along the streams the timber originally was rather heavy, but much of it has disappeared before the woodman's ax. The principal water-course is Big Muddy Creek, which flows in a southward direction almost through the center of the township, and Rayse Creek, passing through the southwest corner, and emptying into Big Muddy a half mile north of the township line. A few small and nameless branches feed this stream and contribute their share to the drainage of the township.

The first settlement in this township was among the first in the county. Isaac and William Hicks settled in the northeast part in the fall of 1817. The Hickses were natives of South Carolina, but had been living down on the Ohio River for some time before coming here. Isaac Hicks had a son—Thomas—born soon after he moved here, and supposed to have been the first child born in the county. He (Isaac Hicks) was an exemplary man and a member of the Baptist Church. John Lee came in 1819, and was from Tennessee, but was a native of South Carolina. He settled where his son, John Lee, now lives, and had a large family of children. Israel Lanier was, perhaps, the next settler in the township to the Hickses, but of him we learned little beyond his settlement. A man named John Stillwell came about 1821 and settled in what is now McClellan Township. He is described as quite a sociable sort of a man, one who cared little for the world's wealth and took but little pains to accumulate property. He was fond of hunting, and to range the woods with his gun upon his shoulder was the sum total of his earthly happiness. But once upon a time he took his last hunt. He and the Abbotts went into the woods one day in pursuit of game in the vicinity of John Lee's, and during the day he became separated from them. This caused no uneasiness, as he was an experienced woodsman, and they expected him to make his appearance at any time. But a heavy snow storm came on, and when his prolonged absence had excited strong apprehensions of his safety, search was made. He was never found, however, and the supposition was that he became confused in the snow storm, lost his course and wandered about until he perished with the cold, or else fell a prey to wolves. Several years after, a gun barrel was found in Elk Prairie together with a few bones. These were always believed to be poor Stillwell's. After search for him was given up, a little fund was raised by the neighbors for his wife, and she returned to Indiana, whence they had come.

James Dickens settled here about 1821-22, in Section 12, and was a cooper by trade. He started a cooper shop in 1825-26, and did a considerable business in that line. He, too, was quite a hunter, and spent much time in the woods. He afterward moved up and for some time had charge of Tunstall's mill. His death is described as novel and peculiar. He was at the house of one Harlow, at some kind of a public gathering, and while at dinner choked to death with a piece of pie. It seems he was a rather rapid and hearty eater, and having his mouth well filled with pie, something amusing occurred, when throwing back his head to laugh, the pie went the wrong way, choking him, and he died at the table in a very few minutes.

William and Jonathan Wells came into the township in 1823 and settled in Wolf Prairie. Jonathan was a blacksmith and had the first shop in the township. He did the work for the entire community for several miles around. William Wells, Jr., still lives in the township and is in good circumstances. Simon McClellan settled here in 1823, on the place now owned by Samuel Jones, and it is said the township was named for him. He has a son now living in Texas. Other additions to the settlement of the township were James Quinn, James Bodine, Philip Osborne, Joseph Hays, Solomon Ford, Thomas Porter, and perhaps others, whose names we have failed to obtain. Quinn came in 1826 and settled in the north part of Elk Prairie, where his son Washington now lives. Bodine settled near Quinn and is still living.

Osborne first settled in Dodds Township, but moved into this about 1830 and settled in the north part of Elk Prairie. Hays settled on the place where Dickens had lived. His death is supposed to have been the first to occur in the township. He was among the early pioneers laid away to their last sleep in Old Union Cemetery. Ford settled in the western part of the township and is still alive, and one of the old landmarks of the county. Proctor came in 1830; he was a plain farmer and lived well.

The pioneers lived what we would term, in this fast age, a hard life, but most of the few still left will tell you that times generally were better than they are now; that people were more social, more disposed to help one another, far more honest and confiding than in the present degenerate times. A neighborhood was a kind of brotherhood—a mystic band of Freemasons, ever ready to lend a helping hand to the needy. They were brave, generous and strictly honest, and despised meanness in any shape it might present itself. It was true there were neighborhoods with a rough element in them always ready for a disturbance. These, upon the slightest provocation, would get up a fight, and in the old rough-and-tumble-knock-down-and-drag-out style. Yet, the fight once over, they were ready to drink friends, get roaring drunk and savagely friendly. The bill of fare was often meager, and consisted of coarse and homely food. The pioneer's rifle supplied the meat; bread was provided often from meal pounded in a mortar. In summer, there were plenty of berries on the prairies and in the woods, and crab apples and wild plums were abundant. Crab apples were gathered and buried in the ground for winter use. These, cooked in honey, made delicious preserves, and wild honey was plenty and to be had for the finding. Thus the life of the pioneers passed, if not always in peace and plenty, at least enjoyable to a certain degree.

Among the pioneer improvements of McClellan Township were roads and mills. The first roads were merely by-paths through the forests and over the prairies. As the people increased in wealth and provided themselves with wagons and teams, roads became necessary, and were made by cutting out the timber along these trails where they passed through the forests. At first and for a number of years there were no bridges over the streams, but as the people could afford it, bridges were built and travel thus rendered more safe. There are now some three or four substantial bridges spanning the streams in the township.

One of the first mills was a little horse-mill built by Jonathan Wells, which had a capacity of only a few bushels of corn per day. Prior to this, some of the early settlers used to go to the Ohio River near Barker's Ferry to mill. A number of neighbors would join together, and with teams and pack horses take the corn of the neighborhood and get meal in return. It took about three weeks to make a trip, and while they were gone the men who were left in the settlements would visit every family daily to see that they were not molested by Indians or wild beasts. This means of procuring the "staff of life" was resorted to until mills at home rendered it no longer necessary. A saw mill was started in the township a few years ago, and sawed up considerable of the timber, which was used mostly by the people on their farms.

John Lee put up a distillery in 1866, which he used exclusively in distilling fruit. It closed business in 1878, and, to the credit of the township be it said, it is the only enterprise of the kind ever within its limits.

To educate the masses is the grand aim of this great country of ours. That every child shall have a chance to obtain an education is the great object of our excellent common school system, and the times are near at hand when every child will not only have a chance, but will be compelled to attend school. Many of the States are passing compulsory educational laws, and soon these laws will be enforced. This is as it should be, for, while education leads to enlightenment and prosperity, ignorance is a direct road to crime and all sorts of lawlessness.

The people of McClellan Township took an early interest in educating their children.

When the settlements were still very sparse, schools were established. These were rude, when compared to our present system, but they were better than no schools at all. The first teacher, or one of the first to wield the birch in this section was Judge Baugh. He taught in a small log cabin on J. W. Lee's farm. It was of small round logs, about 18x20 feet in dimensions, and had been built by the Christian Church for a temple of worship in 1837. A second schoolhouse was built on Silas Rogers' place very early. At present there are six schoolhouses in the township, conveniently located, comfortable in arrangement and well furnished. They are located respectively on Sections 1, 8, 14, 17, 24 and 26. In these, schools are maintained each year for the usual terms.

There are not many church buildings in the township, but it does not follow that the people are not religiously inclined. Several of the schoolhouses are used for church and Sunday school purposes. The first church edifice erected was the one already referred to as having been used for school purposes. It was, as already stated, erected by the Christian denomination, and among the early members were John Lee and wife, Rev. William Chaffin and family—they were from an adjoining township—and John Scott and family, from what is now Dodds Township. The Christians now have a church in Wolf Prairie—a frame building about 40x60 feet. Services are held in it every Sunday, either by the Christians, Baptists, Methodists or Universalists. A Sunday school is carried on, which is attended and supported by all denominations.

John A. Merrill was a clerical fraud in the early days of the township. He came into the community early and represented himself as a Baptist preacher. He stopped at Isaac Hicks', and held meetings in the neighborhood for several days. While this was going on, he stole Hicks' books, passed several dollars of counterfeit money, and, instead of making himself the exemplary shepherd of a flock, he turned out to be one of the very blackest sheep.

McClellan Township is thoroughly an agricultural region. The people are beginning to pay some attention to stock and to fruit. It was for many years that sheep could not be raised on account of the wolves, and even now the worthless dogs of the county prey on them nearly as fatally as the wolves used to do. The early settlers invented many devices for ridding themselves of the wolves that infested the country in the early days, and trapping wolves and wolf hunts were among the most exciting sports of the pioneer. After a premium was offered for wolf scalps, the animals began to disappear rapidly. As the dangers from them were lessened, farmers paid more attention to sheep raising. Were they to carry it still further, it would be so much the better for them. There is but little question that Southern Illinois is better adapted to sheep than wheat raising. The sooner the farmers here turn their attention to stock and fruit, the more remunerative they will find their farms.

As a matter of some interest to our readers, we append a list of township officers since township organization, which took place in 1869. The first officers, however, were elected the next year. The list is as follows:

Supervisors.—W. A. Davis, 1870; D. C. Jones, 1871 to 1873; L. Allen, 1874; S. Ford, 1875; S. Allen, 1876 to 1878; W. A. Davis, 1879-80; D. C. Jones, 1881; W. A. Davis, 1882; and E. Collins, 1883.

Town Clerk.—W. A. Davis, 1872-73; J. M. Hays, 1874-75; D. Millner, 1876; R. A. Dale, 1877; T. B. Ford, 1878-79; R. A. Dale, 1880-81; J. M. Hays, 1882; and R. A. Dale, 1883.

Assessors.—J. W. Bradly, 1872; J. P. Downer, 1873; W. A. Davis, 1874; J. W. Robinson, 1875; J. M. Hays, 1876; V. G. Rosenberger, 1877; G. W. Bodine, 1878; J. M. Hays, 1879-80; J. W. Davis, 1881; G. W. Bodine, 1882; J. M. Hays, 1883.

Collectors.—J. E. Farthing, 1872; J. C. Quinn, 1873; V. G. Rosenberger, 1874 to 1876; G. W. Bodine, 1877; G. W. Dickerson, 1878; G. W. Bodine, 1879; A. Barrister, 1880; G. W. Bodine, 1881; J. E. Gilbert, 1882; J. W. Davis, 1883.

School Treasurers.—J. W. Mayfield, 1872 to 1878; Thomas Gray, 1879; J. W. Mayfield, 1880 to 1883.

Highway Commissioners.—Benjamin Parsley, 1872; Samuel Lacy, 1873; S. E. Gilbert, 1874; J. E. Farthing, 1875; Samuel Lacy, 1876; H. McLaughlin, 1877; J. D. Quinn, 1878; J. M. Rutherford, 1879; S. Ford, 1880; J. M. Hicks, 1881; E. Collins, 1882; and G. A. Lambert, 1883.

Justices of the Peace.—John W. Hagle and S. Reeves, 1870; Peter A. Bean and S. Reeves, 1872; E. W. Gilbert and D. S. Gray, 1874 to 1876; W. A. Davis and D. S. Gray, 1877 to 1880; J. M. Rutherford and W. A. Davis, 1881 to 1883.

McClellan Township is without villages, towns, manufactories or railroads. Its shipping point is Mount Vernon, which is but a mile or two from the northeast corner of the township, and by hauling to that city railroad facilities can be obtained for all the best markets of the country. To sum it up, the farmers of McClellan Township have a prosperous future before them, and they only need to be true to themselves and to guard their interests faithfully to reap a golden harvest at no distant period. They have good lands and valuable farms, and must sooner or later attain all else that is desirable, if they only work to their own advantage. To this end, then, they should look more to stock-raising and fruit-growing and less to grain.

CHAPTER XVII.*

FIELD TOWNSHIP—TOPOGRAPHICAL, GEOGRAPHICAL, PHYSICAL, ETC.—SETTLEMENT BY WHITE PEOPLE—LIFE ON THE BORDER—EDUCATIONAL FACILITIES—CHURCHES AND CHURCH BUILDINGS—AN INCIDENT—TOWNSHIP OFFICERS—SUMMARY, ETC., ETC.

> "And the names he loved to hear
> Have been carved for many a year
> On the tomb."
> —*Holmes.*

IN the rush of invention and discovery, men give but little time or care to the preservation of facts and incidents that render history valuable and instructive. As the period of mortality shortens, activity increases and selfishness becomes a predominating motive. The dead and the past are too quickly forgotten in the hurry of the present and the anxiety for the future. But the reflecting mind always derives satisfaction in reviving the events of preceding years and forming a mental contrast between the then and now. Could we but again go back to our boyhood days, and handle the old wooden plow, the sickle and cradle, and once more listen to the hum of the spinning-wheel in the old log cabin, after so long enjoying the benefits of modern implements and machinery, it would seem to us impossible that the people of the olden time could live as contentedly as they did. But the old settlers have, many of them, passed away. The slow plodding ox team has given place to the more rapid Norman span. The reaping-hook of our fathers has become a curiosity to our children. And so in their turn, perchance, our grandchildren may laugh and wonder at the implements and machinery which we now use and consider so perfect. The methods of harvesting and machinery in use by the coming generation may put our boasted self-binders and steam threshers to shame. These changes are inseparably blended with the changes in population and with the progress in civilization and social life. It is the duty and task of the historian to make note of all these transitions, and the history of Field Township would be imperfect without this reference to the old-time ways and customs, which are yet dear to the memory of many still living.

Field Township is situated in the north tier of townships, and is bounded on the north by Marion County, on the east by Farrington Township, on the south by Mount Vernon Township, on the west by Rome Township, and is Congressionally known as Township 1 south of the base line, and Range 3 east, of the Third Principal Meridian. It is divided between woodland and prairie, the former predominating. The timber is mostly oak and hickory, with a few other kinds common to this section of the country. Casey's Fork of the Big Muddy is the principal stream, and flows south through the west

* By W. H. Perrin.

side of the township. Adam's Fork has its source in the northeast part and flows westwardly. These, with a few other small brooks, constitute the natural drainage.

Field Township has no railroads or manufactories, but is thoroughly an agricultural region, and many prosperous farmers, whose well-kept farms are proof of their enterprise, are found here.

The settlement of Field Township is of much more modern date than some other portions of the county. Among the early settlers were the Fields, for whom the township was named. Jeremiah Field, the patriarch of the family, came to Marion County in 1826, but never lived in this township. Several of his sons, however, came here, among them Nathan, James and Henry Field. Thomas McCrary settled the farm now owned by John Osborne, in Section 17, and was from Alabama. He died about 1877-78, and left several children.

Thomas Jordan settled here very early, and lived near the line, in the prairie which bears his name, and which lies in this and Rome Township. He kept a tavern on the old Goshen road, and had a large family of children. The Jordans were among the earliest settlers in this portion of the State, but they first located in Franklin County, where they lived for some years and built a block-house. They afterward scattered out, and several of the name became settlers in different portions of Jefferson County, Thomas locating in this township, as above. James Foster was an early settler, and improved the place where John McConnell now lives. Mr. Maxwell and David Garrison settled early; W. J. Garrison, a descendant, has always lived here. D. Easley settled the place now occupied by Alfred Finn. John and Benjamin Hawkins came in about 1840, and settled in Section 8. They were good farmers, and came originally from Indiana. Thomas Minor settled in the southeast part of the township prior to 1840, and still lives there. W. D. Claybourn came about 1840, from Tennessee, and is still here. Thus the township settled up, and the land was all entered and improved within a comparatively short time from the first settlements.

Field Township, as we have said, was of more modern occupation than some of the contiguous portions of the county, and hence the first settlers did not experience as great trials as some of the first pioneers did. Mills had already sprung up in many localities, and life was becoming quite easy to what it was when the first whites settled in the county. It was not all flowers and sunshine here, however, for a number of years. The people had their hardships and dangers, and enough of them, too, but they managed to outlive them and to see peace and plenty around them.

The old Goshen road was one of the first highways through Field Township, but so much has already been said of it that we will but make this reference to it here. As the township settled up, other roads were opened to accommodate the increasing population, and substantial bridges were built where they were needed. There are now some three or four good bridges in the township.

An amusing incident is related of the early history of Field Township, which is somewhat as follows: Thomas McCrary, who is mentioned as an early settler, was what was termed in those days an Abolitionist. He used to burn charcoal for a blacksmith named Storman, and the pit where he burned it was on big Muddy Creek. He burnt all the coal Storman used for several years. Blacksmiths then used charcoal entirely in their shops. Being an Abolitionist, McCrary, of course, kept a station on the underground railroad, a line that trafficked between the Slave States and Canada, and was more or less obnoxious to his neighbors, according to their political sentiments. A man named Harmon living just over in Rome Township, had boasted that if any negroes came about him they would be roughly treated, etc. One day Andrew and William McCray, two of Tom McCrary's boys, blacked their faces at the charcoal pit and went to Harmon's. The women were washing at the spring, and when they saw the "niggers," they ran to the house for protection, very much frightened. The boys disappeared into the woods, and at the first branch washed the black from their faces and then joined the immense crowd that had turned out to hunt the "niggers," whom, we may add, they did not succeed in finding. The joke was too good to keep, and the McCrary boys finally told it. This led to a regular "Donnybrook fight" on the next election day, between the friends of Harmon and the McCrarys.

The first schoolhouse in Field Township was built on Big Muddy on the McCrary farm. It was a log cabin about sixteen feet square, and of the usual pioneer pattern, with its slab seats, puncheon floor and old-time fire-place. There are now in the township six good, commodious schoolhouses, well furnished and well patronized during the school terms.

Field Township is well supplied with churches, and if its citizens are not religious it is for no lack of church facilities. Oak Grove Baptist Church, on Section 28, is a neat and tasty frame building. New Mount Zion Methodist Episcopal Church, on or near the line of Section 25, is a handsome frame edifice. Panther Fork Baptist Church, on Section 11, is an excellent frame building. The Campbellites, or Christians, have a new frame church on Section 18, near the line of Rome Township. Thus, as we have said, the people do not lack for church facilities.

As a matter of some interest to our readers, we append the following list of township officials since the adoption of township organization in 1869:

Supervisors—John McConnell, 1870; John McConnell, 1871; John Sprowle, 1873; W. J Garrison, 1874; W. J. Garrison, 1875; W. F. McConnell, 1876; W. F. McConnell, 1877; John Hawkins, 1878; W. F. McConnell, 1879. W. J. Garrison, 1880; W. J. Garrison, 1881; W. J. Garrison, 1882; W. J. Garrison, 1883, the present incumbent.

Township Clerks—Thomas Rollinson, 1872; Thomas Rollinson, 1873; B. R. Carpenter, 1874; Thomas Rollinson, 1875; Thomas Rollinson, 1876; L. Frazier, 1877; H. Hawkins, 1878; Thomas Rollinson, 1879; E. McMeens, 1880; W. F. Simmons, 1881; W. F. Simmons, 1882; W. D. Deane, 1883, now holding the office.

Assessors—J. V. Garrison, 1872; James Brown, 1873; T. B. Cady, 1874; J. M. Bennett, 1875; B. J. Hawkins, 1876; B. J. Hawkins, 1877; E. H. Howard, 1878; E. H. Howard, 1879; R. Raynor, 1880; R. Raynor, 1881; C. F. Hawkins, 1882; R. Raynor, 1883, now in office.

Collectors—B. F. Wimberly, 1872; B. R. Carpenter, 1873; T. Rollinson, 1874; J. F. Satterfield, 1875; J. F. Satterfield, 1876; J. G. Howard, 1877; J. G. Howard, 1878; D. Thompson, 1879; James Brown, 1880; T. H. Wimberly, 1881; James Brown, 1882; J. D. Simmons, 1883, now holding the position.

School Treasurers.—Elias Howard, James Brown. T. H. Wimberly, J. A. Donahoo, M. M. Howard, D. Price, W. F. McConnell, J. Sechrest, D. Price.

Highway Commissioners—John Hawkins, C. D. Frost, S. W. Maxey, John Hawkins, W. J. Garrison, R. Smith, J. J. Williams,

W. J. Hawkins, R. Padget, J. J. Williams, J. J. Connoway, R. Pagdet, etc.

Justices of the Peace—John Sprowle, Joseph Hawkins, J. T. Hutchinson, Joseph Hawkins, J. G. Darnell, Joseph Hawkins, C. M. Whitsen, J. G. Darnell, C. M. Whitsen, etc.

Constables—William Myers, F. C. Quick, T. H. Wimberley, J. J. Hawkins, H. P. Field, M. Bradford, J. E. Gibson.

Field Township contains little to write about, except the mere fact of its settlement, as it is without towns, without railroads and without manufactories. Its population is devoted chiefly to farming and stock-raising, and are an industrious and prosperous people. One of the largest stock-raisers in the township is John McConnell, who devotes his attention to horses, cattle and Cotswold sheep, of which he has some fine animals. Others, also, devote more or less time and attention to stock, and every year stock-raising, as a business, is increasing in interest.

CHAPTER XVIII.*

CASNER TOWNSHIP—TOPOGRAPHY AND PHYSICAL FEATURES—EARLY SETTLEMENT—ROUGH FARE OF THE PIONEERS—SCHOOLS AND CHURCHES—LIST OF TOWNSHIP OFFICERS—POLITICS, ETC.—ROACHVILLE VILLAGE, THE CHICAGO OF THE COUNTY, ETC., ETC.

"Ha! how the woods give way before the step
Of these new comers! What a sickening smell
Clings round my cabin, wafted from their town
Ten miles away."
—*Boone.*

THERE are few now living who were here when Jefferson County was formed. Could you, who have only seen the country as it now is, borrow their eyes, and through them look back over the long past, what an amazing sight it would be to you! The wonder of Rip Van Winkle was not greater when he woke from his long nap in the Catskill Mountains, and discovered himself no longer the loyal subject of George III, but the free and sovereign citizen of the greatest country upon which the sun shines, than would be yours could you look back and take in at a glance the then state of the country in all its primitive glory. What illusions it would dispel, what a change it would produce in your conclusions regarding your county, and the pioneers who settled it and wrought the wonderful changes that have taken place. Men are great and good in this world according to the lives they have lived, and the work they have performed. The true story of the early settlers of Southern Illinois has never been told. It should be; and when it is, they will receive their just meed of praise. Then it will be seen that they are true heroes and heroines. They were not seeking fortunes, nor fame; they were intent only upon making a home for their children, and they loved freedom to that extent that they took their lives in their hands and faced death in all its forms, and laid the foundations of all this splendid structure of civilization we see around us, that brings us all our pleasures, our wealth and our joys. Compared to the battles and victories of the celebrated warriors of the world, the work of these unpretentious, unassuming, unambitious men should tower above the warriors and states-

* By W. H. Perrin.

men in the annals of the great, as does the mountain above the mole-hill. Better men and women never lived than these noble-hearted pioneers, and it is simply shocking—almost criminal—that their descendants are so utterly ignorant of the true story of their great lives. They had no churches, no schools, no courts, no officers of the law. Their law was the imperial court of an honest, healthy public sentiment, and if in the course of their lives they found a dishonest man, they punished him to that extent, and so swift and unerring were their judgments and convictions that they either drove the wrong-doer from the settlement or cured him completely and made an honest man of him. This was the way they lived out their great lives, doing good and building wise in their day and generation. They are gone now, and we shall nevermore behold the like of them; we can only put upon record their lives and their acts, and thus preserve them from being utterly lost to their descendants.

Casner Township, to which this chapter is devoted, is situated west of Mount Vernon, and contains some as fine farming land as there is in the county. The surface is generally level, with gentle, undulating swells, resembling the ocean after a storm. The western part of it, along the Washington County line, is fine prairie land, while the remainder was originally covered with timber, among which were to be seen the varieties of oak, walnut, wild cherry, hickory, ash, locust, a good deal of hazel, sumac, etc. The township is bounded on the north by Grand Prairie Township, east by Shiloh, south by Blissville, west by Washington County, and forms Congressional Township No. 2 south, and Range 1 east. The principal stream is Rayse Creek, a branch of Big Muddy, and which flows nearly through the center of the township; a few unimportant branches flow into this stream, but they are without names on the maps.

The history of the settlement of this township by white people is but that of the settlement of the entire county. The name of the very first settler of Casner Township is somewhat indefinite; but among the first settlers was George Casner, for whom the township was named. He settled on Section 19 or 20 about the year 1824, and was from Virginia. He had quite a large family of children, and was twice married. He died only a few years ago, and his widow is still living on the old homestead. Mr. Casner is described as a most estimable man, somewhat quick and loud spoken, but kind and affectionate in his family. He accumulated quite a little fortune, but through misfortune lost much of it, and died comparatively poor. About the time Casner came to the township, there came a man named Howell, and shortly after him Alva Clark. The latter settled near Casner and died in 1847. William Burris also settled near by. He died, leaving a large family of children—among them a son who died in the late war. Solomon Patterson came here from Monroe County, and settled in Section 31, about the year 1837. He lived here awhile, and then moved into Moore's Prairie, where he, later, died. Harvey Creel also settled here in 1837. He came from Clinton County, had a large family, but all or most of them have moved away. A. M. Daniels settled on Section 6, and died in 1845. T. B. Lacy came from St. Clair County with his father, in 1834, to "move" a man named John Holt, whose father, Robert Holt, lived in Shiloh Township. A man named Johnson was then living on the place where Mr. Lacy now lives. Johnson has moved away from the township. The place was originally settled by Walter Bean, who was a regular Daniel Boone for hunting. He was also very fond of bees, and spent much time in hunting "bee-trees" and gathering wild honey. Mr. Lacy first settled in Blissville Township, but afterward in this. William Champ was among the early settlers in the eastern part of the township. Other families came in, and the land was rapidly settled.

In illustration of pioneer life, we make the following extract from a sketch by Mr. Johnson. " Coffee was not much used, as it cost 50 cents a pound, and had to be brought from Shawneetown or Kaskaskia at that. Meat was plenty, but bread was scarce. Meal had, at first, to be brought from the Wabash River. William and Isaac Casey constructed a little hand mill that would grind a bushel or two in the course of a day, and they did well. But many of the first settlers had to beat their meal in a mortar. One family had a big kettle, which they used for a mortar; but generally the mortar was a stump with a basin burnt in the top of it. Over this was suspended, by a sweep, a huge billet of wood. This billet of wood was brought down upon the grain in the mortar, the sweep raised it, and so thump, thump, the pounding went on till the grain was broken small enough to make bread. Another style of mortar was a huge block, and the pestle was a maul with an iron wedge in the end of it. This was used in bad weather, as it could be brought within doors. The meal was sifted and bread made of the finest, while the coarser was made into hominy. In early autumn, meal was grated and bread made of this meal was baked on a board or in the ashes, and was very delicious." What would the young people of the present day think of such fare? But even this was relished and enjoyed by the people then. However, we would think ourselves on the eve of starvation were we forced to live on it now, in this fast age of the country.

As population increased, mills were built, and the mortar and pestle were "laid on the shelf." Severs had a mill near Muddy Creek, and a Mr. Carroll started a tannery about 1849-50, in the western part of the township. He was finally killed in a saw mill. One of the first roads through the township was the road from Shawneetown to St. Louis, passing through Mount Vernon and this township. Several good, substantial bridges span the streams, thus rendering local travel safe and pleasant. George Casner was a blacksmith, and started the first shop of the kind in the township.

Since the adoption of township organization in 1869, the following is the complete list of township officers:

Supervisors—E. B. Harvey, 1870; W. H. Brooks, 1871; E. B. Harvey, 1872; William R. Champ, 1873; William Goaker, 1874; T. B. Lacy, 1875-76; J. P. Morgan, 1877; T. W. Harvey, 1878; J. H. Watkins, 1879; W. B. Pickett, 1880; W. P. Champ, 1881-82; W. J. Bledsoe, 1883, the present incumbent.

Township Clerks—W. R. Champ, 1872; Thomas Kelly, 1873; J. H. Spillers, 1874; W. J. Bledsoe, 1875-76; J. Fairchild, 1877; William J. Bledsoe, 1878; C. P. Schmidt, 1879; C. P. Schmidt, 1880; William J. Bledsoe, 1881; C. P. Schmidt, 1882; J. W. Fuller, 1883, now in office.

Assessors—James Wood, 1872; J. H. Watkins, 1873-74; F. M. Wright, 1875-76; M. A. Bond, 1877-78; T. P. Champ, 1879; F. M. Wright, 1880; T. W. Harvey, 1881; M. A. Bond, 1882-83, now holding the position.

Collectors—Hiram Casey, 1872; A. J. Baldridge, 1873; W. R. Champ, 1874; W. R. Champ, 1875; F. Champ, 1876; R. J. Burch, 1877; R. J. Burch, 1878; M. M. Clark, 1879; M. M. Clark, 1880; R. J. Burch, 1881;

William Cobb, 1882; W. R. Champ, 1883, the present incumbent.

School Treasurers—William Gray, Hugh Flanagan, A. Carroll, Thompson Lacy, J. M. Severs, Thompson Lacy, A. Hogshead, W. R. Champ, now in office.

Highway Commissioners—Henry Williams, A. W. Downs, T. J. Gaskins, S. P. Creel, M. C. Knowlton, S. White, W. H. Edwards, H. M. Smith, H. H. Matthis, J. Watkins, J. C. Carson, H. Williams.

Justices of the Peace—W. B. Pickett, Joseph Turney, W. B. Pickett, H. Wood, W. J. Bledsoe, T. Kelly, present incumbent.

Constables—Joseph Harvey, J. B. Moore, W. H. Gardner, John Severs, James P. Carroll, J. P. Morgan, William Rogers, J. H. Hicks, J. M. Severs, Byron Moore.

The voting place of the township is at Roachville, and the sturdy yeomanry poll a large majority at all important elections for the Democratic party. Indeed, it is said that many still vote for Thomas Jefferson and Gen. Jackson, and as for Stephen A. Douglas, he could be elected to any office in Casner, from Constable to President of the United States, by an overwhelming majority.

The schools of the township are scarcely up to the standard. The log schoolhouse may still be seen here, though there are several neat frame schoolhouses. There are in the township six, all told, and in these schools are maintained for the usual terms each year.

The first religious meetings were held in a grove near Casner's. Preaching used to be had at Mr. Patterson's before there were any churches built. Reynolds Chapel, a Methodist Church, was organized in 1876. It is a frame building, and has but a small membership. Samuel Reynolds made a profession of religion on his death-bed, and in honor of him the church was organized and given his name. Elijah Lacy was among the early ministers. Religious meetings were also held by the Methodists at the house of Mr. Bean, on the farm where T. B. Lacy now lives. Rev. Mr. Striblin was also an early preacher in this section. A flourishing Sunday school is held in the schoolhouse at Roachville.

Roachville, on the Louisville & Nashville Railroad, about ten miles west of Mount Vernon, is somewhat larger—smaller, we mean—than Chicago. It was laid out April 6, 1870, by John D. Williams, for David Roach, the owner of the land upon which it is located. The place comprised four blocks and forty lots. A storehouse was built by Roach, in which Frank Pease, from Ashley, opened a store. He was followed by Mr. Woods. Benjamin Cole opened a blacksmith shop. A Mr. Quackenbush built a mill and sold it to Abram Severs; the latter afterward sold it to Mr. Fairchild. This, with a few dwelling-houses, comprises all that has ever been of Roachville. It probably never will be much greater, though it is surrounded by an excellent country, particularly on the west.

Casner Township ought to be one of the finest farming regions in the county. It has considerable good land, that is well adapted to grain and fruit. Stock-raising, too, might be made profitable. Energy and enterprise alone is needed to make Casner one of the leading townships of the county.

CHAPTER XIX.*

DODDS TOWNSHIP—DESCRIPTION AND TOPOGRAPHY—COMING OF THE WHITES—EARLY FACTS AND INCIDENTS—THE MAIN SETTLEMENT—ROADS, FIRST MILLS, ETC.—EARLY SCHOOLS—MODE OF PAYING THE TEACHERS—FIRST PREACHERS AND CHURCHES—TOWNSHIP OFFICERS, ETC., ETC.

"Go, till the soil," said God to man,
  Subdue the earth, it shall be thine;
  How grand, how glorious was the plan!
  How wise the law divine;
And none of Adam's race can draw
  A title, save beneath this law,
  To hold the world in trust;
Earth is the Lord's and He hath sworn
  That ere Old Time has reached his bourn,
    It shall reward the just."—*Mrs. Hale.*

RECORDS of the olden time are interesting, and they are not without lessons of instruction. We follow in the footprints of the adventurous and enterprising pioneer, and see him, as it were, and his labors and struggles in the wilderness as he converts it into a fruitful field. We sit by his cabin fire and listen to the accounts which he gives of frontier life, and the hardships, trials, dangers and sufferings of himself and family in their efforts to make for themselves a home in regions remote from civilization, and unexplored hitherto by the Anglo-Saxon. Through these pioneer recitals we make our way to the present, and from small beginnings we come to the mighty achievements of industry. Following on in the path of improvement, we see the once waste places rejoicing under the care of the husbandman; arable farms are spread out before us; schools have been established, churches built and a Chrsitian ministry sustained. All this and more, but space will not allow elaborate reflections.

———

* By J. M. Runk.

The division of the county to which the reader's attention is now directed is the outgrowth of later development. As the inhabitants of other States flock in and make settlements, precincts are formed, which are afterward divided and subdivided, and in 1869 the present township of Dodds was organized. Jefferson County, for many years prior to its division into townships, comprised a number of precincts, and the territory that now constitutes Dodds Township was known as Jackson's Precinct. The township thus designated includes thirty-six sections, and is known as Township 3 south and Range 3 east. It is bounded on the north by Mount Vernon, on the east by Pendleton, on the south by Spring Garden and on the west by McClellen Township. The original character of the country included within these limits was part "barrens" and part true prairie. Moore's Prairie includes a portion of the southeast sections of the township. Another, named "Cub" Prairie, from the amount of cubs seen and caught there by the early inhabitants, is of considerable importance. The soil of the woodland is a light yellow clay, which is particularly adapted to wheat-growing. The prairie soil is rich and productive of wheat, corn, rye, oats, and almost all kinds of vegetables. The natural drainage is toward the southwest. The Casey Fork, one of the prominent affluents of "Big Muddy Creek," enters near the center of the northern boundary and takes a diagonal and zigzag course to the southwest corner. Seven-mile Creek is a stream of some importance and empties into Casey's Fork. On the high grounds and along the streams are to be found considerable timber, such as white, jack and black oak, hickory, sycamore and various kinds of shrubs. But little attention has ever been paid to stock-raising, but the farmers have engaged in a kind of mixed husbandry. Within the last few years, they have conceived the idea that stock-raising could be made remunerative, and they are adding to and improving their flocks and herds as fast as their means will allow. Samuel Gibson is the principal dealer in cattle in the township. He has lately purchased a few short-horn and Durham cattle and some fine Cotswold sheep. In the early days, there was an abundance of game, as was found everywhere in the county. Deer and small game abounded and contributed to the early settlers' larder as well as to their sport. Wolves infested these wooded slopes and made havoc with the young stock; but the bustle and hostility of the new-comers soon drove them out of the country.

A generally accepted tradition is that the first settlement made and the first cabin raised in what is now Dodds Township was by James Dodds, whose advent into this new territory was prior to the year 1818. After him the township was named, and it is not too much to say that his namesake has done him justice. It to-day ranks among the most valuable districts of the county. Dodds' first important business was the same as that of all other adventurers upon their arrival in a new territory—that of building a house. Until this was done, himself and family had to camp on the ground or live in their wagons—perhaps the only shelter they had known for weeks. So the object of building a house, which was also to be a home, was one that gave zest to the rough toil and to the heavy labors. The style of the house was not considered. It was shelter they required and protection from the weather and wild animals. The settlers had neither the money nor the mechanical appliances for building themselves a house. They were content in most instances to have a mere cabin or hut. Their cabins were usually made to resemble a human habitation, and were of round logs, light enough for two or three men to lay up, about fourteen feet square, roofed with bark or clapboards and sometimes with the sod of the prairie. For a fire-place, they made a wall of earth or stone, in an opening in one end of the building, extending outward and planked on the outside by bolts of wood notched together to stay it. Such were the hardships to which most of the early settlers of Dodds Township were exposed. Some of these we shall briefly notice in the following pages, which are framed not from records but from vague tradition, with here and there a fragment of personal reminiscence, which serves us as a guide through the obscurity which the shadows of sixty-five years have thrown around the early times. To say that in this chapter it is proposed to write the history of every family in the order in which they came into the township would be promising more than lies in the power of any man to accomplish. But to give a sketch of some of the pioneers and representative men of the times is our aim, and to transmit them in a durable form to future generations.

Joseph Jordan settled in 1818 on the land now owned and occupied by Isaac Garrison. Jordan was a man of considerable enterprise and tact, and had an eye to business. Although his settlement in the county was made one year before Jefferson County was organized, yet he had almost formed in his mind the extent of the prospective county and calculated the distance, and probably being enthused by a delightful view from a high part of that then uncultivated landscape, he treasured the thought that the county seat migth be located there. He raised his first cabin, dispensed his hospitality to those who came that way, and with heroic patience and fortitude endured the hard life of the pioneer. Only a short time elapsed before he was forced to see his plans and prospects vanish like a morning dew before the rays of the sun. The county seat was fixed at another place. Burdened with disappointment, he let his roving disposition get the better of him, and he sold his claim at a small compensation to William Frizell and moved to Texas.

The Frizell family was a valuable acquisition to the territory, and the impress of their energy is yet visible. Their sad death by the cholera in 1847 is still remembered. William Frizell, wife and children, Joseph and Martha, were the victims of this terrible disease.

The old Jordan farm went into the hands of Isaac Garrison in 1853, and by his industry it has been improved until it now ranks among the first of the county. Some time after Jordan's advent came Dr. Willoughby Adams, who was an excellent physician. He located first in the then small village of Mount Vernon, where he followed his profession, and subsequently on Section 23 in Dodds Township. His services were valuable, as the ague was a frequent visitor in every household. His popularity grew in the estimation of the people, and as early as 1841 he was chosen as one of the County Commissioners, in which capacity he served with honor, and was frequently re-elected. In 1849, he was chosen Associate Justice of the County Court. This position he filled for many years. He was the first practicing physician in Dodds Township, and was also the first County Surveyor. At his own request, he was buried a short distance from his residence, where more of his family are sleeping the sleep that knows no waking.

Frank Hicks settled at a later date on Section 27. He was a rough-spoken man, fond of drink, and participated in shooting matches and hunting sprees, which were very frequent in those days. He was, however, true to a promise, and always fulfilled his contracts. He reared a large family. One son—John R. P. Hicks—lost the use of his lower limbs over forty years ago and is a resident of Mount Vernon. He employs his time in knitting upon some kind of a machine. Another son—William—was a bright, industrious boy, and among the strongest lads in the neighborhood, but was running one day, when he was suddenly taken with a pain in his feet, which resulted in his being a complete reel-foot. He is also living.

Stephen Arnold came from Tennessee among the first, and settled on Section 14. Here he experienced all the hardships incident to the life of the then few inhabitants. Seth, the only living member of his family, resides on the old homestead. John Smith was an early settler on Section 15. He was a man of careless habits, and never accumulated much property. A few of his posterity survive. Absalom Estes settled on Section 10 some time between the years 1820 and 1822. He remained there but a short time, and sold his improvment to his brother Joseph. The latter was the father of sixteen children, all of whom grew to maturity and reared large families. Some of the Esteses accumulated large fortunes. It is said of the Estes family that they were sociable, industrious and energetic. Joseph Pace settled on Section 8. He was among the first surveyors in Jefferson County and surveyed some of the early roads, among which was the old Goshen road, and together with the Benton road, branching from the former on the farm of Isaac Garrison, leading thence to Vienna, Cairo and other old Southern cities in this State, were the only early roads in Jackson Precinct. Joseph Pace was the twin brother of Joel Pace, who was the first County and Circuit Clerk, and among the early teachers of this county. It was extensively discussed a few years since by the leading newspapers of America, and a conclusion finally arrived at to the extent that they lived longer than any twins ever known, Joel having died at the age of eighty-eight years and Joseph four years later. Joseph Rogers settled pretty early on Section 7 and became the possessor of considerable property. William Davis settled what is known as the Harper place. He was a minister of the Baptist Church, and was among the first preachers in the precinct. He died in the county, leaving his family in affluent circumstances. John Stewart came to Jackson Precinct at an early period. Stewart had the "big head" in reality. It was so large that he could not purchase a hat to fit it, and was compelled to have a hat block and employ a hatter to make his hats, which was done at his residence. David Shaffer located very early in the township and was content to live for awhile in a tent. On one occasion a fire swept over the prairie like a whirlwind, respecting nothing in its course, and it was only by the strongest efforts that Mr. Shaffer's tent was saved from the conflagration. He erected his first horse grist-mill in the township about 1838, near where is now the residence of W. T. Sanders. It was here that the inhabitants came early and stayed late to get crushed their little bag of corn, while the wife and little ones awaited with anxiety and eagerness their return. Frank Hicks also put into operation a horse mill on Section 27, and did considerable grinding for several years. Isaac Watson was a real pioneer of what is now Dodds Township.

From the earliest period of the world's history, the people of every civilized nation have realized the importance of learning. Education in its fullest sense comprehends the development and cultivation of the various physical, moral and mental faculties of man. Hence it is that the standard of a people's morals, civilization and progress is indicated by the degree of interest manifested in developing and cultivating the moral, social and intellectual faculties of its masses. Society in every age and every nation upon which the refining hand of civilization has been laid, has been ever ready to realize and accept the truth of this.

Thus from remote antiquity to the present time, we find associated with other beneficent institutions for the elevation and advancement of mankind, institutions embracing every grade of instruction, from the elementary school, where the first rudiments of an education are taught, to the university and college, where art, science and literature are disseminated. The history of education in Jefferson County finds its duplicate in the school history of other counties in Southern Illinois. The pioneers, as soon as they had each prepared a habitation and inclosed a "patch" of land on which to raise the necessaries of life, turned their attention to the erection of a schoolhouse. In 1838, the pioneers of Jackson Precinct, now Dodds Township, erected a log cabin on Government land, which is now the property of W. T. Sanders. Some one took the initiatory step by notifying the settlers within a radius of three or four miles that, on a certain time at a designated place, they would meet for the purpose of erecting a schoolhouse. Punctual at the time and place, armed with their "working tools," they assembled, and in a short time, considering the disadvantages under which they labored, their work was consummated. The structure would not compare with the excellent [temples of learning of the present day, but it afforded them an accommodation for their early schools. This building was about fourteen feet square. The walls were made of rough round logs from the forests; the chimney was of earth and sticks, and the roof of clapboards. Slabs split from trees, the rough edges smoothed with an ax, constituted the floor. The windows were made by cutting out a log and pasting a greased paper over the aperture, which admitted all the light that was afforded the pupils. The furniture consisted of "benches" made from large "puncheons;" "desks" or writing tables were formed by placing against the wall at an angle boards or "puncheons." Could the pupil of this early school have entered the spacious and elegantly furnished school rooms of to-day; could he have sat in the easy patent seat; could he have gazed upon the modern school apparatus and have listened to the sound of the "school going bell," he would, doubtless, have imagined that he had been magically transported to another sphere. After this cabin was finished and furnished, a school was the next thing in order. Some one of the settlers canvassed the neighborhood and determined how many pupils would attend the school at a stated sum *per capita*.

It is thought that W. T. Sanders taught the first school in this cabin, and it is not remembered that he went through any examination. The qualifications required in those days were that the teacher possessed the physical ability to govern the school and be sufficient scholar to teach reading, writing and ciphering, especially the latter, as far as the "double rule of three." Mr. Sanders was very successful. From the beginning of this school, a new impetus was given to education, and each succeeding year the advantages have improved in this direction. About the year 1850, A. C. Johnson taught a school at a private residence, and not far from the same time a log cabin, similar in construction to the one mentioned above, was built on the line between Sections 10 and 11. In this schoolhouse Moses Smith and A. C. Johnson taught. As we have already stated, the interest in education began to grow. It is true there were some who thought education was not essential to farm life, but they were few, and the masses were warmly in favor of schools. There are now six good frame school buildings in the township, and the best teachers are employed to instruct the young.

In the pioneer cabins of the township, Revs. Rhodam and George Allen, two early ministers, held meetings and added cheering words to those gathered from near and far. Services are now held in almost every schoolhouse in the township, besides in two fine frame church buildings. The Lebanon Missionary Baptist Church is located at the intersection of Sections 2, 3, 10 and 11. E. M. Knapp and Isaac Garrison are the present Deacons, and Rev. C. Richardson is pastor. The organization has an enrollment of about 140 members. A good Sunday school is kept up, with an attendance of more than fifty. Samuel Meadows is Superintendent, and through his efforts the interest is gradually growing.

A Methodist Episcopal Church was organized in the township at an early date, but the precise spot and time we have been unable to learn. That kind-hearted and good old pioneer, Joseph Pace, was an early member of this church, and during his life its financial interests were not allowed to suffer through his influence. John Rogers, William Edgington, and James Bradford and their respective families were members of the first organization. Some time subsequently, a large frame building was erected at considerable cost on Section 7, and is known as "Bethel Church." The membership of the same is very large, and regular services are kept up during the year. Like the most of the Methodist Churches, it keeps up a first-class Sunday school.

The first voting place in the precinct was the old James Dodds house. The ballot box used then is the same one that now on election days holds the vote of the determined Democrat, the ardent Republican and aggressive Greenbacker. The present voting-place is the "Hebron Schoolhouse," situated on the line between Sections 10 and 11. The township polls about 250 votes, of which nearly 103 are Republicans, 110 Democrats and the remainder the Greenback and Independent votes.

John Baugh and Henry Gorham were the two first Justices of the Peace in the precinct. George W. Bliss succeeded one of them, and no other change was made until the township was organized. The following is a list of officers since township organization:

Supervisors.—R. D. Roane, 1870; W. H. Smith, 1872–73; M. C. Garrison, 1874; S. Gibson, 1875; R. D. Roane, 1876 to 1879; A. Newby, 1880; S. Bumpus, 1881 to 1883, the present incumbent.

Justices of the Peace.—G. W. Bliss and W. Adams, 1870; S. Gibson and W. Adams, 1873; J. B. Bradford and W. Adams, 1874–76; J. W. Bradford and S. Gibson, 1877 to 1883 the present incumbent.

Township Clerks.—None 1870; Ambrose Adams, 1872; J. M. Frizell, 1873; A. Adams 1874–75; J. Mills, 1876; J. W. Estes, 1877 to 1883, and now in office.

Assessors.—W. M. Hicks, 1872–73; J. G. Daniels, 1874; A. Newby, 1875; J. G. Daniels, 1876–77; A. Gibson, 1878 to 1880; T. J. Mills, 1881; J. W. Estes, 1882; A. C. Cullie, 1883, present incumbent.

Collectors.—F. E. Patton, 1872; N. F. Meredith, 1873; F. E. Patton, 1864; J. D. Downer, 1875 to 1877; W. S. Bumpus, 1878 to 1880; A. Gibson, 1881; S. T. Pace, 1882; E. Roane, 1883, now in office.

Highway Commissioners.—Isaac Garrison, 1872; S. Duncan, 1873; J. M. Frizell, 1874; A. D. Harper, 1875; N. F. Meredith, 1876; J. M. Frizell, 1877; Isaac Garrison, 1878; S. Duncan, 1879; William Hicks, 1880–81; C. Jenkins, 1882–83, at present in office.

School Treasurers.—S. T. Pace, 1872–73; J. A. Johnson, 1874–75; G. M. Bliss, 1876; S. T. Pace, 1877; S. Duncan, 1878; R. D. Roane, 1879; S. Duncan, 1880; R. D. Roane, 1881; J. L. Hinkle, 1882; S. T. Pace, 1883, now holding the office.

Constables.—T. J. Mills and W. T. Hicks, 1874 to 1876; W. Blythe, 1877; Thomas Mills, 1878 to 1881; M. Bradford and J. E. Gibson, 1882–83, the present incumbents.

CHAPTER XX.*

BLISSVILLE TOWNSHIP—DESCRIPTION AND TOPOGRAPHY—KNOB PRAIRIE—SETTLEMENT—HOW THE PEOPLE LIVED—NAME OF TOWNSHIP AND ITS LIST OF OFFICIALS—ROADS, BRIDGES, ETC.—THE VILLAGE OF WILLIAMSBURG—CHURCHES AND SCHOOLS—RETROSPECTION, ETC.

"Nothing so dear as a tale of the olden time."

TRANSCRIBING recollections of the aged, wavering memory, we do not seek to reconcile discrepancies, but to embody here the names and deeds of those whose like can nevermore be seen. We dimly outline, from our signal-point, the history which meets our eye, and steer our course between extremes of dates and happenings, but more often than otherwise the greatest incompleteness marks the narrative.

The most of those pioneers who came here half a century or more ago have passed to their reward, while upon the few still left the rolling years have written their record and left them trembling on the brink of the tomb. They left friends and civilization behind them and came here to build for themselves a home. Ah, a home! Home, celestial home of the world-weary, laboring heart, the sacred asylum of the wandering soul! It is the only type and symbol left on earth since the portals of paradise closed on our ruined race. And to make them a home in this wild waste, these people exposed themselves to the dangers of "flood and field," of savages and wild beasts and perils before which we, their successors, would quail. The history of their lives is one of noble heroism, by the side of which that of the warrior and the statesman pale with insignificance.

* By W. H. Perrin.

"A song for the early times out West,
And our green old forest home,
Whose pleasant memories freshly yet
Across the ocean come."

Blissville Township, which forms the subject matter of this chapter, is one of the west tier of townships, and is situated southwest of Mount Vernon. It lies south of Casner Township, west of McClellan, north of Bald Hill, east of Washington County, and is designated as Township 3 south, and Range 1 east. The surface is rather broken, and diversified between prairie and woodland. An arm of Grand Prairie extends into the township. There are also several other small prairies—notably Knob Prairie, in the southeast part, which receives its name from the elevation of the ground, it being about as high as the site of Mount Vernon. In the timbered section are found black, white and post oak, wild cherry, black walnut, hickory, sassafras, together with hazel and other shrubs. The principal stream is Rayse Creek, or the west fork of Big Muddy. This passes through the northeast corner of the township and is fed by a few small brooks and branches which form the natural drainage of the township.

The settlement of Blissville Township dates back to 1822-23. About that time Sherman Ross and Jesse Green, Sr., came and settled in the northeast corner. Jesse Green died in the township and left a large family. Ross moved to Shelby County, taking his family with him. He was a thriftless sort of a fellow, with but little energy, but not of real bad habits. Green was fond of hunting, and participated freely in all kinds of backwoods sports and pastimes. John Hailes settled in the timber along Big Muddy, and was among the first comers in that section. He was a good, easy, harmless man, who never did much for himself or for any one else. He cleared a small "patch" of ground, and put up a cabin of poles. About two years afterward, he sold his improvement to Jesse P. Dees, an uncle of Judge Jesse A. Dees, of this township, and moved up to Gun Prairie. Jesse P. Dees, however, soon settled in another part of the township, where he died. He made an extensive improvement, and opened quite a large farm for that early day, and was in good circumstances at the time of his death. John Finch bought the first improvement of Jesse P. Dees, and settled here about 1826, but afterward sold out and moved to Missouri. He was a farmer and gunsmith; a rude, rough fellow, of the true frontier type, but finally professed religion at a camp meeting in Washington County, and was afterward licensed as a preacher by the Methodist Church. William Linsey was an early settler in the neighborhood of Jesse P. Dees. He was a good, honest man, and sold his improvement to Reuben Green and moved back into Washington County. Reuben Green, who bought his improvement, raised a large family, who settled around him.

An early settler was Mr. Herron, on Grand Prairie. He afterward moved into Washington County. Peter Sibert afterward settled on the place where Herron first located. Erastus Fairchild settled in Grand Prairie, near the north line of the township. He was a common farmer, and sold out to Thomas Bagby. The latter occupied it several years, and then sold out and moved into Washington County, and afterward to Texas. Samuel Hunter also settled in Grand Prairie about 1840, and is living there yet. James Welch settled in the same neighborhood about the same time. He was from Ohio, and was a large land owner. He lost part of his family here in 1844 and returned to Ohio, but afterward made several trips between Ohio and Illinois, and was finally lost on the Ohio River in a steamboat disaster. A son of his had come here in 1839, and is still living in the township.

Jesse A. Dees, one of the prominent and wealthy farmers of the township, came to Jefferson County in 1824, with his mother and step-father, Lewis Green. They settled in what is now Casner Township, where James Wood lives. Mr. Dees is one of the oldest living settlers of the county, having been here almost sixty years. Joseph Laird came in about 1840, and settled in Grand Prairie. Knob Prairie was settled by David Fairchild, who sold to B. L. Herrons, who came here about 1822. He was from Ohio, and was a brother of Erastus Fairchild, already noticed. H. Hackett was here some time, but was a kind of a transient character. Eli Gilbert settled in Knob Prairie about 1840, and was from Ohio. He opened a store soon after settling here, and sold goods for several years; he died here and left a large family. Another Ohio family was the Places—Isaac and Sidney—who settled in Knob Prairie in 1840-42. The latter is still living here. Henry Bushon came in about 1845, and settled between Knob and Grand Prairies. Such were some of the settlements and the people who made them in this particular division of the county. When we ponder on those olden times, rude and rough as they were, we almost wish for their return. Those good old days when the girls rode behind their sweethearts to church or dance, and when the horses always "kicked up," and the girls held tightly on (then the girls hugged the boys—now the case is reversed); when husband and wife visited on the same nag, and the wife carried her babe snugly cuddled up in her lap. Those good old days when the hypocrisy, shams and selfishness of modern society were unknown; when the respectability of men and women was not measured by their bank accounts, nor by display of shoddy finery, but by the simple standard of worth and merit, by their usefulness in the community, by their readiness to aid the suffering and to relieve the distressed; when there were no social castes or distinctions, and when honesty and uprightness were the livery of aristocracy. Ah! those were the times of free-heartedness and genuine honesty.

The pioneer's first thought is something for his family to eat, and hence a mill in a new country is an object of supreme interest. One of the first institutions of this kind was a tread mill owned by Maj. Herron on land now the property of Samuel Johnson. It was a rude affair, but was much better than no mill at all, and the settlers used to come from a considerable distance to it to get their corn ground. Eli Gilbert had a mill very early. He built a water mill on Big Muddy, but it was never much of a success and soon disappeared altogether. He found it impossible to dam the stream, and so he *damned* the whole thing and gave up the enterprise. A grist and saw mill; operated by steam, was put up near Williamsburg. It passed through different hands, and was finally moved to Saline County.

Blissville Township was named in honor of Augustus Bliss, who settled in Casner Township and made an attempt to lay off a village, which never improved. He started to California during the gold fever excitement, and died of cholera on the way, leaving a wife and five children. The first voting place was an old house on the place where Samuel Johnson now lives; the regular voting place at present is at Locust Grove. The following is a list of the township officers since the county adopted township organization:

Supervisors—S. R. Johnson, 1870-73; J. A. Dees, 1874; Samuel Johnson, 1875-6; T. H. Mannen, 1877; S. Johnson, 1878-79; O. P. Norris, 1880; A. Welch, 1881-82; J. D. Norris, 1883.

Town Clerks—J. R. Dunbar, 1871-73; J. Lemmon, 1874-75; L. E. Denslow, 1876; E. Bagsby, 1877; J. D. Norris, 1878-80; W. D. Hicks, 1881; J. Perry, 1882; W. D. Hicks, 1883.

Assessors—D. T. Campbell, 1872-73; W. H. Norris, 1874; William Robinson, 1875-76; E. Green, 1877-79; J. W. Robinson, 1880-81; J. Hicks, 1882; E. Green, 1883.

Collectors—D. J. Hicks, 1872-73; H. P. Daniels, 1874-75; W. Gilbert, 1876; W. Norris, 1877; M. F. Norris, 1878; W. Gilbert, 1879; Isaac Hicks, 1880-81; J. D. Norris, 1882; W. Gilbert, 1883.

School Treasurers—Edwin Green, 1872-73; E. Fairchild, 1874; L. E. Dunbar, 1875; John Gaddis, 1876; J. Tuttle, 1877; J. M. Gaddis, 1878; J. M. McConneoughey, 1879-81; J. V. Wingard, 1882; G. A. Baldridge, 1883.

Highway Commissioners—W. M. Elliston, J. B. McConneoughey, J. P. Anderson, J. B. McConneoughey, W. Gilbert, A. Welch, D. P. McConneoughey, A. Snider, A. J. Shurtz, D. H. Keller, J. Jones, R. Green, C. Gilbert, W. B. Elliston, James Reed, R. Gilbert, A. J. Shurtz.

Justices of the Peace—A. J. Shurtz and B. L. Bowmaster, 1870-72; A. J. Norris and J.

R. Dunbar, 1873-74; J. McConneoughey and J. R. Dunbar, 1875-76; S. Johnson and H. P. Daniels, 1877-80; S. Johnson and E. Green, the present incumbents.

Constables—Cyrus Gilbert, 1870-72; R. Green, 1873-76; A. J. McConneoughey, 1877-79; T. McAtee, 1880; J. Land, 1881; J. Wingard, 1882; J. Lemmington, 1883.

The first public highway in the township was called the Mount Vernon & Nashville road, or Jefferson County & Washington County road. J. A. Dees made the first trail where this road was laid out. There were nothing but a few paths and trails before this road was made. Good, substantial wooden bridges now span the streams where they are needed.

Among the prominent stock-dealers are Joseph Mannen, Josiah Tuttle, Andrew Welch, Jesse A. Dees, A. Gilbert, etc., etc. They buy and sell and deal in cattle, mules and hogs. Mr. Dees has some very fine cattle, and deals largely in mules; he has on hand at present some sixty odd head of mules. Mr. Gilbert also has a large number of mules.

Williamsburg.—The village of Williamsburg is situated in Knob Prairie, on the northeast quarter of Section 35. It was laid off by Drs. Moore & Peavler December 17, 1867, into four blocks, one of eleven lots, one of twelve lots, and two of ten lots each. John Hagle built the first storehouse, and David Hicks the first residence. His sons opened a drug store, and also built a residence, into which Thomas Westcott moved. The Mannings came a little later, and then Place. Henry Willis erected some brick buildings, the first in the village. About the year 1864, Anderson built a mill, but soon afterward sold it to Boswell, and Boswell sold it to James Dare. A good schoolhouse has been built in the town. At present, J. D. Norris keeps a general store, J. W. Robinson a drug store and William Hicks a drug store. Dr. O. P. Norris is Postmaster. The usual number of shops are operated. The place has about one hundred inhabitants. The town is called Williamsburg, but the post office bears the name of Laur.

Blissville Township was not backward in educational matters, and schools were early established and schoolhouses built. One of the first schoolhouses in the township was built near where Eli Gilbert settled. It stood on the farm now owned by Cyrus Gilbert, and was of logs 16x18 feet, the cracks daubed with mud. The first teacher was of the name of Bellis. Another pioneer schoolhouse was on the land now owned by R. Gilbert, and A. Welch was one of the early teachers here. A schoolhouse was built on the land of G. J. Hoyt, in Grand Prairie, and another on the land owned by the heirs of Reuben Green, Jr. The township has at present six schoolhouses, conveniently located on Sections 7, 10, 16, 18, 24, 28. In these, schools are taught for the usual term each year by competent teachers.

The church history of Blissville Township is extensive, and dates back to an early period of the settlement of the country. At first, meetings were held in dwelling-houses, and in the woods in summer. The Grand Arm Methodist Church was the first church built in the township. It was put up about 1840. Among the early members were Abner Minson and wife, Jacob Freeman and wife, Susan Eubank, Jesse P. Dees and wife, Naomi Dees, John Freeman and wife, and perhaps others. Among the early preachers here were Simeon Walker, T. W. Williams, James Johnson, Files and J. Barnes. The organization is still kept up, and the society has a good frame building. A graveyard is adjacent, in which slumber many of the early members of this pioneer church. The membership of the church is about sixty, and an excellent Sunday school is maintained during the summer, of which J. Tuttle is Superintendent. Rev. Mr. Root is pastor of the church at the present time.

Mount Zion Church is located in the northern part of the township, and has but a small attendance. Pierce's Chapel now has no regular attendance or organization.

At Williamsburg, there is a Methodist Church with an interesting membership of about forty. Rev. Root is the pastor. A good Sunday school is maintained.

There is also a Universalist Church at Williamsburg, with some forty members, under the spiritual supervision of Rev. Mr. Maddox.

Blissville Township has no railroads, nor no manufacturing interests. It is decidedly an agricultural and stock-raising region. Its nearest shipping point is Woodlawn, on the Louisville & Nashville Railroad, located a couple of miles from the northeast corner of the township. This road, though not touching the township, has been of great benefit, by increasing the value of property and real estate, as well as in affording the farmers transportation facilities.

With all the growth and activity, which assumes larger proportions in the recital than in the actual experience, the community which gathered in this township was really on the frontier at the time of which we have been writing. While not so completely isolated as some of the other earlier settlements in Southern Illinois, the people experienced many of the hardships and discomforts incident to frontier settlements. Mills were early built near by, but from lack of power or adequate machinery most of the flour and much of the meal was procured at Carmi and other and even more distant points, enduring long, tedious delays. As a farming district, the settlements in what is now Blissville Township were of slow growth; the village of Mount Vernon, some ten miles distant, seemed to absorb the floating population. Here and there the smoke curled upward in the air from the scattered log cabins, and the busy pioneer protracted the day long into the night in clearing up his farm.

Deer were plenty, and were shot in large numbers, while wolves, panthers, wild cats an occasional bear, and the whole class of small game that was found in this section in early times, afforded wholesome meals and rare sport to those fond of hunting. Most of the early settlers were from the Southern States, and brought here with them many of their social characteristics. Saturday afternoons, as they are still, were a general holiday, and the farmers repaired to the neighboring village. But few in the community had very strong scruples then against the use of whisky, and strong potations tended to make fun lively, and not unfrequently caused rough-and-tumble fist fights.

Thus time passd in the early years of the country, the people enjoying themselves in a rough kind of way. They were rude, but generous to a fault, and always ready with their time and labor to assist a new comer or a friend in his time of need.

CHAPTER XXI*

BALD HILL TOWNSHIP—ITS GEOGRAPHICAL AND PHYSICAL FEATURES—ADVENT OF THE PIONEERS—THEIR TRIALS, TRIBULATIONS, ETC.—MILLS AND ROADS—ORGANIZATION OF THE TOWNSHIP AND THE LIST OF OFFICIALS—SCHOOLS, CHURCHES, ETC., ETC.

"The sound of the war-whoop oft woke the sleep of the cradle."

AMONG the first settlers there was but little law and Gospel, and but little was needed. Industry in working and hunting, bravery in war, candor, hospitality, honesty and steadiness of deportment received their full reward of public honor and public confidence among these our rude forefathers to a degree that has not been fully sustained by their more polished descendants. The punishments they inflicted upon offenders were unerring, swift and inexorable in their imperial court of public opinion, and were wholly adapted for the reformation of he culprit or his expulsion from the community. Any petty misdemeanor was punished with all the infamy that could be heaped upon the offender.

With all their backwoods rudeness, these early settlers were given to hospitality, and freely divided their rough fare with a neighbor or stranger, and would have been offended at the offer of pay. In their settlements they lived, they worked and sometimes they fought—for fun; and they feasted or suffered together in cordial harmony. They were warm and constant in their friendships, and the cold selfishness of the present day was utterly unknown. The world has changed greatly in the past fifty years, and the people have changed with it. The change may have been imperceptible, but nevertheless it has been made.

Bald Hill Township is situated in the extreme southwest part of the county, and comprises a full Congressional township. It is bounded on the south and west by Franklin and Perry Counties, on the north by Blissville Township, on the east by Elk Prairie, and is designated in the Government survey as Township 4 south, and Range 1 east. It is a good farming region and boasts some good farms and some energetic farmers. Its surface features are much the same as other townships described in this work. There are no large water-courses, and the land is generally rather level. The township is without towns and railroads, and devoted chiefly to farming.

Following close upon the heels of the retreating savages came the early settlers of Jefferson County. This township was not settled as early as Moore's Prairie and the country around Mount Vernon. In fact, those sections were considered old settlements before any white man ventured into this division of the county. The first settlers who came here were not well-to-do. Most of them brought sufficient capital only to improve a farm in a country where but little more than energy and frugality were required, and these were, fortunately, sufficient to found a home here. After the first arrivals, emigrants found open doors and willing hands to assist in raising a cabin. A single

---
*By W. H. Perrin.

day sufficed for the united neighborhood to erect the rude structure, build a fire-place and chimney and saw out the logs for doorway and windows. Into houses in this condition the new arrivals were generally glad to remove, for free as the hospitality of the pioneer may have been, it had no power to increase the capacity of the cabin, and two families packed a little dwelling designed for one to overflowing. Blankets supplied the place of windows and doors, and furs, skins and blankets spread on brush or on the puncheon floor supplied the beds. Each man was the "architect of his own fortune;" and while the whole neighborhood lent willing assistance in case of special need, each one was too busy with his own affairs to ply any trade for general hire.

The first settlement of this township is somewhat obscure, nor can the exact date of the advent of the first pioneer be given.

Among the first settlers here were Abraham McGinnis, John G. Turmon, James Bellows, Willis Hardwick, Isaac Smith, William Steerman, Samuel Irvin, the Scroggins, Solomon Goddard, Nathaniel Morgan, etc., etc. McGinnis afterward went to Texas, but left two sons here—James and Richard. Turmon went North, where later he died, leaving a son named Grant. It may be that all of the settlers mentioned above did not settle at first in what is now Bald Hill Township, but they settled in the immediate vicinity. It is a difficult matter, after so many years, to locate every early settler upon the proper section, and they were coming in now so rapidly that it is impossible to keep trace of them.

The abundance of game was a somewhat mixed evil. When the crops of the early settlers were first planted, they were subject to the attack of crows, blackbirds and squirrels, and when further advanced the thousands of wild geese and turkeys threatened to take all that was left. Deer were numerous, so were wolves, while the timber swarmed with the chattering game that found shelter there. "Painters" were numerous—too much so for a very great feeling of security, though as a general thing they were easily frightened away. A story is told of a person, on a certain occasion, riding along a trail on horseback through the woods, when he was very much frightened and his horse considerably scratched by a panther springing upon him from a tree, but it lost its hold and was soon left in the distance. Women out picking wild berries were often startled by seeing these treacherous animals crouched in trees, meditating the chances of an attack, but no serious results are known to have occurred in this immediate section.

The people of this settlement, like those surrounding it, and which were removed somewhat from the older settlements, learned early to depend upon their own resources for the comforts of life. This was especially marked in the clothing of the people and the adornment of the home. Deer skins were largely utilized by the men, and even the women sometimes made their own garments of them. Buckskin breeches and buckskin hunting-shirts were more common then than the farmers' "overalls" are now. A buckskin suit was not a very inviting thing to jump into of a cold morning, or to wear after getting wet, but these were minor discomforts, and were not allowed to stand in the way of daily duties. This was the way the people lived in the early days of the country—days we know nothing of except as we gather it from the "traditions of the fathers."

The early settlers of Bald Hill Township had the same hard times in procuring bread as in other portions of the county. The mortar and pestle, the hand mill, and later the horse mill served them. Now, mill facilities are all that can be desired. The township has as good roads as any other portion of the county, but in reality this is not saying much to the credit of roads in general. As there are few streams in the township, bridges are not much needed.

Originally, Bald Hill was a part of Elk Prairie Election Precinct; but after township organization, it became Bald Hill Township. It is Democratic in politics, and has always been of that faith. Since the time of township organization, the following is a list of township officials in Bald Hill:

Supervisors—John B. Ward, 1870; John B. Ward, 1871; John B. Ward, 1872; John B. Ward, 1873; R. J. D. Allan, 1874; S. B. Gilbert, 1875; R. J. D. Allan, 1876; J. B. Ward, 1877; J. B. Ward, 1878; J. B. Ward, 1879; J. H. Johnson, 1880; L. A. Johnson, 1881; L. A. Johnson, 1882; R. T. Wright, 1883, the present incumbent.

Township Clerks—G. B. Johnson, 1872; H. F. White, 1873; W. Clampit, 1874; W. H. Hudson, 1875; W. H. Hudson, 1876; J. H. Wilhaite, 1877; J. H. Wilhaite, 1878; J. Lemmon, 1879; J. Lemmon, 1880; J. Lemmon, 1881; W. H Baldwin, 1882; Thomas Dennington, 1883, now in office.

Assessors—William Clampit, 1872; William Clampit, 1873; S. B. Gilbert, 1874; William Clampit, 1875; T. S. Johnson, 1876; W. E. Ward, 1877; W. E. Ward, 1878; S. B. Gilbert, 1879; B. W. Laur, 1880; J. J. Baker, 1881; B W. Laur, 1882; O. E. Baldwin, 1883, the present incumbent.

Collectors—S. B. Gilbert, 1872; S. B. Gilbert, 1873; H. Foreman, 1874; W. E. Ward, 1875; W. E. Ward, 1876; W. E. Ward, 1877; W. J. Cook, 1878; B. W. Laur, 1879; H. Foreman, 1880; W. J. Cook, 1881; W. J. Cook, 1882; S. M. Gilbert, 1883, now holding the position.

School Treasurers—R. J. D. Allan, W. H. Benthall, W. H. Baldwin, G. B. Johnson, W. H. Benthall, S. S. Warren.

Justices of the Peace—W. H. Cunningham, S. B. Gilbert, J. F. Kirkpatrick, R. J. D. Allan, W. S. Jenkins, W. J. Cook, S. B. Gilbert, R. T. Wright, R. J. D. Allan.

Constables—J. R. Fagan, W. H. Baldwin, J. Warren, W. H. Allen, S. O. Nowland, J. Johnson, R. T. Wright, J. F. Walker, W. H. Baldwin, A. J. Duglett, J. R. Fagan.

Highway Commissioners—Isaac Fleener, C. B. Hamby, A. C. Wheeler, William Dudley, H. C. Foreman, W. Harris, J. B. Johnson, H. F. White, R. D. Webb, J. B. Johnson, F. M. Baldwin, M. M. Fitzgerrell, W. A. Ward, A. J. Duglett.

Educational and church facilities are somewhat meager in this township to what they are in other portions of the county. The early history of education here is but a sample of what it was elsewhere in the early days. It cannot be said now who taught the first school, or where the first schoolhouse was built. The township now has five schoolhouses, a smaller number than any other township in the county. These schoolhouses stand on Sections 2, 8, 23, 29 and 36, and in them schools are taught for the usual period each year. There is but one church building in the township, and that is Bald Hill Methodist Episcopal Church, near the north line of the township. It is a frame building, and has a very good membership for a country church. Religious services are held in several of the schoolhouses.

Bald Hill Township contains some very fine farming lands. It is diversified between woodland and prairie. Horse Prairie lies mostly in Bald Hill, while the four townships of Bald Hill, Blissville, Elk Prairie and McClellan corner in Knob Prairie. In these prairies may be seen some as fine farms as are found in the county. Stock-raising is beginning to occupy the minds of the farmers much of late years, and judging from present indications the time is not far distant when this will be quite a stock-raising region. No railroad taps the township, but the Illinois Central passes so near it that it affords the farmers here excellent shipping facilities. There is nothing to prevent this township from being one of the most prosperous communities in the county. Nothing is required but plenty of energy and enterprise.

With this chapter we close the historical part of this volume. To the many friends who have lent us their kindly smiles and assistance, and particularly to the old settlers, we wish them health, long life and happiness. *Addio!*

PART IV.

BIOGRAPHICAL SKETCHES.

PART IV.

BIOGRAPHICAL SKETCHES.

MOUNT VERNON CITY AND TOWNSHIP.

JOHN R. ALLEN, farmer, P. O. Mt. Vernon, was born June 16, 1840, in Jefferson County, Ill., son of John W. Allen, of Sumner County, Tenn., since of Jefferson County, Ill., was educated in Washington County, Ill., and is a member of the Methodist Episcopal Church. He served three years in the late war in Company A, One Hundred and Tenth Illinois Volunteer Infantry. He works at the wagon trade and runs a grist mill, but was a blacksmith by trade. Was married, August 11, 1860, to Miss Sarah M., daughter of William Tate, of Jefferson County, and has had six children, five of whom are living—Eli W., Perdita R., Nina, U. S. and Henry D. Mrs. Allen died July 23, 1875, and was buried at Pleasant Grove. Mr. Allen was again married September 26, 1875, to Eliza J. Mitchell of Mississippi, by whom he has had one child—Edward C. He owns 161 acres of land, and is engaged in farming and stock-raising. Politics, Republican.

HON. WILLIAM B. ANDERSON, County Judge, Mt. Vernon. (A sketch of Judge William B. Anderson will be found in the chapter on the War History.)

JOHN W. BAUGH, express agent, Mt. Vernon, was born Febr. 11, 1836, in Mt. Vernon, Ill. He is a son of Judge Downing Baugh, a native of Barren County, Ky., an attorney at law, who came to this county about 1821, teaching school for several years, after which he entered the mercantile business, and then served as Justice of the Peace for many years; also served as Probate Justice. At the age of forty-five, he commenced the study of law, and was admitted to the bar in Mt. Vernon, where he followed his profession, and in 1854 was appointed Judge of the Circuit Court, to fill the unexpired term of Judge Marshall. In 1857, he moved to McGregor, Iowa, where he followed his profession, and was elected Judge of the City Court. He is now virtually retired from active life. He was an active member of the Masonic fraternity, Mt. Vernon Lodge, No. 31, holding the office of Master for many years. In his new home in Iowa, he has also been prominently connected with the higher order of Masons, and now holds the office of Grand Prelate of the Grand Commandery of the Knights Templar, and also Grand Chaplin of the Grand Chapter. He was born in April, 1798, and is yet living, a grand old man, although he has lost his eyesight. He has seen more than two generations rise and pass away. He is a Democrat in politics, and a warm supporter of the Methodist Episcopal Church. His whole life is an example worthy of imitation. His father, John Baugh, was also a native of Kentucky. He was a minister of the Christian

Church. He was also a merchant in Bowling Green, Ky., and Mt. Vernon, Ill., to which latter place he came about 1821, and died here in 1854. The mother of our subject, Milly (Pace) Baugh, was a daughter of an old pioneer, Joel Pace, who was formerly a soldier in the Revolutionary war. He died here. Her mother, Mary (East) Pace, was a fine old lady, a true type of our American women; she reached the good old age of eighty-three years. Our subject was educated in Mt. Vernon. In early life he learned and followed the harness-maker's trade. In 1861, he enlisted in the Eighteenth Regiment Illinois Volunteer Infantry as a musician, and was mustered out in the spring of 1862, when he re-enlisted in Company F, of the Fortieth Illinois Infantry Volunteers, as a private, but through his own exertion and ability was promoted several times, till he held the office of Adjutant. He resigned in the fall of 1864, and returned to Mt. Vernon, where he served in the Circuit Clerk's office for eleven years, and then served four years as Police magistrate. Since then he has been express agent for the Adams Express Company. Our subject was married in May, 1862, at Mt. Vernon, Ill., to Miss Amelia J. Hill, born April 1, 1842, in Clay County, Ill. Her father, Rev. J. H. Hill, was a native of Ohio. Her mother was Eleanor (Williams) Hill. Mrs. Baugh is the mother of two children—Frank C., born July 5, 1865; and Milly E., born October 21, 1867. Mr. and Mrs. Baugh and children are members of the Methodist Episcopal Church. He is an A. F. & A. M. and an active worker in the Sunday school, of which he is the Superintendent. In political matters, he is a Democrat.

WILLIAM BAWDEN, farmer, P. O. Mt. Vernon, was born in Cornwall, England, July 9, 1834, and is a son of John Bawden (deceased), also a native of Cornwall. He married Louise Quilliam, a native of the Isle of Man, and a daughter of John Quilliam. Mrs. Bawden has in her possession a photograph of the Laxey Water Wheel, on her native Island, which is the largest water wheel in the world, being thirty-seven feet in diameter. Mr. and Mrs. Bawden have eight children—Nellie, Hannah L., Willy R., John H., Thomas E., Emma Maud, Herbert M. and Mabel M. Mr. and Mrs. Bawden came to North Michigan in 1857, and to St. Louis, Mo., in 1864, but in eighteen months went back as far as Jo Daviess County, Ill., where he bought a half interest in a lead mine, since known as Bawden's Tunnel, which he ran for about nine years. He then went to Utah Territory, and worked in the celebrated Emma Mine, in Little Cottonwood Cañon for eighteen months, when he returned to Jo Daviess County, and engaged in farming, which he still pursues. He removed to this county in March, 1881, and settled on Section 15, in Mt. Vernon Township, where he owns 160 acres of land.

LEWIS N. BEAL, farmer, P. O. Mt. Vernon, was born in Lehigh County, Penn., April 28, 1844, and is a son of Jacob Beal (deceased), a native of Bavaria, who emigrated to America about the year 1836. Our subject spent his boyhood days on the farm, and attended the common schools. He came to St. Clair County, Ill., with his parents in 1851, and in 1855 to Centralia. He came to Jefferson County in 1858, where he has since resided, except two years that he spent in Kansas, which was during 1864 and 1865. He married Sarah M. Casey January 20, 1872. She is a daughter of the well-known Franklin S. Casey (deceased). They have three children—Alvin C., John F. and May E. Mr. Beal owns eighty-five acres of very valuable land, and is engaged in general farming. He is a member of the Methodist Episcopal Church. His farm lies in Section 30, and adjoining the city of Mt. Vernon.

GEORGE H. BITTROLFF, merchant, Mt. Vernon. This gentleman was born April 18, 1852, in Evansville, Ind. His father, Louis

Bittrolff, was a native of Baden, Germany. He is a jeweler by occupation, having learned his trade with his father, John L. Bittrolff, who also had the first jewelry store in Evansville, Ind. The mother of our subject, Anna (Grossman) Bittrolff, is a native of Wurtemberg, Germany. She is the mother of seven children, viz.: George H., Louis H., Annie Wright, Mollie Ford, William, Eliza and Walter, deceased. Our subject was educated in Evansville, where he learned and followed book-keeping till 1878, when he came to Mt. Vernon, where he, in partnership with R. E. Ryan, opened a dry goods store on a small scale, but added to the stock from time to time till at present they carry a stock of from $12,000 to $15,000, including a stock of boots and shoes. Owing to his energy, honesty and perseverance, he has established for himself a good reputation as a thorough business man. His store occupies the first and second floors of a fine building on the south side of the square. He was married, October 10, 1872, in Evansville, Ind., to Miss Willa Nall, born August 24, 1854, in Rumsey, Ky. She is a daughter of William J. and Rebecca Nall. Four children were the result of this happy union, viz.: Hallie A., born November 3, 1873; George Nall, born July 10, 1877; Ray, born November 30, 1879; Clyde, born June 6, 1882. Mrs. Bittrolff is a member of the Baptist Church. He is a Knight of Pythias, and in politics is a Republican. The Bittrolffs came originally from France, from whence they fled to Germany on account of religious persecution, about the time the Huguenots came to America.

DR. ROBERT BLUM, dentist, Mt. Vernon. It is an encouraging phase of our present age that the prizes awarded honest work and vigorous energy are open to all, and that the young man may win the highest honors and emoluments equally with the man of large and varied experience. Dr. Blum, though only just in middle life, has risen to the higher rank of his profession, and sustains a reputation worthy only of the highest ability. He was born July 23, 1842, in Southeastern Russia, and is a son of A. and Julia (Schultz) Blum, both natives of Russia; he born in 1812, and she in 1818. The parents came to this country, with their family, in 1844, and first settled in Galveston, Texas, where the father dealt in furs for a number of years. At present he is a merchant in Tarpen Springs, Fla., and since his advent in this country he has made and lost three good fortunes. Subject is the youngest of three living children—Edward A., Amalia G. and Robert—out of a family of fourteen children. The schools of New Orleans and St. Louis afforded our subject his means of education. While in the latter city, he apprenticed himself to a dentist there, and there learned his profession. He afterward practiced dentistry in Du Quoin and Cairo, and in 1872 he came to Mt. Vernon, where he has followed his profession since. He was married, June 4, 1867, in Du Quoin, to Miss Alice Spotts, born February 8, 1844, in Greene County, Ill., and a daughter of Samuel Spotts, born May 7, 1812, in Delaware, an architect and builder by profession. He died July 31, 1864. Five children have come to bless this union—May O., born May 5, 1868; Albert and Alfred, twins, born September 2, 1869; Robert A., born January 1, 1874, and Guy E., born February 6, 1881. Mr. Blum is a member of the A. F. & A. M., and in politics is a Democrat.

JOHN S. BOGAN, Circuit Clerk, Mt. Vernon, was born in Woodstock, Shenandoah Co., Va., on the 6th of March, 1820. His father, Benjamin Bogan, was born in Spottsylvania County, Va., December 30, 1795. He was reared in Alexandria, Va., and graduated from the theological seminary of that city; he there served an apprenticeship at the printer's trade with John Stewart, and subsequently removed to Woodstock of that State, when he became engaged in the publication of a paper, he himself acting as editor; he continued this for a number of years and then removed to Mt. Vernon, Ohio, where he published a paper for four years. At the expiration of this time he returned to Woodstock, and soon after was appointed clerk of the Second Comptroller's office, Washington, D. C., and soon after was transferred to a clerkship in the general post office. He held this position for ten years, and was then appointed chief clerk of the Senate document room, where he remained for twenty-two years, and was then removed on the commencement of Grant's Presidency. He was a Captain in the war of 1812. At the time of his newspaper career, he became noted as one of the leading writers of the east, and was afterward a corresponding editor of five or six of the leading journals of our country. He was an Elder of the Presbyterian Church. His death occurred in Fairfax County, Va., on the 25th of July, 1870. He was a son of John Bogan, of Scotch-Irish descent, and a soldier in the Revolutionary war. Sarah A. (Ott) Bogan (subject's mother) was born at Woodstock, Va., April 18, 1801, and died in Fairfax County, Va., September 26, 1867. She was a daughter of Michael and Mary (Zaron) Ott, natives of York, Penn., who subsequently settled in Virginia. He was a soldier in the French war. Our subject's parents had twelve children, of whom the following six are living: Dr. Vanburen, of Washington City; Susan S., wife of Hon. George H. Varnell, of Mt. Vernon, Ill.; Samuel W., of Washington, D. C.; Anna, wife of Samuel Butt, of Fairfax County, Va.; Charles J., of the Treasury Department, Washington, D. C., and John S., our subject, who is the oldest child. He was reared in Woodstock until he was twelve years of age, when he was removed by his parents to Washington. When about fourteen years of age, he entered upon a six years' term of apprenticeship in the *Globe* printing office of Blair & Reed, Washington, D. C. He remained in this position until 1843, when, on account of his failing health, he engaged in farming near Washington, and continued the same until October 30, 1846; he came to Jefferson County, Ill., in Grand Prairie Township, where he continued the occupation of farming until August, 1851, when he removed to Mt. Vernon, and started the first newspaper of the town, the *Jeffersonian*. In the fall of 1854, he sold his paper to Bowman & Robertson, and the same year was elected Circuit Clerk of the county, a position he still retains, and fills to the entire satisfaction of the citizens of Jefferson County. Previous to 1854, while engaged in farming, he held the offices of School Director, Constable and Deputy Sheriff. He was married in 1842 to Miss Louisa Margaret Brunette, a native of Alexandria County, Va. She is the mother of five children, viz., Sarah E., wife of Marcus L. Goodale; Mary C., wife of William T. Goodrich; Hannah, wife of Newton C. Pace; William and John F. Mr. Bogan has been connected with the Jefferson County Fair Association as Secretary or President since 1860; he is a charter member of the I. O. O. F., and also belongs to the "Iron Hall." He and wife are connected with the Presbyterian Church.

RUFUS J. BOND, druggist, Mt. Vernon, was born Nov. 11, 1847, in Shiloh Township, Jefferson County, Ill. He is a son of Michael Bond, a native of North Carolina, but reared in Tennessee. He came to this county in the fall of 1829, and the next year moved his family here, he following his vocation, and dying in 1880, being the son of Louis Bond. The mother of our subject, Maria (Fuller) Bond, was the mother of ten children, of whom five boys and two girls are now living. Her parents were Levi and Elizabeth Fuller, he a native of New York, and she of New Jersey. Our subject was educated in this county, where he also tilled the soil till after he was twenty-two years old, when he commenced clerking in Mt. Vernon in the drug store of Samuel S. Porter. He is now a partner of Mr. Porter, having a half interest in the store. Our subject was joined in matrimony to Miss Mary J. England, who has been blessed with five children—Norman A. and Maude, deceased; Harry, born December 1, 1878; Anna L., born November 19, 1880, and Neal, born May 27, 1883. Mrs. Bond is connected with the Baptist Church. Mr. Bond holds the responsible office of City Treasurer, and in politics is identified with the Republican party.

HON. THOMAS S. CASEY, Circuit Judge, Mt. Vernon. For sketch of Judge Casey, see chapter on Bench and Bar.

W. B. CASEY, liveryman, Mt. Vernon, was born in June, 1820, in Jefferson County. His father, William Casey, Esq., was a native of Tennessee, but reared in Kentucky; he died in this county. When about twelve years old, while living at Cave-in-Rock, Ill., he and his aunt killed a bear which was swimming the Ohio River. He was also married at Cave-in-Rock, to Amy Barker, a daughter of Hon. Louis Barker, one of the most prominent pioneers of Southern Illinois, who was elected to the Legislature when Illinois was a Territory, and was afterward elected to the Senate. His father, Isaac Casey, who was the grandfather of our subject, was a brother of Gov. Casey. He came here about 1817. (See General History about the Casey family.) Squire William Casey was a farmer by occupation and at one time was considered the wealthiest man in Jefferson County, donating the ground on which Mt. Vernon was built. He held the offices of Commissioner and Justice of the Peace. The past record of the Casey family is such that their descendants can well be proud of it. Our subject was educated in Mt. Vernon, where he spent a great deal of his time. His main occupation in life has been that of a United States Mail Contractor; even as late as eight years ago he got sixteen contracts from the Government. He has never held nor sought public office, and may yet be considered a type of the old pioneers. Mr. Casey has been married twice, his present wife, Sarah C. Hamlin, being born in Ohio. She is a daughter of Rhoderick Hamlin. The result of the union is three daughters—Lora, deceased; Cornelia, wife of John McGuire, and Virginia. Mr. Casey is identified with the Democratic party, and during the war belonged to the United States recruiting service.

WILLIAM C. COWGER, deceased, was born in Wilson County, Tenn., February 15, 1828, and was a son of Adam Cowger, deceased. The subject of this sketch came to this county in 1850, where he lived until his death, which occurred February 15, 1883. He followed teaming several years, and ran a livery stable in Mt. Vernon about twelve years. He was married in July, 1849, to Abigail Suter, by whom he had one child—William A., born June 29, 1850, and died January 24, 1874. Mrs. Cowger was born in Bedford County, Tenn., in 1833, and is a daughter of William Suter, deceased.

RUSSELL DEWEY, miller, Mt. Vernon, born February 11, 1833, in Erie County, Penn. He is a son of Russell Dewey, Sr., born January 2, 1800, in New Canaan, N. Y. He was also a miller, and died near Quincy, Adams County, Ill. The mother of our subject, Elizabeth (Miks) Dewey, born March 5, 1805, in Hocking Ohio, and died in Adams County, Ill. She was married September 17, 1821, at Hocking, Ohio, by Rev. Mr. Spurgin, at the age of fifteen. She was the mother of twenty children, of whom seven are now living. Our subject was educated in Pennsylvania and New York, and in early life devoted his attention to milling, and has followed it in Erie, N. Y., near Cincinnati, Ohio, in Missouri and in Mt. Vernon, to which place he came in 1860. He was married twice. His first wife, Rebecca Kimmons, died in Adams County. His present wife, Eunice (Mills) Dewey, was born January 28

1841, in Hardin County, Ill. Her parents were George and Hannah (Pollard) Mills, the latter a native of England. George Mills lived eighteen years in Mt. Vernon, merchandising most of the time, but at one time acting as Deputy Sheriff of Jefferson County, in which he died. Mrs. Eunice Dewey is the mother of eleven children, viz.: George W., deceased; Addie, born March 14, 1864; Mary O., born October 20, 1865; Emma L., born December 2, 1867; Eliza G., born October 26, 1869; Edgar A., born March 12, 1871; Mattie, born December 27, 1873; Charles L., born November 16, 1875; Lucy A., born May 26, 1878; Harry R., born April 9, 1880; Frank M., born September 13, 1882. Mrs. Dewey is a member of the Presbyterian Church. He is an A. F. & A. M.; also a Royal Arch Mason, and a member of the Iron Hall. At present, he holds the office of Alderman.

SILAS DOWNER, wagon-maker, Mount Vernon, was born July 15, 1831, in Vermont. His father, John Downer, was a native of New Hampshire. He was a farmer by occupation, but in early life taught school. In the fall of 1832, he came to Jefferson County, and for many years followed teaching as a vocation. He is yet living with the subject of this sketch, whose grandfather, Silas Downer, was a native of New Hampshire, but died in Jefferson County, to which he came about 1830. The mother of our subject, Sarah (Neil) Downer, was a native of Vermont; she was a daughter of Walter and Hannah Neil, and the mother of eight children, of whom four are now living in this county; she died May 1, 1882. Our subject was educated in this county, where he has made his home most of his life. In early life he farmed. At the age of nineteen, he commenced working at the blacksmith trade, to which he devoted a great deal of attention. He is a natural mechanic, and most of his life has been spent in shops and mills, of which latter he has built and repaired a great many. The last three years, however, he has spent in his wagon shop. Our subject was joined in matrimony, April 13, 1852, in Mount Vernon, to Miss Harty L. Schanck, born July 9, 1825, in New York; she is a daughter of Samuel Schanck, a native of New Jersey, born in 1799. He came here in 1839, following different occupations, and is one of the oldest living men in the county; he was also the oldest man in his regiment while serving in the Mexican war. Mrs. Downer's mother, Abigail (Cole) Schanck, was a native of Oneida County, N. Y. She was the mother of seven children, of whom four are now living. Mr. and Mrs. Downer are members of the Methodist Episcopal Church. He is an A., F. & A. M., also a member of the H. W. Hubbard Chapter of R. A. M.; has been Alderman of the Third Ward, and is a Democrat in politics.

COL. GEORGE W. EVANS, banker, Mount Vernon. This gentleman is a son of Nathaniel and Mary Evans, both deceased, who were natives of Wales, and who came to America when they were both young, and were reared by their parents in Eastern Virginia, where they died, the former in 1846, aged fifty years, and the latter in 1849, aged fifty years. They were the parents of two children, viz., Jonathan and George W., our subject. He was born in Preston County, Va., December 20, 1832, and was there reared on a farm, being bound out to work after his father's death. When he was seventeen years of age, he accompanied an overland emigrant train to California, and there spent four years in merchandising and mining. In the fall of 1850, he returned to Jefferson County, Ill., and the following spring began a roving life, which he continued until the breaking-out of the late war, when he enlisted in Johnson County, Ill., and raised Company E, of the Sixtieth Illinois Volunteer Infantry, and entered the service as Captain of the same. He served through the war, and passed through the general rules of promotions, and when he was mustered out of the service he held the rank of Colonel. After the war, he settled permanently in Jefferson County, Ill., and engaged in farming in Elk Prairie Township; he is now one of the largest land owners of the county, and has been very successful in farming. In 1873, he engaged in the banking business, under the firm name of Evans, Wilbanks & Co. In 1865, he married in Jefferson County, Ill., Miss Martha C. Anderson, daughter of Gov. Stinson H. Anderson, whose history appears elsewhere in this work. This union has been blessed with three children. Col. Evans is a wide-awake, public-spirited and self-made man, and enjoys the highest respect of the community in which he lives. He is an active member of the A., F. & A. M. and K. of H.

J. E. FERGERSON, merchant, Mt. Vernon, was born August 1, 1819, in Sumner County, Tenn. He is a son of Nelson Fergerson, a native of Virginia, and a blacksmith by occupation. He came here in the fall of 1819, following his trade, mostly. He moved back to Tennessee in 1822, and died there in 1825. His father, Edward Fergerson, was also a native of Virginia, but died in Tennessee. The mother of our subject was Roxoda (Tyler) Fergerson, a native of Tennessee, where she died. She was married three times, her second husband being Gideon Pitt, who died in Tennessee. Her third husband was Carter C. Hall. She was the mother of eight children, viz.: James E. Fergerson, John W. Fergerson, Matilda A. Fergerson (deceased) Nelson Fergerson (deceased) Sarah E. Pitt, William H. Hall, Andrew Hall and Catharine Hall. Our subject only went a few months to the old subscription schools in Tennessee. At the age of thirteen years, he was bound out eight years, by the courts, to learn the blacksmith trade with B. F. Simpson. After four years, he took the white swelling in his ankle, and was laid up almost two years, and finally was cured, his employer paying all expenses and giving him his liberty. In the fall of 1836, he returned to Jefferson County (where he had lived several years during his infancy), and in Mt. Vernon worked at his trade as a blacksmith with Burton Affleck, till August, 1837, when he returned to Bedford County, Tenn., where he stayed with his uncle from 1837 till 1841, when he got married and moved to Sumner County in 1843, where he carried on farming with good success till 1852, when he lost his first wife, Ann S. Ventress, who was the mother of eight children, of whom three are now living, viz.: James M., Frank L. and John L. In the spring of 1852, he again came to this county, where he engaged in farming and merchandising. He was married the second time to Mrs. Margaret S. Westcott, who died in 1858. After Mr. Fergerson was married, he went back to Tennessee in order to bring his children to his new home. Mrs. Margaret S. Fergerson was the mother of five children, viz.: Mary A. Westcott, wife of William T. Williams; James Westcott; Hon. John W. Westcott, a prominent merchant and politician of Xenia, Clay County, Ill.; Elizabeth Westcott, present wife of T. J. Gaston, and William B. Westcott, a commission man in St. Louis, Mo. Our subject was married a third time, to Sarah F. Allen, born in Jefferson County. Her father, Rev. George Allen, is a local minister of the Methodist Episcopal Church. She is the mother of six children, viz.: Glendora B., born May 2, 1860; Juliette E., born September 18, 1863; Edith L., born January 6, 1869; George E., born July 20, 1872 (he died, July 6, 1883, from wounds received by the explosion of a coal oil can on July 5), Fannie E., born August 5, 1876, and Carrie M., born October 25, 1881. Mr. and Mrs. Fergerson are members of the Methodist Episcopal Church. Mr. Fergerson has no aspiration for office, but devotes his attention strictly to business. He has been engaged as a merchant, farmer and manufacturer since 1852. He now owns a harness store and an interest in Hudspeth, Taylor & Co.'s dry goods store; also, an interest in the woolen factory, and for many years had an interest in the milling business. In politics, he is a Republican to the core.

JOHN GIBSON, farmer, P. O. Mt. Vernon, was born October 22, 1829, in Monroe County, Ohio, the son of James and Mary (Gorley) Gibson. The grandfather of our subject, Joseph Gibson, was a native of Scotland. He was a farmer by occupation, and settled in the North of Ireland, where he died. The father was a native of County Tyrone, Ireland. He was a farmer by occupation, and came from Ireland in an early day, and was one of the earliest settlers in Monroe County, Ohio, where he entered Government land. He finally moved to Mt. Vernon, where he died. The mother was a native of County Dublin, Ireland, and was the mother of eight children, of whom seven are living. Our subject's education was received in the schools of his native county, and, in 1853, he went to California, where he mined for a year and then returned to the States. In 1855, he came to Jefferson County, Ill., and farmed for three years, and then went to Pike's Peak, Colo., crossing the plains with two yoke of oxen. He mined in what was called the California Gulch until 1860, and then returning to Illinois, he farmed in this county until October, 1861. He then enlisted in the Sixtieth Illinois Volunteer Infantry, Company I, and served until the close of the war. He entered the army as a private, but was soon afterward elected to First Lieutenant. He was next promoted to Captain, and held that position to the close of the war. Among the battles in which he participated were the battles of Shiloh, Corinth, Stone River, siege of Nashville, Mission Ridge, Atlanta campaign, Sherman's "march to the sea," and was finally mustered out at Goldsboro, N. C. Since the war, he has been actively engaged in farming. He owns 134 acres, part of which is situated in the corporate limits of Mt. Vernon. He was married, in this county, October 10, 1833, to Mrs. Mary Adeline Coleman, who was born in Morgan County, Ohio, October 10, 1833, and is a daughter of Charles and Sarah Jane (Webster) McClure. This lady is the mother of four living children—C. C. Coleman (by her first husband), born June 12, 1860; Armettie, born February 13, 1867; James A., born November 4, 1869; Emily B., born May 27, 1872. Mr. and Mrs. Gibson are members of the M. E. Church. He is a member of the A., F. & A. M. fraternity of Opdyke, and the Union Lodge, No. 13, I. O. O. F., of Mt. Vernon. He has filled the various chairs in both lodges, and has been Grand Representative to the Masonic Grand Lodge twice. In politics, he has been identified with the Republican party.

JUDGE ANGUS McNEIL GRANT, banker, Mt. Vernon, was born in Christian Co., Ky., May 26, 1810. His parents, Joshua and Henrietta (McNeil) Grant, originally of North Carolina, and of Scotch parentage, settled in Kentucky in the early part of the present century. He received in his boyhood an ordinary school education, perfected by a subsequent two-years course of study in the higher branches of learning, at Princeton College, in his native State. Upon abandoning definitely student life, he became engaged in clerking for an uncle, with whom he remained for a period of about four years. He was afterward occupied in farming and agricultural pursuits, at which he continued until 1836. At this date he moved to Mount Vernon Ill., and for two years was employed in merchandising, at the expiration of which time he became identified with the hotel business and also with farming operations. In 1867, he abandoned the hotel business; continued busy with farming, however, until 1872. In this year, the organization of the Mount Vernon National Bank was effected, he being the prime mover in the enterprise, and to him by election was awarded the presidential chair, which he continued to fill with fidelity and ability until a serious attack of sickness, in

1879, compelled him to resign the position. During the days of the Whig party, he was one of its adherents and supporters, but since its dissolution has been a zealous and consistent Democrat. In 1837, he was elected County Surveyor, and filled that office for many years. He was afterward elected County Judge, but resigned before the expiration of his term. He was one of the earliest pioneers and settlers of Mount Vernon, and is honored as one of its most enterprising citizens; upon his arrival, there were but four or five houses in the place, and from that time to the present he has constantly and ably exerted himself to aid in securing to it the full development of its resources. He was united in marriage in October, 1836, to Miss Martha Anderson, a native of Tennessee, and a daughter of William B. and Ann (Galaspie) Anderson. She was born in 1810, and died in Mount Vernon, Ill., May 8, 1883. She was the mother of the following children: Edward Henry, who died at the age of six years; Lena, wife of C. D. Ham; Amanda C., wife of M. M. Poole, a prominent banker of Shawneetown, Ill., and Augusta May, wife of William C. Pollock. Judge Grant is a member of the Presbyterian Church of Mount Vernon, and enjoys the highest esteem of the community in which he lives.

WILLIS DUFF GREEN, M. D., Mt. Vernon, was born in Danville, Ky., January 18, 1821. His father, Dr. Duff Green, an eminent physician of that place, was the eldest son of Willis Green, who emigrated to Kentucky from the Shenandoah Valley of Virginia about the year 1780. He is a brother of Judge W. H. Green, of Cairo, Ill. He was educated primarily at Center College, in his native town, and was a classmate of Gen. John C. Breckenridge. Upon relinquishing college life, he began the study of medicine with his father, remaining under his preceptorship for a period of two years. He then, at the expiration of this time, attended the Medical Department of the Transylvania University, and graduated from the Medical College of Ohio. He then began the practice of his profession at Hartford, Ky., where he resided for a year and a half. He afterward practiced for two years in Pulaski, Tenn., removing subsequently, in 1846, to Mount Vernon, Ill., which has since been his home, and where he has been constantly and successfully occupied in the practice of his profession, which extends over the entire southern portion of the State. In politics, he has invariably and consistently supported the principles and platforms of the Democratic party, and as the Breckenridge candidate for Congress, was defeated with the head of the ticket. He is a prominent member of the Odd Fellows of Illinois, and has officiated as Grand Master, also as a Representative to the Grand Lodge of the United States. He is noted for his generosity in charitable enterprises, and has always been an active and a zealous member of benevolent societies and organizations. He was President of the Mt. Vernon Railroad Company, until it was merged in the St. Louis & Southern Railroad, and in the performance of the important functions attendant on that office evinced the possession of admirable administrative powers. He is a man of scholarly attainments, a skillful and reliable physician, and a useful member of the community amid which he is an esteemed and loved townsman. He was married, in 1844, to Corinne L. Morton, of Hartford, Ky.

BLUFORD HARLOW, farmer, P. O. Mt. Vernon, was born in Wilson County, Tenn., December 27, 1814, and is a son of Overton Harlow (deceased), a native of Virginia, who brought his family to this county in 1818, and settled in Mt. Vernon Township, where our subject has since resided. Mr. Harlow was married, January 7, 1841, to Emma Branson, a daughter of Brisco D. Branson, an early settler of this county. They have had eleven children, nine living—Noah H., John H., William T., Mary E., Martha C., Stephen A. D., James O., Joel

J. and Sarah E. Mr. Harlow owns 160 acres of land, and has always been a farmer.

ROBERT HARLOW, farmer, P. O. Mt. Vernon, was born December 15, 1816, in Wilson County, Tenn., a son of Overton Harlow, of Virginia, who married Elizabeth Hunt, of Tennessee, by whom he had seven children—Joel, Bluford, Robert, Mary, Henderson, Charles and Elisha. Our subject came to Jefferson County, Ill., in the fall of 1818, where he still resides. He was educated in Jefferson County, Ill., and is a member of the Baptist Church. He was married May 1, 1844, to Serena, daughter of William Lisenby, of Tennessee. Our subject has had ten children, seven living—Charles, Thomas, Mollie, William, Ellen, Henry H. and Ida. He owns 165 acres of land, and is engaged in farming and stock-raising. Politics, Democrat.

WILLIAM J. HARLOW, farmer, P. O. Mt Vernon. The subject of this sketch is a native of Jefferson County, and was born in Mt. Vernon Township May 8, 1844, son of Joel Harlow, of Texas, who removed to Arkansas when our subject was quite small, and later to Missouri. William J., returned in 1863, and has since resided in Jefferson County. He was in the late war in Company A, Eighth Missouri Cavalry, in the State militia. He was married October 9, 1868, to Rosella Warren. They had one child—Earl (deceased). Mr. Harlow owns forty acres of land, and is engaged in general farming. He is a member of the Baptist Church.

JOHN Q. HARMON, a son of John M. and Christina (Brown) Harmon, was a native of Campbellstown, Lebanon County, Penn., born on the 10th of August, 1830. During his early life, he had a severe and protracted struggle with poverty, and when a boy received but a limited common school education. On beginning his business career, he was almost wholly uninformed in literature, language, books and principles, and had a passionate temper, but was blessed with a resolute will, and he then determined to overcome these obstacles, and by industry, energy and patience he accomplished the work and learned to govern himself. Leaving home when but a boy, he embarked on his career in life as a clerk in a country store, and the few months of his stay in that position received the first lessons of an active life. After leaving the store, he apprenticed himself to the saddler's trade, but for some reason unknown to the writer he soon gave it up and began teaching the country schools, and continued thus until he was offered a position under the late John B. Irvin, contractor on the Pennsylvania Railroad. He was connected with different railroads, holding different positions, for a number of years. He afterward located permanently in Newark, Ohio, and was there employed in the County Clerk's office until 1850, when he came to Cairo, Ill., accepting a clerkship with Ellis, Jenkins & Co., contractors in building the levees that surround that city. In 1851, he went out in the Lopez expedition for the liberation of Cuba, with Joseph I. Abell, of Cairo, and Frank Livingston, of Paducah, and was sentenced to be executed, and once taken out to be shot, but through the efforts of Daniel Webster those of the expedition, who were not already executed were finally pardoned, Harmon among the number. In 1852, he went to Jonesboro, Ill., and began clerking in a general merchandising store for C. D. Finch, and remained thus engaged for about two years. In 1854, he returned to Cairo and engaged as book-keeper for Fowler & Norton, wharfboatmen, and later with Williams, Stephens & Co., wholesale grocers. At the organization of the Court of Common Pleas in 1856, he was appointed Clerk of that court, and the following spring was elected City Clerk; he held these positions until 1861, when he resigned and declined a re-election. On the 30th of April, 1860, he was appointed Clerk of the

Circuit Court to fill a vacancy in that office, and was elected to the same office the following fall and re-elected in 1864 and 1868. In 1861, he was elected County Clerk and served one term. He was Secretary of the State Constitutional Convention of 1870, and Clerk of the House of Representatives of the session of 1863 and 1864 of the General Assembly. He was appointed Consul to Chihuahua in Mexico, by President Buchanan, but declined the appointment. He also held the office of Master in Chancery of the Circuit Court, and Court of Common Pleas. In 1878, he was elected Clerk of the Appellate Court for the Eighteenth District of Illinois, and during his term of office, in the year 1882, died of Bright's disease, at Eureka Springs, where he had gone in the vain hope of regaining his health. He was married on the 24th of June, 1858, to Mary H., daughter of Joseph and Henrietta McKenzie, who still survives, and is the mother of the following children: Mary C., Rob Roy, Frank B., Kate I. and Gertrude P. Mr. Harmon was a Democrat in politics, and was one of the best known and most popular men that ever lived in the county. Of an impulsive, warm and generous heart, his whole nature was as genial as sunshine; of blood pure and gentle, his companionship was an unmixed pleasure to all his large acquaintance, which extended throughout the entire State. His warm heart went out in sympathy to the afflicted, and his purse-string was never tied when the appeal of charity came. His integrity stood every test of life, and was never questioned; brave, chivalric and impulsive, he would resent instantaneously any real or fancied reflection upon his own or his friend's integrity, but his pure soul never harbored malice, hate or revenge a moment, and he was as ready to forgive and forget as he had been to feel and resent the wrong. His ideal of moral integrity was placed in the highest niche, and yet his whole life was marked by no deviation from the high standard he had placed before him when a boy. His life was pure and cleanly—both morally and socially. He was a loving and affectionate husband and father, and when the cruel and irreparable loss came to his loved household, with its great and incurable affliction, the sympathy and condolence—sincere and heartfelt—of all his wide circle of friends went out to them in their hour of severe trial. At the head of his grave the sons and daughters of posterity may stand and truly say the world is brighter and better that he lived. His memory will be cherished, and his good deeds not forgotten.

GEORGE M. HAYNES, attorney at law, Mt. Vernon, was born in Mt. Vernon, Ill., August 27, 1847, and when some two years old removed with his family to Washington County, where he remained until 1865. He then returned to Mt. Vernon, for the purpose of attending school, and has since made it his home. By the aid of friends, he was enabled to attend McKendree College, at Lebanon, Ill. for six months, which, with previous schooling, gave him a fair English education. While engaged as a clerk, he found time to read law under the direction of the late Judge T. B. Tanner, and in March, 1870, was admitted to the bar. He did not, however, enter upon the active duties of the profession, but pursued his studies until March, 1872, when he, with Mr. R. A. D. Wilbanks, purchased the Mt. Vernon *Free Press*, the Democratic organ of the county. Mr. Haynes took charge of the paper, and under his management it became a strong and vigorous element in the campaign of 1872. In October, Mr. Haynes sold his interest in the paper to W. H. Mantz, and in June, 1873, formed a law partnership with Seth F. Crews, which continued for nearly eight years. They at once took a front rank in the profession, and held it until 1880, when the partnership was dissolved. Since that time, Mr. Haynes has enjoyed as good a practice as any member of the bar of Jefferson County. From 1873 to 1879, he was Master in Chancery, an office he filled with acceptance. At the December term of court, 1877, the State's Attorney was sick and Judge Allen appointed Mr. Haynes in his place. In politics, he has always been an unflinching and uncompromising Democrat, permitting nothing to move him out of line. Mr. Haynes is still young in years, and has a useful future before him. A man of more than ordinary intelligence, a lawyer of ability and experience, he will yet make his mark in the profession. He has written much for publication, and is a good, though not a brilliant writer. One of his best efforts is his chapter on the bench and bar of Jefferson County, written especially for this work. Mr. Haynes was married, August 22, 1876, to Miss Ada Buckingham, of Hamilton County. They have two children living—Maggie and Florence—the latter born on the day President Garfield was shot—and Ada Louise dead.

W. H. HERDMAN, blacksmith, Mount Vernon. Among our quiet, steady and reliable citizens who deserve mention in this work we class him whose name heads this sketch. He was born January 25, 1828, in Allegheny County, near Pittsburgh, Penn. His father, Robert Herdman, was a native of Pennsylvania, and a farmer and miller by occupation; he was a prominent man in his county, and drowned at the age of thirty-eight in the Muskingum River. The father of Robert was William Herdman, a native of Ireland, though the family originally is of Scotch descent. The mother of our subject, Jane Hanson, is a native of Pennsylvania; her father was Thomas Hanson; she is yet living, aged eighty years, the mother of seven children, of whom six are now living, viz.: William H., our subject; Prof. Thomas H., now Presiding Elder at Lebanon, Ill.; John R., a carpenter and farmer in Clay County, Ill.; James H., County Treasurer of Warren County, Ill.; Mary A., wife of Dr. Elli- ott, of Hagerstown, Ind., and Jane E., wife of Dr. Givens, of Paxton, Ford Co., Ill. Our subject went to school in Ohio; in early life, he farmed and then learned the blacksmith trade, which he has followed all his life; he has also manufactured plows, wagons, buggies, etc.; he came to Mt. Vernon in 1850, and there has followed his occupation; he was joined in matrimony, on the 24th day of November, 1850, to Miss Mary A. Kirby, born May 3, 1836, in Louisville, Ky. Her parents, Moses and Lydia (Williamson) Kirby, were natives of Cincinnati, Ohio. This happy union was blessed with eight daughters—Ada I., Ina B., Lydia J. (deceased), Florence V., Ella A., Etta, Grace and Octavia. Mr. Herdman is an I. O. O. F., having filled all offices, and also been a Representative to the Grand Lodge and Encampment; he has been a member of the Town Council and Supervisor and School Director. In politics, he is a liberal Republican.

F. W. HERMANN, merchant tailor, Mount Vernon. Among the energetic young business men of Mt. Vernon we must count Mr. Hermann, who was born March 24, 1841, in Loeban, Prussia, Germany. His father, F. W. Hermann, Sr., was a native of Germany, where he died; he also served as a soldier in the German Army. The mother of our subject, Louisa Heske, an estimable lady, was also a native of Prussia, where she died, leaving six children to mourn her departure, and of those, five brothers are now living. Our subject was educated in Germany, where he learned his trade; becoming imbued with a desire to see America, the land of wealth and wonder, he, like many of his sturdy countrymen, who make such excellent citizens, emigrated to the United States August 12, 1872, landing in New York. He worked at his trade four and a half years in Little Falls, Herkimer Co., N. Y. From there he went to St. Louis, and finally, August 16, 1877, he came to Mt. Vernon, where he has followed his trade ever since. He was joined in marriage twice; his first wife, Matilda A. Wachter, was born in Germany; she died in Mt. Vernon, leaving three children, viz.: E. R. August, born January 27, 1871; F. William, born August 3, 1876, and Emma, deceased. His present wife, May Stoker, was born May 8, 1855, in Nashville, Ill. She is the mother of Laura L., born October 18, 1882. Mr. Hermann is identified with the Democratic party.

COL. STEPHEN G. HICKS, deceased. A sketch of Col. Hicks will be found in the chapter on the war and military history of the county.

ROBERT N. HINMAN, Postmaster, Mt. Vernon, is a native of Jefferson County, Ill., born on the 18th of December, 1854. His father, Harmon D. Hinman, was a native of Vermont, born in 1804. Here he spent his early life and received a limited education in the common schools. In 1825, he moved to Zanesville, Ohio, and there served an apprenticeship at the brick mason's trade, and was, in November, 1830, married to Cynthia Eddy, who died in 1851, leaving three children as the result of their union—Safford E., deceased; William H., and Mary J., wife of D. C. Groves, of Richland County, Ill. In 1833, he removed to Madison County, Ind., and subsequently, in 1841, to Jefferson County, Ill., and settled on a farm one and one-half miles northwest of the city of Mt. Vernon, where he remained engaged farming and working at his trade until 1859, when he removed to Mt. Vernon, and erected by his own design a large and commodious brick residence, intending to spend his remaining years in the enjoyment of his past labor. His death occurred in the fall of 1860 from an injury received by being thrown from a horse. He was an industrious man, of good standing in the community, a member of the Presbyterian Church, and an active worker for the Republican party. His second marriage occurred in this county, in 1851, to Elizabeth Moss, a native of Jefferson County, Ill., born January 30, 1832, and died December 29, 1871. She was the mother of five children—Robert N., our subject; Alma, wife of J. C. Moss; and Rosa, John and Alice (deceased). Robert N. Hinman was reared in Mt. Vernon and educated in the city schools. When he was fifteen years of age, he engaged as clerk for S. K. Latham, Postmaster, and remained thus engaged for nine years, and at the expiration of that time was appointed Postmaster, which position he has since filled. In Ashley, Ill., in 1875, he married Miss Elizabeth E. Burghardt, a native of New York, who has borne him the following children: Eugene, Earl, and an infant unnamed. Mr. Hinman is an enterprising young man, well worthy of the confidence the people place in him. He is a Republican politically, but takes no active interest.

EDWARD HITCHCOCK, editor and publisher of *Exponent*, Mt. Vernon, was born in Evansville, Ind., February 3, 1841. He is a newspaper man, and has been in that business nearly all of his life. At the age of twenty, he published the *Temperance Guide* in Terre Haute, Ind., in conjunction with J. M. Pool, the editor. The war of the rebellion breaking out, the patriotic ardor of Mr. Hitchcock was so wrought upon that, leaving an edition of the paper incomplete still upon the press, he volunteered "for a soldier" under the first call of the President for 75,000 volunteers to suppress the rebellion, and April 19, 1861, at Indianapolis, was mustered into the service. In the following August (his term of enlistment having expired) he received his discharge. August 18, 1862, he "donned the blue" again, for "three years or during the war," as Orderly in Company E, Seventy-first Indiana Volunteer Infantry, and two days later was commissioned Second Lieutenant, and subsequently promoted to First Lieutenant, Company E, Sixth Indiana Cavalry. (The regiment, in 1863, was transferred from the Infantry to the cavalry arm of the service.) After passing through the usual privations and trials incident to those stirring times (having once been taken prisoner and paroled) and the rebellion having been crushed—in 1865, he was mustered out at Indianapolis. He located in the fall of 1865 in Olney, Richland County, Ill., and there engaged in the combined business of provision dealer and job printer. Subsequently moving his job office to Flora, Ill., he bought, in 1866, a half interest in the *Clay County Union*, with S. P. Connor as associate, and moved to Louisville, the county seat. Some months later, Connor having "Andy Johnsonized," Mr. Hitchcock, under political compulsion, bought the former's interest in the office. For seven years thereafter he had sole editorial control of the paper, which he had christened *The Voice of the People*. In 1871, he bought an interest in the Greenup *Mail*, and for a year or so edited both journals. Leasing *The Voice* to one of his pupils, Mr. C. R. Davis, in 1872, he moved to Greenup, and there in person conducted *The Mail* during the memorable Grant-Greeley campaign. In 1873, he again assumed charge, personally, of *The Voice of the People*. A few months later, by purchase, H. R. Miller, another pupil, took control, changing the name to the *Tribune*. The parties who had taken *The Greenup Mail* in twelve months suspended publication, and in 1874 Mr. Hitchcock was induced to lease and resurrect it. He moved the office to the county seat, Prairie City (now Toledo), and began at "No. 1, Vol. I," the publication of the *Cumberland Republican*. Placing the paper upon a sound footing, at the end of his lease, he repaired to Effingham, subsequently at Terre Haute, Ind. (his old home); he found a better opening in the *Express* office, where, later, a company was formed, with our subject as its President, for the purpose of publishing a daily and weekly newspaper. It was named the *Republican* and he was its political editor. This was in the winter of 1875-76, and during the early months of the Hayes-Tilden campaign. Disposing of his interest in the *Republican*, Mr. Hitchcock took charge of a job office on Main street. His friends offering sufficient inducement, he, in December, 1876, removed to Casey, Clark County, Ill., and under a lease, established the *Exponent*. Having been appointed Postmaster of the thriving town, he managed both offices with Mrs. Hitchcock's assistance. In November, 1878, the Republicans of Jefferson County invited Mr. Hitchcock to locate at Mt. Vernon, and to bring hither his printing material. He did so; and on the 5th day of December, of that year, the first number of Vol. III, of the *Exponent* was issued in Mt. Vernon. Since that date, now nearly five years, the paper has regularly appeared, notwithstanding difficulties and trials that possibly are not appreciated by those who never tried to stem the tide of an adverse political sentiment that uniformly at elections sweeps over Jefferson County. Mr. Hitchcock was married May 27, 1863, to Miss Henrietta Barber. Five children is the result of this marriage—Edward, Kate, Clyde, Andrew H. and Grafton.

JAMES HITCHCOCK, photographer, Mt. Vernon. The subject of this sketch was born in Terre Haute, Ind., Dec. 15, 1842, and is the son of Dr. J. W. Hitchcock, of Mt. Vernon, Ill. Our subject received his education in the schools of Terre Haute, Ind. In early life, he learned the drug business, and followed the same till August 12, 1862, when he enlisted in Company E, Sixth Indiana Cavalry, under Capt. Welsh and Col. James Biddle. The regiment served in the Army of the Cumberland. During the first engagement of the regiment at Richmond, Ky., Mr. Hitchcock received a flesh wound. August 6, 1864, he was captured and lay in Andersonville Prison till April 28, 1865. June 10, 1865, he was mustered out at Camp

Chase, Ohio, and at that time was Sergeant of his company. After returning from the army, he went to Olney, Ill., where he was again employed in his old business as druggist, but after a short time he begun in his present profession of photographer. Till 1870, he traveled and did photographing; he then located at Mt. Vernon, Ill., and through his superior workmanship has built up an extensive trade, receiving work from Cairo and other cities at a distance. May 3, 1868, he was married, in Olney, Ill., to Miss Annie E. Gardner, a native of Maryland, and daughter of George Gardner. In early life, she was left an orphan, and during the war was Assistant Postmaster at Petersville, Md., where she was subjected to the experiences found in being in the midst of contending armies. Three of her brothers were soldiers in the Union army. Mr. and Mrs. Hitchcock have three children, viz.: Ruby E., Ray and Ethel. He is a charter member of Ivanhoe Lodge, No. 683, K. of H.; also Rowena Lodge, No. 283, K. & L. of H. He is also member of the Royal Templars of Temperance, Mt. Vernon Council, No. 7. In politics, he is a Republican.

THOMAS H. HOBBS, miller, Mount Vernon, was born in Sumner County, Tenn., on the 18th of May, 1820, to David and Chloe (Hunt) Hobbs. The elder Hobbs was born in North Carolina February 6, 1783, and when a small boy was left an orphan, and was bound to Jesse Hunt to learn the saddler's trade, and was removed by him to Sumner County, Tenn., and there principally reared and educated. He subsequently married a daughter of Mr. Hunt, and in the spring of 1826, with his wife and seven children, removed to Illinois and settled in Williamson County, and the fall of the same year came to this county, bought a small improvement of land, and engaged in farming to the time of his death, which occurred February 15, 1852. He was a volunteer of the war of 1812, and a member of the Methodist Episcopal Church for over fifty years His wife and subject's mother was born in North Carolina May 19, 1783, and died in Jefferson County, Ill., January 8, 1854. She was the mother of eight children, of whom six are living. Thomas H. Hobbs was principally reared in this county, and here received such an education as the schools of the county afforded. In 1849, he left his home and went to California by overland route, and remained there engaged in mining in the mountains for over two years, and returned home in 1851, after an absence of two years two months and twelve days. During the years of 1851 and 1852, he was engaged in contracting and superintending the track-laying on the Illinois Central Railroad. He then bought a farm in Washington County, near Ashley, and engaged in farming, and continued the same only one year, and removed to Ashley and engaged in merchandising. In 1855, he sold his business, returned with his family to Mount Vernon, and engaged in the hotel business in connection with farming. In 1860, he engaged in merchandising, and continued in this business until 1867. The year previous to his selling out, he bought the flouring mill, which has since chiefly occupied his time in connection with stock-feeding, trading and shipping. In February, 1843, he married Miss Malinda Holtsclaw, who died in 1852, leaving two children as the result of their union. Of these, one is now living—James H., a machinist of Mount Vernon. In 1854, Mr. Hobbs married Eliza E. Guthrie, who has borne him five children, of whom the following are living: Charles A., Alva L., Thomas Edward and Homer. Mr. and Mrs. Hobbs are Methodists; he is a Republican in politics, and a member of the A., F. & A. M. and I. O. O. F.

THOMAS HUDSON, farmer, P. O. Mount Vernon, was born in this county June 18, 1854, and is a son of Joel Hudson (deceased), a native of Tennessee, and a soldier for the

B

United States Government in the late war. Our subject spent his early life, from the time he was seven years old, in Mount Vernon, working in the flouring mill of Hobbs & Guthrie. He was married, January 20, 1878, to Miss Martha S., daughter of Stephen D. C. and Elizabeth L. Davis, of this township. Mr. Davis is a boot and shoe maker in Mount Vernon. Mr. and Mrs. Hudson have had three children, two living—Samuel C. and Alvar T. Mr. and Mrs. Davis had ten children, four living—Matilda R. (Foster), Lutitia A. (Winters), Alevia (Smith) and the wife of our subject. There were ten children in the Hudson family, four of whom are living—Joel, Newton, Charles and our subject. Mr. Hudson is a member of the Methodist Episcopal Church, owns eleven acres of valuable land on Section 18, where he now resides, having recently abandoned the milling business.

JOHN B. HUDSPETH, merchant, Mount Vernon, was born December 16, 1824, in Warrick County, Ind., son of Thomas Hudspeth, a native of North Carolina. He was a farmer in early life, and a merchant in the latter part of his life, he dying in Booneville, Warrick Co., Ind., his father being Charles Hudspeth, a farmer. The mother, Susannah (Boone) Hudspeth, was a native of Warren County, Ky. She is a distant relative of old Daniel Boone, the famous hunter of Kentucky. Her father, John Boone, was a farmer in Kentucky. She was the mother of nine children, of whom five are now living, viz.: Mary, wife of William Hudson; Thomas J., George P., John B. and Joseph M. Our subject was educated in Bloomington, Ind., at the institute. In early life, he worked in his father's store, then learned and followed the cooper's trade five years, and then entered the mercantile career and has followed it ever since. He, in partnership with his brothers, started a general store in Booneville, Ind., buying and shipping large quantities of tobacco. They were also engaged in the milling business, building two flouring mills and one saw mill. In 1865, he severed connection with his brother and went to Evansville, Ind., where he was connected with the firm of Hudspeth, Adams & Co.; afterward it was changed to Hudspeth, Miller & Co. In 1878, Mr. Miller sold out and Mr. Curtis took his place. The firm is now known as Hudspeth & Curtis; they are running two large retail dry goods houses. A year ago last February, our subject sold out to his younger brother, Joseph M., and in December, 1882, came to Mount Vernon, and in April the following year he formed a partnership with A. F. Taylor, and runs a dry goods store. He was joined in matrimony at Bloomington, Monroe Co., Ind., to Miss Mary E. Denny, born April 13, 1821, near Lexington, Ky., daughter of James and Harriett (Littrell) Denny, natives of Kentucky. Subject has three children now living, viz.: Lily, wife of F. M. Barbour; Eugene E., March 29, 1857, and Birdie, October 18, 1866, and twins (deceased), Thomas B. and James L. Mr. Hudspeth is an A. F. & A. M., and also an I. O. O. F. While in Indiana, he was Sheriff of Warrick County, and filled other town offices. Had been a Democrat till Fort Sumter was fired on. He is now a stanch Republican.

MAJOR NOAH JOHNSTON, banker. A sketch of Major Johnston will be found in chapter on the political history of the county.

JAMES D. JOHNSON, merchant, Mt. Vernon, a descendant of one of the oldest pioneer families of Jefferson County, and a prominent business man of Mt. Vernon, was born in Jefferson County on the 20th of June, 1838, to John N. and Sarah T. (Hobbs) Johnson. John N. Johnson was born in Tennessee, and there reared and educated. In 1819, with his parents, he emigrated to Illinois, and settled in this county In 1834, he married, and soon after began the study of medicine in the office of Short & Frost, and subsequently graduated at the Ohio Medical College. In 1850, he gave up his professional practice and engaged in the mercantile business, and continued the same with good success until the time of his death, which occurred in November, 1855. He was a consistent member of the Methodist Episcopal Church for over thirty years, a liberal contributor to churches and all charitable purposes. He was a son of James Johnson, a native of Virginia, who removed to Kentucky, being one of the early settlers of that State, and afterward to Tennessee, and subsequently to Illinois, and settled in Jefferson County, where he engaged in farming during the remainder of his life. Our subject's mother was born in Sumner County, Tenn., and is now residing in Mt. Vernon. She is the mother of seven children, of whom the following are now living: James D., our subject; Mary P., wife of Henry F. Waters; Chloe C., wife of David H. Warren; A. Curt, and John N. James D. Johnson was reared in Mt. Vernon, and was educated in the schools of the county. In 1857, he engaged as clerk in a store for James M. Pace, for three years, and at the expiration of that time engaged in merchandising on his own account, continuing the same until August, 1862, when he entered the late civil war as a private in Company B, of the One Hundred and Tenth Illinois Volunteer Infantry, under command of Col. T. S. Casey, and was mustered out of the service in May, 1863. He then returned home, and engaged in merchandising, and is at present engaged in the same business, on the east side of the public square. His stock of goods comprises everything found in a first-class general store. He was one of the gentlemen who built the large wollen mills of this city, and was a partner of the same for fifteen years. In October, 1860, he married Miss Martha Boswell, a native of Princeton, Ind., who died in September, 1870, leaving three children, viz.: Lucius H., Sarah A. and Alva C. In June, 1875, he married a second time, Miss Arabella Courtney, a native of Danville. Ill. This union has been blessed with two children, of whom one is now living, viz., Leroy C. Mr. Johnson and wife are members of the Methodist Episcopal Church; he is a Republican in politics, and has served the people in many of the town offices.

DR. A. C. JOHNSON, druggist, Mount Vernon, a son of John N. and Sarah T. (Hobbs) Johnson, was born in Mount Vernon, Jefferson Co., Ill., on the 17th of August, 1847. He was reared in this county, and was educated in the Mount Vernon High Schools. After his father's death, he engaged as clerk in the mercantile establishment of James M. Pace, and remained with him for a period of two years. He then engaged as clerk in a drug store for Dr. E. Welborn, and remained thus engaged for three years. In 1865, he engaged in the grocery business on his own account. In 1866, he began the study of medicine with Hiram S. Plummer, M. D., and after one and one-half years' study, entered the Miami Medical College at Cincinnati, graduated, and entered upon the practice of his profession in Elk Prairie Township, Jefferson County, and the following year came to Mount Vernon and engaged in the drug business, at which he still continues. In October, 1868, he married Miss Amelia R. Stratton, daughter of Capt. S. T. Stratton. They have two children. Politically, he is a Republican, an enterprising and public-spirited citizen.

JAMES K. JONES, farmer, P. O. Mount Vernon, was born August 14, 1816, in Virginia. He is a son of George Jones, also a native of Virginia, and a farmer by occupation. He died in Jennings County, Ind. The mother of our subject, Prudence (Keith) Jones, was a native of Virginia, but died in Jennings County, Ind. She was a daughter of Rev. Keith, a farmer and minister by occupation. She was the mother of nine children, of whom five are now living. Our subject was educated in Indiana. He came to this county in the fall of 1864, and has followed farming with good success. He built and owned the Opdyke Mills, managing it for some time with good success; he finally rented it to other parties, and afterward ran it again himself for four years, when he sold out and came to live at Mount Vernon. Our subject was joined in matrimony twice. His first wife, Hannah S. Keller, was a native of Indiana, and died in March, 1872, in this county; she was the mother of the following children: Isabella Stonemetts, Mary Stratton, Jessie D., Frederich C. and Virginia H. Kline. Mr. Jones' present wife, Miss Hannah A. Montgomery, is a native of Ohio, but was reared in Indiana. Her father, Alexander Montgomery, was a native of New Jersey. Mr. and Mrs. Jones are members of the Methodist Episcopal Church. He is a Democrat and an A., F. & A. M. They are raising a little grand-daughter, whose name is Eva C. Yost.

WILLIAM A. JONES, physician, Mount Vernon, was born December 24, 1857, in Shiloh Township, Jefferson Co., Ill. His father, Samuel W. Jones, was a native of Indiana, where he was a farmer by occupation. He came here in the fall of 1857, farming nine years on Moore's Prairie, and finally moved back to Shiloh Township, where he had first settled. His father, George Jones, was a native of Virginia, but died in Indiana. More about the Jones family is found in another part of this work. The mother of our subject, Mary A. (Henry) Jones, was a native of Indiana; she is a daughter of John Henry; she is yet living, loved and respected by all who come in contact with her, and is the mother of nine children, viz., Nanny P. Wells, George H., Gilbert D., William A., John C., Mary E., Minnie M., Anna M., and Samuel S. (deceased). Our subject was educated mostly in the common schools of Jefferson County. He attended medical lectures at the Missouri Medical College, St. Louis, Mo., where he graduated March 4, 1880. After practicing ten months he removed to Mount Vernon February 1, 1881, where he is now engaged in the practice of his profession, enjoying the confidence and esteem of a large number of people in both town and country, and building for himself an enviable reputation. He is a member of the A., F. & A. M., Marion Lodge, No. 31. In politics, he has been identified with the Democratic party, and for the last two years has filled the office of County Physician with tact and ability.

WILLIS A. KELLER, farmer and livery stable, P. O. Mt. Vernon, was born in Lincoln County, Tenn., July 1, 1826. His father, John Keller, was born in North Carolina July 17, 1804, and moved with his parents to Bedford County, Tenn., in 1814, where he received his education and married. In December, 1841, he moved with his family to Jefferson County, Ill., and settled in Elk Prairie Township. He was a farmer by occupation, but in the winter often worked at shoe-making and coopering. In 1847, he enlisted in the United States service of the Mexican war, and died in Jalapa, Mexico, in January, 1847, from a disease contracted while in the service. His wife, Mary (Nees) Keller, was a native of Lincoln County, Tenn., born in 1805, and died in Jefferson County, Ill., in December, 1869. She was the mother of ten children, of whom Elizabeth, Jane, Willis and Jesse are now living. Willis A. Keller was reared on the farm, and received but a limited education. At ten years of age he began working out on a farm by the month, and continued the same until he was nineteen years of age, when he married and engaged in farming on his own account. He commenced on a capital of less than $10, and rented land; but by good management, economy and integrity he became very successful, and accumulated over 1,000 acres. In connection with his farm, he has, for two years, been engaged in the livery business in Mt. Vernon. He was married, January 7, 1846, to Miss Mary Dodds, a native of Kentucky, born November 29, 1829, and died in Jefferson County, Ill., July 1, 1865, leaving four children, viz.: Sarah E., wife of George W. Yost; Judge C A. Keller; Amanda, wife of Robert Lloyd, of Kentucky, and Minnie E., wife of Julian, Frochock. Mr. Keller married a second time in 1866, Mrs. Lucy Rentchler a native of Mt. Vernon. She has borne him three children, viz.: Mary J., Luthema and Charles R. Mr. Keller is a self-made man, a Democrat in politics, and a member of the I. O. O. F. and A. F. & A. M.

JUDGE COLUMBUS A. KELLER, lawyer, Mt. Vernon, is a native of this county, having been born about three miles southwest of Mt. Vernon, November 24, 1851. He was raised on the home farm, and during his youth gave his attention to farming pursuits. In the common schools of the vicinity he obtained his early schooling, which he supplemented by a three years' course of study, under the preceptorship of Prof. T. H. Herdman, then of Mt. Vernon, now a Methodist clergyman residing near Vandalia, Ill. Becoming dissatisfied with life on the farm, he evinced an early desire to cast his lot with some of the higher profession. That of law appeared to possess greater attractions for him than any other, and he resolved to give both time and money to the prosecution of studies in this direction, and accordingly, in 1869, he entered the McKendree College, Lebanon, Ill., where he subsequently passed the required examination, and graduated with honor in 1871. He returned home and continued his studies under Judge James M. Pollock, and in the fall of 1872 entered the Ann Arbor Law University, where he acquired such a proficiency in his studies, that he was enabled to creditably pass a rigid examination in open Supreme Court at Ottawa, Ill. Judge Pollock took him in as a partner, the partnership lasting until 1877, when our subject was elected County Judge of Jefferson County for four years, during which time he discharged the duties thereof to the credit of himself, and to the satisfaction of the people at large. Upon his retirement from office, he resumed the practice of his profession, and is at present thus engaged. September 16, 1873, he married, in Lebanon, Ill., Miss Nellie F. Raymond, a native of California, and a daughter of Charles R. and Jennie L. Raymond. This union has been blessed with three children, viz., May, Raymond and Willis. In politics, the Judge takes an active interest, being identified with the Democrat party. He is Grand Master of the Grand Lodge, I. O. O. F., and is also a member of the A. O. U. W., K. of H., and R. T. of T. It is seldom that we find one who has ascended the ladder of fame with more rapid strides than has Judge Keller. Rising from the lowly position of a farm boy to that of Judge of a wealthy and populous county, and that, too, at an age which made him by far the youngest in the State of Illinois, entitles him to that honor and praise which is due to those whose pathway is strewn, not with flowers as some might suppose, but at whose every step are met obstacles and adversities which determination and perseverance can only surmount.

C. KOONS, physician, Mt. Vernon. Among the young and rising physicians of this county who owe their high standing and the confidence that the people place in them not to inherited wealth or fame, but to their own exertions and go-ahead spirit, we are glad to count him whose name heads this sketch. He was born July 16, 1849, in Athens, Ohio. His father, Jonathan Koons, is a native of Pennsylvania, and a farmer and mechanic by occupation. He came to Illinois in 1855, and is yet living in the north part of Franklin County. His father, Peter Koons, was a native of Bedford County, Penn., near the old battle-field of Bloody Run. He was a farmer and died in Pennsylvania. The mother of our subject, Abigail (Bishop) Koons, was a native of New Hampshire, and died in Franklin County, Ill. She was a daughter of Rev. G. Bishop, a minister of the Baptist Church and one of the greatest revivalist in his day. Eight boys and two girls were the result of this happy union. Seven are now living—Nahum W., James R., John A., George E., Joseph B., Quintillia Taylor and Cinderrellus, our subject, who received a common school education at Taylor's Hill in Franklin County, and received his medical education at the American Medical College, St. Louis, Mo., graduating May 16, 1876, after which he followed his profession two years in Franklin County, and since 1878 in this county, being located at Belle Rive. June 8, 1883, he located in Mt. Vernon, where he now follows his profession. Dr. Koons was joined in matrimony, October 9, 1870, to Miss Sarah J. Border, born May 29, 1846, in Athens County, Ohio. Her parents, Joseph and Jemima (Jones) Border, were natives of Ohio. Two children blessed this union—Alice, deceased, and Nellie, born January 1, 1880. Dr. Koons has always been an ardent Republican. His two older brothers, S. B. Koons and J. R. Koons, were soldiers in our late war. The former died while in the army.

SAMUEL K. LATHAM, farmer, P. O. Mt. Vernon, was born April 14, 1839, in Jefferson County, Ill. His father, James Latham, was a native of Ireland, but reared in Vermont. The mother of our subject, Anna (Johnson) Latham, was born in 1798 in Virginia, but reared in Tennessee, and at the age of twenty-one came to this county with her parents, Louis and Frankie (Stone) Johnson, natives of Virginia. Mrs. Anna Latham is yet living, and, although in her eighty-fifth year, is quite strong, and at this writing does a great deal of work. She is the mother of nine children, of whom eight were with her first husband, Ransom Moss, a native of Virginia. He died in this county. She has altogether 150 offspring, including children, grandchildren and great-grandchildren, of whom a few are deceased. She is a lady who is loved and cherished by all with whom she comes in contact. She has seen almost three generations rise and pass away. Our subject went to school when the subscription plan was in vogue. He farmed till November 10, 1861, when he enlisted in Company C, of the Sixtieth Illinois Volunteer Infantry. After the second year, he veteranized and re-enlisted, serving till 1864, when he was honorably discharged on account of disability. Since then he has been looking after his farm interest. He has also been Postmaster of Mt. Vernon for thirteen years. He was joined in matrimony August 12, 1858, in this county, to Miss Emeline T. Dukes, born October 21, 1838, in Tennessee. Her parents, Jackson and Elender (Rife) Dukes, were natives of Tennessee, having come to this county almost forty-five years ago. Eight children now living are the result of this happy union—Emma A., John S. and Clara A. (twins), Charles L., Della M., Mandy, Nora and Nina. Mr. and Mrs. Latham and three children are connected with the M. E. Church. In politics, Mr. Latham is a Republican, casting his first vote for Old Abe.

C. W. LINDLEY, merchant, Mt. Vernon, was born August 20, 1847, in Lincoln County, Tenn., son of Thomas J. Lindley, who was a native of Vermont, and a millwright and machinist by occupation, who died in Franklin County, Ill., his father being Oliver Lindley, a native of Connecticut, and a farmer by occupation. The mother of our subject, Virginia (Timmons) Lindley, a native of Tennessee, was the mother of ten children. At the age of two years, our subject was crippled by paralysis, and up to the age of twelve he could not walk. He read a great deal, and attended school in different places, viz.: Oakhill Seminary and Manchester, Tenn. After that, in 1863, he came to Illinois and attended school in Shawneetown, Springgarden, and then at Mt. Vernon, where he clerked about sixteen years, and then was elected County Treasurer in 1879, serving till

December, 1882, filling the office with tact and ability, being the only Republican that has ever filled that office. Previous to that, he had been Township Collector for two years. In March, 1882, he opened a grocery store, which he has continued ever since. He was married, in Mt. Vernon, to Miss Kate Hitchcock, born July 14, 1847, in Terre Haute, Ind., daughter of Dr. John W. Hitchcock, and is the mother of two children, viz.: Neil (deceased) and Cliff, born February 12, 1881. Mrs. Lindley is a member of the Congregational Church. He is a member of the Christian Church, and also a member of K. of H., I. O. M. A., and Iron Hall; has been City Treasurer for four years; is a Republican in politics.

C. B. LINDSEY, merchant, Mount Vernon, was born April 15, 1853, in St. Louis, Mo., son of John Lindsey, a native of Washington, N. Y., born October 23, 1815, a harness-maker by occupation. He is yet living in Weatherford, Tex. He came to Illinois in 1840, but for the last nine years has lived in Texas. His father, Theodore Lindsey, and his grandfather, John Lindsey, Sr., were soldiers in the war of 1812. The latter died from wounds received in the war. John Lindsey learned his trade in Troy, N. Y.; he finished in Utica, N. Y., and followed it in Buffalo, Cleveland, Troy, N. Y., and Troy, Ill. In 1844, he went to St. Louis, and in 1849 went to California, returning to St. Louis in 1851, and to Madison County, Ill., in 1853. From there, in 1859, he went to Montgomery County, Ill., and then, in 1875, he went to Texas, where he now resides. The mother of our subject, Caroline (Smith) Lindsey, was a native of New York. She is a daughter of Amos Smith, who lived to be ninety-six years old, dying the centennial year. She is the mother of ten children, of whom five are now living, viz.: Julia A. Whitzell, Rebecca J. Huey, Lottie M. Campbell, Charles B., our subject, and Jennie L. Fouke. Our subject was educated in Illinois. He studied pharmacy in the New York College of Pharmacy, New York City, returning to Illinois in 1878, clerking in Taylorville, Christian County, one year, when he went to Warrenton, Mo., where he opened a drug store, continued it one year, then sold out and started for Texas; was wrecked in a railroad disaster, and returned to Illinois, where he clerked in McLeansboro till June, 1881. August 17, 1881, he was married, in Mt. Vernon, to Mrs. Belle Reardon, and went to Fort Worth, Tex., where he clerked in a drug store till March, 1883, when he returned to Mt. Vernon, where he now runs a harness shop. Our subject is a member of three societies, viz.: Knights of Honor, Odd Fellows and Ancient Order of United Workman. In politics, he has never taken an active part, and is identified with no particular party, voting for the best man. Mrs. Lindsey is the mother of one boy, Edgar B., born September 5, 1882.

JOHN P. LISENBEY, farmer, P. O. Mt. Vernon, is an old settler of Jefferson County, and therefore is entitled to more than a passing notice. He was born in East Tennessee May 19, 1822, and is a son of William Lisenbey (deceased), a native of Tennessee also. Our subject spent his boyhood days on his father's ferry boat at Walton's Ferry, on the Tennessee River, in Ray County. He came with his parents to this county in 1833, where he has since resided. He served one year in the Mexican war, in Company H, Third Regiment Illinois Volunteer Infantry, and participated in the battles of Cerro Gordo and Vera Cruz. Mr. Lisenbey was married, August 31, 1847, to Miss Frances Hawkins, a daughter of Meredith and Martha Hawkins. This union has been blessed with eight children, six of whom are living—Laura. Huldah M., Idelia, William M., Benjamin and Charles M. One daughter, Clara, died at the age of fourteen years; the other one, Martha J., died at the age of four years. Mr. Lisenbey owns forty acres of valuable land, and is engaged in general farming. He is a member of the Methodist Episcopal Church South.

JOHN W. LOCK, D. D., minister, Mount Vernon. The subject of this sketch is another exemplification of the truth that character does not die; that traits of mind, as well as physique, are handed down for generations, sometimes obscured, sometimes marvelously developed by circumstance. Dr. Lock was born February 12, 1822, in Paris, Bourbon Co., Ky., and is a son of Rev. George Lock. The grandfather of our subject, David Lock, was a native of the North of Ireland; his father, grandfather and great-grandfather were all ministers of the Established Church of England; he was also educated for the ministry, but after his arrival in this country he followed the profession of teaching in Pennsylvania and Kentucky, and finally died in Kaskaskia, Ill. The father was born in Pennsylvania in 1797, but was raised and educated principally in Kentucky. In 1816, he entered the ministry at an early age. The first year of his ministry was spent in the mountains of Tennessee. He afterward removed to Indiana, and was finally elected Presiding Elder of a district that was 200 miles long and 100 miles wide. It extended on both sides of the Wabash, through Illinois and Indiana, with headquarters at Mt. Carmel, Ill. He died in 1834, and his memory is fondly cherished by the people over whom he watched as a tender shepherd for so many years. The mother of our subject, Elizabeth B. McReynolds, was born in 1802, in Virginia, and was a daughter of Robert McReynolds, who was also a native of that State and a farmer by occupation; she was a teacher by profession, and followed it after her marriage; she died at New Albany in 1858. Subject is the only one living of a family of six children. His education was received at the Augusta College, Kentucky, where he fitted himself for the ministry. He commenced to preach in the fall of 1843, at Bainbridge, Ohio. In 1850, he was transferred to the Indiana Conference, and served at Bevay and Rising Sun. Was next appointed President of the Brookville College, and served in that institution four years, and was then appointed the Presiding Elder of that district. In 1860, he was elected to the Chair of Mathematics in the Indiana Asbury University, and filled that position creditably to himself and the institution for twelve years. In 1872, he resigned from the faculty, and was appointed to the pastorate at Jeffersonville, Ind. After two years' service there, however, he was elected President of the McKendree College at Lebanon, Ill. He resigned that capacity after four years of service, and was appointed Presiding Elder of the Lebanon, Ill., district. In 1881, he was transferred to the pastorate of the M. E. Church at Mt. Vernon, where he is still stationed. His life thus far has been a very busy one. In connection with his other ministerial duties, he has served from his conference as delegate to the general conference four times. In connection with the degree of B. A., which he received from his *Alma Mater* at the time of graduation, he also took a post graduate course, and in 1845 was given the degree of M. A., and while professor in Asbury was given the degree of D. D. Dr. Lock was joined in matrimony, in Jacksonville, Ohio, on June 11, 1846, to Miss Matilda Wood. This lady was born in Adams County, Ohio, on April 20, 1827, and is a daughter of Col. Samuel R. Wood (a soldier of the war of 1812 and a native of Kentucky) and Ruth (Shoemaker) Wood, a native of Ohio. Seven children have come to bless this union, of whom three are now living, viz.: George W. (a lawyer in East St. Louis), Bettie L., wife of Mr. Hamilton, of Jerseyville, Ill., and Rev. Edwin, now preaching at Sebetha, Kan. Subject is a member of the A. F. & A. M. and I. O. O. F., and in politics is a Republican.

CHARLES HARDY MAXEY, farmer, P. O. Mt. Vernon, was born in Sumner County, Tenn., July 26, 1805, and is a son of William Maxey, deceased, a pioneer of Sumner County, Tenn., and one of the first settlers of this county. Our subject's grandfather, Jesse Maxey, was a native of Virginia, and a pioneer of Tennessee, where he was at one time scalped, tomahawked and left for dead by the Indians, but recovered and lived several years. Mr. Maxey came with his parents and settled among the Indians and wild animals in this county in 1818. He attended the first school ever taught in Jefferson County. Joel Pace was the teacher, and the house was a log cabin, with a dirt floor, split poles, with pins in them for seats, and a puncheon writing desk fastened on pins in the wall, just beneath a crack in the wall, used for window. Mr. Maxey was married, April 1, 1824, to Sallie Bruce, a daughter of Azariah B. Bruce (deceased). They have had eight children, five of whom they raised to maturity, viz.: Artamissa C. (deceased, leaving four children), Mary E., Martha E., Susan B. and Druscilla J. Our subject owns 136 acres of land, and has always been a farmer. He is a consistent member of the Methodist Episcopal Church South.

SAMUEL T. MAXEY, farmer, P. O. Mt. Vernon. The subject of this sketch was born in Mt. Vernon Township August 29, 1834, on the old Maxey homestead, on Section 6, and is a son of Dr. William M. A. Maxey, of whom we make further mention elsewhere in this work. Our subject was reared on the farm and educated in Mt. Vernon. He worked for six years at the carpenter and builder's trade. He served four years and two months for Uncle Sam during the late war. He was twice a Lieutenant, and twice a Captain, having been promoted for gallantry. He served one year as a private in Capt. R. D. Noleman's Company, First Illinois Cavalry. After that, he was promoted to the Lieutenancy, then to the Captaincy. He participated in the battles of Stone River, siege of Nashville, Franklin, siege and taking of Memphis, Perryville, Ky., and others, twenty-one in all. His brigade was the only one that held its ground all through the battle of Stone River; and in honor of that fact the United States Government placed the cemetery on the spot of ground where this transpired. It would be in keeping here to remark that the Captain also participated in the taking of Island No. 10. After the war, he engaged in farming for two years, when he engaged in the ministry, spending eleven years in the itineracy in the Southern Illinois Conference of the Methodist Episcopal Church. When having failed in health, he again settled on the old homestead. Mr. Maxey was married, January 12, 1855, to Miss Lucinda, daughter of the eminent Dr. Joseph Frost (deceased). She was born in Monroe County, Ill., near Waterloo. Our subject still resides on the old homestead, where he owns 310 acres of valuable land, and is engaged in farming and raising of graded stock. Although the Captain has been often solicited, he has never held a civil office. He is a member of the Odd Fellows society, in good standing, and has been a member of that order since he was twenty-one years old. Mr. Maxey has always been identified on the side of temperance and total abstinence. In politics, he is a stanch Republican.

DR. J. H. MITCHELL, physician, Mt. Vernon. The profession is always below the man. He is not the best lawyer who lives only among the books and dusty documents of his office, nor is he the most successful physician whose knowledge is confined to his drugs and the narrow range of his daily routine. The man makes the profession and the respectability depends upon the manner in which it is used. Dr. Mitchell, the subject of this sketch, is a man who, though most thoroughly qualified in every particular of his calling, does not allow his profession to tyrannize over him. He was born March 15, 1850, in Blairsville, Ind., and is a son of Dr. S. M. and Martha A. (Harrison) Mitchell. The grandfather of our subject, Sion H. Mitchell, was a native of North Carolina, and was a teacher by profession. He came West and died in Raleigh, Ill. The father was born in Tennessee ; received his medical education in the Rush Medical College, Chicago ; has practiced in Corinth and Blairsville, Ind., and at present leads in the latter place a retired life, his practice being carried on by his son Henry C. The mother was a native of Evansville, Ind. Subject is one of six children —John H., Audubon Q., Martha J. Jones, Henry C., George O. and Thomas M. His education was received in Corinth, Ind., and afterward at McKendree College. His professional learning was obtained at the Rush Medical College, from which institution he graduated in 1874. He first located at his home, where he shared his father's practice until 1879, and then came to his present location at Mt. Vernon, Ill., where he has followed his profession ever since. Mr. Mitchell was married April 30, 1874, in Elk Prairie Township, Jefferson County, Ill., to Miss Sarah E. Fitzgerrell—a native of this county, being born here December 9, 1854, and a daughter of James J. and Patsey A. (Martin) Fitzgerrell (whose sketches appear elsewhere in this work). Three children have blessed this union—James M., born February 16, 1875 ; John S. and Thomas J., twins, born August 10, 1877. Mr. and Mrs. Mitchell are both members of the Mt. Vernon Methodist Episcopal Church. Subject is a member of the A. F. & A. M and I. O. M. A. fraternities and of the Iron Hall, Mt. Vernon Lodge, No. 68. In politics, he is a Republican. At present is a member of the Board of Education of the Mt. Vernon Public Schools.

RUFUS A. MORRISON, farmer, P. O. Mt. Vernon, was born in Hardeman County, Tenn., December 20, 1844, and is a son of Adlai S. Morrison (deceased), a native of Wilson County, Tenn. Our subject was reared on the farm and attended the common school. He served three years in the late war in Company A, Sixth Regiment, Tennessee Cavalry. After the close of the war, in 1865, he came to Jefferson County, where he has since resided, and engaged in farming. He was married September 4, 1873, to Mary, daughter of William T. Williams of this township. They have four children—Charles, Walter, Robert and John. Mr. Morrison owns forty acres of land, and resides on the northeast quarter of Section 19.

NORMAN H. MOSS, lawyer, Mt. Vernon, was born in Jefferson County, Ill., March 25, 1856, and is a son of Capt. John R. and Parmelia C. (Allen) Moss, whose history appears in the department devoted to Shiloh Township. His early life was spent on the home farm, and received the benefits of the common schools of the county; besides attended the Agricultural College at Irvington, Ill., and the Southern Illinois Normal University. In 1875, he began teaching school in the county, and continued the same until 1879, when he entered upon the study of law in the office of Crews & Haynes. He was admitted to the bar May 5, 1882, and immediately engaged in the practice of his chosen profession in the office with Mr. Seth F. Crews, and continued with him until January 1, 1883, when he opened his present office. Mr. Moss is a member of the Royal Templars of Temperance and the Iron Hall Lodge ; is Independant in politics, and in 1880 was a delegate to the National Convention for the Greenback party.

CHARLES H. PATTON, lawyer, Mount Vernon, is a native of Hartford County, Conn., born on the 9th of May, 1834. His father, Eliphalet W. Patton, was a native of the same county, born October 5, 1805, and was there reared, educated and married. During his younger life he followed boating on the river, and subsequently engaged in agricultural pursuits. In 1835, he emigrated with his family to Ashtabula County, Ohio, where he remained until 1862, when he came to Illinois and settled in Jefferson County, on a farm in Dodds Township, one and one-half miles south of Mount Vernon, and which he had purchased the year previous. He remained in this county, actively engaged in farming, to the time of his death, which occurred December 5, 1881. He was a member of the Christian Church, a Democrat in politics, and a man who took but little interest in political affairs. His wife, and subject's mother, was Ladora A. Griswold, a native of Burlington, Vt., born February 6, 1814; she is now residing with her son, Frank E. Patton, Deputy County Treasurer, in the city of Mount Vernon. She is the mother of six children, of whom five are now living, viz., Albert W., Arthur W., Adelaide M. (deceased, who married Charles A. Kinney, of Mount Vernon), Byron E., Frank E., and Charles H., our subject, who is the oldest child. He was reared on the farm, and was educated in Ohio, under the preceptorship of Zuinglas C. Graves, now President of the Lebanon, Penn., Female College. At eighteen years of age, he left his home and engaged as a sailor upon the lakes, and followed the same for three years. When he was twenty-one years old, he began teaching school, and by close economy he was enabled to save enough that would defray his expenses while studying law under the preceptorship of Judge L. A. Leonard, of Pierpont, Ohio. He was admitted to the bar March 12, 1862. He came to Jefferson County in 1861, and settled on his father's farm, and the same winter taught school. In 1862, on the arrival of his parents to take charge of the farm, he removed to Mount Vernon, entered into the practice of law in partnership with Judge James M. Pollock, and continued with him until 1865, when he was elected to the office of County Clerk, and served in that position until 1869; he again returned to the practice of his profession. In 1870, he formed a partnership with Judge Thomas S. Casey, and continued with him until 1873. In 1880, he took in as a partner Mr. Albert Watson, a former student, and a young man who promises to become a prominent and worthy member of the bar. Mr. Patton was married, November 17, 1854, to Miss Charlotte Shave, a native of Bere Regis, Dorsetshire, England, who came to America with her parents at the age of eleven years, in 1847. She is the daughter John and Charlotte (Lane) Shave, both deceased. Mr. and Mrs. Patton have the following children: Fred W., Lulu L. (wife of Stephen G. H. Taylor), Lillie W. and Otto Charles. He and wife are members of the Methodist Episcopal Church. He is a member of the bar of the United States, District, Circuit and Supreme Courts, and is a member of the orders K. of H. and A., F. & A. M.

COL. C. W. PAVEY, Collector Internal Revenue, farmer, etc., P. O. Mount Vernon, was born in Highland County, Ohio, November 8, 1835, and is a son of C. T. Pavey, a native of Kentucky. He was a prominent farmer and stock-raiser, and removed to Highland County, Ohio, where he died in 1848. Politically, he was a Whig, and a great admirer of Gen. Harrison, and took an active interest in everything pertaining to the good of the county in which he lived. His father, Isaac Pavey, was also a native of Kentucky, but died a citizen of Ohio; his death was caused from the effects of a fall from his horse, and occurred when he was eighty years of age. The mother of Col. Pavey, our subject, was Lucinda (Taylor) Pavey, and sprang from a branch of the old Zachary Taylor family; she is still living, at the age of eighty-four years, and is the mother of six children, of whom D. D. Pavey, of Sedalia, Mo., and our subject are the only two now living. Col. Pavey spent his early life, until twelve years of age, on his father's farm. He was educated in the common schools, and at Greenfield and Athens, Ohio, and after leaving school engaged in merchandising, which he has followed the greater part of his life. He remained in Ohio until 1859, and then came to Mount Vernon, Ill., where he opened a grocery store, which he carried on successfully until the spring of 1862, when he assisted in raising Company E, of the Eightieth Illinois Volunteer Infantry, of which he was elected Second Lieutenant. He went to Louisville, Ky., with his regiment, and in September was detached to the Fourth United States Battery, and placed in charge of a section. He remained with it until the battle of Perryville, Ky., when it was so decimated and shattered it was ordered to be disbanded, and he ordered to report to Gen. McCook. He soon obtained permission to join his company, and remained with it until its arrival at Murfreesboro, when he was ordered to brigade headquarters for staff duty. He served as Brigade Inspector until the spring of 1863, when the expedition was organized, under the command of Gen. Straight, to go to the rear of Bragg's army. He was placed in command of a battery upon his arrival at Nashville, and participated in the battle of Sand Mountain, or Day's Gap, in Alabama, where he was wounded and left on the field. He was captured by the enemy, and kept in the prisons of Knoxville and others, then sent to Libby, and finally exchanged. He was kept at Libby for twenty-two and one-half months, and with five other officers held as hostages. At one time they were sentenced to death, and were placed in close confinement in a cell under the prison for 105 days, and then sent to the North Carolina Military Penitentiary. He remained there until the outbreak of the prisoners in 1864, when they were removed to Danville, Va. He was charged with being one of the instigators of the outbreak. At Danville he was engaged again in an outbreak, and was placed under a heavy guard and again sent to Richmond, and put in the old cell in close confinement. He stayed there until February, 1865, when they were exchanged, as the parties for whom they were held were not executed. The exchange was brought about by Gens. Oglesby and Logan, of Illinois, and friends of the other parties. Upon his arrival in Washington, President Lincoln did not think him fit for duty, and granted him a leave of absence, and a permit to visit the Northern prisons. After the battle of Nashville, he reported to Gen. Thomas for duty. But Gen. T. not thinking him able for field duty, ordered him to report to Gen. Rosseau for light duty. He remained there until the close of the war, and then came home to Mt. Vernon, and engaged in milling, grain and general merchandise, which he followed until the spring of 1880, when the firm sold out to Stratton, Fergerson & Co. Since then he has been devoting his attention to farming and stock-raising, and owns 380 acres of land in this county. He is an energetic and active business man, and takes great interest in every enterprise for the good of his county, and the Republican party, of which he is an ardent supporter. In August, 1882, he was appointed by President Arthur Collector of Internal Revenue of the Thirteenth District of Illinois, with headquarters at Cairo. He was one of the delegates from the Nineteenth District to the National Republican Convention at Chicago, which nominated Garfield and Arthur. He was a candidate for Congress against R. W. Townsend, but was defeated, owing to the minority of his party. He was appointed by Gov. Cullom Commander of the Third Brigade of the Illinois National Guards, located on and south of the Ohio & Mississippi Railroad, and held the position for four years. His wife, Isabella F., is a daughter of Joel Pace, one of the old settlers of the county. She is the mother of five children, all living, as follows: Eugene M., Lewis G., Neil P., Mabel and Alice. Gen. and Mrs. Pavey are members of the Methodist Episcopal Church.

JOHN C. PIGG, farmer, P. O. Mt. Vernon, was born in Warren County, Tenn., March 26, 1831, and is a son of John Pigg (deceased), a native of Tennessee. Our subject was brought to this county by his Grandfather Smith in 1834, where he has since resided, except six months in Arkansas. He served about three years in the late war, in Company B, One Hundred and Tenth Regiment Illinois Volunteer Infantry. He was on detached duty as teamster from the first, and he was promoted to Wagonmaster after the battle of Bentonville. He was married, March 15, 1849, to Polly M. Newbey, by whom he has had nine children, seven living, four boys and three girls, viz.: Henry, James T., William P., Frances E., Ellen C., Hardy and Mary Belle. Our subject owns eighty acres of land, and resides on Section 17.

A. W. PLUMMER, retired, Mount Vernon, was born December 24, 1826, in Goshen Township, Champaign Co., Ohio, son of Joseph and Eunice (Cummings) Plummer. She was a native of Massachusetts, and he of Vermont. She removed to Ohio with her parents when quite young, and died there. He came to Ohio in early manhood, and died in Mt. Vernon, Ill. They were the parents of six children, of whom five still survive. Our subject early turned his attention to farming, and followed it for many years. In 1866, he came to Jefferson County, Ill., settling on a farm which he yet owns. It contains 120 acres, and is situated two miles south from Mt. Vernon. He was the second owner, the land having been entered during Tyler's administration. About the year 1868, he formed the acquaintance of G. S. Winslow, and he in partnership with that gentleman assisted in the construction of the Southeastern Railroad. After its completion, they became contractors on the Burlington, Cedar Rapids & Northern Railroad. After a five years' sojourn in the Northwest, he returned to his family in Mt. Vernon, Ill., where he yet resides, looking after the interests of his farms. Our subject was married, November 11, 1847, in Ohio, to Miss Maria Flemming, who was born and reared in Clark County, Ohio. Her parents were James and Elizabeth (Bunnell) Flemming. She is the mother of four daughters, viz.: Malvina C., wife of L. E. Legge, of Sedalia, Mo.; Janette, deceased, wife of James Bussell; Olive, wife of James Tyler, and Alice L. In 1864, he enlisted in Company C, One Hundred and Thirty-first Ohio Volunteer Infantry, for the 100-day service; served as color-bearer of the regiment under Col. Armstrong, of Champaign County, Ohio. The regiment joined Gen. Butler at City Point, on James River. Mr. Plummer is a member of A. F. & A. M., Mt. Vernon Lodge, No. 31, and while in Ohio represented his lodge in the Grand Lodge of the State. Since the breaking-out of the war, he has been associated with the Republican party.

HIRAM S. PLUMMER, M. D., Mayor of Mt. Vernon. The spirit of self-help is the root of all genuine growth in the individual, and as exhibited in the lives of many it constitutes the true source of national vigor and strength. The record of Dr. Plummer is such as to entitle him to a prominent place among the self-made and successful men of Illinois. His life is an example of the power of patient purpose, resolute working and steadfast integrity, showing, in language not to be misunderstood, what it is possible to accomplish, and illustrating the efficacy of self-respect and self-reliance in enabling a man to work out for himself an honorable competency and a solid reputation. He is the third child of Joseph and Eunice (Cummings) Plummer, and was born in Marysville, Union Co., Ohio, on the 25th of February, 1831. Joseph Plummer was a native of Rutland County, Vt., born in 1794, and was there reared until he was eighteen years of age, and with his parents then removed to Lower Canada. Here he remained with his parents until he reached his majority, and then moved to Union County, Ohio, where he engaged in farming. In 1871, he came to Mt. Vernon, Ill., and resided with the Doctor until he died, which sad event occurred in 1873. His wife, and mother of our subject, was born in Marietta, Ohio, in 1802, and was married on the 3d of February, 1820; she died in Mechanicsburg, Ohio, in 1865. Hiram S. Plummer spent his early life at home, assisting to till the farm, and receiving the benefit of the common schools. At twenty years of age, he left his home and began the study of medicine under the preceptorship of Dr. Andrew Wilson, of Urbana, Ohio, and remained with him three years, subsequently graduating from the Cincinnati College of Medicine and Surgery with the degree of M. D. He immediately entered upon the practice of his chosen profession, and continued the same until the breaking-out of the late rebellion in 1862. He yielded to the promptings of patriotism, and enlisted as Assistant Surgeon of the One Hundred and Tenth Illinois Regiment. After the battle of Perryville, he was detached to take charge of the wounded, and subsequently, in June, 1863, he was appointed Surgeon in charge of the hospital at Nashville, Tenn., and on the consolidation of his regiment in November of the same year, he was mustered out of the service, but remained in charge of the hospital under contract until the spring of 1864, when he resigned his position, returned to his home in Mt. Vernon, Ill., and resumed his practice, continuing the same until February, 1865, when he again entered the service, this time as Surgeon of the One Hundred and Fifty-second Regiment. In October of the same year, he returned home and has been engaged in his professional work, doing a large and lucrative practice. He was married, in September, 1860, to Miss Martha, a daughter of Harvey T. Pace, one of the old pioneers of the county. Mrs. Plummer is a native of the county, and is the mother of the following seven children: Hollie, Grace, Minnie M., Nanie, Ada R., Leelah and H. Gale. Dr. Plummer is an active worker for the Republican party, and has held several official positions. He is now Mayor of the city, is a member of the order A. F. & A. M., and a member of the Southern Illinois Medical Association.

JUDGE JAMES M. POLLOCK, lawyer, Mt. Vernon, was born in County Down, Ireland, and is a son of William and Mary Ann (Corrough) Pollock. William Pollock was born, reared and educated in Scotland, and during the war of his native country, he with his parents removed to Ireland, and was there married and engaged in farming. He subsequently emigrated to America, locating in Allegheny County, Penn., bringing with him at the time his wife and seven of his children. He died in Pennsylvania. His wife was a native of Ireland and died in Pennsylvania. She was the mother of nine children, of whom six are now living, James M. Pollock, our subject, being the fifth child. He emigrated to America alone at the age of sixteen years, and joined his brother, who resided in Pennsylvania. He spent his early life in farming, as a hired hand, and by his industry and economy he was able to save enough means to receive an education. He entered the Meadville (Penn.) College, and graduated with honor in the class of 1849. Previous to this, and while working on the farm, he had purchased some law books, and so diligently did he study that in 1850 he was admitted to the bar. He then began the practice of his profession, at New Castle, Lawrence County, Penn. In 1852, he was elected State's Attorney for Lawrence County, and served four years. In 1857, on account of his failing health, caused by the close confinement to his profession, he turned his face westward, determined to find a more healthful climate. On the 20th of April, 1857, he came to Mt. Vernon, and finding the climate beneficial to his health, he decided to remain, and immediately began the practice of law. In 1863, he was elected Circuit Judge, and filled that office until 1872. He is now engaged in a large and lucrative law practice in partnership with his sons. He was married in Meadville, Penn., in 1848, to Carolina M. Lyon, a native of Canada, but who was reared in Pennsylvania. She is the mother of three children—William C., James L., and Alice, who died at the age of nine years. Judge Pollock is a member of the I. O. O. F; a Democrat in politics, and with his wife unites with the Presbyterian Church.

GEORGE WILLIAM REID, jeweler, Mt. Vernon, was born in Woburn, Mass., May 19, 1854, and is a son of J. B. and Emma T. (Holden) Reid. The father is a native of Ireland, is a shoe-maker by trade, and is living in Greenville, Ill. The mother of our subject is a native of Massachusetts, and a daughter of William and Catharine Holden. The parents are also natives of that State. To her has been born ten children, nine of whom are now living—William G., Lizzie (wife of a Mr. Dickey), Ward J., Katie (wife of a Mr. Rodgers), John D., Susie, Lilly, Frank and Tina. Subject received his education in Greenville, Ill. In early life, he farmed and clerked, and finally came to Mt. Vernon, where he learned the trade of a machinist, and afterward that of a jeweler under Mr. Morgan. He afterward formed a partnership with his employer, which still exists. In Greenville, on May 19, 1875, he was married to Gertrude A. Schank, who was born in Rochester, N. Y., November 26, 1852, and is a daughter of Lafayette and Delia (Wilson) Schank, also natives of New York. Four children have come to bless this union—Delia E. (born October 14, 1876), Katie W. (born June 28, 1878), John B. (born January 26, 1880), Minnie G. (born December 13, 1881). Mr. and Mrs. Reid are members of the Baptist Church. Subject is a member of the A. O. U. W. In politics, he is a Republican.

JOHN A. ROBINSON, farmer, P. O. Mt. Vernon. Among the enterprising and substantial farmers of Mt. Vernon Township is Mr. Robinson. He is a native of this county, and was born in Spring Garden Township July 18, 1841. His father, John Robinson (deceased), was a pioneer of this county and a native of South Carolina. He was a soldier in the war of 1812, and, in 1815, came to Franklin County, Ill., and helped build the first house in old Frankfort, in that county, and a short time afterward came to this county and settled the old Wescott farm in Shiloh Township, on the Centralia road. He was a blacksmith, and struck the first lick on the forge in Jefferson County. He was a hard-working man, and cleared up several farms. In stature, he was six feet and seven inches. He married Rhoda Sanders, who survives him. She was born in North Carolina; came to Rutherford County, Tenn., when a girl, where she became acquainted with Mr. Robinson; they grew up children together, and married in that county. The old folks had fourteen children, seven boys and seven girls, of whom the subject of this sketch is youngest. But three of them are living—Jemima Malone, of Mt. Vernon; Theresa Phelps, near Creal's Springs, Williamson County, Ill.; and John A. The father died during the cholera plague in 1852, of that dreaded disease. John A. Robinson has been a druggist thirteen years, but had to abandon it on account of failing health. He was married, August 6, 1863, to Susan, daughter of Isaac Dodson, and by her he has had seven children, five living—Edward M., eighteen years old; John S., Lulu, Frankie M., and George N. Mr. Robinson owns eighty acres of valuable land, and is engaged in farming and trading. He is turning his attention to short-horn cattle. He is a member of the Odd Fellows order, and of the M. E. Church. In politics, a Republican. For seven years he superintended the County Infirmary and discharged his duties faithfully.

R. E. RYAN, merchant, Mount Vernon. It is admitted that a poet is *born* not *made*, and of a true painter the same may be said. A strong natural bias or inclination for a special course in life will struggle for development and in most cases with success, and the gentleman whose name heads this sketch is an example of both of these principles. Among the self-made men of Mount Vernon, none deserve a more honorable mention than Mr. Ryan, who was born in Princeton, Ind., July

21, 1852. Our subject is of direct Irish descent, his father, John M. Ryan, having come from Ireland at an early age. The latter is also a merchant by occupation, and is at present engaged in business in Evansville, Ind. Ellen (Little) Ryan, the mother of our subject, was a native of Charleston, S. C., and died in Princeton, Ind., in 1867. Subject is the second of five children, viz., Mary J. (wife of a Mr. Page, of California), Robert E. (our subject), James L., John M. and Margaret. As far as his education goes, it was received in the common schools of his native town. When quite a boy, he commenced life in a woolen mill, and then clerked in a general store. He remained in that town five years, and then went to Evansville, Ind., and clerked three years for Miller Bros., of that place. In the spring of 1878, he came to Mount Vernon, and, in company with George H. Bittrolff, opened a general store. It was a stock of about $1,500, and consisted mainly of dry goods and boots and shoes. Since then, by careful industry and perseverance, the stock has been increased to about $15,000, and the firm now occupy one of the most commodious and handsome store rooms in Mount Vernon. Mr. Ryan, in his business career, has proved himself to be truly a self-made man—one that can rely entirely upon his own ability; and he has made a mark for himself in the business circles of the city. Our subject was joined in matrimony in this city, April 28, 1881, to Christina May Harmon, who was born in Cairo, on May 7, 1859, and is a daughter of John Q. and Mary (McKenzie) Harmon, the father being among the pioneers of Southern Illinois. The mother was a native of Pittsburgh, Penn. Mrs. Ryan is a member of the Episcopal Church of Mount Vernon. Mr. Ryan is a member of the K. of P. and I. O. M. A. fraternities. In politics, he is a Democrat.

JUDGE JOHN R. SATTERFIELD, Justice of the Peace, Mount Vernon, was born in Pendleton County, Ky., September 28, 1809, to Jeremiah and Elizabeth (Breshiers) Satterfield. When he was eighteen months old, he was adopted by Edward Maxey, by whom he was reared. He was brought to Jefferson County, Ill., in October, 1818, and here he received the principal part of his education. He engaged in farming, and continued in that vocation until 1843, when he was elected to the office of Justice of the Peace, which he still continues to hold, having served in it for over forty years. In 1843, he was also elected County Recorder, and served in that office for a number of years. In 1845, he was elected School Superintendent, and held the office one term. In 1842, he served as Deputy Sheriff, and also in 1846 and 1847. In 1850, he was elected Sheriff for two years. In 1850, he was elected County Judge, and held the same position for twenty-three years. In all his official positions, Judge Satterfield did his duty, and won the highest esteem of the people at large. He was married in Jefferson County, Ill., January 30, 1833, to Elizabeth P. Johnson, a native of Tennessee, born in 1815. She came to the county with her parents in May, 1818. She is the mother of nine children, of whom the following are living—Edward V., John N., Prudence (wife of Frank Fry, of Colorado), Martha (wife of Samuel D. Cooper) and Laura. The Judge was in the Black Hawk war for three months, and held the office of Sergeant. Politically, he is a Democrat.

JOSHUA SHORT, farmer, P. O. Mount Vernon, was born in Clinton County, Ill., March 23, 1830, a son of Thomas J. Short, of Clinton County, Ill. He was educated in Jefferson County, and was in the late war, in Company I, Forty-eighth Illinois Volunteer Infantry; he was in the battles of Fort Donelson, Shiloh and several skirmishes, serving nine months. He was married, November 24, 1857, to Abigail Williams, of Ohio, by whom he had one child—Martha Jane. Mrs. Short died July 1, 1862, and was buried in Jefferson County. He was again married, May 26, 1864, to Lucinda Turner, by whom he had eight children, six living, viz., Sarah S., Lena L., John T., George W., Alice I. and Albert A. Mr. Short owns sixty acres of land and is engaged in farming and stock-raising. Politics, Republican.

THOMAS H. SIMONDS, farmer, P. O. Mount Vernon, was born in Rutherford County, Tenn., February 25, 1833, and is a son of Richard Simonds (deceased), a native of Virginia. Our subject attended the subscription schools in the old log schoolhouse, sat on a split pole seat, and wrote on a slab. He came to this county in March, 1852, where he has since resided. On the 1st of February, 1854, he married Sarah Vance, by whom he has had eight children, seven living—John, William, James E., Mary E., Susan E., Robert and Rebecca. Mr. Simonds owns eighty acres of land, and is engaged in general farming on Section 23.

MAJ. W. H. SUMMERS, Mt. Vernon, was born June 22, 1821, in Muhlenburg County, Ky. He is a son of David Summers, a native of North Carolina and a farmer by occupation, who came to Jefferson County in 1828, and died here after a useful career, in which he filled the office of Justice of the Peace for a number of years. His father, William H. Summers, Sr., was also a farmer. The mother of our subject, Mary A. (Cash) Summers, was a native of North Carolina. She is yet living, and was the mother of six children who reached maturity, and of whom Emeline, wife of M. Redmond, and our subject are the only ones now living. The latter was educated in this county. In early life he farmed. He has distinguished himself as a soldier in two wars. He fought in the Mexican war and in our late war, enlisting in the summer of 1861 in the Fortieth Illinois Volunteer Infantry, Company E. He was elected Second Lieutenant, and from that rose rapidly through his merit and bravery to the rank of First Lieutenant, then Captain and finally Major, and as such mustered the regiment out at the close of the war, at Louisville, Ky. Maj. Summers participated in many thrilling scenes and famous battles, among others those of Shiloh, Jackson, Chattanooga, Mission Ridge, the Atlanta campaign, and was with Gen. Sherman in his famous "march to the sea," and while on the route he and his regiment participated in what they called the "side-show at Griswoldville," and afterward in the battle of Bentonville and other minor engagements. At the battle of Shiloh, he was shot in the right leg, and for three months did not know that the bullet was in the leg. It is in there yet, a fit memento of the hardships gone through. He was also wounded at the engagement of Griswoldville. At the battle of Mission Ridge, he was stunned by a shell, which shock impaired his hearing and otherwise injured him. The United States Government has granted him a pension for his faithful and valuable service. After the war, Maj. Summers returned to this county, where he engaged in farming and milling, and at present keeps the "Farmers' House" in Mt. Vernon, where he intends to pass his days. He was joined in matrimony twice. His first wife, Theresa Lisenbey, died in this county. This union was blessed with two children, viz.: Charles F., deceased, and John D., a farmer in Moore's Prairie. His present wife, Loviza J. (Short) Summers, is a native of Tennessee. She is the mother of three children, viz.: Nebraska Van Dyke, William S. and Thomas J. He and his estimable wife are connected with the Methodist Episcopal Church. He has filled the office of Justice of the Peace, and in politics has been identified with the Republican party.

JOHN W. SUMMERS, deceased. Among the worthy and once useful men of this county was Mr. Summers. He was a native of this county and was born in this township July 2, 1825. His father, John Summers, was a native of Scotland, but spent most of his life after coming to this country in Jefferson County, except one year, which time he spent in Texas. He was engaged mostly in the milling business. He owned a saw and flouring mill and carding machine, in partnership with his father. He also made some furniture, and was a kind of general mechanic. He married Wincy J. Hutchison September 22, 1847; she is a daughter of William Hutchison, deceased. This union was blessed with nine children, eight of whom are living, viz.: John W., Linda W., Rufus A., Margaret F., James C., Wincy C., Thomas E. and Bertha L. Mr. Summers was a consistent member of the Methodist Episcopal Church. He died July 14, 1864, loved by all who knew him. Mrs. Summers married William Finley December 30, 1866, and by him had one child, Everard W. Mr. Finley is also dead. The latter was a Presbyterian minister, and a native of Warren County, Ky., born November 30, 1800.

JEREMIAH TAYLOR, banker and farmer, P. O. Mount Vernon, was born in Warren County, Ky., on the 26th of November, 1816. His early life was spent at home, assisting to till the soil of the farm, and receiving such an education as the subscription schools of that period afforded. At seventeen years of age, he began teaching school, following the same during the winter months, and in the summer divided his time in working on the farm and trading in stock, shipping by flatboats to New Orleans. The exposure incident to such a business so impaired his health that in 1842 he was obliged to give up trading and seek other pursuits. He began the study of chemistry and daguerreotyping for the purpose of securing a business that would enable him to travel and thereby regain his health. After six months of laborious study and practice, he became master of the art, and immediately began traveling in the interests of his business, making a tour through the following States: Kentucky, Indiana, Tennessee, Missouri and Illinois, which occupied five years of his life. He is now one of the oldest artists in the United States. On the 13th of June, 1848, he arrived in Mount Vernon, and became one of Jefferson County's permanent settlers. He worked at his trade in the city of Mount Vernon until the following September, and then married and engaged in farming and stock-raising on a farm nine miles south of Mount Vernon. He proved to be a very practical and successful farmer, and by economy and good management he soon acquired sufficient means to start a tanyard, saddlery and shoe shop, which he operated in connection with his farm duties, continuing thus until April, 1867, when he retired and removed to Mount Vernon. Having always been a man of active business qualities, he soon tired of this easy life, and after three months engaged in the mercantile business, taking in as a partner his step-son, Mr. C. D. Ham. This business was continued for five years, and with good success. In 1872, after selling his mercantile interests, he, in company with several other prominent men of the county, organized the Mount Vernon National Bank, and which has occupied a great portion of his time since. He has, however, managed his farm during all this time. In September, 1848, he married Mrs. Frances Ham. He and wife are connected with the M. E. Church; he is a member of the A., F. & A. M. and I. O. O. F., and politically is a Republican.

A. F. TAYLOR, merchant, Mount Vernon. As a worthy example of Western enterprise, no better can be found than he whose name heads this article, a man who, beginning life without wealth or position, with no other help than a determined will and native abilities, has amassed quite a fortune, and has risen to a position of honor among his fellow-townsmen. Mr. Taylor is a native of this State, and was born in Schuyler County, Ill., on November 22, 1832. He is son of Rev. W. H. and Elizabeth (Spohnhimmore) Taylor. The grandfather of our subject was a native of England, and came to this country in an early day and settled in Vermont, where the father was born August 27, 1800. The latter came West in 1818, and settled in what is now Schuyler County, Ill., and became minister of the M. E. Church. In 1847, he came to Jefferson County, where he followed his noble calling until his death, which occurred in this county on April 3, 1872. The mother was a native of Kentucky, and a daughter of Philip Spohnhimmore, a native of Pennsylvania Subject was one of a family of eight children; his education was received mostly in this county. At the age of sixteen, he commenced clerking in Mount Vernon, and remained there until the spring of 1861, when he enlisted in the Fortieth Regiment Illinois Volunteer Infantry. In that regiment he served as Quartermaster for two years, with the rank of First Lieutenant. He was then detached to serve on the staff of Col. Hicks, with the rank of Brigade Adjutant. He afterward served in the same capacity under Gen. Meredith, who commanded the district of Western Kentucky. In that line of duty he served until the close of the war. Among the battles in which he participated was that of Shiloh, Vicksburg, Jackson (Miss.), and many other smaller skirmishes. After the war, our subject returned to Mount Vernon, when he again devoted himself to the mercantile business. He first opened a clothing store, in company with S. H. Watson. At the end of one year the partnership was dissolved, however, and he went into the dry goods trade with J. F. Watson. This firm continued in operation about five years. The firm was then changed to Johnson, Taylor & Co., and at present the business is being transacted under the name of Hudspeth, Taylor & Co. In Mount Vernon, Ill., he was wedded to Miss E. A. Hicks, who was born January 16, 1834, near Edwardsville, Ill. This lady is the daughter of Stephen G. and Eliza R. (Maxey) Hicks, the father being a native of Georgia, the mother of Tennessee. The result of this union has been three children, two of whom are now living—Stephen G., born May 21, 1859; Nellie A., July 16, 1866, and William W. (deceased). Mr. and Mrs. Taylor are both members of the M. E. Church. Subject is a member of the A. F. & A. M. fraternity, and has filled most of the offices of that organization. It is Mr. Taylor's desire to bend all his faculties and abilities to his business, and, in consequence is no office seeker, but as far as his political feelings and principles go, he gives his influence to the Republican party.

S. G. H. TAYLOR, merchant, Mt. Vernon. Among the many successful business men of Mt. Vernon, there are none whose career affords a much better example of what steady perseverance will accomplish than the gentleman of whose life this is a brief sketch. Still a young man, Mr. Taylor has already made himself a mark among the business men of this city. He is a native of the town in which he is doing his duty as a good and true citizen, being born here March 21, 1859. He is a son of Albion F. and Elmira A. (Hicks) Taylor, whose sketches appear elsewhere in this work. Our subject's education was received in the schools of this city, and then took a course in the McKendree College at Lebanon, Ill. After his return from that institution, he clerked in his father's store for a short time, and then in 1881, he having chosen the mercantile profession as his calling for life, he opened a grocery store, where so far he has had a fair share of the patronage of Mt. Vernon and vicinity. In the pleasant little city of Mt. Vernon, on September 8, 1881, he was wedded to Miss Lulu L. Patton, who was born in Ohio and is a daughter of Charles H. and Charlotte (Lake) Patton, the father a native of Ohio, the mother of England. Both Mr. and Mrs. Taylor are members of the Methodist Episcopal Church of this city. He is a member of Marion Lodge, No. 31, A.

F. & A. M., and the I. O. O. F. In politics, he is identified with the Democratic party.

ALLEN C. TANNER, County Clerk, Mt. Vernon. The grandfather of our subject, Allen C. Tanner, a merchant, and connected with many of the best families of Virginia, emigrated to Missouri in 1824, and there engaged in frontier trading. His wife, Martha (Bates) Allen, was of a highly respectable family. Tazewell B. Tanner, subject's father, was born in Danville, Va., November 6, 1821. His education was acquired in the McKendree College, located at Lebanon, Ill., although his home was in St. Louis. After leaving college, he engaged in school teaching, and continued at that avocation during the ensuing four years. He then went to California in search of gold, remaining on the Pacific slope for one year. Upon his return to Illinois, he was elected Clerk of the Circuit Court of Jefferson County, serving two years, at the expiration of which time he resigned his position. He was subsequently elected to the Lower House of the Illinois Legislature, and in the following year conducted the *Jeffersonian* newspaper, a journal intended to educate the people upon the question as to the propriety of donating swamp lands to aid in the construction of railways, a mission which it ultimately accomplished. In the meantime, he studied law with the Hon. William H. Bissell, and later under the supervision of Judge Scates. While conducting the *Jeffersonian*, he was occupied also in practicing law, meeting with much success. At the end of fifteen months, he sold out his interest in the newspaper and devoted himself exclusively to the increasing calls of his profession. In 1862, he was elected a member of the Constitutional Convention, and served prominently and ably with that body until its dissolution. He was while thus engaged Chairman of the Committee of Revision and Adjustment, and while officiating in this capacity elicited the praise and encomiums of all concerned, and was especially complimented for the masterly manner in which bills were revised and adjusted, and redeemed from bareness by the elegant language in which they were expressed. In 1873, he was elected Judge of the Twenty-fourth Judicial District, which position he held to the time of his death, which occurred March 21, 1881. He was always associated with the Democratic party, and was one of its most esteemed supporters. His skill and judgment as a legal practitioner and as an expounder and definer of the law was unimpeachable. He enjoyed the respect and confidence of the entire bar, and was highly commended for the fairness and soundness of his decisions. He was married, May 22, 1851, to Sarah A., daughter of the late Gov. Anderson, of Illinois, whose history appears elsewhere in this volume. Mrs. Tanner was born on the 11th of April, 1831, in Jefferson County, Ill., and is now residing in the city of Mt. Vernon. She is the mother of the following children: Allen C., our subject; Winona, wife of R. A. D. Wilbanks, Mary, Blanche and Neil. Allen C. Tanner, whose name heads this sketch, was born in Jefferson County, Ill., August 4, 1854. He was educated in the Union School of Mt. Vernon, Champaign University of Illinois, and the Christian Brothers' College of St. Louis. At eighteen years of age, immediately after leaving school, he began the study of medicine under the preceptorship of Dr. W. Duff Green, of Mt. Vernon, but at the end of two months was compelled to relinquish his study on account of poor health, and immediately started West to Colorado and spent a considerable time in fishing and hunting, and afterward went North to Minnesota, where he remained thus engaged for the benefit of his health, and in 1874 returned home to Mt. Vernon. He immediately engaged with Circuit Clerk Bogan and remained in his employ until, December 14, 1880, he was appointed County Clerk to fill a vacancy, and was elected to the same office in the fall of 1882, for a term of four years. Mr. Tanner, like his father, is an active worker for the Democratic party. He is an active member of the orders I. O. O. F. and A. O. U. W. He was married, on the 28th of September, 1880, to Miss Mabel W. Pace, who has borne him one-child, Florence.

HON. GEORGE H. VARNELL was born in Georgetown, D. C., February 2, 1833, the second child in a family of ten children of George W. and Mary Ann (Gibson) Varnell. George W. Varnell was a native of Alexandria, Va., born in 1808, and Mary Ann Gibson, born in St. Mary's County, near Leonardstown, Md., in 1813; she died in 1854, leaving her husband and the father of her ten children a citizen of Georgetown, where he now is spending the evening of his green old age, residing in the same house where he has spent the past forty years of his life. In early life, he was a hard-working brick mason, and worked and struggled hard for his large young family. For some years now, he has retired from the active business of life, and is enjoying the fruits of his early labors, and the loving care of his children and friends. The childhood of Hon. George H. Varnell was spent in Georgetown, where he passed through the various phases of infancy, and when old enough did "with shining face trudge unwillingly to school"—to the Benevolent Catholic School—but at the premature age of thirteen years this childhood was cut short, and he found himself launched upon a rather selfish world and forced to enter upon the great struggle for existence—a mere child taking up the cast-down gauntlet, and in steady-eyed confidence entering the lists where every hour for so many thousands of years have gone down in despair and gloom so many and such strong, well-developed men—dashed to pieces upon the rocks of strife warring with their fellow-men. He embarked on his career in life as a mule-driver for a canal boat on the Chesapeake & Ohio Canal, and worked at the same for two years. He then went to Washington, and there spent his first week walking the streets and asking for an apprenticeship at some trade, and at the expiration of the above-named time his ambition was rewarded by being taken as an apprentice to Harvey & Hay, house and sign painters. He was bound to this firm for a term of three years, and faithfully served it out, not losing a day, and even remained one month longer than his allotted time to benefit himself. He then borrowed $25, which enabled him to buy a small stock of brushes, paints, etc., for the purpose of opening a business of his own. He worked in this way diligently for ten years, from the first getting all the work he could do; in fact, very soon began to hire assistants and widen his business, and soon was enabled to take contracts, and rapidly rose to the position of chief workman and contractor in the city, until he secured the work of painting the public buildings, and often had a hundred men in his employ. In this time, his untiring industry was rewarded with a net profit of $75,000, when he closed up his business and turned his face westward and came to Illinois, arriving in Mt. Vernon, his present home, October 20, 1861. On his arrival here he completed his arrangements to study law, and immediately entered the office of Tanner & Casey. He was admitted to the bar subsequently, and after being engaged to defend two cases, and after having painted his own sign, which he never hung up, he became dissatisfied with his profession and gave it up, determined to engage in a more active business that would be more adapted to his ambitious life. He engaged in mercantile pursuits in Mt. Vernon, which he continued for five years, and from its commencement began erecting some of the most substantial buildings—business houses, mills, residences and manufacturing establishments, which now stand as a monument to his memory, showing how much he has done to beautify and improve the city. Among these edifices might be mentioned the large mill of Hobbs & Sons, and the Continental Hotel, which was built at a cost of $30,000. During the war, he also carried on mercantile establishments in Cairo and McLeansboro, and was also engaged in farming and conducted a large tannery. In the twenty years' stay in this county, he has bought several thousand acres of wild land, and, after making all modern improvements, would sell again, and it might be said to his honor that in this way he has undoubtedly done more to improve Jefferson County than any other one man. He now owns 600 acres of land, one of the model farms of the county, which is located within one mile from the limits of Mt. Vernon. At the time when the St. Louis & Southeastern Railroad was talked of intersecting this portion of Southern Illinois, he became one of the most active workers toward the enterprise, and besides using his money freely, he made many enthusiastic speeches at points between St. Louis and Shawneetown, which at once caused the people to wake up to the importance of such an enterprise, and he was successful in his object. He has also been engaged extensively in the lumber and saw-mill business, and during the last ten years he has furnished different Western railroad companies with timbers and ties. During the summer months of 1882, he furnished over 2,000 car-loads of ties and timbers for railroad companies; being well experienced in this line of business, he has made it a financial success. For all he has been engaged so extensively in business, he has found time to serve his people in several different positions of trust. He was Trustee of Mt. Vernon for a number of years, a member of the Board of Supervisors; Superintendent of the County Almshouse, and the manner in which this institution was conducted under his management brought to him great credit; Mayor of the city for four consecutive terms, and, in 1882, was elected to his present office, to the General Assembly. He has been President of different associations, one of which was the Jefferson County Fair Association. He is now an active member of the orders, I. O. O. F., K. of H. and K. & L. of H. He is a liberal contributor to all charitable enterprises, and has donated largely to the building of many of the churches of the county. He was married, on the 18th of November, 1852, to Miss Susan S. Bogan (see history of John S. Bogan). This union has been blessed with eleven children, of whom the following are now living: Mrs. Anna (Frank) Patton, born July 25, 1857; George L., born June 19, 1859; John G., born April 9, 1862; Mary Nellie, born June 7, 1865; Daisy, born March 3, 1874, and Elbert Leo, born December 15, 1877. In politics, he has been a consistent Democrat, yet he has never forfeited the respect nor confidence of even his most earnest political adversaries. His broad and just benevolence and liberal charity have shed their blessings upon his fellow-man, his prudent foresight and active, liberal business transactions have immeasurably benefitted the county, and his whole life work has helped mankind in that great human contest where fate is on one side and fortune on the other. He has won the goal, and the "well done thou faithful servant" is stained with no shadow of a dishonored life, is blistered with no tear of widow or orphan. An inactive or uneventful life may easily drift with the current and attract neither attention nor temptation, and to say of it when it is over that it was steered successfully between Scylla and Charybdis, is but a commonplace that is idle and means but little, but when we look back over a great and active life, one that has stood in the foreground, breasting life's rudest storms and attracting the attention of the most cunning tempter, and yet has never fallen, never faltered, but has gone onward and upward, carrying the feeble, sustaining the weary and faint-hearted, feeding the hungry, clothing the naked, and winning life's chiefest victories.

We have a picture—a biographical sketch, so to speak, worthy the study and contemplation of the youths of the country, where they may read the most valuable lesson of their lives. Such we esteem the story of the Hon. George H. Varnell's life, and we give it to the world, only too briefly, as a most valuable paragraph in the history of Jefferson County.

G. F. M. WARD, clothier and gents' furnisher, Mount Vernon. The successful man is he who chooses his life-work with reference to his native ability and tastes. The men who fail in their calling are not men without ability; often they are men of brilliant genius, but they are they who have turned the current of their life force into a wrong channel. Mr. Ward is a successful business man. His success has followed his work naturally as effect follows cause. His early tastes inclined him toward a mercantile life. He cherished this feeling till it became inwrought in the very fiber of his being, so that when he began active life he had little to decide; the atmosphere of mercantile life has become his native element. Our subject was born in Harrington, Litchfield Co., Conn., on October 11, 1854, and is a son of Henry and Lucy A. (Todd) Ward. The father is a native of Waterbury, Conn., and is a farmer by occupation. In 1858, he came to Illinois, and first settled near Carbondale. He is at present living near Duquoin. The mother was a native of Connecticut, and is still living. To her have been born six children, viz.: Elmira (deceased), Julius H., William D. (both in business in Duquoin, Ill.), George T. M., John N. (deceased), and Samuel (a merchant in Carbondale). The education of our subject was received principally in the schools of Carbondale. When young, he lent an assisting hand on his father's farm. On April 7, 1874, he commenced clerking for M. Goldman, at Carbondale. He remained with this gentleman until May 10, 1875, and then formed a partnership with John Hayden, and put in operation the Carbondale Marble Works. In August, 1875, he, however, sold out his interest in that concern and came to Duquoin, where he clerked for Joseph Solomon, until his arrival in Mount Vernon, on August 1, 1879. In this city he formed a partnership with his employer, and opened a clothing house under the firm name of Ward & Solomon. This firm continued in operation until January 1, 1883, when the firm dissolved by mutual agreement, and since then our subject has carried on the business alone, and at present has in stock one of the most complete assortments of gents' furnishing goods in the city. In Duquoin, Ill., on June 2, 1880, Mr. Ward was married to Miss Sarah E. Pope. This lady was born July 31, 1857, in Franklin County, Ill., and is a daughter of Dr. B. F. Pope, of Duquoin. Two children have blessed this union—Todd P., born February 16, 1881, and Leota, born September 4, 1882. Mrs. Ward is a member of the Christian Church of Duquoin. Mr. Ward is a member of Marion Lodge, No. 13, I. O. O. F., and Jefferson Encampment, No. 91. He at present represents the Third Ward in the Mount Vernon Common Council. In politics, he is a Democrat.

JOEL F. WATSON, capitalist, Mount Vernon, was born in Pendleton County, Ky., on the 26th of March, 1821. His father, John W. Watson, was a native of Maryland, born in 1771. He was removed by his parents to Virginia when a small boy, and was there reared. He studied medicine, and was a graduate of the Jefferson Medical College. He married in Virginia, and, in 1811, removed to Bourbon County, Ky., and soon after to Pendleton County of the same State. After about ten years, he turned his face Westward and came to Illinois, arriving in Mount Vernon in November, 1821. His journey was made overland, with a two-horse wagon, which carried his family and all of his earthly possessions. He settled on a farm known as Mulberry Hill, and the following year (1822) bought land one-half mile north of Mount Vernon, on the Vandalia road, where he remained and managed his farm, in connection with the duties of his profession, until he died, which sad event occurred June 3, 1845. He was the first physician of the county, and his ride extended over a great portion of this part of the State. He often made rides of fifty and one hundred miles, on horseback, in one day. In 1828, he was called on a professional visit to Williamson County, and, from the long ride, his horse became exhausted and died on his arrival at his journey's end, and he was obliged to borrow a horse to get back to his home. He was of Welsh descent, a Democrat politically, and a man of unswerving honesty and integrity. His wife, Frances (Pace) Watson, was born in Virginia in 1785, and died in this county on the 3d of March, 1845. She was the mother of nine children, of whom Joel F. Watson, our subject, is the only surviving child. He was brought to the county by his parents when an infant, and was here reared on his father's farm. His education was limited to the subscription schools of that early day, supplemented by one term in the Mount Vernon Academy. In 1842, he engaged in teaching in the common schools of Franklin County, and, in 1843, was elected to the office of County Clerk of Jefferson County, and held the office for fourteen consecutive years. In 1849, in conjunction with his official duties, he engaged in merchandising in Mount Vernon on a small scale, as his capital at that time was small; he was engaged in this business most of the time until 1876, when he retired from active business. He is the owner of large tracts of land, and, at the present day, is undoubtedly the wealthiest man of the county. He commenced life a poor boy, and now, in the latter years of his life, he is surrounded with those comforts, and enjoys those pleasures that are ever the result of honesty, industry and economy. He was married, on the 2d of January, 1849, to Sarah M. Taylor, a native of Pike County, Ill. She died in March, 1859, leaving four children as the result of their union. Of these, Walter, Howard and Albert are now living, and all enterprising young men. In December, 1860, he married Mrs. Sarah E. Page. He and wife are connected with the Methodist Episcopal Church. He is a member of the order of A., F. & A. M., and a Democrat in politics.

S. H. WATSON, dealer in agricultural implements, Mount Vernon. From one of the oldest families in this county the gentleman whose name heads this sketch is descended. He was born here November 5, 1838, and is a son of John H. and Elizabeth M. (Rankin) Watson. The grandfather of our subject, Dr. John W. Watson, was born in Maryland in 1791, and was removed to Virginia at an early day by his parents; he was educated in that State, then read for a physician, graduated from the Jefferson Medical College, and practiced medicine the rest of his life. About 1803, he married Frances Pace, and to them the father of our subject was born in 1805. In 1811, the grandfather with his family moved to Bourbon County, Ky., but soon after moved to Pendleton County, same State, where the family lived until 1821, when he started to Jefferson County, Ill. His journey was made overland in a two-horse wagon, which contained his family and all of his earthly possessions; they camped out nights, and experienced great fear from the wild animals. Arriving in this county, the Doctor first settled on a farm on what is called the "Mulberry Hill," where he resided one year and then removed to a farm on the Vandalia road, one and one-half miles from Mt. Vernon. Here he resided for a number of years, and, in connection with the management of his farm, he followed his profession. He was the first physician in the county, and was kept very busy, his practice extending over this as well as adjoining counties, and he was obliged to make on horseback a trip of from 50 to 100 miles long. On June 3, 1845, he departed this life, and left an example worthy of imitation by the coming generation. He was of Welsh descent, and was a man of unswerving honesty and integrity. The father of our subject grew up to manhood in this county, receiving his education in the subscription schools. In 1827, he was married to Elizabeth M. Rankin. In his youth, he learned the trade of a carpenter and made that his occupation through life. He served as Justice of the Peace in this county for twenty-four years in succession, and also served one term as County Treasurer. He was an upright member of the M. E. Church, and was one of the pillars of the organization in Mt. Vernon, having been one of the organizers of the church. In politics, he was a Democrat, as his father had been before him. He died September 26, 1860, and was buried by the Masonic fraternity, of which he was a member. The mother of our subject was a native of Tennessee, and to her were born nine children, of whom seven are now living. Our subject was educated partially in Mt. Vernon, and at the age of ten he went to St. Louis, and there clerked until he was eighteen; he then came to Tamaroa, Ill., and there clerked until 1860, and then came to Mt. Vernon. Here he clerked until the summer of 1861, when he enlisted in the Fortieth Illinois Volunteer Infantry, Company G. Entering as private, he served first as Quartermaster Sergeant; then, on April 1, 1862, was elected Second Lieutenant, and was next promoted to First Lieutenant. On January 26, 1863, and while serving in that capacity, he was detailed to act as Aid on the staff of the General commanding. On March 5, 1864, he was promoted to the Captaincy, and afterward was appointed Inspector of the brigade, which position he held until the close of the war. He participated in many thrilling scenes and famous battles, among which were the battles of Shiloh, capture of Vicksburg, Knoxville, Mission Ridge, Jackson (Miss.), Atlanta campaign, and Sherman's march to the sea. After the war, he returned to Mt. Vernon, where he engaged in the drug business for a short time, and then embarked in the clothing business. He followed that for about a year and a half and then went to Ashley, Washington County, where he resided about eleven years. In that place, his principal business was dealing in stock, also running an agricultural implement store. In 1879, he returned to Mt. Vernon, and opened an implement store here. This he still carries on, having on hand besides a full stock of farm machinery, wagons, buggies, pianos and organs. Mr. Watson was married in Mt. Vernon, on October 1, 1860, to Anna A. Goetschius. This lady is a native of Massachusetts, and a daughter of Isaac D. and Elizabeth (Tucker) Goetschius, who were natives of New York. The result of this union was Fred P., born July 22, 1865, and Harry W., born December 16, 1867. Mr. and Mrs. Watson are both members of the M. E. Church. Subject is a member of the A., F. & A. M. fraternity of Mt. Vernon. In politics, he is a Republican, and is at present Chairman of the Republican County Central Committee.

WALTER WATSON, M. D., Mt. Vernon, was born on the 14th of May, 1851, in Mt. Vernon, Ill., and is the oldest of three children born to Joel F. and Sarah M. (Taylor) Watson. He was educated in the High Schools of Mt. Vernon, supplemented by a four years' course in the McKendree College, Lebanon, Ill., graduating from that institution with honors in June, 1872. Returning home, he immediately began reading medicine in the office of Dr. W. Duff Green, of Mt. Vernon, Ill., and in September of the same year entered Ohio Medical College at Cincinnati, and graduated from that institution with the degree of M. D. in March, 1875. At this time he was successful in winning a prize of $50, which was offered for the one most successful in the examination in ophthalmology. After his examination, he entered a competitive examination for the position of resident physician of the Good Samaritan Hospital of Cincinnati. Being successful, he entered upon the practice of his profession in that position and continued the same for one year. In 1876, he was elected to fill the chair of Demonstrator of Anatomy in the college where he graduated. In 1877, on account of the failing health of his father and the importance of being with him to attend to his business, he resigned his position and returned home to Mt. Vernon, where he has since remained engaged in the practice of his profession. During 1877–78, he was practicing in partnership with Dr. Green, but since that time he has practiced by himself. He was married in September, 1880, to Miss Nettie Margaret Johnson, of Champaign, Ill., and a daughter of George W. and Margaret G. (Lawder) Johnson. This union has been blessed with one child, Margaret. Dr. Watson is a Democrat in politics, a member of the A. F. & A. M. and K. of H., and is State Medical Examiner for the latter.

ALBERT WATSON, lawyer, Mt. Vernon, is the youngest of a family of three sons born to Joel F. and Sarah M. (Taylor) Watson, whose history appears elsewhere in this work. He was born in Mt. Vernon, Jefferson Co., Ill., on the 15th of April, 1857. He attended the schools of Mt. Vernon and the McKendree College at Lebanon, Ill., graduating from the latter place with honors in 1876. He then began teaching school and continued the same for two years, when he began reading law under the perceptorship of C. H. Patton, Esq., and passed his examination in July, 1880, receiving his admittance to the bar in September of the same year. Since then he has been engaged in the practice of his chosen profession, in partnership with Mr. C. H. Patton. He was married in Mt. Vernon on the 12th of August, 1880, to Miss Mary E. Way, a native of Washington County, Ill., and a daughter of Newton E. and Lizzie H. (Heaton) Way, both natives of Ohio, the former deceased and the latter resides in Mt. Vernon. They have been blessed with one child, Marena.

T. E. WESTCOTT, dry goods merchant, Mt. Vernon. One of the most prominent dry goods merchants of Mt. Vernon is the gentleman whose name heads this sketch. Mr. Westcott is a native of this county, being born here March 4, 1846, and is a son of James and Telihat (Downer) Westcott. The grandfather of our subject, David Westcott, was a native of New Jersey, and came West when a young man and settled in Ohio. There he married Margaret S. Willis, who was a native of Maryland. To them the father of our subject was born, June 12, 1826. In 1838, the grandparents came to this county, and settled in the south part of it. There the father grew to manhood and married Telitha Downer, who was born August 22, 1827, in Vermont. The result of this union was seven children, four of whom are now living, viz.: Thomas E., Sarah M. (wife of a Mr. Dare), James and George. The father is at present following the trade of a carpenter. In his life he has held many responsible offices, among which are that of Sheriff, Treasurer, Assessor, and Commissioner of Highways. In politics, he has been a life-long Democrat. The common schools of Jefferson County afforded our subject his means of education, and when not in school when a youth he would assist his father in running the old homestead. He commenced life for himself as a clerk in Ashley, and remained in that town twelve years, and finally he came to Mt. Vernon, and in this city he clerked for two years, and then in company with his uncle, W. B. Westcott, he opened a general store. At present, he carries a complete stock of dry goods, groceries, and boots and shoes. In McLeansboro, Ill., Mr. Westcott was wedded to Miss Nannie Shoemaker. This lady was born April 1, 1847, and is a daughter of Joshua and Artimissa (Maulding) Shoemaker. This marriage has resulted in six children, viz.: Freddie L., Bertram E., Robert L., Walter, Clarence and Thomas E. Mrs. Westcott is a member of the Mt. Vernon M. E. Church. Mr. Westcott is a member of the A., F. & A. M. fraternity and in politics is a Democrat.

W. N. WHITE, State's Attorney, Mt. Vernon. It is an encouraging phase of our present age that the prizes of honest work and vigorous energy are open to all, and that the young man may win the highest emoluments equally with the man of long and varied experience. Mr. White, though but a young man, has risen to a high rank in his profession, and sustains a reputation worthy only of the truest ability. He was born on the 17th of October, 1856, near Mt. Vernon, in Jefferson County, Ill. His early life was passed on a farm, but, unlike many whose boyhood is thus spent, he so economized his time and improved his opportunities as to gain a knowledge of a wide range of studies. He began the study of law in 1876, with Green & Carpenter, of Mt. Vernon, and was admitted to the bar in February, 1879, having passed his examination before the Appellate Court. He immediately engaged in the practice of his profession, and has continued the same with marked success. In November, 1880, he was elected to the office of State's Attorney, and is now filling the same office with the approval and satisfaction of all. In Mt. Vernon, May 26, 1881, he married Miss Laura Casey, daughter of Samuel K. and Anna L. Casey, both deceased. Mr. White is an active member of the orders I. O. O. F. and "Iron Hall," and a Democrat in politics.

ROBERT A. D. WILBANKS, Clerk of Appellate Court, Mt. Vernon, was born in Jefferson County, Ill., June 23, 1846. His grandfather, Daniel Wilbanks, was a native of North Carolina, and emigrated from South Carolina to Illinois in about 1820, and settled on Turkey Hill in St. Clair County. Being a practical surveyor, he was employed to survey lands in that county. In 1824, on account of being afflicted with malarial chills in St. Clair County, he removed with his family to Jefferson County, Ill., and settled in Moore's Prairie Township. Our subject's father, R. A. D. Wilbanks, was born in South Carolina in 1805, and was there reared and educated. He came to Illinois with his parents, and while residing in St. Clair County was employed to carry the mail from Belleville to Metropolis, making the trip on horseback. Soon after coming to Jefferson County, he engaged in agricultural pursuits, and after the death of his father purchased most of the home farm, and subsequently became the largest land-owner of the county. In 1828, he married Miss Sarah Ham, who bore him the following children: Thomas J. (deceased), Nancy, widow of Robert E. Yost, she resides in Cairo, Ill.; Judith Ann, who married William K. Parish, and is now the wife of Dr. Venson S. Benson, of McLeansboro; Mary, who married C. C. Campbell, a lawyer, both deceased. He married a second time, Madaline (Arington) Wilbanks, a native of Ballard County, Ky., who died in Benton, Ill., April 13, 1849. This union was blessed with two children—Sarah Illinois, wife of Judge M. C. Crawford, of Jonesboro, Ill., and Robert, our subject. Mr. Wilbanks was an enterprising man, a kind, indulgent father, and his taking away by death July 7, 1847, was mourned by all. He had represented his district in the State Senate, and had held many of the county offices; was a Democrat in politics, though he took no active part.

WILLIAM T. WILLIAMS, Sr., minister and farmer, P. O. Mt. Vernon, was born in Montgomery County, Ky., May 29, 1810, and is a son of John Williams, deceased, a native of Virginia. Our subject was brought up on the farm and attended a subscription school. He came to this county in 1840, where he has since resided. He was married to Mary A. D. Westcott September 10, 1840, and has had four children, three living—John D., School Superintendent of this county; William T., Jr., present County Surveyor of Jefferson County, and Mary A. Morrison. Mr. Williams owns forty-eight acres of land and resides on the southeast quarter of Section 18. He is a minister in the Christian Church, in which capacity he has served for fifty years. He has always been an earnest worker in the Master's cause, and has given thousands of dollars to promote the cause.

ELISHA R. WILLIAMS, brick-mason, Mt. Vernon, was born in Hamilton County, Ill., October 20, 1842, and is a son of Wylie Williams, of Hamilton County, Ill., and a native of Tennessee. Our subject was reared on the farm and attended the common schools. He came to this county in February, 1882. He manufactures brick and also raises a crop each year. He served three years in the late war, in Company A, Eighty-seventh Regiment Illinois Volunteer Infantry, and participated in the battles of Vicksburg, Wilson's Hill, Saline Cross Roads, Pleasant Hill and others. Mr. Williams was married, December 27, 1858, to Mary Daily, by whom he had eight children, seven living—Alice L., Elisha M., Emily R., Mahala D., Celia J., Elnora and Zora Z. Mrs. Williams died June 2, 1879. He again married, September 14, 1880; this time to Margaret J. Gordon, by whom he has had two children, one living, Mary E. He is a member of the Odd Fellows and the United Workmen societies, and the Baptist Church. Mr. Williams' father was a soldier in the Black Hawk war, and helped to drive the Indians out of the northern part of Illinois. He was tomahawked in the right arm during that campaign, not far from Vandalia, and was in the battle of Carlough's Grove, and now draws a pension.

DAVID H. WISE, merchant, Mount Vernon. The gentleman whose name heads this sketch was born September 20, 1846, in Hungary, and is a son of Lefko and Amalia Wise. Both the mother and father are still living in Hungary; the father is a hotel-keeper. To the mother have been born seven children, who are now living. Our subject was educated in the Hungarian language. When thirteen years old, he went to Pesth, the capital of that province, and there remained about five years, where he learned the trade of a tailor. In 1865, he came to the United States, and first settled in Tennessee. In that State he first made his start, carrying his goods on his back, and selling them from house to house. After four years of traveling, he became tired of wandering, and obtained a situation as salesman in Uniontown, Ala., with the firm of Edler Brothers. After a residence of three years in that city, he went to Yazoo City, Miss., where he opened a general store. In 1874, he sold out his stock of goods and went to Europe. After six months sojourning in that country, he returned to the United States, and came direct to Mount Vernon. In this city he opened a clothing store, in which he still engages, now carrying a very fine stock of clothing and gents' furnishing goods. Mr. Wise was joined in matrimony, in Duquoin, in 1876, to Miss Augusta Hammer. This lady was born, in 1860, in Prussia, and is the daughter of Samuel Hammer. She is the mother of three children, viz.: Morris, born December, 1877; Joseph, born January, 1879, and Rosa M., born May, 1881. Our subject is a member of the I. O. O. F. fraternity. In politics, he is a Democrat. The youngest child, Rosa M., was burnt with concentrated lye when one year old, and exactly one year from that day she broke her left arm. Mr. Wise is a member of the Masonic fraternity.

HENRY WLECKE, proprietor of Central Hotel, Mount Vernon, was born June 5, 1837, in Hanover, Germany. His father, Ernst H. Wlecke, was also a native of Hanover, a carpenter by occupation; he died, in 1865, in

Washington County, Ill. His father, Ernst Wlecke, the grandfather of our subject, was born and died in Hanover, where he was a tailor by occupation. The great-grandfather of our subject was a native of Sweden, and came to Germany as a soldier under their beloved leader, Gustavus Adolphus, King of Sweden, who was a Protestant, and came to Germany to assist his brethren against the Catholics in the thirty years' war. Even after his death, at Lutzen, the Swedes stayed in Germany, and many stayed after the war, marrying in that country. Among them was the great-grandfather of our subject. The mother of our subject, Maria H. (Wulff) Wlecke, was a native of Hanover, born April, 1797. She died November 20, 1882, in Washington County, Ill. She was the mother of two children, viz.: Henry and Mary Wlecke. The mother of our subject was a woman who was only known to be loved by all. Our subject was educated in the place of his birth, and, at the age of seventeen, came to the United States with his father. He worked on the farm till 1867, when he kept a saloon in Hoyleton, Washington County, Ill, serving as Constable at the same time. He finally removed to Okawville, where he entered the general merchandising business, and continued it till he came to Mount Vernon, in 1881, where he now keeps the Central Hotel. Our subject was joined in matrimony, January 31, 1861, to Miss Wilmina Rolfing, a native of West Farling, Alswede, by Lubke. She was a resident of St. Louis at the time of her marriage. She was born July 25, 1836, yet living, the mother of nine children, of whom five are now living, viz.: Mary, born August 2, 1863; Caroline, born April 8, 1866; Fred, born January 26, 1868; Anna, September 16, 1869, and Lizzie, born May 18, 1872. Mr. and Mrs. Wlecke are members of the Evangelical Church. Mr. Wlecke has, by dint of hard toil and perseverance, succeeded in gaining enough of this world's goods to make him comfortable, and he enjoys the esteem of all with whom he comes in contact. In politics, he is identified with the Democratic party.

PENDLETON TOWNSHIP.

CHARLES A. BAKER, operator, Belle Rive, was born August 19, 1853, in Bennington, Ill., son of William H. Baker, a native of Boston, Mass., where he was a merchant. He came West about 1852, and engaged in the mercantile business till his death, which occurred in 1858. The mother of our subject was Emily Moore Baker, a native of Ohio. She is yet living, and the wife of John Robinson. She is the mother of five children, viz., Charles A. (our subject), Mary Harvey, Effie Seely, Louella Robinson and Lunetta (deceased). Our subject was educated at Olney, Ill., where he also clerked in a grocery store for three years. In 1872, he went to Madisonville, Ohio, where he learned telegraphy, and secured a position on the Louisville & Nashville Railroad, working at Dahlgren, New Memphis and Belle Rive, where he is now following his occupation, also acting in the capacity of station agent, filling the office with tact and ability. He is an active member of the Masonic fraternity, Belle Rive Lodge, No. 696; also Good Templars. In politics, he is identified with the Republican party. In the spring of 1883, the people honored him by electing him a member of the Board of Trustees of Belle Rive.

AMOS B. BARRETT, farmer, P. O. Belle Rive. This gentleman is another type of our self-made, enterprising men. He came to this county in 1840, with his father, Joshua P. Barrett, who was a native of Illinois. He was a tanner by trade in early life. He died in Mount Vernon in 1852, being retired from active life. His father, Thomas Barrett, was a native of Hagerstown, Md. He was of English descent. The mother of our subject, Priscilla Long, was born in the same neighborhood that her husband was. She died in 1879. She was a daughter of William Long, born August 9, 1756, near Mount Vernon, the old home of George Washington. He died in 1850, in Mount Vernon, Ill., aged ninety-four years; also of English descent. He was a brave soldier in the Revolutionary war. He was one of the first to espouse the cause of the Colonies, and fought through the whole conflict. He participated in many thrilling scenes and battles, among others that of Brandywine and Germantown. He was one of Gen. George Washington's body guard. He was the father of twenty-six children, of whom twenty-two reached maturity. Thirteen with his first wife, Eleanor Ford, and thirteen with his second wife, Elizabeth Thomas, daughter of Capt. John Thomas, of Baltimore, Md., a very noted family, filling then and now some of the most important offices in the State, one of them having been Governor of Maryland. Mrs. Priscilla Barrett was the mother of seven children, who reached maturity, viz., Hiram G. (deceased), Julia A. T., Eliza H., Amos B., Cyrus A., Horace O. (deceased) and Mary E. Our subject was educated at Mount Vernon. In early life he farmed, taught school one year, and after marriage farmed again till 1859, when he again moved to Mount Vernon, where he was appointed Postmaster in 1861, filling the office four years, when he resigned in favor of a crippled Union soldier; after which he went to merchandising till 1877, when he bought a farm of 200 acres near Belle Rive, where he now resides, owning now 260 acres of fine land. He was married, April 11, 1852, to Helen M. Eldridge, born February 22, 1830, in Cincinnati, Ohio, daughter of Charles and Sopronia (Hinman) Eldridge. She is the mother of three children, viz., Martha C., wife of L. C. Thompson: Charles W., he married Nellie B Foster, daughter of Judge J. Foster; Mary J., wife of George W. Meyers, a miller by occupation. Mr. and Mrs. Barrett are religiously connected with the Methodist Episcopal Church. Mr. Barrett is a member of the I. O. O. F. fraternity, Marion Lodge, No. 13. He has filled minor offices, and was elected to the Twenty-ninth General Assembly by the Republican party, filling the office with tact and ability. In politics, he has always been identified with the Republican party, and is the only one living of the six men who organized the Republican party in this county in 1856.

J. W. BROUGHER, farmer, P. O. Opdyke, was born October 17, 1827, in Jennings County, Ind., son of Jacob Brougher, a native of Pennsylvania, a farmer; he died in Indiana, and was well known as an industrious, well-doing man. The mother of our subject, Isabella Foutz, was a native of South Carolina; she was a daughter of Louis and Sarah Foutz, natives of South Carolina, and was the mother of nine children; she died in Indiana. Our subject was educated in Jennings County, in the old-fashioned pioneer subscription schools. He has farmed all his life. In 1859, he came to Jefferson County, and here owns 310 acres of land. He is no office-seeker, and in politics he is identified with the Republican party. His wife, Nancy Hilton, born in Indiana, daughter of James Hilton, is the mother of two children, now living, viz., Alvin L., born September 22, 1860; Jacob C., born July 28, 1864. Mrs. Brougher is a member of the Methodist Church. He believes in no particular church, but believes it right to do to others as he would have them do to him.

RUSSELL BROWN, farmer, P.O. Opdyke, was born June 9, 1824, in Genesee County, N. Y., son of Samuel Brown, a native of Vermont. He was a farmer by occupation. He lived twelve years in this county, but is now living in Fulton County, Ill. His father, Thomas Brown, was a native of New Jersey. His four brothers were soldiers in the Revolutionary war, of whom three were killed—one at the battle of Yorktown. The mother of our subject, Mary E. (Burr) Brown, was born in Steuben County, N. Y. She was the mother of a large family, of whom eight children are now living. Our subject was educated but little in early life. He came to Illinois one year after the Black Hawk war. He lived in Tazewell County till 1851, when he came to Jefferson County, where he has farmed ever since. In the summer of 1861, he enlisted in the Forty-fourth Illinois Regiment Volunteer Infantry, Company I, as private, and after standing guard one night he was promoted to Fourth Sergeant; after a few days was promoted to First Lieutenant; for two years he was Quartermaster. He served three years and two months, being mustered out at Atlanta, Ga. He participated pated in many thrilling scenes and famous battles, viz., Perryville, Ky., Pea Ridge, Ark., Stone River, Chickamauga, Mission Ridge, the Atlanta campaign and others. After the war, he came home and went to farming. He was joined in matrimony, September 22, 1853, to Miss Mary E. Bennett, born August 4, 1836, in this county, daughter of Levi and Nancy (Myett) Bennett, both natives of Tennessee.

They came here in a very early day, and were highly esteemed people. This union was blessed with four children now living, viz., Shelby C., born March 4, 1855; his twin brother, William O., being deceased; Thomas E., born October 12, 1857; Estella C., deceased; Gideon S., born November 18, 1865, and Rodia C., born July 4, 1868. Mrs. Brown is a member of the Methodist Episcopal Church. He has 200 acres of land, and in politics is a Republican. He is an A., F. & A. M., also an I. O. O. F. He has been Township Collector and Supervisor for many years.

JOHN E. CALHOUN, mechanic and railroad engineer, Opdyke. Among the self-made and enterprising men on Long Prairie, we must count him whose name heads this sketch. He was born May 24, 1830, in Chittendon County, Vt. His father, Samuel Calhoun, was a native of Massachusetts, and died at Oplain River, eight miles west of Chicago, supposed to have been murdered, about the year 1833. He was a self-made, energetic man. His father, Samuel Calhoun, Sr., was a native of New England. The mother of our subject, Luthera Farnsworth, a finely educated lady and teacher, was a native of Vermont, yet living near Chicago, and the mother of eight children—of whom our subject is the only one living. Her parents, Josiah and Judith (Lynde) Farnsworth, were wealthy and highly respected people; they were natives of New Hampshire and Connecticut, but died in Vermont. Our subject was educated at Maria Four Corners, Essex Co., N. Y. In early life he clerked and farmed, and then learned the machinist trade at Rutland, Vt. This trade he followed from 1848 to 1873; then left it four years to follow milling, farming and selling goods. In 1878, he sold out, and again followed his trade for two years, after which he followed farming on account of incipient locomotor ataxia. He has dealt largely in real estate for the last twenty years, owning at present nearly 600 acres, having owned at times 1,600 acres of land in different States. Mr. Calhoun was married twice. His first wife, Fannie Peas, died in 1856. His present wife, Ellen (Dow) Calhoun, was born February 23, 1842, in Governeur, N. Y. She is a daughter of John D. and Charlotte (Hawley) Dow, natives of Vermont, and is the mother of four children, viz., John E., Jr., born November 3, 1859; Fannie D., born December 26, 1861; Charlotte L., born October 2, 1863, and Samuel T., born January 4, 1878. Our subject is a member of the Masonic fraternity, being a Royal Arch; is an I. O. O. F.; also a member of the Brotherhood of Locomotive Engineers. In politics, he is a high tariff man, or Henry Clay Whig. While engineering, he has filled the positions of Master Mechanic for years, and the last two years was Locomotive Inspector for the United States Rolling Stock Company.

JESSE M. CATRON, farmer, P. O. Belle Rive, was born May 7, 1860, in this county. We count Mr. Catron among our thrifty young farmers on Long Prairie. He is a son of Jonathan Catron, a native of Pennsylvania. He was a farmer by occupation, and died in Greencastle, near Nashville, Tenn., while a soldier in the late war. He went to the war with the regiment raised in Jefferson County to protect the stars and stripes. He was a gallant soldier and good citizen, participating in many thrilling scenes and battles. The mother of our subject, Martha Moore, was a native of Tennessee; she is yet living, the wife of William Richardson. Our subject was educated in this county. In 1872, he went to Kansas, living there till September, 1880, when he returned to his native county, where he now cultivates his farm of 181 acres. He was joined in matrimony, February 15, 1883, to Miss Mary Ellen Green, born March 2, 1866, in this county. She is a daughter of Wiley and Minerva (Flint) Green. Mrs. Catron is a member of the Baptist Church. Mr. Catron is identified, politically, with the Democratic party.

L. D. DAVENPORT, dealer in lumber and farm implements, Belle Rive, born November 14, 1838, in Indiana, son of Edmund Davenport, of English descent, born in Virginia, where he farmed. He came to Jefferson County in about 1835; he farmed till his death, which occurred in 1848. The mother of our subject, Mary Davis Davenport, a native of Kentucky, died in this county, leaving seven children, viz., Thomas, Sarah J., William, Serena, Edmund, Lorenzo Dow (our subject), Martin, Lydia C. and Eliza; of whom Sarah J., Thomas and Edmund are deceased. Our subject went to school mostly in Jefferson County. In early life he farmed, and then learned the blacksmith trade, which he followed twenty-five years. In 1882, he formed a partnership with William Hunter, and engaged altogether in the lumber and agricultural implement business, having, previous to that time, been engaged in various occupations. He was married twice. His first wife, Mary C. Estes, died October 27, 1873, leaving five children, viz., Minnie E., born January 11, 1863; Nellie T., born December 16, 1866; Mary M., born June 8, 1869; Josie C., born November 2, 1870; Lydia C., born September 29, 1873. His second wife, Louisa S. (Bunnell) Davenport, born March 12, 1851, in Ohio, daughter of Jessie and Julia F. (Stratton) Bunnell. He was married to his second wife December 24, 1874. She is the mother of three children, viz., Jessie, deceased; Otis, born December 26, 1878, and Evaline, born March 11, 1881.

Mr. Davenport is an A., F. & A. M. In politics, he is a Republican.

JOHN ESTES, farmer, P. O. Opdyke, was born May 28, 1826, in Osage County, Mo., son of John Estes, Sr., farmer, a native of Tennessee; he died in Missouri. His father was also called John Estes, and lived to be one hundred and one years old. The mother of our subject, Dicy Jordan, was a native of Tennessee. She died here, and was the mother of ten children, of whom only five are now living. Our subject was reared in this county, being brought here by his mother in 1828, and has been identified with the county most of the time. He was married, in Hamilton County, Ill.—where he also lived four years —to Caroline Irvin, born in Hamilton County, daughter of Runyon and Harriet (Allen) Irvin, and is the mother of five children, viz.: William H., Sarah F., Runyon I., James W., Delbert J. Mr. and Mrs. Estes are members of the Methodist Episcopal Church. He has a farm of eighty acres, and in politics is a Democrat. He is a member of the Opdyke Lodge, A., F. & A. M., No. 368.

JAMES W. ESTES, merchant, Opdyke, This gentleman is a descendant of one of our old settlers. He was born January 7, 1856, in Hamilton County, Ill., son of John Estes, a native of Missouri. The mother of our subject, Caroline Estes, is a native of Illinois, and the mother of five children. Our subject was educated in the common schools of Jefferson County, where he farmed in early life, and in 1874, he, in partnership with his brother, Runyon J., started a general store in Opdyke, continuing in it till 1882, when they started a hardware store. Our subject was joined in matrimony, March 24, 1880, in Opdyke, to Miss Rosie L. Jones, born June 22, 1857, in Indiana. She is a daughter of George D. Jones, deceased, and is the mother of two children, viz., Harry, born January 20, 1881, and Otto, born February 8, 1883. Mr. Estes is identified with the Democratic party in politics.

JUDGE JARED FOSTER, Belle Rive, was born January 25, 1807, in Ontario County, N. Y., son of Jonathan Foster, a native of Massachusetts. He was a farmer, and died in New York. His father, Jonathan Foster, Sr., was of English descent. The mother of our subject, Elizabeth (Wright) Foster, was a native of Massachusetts She died in New York. She was the mother of seven children, of whom two are now living, viz., Riley Foster, of Indianapolis, Ind., and our subject, who was educated in Indiana, studying law with William A. Bullock, attorney at law. At the age of nineteen, he learned and followed the trade of millwright, mostly till he came to Jefferson County in 1861. Here he farmed principally, and yet owns almost four hundred acres of good land. He was a magistrate for many years in Indiana. In 1873, he was elected County Judge in Jefferson County, filling the office with tact and ability for four years. He is now principally retired from active life, and enjoys the quiet of his comfortable country residence, as well as the esteem of all his fellow-men. He has been married four times. His first wife, Polly Branhan, was the mother of two children, now living, viz., Jonathan and Mary E. Marsh. His second wife, Jane Branhan, a sister to his first wife, was the mother of Lucy Cornelius. His third wife, Jane Sweet, was the mother of Eli Leavett. His present wife, Orpha Ann Denison, is a native of Hamilton County, Ohio. She is a daughter of Daniel and Orpha (Sweet) Denison. She is the mother of eight children, living, Denison, Clark and Cornelia W., deceased; Alice Metz, Frank E., Emily Tucker, Nellie V., Barrett and Marcus C. Judge Foster and wife and five children are mem-

D

bers of the Christian Church. He is a Royal Arch Mason and also an I. O. O. F., in high standing in both orders. In politics, he has always been identified with the Republican party. Mr. Daniel Denison was a native of Connecticut, but reared in Vermont, and his wife, Orpha Sweet, was a native of Rhode Island.

GEORGE W. GARRISON, teacher, Belle Rive. We take great pleasure, in writing the history of Jefferson County, to record in the list of young, intelligent men, him whose name heads this sketch. He was born August 4, 1847, in Hamilton County, Ill.; son of Jefferson Garrison, a native of Northwestern Virginia, of Scotch descent. He was a farmer and merchant by occupation, a well-known and prominent man in that country. He came to Hamilton County in 1830, where he died in 1874. The mother of our subject was Francis Drew Garrison, a native of North Carolina, but reared in Indiana. She was of English descent, and the mother of seven children, viz., Mastin E., deceased; Caleb, John, Thomas J., all farmers; George W., our subject; Elizabeth Buck and Sarah McColgan, now resident of the Indian Territory. Our subject was educated in Bloomington and Southern Illinois College, then located at Carbondale. After his school days were over, he commenced to teach school, and devoted all his time to his profession till 1878, when he opened a lumber and general agricultural house in McLeansboro; continued it till the fall of 1880, when he became Principal of the McLeansboro School, with six assistant teachers. In February, 1882, he came to Belle Rive, where he took charge of the schools, and is yet its Principal. Our subject was joined in matrimony, October 2, 1872, in McLeansboro, Ill., to Miss Letha E. Baily, daughter of Gephart and Elizabeth (White) Baily, he a native of Baden, Germany, she a native of Kentucky. Mrs. Letha E. Garrison was born December 26, 1851, in Hamilton County, Ill. She is the mother of one little boy—Chalon, born March 18, 1882. Mr. and Mrs. Garrison are members of the Christian Church. He is a member of the A., F, & A. M., Belle Rive Lodge, No. 696, and also an I. O. O. F., McLeansboro Lodge, No. 191. In politics, he is identified with the Democratic party.

S. F. GRIMES, merchant, Belle Rive, born January 26, 1838, in Gibson County, Ind., son of William H. Grimes, born 1801, a native of Frankfort, Ky. He died February 21, 1863, in Wayne County, Ill. He was a house carpenter by occupation, coming to Wayne County in 1850, and his father, Steven Grimes, was a soldier of the Revolutionary war, the Florida war and the Black Hawk war. He was famous as an Indian fighter, and was scalped and tomahawked, but survived, although he lost his eyesight. He died at a ripe old age near McLeansboro, Ill. The mother of our subject, who was a native of Lexington, Ky., was born 1811; she died 1872, in Wayne County, Ill. She was the mother of eleven children, of whom five are now living, viz., Mary A. Jewell, Martha Millner, Steven F. (our subject), William W. and Robert O. Our subject was educated in different counties in Illinois and Indiana. He farmed in early life; worked at the printer's trade one year; then studied medicine three years, and then, September 15, 1861, he enlisted as private in the Forty-eighth Illinois Volunteer Infantry, Company I; was commissioned as Second Lieutenant, and after the battle of Shiloh was promoted to First Lieutenant; he was wounded, and after his recovery was promoted to Captain of Company A, serving in that capacity till after the battle of Ft. McAllister, where he was wounded a second time; and finally, at Savannah,

Ga., was honorably discharged and returned home. He participated in many thrilling scenes and famous battles, among others, those of Fort Donelson, Shiloh, Vicksburg, Jackson, Miss., Mission Ridge, with Gen. Sherman in his world-famed "march to the sea," and the battles which occurred in that march and after reaching the coast. Our subject has been merchandising ever since the war, keeping a general store in Piatt County, Ill.; at Spring Garden, this county, where he moved in 1866; stayed there till the spring of 1873, when he came to Belle Rive, where he now keeps a general store. He is a man that stands high in the community in which he lives. He is an A., F. & A. M., and also an I. O. O. F. He is no politician, and votes the Republican ticket. Our subject married Miss Laura A. Hoskinson, born January 26, 1847, in Mount Carmel, Ill., daughter of William W. and Emeline (Geddis) Hoskinson, both natives of Ohio. This union was blest with three children, viz., Florence B., born November 26, 1864; Minnie M., born December 2, 1867, and Lora A., born January 26, 1873. Mrs. Laura Grimes is a member of the Methodist Episcopal Church.

S. C. GUTHRIE, druggist, Belle Rive, born May 16, 1858, in Adams County, Ohio. We count him whose name heads this sketch among our most wide-awake and intelligent young business men. He is a son of James Guthrie, a native of Virginia, born 1801, who died here in 1874; he was a shoe-maker by occupation, but followed farming here. The mother of our subject, Sarah Huff, born in 1825 in Ohio, is yet living, and the mother of six children now living, viz., Marion D., John E., Emmerson L., Sebastian C., Frank S., Louella. Our subject received a common school education in this county. At the age of fifteen, he entered R. J. Eaton's drug store, where he clerked about six years, when he took stock in the store and continued the business himself, being the successor of Dr. R. J. Eaton. He keeps the only drug store in Belle Rive. He is Township Clerk, having been elected twice. He was joined in matrimony, February 26, 1880, to Miss Mary A. Grant, born November 7, 1861, in Pendleton Township. She is a daughter of William M. Grant, a native of Illinois, where he was a farmer. Mrs. Mary A. Guthrie is the mother of one little girl—Lela Anna, born June 30, 1881. Mrs. Guthrie is religiously connected with the Methodist Episcopal Church. Mr. Guthrie is a member of the A., F. & A. M. fraternity, Belle Rive Lodge, No. 696. In politics, he is identified with the Democratic party.

ORLANDO M. D. HAM, farmer, P. O. Opdyke, was born July 4, 1840, in Jefferson County, Ill. His father, James Ham, was born 1805, in Kentucky; he died in 1845. He was classed among our best citizens. His father, Moses Ham, was also a native of Kentucky. James Ham followed farming, tanning and merchandising as his occupation. The mother of our subject, Frances T. Crisel, a native of Gallatin County, Ill., was born February 8, 1817. Her parents, Henry and Sally (Truss) Crisel, were natives of North Carolina. Our subject has one brother living—Christopher C., who is connected with the Mount Vernon National Bank. Mr. Ham early turned his attention to farming, and at present owns 160 acres of good land. He was joined in matrimony, February 10, 1862, in this county, to Marinda E. Goodner, who was born June 28, 1838, in Washington County, Ill. She was a daughter of Elijah Goodner, and is the mother of three children, viz., Charles R., born November 22, 1862; Orley T., born January 18, 1868, and Ulah Dove, infant girl, deceased. Mr. and

Mrs. Ham and children are esteemed by the community in which they live. They are members of the Methodist Episcopal Church. Mr. Ham holds the office of Township Collector, and in politics is identified with the Republican party.

THOMAS G. HOLLAND, farmer and stockman, P. O. Belle Rive. This gentleman is one of our old settlers and self-made men, who have made their way up in the world by hard work and perseverance. He was born October 6, 1814, in South Carolina. His father was Hugh Holland, a native of South Carolina, where he farmed. He was a soldier in the war of 1812, with a good record as a brave soldier. He never came home, and was numbered among the missing heroes. The mother of our subject was Priscilla Brown, a native of Richmond, Va. Her father, Austin Brown, was a silversmith by occupation and a native of Scotland. She was married a second time, to J. Bowyear, a shoemaker, who was the father of two children, of whom William Bowyear is now living in Missouri. Our subject only went to the old-fashioned subscription schools of Tennessee about twelve months. He has been with strangers all his early life, having to work on the farm for his living, and for very small wages. He came to Jefferson County, Ill., in the spring of 1837, working for small wages, till he was married, July 23, 1840, to Armilda Goodrich, born June 20, 1820. She is a daughter of Samuel and Calender Goodrich. Mrs. Holland reared ten children, viz., Callie A. Dixon, a widow lady; Mary, wife of I. M. Casey; Priscilla, wife of Thomas J. Smith; John G., who married Hattie Baker; Minnie, wife of J. H. Wheeler, M. D.; Douglas, married Nettie Kirkpatrick; India Viola, wife of C. J. Riddle; Laura, William St. Clair and Thomas G. are deceased. After Mr. Holland got married, he settled on Government land. He was poor in purse, but rich in muscle and perseverance. After raising nine crops, he sold his claim, and then moved to Moore's Prairie, and there bought an improvement and deeded 160 acres of land with a Mexican land warrant, and then commenced to farm and raise stock in earnest, with good success. He has now a good farm of 240 acres in this county, having deeded his son 120 acres of land. He also owns forty acres of timber land in Hamilton County. Mr. Holland has been elected twice as Township Supervisor, and also filled minor offices. Mr. and Mrs. Holland are religiously connected with the Methodist Episcopal Church. In politics, he is a Democrat. He is a stockholder, and at present Vice President of the Mount Vernon National Bank.

W. A. HUGHEY, physician, Belle Rive. Among our medical men in this county we are proud to record him whose name heads this sketch. He was born March 9, 1836, in Crittenden County, Ky., son of John R. Hughey, a native of Virginia, a farmer. He came to this county in 1869, and is yet living here, having reached the ripe old age of seventy years. The mother of our subject is Polly Ann (Crider) Hughey, a native of Kentucky; she is yet living, and the mother of nine children. Our subject is principally self-educated, receiving his primary education in Kentucky. At the age of twenty-one, he commenced to read medicine with his uncle, Dr. C. M. Hughey. After reading two years, he commenced the practice of medicine in Wayne County, Ill. He came to this county in 1857, and has been here most of the time since. He is yet following his profession in Belle Rive. In September, 1861, he enlisted in the Forty-eighth Regiment Illinois Volunteer Infantry, Company F, serving three years and three months. He participated in many thrilling battles, among others that of Ft. Donelson, Jackson, Mission Ridge, Atlanta and others. The Doctor taught one term of school after the war, and then farmed one year and finally took up the medical profession. He was married, in 1859, to Lois Smith, a native of this county, born November, 1840. She is the mother of eight children, viz., Rosa V., Isaac A., Thomas L. M., Sarah B. (deceased), John S., Lenora L., Joanna M. and Benjamin F. Mr. and Mrs. Hughey are religiously connected with the Cumberland Presbyterian Church. He is a Republican.

WILLIAM H. HUNTER, lumber and farm implement dealer, Belle Rive, born June 5, 1846, in Rush County, Ind., son of William Hunter, a native of Pennsylvania, a farmer; he died in 1878 in this county. His father was John Hunter, a native of County Donegal, Ireland. The mother of our subject was Elizabeth Kirk, a native of Maryland, yet living, and the mother of nine children, of whom two are now living, viz.: David S., and William H., our subject, who received a common school education in Tazewell County, Ill., and attended one year at the Vermillion Institute, Ohio. In early life, he farmed till he was seventeen years old, when he enlisted, March 12, 1864, in the Ninety-fourth Illinois Volunteers, Company I; served as a private in that company till June, 1865, when he was transferred to the Thirty-seventh Illinois Volunteer Infantry, Company G, and was promoted Corporal of the Color Guard. He was not discharged till May 30, 1866. He participated in the siege of Fort Morgan, Ala., Franklin Creek, Miss., Spanish Fort, Ala. After he came home, he farmed and taught school. In April, 1881, he came to Belle Rive, where he has been in the lumber and harness businesses, and is now engaged in the lumber and farm implement business, in partnership with L. D. Davenport. Our subject was married, October 5, 1871, to Miss Olive H. Rotramel, born December 29, 1852, daughter of David and Mary (Myres) Rotramel. She is the mother of two children, viz., Harry (deceased) and Fred, born May 7, 1875. Mr. and Mrs. Hunter are members of the Methodist Episcopal Church. He is an A., F. & A. M., also an I. O. O. F., and I. O. G. T. and O. I. H.; has been Assessor of Moore's Prairie Township, and in politics is identified with the Republican party.

WILLIAM A. JONES, merchant, Opdyke. This gentleman represents one of the Jones families who came here when the southwest part of Jefferson County was a wilderness. He was one of that class who helped, by his industry and perseverance, to make out of a wilderness a beautiful and productive country. He was born May 10, 1810, in Virginia, but was reared principally in Indiana. He was a farmer and merchant in Indiana, and in 1858 moved to this county, where he tilled the soil for about fourteen years, breaking up the very soil on which the village of Opdyke now stands, having built the first substantial frame house on this prairie. About ten years ago, he again embarked in the mercantile business, which he now follows. He was joined in matrimony to Sarah Ann Conner, a native of Ohio, but reared in Indiana. She was a daughter of Willoughby and Rachel (Johnson) Conner, and is the mother of ten children, of whom four are now living, viz.: George W. and James W. are twins (they were born July 3, 1836, both are married and mechanics by occupation); Alanson C. (born January 10, 1844, and is married to Martha Foster, a grand-daughter of Judge Foster, and the mother of four children, viz.: Melnotte, born November 18, 1876; Pearl M., born June, 1878; Augusta, born June, 1880, and Royal

H , born 1882); Mary Maria Jones (who is yet living with her parents). The father of our subject, George Jones, was a native of Virginia, a farmer by occupation. He came to Indiana in 1816, and died there in his seventy-fifth year. The mother of our subject, Prudence Keith Jones, was a native of Virginia; she died in Indiana, and was the mother of eight children, seven sons and one daughter. All the boys have been residents of this county. Our subject and wife are members of the Methodist Episcopal Church, of which he is also a local minister. He is an I. O. O. F., and in politics has always been a Democrat. He was a member of the County Board who built the court house. He has been no office-seeker nor politician.

MRS. SARAH J. JONES, Opdyke, was born July 29, 1821. She is a daughter of Jacob Brougher, who was a native of North Carolina, but was reared in Indiana, where he died July 23, 1853. The mother of our subject, Isabella Foutz, was born in 1804, in North Carolina; she died August 23, 1879, in Jennings County, Ind., and was the mother of nine children. Her parents, Lewis and Sarah Dougan, were natives of North Carolina, but reared a large family in Clark County, Ind. Mrs. Sarah J. Jones went to school in Jennings County, Ind. She was married in 1841, in Indiana, to George D. Jones, born May 12, 1821, in Indiana, dying May 14, 1879. He was a son of George and Prudence Jones, of Virginia. George D. Jones, deceased, was a man of considerable intelligence. He was identified with the affairs of the county to a great extent, acting as Justice of the Peace for many years; also was Notary Public, and filling many minor offices. Among the secret societies he was well-known. The A., F. & A. M. fraternity counted him among her active members, as did also the I. O. O. F. Commencing with small means, he accumulated wealth. The family lost in him a true husband and a good father, and the county an exemplary citizen. He was the father of seven children now living, viz., Lewis E., Silas W., Jacob B., Sarah C. (the widow of A. J. Wilkerson), Rosa (wife of James Estes), Isaac N., Clement L V. (born July 25, 1863). Our subject has a farm of 165 acres of good land, left her by her industrious husband. Mrs. Jones is a member of the Methodist Episcopal Church. Her husband was formerly a member of the Methodist Epicopal Church (South). He came here in 1865.

ALONZO JONES, farmer, P. O. Opdyke, was born December 24, 1843, in Jennings County, Ind., son of Jonathan C. Jones, a native of Indiana and a farmer. He died in 1878, in this county, to which he had come in 1858. He was a wide-awake, intelligent farmer, and has set an example worthy of imitation. He was prominently connected with the Methodist Episcopal Church South. In politics, he was Democratic. His father was George W. Jones, a native of Virginia. The mother of our subject, Delilah Keller, was a native of Indiana. She was a daughter of Adam Keller, from New Jersey, of German descent. She is yet living, and the mother of twelve children, of whom our subject is the oldest. He was educated in Indiana and Illinois. He has now a farm of 136 acres, which he keeps in a high state of cultivation. He was married, November 19, 1875, to Miss Ellen Newby, born September 28, 1847, in Jefferson County, Ill. She is a daughter of Hezekiah B. and Nancy (Brown) Newby, he a native of North Carolina and she a native of Tennessee. This union was blessed with two children now living, viz., Curran N., born August 14, 1878, and Rado, born November 1, 1881. Mr. Jones is a member of the I. O. O. F., Moore's Prairie Lodge, No. 397. In politics, he is identified with the Democratic party.

J. D. JONES, merchant, Opdyke, born May 22, 1846, in Jennings County, Ind., son of James K. Jones, a native of Virginia. He was a farmer, principally, and is yet living in Mount Vernon. His father, George Jones, was a native of Virginia. The mother of our subject, Hannah S. (Kellar) Jones, was born in 1819 in Indiana. She died in 1874 in this county. She was of German descent, and the mother of five children now living, viz., Isabelle D. Stonemetz, Mary L. Stratton, Jesse D., Frederick C. and Virginia H. Our subject was educated principally in Mount Vernon. In early life he tilled the soil. In 1878, he engaged in the mercantile business in Opdyke, where he now keeps a general store. Our subject was joined in matrimony, October 24, 1869, to Sarah F. Estes, born May 1, 1854, daughter of John and Caroline (Irvin) Estes. She is the mother of four children, viz., Carrie A., born September 21, 1870; Nellie J., deceased; John K., born November 8, 1875; Jessie R., born October 4, 1877. Mrs. Jones is an active member of the Methodist Episcopal Church. Mr. Jones is a member of the I. O. O. F. fraternity, Moore's Prairie Lodge, No. 397. In politics, he is identified with the Democratic party.

F. C. JONES, farmer, P. O. Opdyke. This gentleman is a member of the Jones family, who settled in this part of the county in an early day, and who have done much for the advancement of education and the general prosperity of the country. He was born March 15, 1848, in Jennings County, Ind., son of James K. and Hannah S. (Keller) Jones. Our subject received his education partly in Indiana, and the rest in Jefferson County, Ill., where he follows farming, owning sixty acres of good land, which he keeps in a high state of cultivation. He was joined in matrimony twice. His first wife, Ella A. Brittin, died, leaving five children— Myrta I., Jesse M., Anna A.; Sophia and Freddie are deceased. His present wife, Mrs. Catharine J. Wood, was born in 1851, in Columbus, Ind. She is a daughter of James McEndree, a farmer by occupation. She is the mother of two children—James and Flora Wood. Mrs. Jones is a member of the United Brethren Church, and Mr. Jones is religiously connected with the Methodist Episcopal Church. In politics, he is identified with the Democratic party.

JESSE LAIRD, farmer, P. O. Belle Rive. This gentleman is one of our self-made and most enterprising and successful men in Jefferson County. He started in life without a dollar and without an education. Yet, eleven years after he started he had accumulated $20,000. He is not known for style, but for solid business qualities. He was born April 7, 1825, in Macon County, N. C., son of David Laird, a native of Virginia. He died in this county, to which he had come in about 1837. He was a farmer. The mother of our subject was Elizabeth (Tumbleson) Laird, a native of North Carolina. She died here. She was the mother of ten children, of whom three are now living—Samuel, of Ottawa, Kan.; Nancy Cofield and Jesse. Our subject went to school only about three months, to the old-fashioned subscription school. He worked on his father's farm till he had reached his majority, when he went to the American bottoms, where he worked for Blair & McLean; finally came to Jefferson County, where he bought hogs and drove them to St. Louis, where he sold them. Getting an insight in the stock business, he devoted his whole attention to it, and amassed quite a fortune. He was the most successful stockman in this county in his day, and to-day owns 280 acres of good land. He is, to a great extent, connected with the railroad history of Jefferson County. Our subject was married June 18, 1856, in this county, to Miss Martha J. Goodmer, born November 18, 1828, near Belleville, St. Clair County, Ill. She is a daughter of Elijah and Mary (Gore) Goodmer. Mrs. Martha Laird is the mother of six children—an infant daughter (deceased; Clara L., born February 23, 1859, wife of Dell Guthrie, of Belle Rive; Samuel T., born July 11, 1861; Sarah A., wife of H. A. Shields; Flora B., born July 23, 1866, she died October 10, 1882; Cora E., born February 9, 1868. Mr. and Mrs. Laird are members of the Methodist Episcopal Church, of which he was once a local preacher for two years.

JACOB METZ, farmer, P. O. Opdyke. This gentleman was born June 19, 1849, in Dayton, Ohio, son of Jacob Metz, Sr., a native of Hessen, Germany, where he was a weaver in silk and satin, and after coming to the United States he followed carpet weaving for about twenty-three years, but for the last twenty-five years has followed farming in Warrick County, Ind. The mother of our subject, Anna Fischbach, was a native of Germany; she died in 1856, in Dayton, Ohio. She was the mother of six children now living—Henry, Belle, Matilda, Julius, Jacob and Emma. Our subject attended school mainly in Indiana; also took a commercial course at Evansville, fitting himself for the mercantile business, of which he followed various branches in Evansville, Ind. In 1874, he came to Belle Rive, Ill., where he was engaged in the lumber and saw mill business till 1878, when he was married and settled down on a farm, where he is considered a practical farmer. September 26, 1877, at the residence of Judge Foster, he was married to Alice Foster, who was born June 9, 1855. She is the mother of two children now living—Harry Foster, born September 22, 1880, and Ruby Nell, born September 24, 1882. Mr. Metz is a member of the Methodist Episcopal Church, and his wife is religiously connected with the Christain Church. He is a strong Prohibitionist, and in politics he is connected with the Republican party.

ED MILLER, physician. This gentleman, who may be counted among our wide-awake physicians, was born August 16, 1847, in Jefferson County, Ill., son of John W. Miller, a native of Ohio, where he was a carpenter. He is now in the furniture business in Belle Rive, and his father, John J. Miller, a farmer and miller by occupation. The mother of our subject, Harriet N. Dodridge Miller, was a native of Ohio, and daughter of Enoch and Elizabeth (Miller) Dodridge. He a native of Virginia, a saddler, and she a native of Ohio, and born 1820, in Lawrence County, and died January 7, 1880. She was the mother of nine children, of whom three are now living —John E., Dr. Merritte S. and Edward, our subject. Dr. Miller received his primary education in his native county He worked on his father's farm till he was eighteen years old; he then worked at the carpenter's trade three years, and then kept a drug store in partnership with his brother, Dr. Merritte Miller, in Mt. Vernon. At the end of two years, they sold out to Ed Shephard, and both went to Kansas, where they remained about two years. In 1871, he returned to Jefferson County, where he read medicine with Dr. Eaton, and the following year entered the College of Physicians and Surgeons at Keokuk, Iowa, graduating in February, 1878, after which he returned to Belle Rive, where he commenced the practice of his noble profession. He is yet following it, enjoying the esteem and confidence of the people. He was joined in matrimony, August 8, 1876, in Opdyke, to Miss Anna J. Barbee, born June 17, 1858, in this county, daughter of William and America (Harshbarger) Barbee. She is the mother of two children—Walter F., deceased, and Lizzie A., born July 24, 1878. Dr. Miller is an active member of the Masonic fraternity, Belle Rive Lodge, No. 696, also a member of the O. I. H. He is identified with the Republican party.

M. V. B. MONTGOMERY, physician, Opdyke. This gentleman is a native of Ohio, being born near Cincinnati March 4, 1837, on the day President Martin Van Buren was inaugurated, and whose initials he bears. His father, Alexander Montgomery, was a native of New Jersey, of Scotch descent; he was a farmer, and died in this county, to which he had come in May, 1869. The mother of our subject, Catharine (Jaggers) Montgomery, was a native of New Jersey. She was also of Scotch descent, and the mother of twelve children; she died in this county. Our subject is the youngest of the twelve children, who are all living and married except one. He was educated in Indiana, and received his medical education in the Ohio Medical College at Cincinnati. Dr. Montgomery followed his profession two years in Indiana, and then in 1863, came to Jefferson County, Ill., settling near Lynchburg, and in 1870 removed to Opdyke, where he now follows his profession, enjoying the esteem of the people. The Doctor was joined in matrimony, April 25, 1861, in Jennings County, Ind., to Miss Serena P. Jones, born January 8, 1840, in Jennings County, daughter of David C. and Susan C. (Prather) Jones, he a native of Virginia, and she a native of Indiana. Mrs. Dr. Montgomery is the mother of two children now living—George W., born May 10, 1866, and Lena L., born March 7, 1869. Dr. Montgomery is an A. F. & A. M., also an I. O. O. F. He owns a fine farm of 160 acres near Opdyke. In politics, he has always been identified with the Democratic party.

W. H. POOLE, merchant, Opdyke, was born May 10, 1842, in Robertson County, Tenn., son of William Poole, a native of that State, a farmer by occupation, who is now living at Mount Vernon. His father, Ephraim Poole, was a miller. The mother of our subject was a descendant of the Chambless family. She was the mother of twelve children, of whom nine boys are now living. Our subject was educated in Montgomery County, Tenn. At the age of twenty-two, he left Montgomery County, and came to Washington County, Ill.; this was in 1866; he ran a grocery store there one year, then sold out and came to Jefferson County, where he ran a wagon shop in Mount Vernon for about twelve years, and then came to Opdyke, where he ran a wagon shop till the fall of 1880, when he engaged in the mercantile business with J. C. Tucker, keeping a general store till July, 1883, when he bought his partner out and continued in the business himself, keeping a large and good stock of goods and doing a cash business. Our subject was married, August 15, 1867, in Mount Vernon, Ill., to Miss Amelia V. Davison, born May 3, 1851, in Jefferson County, Ill., daughter of Hardin Davison, and is the mother of five children—Fannie E., Gertie, Edith, Judson C. and Ida. Mr. and Mrs. Poole are members of the Methodist Episcopal Church. He has always been identified with the Democratic party.

JAMES W. RENTCHLER, merchant, Opdyke, was born October 22, 1856, at Hams Grove, Jefferson County, son of John Rentchler, a native of Pennsylvania. He was a farmer, and died in this county, to which he had come about 1852. His father, Jacob Rentchler, Sr., was a native of Pennsylvania and of German descent. The mother of our subject, Lucy J. (Adams) Rentchler, was a native of Jefferson County. She is a daughter of Dr. W. W. Adams, a native of the South. She is yet living and the mother of eight children—John D., James W., William D., Ella E., Clara A., are from her first husband. Her second husband, W. A. Keller, was the father of Mary, Lulu and Charles. Our subject received his education in Belleville, Ill. In early life he farmed. He afterward worked for his uncles, D. & H. Rentchler, in the manufacture of agricultural implements. He afterward became cashier of the St. Louis Bridge & Tunnel Company. January 1, 1882, he came to Opdyke, where he engaged in the mercantile business, in company with D. D. Smith. He was married December 22, 1880, to Miss Flora D. Kerr, born July 6, 1859, in Edinburgh, Scotland. She is a daughter of John and Jane (McDonald) Kerr. Mr. Rentchler is a member of the Legion of Honor, St. Louis, Mo., "Alpha Council." In politics, he is identified with the Republican party.

W. R. ROSS, physician, Belle Rive. Of the wide-awake physicians in Jefferson County, who are a benefit to the human race, we count him whose name heads this sketch. He was born June 11, 1855, in Jefferson County, Penn., son of James M. Ross, a native of Pennsylvania, an architect by occupation, which he yet follows, though quite aged. He was the builder of the Grand Pacific Hotel, San Francisco, Cal. His father came from Scotland. The mother of our subject, Mary (Herrin) Ross, a native of Pennsylvania, is also living, and the mother of five children—Maggie B. Hopkins; John H., deceased; William R., our subject; Samuel M. and James B. Our subject was educated in Marietta, Ohio; he received his medical education in the College of Physicians and Surgeons and Maryland Women's Hospital, at Baltimore. After he graduated, he came to Wayne County, Ill., settling on Long Prairie; practiced there two and a half years, and then came to Belle Rive, where he now follows his profession. He was joined in matrimony September 13, 1882, in South Bend, Ind., to Miss Jennie M. Thomas, a native of New York State, born February 23, 1861, daughter of Ephraim P. and Saphora (Shepard) Thomas. He is of Welsh descent and a native of New York State, and she also a native of New York State. Mr. and Mrs. Ross are members of the Presbyterian Church. He is a member of the Armstrong County Medical Society. In politics, he is a Republican.

HENRY A. SHIELDS, section boss, Belle Rive. This gentleman was born December 18, 1851, in Pittsburgh, Penn., son of Henry C. Shields, a native of Ireland. He was a soldier the best part of his life while in Ireland, occupying the office of Lieutenant in the same regiment in which his father, Maj. Henry Shields, served all his life, who participated in the Crimea war and also in the Sepoy insurrection in India. Lieut. H. C. Shields came to the United States in about 1851, but was drowned in the Ohio River in 1852, while on his way to Cincinnati. The mother of our subject, Minnie (Shute), a native of Ireland, died in 1879 in Louisville, Ky. She was married a second time to Charles Moore, and was the mother of ten children, of whom six are now living —Charles, Lewis, Walter, Lizzie, Albert, and Emma. Our subject was the only child from the first marriage; he received five weeks' schooling in Louisville, Ky., but by reading has acquired a large fund of useful knowledge. In early life he worked in a tobacco factory in Louisville, Ky. From 1869 to 1873, he worked at railroading, and then entered the regular United States Army, serving till 1878, when he again took to railroading, coming to Belle Rive in 1879. He has charge of a section. He is the Superintendent of the Sunday school. Mr. Shields was married, December 31, 1879, in Belle Rive, to Sarah Alma Laird, daughter of Jesse Laird. She is the mother of Henry L. Shields. Our subject is a member of the A. F. & A. M., and also an I. O. G. T. In politics, he is a Republican.

JACOB STONEMETZ, physician, Opdyke. Among our wide-awake physicians in this county we are proud to record him whose name heads this sketch. He was born May 13, 1825, in Montgomery County, N. Y. His father, John Stonemetz, was a native of New York, born 1796, where he farmed till his death, which occurred October 12, 1865. His father was born in Germany. The mother of our subject, Leah Dingman Stonemetz, was a native of New York, born 1797. She was the mother of nine children, of whom four are now living, viz., Mary Nelson, Eliza Moore, James M. and Jacob. The following are deceased: Philip, John, Hannah Rector, Gitty Freeman and Catharine. Mrs. Leah Stonemetz died August 29, 1861. Our subject was educated in Jefferson County, Ind., and graduated at the Medical College of Ohio at Cincinnati. Having previous to this read medicine with Dr. John H. Reynolds, of Wirt, Ind., Dr. Stonemetz commenced to practice at Azalia, Bartholomew Co., Ind. After one year, he returned to North Vernon, Ind., and vicinity, where he remained ten years, and then, in 1859, emigrated to Moore's Prairie, in Jefferson County, where he yet follows his profession, enjoying the confidence and esteem of his fellow-men. He built the first house in Opdyke, and is, therefore, one of the first settlers in this town. Dr. Stonemetz was joined in matrimony, August 4, 1852, in Jennings County, Ind., to Lucinda J. Wilson, born April 29, 1833, in Jennings County, Ind. She was a daughter of Samuel and Sarah (Chapman) Wilson, he a native of West Virginia and a merchant by occupation, and she was a native of Kentucky. Mrs. Stonemetz was the mother of five children, viz., Alice C., born May 25, 1853, wife of Andrew J. Cook; William E. and Elva M., deceased; Guy Nelson, born March 8, 1863; and Leah M., born February 26, 1868. Dr. and Mrs. Stonemetz are members of the Methodist Episcopal Church. He is an A., F. & A. M., also been an I. O. O. F. for thirty years. In politics, he is identified with the Republican party.

LEWIS CAMPBELL WATERS, Belle Rive, was born May 17, 1850. His father, Moses Waters, a farmer by trade, was born in Wilkes County, N. C., in 1806, from which State he emigrated with his father: Isaac Waters, to Tennessee, where he remained until 1834, the year from which dates his location in Jefferson County, Ill. Soon after his arrival at the last-named place, he was married to Elizabeth Campbell, daughter of Scotch parents, her father, Dougald Campbell, being a descendant of the famous Campbell family of Scotland. This union was the result of six children—Elizabeth, John C., Isaac N., George W., Lewis C. and William D. Waters. Of these, the first two died at the ages of three and five years respectively. The remaining four—except Isaac N., who now resides in Southern Kansas—are at present residents of this county. But few of the early settlers of this county did more to encourage the cause of education in their respective localities than Moses Waters. With him the student was always a welcome guest. He died at his farm residence, half a mile north of the present site of Belle Rive, Ill., February 14, 1875, in the sixty-ninth year of his age, his wife, Elizabeth, having departed this life March 10, 1864. George W., now one of Jefferson County's most experienced teachers divides his time alternately between his profession and farm. W. D. Waters, the youngest of the family, is a man of liberal education, having studied three or four different languages, including the German, which language he speaks with ease and fluency. The last six years of his life have been devoted to the study of medicine, upon the practice of which profession he expects soon to enter. Lewis C. Waters, the true subject of this sketch, is next youngest of the family. His father sent him to the district school until he was nineteen years of age, by which time he had completed the common school branches, including the elements of algebra. During the winter of 1870, he was engaged in the business of teaching, and thus earned sufficient means to defray his expenses at the select school of Prof. John Turrentine, who afterward founded the Enfield High School. Here his time was devoted to the study of the elements of the natural sciences and higher algebra. In 1873, he entered Ewing College, where he spent several terms, teaching at intervals to defray expenses. In the spring of 1876, he entered upon the study of the law with Judge T. B. Stelle, of Hamilton County, as his preceptor. August 30, 1877, he was married to Miss Hettie E. Vance, daughter of the Rev. T. M. Vance, of Franklin County, Ill., the result of which marriage is two daughters—Lottie and Maud, aged respectively four and two years. The year following his marriage, Mr. Waters resided in the village of Belle Rive, continuing his legal studies with the Hon. T. S. Casey, now Presiding Judge, as his preceptor. It was here he first engaged in the practice of his profession. In the fall of 1879, he removed to Benton, Franklin County, this State, where he was engaged in the practice of the law till January, 1883, being admitted to the bar in the spring of 1880. He now resides with his family at Belle Rive, Ill., and is numbered with the bar of his native county. His energies in the future will chiefly be devoted to the study and practice of criminal jurisprudence.

Q. A. WILBANKS, farmer, P. O. Belle Rive. Of the many men in the county who are descendants of the old pioneers, and who have given strength, stamina and prosperity to their immediate neighborhood, we count him whose name heads this sketch. He was born in February, 1825, in St Clair County, Ill. His father, Joseph Wilbanks, a native of South Carolina, he came here about 1825, in company with his father, Daniel Wilbanks, who was a mechanic by occupation. He settled on Moore's Prairie, fourteen miles southeast of Mount Vernon, where he died. Joseph Wilbanks died in South Carolina, where he had gone on account of his health. The mother of our subject, Candace Pickering, is well remembered by many old settlers as one of the noblest women in this county. She was the mother of four children, viz., John, Luke, Quincy A. and Margaret (deceased). Her second husband, S. H. Anderson, was the father of five children, viz., William B. Anderson, our present County Judge; Sarah, the widow of Judge T. B. Tanner; Dewitt C. Anderson; Nebraska, deceased, former wife of R. A. D. Wilbanks, and Edward Anderson, deceased. Our subject was educated in our old-fashioned log house subscription schools, and in early life tilled the soil on his uncle, R. A. D. Wilbanks, Sr.'s farm. After he had attained his majority, he went to the Mexican war with the Third Illinois Regiment, Capt. Hicks, of Company H. After one year's service, he returned to Moore's Prairie, where he engaged in the mercantile business and farming, with splendid success, which is the sure result of honesty, industry and frugality. Since 1873, he has been identified with Belle Rive, then a mere station on the L. & N. Railroad. In January, 1883, he sold out his mercantile interest, and now devotes all his attention to farming, owning 150 acres of good land. He is an I. O. O. F., and in politics is a Democrat. He also served one term as Township Supervisor. He has been married twice. His first wife, Hester Wilkey, died in 1861. She was a daughter of Dr. Wilkey, and was the mother of Eldorado C., deceased; William H., born December 3, 1851, he married Josie Parks, and is now a resident of Texas; Douglas P., deceased; and Sallie N., born July 30, 1856, wife of Dr. R. J. Eaton. His present wife, Mary Riddle, born June 28, 1850, in Hamilton County, Ill., is a daughter of Charles and Harriett (Ivrin) Riddle. Her grandfather, Abraham Irvin, was a native of New York. He came to Illinois about the time it became a State. Mrs. Wilbanks is the mother of three children, viz., Lena, born December 8, 1872; Robert E. J., born February 3, 1875, and Lottie Lee, born July 2, 1879. Mrs. Wilbanks is religiously connected with the Christian Church.

PATRICK WILLIAMSON, farmer, P. O. Belle Rive, was born August 14, 1829, in Wayne County, Ill. His father, Henry Williamson, was born in North Carolina, but died in this county, a true type of our old pioneers. The mother of our subject, Nancy (Nothen) Williamson, was the mother of nine children. Our subject came to this county when quite young. He never enjoyed the advantages of an education and followed farming for a livelihood. He was joined in matrimony to Sarah Ann Dow, a native of Illinois. She is the mother of seven children, viz., David H., Joel, Lewis, Charley, Ella M. and Albert. Mr. Williamson lives on his farm of 240 acres of land. He is no more a young man, and although life's embers are burning low, he yet, with a youthful heart, loves to recall the days of the old pioneers. In political matters, he is connected with the Democratic party.

J. W. WRIGHT, merchant, Belle Rive, born September 20, 1849, in Hamilton County, Ill., son of James H. Wright, a native of Tennessee, an active, energetic man. He came to Hamilton County in an early day, and there was engaged in the mercantile and milling business. He is yet living, in the Black Hills, where he is now mining. The mother of our subject was Elizabeth Webb, a native of Kentucky. She died in April, 1882, near McLeansboro, Hamilton Co., Ill. She was the mother of nine children, of whom six are now living, viz., Thomas B., a large and wealthy business man in McLeansboro, Ill.; James H., of Chicago; Andrew J., a farmer in Hamilton County; Mary E., Arminta Smith, and Joseph W., our subject. Sallie C., Henrietta and Eliza J. are deceased. Our subject was principally educated in McLeansboro, Ill. In early life he clerked for his father in the mill and store. At the age of twenty-two, he embarked in the mercantile business on his own account, keeping a grocery and dry goods store in Belle Rive, to which place he had come in 1873. He is yet engaged in the same business, and is also the principal grain dealer of Jefferson County. He is now Superintendent of Construction of the T. T. & R. G. Railroad, and also General Contractor of timbers on this division. He is identified with the Republican party. He is no office-seeker nor politician. He was married, October 6, 1871, in Hamilton County, Ill., to Miss Artemesia Maulding, born September 7, 1852, in Hamilton County, Ill., daughter of Jarrett and Julia (Hall) Maulding; they were very old settlers. Mrs. Wright is the mother of two children now living, viz., Commodore, born January 1, 1874; Edward, born March 6, 1878. Mr. and Mrs. Wright are both religiously connected with the Methodist Episcopal Church.

SHILOH TOWNSHIP.

TOBIAS K. BUCK, farmer, P. O. Mount Vernon, was born in Blair County, Penn., June 13, 1832, and is a son of Abraham Buck, a native of Juniata County, Penn. Our subject was raised on the farm and educated in the common schools of Ogle County, Ill., where the family removed in 1842. He was married, November 27, 1863, to Maggie M. Miller, a daughter of Otho D. Miller. They have had eight children, seven living—Otho M., Alma E., Walter S., Hattie D., Grace, William and Gaylord W. Mr. Buck came to this county in December, 1877, and now owns eighty acres of land; is engaged in general farming.

CLINTON M. CASEY, farmer, P. O. Mount Vernon, is a son of Thomas M. and Harriet (Maxey) Casey, whose history appears in another part of this work, and was born near his present residence on the 14th of December, 1821. His early life was spent at home, receiving the benefits of the subscription schools of the period, and assisting to till the soil of his father's farm. When he was of age, he engaged in farming on his own account, at which he is still actively engaged. He is the owner of 525 acres of well improved land, upon which he has a good home. In 1864, he responded to the call of his country and enlisted in Company G of the Second Infantry, and served nine months and was in the battle of Wise's Cross Roads. He was married, November 16, 1845, to Miss Artemisia, daughter of Thomas L. and Agnes Harrel. He is a native of Gallatin County, Ill., and she of Kentucky. They died in Missouri, he September 5, 1831, she August 15, 1831. Mr. and Mrs. Casey have three children living, viz., Thomas Alexander, Lucy J. Gaddis and McKendree Ames. Also three sons and three daughters dead, three of whom passed away almost at the same time. Mr. Casey is Republican in politics and has held different offices in the county. For seven years he was Revenue Assessor of this county for the Government.

JAMES H. CLAYBOURN, saw mill, Woodlawn, was born in Rome Township, Jefferson County, Ill., April 27, 1843, and was a son of William D. and Frances A. (Haulker) Claybourn. They were both natives of Tennessee, the father of Knox County, the mother of DeKalb County, where the marriage was solemnized. In 1838 or 1839, they came to Gallatin County, then to this county, where the father still resides and gives his attention to farming. The result of this marriage was eight sons and six daughters, and of this number eleven are now living. The mother died in 1863, and the father was again married, and has since had two children. During his life, our subject has made this county his home most of the time, except for a two years' residence in Franklin County. He was reared on the farm, but has given the most of his attention to other business pursuits. Has been engaged principally in saw and grist milling; is at present engaged in saw-milling, in partnership with J. V. Bruce, at Woodlawn. The mill is fitted with a fifteen-horse-power engine, a sixty-inch saw and a capacity for 6,000 feet per day. The firm also runs a thresher and engine in the summer. Mr. Claybourn was married in Shiloh Township in November, 1865, to Miss Polly A. Yandell. She was born in this county, and a daughter of James Yandell, deceased. The result of this union was one child, Mrs. A. V. I. Lacy. This Mrs. Claybourn died in December, 1866, and in August, 1867, he was again married to Miss H. A. Maxey, a daughter of King Maxey, one of the oldest families in this part of the county. This union resulted in seven children, six of whom are now living, viz., Eva M., Alma B., Nora M., Orley F., Bertie M. and Libby F. May 9, 1861, he enlisted in Company C of the Twenty-second Regiment Ohio Volunteer Infantry, but soon afterward re-enlisted in the First Illinois Cavalry, Company H, under Capt. Noleman, of Centralia. He served one year with this company, when they were mustered out. He again enlisted, this time in the Eightieth Illinois Volunteer Infantry, Company H, and served until July, 1864, when he was wounded, and in September of the same year was transferred to Company C, Eighth Veteran Reserve Corps, with headquarters at Chicago. There he remained on duty until July, 1865, when he was mustered out. In politics, he is a Republican.

WILLIAM COLEMAN, farmer, P. O. Mount Vernon, was born in Delaware County, Ohio, September 15, 1844. Is the son of Valentine and Mary (Worline) Coleman. He was born in Pennsylvania, she in Ohio. He is still living and resides in this county. To them six children were born, three of whom still survive, viz., Mrs. Elizabeth Shultz and Mrs. Isabelle Strattan, both of Marion County, Ohio, and our subject. In 1855, our subject was brought to Stark County, Ill., and two years later to this county, where his father settled on the present farm, which contains 123 acres, our subject having charge of the same. He was reared on a farm and such has been his occupation during life. December 9, 1869, he was married to Miss Maria Pettit, daughter of Windsor and Nancy (Burger) Pettit. Mr. and Mrs. Coleman have two children living and one dead, viz., Luetta, Effie, and Estella (deceased). In politics, Mr. Coleman is Republican, but in local elections votes for the man.

JAMES R. DRIVER, farmer, P. O. Woodlawn, was born in Wilson County, Tenn., February 21, 1831, to John and Mary (Campbell) Driver. He was a native of North Carolina and she of Virginia; they emigrated from Tennessee to Jefferson County, Ill., in 1841. He, born in 1809, died in 1863; she, born in 1809, died in September, 1852. They were the parents of ten children, four of whom are now living. Our subject was brought to the county by his parents in 1841, and since that time has principally resided in the county. He commenced his career in life in the saw mill business, and continued the same for twenty-seven years, operating mills in Jefferson, Christian, Alexander and Union Counties during different periods. In 1878, he began farming, at which he is actively engaged, and is the owner of 335 acres of good land. In response to the call of the country for volunteers of the late civil war in 1861, he enlisted on the 10th of December, in Company C of the Sixtieth Illinois Volunteer Infantry, under Col. Toler and Capt. Moss. In September, he was discharged on account of physical disability, having been injured in the back. In August, 1852, he was married to Miss Matilda C. Allen, who died in February, 1858, leaving four children, of whom John M. is still living. He was married a second time, October 10, 1860, to Mrs. Evaline Pate, widow of Lewis Pate, and a daughter of John Roberts. Mr. Driver is a wide-awake, public-spirited citizen, a Republican in politics and has served as Justice of the Peace for sixteen years. He and wife are members of the Baptist Church. Mr. Driver's son was born February 10, 1857, was educated for the ministry, and for five years has been thus engaged, now being pastor of a Methodist Episcopal Church of Boston.

JOHN L. FERGERSON, farmer, P. O. Mount Vernon, was born in Sumner County, Tenn., June 23, 1844, and is a son of James E. and Anna (Ventress) Fergerson. The father was born in this county, but when a small boy he went to Tennessee, where he remained until 1851, when he again returned to this county, where he has since given his attention to farming and the mercantile profession. He is at present engaged in business in Mount Vernon. The mother was born in Tennessee and died there prior to her husband's removal to this county. Our subject received his education principally in the schools of this county, and has since that time given his attention to farming. He now owns 160 acres, most of which is under cultivation. It is the same farm that was settled by Rev. Rhodam Allen. Mr. Fergerson was married, March 29, 1869, to Miss Rose Moss, a daughter of Thomas L. Moss. The result of this union was five children—Lena, Charles, Minnie, Homer and Flora. Mr. and Mrs. Fergerson are both members of the Methodist Episcopal Church. In politics, he is a Republican.

S. B. GILBERT, farmer, P. O. Woodlawn, was born in this county, February 25, 1841, and was a son of Eli and Lucy (Fairchild) Gilbert. The father was born March 2, 1809, in Waterbury, Vt., the mother June 10, 1805, in Preston, Mass. The twain came to this county in 1839, where they lived until their death, which occurred January 20, 1878, both dying on the same day. The father was a farmer by occupation, and to them were born five sons and two daughters, and of that number five are now living. Our subject has made this county his residence all his life. His education was of the common school character, and since then he has been engaged in farming, now having a farm of 100 acres. He also deals in stock. In the spring of 1865, he entered the service, enlisting in the Forty-ninth Regular Infantry, Col. Moore, Company G. Our subject was stationed at Paducah, Ky., where he remained until the close of the war. Mr. Gilbert was married in 1862, to Mary A. Rightnowar, a native of this county, and a daughter of Henry Rightnowar, one of the leading farmers of this county. The result of this marriage has been ten children, nine of whom are now living—James H., David P., Mary E., Martha A., Hiram E., Robert H., Lucy M., Lavina J., Ida E. and William I. Samuel B. is the one deceased. Our subject is a member of the A. F. & A. M. of Mount Vernon, No. 31, and has acted as representative of this organization to the Grand Lodge. In politics, he is a Democrat; has served his county and township in numerous offices, among which are Justice of the Peace, Constable, Supervisor and Assessor.

C. B. HARPER, farmer, P. O. Mount Vernon, was born in Wilson County, Tenn., May 11, 1821. He is the son of John and Elizabeth (Bracket) Harper. They were from Virginia and Tennessee, moving there after their marriage. In 1831, they moved to Illinois and settled on the farm now owned by our subject. He was born December 25, 1773, and died December 11, 1875, being nearly one hundred and two years of age. She died some years before at the age of about eighty years. Both retained perfect health and their mental faculties till their final sickness. They were the parents of three children, our subject being the youngest, and only one now living. Our subject was reared in this county, and in the pioneer style, his father, having settled on an improved farm, and entering Government land. Our subject in early life attended school in the rude schoolhouses of the day, and when embarking in life for himself, he chose the same occupation as his father—that of farming—and has continued in the same business all his life on his present farm, which contains 140 acres, and is in a high state of cultivation, with good farm buildings. He was married in this county, October 22, 1843, to Miss Matilda Bateman. She was born here October 21, 1823, daughter of Asahel and Millie Bateman. They were both of Tennessee, coming here at an early date—1819 —her mother being a daughter of Rev. Lewis Johnson. Mr. Bateman died about 1848, and his widow January, 1883, at over eighty-six years of age. Mr. and Mrs. Harper have five children, living, viz., Isabelle, Mary J., Thomas B., Mattie and C. M. He and wife are members of the Methodist Episcopal Church. In politics, he is a Republican.

HENRY J. HOLTSCLAW, farmer, P. O. Mount Vernon, was born in Barren County, Ky., June 27, 1815, and is a son of James and Rhoda (Brooksher) Holtsclaw, the latter a native of South Carolina and the former of North Carolina, and his father, Henry Holtsclaw, was a genuine Pennsylvania Dutchman, who emigrated to North Carolina and thence to Kentucky. In 1827, both he and his son (father of our subject) came to Illinois and settled in this township, where both died, the latter in 1831 or 1832, and his wife about the year 1860. They were the parents of ten children, only three of whom are living—Mrs. Margaret Booth, near Centralia, Ill.; Richard J., residing in Xenia, Clay County; and our subject. Mr. Holtsclaw was left to battle for himself at an early age, his father dying soon after his removal to Illinois, and leaving his wife with a large family of children. He had but few chances for receiving an education, as he says it was "root little pig or die." But by the most persevering industry he won his way in the world, and after helping his mother to rear the younger children, he commenced to work for himself. He owns the old homestead, upon which the third generation of the family now lives. It embraces 360 acres of land, well improved and in a fine state of cultivation. Indeed, it is one of the finest farms in the county, and probably the finest barn in the county is on it. Mr. Holtsclaw's Pennsylvania Dutch blood shows in this, as it is a maxim with them, that "a good barn will soon pay for a residence, but a fine residence will not pay for a barn." He was married, in 1859, to Miss Elizabeth Johnson, a daughter of Rev. Lewis Johnson, an early pioneer of Jefferson County. They have four children—Martha Ann, Thomas Jefferson, John Henry and Ida A., all of whom are living. He and his wife are members of the Baptist Church. Mr. Holtsclaw has never sought office, but takes an active interest in politics, as all patriotic citizens should, and is a Democrat of the Jackson school. He has a great veneration for that old hero of New Orleans, under whom his father served as a soldier. Mr. Holtsclaw came here a small boy, when the country was new and wild, and game of all kinds was plenty. He is an old man now, and has seen the country improved and civilized and the wilderness made to rejoice and blossom as the rose. For more than fifty years he has lived upon one place, and by his own hard work has gathered plenty around him, and now in his old age he is prepared to live at his ease.

THOMAS C. JOHNSON, farmer, P. O. Mount Vernon, was born in Jefferson County, Ill., June 14, 1827, and is the son of James Johnson, Sr. (deceased), who came with the Maxeys and Caseys from Tennessee in 1818, and was a native of Virginia. His wife was Clarissa Maxey. They were the parents of fifteen children, six of whom are now living. Our subject was educated in the early schools of this county, and assisted in developing the resources of the country. January 14, 1847, he was married to Miss Sarah J. Frost, daughter of Dr. Joseph Frost. Mr. and Mrs. Johnson have eight children, seven of whom still survive, viz., Mary E., Eliza C., Laura A., John S., Alice A., Lucy J., Sarah E. and Joseph M. (deceased). Mr. Johnson's farm contains ninety acres of well improved land, good farm buildings, etc. He and family are members of the Methodist Episcopal Church; in politics, he is a Democrat.

JEHU G. D. MAXEY, farmer, P. O. Mount Vernon, the youngest son of William Maxey (deceased), was born in Sumner County, Tenn., March 16, 1814, and came to this county with his parents in May, 1818, where he has since resided. Fifty-two years of this time he has spent on the farm he now occupies, which is on the southeast quarter of Section 12. He attended a subscription school, the first in Jefferson County, in a log cabin, dirt floor, clapboard roof, with a log left out and with nothing in the opening for a window. He was married, January 12, 1832, to Mary A. Bruce, a daughter of Azariah B. and Martha Bruce. They had but one child—James Henry—(deceased). Mr. Maxey owns 154 acres of land, and is engaged in farming and stock-raising. He is a worthy Methodist, of which church he has been a member since a boy, and has been a licensed exhorter in the church since 1841. He has been President of the Pioneer Association of Jefferson County for the past twelve years. Mr. Maxey spent much of his time for twenty years in hunting. Has shot many a deer standing in his saddle; shot deer running and his horse running also at full speed.

THOMAS L. MOSS, farmer, P. O. Mount Vernon. Among the more active, upright and highly respected citizens of Shiloh Precinct who have, by their honesty, industry and indomitable energy, carved out a successful career, is Mr. Thomas L. Moss, whose name heads this sketch. He was born in Jefferson County, Ill., on the 30th of November, 1823. His early life was spent on the farm, experiencing all of a pioneer's life and receiving such an education as the log schoolhouses of the period afforded. Arriving at his majority, he embarked on his career in life as a farmer upon his own account, with a farm of forty acres of unimproved land. He still resides on the same farm, but by hard work and close economy, he has been able to make the necessary improvements and to add to it until now he owns 1,000 acres of well improved land, upon which he has a large and commodious residence, which was erected from his own designs. He was married in this county, September 27, 1842, to Miss Sarah Brock, a native of Missouri, born June 7, 1824. Her parents, Tarlton F. and Susan (Antrobus) Brock, were natives of Virginia and early settlers of Missouri. She is the mother of the following children: Thaddeus C., Mahala A., Rose, Lafayette B., Walter D., Ella and Elsah, all of whom are married except the youngest child, and are all residents of Jefferson County except Thaddeus C., who resides in Missouri. Since their marriage, Mr. and Mrs. Moss have been leading members of the Methodist Episcopal Church; in politics, his sympathies are in accord with the views of the Republican party, and he has held numerous offices of the county. Ransom Moss, his father, was a native of Virginia, where he was raised and educated, and where, when a young man, he removed to Tennessee, where he was married. He emigrated to Illinois and settled in Jefferson County in 1819, and here engaged actively in farming to the time of his death, which occurred on the 2d of August, 1835. His first wife was Charlotte Clark, who bore him two children, a son now residing in Ashley, Ill., and a daughter, who married Hon. Washington Ewing, a native of Rensselaer County, Ky. He married for his second wife Anna Johnson (subject's mother), a daughter of Rev. Lewis Johnson, an early settler of the county, who came in 1819. This union was blessed with eight children, of whom four are now living. Mrs. Moss is still living, and is the widow of James Latham, by whom she had one child, S. D. Latham, a resident of Mount Vernon.

HON. JOHN R. MOSS, farmer and breeder of thoroughbred stock, P. O. Mount Vernon, was born May 13, 1830, in Jefferson County, son of Ransom Moss (deceased). (See sketch of Thomas L. Moss.) Our subject was educated in this county, and has made farming and stock-raising his occupation. His farm contains 250 acres of land, and his homestead is that which was first settled by ex-Gov. Zadok Casey, and is known as the Redbud Hill Stock Farm. In 1879, Mr. Moss imported the first sheep ever brought to this county, at that time bringing them from Canada—four ewes and one buck of the Cotswold breed. He now is engaged in raising thoroughbred short-horn and Jersey cattle, Berkshire swine and Cotswold sheep. His son, Angus Moss, is also a breeder of thoroughbred cattle, having one of the finest herds of short-horn cattle in Southern Illinois. January 30, 1853, Mr. Moss was united in marriage with Miss Parmelia C. Allen, daughter of Rev. George W. Allen (deceased), and grand-daughter of Rev. Rhodam Allen. This union has been blessed with six children, viz., Angus, Hannah H., Adda M., Anna E., Harry C. and Grace S. October 10, 1861, Mr. Moss enlisted in the service of his country in Company C, Sixtieth Illinois Infantry, and was made Captain of the company. On account of physical disability, he was discharged in 1863, and was appointed Deputy Provost Marshal for the Eleventh District, and in this capacity served till the close of the war. Capt. Moss served in the Thirty-first General Assembly of the Illinois Legislature, having been elected by the Independents, in 1878, but when necessary co-operated with the Republicans, to which party he belongs, and has taken an active part in furthering the interests of the Republican party in this district. He is a

Royal Templar of Temperance and a strong Prohibitionist, and a prominent member of the Methodist Episcopal Church.

J. H. PAYNE, merchant, Woodlawn, is a native of Jefferson County Ill., born October 27, 1837, to Joseph and Harriet (Stanford) Payne, both natives of Tennessee, who emigrated from Smith County to Illinois, locating in Jefferson County in 1835, where they engaged in farming till the time of their death. They were the parents of seven children, of whom three are now living, viz., J. H., Essex and J. T. Our subject spent his early life at home, assisting to till the soil of his father's farm, and during the winter months attending the common schools. Arriving at his majority, he embarked upon his career in life as a farmer, and continued the same uninterruptedly until 1874, when he engaged in the mercantile business, at which he is at present engaged, doing a large and thriving trade at the town of Woodlawn, and where he and his partner, Mr. Sharp, buy the most of the grain and general produce of the surrounding country. He was married, on the 2d of November, 1862, to Miss Mary Webb, a native of the county and a daughter of Bennett Webb, a prominent farmer of the county. Mr. and Mrs. Payne are members, he of the Methodist Episcopal Church (South), and she of the Baptist Church. In politics, he is a Democrat. Like his partner, Mr. Payne is a self-made man, who depends upon his own resources for a livelihood.

J. N. PETTIT, farmer, P. O. Mount Vernon, was born in Crawford County, Penn., April 22, 1844, a son of Windsor and Ann Eliza (Burger) Pettit. The father was a native of Crawford County, Penn., and the mother of New York. The former is still living, but the mother died in this county March 27, 1882. Of the family there are three sons and five daughters now living. In 1846, our subject's parents came to Illinois, and in a few years after removed to Iowa, where subject received his education. There he also remained until August 15, 1862, when he enlisted in Company I, Twenty-seventh Iowa Volunteer Infantry. A part of the Second Brigade of the Second Division of the Sixteenth Army Corps, Gen. A. J. Smith commanding. He was in the battles of Nashville, Red River expedition and others of less importance. He was discharged at the close of the war, after having been out three years, less six days. At the close of the war, he came to this county, where he has since given his attention to farming. He now owns a farm of forty-nine acres. Mr. Pettit was married, February 14, 1869, to Miss Eliza C. Johnson, a daughter of Thomas and Sarah (Frost) Johnson, both of whom are now residents of this township. This union resulted in three children—Mary F., Charles A. and Thomas W. Our subject is a member of the Methodist Episcopal Church, and in politics is a Republican.

SHERWOOD PIERCY, physician, Mount Vernon, was born in Greene County, Ill., April 1, 1837, and is the son of Anderson and Catherine (Lasator) Piercy. He was a native of Virginia, she of South Carolina, but died in this county at an advanced age. They were the parents of twelve children, six of whom are still living, our subject being the youngest of the six. In about 1844, they came to this township, and here our subject was reared and educated. At about the age of twenty-five years, he began reading medicine under Dr. Peavler, of Mount Vernon, and then with Drs. Green & Peavler, continuing with them for about four years. In 1866, he began the practice of his profession in Belle Prairie City, Hamilton County, and remained till 1879, when, on account of ill health, he had to leave, so purchased the present farm, but gives his attention to the practice of his profession and has built up a good business. He was married in August, 1861, to Miss Mary F. Mangrum. She was born in Tennessee, but came to this county when small. Dr. and Mrs. Piercy have five children living and one dead, viz., Lovona E., Lovina C., John Anderson (deceased), W. Duff, Annie Jane and Cora Agnes. Dr. Piercy is a member of the Masonic fraternity. He and wife are members of the Methodist Episcopal Church. In politics he is a Democrat. During the civil war, he saw some active service, enlisting in 1861 in Company D, One Hundred and Tenth Illinois Volunteer Infantry.

JOHN A. REED, farmer, P. O. Woodlawn, was born in Jefferson County, Ill., September 10, 1842, son of Bird and Emily (Piper) Reed. They both were natives of Tennessee, and came to this county in 1839, and died here—she September 24, 1872, he December 13, 1878. They were the parents of thirteen children, eleven of whom still survive. Our subject obtained his education in the common schools of this county, and his occupation has been various, but mostly that of farming and stock-dealing. His present farm contains eighty acres of land in a high state of cultivation. September 1, 1863, he was first married to Miss Eliza E., youngest daughter of Isaac and Sophia Hicks. Mrs. Reed died September 23, 1882. Seven children were the result of this union, four of whom still survive, viz., Cora, Minnie, Fannie and Joseph Carl. Mr. Reed was again married. He is a member of the Independent Order of Odd Fellows, being initiated into the Marion Lodge June 7, 1875. Now is a member of Woodlawn Lodge, No. 522, and has held all the offices and represented his lodge in the Grand Lodge. In politics, he is a Democrat, and has held various township offices—Assessor, Collector, etc., and for years has been Chairman of the Democratic Central Committee of the township. In 1861, he entered the service, Company I, Sixty-eighth Illinois Volunteer Infantry, Col. Taylor, and served in the East till discharged.

LEWIS S. SEWARD, farmer, P. O. Mount Vernon, was born in Montgomery County, this State, April 28, 1845, and is a son of George C. Seward, of Montgomery County. Our subject was raised on the farm and educated in the common schools; he has always been a farmer. His mother died when he was quite small, and he was brought here and raised by his grandparents. Mr. Seward was married, July 21, 1878, to Margaret Frost, a daughter of Newton L. Frost, of this township. They have one child—Lillian—a bright little girl of four years. Mr. and Mrs. Seward are members of the Methodist Episcopal Church. Mr. Seward owns eighty acres of valuable land.

J. F. SHARP, merchant, Woodlawn, was born in Gibson County, Ind., October 19, 1823, to Micajah and Nancy (Wright) Sharp, both of whom were natives of Maryland and early settlers of Kentucky, and afterward removed to Indiana, where they remained to the time of their death. He was a cabinetmaker, but followed the occupation of farming during the principal part of his life. They were the parents of ten children, our subject being the only living child. He was reared and educated in his native county, and, arriving at his majority there, engaged in farming until 1873, when he came to Illinois and located at Woodlawn, his present residence, and engaged in the mercantile business. Their stock comprises a general line of merchandise, and they do a $25,000 business annually. In connection with this business, the firm of Payne & Sharp do a general grain business and also handle railroad ties. Mr. Sharp was married in Gibson, Ind., October 25, 1847, to Miss Margaret A. Yerkers, a native of Pennsylvania; the result of this union is one child. He and wife are members of the Presbyterian Church. He is a member of the I. O. O. F., and a Republican politically. He is a self-made man in every respect, being left an orphan when quite young; he has by his honesty, industry and economy, accumulated his property and the worthy name he bears.

WILLIAM SIDES, blacksmith, Woodlawn. The subject of this sketch was born in 1842 in Cape Girardeau County, Mo., son of Samuel and Margaret (Miller) Sides. He was a farmer, who was born in North Carolina, came to Cape Girardeau County, Mo., and then to Union County, Ill., where he died. She was a native of Cape Girardeau County, Mo., and died in Union County, Ill. They were the parents of eight children, only two of whom are now living, viz., Sapora Ann, wife of Jacob Reynolds, and our subject. William Sides was left an orphan at nine years of age, and from that time he was thrown among strangers. He gained such an education as the circumstances would permit, having the opportunities of attending school but about six months. In early life, he worked on a farm, but when he grew older he commenced learning the blacksmith's trade. Although still a boy, he wished to defend the stars and stripes when the rebellion broke out, so in June, 1862, he enlisted at Ashley, Ill., in the Sixteenth Illinois Volunteer Cavalry, and participated in numerous engagements, among which was the battle at Jonesville, Lee Co., Va., and there was taken prisoner, January 3, 1864. For nearly fourteen months he suffered untold miseries in Southern prison pens, being at Belle Isle, Andersonville, Ga., Charleston, S. C., Florence, S. C., and finally Richmond, Va. At Charleston, they were put under fire while the Federals were shelling the city. February 14, 1865, he was exchanged, but was taken sick and laid in the hospital at Columbus, Ohio. Finally, when able, he returned to Ashley on furlough, and in June, 1865, rejoined his regiment. August 17, 1865, was mustered out at Nashville, Tenn. After returning to Ashley, he completed his trade of blacksmith, and remained there till June, 1867, when he came to Jefferson County, and in 1870 settled in Woodlawn, his being the third family in the village. Mr. Sides has a large shop in Woodlawn, and is partner in the flouring mill here. He deals in grain, agricultural implements, etc. Mr. Sides is a self-made man, and through his personal integrity has made a name respected and honored by his many acquaintances. His life has been one of activity, but his labor here has had its reward—coming here with only $2.50 in money, and now having amassed a property of upward of $20,000. He is identified with the Republican party. March 18, 1866, near Ashley, he was married to Miss Nancy E. Eubank. She was born in Washington County, Ill., daughter of Spencer S. and Sallie (White) Eubank. This union has resulted in seven children, viz., Adria Oscar, Samuel Wiley (deceased), Albert, Ollie, Adda and Edda, twins, and William, the youngest. Mrs. Sides is a member of the Methodist Episcopal Church.

JOHN T. SMITH, farmer, P. O. Mount Vernon, was born in Sumner County, Tenn., November 2, 1827, and is a son of James Smith (deceased), a native of Clark County, Va., who brought his family to this county in 1829. Here our subject was brought up in a thinly settled country, where there was plenty of game, shooting deer from their door. He attended a subscription school, taught in a log cabin, with slab seats and greased paper over a crack in the wall for a window. He married Polly, daughter of Green Casey, in 1867. They have two children—Eugene and Walter N. Mrs. Smith was born in this county; both are Methodists. Mr. Smith was School Trustee for four years. He now owns 223 acres of land.

J. C. TYLER, farmer, P. O. Mount Vernon, is a native of Jefferson County, Ill., born on the 28th of March, 1829. His father, James H. Tyler, was a native of Sumner County, Tenn., and was one of the early settlers of this county. He died here in the spring of 1877, having been a resident of the county for about sixty years. His wife, Catherine (Casey) Tyler, is one of the oldest living settlers of the county. She was born December 15, 1809, and is the mother of five children, of whom two sons and one daughter are now living. Our subject was raised on a farm and educated in the common schools. He is one of the successful farmers of Jefferson County, and is the owner of 165 acres of good land. He was married, October 30, 1850, to Miss Martha H. Maxey, who has borne him six children, all of whom are dead except Ida M. Mr. Tyler is now serving his third term as Township Supervisor. He is a Republican in politics, an active member of the A., F. & A. M. and I. O. O. F., and, with his wife, unites with the Methodist Episcopal Church.

JOSEPH V. WARD, farmer, P. O. Mount Vernon, is a native of Lawrence County, Ohio, and was born April 7, 1832. His father, William Ward (deceased), was a native of Maryland and came to this county with his family in 1844. Our subject attended the old-fashioned subscription school, taught in a log cabin with split-pole seats, puncheon floor, a log out for window and a stick and clay chimney. He was married, November 4, 1852, to Nancy Hales, a daughter of Thomas Hales. They had seven children born to them, of whom five are living, viz., William T., James W., John H., Joseph M. and Hiram Ulysses. Mr. Ward was a soldier of Uncle Sam in the late war, in Company C, Sixtieth Regiment Illinois Volunteer Infantry, under Gen. Morgan and Col. Anderson. He served in this capacity for two years, and was Sergeant eighteen months in Company H, First United States Engineers. He was hurt at Chattanooga by a falling timber when assisting to erect a magazine He now draws a pension in consequence of said injury. Mr. Ward owns 162 acres of valuable land, and is engaged in farming and stock-raising. He is a Methodist and a Mason. For the past six years he has filled the office of Highway Commissioner.

DR. J. H. WATSON, Woodlawn Among the able practitioners of *Materia Medica* in Shiloh Township is Dr. J. H. Watson, whose name heads this brief biography. He is a native of the county, born July 31, 1846, and is a son of John H. and Elizabeth M. (Rankin) Watson. The father was a carpenter by occupation, and in his latter years gave his attention to the office of Justice of the Peace at Mount Vernon. He was a native of Virginia, and son of Dr. Watson, a native of England, who first settled in Virginia and afterward in Jefferson County, Ill. She is a native of Tennessee and the mother of nine children, of whom seven are now living, our subject being the youngest child. He was reared and educated in the city of Mount Vernon, and where he studied medicine with Dr. Green. He afterward attended medical lectures in Cincinnati and St.

Louis, and graduated from the medical college of the latter place in 1880. He first began the practice of medicine in 1867 in Dunklin County, Mo. In 1868, he returned to his native county and located in Woodlawn, where he has since remained, with the exception of two years spent in Colorado. He was married in Woodlawn in 1870, to Miss Melissa, daughter of William Wood, for whom the town of Woodlawn was named. This union has been blessed with the following children: Elizabeth Neva and Thomas Bertrand. The Doctor is an enterprising, public-spirited citizen, and is an honor to the profession to which he is devoted. He is a member of the A., F. & A. M., and a Democrat in politics.

W. C. WEBB, farmer, P. O. Woodlawn, was born in Wilson County, Tenn., October 27, 1830, son of Bennett and Martha (Hall) Webb. They were natives of North Carolina, but came to Tennessee when young, and in 1844 came to Jefferson County, Ill., where they died. Of their family of ten children, seven still survive. Our subject's opportunities for an education were very limited. His occupation has always been that of farming. In January, 1872, he was married to Miss Mary Frost, daughter of Newton Frost and grand-daughter of Dr. Frost, an early settler of the county. Mr. and Mrs. Webb have two children, viz., Wilford Bennett and Newton Eldridge. Mr. Webb's farm contains 320 acres, about 200 in cultivation. For twenty years he has been an active member of the Baptist Church. He holds to the principles of the Democratic party, and has held different offices of the township. Mr. Webb is one of the successful farmers of Shiloh Township, and has made his success through his own efforts.

WILLIAM WEATHERFORD, farmer, P. O. Woodlawn, was born in White County, Tenn., April 15, 1832, son of James and Rebecca Weatherford, natives of South Carolina, who came to this county in 1856 from Tennessee. She died when our subject was small, he March 5, 1875. Our subject was reared in Tennessee, and his life has been spent in different places and engaged in various business pursuits. For a number of years he lived in Mount Vernon and in Colorado, etc. In the fall of 1866, he bought his present farm in partnership with his brother, M. C. His brother died in 1876, and our subject has since purchased the entire farm of 240 acres. He did not remain on the farm all the time till 1880; now, however, he gives his entire attention to it. Mr. Weatherford is not a member of any society, but is always ready to aid the furtherance of any good enterprise. In politics, he associates with the Republican party.

JOHN N. WHITE, farmer, P. O. Mount Vernon, was born in Brown County, Ohio, June 11, 1831, to Warner and Elizabeth (Daniel) White. He was born in Virginia May 21, 1801, and was reared on a farm in his native State. Upon reaching his maturity, he removed to Brown County, Ohio, where he was married to the mother of our subject in 1831. For some time he was engaged at his trade of shoe-maker, but soon after marriage began farming, and has followed the same since. In the spring of 1843, he emigrated with his family to this county and now resides on the farm on which he moved soon after coming to the county. In politics, he is Republican, and for many years has been an active and liberal member of the Presbyterian Church. He is the son of Warren White, a descendant of one of the Pilgrims who came in the Mayflower. The mother of our subject, who also is still living, was born January 14, 1811, in Ohio, a daughter of Joseph Daniel, a native of Virginia, who settled in Brown County, Ohio, when reaching manhood. To Mr. and Mrs. Warren White six children were born, five of whom still survive, viz., our subject, William, Sarah (widow of Charles H. Maxey), Robert and James. Our subject remained on the farm till about 1849, when he began working at the carpenter's trade, and has followed the same for many years since. In 1854, he was married to Miss Eliza H. Maxey, who was born in Jefferson County in 1837, and is the mother of two children—Warner N. and Lora E. In January, 1862, he enlisted in Company H, First Illinois Cavalry, under command of Capt. Noleman, of Centralia. In July of the same year, he was mustered out. In August, 1862, he again enlisted in Company B, One Hundred and Tenth Illinois Volunteer Infantry, and served in that till in the spring of 1868, when he was mustered out. While in the service, he received a wound in the ankle while making a charge, from the effects of which he still suffers. After returning from the service, he again engaged at his trade, but in 1876 began farming, at which occupation he is now engaged. In politics, he is a Republican.

WEBBER TOWNSHIP.

WILLIAM T. ADAMS, farmer, P. O. Bluford. This gentleman is one of those self-made, energetic men who have worked their way up in the world by hard work and perseverance. He was born June 22, 1826, in this county. His father, Willoughby W. Adams, was a native of North Carolina and reared in Alabama, who died in Jefferson County, Ill., where he was classed among the most highly respected citizens. The mother of our subject was Jane (Tunstel) Adams, a native of Kentucky, who died in this county. Our subject was educated in the common schools of Jefferson County, and there married Harriet A. Wright, born April 15, 1832, in Kentucky, daughter of Robert S. Wright, a native of that State. Her mother, Rachel Davis, was also a native of Kentucky. This union was blessed with twelve children, of whom eight are now living—Robert W., born July 12, 1852; George W. born November 1, 1854; Lydia F., born November 4, 1856 (wife of William Nation, and the mother of four children—Oliver R., Lula L., Julia A., Lizzie B., deceased, Thomas J., born May 24, 1859; Charles H., born May 7, 1863; John Q., born July 31, 1865; Nancy M., born January 7, 1868; Jacob D., born November 31, 1873. Mrs. Adams is a member of the Christian Church, and has one little girl adopted, Minna M., born May 17, 1878. Mr. Adams has a farm of 320 acres. In politics, he is a Democrat.

CHRISTOPHER BROOKMAN, farmer, P. O. Pigeon, was born in Pulaski County, Va. The records were burned when he was quite small, and the date of his birth is not certainly known. He was brought by his parents to Clinton County, Ill., in infancy, and to this county when about twelve years old, where he has since lived. Married, in 1858, Rosetta Sledge, by whom he had six children, five living—John F., David, William L., Minnie and Lillie. He owns 166 acres of land, and is engaged in farming and stock-raising. He served in the late war, Company C., Eighth Illinois Volunteer Infantry, one year, and participated in the charge at Mobile.

LEONARD W. BRUCE, farmer, P. O. Marlow, the pioneer of Webber Township, was born in Wilson County, Tenn., March 13, 1819, and is a son of Azariah Bruce (deceased), a native of Virginia, who brought his family to this county in 1826. Our subject attended school in a log cabin, sat on a split, and wrote on a slab, supported on pins in the wall. The cabin had no floor except "mother earth," and the window was the aperture made by removing a log. In 1850, he married Caroline, daughter of James Bridges. They had nine children, eight living—Mary, Rebecca, Adda, Roland, Hardy, Nannie, Ellen and Peter. Mr. Bruce owns 200 acres of valuable land. Is a member of the Masonic fraternity.

JESSE J. CLARK, farmer, P. O. Pigeon, was born born in Robertson County, Tenn., May 28, 1828, and is a son of Jesse Clark (deceased), a native of Virginia. Our subject was brought up on the farm, and has always been a farmer. Came to this county in 1856. Married, December 27, 1855, to Fannie Winters, by whom he has had eight children, six living—Mollie, Fredonia, Wade, Nannie, Della and Mertie. Mr. Clark owns ninety-eight acres of land. Is a member of the Baptist Church.

JOSEPH F. CLARK, farmer, P. O. Pigeon, was born in Robertson County, Tenn., September 8, 1831, and is a son of Jesse Clark (deceased). Came to this county in 1856. Was married, February 26, 1857, to Sarah Smith, by whom he had nine children, seven living—Florence, Ardelia C., Edith, Cora, Lillie, George and Thomas. Is a member of the Baptist Church. Owns seventy-seven and a half acres of land on Section 32.

ANDREW J. COOK, stock-raiser, P. O. Pigeon, was born in Germany February 28, 1851. His father, Henry Cook, brought his family to America in 1858, and located in St. Louis. Mr. Cook came to this county in 1860. He married Alice Stonemetz in December, 1873. They had three children—Ola (deceased), Dena (deceased), and Nellie; the latter is six years old. Mr. Cook is extensively engaged in breeding short-horn cattle, and has one of the finest, if not the finest, herd of cattle in Southern Illinois. His bull weighs 2,000 pounds, and is four years old. He owns 180 acres of fine, well-improved land. He began life fifteen years ago without a dollar. His fine cattle and extensive improvements show that he has been eminently successful. He is a hard worker and very industrious.

WILLIAM P. DAVIS, farmer, P. O. Tilford, is a native of Surry County, N. C., and was born May 11, 1827. His father, Reece Davis, deceased, was also a native of Surry County, and brought his family to this county in 1849, where he died in 1854. Our subject attended a subscription school in a log cabin with a dirt floor, and sat upon a split-pole bench. His mother's maiden name was Patsy Harris. She still resides in this township, and is eighty-five years old. Mr. Davis was married, February 14, 1864, to Margaret Dagg, daughter of James Dagg, deceased, a native of Ireland. They had seven children, five living—Mary F., Martha J., Theodosia, Lucinda and William R. Mr. Davis owns 157 acres of land, and is engaged in farming and stock-raising. The family are Baptists.

WILLIAM B. DULANY, farmer and teacher, P. O. Tilford, is a native of Van Buren County, Tenn., and was born November 28, 1849. His father, John P. Dulany, resides at Black Oak Ridge, this county. The family came to this county in 1867. Our subject was educated at Ewing College, Franklin Co., Ill., and has taught school for the past eleven winters, and farmed during the summers. He married Martha A. Bruce September 25, 1873. She is a daughter of S. V. Bruce, of Mount Vernon Township. They have had four children, three living—Edith B., Silas F. and Ina. Mr. Dulany owns 100 acres of land, and makes the raising of fine horses a specialty—the Norman stock. He held the office of Assessor two terms. Is a member of the Masonic fraternity.

BRITTEN D. ESMAN, merchant and farmer, P. O. Tilford, was born in Monroe County, Tenn., July 20, 1847, and is a son of William Esman, deceased, who brought his family to this county in 1858. Our subject preached regularly in the Baptist Church for ten years in this county. In June, 1883, he engaged in the mercantile business at Bluford, and has built up a good trade in general merchandising. He also carries on the farm. He married Cynthia Patterson February 28, 1869. Five children were the fruit of this union, four of whom are living—Rosa E., Mary J., Ida F. and Anne.

SAMUEL H. HILLIARD, physician, Pigeon, was born in Tensas Parish, La., January 10, 1851. His father, John D. Hilliard, is a native of New Hampshire, and resides in Carlyle, Ill. Our subject was educated in Washington Seminary, at Richview, Ill. He graduated from the Medical Institute, of Cincinnati, Ohio, in March, 1877. He came to this county in 1877, soon after graduation, and has built up a large and remunerative practice. Was married in 1879 to Miss Florence, daughter of Joseph F. Clark, of Farrington Township, this county. The Doctor owns 40 acres of land and is a member of the Masonic fraternity.

LANSON K. LAIRD, farmer, P. O. Tilford, was born in Athens County, Ohio, September 28, 1844, and is a son of John Laird (deceased), a native of Greene County, Penn. Mr. Laird was a soldier for Uncle Sam in the late war, in Company G, Ninety-second Ohio Volunteer Infantry, and participated in the battles of Chickamauga, Mission Ridge, Hoover's Gap, Wilderness, Ft. Sumter and others. He came to Effingham County, Ill., in 1866, and to Texas in 1869, traveling through Texas, Indian Territory and Kansas until 1874, when he came to Douglas County, Ill., and in 1881 he came to this county. He was married, September 4, 1868, to Miss Hettie Wintering, who died about eight months later. On the 30th of July, 1879, he married Mrs. Mary Evinger, a daughter of John Woods. She had three children by her first husband, viz.: Emma, Rosa and Eura F. Evinger. Mr. L. owns 120 acres of land. Is a Mason.

LORENZO M. LIVESAY, deceased, was born in Tennessee October 9, 1825. He came to this county in the fall of 1856, where he died June 6, 1876. He was twice married—the first time to Margaret J. Thompson, October 22, 1845. By her he had twelve children, but four of whom are living—Mary C., Ephraim J., Elizabeth P. and Lafayette S. Mrs. L. died October 28, 1868, and on the 16th of May, 1869, he married Sarah S. Lane, daughter of Henry Lane (deceased). She was born in Caldwell County, Ky., and came with her parents to Clinton County, Ill., in 1840. Mr. Livesay was a faithful Methodist, and a useful, honest man.

ABRAM MARLOW, farmer, P. O. Marlow, was born in Wilson County, Tenn., September 8, 1822, and is a son of James Marlow (deceased), a native of Virginia, who brought his family to this county in 1828, and settled on Bullock's Prairie, four miles west of Mt. Vernon. Mr. Marlow attended a subscription school in a log cabin, with stick chimney, and sat on a split pole, with pins in for legs. When the Marlows settled here, there were many deer, turkeys, wolves, wild cats, and a few bears and panthers here. Our subject was married, in 1842, to Elvira, daughter of Burrel Warren (deceased). They had eleven children, seven living—Winfield S., Millard F., Sarah A., A. Lincoln, Lucretia J., Hiram P. and Cora. Mr. Marlow was Justice of the Peace fifteen years, Supervisor three years, Postmaster at Marlow one year, and is Notary Public. Member of the Methodist Episcopal Church and Masonic fraternity.

SAMUEL G. MARTIN, farmer, P. O. Tilford, is a native of Bedford County, Tenn., born November 24, 1838, and is a son of Asa Martin (deceased), a native of North Carolina. Mr. Martin came to this county in 1854. He was a soldier in the late war, in Company B, One Hundred and Tenth Illinois Volunteer Infantry, United States Army, nearly three years, participating in the battles of Mission Ridge, Chickamauga, all through the Atlanta campaign, with Sherman to the sea, and back through the Carolinas, and lastly participated in the battle of Bentonville, N. C. He was married, January 16, 1862, to Mary Schanck, by whom he had seven children, four living—Alcora I., Ina L., Willard W. and Otto C. Mrs. Martin died December 3, 1876, and he again married, April 11, 1879, to Mrs. Hester A. Gibson (maiden name Buroughs). By her he has two children—Marcus and Ruby (twins). She had five children by her first husband—Adda J. (deceased), Mary, Laura M., Margaret and Ettie. Mr. Martin owns 120 acres of land.

JAMES C. MAXEY, farmer and stock-raiser, P. O. Pigeon, was born in Shiloh Township, this county, June 14, 1827. He was brought up on the farm, and received his education in a subscription school in a log cabin. He married Nancy J. Moss October 31, 1850. Her father, Ransom Moss (deceased) is of the large tribe of Mosses (or as some spell it, Morse), whose ancestral lineage can be traced back several hundred years. Ransom Moss came from Virginia to this county about the year 1818, and settled among the Indians and wild animals. Mrs. Moss still resides in this county, and is eighty-five years old, the oldest lady member of the Pioneer Society of this county. Mr. and Mrs. Maxey have had eight children, seven living—John R., Walter S., Oscar S., Albion F., Henry B., Lillie B. and Ransom M. One son, Oliver W., died at the age of nineteen years. Mr. Maxey owns 120 acres of valuable land, and resides on Section 2. His father, Henry B. Maxey (deceased), was a native of Wilson County, Tenn., and a pioneer of this county, having settled here in 1818. He was a mason by trade, and when away building chimneys his wife often had to throw venison to the wolves and bears to prevent their breaking into the cabin. She was a brave woman. On returning late one night he feigned to frighten her by disguising his voice, but she was equal to the emergency, and took the gun down and made ready to shoot as she opened the door at his command, whereupon he ran around the house, holloaing, "Don't shoot, Peggy, it's me."

HARVEY M. MAXEY, farmer and merchant, P. O. Pigeon, was born in this county March 26, 1840, and is a brother of James C. Maxey, of this township (see his biography). Mr. Maxey received a common school education. He taught school about four years, and clerked in different stores in Mt. Vernon several years, but has also carried on his farm. For the past year, he has been selling goods at Keen Station. His oldest son, Albion T., superintends the farm, of which there are over 200 acres (but in different tracts). Mr. M. married, October 24, 1864, Elizabeth Rook, by whom he had seven children, six living—Albion T., Frederick N., Harry R., Edward B., Orvil and Clarence.

THOMAS F. MOORE, stock-dealer, P. O. Tilford, was born in McMinn County, Tenn., April 10, 1839, and is a son of Alexander Moore, of Pendleton Township, who brought his family to Jefferson County in 1840. Our subject spent his boyhood days on his father's farm, and received a limited education. As a business man Mr. Moore has been eminently successful, although at first everything seemed dark. At the age of nineteen years, he engaged in the mercantile business at Lynchburg, in this county, but soon afterward failed; and when he was married he "was not worth anything." He then began to raise stock, which suited his disposition. He has since been prospered beyond his most sanguine expectations, until at present he owns about 2,500 acres of land, besides a large general store at Bluford. He also deals very extensively in poultry and produce as well as in stock. Mr. Moore owns also a first-class flouring mill at Opdyke, in this county. But few men in Southern Illinois handle as much money as does Mr. Moore. He was married, February 7, 1863, to Catherine, daughter of William Scrivner. They have had ten children, eight living—William N., Mollie, Margaret, Thomas F., Lydia, Alexander, Oliver R. and Cora. Mr. Moore held the office of Collector two terms, and is the present Supervisor of Webber Township. He is a stockholder in the Jefferson County Agricultural Society, a member of the Masonic fraternity, and of the Baptist Church.

ALEXANDER MOORE, JR., farmer, P. O. Tilford, was born in this county, September 14, 1843, and is a son of Thomas Moore (deceased), a native of Tennessee. Mr. Moore was brought up on the farm, and has always been a farmer. In January, 1865, he married Nancy Davis, by whom he has seven children—William T., Martha, Annie, Mary, Ford, Freddie and Riley. Mr. Moore owns 120 acres of land, and is engaged in raising and dealing in stock as well as farming.

WILLIAM A. NATION, teacher and Justice of the Peace, Tilford, is a native of Hamilton County, Ill., born November 30, 1852, and is a son of John H. Nation, of Hamilton County. Mr. Nation received a common school education, but is a self-made man. For the past eleven years he has been engaged in teaching. He owns forty acres of land where he resides on Section 34. Is the present Justice of the Peace for Webber Township. He was married, August 15, 1875, to Lydia F., daughter of William T. Adams, of this township. They had four children, three living, viz.: Oliver R., Lula L. and Julia A.

JOSEPH H. NEWTON, physician, Marlow, was born in Robertson County, Tenn., September 9, 1837, and is a son of Anderson Newton (deceased), a native of Orange County, N. C., who emigrated with his parents to Tennessee in 1818, and brought his family to this county in 1852, where he died in 1862. Our subject was brought up on the farm, and received a common school education; but most of his education was obtained at home in a chimney corner. He began the practice of medicine in 1864, in Hamilton County, Ill., and came to this county in 1866, and has built up a large practice. He was married in 1864, to Lovina, daughter of George Starner. They have had nine children, six living—Eva C., Alluna, Ann, Walter H., Kate and Leda. The Doctor is an Odd Fellow.

OSCAR J. PULLIAM, farmer, P. O. Tilford, was born in St. Clair County, Ill., September 28, 1854, and is a son of Richard C. Pulliam (deceased), a native of the same county. Mr. Pulliam was brought up and educated in Belleville, in his native county. He followed railroading for eight years, and for the past five years has been farming in this county, where he came in 1878. He married Miss Adda J. Gibson September 25, 1880, but she died the following November. Our subject's mother, his two sisters and a brother reside with him on the homestead, of which there are eighty acres. Mr. P. is a Baptist, as also are his mother and elder sister. The father died December 12, 1872. He was also a consistent Baptist.

WILLIAM STONE, farmer, P. O. Opdyke, was born in Dearborn County, Ind., January 22, 1843, son of Orman Stone (deceased). Came to White County, Ill., in 1868, and to this county in 1875. Married Melvina Jacobs, by whom he had two children, one living—

Frank. Mrs. Stone died in 1863, and he married, February 13, 1865, Mary M. Dosher, by whom he had three children, two living—Warren H. and Bertha L. Mr. Stone owns 210 acres of land; is a member of the Christian Church.

THOMAS S. VOYLES, farmer, P. O. Pigeon, was born in Hall County, Ga., February 20, 1832, and is a son of David Voyles, who emigrated to Greene County, Ill., several years ago. He now resides with his son, and is ninety-six years old. Our subject was married, July 5, 1860, to Minerva A., daughter of George W. Hunter (deceased). They have had ten children; nine of these are living—Thomas A., James M., Calloway H., Harriet E., Mary A., Sarah E., Lillie M., Amanda J. and John H. Mr. V. brought his family to this county in 1878. He owns 160 acres of land; is a member of the United Brethren Church.

LEWIS C. WORK, farmer, P. O. Tilford, was born in Brown County, Ohio, February 11, 1826, and is a son of William Work, of Ohio, and a native of the same county. Mr. Work was brought up on a farm, but learned the carpenter's trade, at which he worked nine years in Middletown, Ohio. He came to this county in 1875. Married Caroline Lysher, by whom he had seven children—Marnelvia (deceased), Annie, Francis M., Mary, William L., Benjamin L. and Joseph H. Mr. Work owns 160 acres here and 40 acres in Richland County, Ill.

ROBERT S. YOUNG, farmer, P. O. Pigeon, is a native of this township, and was born November 14, 1858. His father, Robert S. Young (deceased), was an early settler of this county. There were ten children in the father's family, of whom the following are living: William L., Mary, Lucy, James B., Robert S. and Nannie H. Their mother's maiden name was Rachel Brown. Our subject owns an undivided third of the homestead, which consists of 240 acres. He is paying some attention to the raising of fine stock. He has been Assessor two terms. Is a member of the United Brethren Church.

ROME TOWNSHIP.

R. B. BALTZELL, farmer, P. O. Dix, was born in Jefferson County, Ill., February 4, 1845, to G. J. and Nancy A. (Bryan) Baltzell. He was born in Ohio, she in Virginia. They were married in Missouri, and moved to Mount Vernon, Ill., about 1842, where he probably manufactured the first hat manufactured in the county. They afterward moved near to Walnut Hill, where our subject was born, and where his mother died of the cholera, in August, 1853. He afterward moved to Centralia, where he still resides. Our subject then was mostly reared and educated in Centralia, and engaged in different business ventures till March, 1874, when he came to his present farm. He had been engaged in the dry goods business, photographing, farming, etc. He bought his farm of ninety acres from M. C. Kell, and is the one first settled by Thomas Kell, and the old store building still stands in which were sold the first goods from this part of Jefferson County. May 20, 1864, our subject entered the service of his country, in Company E, One Hundred and Thirty-sixth Illinois Volunteer Infantry, and did station duty at Columbus, Ky., and St. Louis, Mo., until mustered out, October 22, 1864. December 24, 1867, he was married, in Centralia, to Miss Mary J. Croe. She was born in Ohio, but was left an orphan, almost in infancy, her parents dying in 1853. Mr. and Mrs. Baltzell have six children, viz.: George W., Bertha A., Blanche A., Silas L., Raleigh C. and baby. He is a member of the I. O. O. F., Walnut Hill Lodge, No. 710, and holds the office of Warden. In politics, he is a Republican.

S. B. BOGAN, M. D., physician, Dix. The subject of this sketch was born in Grand Prairie Township, Jefferson Co., Ill., January 24, 1853, and is the son of Henry M. and Elizabeth (Casey) Bogan. He is a native of Virginia, and brother of John S. Bogan, whose sketch appears in this work. She is a daughter of Samuel Casey. Our subject is one of a family of six children, all of whom are still living. His early life was spent in assisting to till the soil on the old home farm. At the age of eighteen years, he was sent to Irving College, where he remained for two years; he then went to Columbia College, Washington, D. C., where he took the degree of B. S. He then attended medical lectures at the same institution, and graduated with honor in the medical department. In 1876, the Doctor, wishing to remain in his native county, located at Woodlawn, and began the practice of his profession. Here he was very successful, but, in 1880, he decided to change his location to Rome, where he now resides, and has built up a good practice in his new field. September 1, 1880, he was married to Miss Louisa Casey, a native of this county, and daughter of Robert Casey, of Rome. The result of this union is one child—Pearl Irene. Dr. Bogan is a member of the Rome Lodge, No. 721, A., F. & A. M., and also the W. H. Hubbard R. A. Chapter of Mount Vernon. In politics, he is a Democrat, having followed in the footsteps of his ancestors.

W. A. BOGGS, farmer, P. O. Dix, was born in Marion County, Ill., January 21, 1833, to S. A. and Martha (Kell) Boggs. He was born in North Carolina in 1801; she in South Carolina about 1808. They were married in North Carolina, and came to Illinois in 1826, settling in Marion County within one-quarter mile of the Jefferson County line. Both died in that county—she in 1856, he in 1873. His occupation had always been that of farming and stock-raising, and at the time of his death owned about 700 acres of land which he had purchased from the Government, and was well known in Marion County as a good business man and stock-dealer. In early life he was a Whig in politics, but in later years was a Republican. He enlisted in the Black Hawk war, but it closed before the company got into the field. For many years he was a prominent member of the Reformed Presbyterian Church, contributing largely toward the construction and maintenance of houses of worship, and for over twenty years was Treasurer of the church. He was the father of fifteen children, there being a triplet of sons who died in infancy. Of the fifteen only three now survive—William A., Hugh, and Mrs. Sarah Telford. Our subject was reared in Marion County, and had the advantages of good common schools. His occupation has always been that of farming. In 1855, he came to his present farm, which contains 150 acres, ten of which are in orchards. October 16, 1852, he was married, in Perry County, Ill., to Miss Sarah E. McMillan, a native of that county, and daughter of James S. McMillan. This union has been blest with seven children, viz.: James A.; Jane, wife of Franklin Campbell; Margaret, wife of John Hayes; Lora (deceased), wife of Elmer Hayes; Lucy, wife of D. Norfleet; Charles and Ada. He and family are members of the church, and all but one son of the U. P. Church. He is an ardent worker in the Sunday school cause. In politics, he is a Republican, and has always taken an active part on political questions, and has held various township offices.

JOSEPH BOLES, farmer, P. O. Walnut

Hill, was born in Indiana September 27, 1841, to Hugh and Lethe (Reed) Boles. He was of Irish parentage, and was either born in Ireland or soon after his parents came to America. She was of English parents, and is still living. He died in this county. Of their family of children, five are still living, and by her second marriage she has one child. Our subject was reared on a farm and mostly in this county, and also educated here. In 1861, he enlisted in Company F, Forty-ninth Illinois Volunteer Infantry, Capt. Jones, Col. Morrison, but served only for about eighteen months, when he was discharged on account of disability, he having contracted rheumatism in the service. In the spring of 1865, he was married to Miss Harriet Breeze, daughter of Owen Breeze, of Centralia, a retired farmer. This union has been blest with six children, viz.: Alice, Owen, Otto, Emmet, and the twins, Maud and Mabel. In 1867, they moved to their present farm, which contains 336 acres, and in high state of cultivation, and on which he raises stock and grain. He is a member of Walnut Hill Lodge, I. O. O. F., No. 710. In politics, he is a Republican. He and wife are members of the Christian Church.

M. D. BRUCE, farmer, P. O. Dix, was born in Wilson County, Tenn., March 19, 1812, to Azariah and Patsy (Keeling) Bruce, natives of Virginia, he the son of Michael Bruce, a native of Scotland. In Virginia, Azariah Bruce was married to the mother of our subject, and in 1801 emigrated to Tennessee. During his residence in Tennessee, he enlisted in the army, serving in the war of 1812, being at the battle of New Orleans. In 1823, he emigrated to Jefferson County, Ill., and continued to follow his chosen profession of farming, taking quite a pride in keeping his farm in perfect order. He died in this county about 1854, his wife having died a short time before. He had passed his seventy-seventh year of age, and had served a number of terms as County Commissioner. He was the father of thirteen children, eight of whom still survive, six residing in this county. Our subject has resided in this county since 1823, and received his education in the early schools of the county. He served during the Black Hawk war, and also in the Mexican war. During the latter, he was engaged in the battles of Cerro Gordo and Vera Cruz. January 12, 1838, he settled on his present farm of 100 acres. He entered land from the Government at $1.25 per acre. February 13, 1834, he was married to Jane Brown, a native of Smith County, Tenn., and daughter of James and Sally (Clayborn) Brown, natives of South Carolina. He died in Tennessee a short time before the birth of Mrs. Bruce. About 1828 or 1830, Mrs. Brown moved to this county, and died about 1854. Mr. and Mrs. Bruce have had ten children, six of whom are still living—Francis M. (deceased), Charlotte, Sally (deceased), Martha A., James D., Malissa, Mary (deceased), Samantha (deceased), Alice and Azariah. For many years he and wife have been members of the Christian order. He is a member of the I. O. O. F., Rome Lodge, No. 394, and has represented his lodge in the Grand Lodge. In politics, he is a Democrat, and takes an active part toward securing the success of his party.

S. W. CARPENTER, miller, Dix, was born in Knox County, Ky., January 5, 1812, son of Benjamin and Melea (Shook) Carpenter. Her father, William Shook, was a native of Germany, and her mother an Englishwoman. Both died in Bedford County, Tenn. Our subject's father was engaged in boating on the Mississippi River at the time of his death, but his family resided in Indiana at the time. His widow then removed to Tennessee with her family to her people, where they resided until January, 1830, when they came to Jefferson County, where she died. She was the mother of seven children, only two of whom still survive—our subject and Jesse W., now of Texas. Our subject has made this county his home since 1830. Till about 1860, he had given his entire attention to farming. He then, in partnership with his son, William R., purchased their present mill, which they have run to do custom grinding. He also has a farm of seventy-seven acres, which he oversees. March 7, 1833, he was married to Lucinda O. Stockton. She was born in Illinois, daughter of Robert and Phœbe Stockton. Twelve children have been born to Mr. and Mrs. Carpenter, nine of whom still survive—Phœbe C. (Maxey), William R., Robert W., Margaret (Spiller), Mary L. (Frost), Jemima M. (Beagle), Sarah T. (Williams), Helen M. (Metzenthin) and Isaac D. Mr. and Mrs. Carpenter are members of the Methodist Episcopal Church, and he has been since he was sixteen years of age. In politics, he is Democratic, and for about forty years has acted as Justice of the Peace. For eight years he was Associate Justice of the county. He is one of the few survivors of the Black Hawk war.

ISAAC CASEY (deceased) was born in Tennessee March 25, 1811, to Abraham and Nancy (Baker) Casey. He was brought to this county at an early date, and was mostly reared and educated here. His occupation was always that of farmer. October 31, 1833, he was married to Tabitha White, present wife of James C. Baldridge. In 1835, he bought a farm in Grand Prairie Township, where he resided till time of death, November 23, 1840. He was the father of three children—Martha A. (deceased), wife of George Davis; Mary A., wife of E. S. Noleman; and Robert F. Mr. Casey volunteered from Mt Vernon during the Black Hawk war, and was at Kellogg's Grove when so many were decoyed from the fort and killed. He helped to keep wet blankets on the fort, so that the Indians could not fire it. Mr. Casey was an energetic and successful business man. In politics, he was Democratic, and before death was a professor of religion.

R. F. CASEY, merchant, Dix, was born in Jefferson County, Ill., August 17, 1838, and is the son of Isaac S. Casey (deceased), whose sketch appears in this work. Through the death of his father, our subject was left an orphan at an early age, but resided with his mother—who subsequently married Mr. J. C. Baldridge, of Grand Prairie—till he was sixteen years of age. He then embarked in life on his own account, engaging for the first year as a farm hand, at $6 per month. A month before the year was out, he decided to attend school, so bought off his time by paying $10 to his employer. In this way he succeeded in obtaining a good business education, working and then studying, attending one year at McKendree College, at Lebanon, Ill. From 1859 till 1865, he was engaged in dealing in stock. In 1866, he embarked in the mercantile business in Rome, but remained in that only till 1868, when he again began in farming and stock dealing. In 1876, he again sold his farm, and has since been doing a prosperous business as a general merchant in Rome. He carries a general stock of merchandise, valued at about $3,000, with annual sales of about $10,000 to $12,000, and also has a farm of eighty acres near Rome, on which he keeps stock, raises grain, etc. June 14, 1860, he was married to Miss Mary E., second daughter of Hiram Milburn. She was born in Gibson County, Ind., but, when about six weeks of age, was brought to this county by her parents. Mr. and Mrs. Casey have three children living, viz.: Louie, wife of Dr. S. B. Bogan; Irene Rose and Mary F. He and wife are members of the Methodist Episcopal Church South. In politics, he is a Democrat, and has held many of the local offices. He is a member of the A., F. & A. M., Rome Lodge, No. 721, and has several times represented it in the Grand Lodge.

RILEY COPPLE, farmer, P. O. Walnut Hill, was born in Clark County, Ind., January 17, 1826, and resided there till 1837, when he came with his parents to this county, and has resided

F

here since. When coming to the township there were no schoolhouses here, so his opportunity for an education was very limited, attending but three months during his life, and that in Marion County. His occupation has always been that of farming, and, when reaching his majority, he embarked in life as a farmer on his present place. Success has not been lacking, and now he owns a well improved farm of 200 acres. He was married, on September 16, 1850, to Miss Sarah C. Dukes. She was born in Tennessee, March 14, 1834, to John and Eleanor (Rife) Dukes. They were natives of Tennessee, and she still survives. To Mr. and Mrs. Copple ten children have been born, seven still living, viz.: Elizabeth E., Mary J., Darthula A., John H., Liley B., James R. (deceased), Sarah E., Hattie (deceased), Ahlute A. and an infant deceased. He and wife are members of the Christian Church. In politics, he is a Republican. He is the son of John and Elizabeth (Garren) Copple, natives of North Carolina, who was twice married, by his first wife having one son, Jacob, who was drowned in the Ohio River when a lad. He was married to the mother of our subject in Indiana, and by her had twelve children, five of whom still survive, viz: Abram, Riley, David, John, Margaret, wife of B. Harvey, now of the Indian Nation. David resides in Missouri, and the other three brothers in Jefferson County, Ill.

DAVID COPPLE, farmer, P. O. Walnut Hill, was born on his present farm, December 1, 1839, to Isaac and Martha (Green) Copple, both natives of Indiana; he the son of John Copple, a native of North Carolina. They moved from Indiana to this county in 1837, and he, Isaac Copple, died in 1843. He was the father of three sons, viz.: David, John R., who was killed in the army, and one son who died small. His widow afterward married M. D. Victory, of Missouri, and now resides there. After his father's death, our subject lived with his mother in Marion County, Ill., and in Missouri till he was grown, and received his education in the common schools. In 1859, he returned to his native county, and in August, 1861, enlisted in the service of his country, Company C, Eleventh Illinois Volunteer Infantry, Capt. George C. McKee, Col. W. H. L. Wallace. He served for three years, and was discharged at Vicksburg, Miss., in August, 1864. During his term of service, he was in some of the hardest fought battles of the war, being at Fort Donelson, Fort Henry, Shiloh, Corinth, Vicksburg, etc. After returning from the army, it was again to this county, and to his occupation of farming, and in 1865 purchased the farm on which he was born. He now owns 104 acres in a good state of cultivation. November 25, 1865, he was married to Miss Hannah Grubb, a native of Indiana, and daughter of Virgil Grubb. She died September 22, 1882, bearing to him four children, viz.: Joel, Benjamin F., Virgil I. and Ida Dora. He was married, December 29, 1882, to Virginia A. Foutch. She was born in Jefferson County, Ill., daughter of William Foutch. Mr. Copple is a member of the Walnut Hill Lodge, I. O. O. F., No 710. He and wife are members of the Christian Church. In politics, he is a Republican.

JOHN F. CORRELL, farmer, P. O. Mt. Vernon, was born in Bedford County, Penn., April 24, 1833, to Abram and Charlotte (Mellott) Correll. Both were born in Pennsylvania, she of German and he of English parentage. In 1845, they came to Jefferson County, Ill., and died here in 1862. His occupation was that of a tanner, having a tan yard in this county for some years. For several years previous to his death, he had been engaged in saw milling. Our subject spent his early life in assisting his father in the tan yard, and continued in the same as long as his father, but then went to farming, and has given his attention to the farm since, now owning 140 acres of well improved land. July 24, 1854, he was married, in this county, to Miss Mary Greer, daughter of William L. Greer, an old settler of this township. By her he has six children living, viz.: Sarah M., wife of John Hall; Joseph, Mary A., Zella, John, and Lottie. His wife died March 18, 1875. January 14, 1876, he was married to Sophia Hill. She was born in Marion County, Ill., daughter of John Hill. She is the mother of three children, viz.: Viola, Lena, and George. In politics, Mr. Correll is a Democrat, but takes no part in political matters.

G. L. CUMMINS, farmer, P. O. Dix. Among the substantial ruralists of Rome Precinct is G. L. Cummins, born October 15, 1833, in Jefferson County, Ill. His father, Samuel Cummins, was a native of Barren County, Ky., born in 1801, and his mother, Elizabeth (Holtsclaw) Cummins, was born in the same borough two years subsequent to the father. The former died in this county in 1867, the latter died in 1845. The father was an active member in the Democratic party, and was selected by that party to fill several offices. He came to this county about the year 1824, in company with his wife and children. His union gave him ten children, six of whom survive, viz.: Patrick; Minerva, widow of H. M. Watson; Mary, wife of W. T. Maxey; G. L.; Abigail, wife of Frank Galbraith; and Martha, wife of I. F. Hamlin. Our subject received a good common school education, and was brought up on a farm. On reaching his majority, he began for himself on his present farm of 140 acres, which is well improved, and on which he makes a specialty of raising grain and stock. He was married, July 4, 1861, to Lucy Andrews, a native of this county, and daughter of Sidney and Margaret (O'Melvaney) Andrews, old settlers in this borough. His union blessed him with two children—Wayne and Omer. He is a member of the A., F. & A. M., Rome Lodge, No. 721, and has held the various offices of the same. He was elected by his party, the Democrats, to the office of County Treasurer in 1877, and has been Supervisor. His grandfather, Henry Holtsclaw, came from Virginia to Kentucky, and thence to this county, while his grandfather, Cummins, removed from Pennsylvania to Kentucky, where he died. The Cummins family is of Scotch origin.

JOHN R. CUNNINGHAM, farmer, P. O. Dix, was born in Perry County, Ill., March 5, 1837, to Matthew J. and Esther E. (Little) Cunningham. He is a native of Kentucky, she of South Carolina. Both are still living, and reside in Centralia. January 27, 1883, they celebrated their golden wedding. His occupation has always been that of a farmer, but for some years has been retired from active life. They are the parents of eleven children, six sons and five daughters, three sons and the daughters still living. Our subject, when about nine years of age, came to this county with his parents, and has made the immediate neighborhood his home since. He received his education in the schools of the county. His occupation has always been that of farming. Mr. Cunningham was probably the first man to enter the service from this county during the civil war, enlisting in April, 1861, with Company G, Twelfth Illinois Volunteer Infantry, from Perry County, Ill., under Capt. Brookins, of Duquoin, and Col. McArthur, of Chicago. Their term of service expired in August, 1861, and our subject returned home and remained till August 12, 1862, when he enlisted in Company H, Eightieth Illinois Volunteer Infantry. Capt. James Cunningham, Col. Thomas G. Allen, our subject being commissioned Second Lieutenant of his company, and afterward First Lieutenant. He remained in the service till June, 1865, when they were mustered out. He participated in from twenty-five to thirty engagements. Was at the fall of Atlanta, but after that was no longer with Sherman, but remained under Gen. Thomas, and was at the battles of Franklin and Nashville, Tenn., etc. Since returning from the service, he has been engaged in farming. December 28, 1865, he was married to Miss Mollie T. Ellis. She was born in Fayette County, Ind., daughter of Lester and Sally E. Ellis, natives of New York State. Both died in this county, he June 26, 1868, she July 8, 1879. Mr. and Mrs. C. have six children, viz.: Carrie M., Lester E., Maud B., Silas A., Theodore B. and Louie B. In politics, he is a Republican, and takes an active part to secure the success of his party. The Cunningham family is of Scotch-Irish descent, the grandfather of our subject coming to the United States when about eight years of age.

J. M. B. GASTON, farmer, P. O. Dix. The subject of this sketch was born in Randolph County, Ill., March 22, 1824, son of William and Elizabeth (Couch) Gaston, both natives of South Carolina. She was born in April, 1803, and her parents removed from South Carolina to Tennessee in October of the same year. About 1806, her parents, James and Elizabeth (McBride) Couch, came to Illinois and died here at advanced ages. The father of our subject removed to Kentucky previous to the war of 1812, and enlisted in that war from the vicinity of Hopkinsville, Ky. Some time after the close of the war, he settled in Indiana, and it was there that he was united in marriage to his first wife, Jane McMillin. By her he had a family of five children, none of whom now survive. He was married to the mother of our subject in Randolph County, Ill., and by her had four sons and four daughters, all of whom are still living, our subject being the eldest. He died September 21, 1869, at the age of eighty-three years six months and some days. He was a son of William Gaston, who was a Revolutionary soldier, as were many other members of the Gaston family of South Carolina. The Gaston family is of French descent, and several generations ago were banished from France on account of religious belief. Our subject was mostly reared in Marion County, where his parents moved when he was small, but his education was obtained across the line in Jefferson County. His leading occupation in life has been that of farming, but for some months worked at coopering, and also about five years at the blacksmith trade. For seventeen months has served in the Mexican war, being under Gen. Price in New Mexico. In 1851, he came to Rome Township, and in 1856, to his present farm, where he has since resided, except three years during the late rebellion. In 1861, he enlisted in Company C, Twenty-second Illinois Volunteer Infantry, Col. Dougherty, and was out for three years, but at the battle of Belmont, Mo., he was so severely wounded that he was unable for further active duty. Mr. Gaston has twice been married, first to Miss Mary Storment, in Marion County, Ill., February 5, 1852. She was the daughter of John Storment, and was born in Jefferson County, Ill. She died September 28, 1866, aged thirty-six years eight months twenty days, and was the mother of four children, one now living, viz.: Margaret E., wife of W. H. Michael. September 12, 1867, he was married to his second wife, Mrs. Nancy J. (Hill) Creel, widow of DeWitt Creel, and daughter of William Hill, who came to Illinois in 1803, landing in the vicinity of Kaskaskia on Christmas Day. By her first husband Mrs. G. has two sons living, viz.: James M. and William D. One son by her present husband, viz., John H., deceased. Mr. and Mrs. Gaston are members of the M. E. Church. In politics, he is a Republican.

H. H. HUTCHISON, farmer, P. O. Dix, was born in Wilson County, Tenn., June 24, 1840, to William and Jane (Williams) Hutchison. They were both natives of South Carolina, and moved to Tennessee after marriage, and in about 1845 to this county, where they remained till death. They were the parents of fourteen children, twelve of whom still survive; of their descendants now living there are about 200. From early life, our subject was reared in this county, and received such an education as the common schools afforded, and afterward attended the college at Lebanon, Tenn., for one year. He then remained in the South for six years longer, engaged in teaching, with excellent results. Since returning North, he has still been engaged in teaching to some extent, having taught in all eighteen sessions of school. August 21, 1875, he started into the mercantile business in Rome, but in latter part of 1876 traded the store to Mr. R. F. Casey for his present farm, on which he has since been actively engaged as a successful agriculturist. His farm contains 100 acres. February 25, 1877, he was married in this county to Miss Minnie F. Davis, born in Centralia, and daughter of George Davis, now a resident of Rome. Mr. and Mrs. Hutchison have three children, and one dead, viz.: Mary Ethel, Maud Eltha and Mona Esther, and an infant deceased. He is a member of A. F. & A. M., Rome Lodge, No. 721. In politics, he is a Democrat.

B. P. MAXFIELD, retired farmer, P. O. Dix, was born in Overton County, Tenn., July 17, 1818, and is the son of John and Sarah (Carpenter) Maxfield. She was a native of Virginia, he of Tennessee. In 1825, they removed from Tennessee to Indiana, and in 1829 to Sangamon County, Ill., where they remained till 1831; then to Effingham County, Ill., and made that their home for ten years, when they located in St. Clair County, Ill., and he died there. His occupation was that of farming. They were the parents of ten children, seven of whom reached maturity. Of the number, but four are now living, viz., B. P., Seth, John and Mrs. Rhoda Finch. In 1846, our subject came to Jefferson County, Ill., and has resided here since. His mother, who also came, died in the county. Until 1858, he was engaged in farming and then embarked in the milling business at Rome, and continued in the same till 1865, when he again went to farming, and has made that his business since. Now, however, he has retired from active life. Mr. Maxfield has been very successful in business, and has done a good part by his children. His farm now contains ninety acres adjoining the village of Rome. November 15, 1840, he was married to Miss Lucinda Galloway. She was born in Kentucky November 15, 1817, daughter of Adam and Sarah (Lock) Galloway. In 1818, they moved to Edwards County, Ill., but afterward to Sangamon County, where he died. She died in Jackson County. They were the parents of twelve children, nine reaching maturity, but three now surviving—Mrs. Maxfield, Mrs. Sarah Flowers and Mrs. Elizabeth D. Stacy. Both the fathers of Mr. and Mrs. Maxfield served in the war of 1812, under Jackson. To Mr. and Mrs. Maxfield six children were born, three now living, viz., Sarah, wife of Matthew Tilford, and Mary A., wife of Robert White, both of this township, and one son, Hiram, now a resident of Effingham County. For over thirty years, Mr. M. has been a member of the Methodist Episcopal Church, of which church his wife is also a member. In politics, he is Republican.

WILLIAM A. McMILLAN, farmer, P. O. Walnut Hill, was born in Perry County, Ill., May 3, 1853, to James and Jane (Cunningham) McMillan. They were both natives of North Carolina, and of Irish descent. His occupation was that of a farmer. Both died in Perry County, Ill. Of their children, six are still living, our subject being the youngest. He was reared and educated in Perry County, Ill., but was left an orphan at an early age, his mother dying when he was but four years of age, and his father about four years later. When our subject was seventeen years of age he started in life upon his own account. He was married August 23, 1870, to Miss Martha J. Brown; she was born in Perry County also; daughter of Andrew and Margaret L. (Brown) Brown, both natives of South Carolina, and neither now surviving. Mr. and Mrs. McMillan have one child dead and four living, viz.: Ira Delbert, born in 1874, died July 1, 1875, at about fourteen months of age; Minnie L., born March 17, 1876; Cora L., born February 14, 1878; Charles B., born July 29, 1880; Frederick, born May 4, 1883. In politics, he is Republican. Mrs. McMillan is a member of United Presbyterian Church. In starting in life for themselves, Mr. McMillan had about $700 in money and his wife 100 acres of timber land. Their farm now contains 93 acres of well-improved land. They came to this county, to their present home, in 1876.

NEWTON MILBURN, farmer, P. O. Dix, was born in Rome Township September 9, 1855, and is the son of Hiram Milburn. Our subject was reared on his father's farm, and educated in the common schools of the county. May 25, 1876, he was married in this county to Miss Mary Douthet, born in Franklin County, Ill., in 1858, daughter of Campbell and Betsie (Fox) Douthet. Mr. and Mrs. Milburn have three children, viz., Lucy J., Hattie and Mary A. Our subject has made farming and stock-dealing his occupation, and in his chosen profession has been very successful by close attention to business. Soon after marriage, he moved to his present farm, which contains 140 acres in a high state of cultivation. Most of his attention is given to buying young stock and keeping it till he can realize a handsome profit through its growth. His father, Hiram Milburn, was born in Indiana January 23, 1816, to Robert and Nancy Milburn. Both had come to Indiana at an early date, and were married there in 1812. By trade, he was a hatter, but for many years was engaged in the milling business, and was one of a company who erected a steam flouring mill at Princeton, Ind., the first built in Southern Indiana. He was an old soldier, having served with Gen. Harrison at the battle of Tippecanoe. He was the father of a large family of children, five of whom still survive. Our subject, Hiram Milburn, came to Illinois in 1839, but settled in Marion County, where he remained until 1854, when he came to his present farm, where he has since resided. June 11, 1836, he was married near Evansville, Ind., to Miss Mary A. McCoy, who was born July 24, 1819. This union has been blessed with the following-named children: Mrs. Rose McWilliams, Mrs Mary E. Casey, Mrs. Malinda W. Meyers, Mrs. Louisa M. Free, Thomas N. and William A.; also two sons deceased, one dying while young, the other, Robert, in 1866, from disease contracted while in the four years' service of his country. Mr. Milburn is associated with the Republican party in political matters, but takes no active part in political life.

JOHN SANDERS, farmer, P. O. Walnut Hill, was born in Marion County, Ill., February 22, 1835, to John and Sarah (Copple) Sanders. He was born in North Carolina; she in Indiana. His parents moved to Indiana when he was about eighteen months of age, and it was there he was reared and educated, and died about July 6, 1875. She is still living. To them nine children were born, five of whom still survive, viz.: Thomas, Elizabeth, John, Charles and Isaac. In 1857, our subject came to this county and settled on his present farm, which contains 280 acres of land. He was married in Indiana, in 1854, to Miss Elizabeth Cook, who was born in Orange County, Ind., daughter of Absalom Cook. Their union has been blessed with nine children living, viz.: Thomas, William R., John A., Absalom, Cena, Samuel, Charles, Ira and Edward; also three dead. Mr. Sanders has been one of the successful farmers of this township, but his success in life has been made through his own energy. From April 7, 1865, till July 29, 1865, he was in the army, and served in Company H, Fifty-third Illinois Infantry. He is a member of Walnut Hill Lodge, I. O. O. F., No. 710. In politics, he is Greenbacker. For over thirty-one years he and wife have been active members of the Christian Church.

JOHN TELFORD, farmer, P. O. Walnut

Hill, Marion County. The subject of this sketch was born in South Carolina September 17, 1824, to Joseph and Martha (Craven) Telford. He was a native of South Carolina, born in 1791; she of Virginia, born 1798. In June, 1831, they moved from South Carolina to Illinois, bringing a family of five children. They settled in Marion County, but the farm lay partly in Marion and partly in Jefferson County. At the time of his death, September 7, 1850, he had 326 acres of land. She died in 1877. They were the parents of nine sons and two daughters. Only two of the family dead; the remainder are living in this and Marion County. In politics, he was a Whig, then Republican, and in religion was connected with the Associate Reformed Church. Our subject was reared on the farm in Marion County, and attended the schools in Marion and Jefferson Counties. The first year after embarking in life for himself, he lived out as a farm hand. February 1, he began the improvement of his present homestead, then having 40 acres of land given to him by his father. His farm now contains 286 acres, besides a farm owned by his wife. He has also deeded 40 acres to each of his three children. April 27, 1848, he was married to Miss Sarah M. Boggs, sister of William Boggs, whose sketch appears in this work.

This union has been blessed with the three following-named children: Julia A., wife of William L. Boles; Joseph C. and Charles R. He and wife are members of the Reformed Presbyterian Church. In politics, he is associated with the Greenback party.

B. F. WIMBERLY, farmer, P. O. Dix, was born in this county June 25, 1843; is the son of Elijah and Maria (Hollin) Wimberly. She was a native of Virginia, he of Tennessee. They came to this county at an early date, and died here. They were the parents of thirteen children, of whom four sons and two daughters are still living. Our subject's early life was spent in tilling the soil, and with but little advantage for a school education. When reaching his majority, he embarked in life for himself, and has through his own exertions been very successful. Most of his life he has been engaged in farming, but for eighteen months was in the mercantile business at Rome. He now, however, is actively engaged in making his present farm of 160 acres a complete success. In 1865, he was married to Miss Sally Walls. She was born in Marion County, Ill., daughter of Henry Walls. Five children are the result of this union, viz.: Alonzo, Emma, Robert, Clarence and Cora. In politics, his views coincide with those of the Democrat party.

DODDS TOWNSHIP.

JOHN H. ARNOLD, farmer, P. O. Mount Vernon, was born October 2, 1846, in Jefferson County, Ill., to which his father, John Arnold, came in 1827, with his father, Steven Arnold, who was a soldier in the war of 1812, his wife, Elizabeth Arnold, coming from Tennessee. John Arnold died October 10, 1878, in this county. The mother of our subject, Elizabeth W., born January 28, 1812, in Tennessee, was a daughter of John W. and Mary McBrian, natives of Virginia, and the parents of eight children, of whom four are now living, viz.: Steven W., John H., Martha T. and Elizabeth A. Prior L. and William J. died while in the United States Army in our late war. The former died January 29, 1863, and the latter died

March 29, 1863. Our subject was educated in his home district, and has carried on the farm of 260 acres. In politics, he is a Democrat.

C. N. BAUGH, farmer, P. O. Mount Vernon, was born November 19, 1840, in Jefferson County, Ill., son of John Baugh, a native of Lookingglass Prairie, Ill.; he died in Texas in 1881. His father, John, was a native of Virginia. The mother of our subject, Elizabeth Bruce, was born in Tennessee, but reared in this county. She is yet living in Texas and the mother of eight children now living. Our subject served in the United States Army during our late war, in the Sixtieth Illinois Volunteer Infantry, Company D; he was a blacksmith a part of the time, but was also in many battles, being wounded twice, and receives a pension. His wife, Sarilda Houser, a native of Union County, Ill., born October 13, 1846, is the mother of six children, viz.: May B., Viola R., Luella R., Millard A., John E. and Scott I. He has a farm of 120 acres, and in politics is a Greenbacker.

PHILLIP BRESACHER, farmer, P. O. Mt. Vernon, was born July 13, 1833, in Alsace, France, but which now belongs to Germany. His father, John Bresacher, was a native of the same place; he was a farmer also. He came to the United States when our subject was only four years old. The mother of our subject was of Germany also. She was the mother of seven boys. Of the boys only two are now living, viz., Henry Bresacher and our subject, who received his education in Centreville, St. Clair Co., Ill., where he was also married March 12, 1856, to Miss Louisa Schramm, born April 9, 1834, in Saxony, Germany, daughter of Michael and Elizabeth (Hugch) Schramm, natives of Germany. This union was blessed with seven children, all of whom are living, viz.: August, born December 2, 1867; Clara, born August 12, 1869; Sophia, born April 17, 1871; Pena, born January 6, 1874; Louisa, born September 14, 1877; Phillip, born November 14, 1879, and Lawrence, born June 18, 1881. Mr. and Mrs. Bresacher are members of the Evangelical Church. Our subject has a farm of 240 acres, and in politics he is a Republican. He and his wife lived among the Indians for quite awhile, and were treated nicely all the time. He came to this county in February of 1879.

WILLIAM S. BUMPUS, Jr., farmer, P. O. Mount Vernon, was born May 22, 1837, in Hanover County, Va. His father, William S. Bumpus, Sr., was a native of Virginia. He was also a farmer, and had also served an apprenticeship at the house-carpenter trade, in Old Virginia. He moved to Kentucky in 1838, and there our subject was reared and schooled. He came to this county about fourteen years ago, and is yet living. His father, Evan Bumpus, was a native of Virginia. The mother of our subject, Charlotte Buckner, was a native of Virginia, and the mother of six children. Our subject was joined in matrimony, in Butler County, Ky., to Miss Elizabeth Sharer, born December 24, 1837, in Butler County, Ky. She was a daughter of John and Rosa Ann Sharer, both natives of Kentucky. This union resulted in seven children, now living, viz.: Charles H., born October 27, 1858; Eugenia C., born July 31, 1860; William, born September 25, 1864; Theodore, born December 28, 1869; Millard, born November 9, 1871; Edgar, born December 26, 1874; Alpheus, born October 21, 1877. Mr. Bumpus is a member of the A., F. & A. M., Mount Vernon Lodge, No. 31; and I. O. O. F., Williams Lodge, No. 242; also a member of the Encampment. He has a farm of 240 acres, and came to this county in 1856. He has been Justice of the Peace four years; was re-elected and resigned. He then was Supervisor, being the first in the township; served three years; then was Collector three years, and is now Township Supervisor. In politics, he is identified with no particular party.

A. D. COWGER, farmer, P. O. Mount Vernon, was born August 13, 1825, in Wilson

County, Tenn., son of Adam Cowger, a native of Pennsylvania, a farmer and blacksmith; he died in Tennessee. The mother of our subject, Keziah Davis Cowger, was a native of Virginia, and died in Tennessee. She was a daughter of Isum Davis, a native of Virginia, and the parent of ten children, of whom only Ann E. F. Walker, Jacob Cowger, of Texas, and Martha P. Watson are now living. Our subject received no education at all, in early life. He came to Jefferson County about 1856, and here he has now a farm of 120 acres of land. He is self-made, and in political affairs is connected with the Democratic party. His first wife, Martha C. McConnell, was the mother of Mary Luster, now living. His second wife, Elizabeth Hunt, is the mother of three children now living, viz.: Ida Luster, Benjamin E. Cowger, now in Texas, and Electra Sursa. His present wife, Vermont Gorham, is a Kentuckian, born July 2, 1848. She is a daughter of Henry S. and Mary (Cooper) Gorham. She is the mother of six children, viz.: Rado, Walter J., Minnie M., Clara, living, and two deceased. Mr. and Mrs. Cowger are connected with the United Baptist Church.

ADAM CULLI, JR., farmer, P.O. Mt. Vernon, was born October 17, 1856, in St. Clair County, Ill., son of Adam Culli, Sr., a native of Alsace, France, a mason by occupation in the old country, but who follows farming in St. Clair County, Ill. His father, Christian Culli, was also a native of France, a tailor by occupation, and now living in St. Clair County, aged ninety-two years. The mother of our subject, Christine Baker, a native of France, is yet living, and the mother of five children, viz., Adam (our subject), Phillip, Christian, Leonhard, and Albert (deceased). Our subject was educated in St. Clair County, where he was joined in matrimony, May 18, 1880, to Miss Eva Dintelman, born July 24, 1860, in St. Clair County. She is a daughter of John and Sophia (Miller) Dintelman. This union was blessed with one child, Adam E., born March 18, 1881. Mr. and Mrs. Culli are members of the Lutheran Church. He has a farm of 320 acres of good land, with good buildings. In politics, he is a Republican.

LAWRENCE CUNIO, farmer, P. O. Mount Vernon, was born October 13, 1832, near Genoa, Italy. He is a son of Andrew Cunio, also a native of Italy, where he was a mason by occupation. The mother of our subject was Isabelle Cunio, also a native of Italy. She was the mother of eight children, of whom John B., Juana and Lawrence are now living. Our subject never went to school in his life, but while in the United States Army obtained the rudiments of an education. He came to this country in November, 1855, landing in Boston. He came to this county in 1859. In March, 1863, he enlisted in the Forty-ninth Illinois Volunteers, Company K, paying his own way to his regiment, which was stationed near Memphis. He served till the close of the war, participating in many thrilling scenes and famous battles, viz., Pea Ridge, Fort Jerusha, La., on the Red River, Alexander, Pleasant Hill, and other engagements. After the war, he returned to Jefferson County, where he was married to Mrs. Parthenia Maneas, born January 19, 1843, on Wolf Prairie, Jefferson County, daughter of Barton and Dorothy (Carter) Wells, of Tennessee. This union was blessed with five children, viz., Charles A., born September 9, 1866; Laura B., December 15, 1868; Plummer E. and Etta May, twins, January 27, 1873; and Johnny, October 31, 1875. Mr. Cunio has a farm of 150 acres, and in politics he is identified with the Republican party.

JOHN DOWNER, farmer, P. O. Mount Vernon, was born March 27, 1834, in Jefferson County, Ill., on Moore's Prairie. His father, John Downer, Sr., was born in New Hampshire in 1802. He is yet living in this county, to which he came in an early day. He was a farmer and teacher by occupation, being one of the first teachers, and also one of the first to organize a Sunday school. His father, Silas Downer, was a native of New Hampshire. The mother of our subject, Sarah Neal, was born in Vermont; she died in this county. She was a daughter of Walter Neal, a native of Vermont, and was the mother of nine children. Our subject went to the schools in this county before the free-school system. He has been a farmer all his life, owning now a farm of 130 acres. Our subject was married in this county to Sarah F. Bradley, born August 13, 1834, in Ohio, daughter of Joseph and Mary (Van Cleve) Bradley, he a native of Delaware and she a native of New York. Mrs. Downer is the mother of nine children, viz.: Mary and Martha, deceased; Oscar M., who married Anna Maltby; O. O., Amy B., Lydia M., Willie B., John F. and Eunice. Mr. and Mrs. Downer are religiously connected with the M. E. Church. In politics he has been Democratic, but during the last few years he has been rather independent. Mr. Downer has been the Collector for three years, and is now the School Treasurer.

JOHN W. ESTES, farmer, P. O. Mount Vernon, was born January 4, 1837, son of James Estes, born 1809, in Tennessee, a farmer, who came to this county when a young man, and died here in 1872; his father, Absalom Estes, died here also. The mother of our subject, Temperance (McBrian) Estes, came from Middle Tennessee. She died in 1871, leaving three children, viz.: John W., Mary C. Davenport, deceased, and James A. Our subject was educated in the common schools in this township, and here he married Miss Susannah B. Lynch, born November 17, 1838, in Jackson County, Ill., daughter of Marmaduke B. and Sarah A. (Wolsey) Lynch, natives of Tennessee. Six children now living are the result of this happy union—Rosella F. Jones, born October 27, 1858; Anna E., born December 11, 1860; James M. W., born December 19, 1862; John E. L., born November 18, 1864; George E., born April 7, 1869; Charles R., born August 16, 1871. Our subject served in One Hundred and Thirty-second New York Regiment, and also the Fiftieth Illinois Regiment; served till the close of the war. He has a farm here of eighty acres. He was the first Constable, was also Township Clerk and Assessor. In politics, he is an Anti-monopolist man.

ISAAC GARRISON, farmer, P. O. Mount Vernon. This gentleman is one of that good old class of settlers who have made their way in the world amid privations and hardships that would discourage the most of our young people of the present day. He started with nothing, and is to-day classed among our well-to-do farmers. He was born January 16, 1814, in Smith County, Tenn.. His father, David Garrison, who is well known to the old pioneers as the owner of a horse mill east of Mount Vernon, was a native of North Carolina, and his father, Moses Garrison, was also a native of that State. The mother of our subject, Elizabeth (Newby) Garrison, was a native of Tennessee. She and her husband died in this county. She was the mother of twelve children, of whom four were twins. Of the children, only three are living, viz.: Rebecca Bridges, Mary Vaughn and our subject, who helped his father in his early life a great deal, and whose early career is remarkable for his privations, perseverance and final success. He never went to school, but learned to read and write from his first wife, Margaret Elder, who was the mother of seven children, viz.: William C., James W., Elizabeth Ackerson and Rebecca Jones, living, and Dr. David Garrison, Nancy and Azariah, deceased. His second wife was Mrs. Margaret Davis, daughter of James Murry, and the mother of Laura and Mary Jackson, both deceased. His third wife was Mrs. Elmyra Estes, daughter of Henry Goodridge, and the mother of Isaac Newton, deceased. Our subject's present wife was Mrs. Mary A. Beasley, daughter of Andrew and Mary (McFall) Clark, both natives of Virginia. Mrs. Garrison was born December 23, 1826, in Smith County, Tenn. Mr. and Mrs. Garrison are connected with the Baptist Church. He has now nearly 600 acres of good land, which, though he is almost seventy years old, he oversees. He is now a well-to-do man, and has helped all his children in life, who are all well to do. In politics, he has been a Democrat. He has split rails for 25 cents per hundred, and worked for $3 per month, being hired out by his father, whom he had helped a great deal in after life. He came here first in 1830, and after one year he went to Gallatin County, Ill., where he first worked the farm of his uncle, and lived in the county twenty years, returning to this county in 1853. While in Gallatin County, he was Captain of the militia for seven years.

WILLIAM C. GARRISON, farmer, P. O. Mount Vernon. This gentleman, who may properly be classed among our thriftiest and well-to-do farmers who are mainly self-made men, without whom no county can be properly developed, and who are the main stays in all moral, financial and religious matters, was born September 7, 1834, in Saline County, Ill. His father, Isaac Garrison, was born January 16, 1814, in Smith County, Tenn. He is yet a farmer in this county, to which he came in 1829; his father, David Garrison, was a native of North Carolina. Our subject was educated in Southern Illinois, but is principally self-educated. He came here with his father, and has been identified with the county ever since, following farming mainly. In 1862, he was appointed Deputy Sheriff by Sheriff J. B. Goodrich, serving two years. He filled the offices of Township Assessor and Supervisor twice, to the entire satisfaction of the people. He has a farm of 220 acres with good improvements and well watered. In politics, he was formerly connected with the Democratic party, but of late years he has been identified with the Greenback and Republican parties. Our subject was joined in matrimony, April 26, 1866, in this county, to Mrs. Mary J. Noel, born February 23, 1839, in Gallatin County, Ill. She was a daughter of George and Hannah (Pollard) Mills, he a native of New York, she a native of Yorkshire, England, and yet living, the mother of seven children. Mr. and Mrs. Garrison have been blessed with four children, viz.: Jennie, born July 4, 1867; William E., born February 3, 1870; John C., born December 15, 1871; James E., born June 5, 1874; and she is also mother of Johnette Noel, born April 11, 1858, daughter of her first husband, John Noel. Mrs. Garrison is a member of the Baptist Church.

J. W. GARRISON, farmer, P. O. Mount Vernon, was born June 21, 1839, in Saline County, Ill., son of Isaac and Margaret Garrison, old settlers, who are mentioned elsewhere. Our subject went to school in our old-fashioned subscription schools in Southern Illinois. He came to this county with his parents, and has been a farmer all his life. He now owns 310 acres of land in this county. In 1862, he joined the army, enlisting in the One Hundred and Tenth Regiment Illinois Volunteers, Company G; he served till the close of the war, and was mustered out at Washington, D. C. He participated in different engagements, and after the war again went to farming. He was married twice. His first wife, Nancy J. Vaughn, was born and died in this county; his second wife, Lydia Hughes, was born August 8, 1850, in Athens County, Ohio. She is a daughter of Cyrus S. and Louisa E. (Dye) Hughes, and is the mother of four children, viz., Louisa May, born September 23, 1876; Ora E., July 17, 1878; Cyrus I., February 23, 1880; and Lee Ann, February 4, 1882. Our subject is identified with the Greenback party, favoring the anti-monopoly movement.

SAMUEL GIBSON, farmer, P. O. Mount

Vernon, was born October 23, 1827, in the southeastern part of Ohio, son of James Gibson, a native of County Tyrone, Ireland. James was a farmer, and came to this county before the war, and died here. His father, Thomas Gibson, was also a native of Ireland. The mother of our subject, Mary (Gourley) Gibson, was a native of Ireland, and died in this county. She was the mother of eight children. Our subject received his education in the common schools of Ohio, but is mainly self-educated, especially in latter years. He learned the blacksmith trade in Zanesville, Ohio. In 1849, he came to this county, following his trade in Mount Vernon when it was a small village; in 1854, he bought 160 acres of land, farmed on it several years, and then returned to Mount Vernon. In 1861, he again moved on to his farm, and the next year entered the army as First Lieutenant in the One Hundred and Tenth Regiment Illinois Volunteers, Company G; the following year he resigned on account of sickness. Since then he has farmed, and served the people in the capacity of Justice of the Peace for about twelve years, filling the office to the present day. He has also filled minor offices, and in politics is independent, voting for the best man. He has now 460 acres of land in this county, besides town property. He was married, November 30, 1851, in Mount Vernon, to Miss Angeline Newby, born July 10, 1835, in Illinois, daughter of Hezekiah B. and Nancy (Brown) Newby, old settlers, and highly respected people. This union resulted in ten children now living—Augustus, Mary I., John E., Oscar N., Thomas O., Adela, William E., Samuel A., Nancy E. and Walter. Mr. and Mrs. Gibson are members of the Presbyterian Church, of which he is an Elder; he is also a member of the I. O. O. F., Marion Lodge, No. 13, Mount Vernon, Ill.

JOHN A. JOHNSON, farmer, P. O. Mount Vernon. This gentleman, who is one of our most energetic and enterprising farmers, is well deserving a place in the history of Jefferson County. He was born April 19, 1842, in Tennessee. He came to this county with his parents when he was quite young. He has been a tiller of the soil all his life, and now owns about 300 acres of land in this township. He was joined in matrimony to Miss Margaret C. Daniel, born November 16, 1846, in this county. She is a daughter of Jacob and Emeline (Scott) Daniel, natives of Kentucky. Mrs. Johnson is well worthy the esteem and confidence with which she is regarded everywhere. She is the mother of six children, viz.: Lillian Z., Vernadell, Laura B., A. Floyd, Gustavus and Virgil. Mr. Johnson is no aspirant for public office and in political matters he has been identified with the Republican party.

JAMES WILLIAM LINDSEY, engineer, Opdyke. This gentleman is a native of Ross County, Ohio, where he was born December 29, 1831, son of Abraham Lindsey, a native of Ohio. The mother of our subject, Nancy Bannon Lindsey, was a native of Delaware, and the mother of one son, our subject, who was educated in Ohio, where he also learned the engineering with his uncle, Sims Davenport. He was joined in matrimony in Columbus, Ohio, December 23, 1854 to Miss Catharine Freck, born November 8, 1833, in Wurtemberg, Germany, daughter of Tilman and Fannie (Harmon) Freck, both natives of Germany. This union was blessed with the following children: Mary I., wife of William Snider; Alice P., wife of Jeptha Jones; Emma L., wife of Owen M. Smith; Charles F., born May 1, 1863; Nancy E., born May 20, 1866; Catharine U, born June 26, 1868; Frank B., born January 14, 1871; Albert R., January 8, 1875; John W., January 17, 1877. Mr. Lindsey came to this county in the fall of 1877. He owns 196 acres of land, but at times follows his trade as engineer. In politics, he is a Republican.

S. T. PACE, farmer, P. O. Mount Vernon, was born August 4, 1833, son of Joseph Pace.

The subject of this brief sketch is one of Jefferson County's most unassuming but worthy citizens. He has made farming his chief occupation and now owns 600 acres of land near Mount Vernon. In the fall of 1861, he enlisted in the Sixtieth Regiment Illinois Volunteer Infantry, Company I. He served three years, participating in many thrilling scenes and famous battles, among others those of Mission Ridge, Kenesaw Mountain and Peach Tree Creek, losing his right arm at Jonesboro, near Atlanta. After the war, he returned home and again turned his attention to farming. In politics, he has been identified with the Republican party.

CORNELIUS PEERY, farmer, P. O. Mount Vernon, was born June 9, 1808, in Tazewell County, Va. His father, James M. Peery, was a native of Virginia, and also a farmer; he died in Perry County, Ill. His father, John Peery, came from Ireland. The mother of our subject, Phœbe Pickens, was a native of Virginia, and the mother of eleven children; her parents, Thomas and Sarah (Brown) Pickens, were also natives of Virginia. Our subject was educated in Kentucky. He came to Washington County, Ill., in 1833; he commenced farming there, and in 1867 he came to this county. He was married more than once. His first wife, Rhoda B. Ayers, was born in St. Clair County; she died in Washington County, Ill. His second wife, Mrs. Polly Gore, is a daughter of Richard Hull. She is the mother of seven children, viz., James M. Gore, Escalana Gore, George M. (deceased, aged one year and sixteen days), Jonathan A., Richard A. (a law student in Belleville, Ill.), Mary M. (deceased) and Martha N. Gibson. Our subject began life with nothing to speak of, and is to-day classed among our well-to-do men in this county. In politics, he has been identified with the Democratic party.

SILAS ROGERS, farmer, P. O. Mount Vernon, was born November 8, 1845, in this county. His father, William A. Rogers, was a native of Tennessee; he came here in an early day, and died January 1, 1874, his father, Abraham Rogers, being also a native of Tennessee. The mother of our subject, Amanda A. Pace, a native of Kentucky, was a daughter of John M. Pace, and is the mother of ten children. Our subject was educated here. He was joined in matrimony, January 11, 1883, in Brighton, Macoupin Co., Ill., to Miss Mollie McKenny, born January 25, 1860, in Union County, Ky., daughter of John B. and Mary (Church) McKenny, natives of Kentucky. Mrs. Rogers is a member of the Methodist Episcopal Church. In politics, Mr. Rogers is a Democrat.

JOHN TIPTON, farmer, P. O. Opdyke, was born January 9, 1838, in Knox County, East Tennessee, son of Isaac Tipton, a native of East Tennessee, where he yet resides. The mother of our subject, Dama Tipton, was a native of East Tennessee, where she died. Our subject has been a farmer all his life. He came to this county in 1860, and the next year he joined the Union army, Forty-fourth Illinois Volunteers, Company I, serving till the close of the war. He participated in many thrilling scenes and battles, among others that of Pea Ridge, Stone River, Chickamauga, Mission Ridge, Strawberry Plains, Nashville, Atlanta, and many minor engagements. He was only about one week away from his command during his entire term of service. After the war, he came back to Jefferson County, where he married Anna Bates, who died after giving birth to four children, viz., Eva (deceased), Emma, Lucinda, Lotta (deceased). His second wife, Mary Ann Presly, was born in North Carolina. She is the mother of two children now living, viz., James and Mima. Mr. Tipton is a member of the Methodist Episcopal Church. He has a farm of 240 acres of land. In politics, he is a Republican. Mr. Tipton is a self-made man in every respect. His great-grandfather, Billy Tipton, was a soldier in the Revolutionary war, being shot through the body, and his son, Jacob Tipton, was a soldier in the Mexican war.

JAMES T. WOLF, coppersmith, Mount Vernon, was born January 23, 1853, in St. Louis, Mo. His father, Abraham D. Wolf, is a native of Pennsylvania. His career in life has been a checkered but a very honorable one. He came West long before Horace Greeley gave his advice on the subject, and has been one of the pioneer boatmen of the Western waters. He started as a ship carpenter, but, through his own exertion and perseverance, he worked his way up to mate, pilot and Captain, acting in the latter capacities almost thirty-five years. He is yet living on his farm of 320 acres. The mother of our subject, Virginia Sexton Wolf, is a native of Virginia. Her parents, John and Phœbe Sexton, were also natives of Virginia. Mrs. Virginia Wolf is the mother of nine children, of whom four are now living, viz., James, George R., Fannie W. (McKnight), and Phœbe S. Our subject was educated in St. Louis, Mo., where he also learned and followed the coppersmith trade. In November, 1876, he came to this county, with his parents and here he has followed his trade part of the time. In politics, he is identified with the Democratic party.

BLISSVILLE TOWNSHIP.

JESSE A. DEES, farmer, P. O. Laur. A life of nearly fourscore years; launched upon its tempestuous sea in circumstances poor and lonely; hardships, trials, temptations on every hand; peace and rest unknown; but he struggles, the tide turns gradually in his favor, he slips, falls back, only to strive again; time and perseverance are not to be baffled; obstacles the most formidable are grappled with at every step, but to his matchless energy they succumb, and are consigned to the rear; onward he strides, the land of peace and plenty is in sight; he is there, the goal of his highest ambition is at last reached, and as he turns and glances backward o'er the rugged pathway he has trod, can it be other than with commingled feelings of just pride and honor. Such is a circumstantial outline of the lives of many of our great and noble men, and it is strikingly applicable to that of the worthy subject of this sketch, the necessary brevity of which compels us to do him but meager justice. Jesse A. Dees was born June 11, 1808, Abbeyville District, South Carolina, being the place of his birth. His father was Robert Gillam, and his mother Naomi Dees, whose name our subject retained. He lived with her until becoming of age, she having in the meantime married Lewis Green, by whom she had one child. His advantages of an early education being extremely deficient, and his mother's circumstances poor, our youth was compelled to rely wholly upon his own resources to obtain the four-and-a-half months schooling, which was all that he ever received. This he paid for by setting bait for bee-trees, and finding two of the latter, he disposed of the honey secured to a Catholic seminary, at $1 per gallon, and was thus enabled to proudly defray the expenses which his limited course of study had incurred. This was in Perry County, Mo., whence his step-father had removed, after living awhile in Arkansas and still previously in Jefferson County, Ill., having first come here during the close of the year 1824. Our subject was hired out by his step-father, and afterward worked out on his own account. He went to St. Louis in his twenty-first year, and was there variously engaged for about six months. He carried a hod to the fourth story of the court house, then in course of construction, dug cellars, labored on the wharves, and worked at anything his eager hands could find to do. He returned to this county, and with his hard-earned savings built a little house, opened a little farm, and last, though not least, married a good little wife, and thus he commenced the journey of life, with fair winds and a clear head. His happy affianced was Naomi Booth, born March 4, 1809. She is still living, and the venerable couple have long since celebrated the golden anniversary of their wedded life. Having no children of their own, they have raised several during their life, most of whom have grown up and started out for themselves. Mr. Dees has farm property to the extent of 1,400 acres of selected land, all in this county, four or five hundred of which constitute the home place, on which he had moved in the spring of 1837. In 1871, he erected a handsome and commodious residence, the finest, perhaps, in the surrounding country. During his life, he has engaged in farming in its various branches, and has given particular attention to stock, having at times large herds of cattle and mules, and at present has a herd of sixty of the latter. Mr. Dees is a member of the A. F. & A. M., Clay Lodge, No. 152, being also a Royal Arch Mason. He has filled most of the offices of his township, and for many years has served as President of the County Agricultural Society, and is a present stockholder therein. Politically, he is a Democrat of the Jacksonian school, but his votes have repeatedly shown that he strives to secure the services of an honest man, be his political faith what it may. We have now given the record dates in the life of Mr. Dees, and as these mark the different periods therein, they but feebly portray the many vicissitudes through which he has passed. Being born to a poor mother, whose humble circumstances permitted her to do but little for her child, he was thus thrown upon his own resources, and the ingenuity and energy which he displayed in his endeavors to secure means to pay for an early schooling and to obtain a start in life, developed traits in his character upon which a solid foundation could rest. He was virtually his own educator, his own genius was his teacher, and he was likewise the architect of his own fortune, for he never inherited a dollar. His life was at first varied. He was a great lover of the chase, and many bear, and hundreds of deer have succumbed to his unerring aim. Still hale and hearty, Mr. Dees and his noble wife have, apparently, years yet to live, and as they go down in the evening of life, the blessings and well-wishes accompany them of the community in whose midst they have lived and toiled for so many years.

ELI FAIRCHILD, farmer, P. O. Laur, is a native of Wabash County, Ind., born December 11, 1829, to Erastus and Elizabeth (Giddings) Fairchild, he of New York and she of England. The father was a farmer. He moved to Ohio, then to Indiana, where Eli was born, and afterward back again to Ohio. He came to Jefferson County in 1839, and located in Blissville Township, but removed again to Bond County, Ill., where he died. He was married a second time to Edith Shelton. By his first wife he had eleven children, of whom three are living—Eli, Melissa and Ann M. Our subject obtained but a limited education, and he has always given his attention to farming pursuits; he has 320 acres of land, and in 1871 he erected a fine frame residence. He was first married to Maranda L. Haines, who bore him one child—Maranda L. His second marriage was with Sarah L. Place, by whom he had nine children—Rhoda, George W., Emily, Luna, Daniel S., Eli W., Dora M., Minnie F. and Eunice. Mr. Fairchild was married a third time, to Susan E. Boswell, who has also departed this life, the mother of one child—Mary E. Politically, Mr. Fairchild is a Republican.

CYRUS GILBERT, farmer, P. O. Laur, was born in Washington County, Ohio, January 26, 1823, a son of Eli and Susanna (Gale) Gilbert, natives of New Hampshire. The father was a cloth dresser by trade, and worked at it for several years in Ohio; he also ran a water mill, and in after years gave his attention to agricultural pursuits. He was a very enterprising man, and after coming to Jefferson County in 1839, built the house where our subject now resides, out of lumber brought from Ohio. The old folks had a family of seventeen children, of whom there are living Ira, Truman, Josiah, Philo, Cyrus, Malissa, Menzis R., Waldo, Lois and Alvin. Our subject received a little schooling in his native State, and after coming to this county with his parents, attended the old schools here. In 1842, he contracted a scrofulous disease, which was cured under the skillful treatment of an Indian doctor, who resided in this State. Mr. Gilbert studied with him a year, and he has since been called upon himself to attend to many cases of this nature, and his knowledge of the various herbs which seem to possess remarkable medicinal qualities has rendered his services of value to the afflicted. Mr. Gilbert has several hundred acres of land, and he engages mostly in farming. He married Eliza J. McClendon, and has a family of four children—Mary E., Stephen U., Mary F. and Annie. Mr. Gilbert has five children deceased. He is a member of the A., F. & A. M., Mt. Vernon Lodge, and with his wife of the Universalist Church. Politically, he is a Republican.

MENZIS R. GILBERT, farmer, P. O. Laur, was born February 23, 1831, in Washington County, Ohio, a son of Eli Gilbert. (See sketch of Cyrus Gilbert elsewhere.) Subject came with his parents to Jefferson County in 1839, and here continued his attendance at school, although his eyes, which had been seriously affected from his birth, prevented him from doing much studying. He was brought up on a farm, and has during his life, given his attention to no other employment. His present farm of 400 acres is under a good state of cultivation, and he engages in mixed farming. He was married, January 19, 1858, to Elizabeth Ford, born January 22, 1841, a daughter of Solomon Ford, of this county. Five children have blessed this union, of whom three survive—Waldo E., born September 30, 1861; Luna O., June 12, 1863, and Tilman I., August 15, 1868. Mr. Gilbert has a good residence, which he built in 1859, and made some substantial additions in 1875. Having a farm especially adapted to the raising of stock, he intends to devote some time to this branch of farming hereafter. He is a Republican in politics, and, with his wife, a member of the Universalist Church.

ALVIN GILBERT, farmer, P. O. Laur, was born in Washington County, Ohio, March 3, 1839 (for parents see sketch of Cyrus Gilbert), coming to this county with his parents in October of the same year. Our subject obtained what little education the common schools of this vicinity afforded. He has given his constant attention to farming pursuits, with the exception of two years, 1858-60, during which period he ran a general store in Ashley, Ill., in partnership with his father. His present farm property consists of 440 acres of land, located mostly in Blissville Township. He was united in marriage, June 4, 1858, to Annie M. Watkins, a daughter of Jacob R. and Ann E. (Anderson) Watkins. Mr. and Mrs. Gilbert are the parents of six children—Walter J., Thomas E. Orloff, Linnie, Maggie M. and Maude. Politically, Mr. Gilbert is a Republican.

EDWIN GREEN, farmer, P. O. Laur, was born December 30, 1823, in this county, to Reuben and Drusilla (Dees) Green, both of whom were natives of Georgia. Reuben Green was one of the first settlers in Jefferson County. He was a farmer by occupation, and he served in the Black Hawk war. The parents were blessed with a large family, eight of whom are living. Our subject obtained but a few months' schooling in his early life, and he started in life as a tiller of the soil, and has always been thus engaged, with the exception of a short period during which he was engaged in business in Ashley, Ill. His first marriage was with Nancy Landrum, a daughter of Henry Landrum. She died December 30, 1870, the mother of eight children, of whom five survive—Sarah, E. F., Mary C., Charles L. and Thomas J. Mr. Green's second marriage was with Jane Outhouse, a daughter of Meredith Outhouse. This union has given five children—William M., Lulu M., Claude E., Harry E. and Andrew F. In February, 1865, Mr. Green joined the One Hundred and Fifty-second Illinois Volunteer Infantry, Col. Stevenson. He was mustered out at Memphis, and came home the first of September of the same year. He has filled many offices in the county, including those of Constable, Assessor, Justice of the Peace, and is at present an officer in the latter capacity. He is a Democrat in politics. He has a farm of 240 acres, which is given to farming in its general branches. Mr. Green and his brothers are among the oldest citizens that were born in Jefferson County.

BARNETT GREEN, farmer, P. O. Laur, is a native of this county, born September 23, 1827, a son of Reuben Green. (See sketch of Edwin Green.) Our subject received but a limited education in his younger years, and farming has always been his occupation. His present farm consists of 160 acres, which is given to mixed farming. He was united in marriage to Martha J. Page, a daughter of William and Margaret (Taylor) Page, and the union has been blessed with eleven children, nine of whom are living—Margaret, Harvey, Mary E., Sarah, Delilah, Marshall, Albert, George and Charlie. Politically, Mr. Green is a Democrat.

WILLIAM HICKS, farmer, P. O. Laur, was born in this county September 16, 1828, to Isaac and Rebecca (Casey) Hicks, both of whom were natives of Kentucky. The father was a substantial farmer; he moved from Kentucky to this county at an early day, and one of his sons, Thomas, was the first white male child born in this county. The parents had six children, only two of whom are now living—James and our subject. The latter obtained but about three months' schooling, in the old subscription schools, and, giving his attention to farming in early life, has been thus engaged most of his life. He has at present a farm of 120 acres, which is given to general farming. He was married, in December, 1848, to Martha M. Ames, and nine children have blessed the union, of whom six are living—Thomas, Mary, George W., Millie, Charlie and Eliza. In 1861, Mr. Hicks enlisted in the Forty-fourth Iowa Volunteer Infantry, Col. Noblesdorf. The first time out he served as Lieutenant. He resigned on account of ill health, came home and in the spring of 1864 volunteered again and rejoined the same regiment, and served until the fall of 1865, being mustered out at Springfield; he fought at Pea Ridge and other battles in Missouri, and was with Sherman thoughout his campaign. Mr. Hicks served also in the Mexican war—a year in the Third Illinois Volunteer Infantry; was at Cerro Gordo, and other severe engagements. Politically, Mr. Hicks is a Republican.

SAMUEL JOHNSON, farmer, P. O. Ashley, came from Washington County, Penn., where he was born October 28, 1822, a son of John and Lydia (Updegraff) Johnson, both natives of the same State. The father, who was a son of John Johnson, came from England, learned the shoe-maker's trade and worked at it many years, but gave his attention to farming pursuits in after life. The parents had thirteen children, of whom five are supposed to be living—Samuel, Henry, Harmon, William and possibly Timothy. Our subject obtained a little schooling in early life, and at the age of ten removed to Ohio, where he remained until coming to this county, in 1865, having the year before purchased 140 acres of land here; he is at present engaged in general farming. He was married to Hester Johnson, a daughter of Thomas J. and Julia (Bruce) Johnson, and the union has given twelve children, seven of whom survive—Jennette, Dennis J., Sarah, John W., Samuel A., George W. and David P. Mr. Johnson has three grandchildren living with him—Allen T., Hester and Elizabeth—children of his daughter Julia, who was the wife of Richard J. Brunson. She died October 17, 1879. Mr. Johnson is an A., F. & A. M., Clay Lodge; he has filled the office of Supervisor, and is at present School Treasurer and J. P., having discharged the duties of the latter office for a period of fifteen years. He is a Democrat in politics.

JOSEPH LAUR, farmer, P. O. Laur, was born in Lower Canada, in the town of Wolf River, March 14, 1814, a son of Charles and Lucy (Deuame) Laur, he of Vermont and she of Canada, of French descent. The parents had six children, our subject being the only one living from all that is known. The father had been twice married before marrying our subject's mother, and by his former wives had seventeen children. Our subject received but a limited education; he could only speak French until he became eighteen years of age. In 1833, he emigrated to Lincoln, Mass., and after farming a few years, served an apprenticeship to the shoe maker's trade, but only worked at it a few years. In 1839, he went to boating on the river, selling general merchandise between Pittsburgh and New Orleans. He came to Jefferson County in 1840, but returned to the river, and three years later came back and settled on his farm, which he had previously come into possession of. He was married in the spring of 1844 to Mary E. Philp, and the union has been blessed with seven children—Charles T., Benjamin M., Laura, Harriett, James W., Mary E. and Elizabeth. In 1850, Mr. Laur went to California overland, and returned in December, 1851, by way of Central America. October 19, 1861, he enlisted in Company K, Forty-ninth Illinois Volunteer Infantry, Col. Morrison. He was shortly afterward elected Captain of his company, and served as such through the war. He took part in the battles of Fort Donelson, Shiloh, Corinth, was in the Red River expedition, and at Vicksburg, etc. His present farm consists of 240 acres. The post office at Williamsburg was named in his honor. He and wife are members of the Methodist Church. Politically, he is a Republican.

THOMAS H. MANNEN, farmer, P. O. Laur, is a native of Bracken County, Ky., born June 24, 1839, eldest child of Sidney S. and Eliza A. (Walton) Mannen, natives of the same State. The father was a tanner by trade, and was thus engaged in his native State and also in Illinois, removing in 1841; he dealt also largely in stock, and in early days followed the river, dealing in horses, etc.; he also farmed in late years, and he died on election day, 1871. His wife is still living in this county. The parents had nine children, one of whom is deceased; those living are T. H., Josiah H., John J., Leslie C., Robert W., Sidney S., Annie E. and Jerome. Mr. Mannen obtained but a limited education in early years. He started out as a farmer, but after some time thus engaged, he went into the mercantile business, and ran a general store in Williamsburg for several years, since which he has given his attention to farming pursuits. He has about 400 acres of land, and raises and deals in cattle and stock largely. He was first married to Isabel Norris, who died in 1870; she bore him five children, four living—Olive M., Annie E., Martha E. and Thomas E. Mr. Mannen's present wife was Margaret (Dodds) Norris, widow of A. J. Norris, and daughter of John Dodds. This union has given one child—Sunie O. In politics, Mr. Mannen is a Democrat.

GEORGE NEWELL, farmer, P. O. Laur, was born in this county about one-half mile from where he at present resides, April 15, 1841, the eldest child of Asa B. and Eleanor (Shuttlesworth) Newell, he a native of Vermont, and she of Ohio. The parents had five children—George, Levi, Lucy, Oscar and Ichabod. The mother died when our subject was about twelve years old, and the father married Margaret Hayes, who is still living. Of this marriage, there were three children, two of whom are living, Philip and Stephen D. Our subject obtained but a meager schooling, and he started out as a farmer. His present farm consists of 120 acres. He was married to Sarah C. Gilbert, a daughter of Stephen Gilbert. This union has been blessed with seven children, of whom six are living—Asa, Laura, Mina, Rufus N., Orla and Minnie. August 2, 1861, Mr. Newell enlisted in the Forty-fourth Illinois Volunteer Infantry. He served out his time of enlistment and was discharged at Atlanta, Ga., in October, 1864. He lay sick for several months in the hospital, and fought afterward at Chattanooga, Chickamauga and Atlanta, and other severe engagements. Politically, he is a Republican.

O. P. NORRIS, physician and surgeon, Williamsburg, was born in Bracken County, Ky., August 29, 1843, a son of Joseph and Rebecca R. West (Morris), the father a native of Kentucky, and the mother of Pennsylvania. The father followed boating in early life, but later he engaged in farming. The parents were blessed with nine children, of whom there are five living—O. P., William H., Millard F., Joseph D. and Edward J. Our subject obtained a little schooling in his native State, and after coming to this county with his parents, about 1851, he continued his studies here, attending in after years the school at Normal, Ill. In September, 1864, he was drafted into the war, and joined the Thirty-second Illinois Volunteer Infantry, which belonged to the Seventeenth Army Corps, under Blair. The regiment joined Sherman at Atlanta, and fought under him at Savannah, Columbia, Bentonville, etc. Our subject returned at the close of the war, and attended the high school at Mount Vernon, Ill. He had a desire for studying medicine, and he read under the instruction of Dr. J. C. Gray, of Mount Vernon. He afterward attended the Ohio Medical College, Cincinnati, and received a full course of lectures, and later the Cincinnati College of Medicine and Surgery, from which institution he graduated, and returned to this county, where he has since enjoyed a liberal patronage; he has given a good deal of attention to diseases of the eye, but of late has given his time to the study of obstetrics, in which branches of the profession he is especially successful. The Doctor has dealt largely in real estate, having at present several hundred acres of land in the county, and also a fine residence in Williamsburg, which he erected in 1873. He has been Postmaster for seven or eight years at this point; has administered several estates, and was engaged in the drug and dry goods business until his practice assumed such proportions as to demand all of his attention. He was united in marriage to Sarah M. Smith, and the union has given four children, three of whom are living—Myrtie E., Lena F. and Verner S. The Doctor is a member of the A. F. & A. M., and has also been an I. O. O. F. for many years. He has filled many of the offices of the township, including that of Supervisor. Politically, he is a Democrat.

SIDNEY PLACE, farmer, P. O. Laur, is one of the old and respected residents of Jefferson County. He was born in Chittenden County, Vt., April 21, 1807, youngest child of John and Lydia (Garland) Place, both natives of New Hampshire. The father was a carpenter by trade, but in late years he engaged in farming. He volunteered, and served six months in the Revolutionary war, and fought at the battle of Bennington; he died April 22, 1828. The parents were blessed with ten children, only two of whom are living—Hannah and Sidney. The father had been married twice, his first wife bearing him three children. Our subject got but a meager education in early life. At about ten years of age, his parents removed to New York, and then to Ohio, where the father died, and afterward to this county in 1839, where the mother died in August, 1845. Mr. Place worked at boat-building several years in Ohio, and after coming to this county engaged in farming; he has a farm of 280 acres. He married Rhoda Dufur, a daughter of David Dufur, of Ohio. This union has been blessed with ten children, five of whom are living—Emily, Luther, Isaac, Rufus and Malissa. Mr. Place had five sons in the late war, one of whom, Stephen, died in Andersonville Prison. Politically, Mr. Place is a Republican. He has nine great-grandchildren living.

ISAAC W. ROBINSON, merchant and Notary Public, Williamsburg, was born in Franklin County, this State, July 20, 1845, the eldest child of Isaac W. and Margaret (Knox) Robinson, he of South Carolina and she of Tennessee. The father was a farmer and stock-dealer during life, and was a strong Democrat in politics. The parents moved to Jefferson County when our subject was about two years old. There were six children in the family, four of whom survive—Isaac W., William A., Mary J. and John A. Our subject obtained his early schooling first in an old log schoolhouse, and he afterward attended a select school for about eighteen months. During his life, he has dealt extensively in stock, and has also given some time to farming pursuits. Thinking that he would take up law as a profession, he studied during his leisure moments in this direction for many years. He, however, went into business in partnership with J. D. Norris, and being burnt out some time afterward, received a considerable set-back, but opened a general store himself in February, 1878, which he still runs, carrying a line of drugs, groceries and dry goods. He has been Assessor in this and McClellan Township, and has also been for several years Notary Public. He married Louvina J. (McConnaughey) Gilbert, widow of William H. Gilbert, and daughter of James McConnaughey, of this county, and this union has been blessed with two children—James W. and Martha J. In March, 1864, Mr. Robinson enlisted in the Forty-fourth Illinois Volunteer Infantry, Col. Opdyke, which regiment was engaged in many heavy battles through the Southern campaign, and was finally sent to Texas, where they remained until mustered out at Springfield, this State; politically, Mr. Robinson is a Republican.

ANDREW J. SHURTZ, farmer, P. O. Ashley, is a native of Warren County, N. J., born February 3, 1834, the eldest child of Robert W. and Hannah (Cole) Shurtz, both of whom were born in Essex County of the same State. The grandfather was Andrew Shurtz, of German descent. Robert W. Shurtz was a blacksmith by trade, and worked at it during odd spells, but was mostly engaged in farming. He was a robust, hard-working man, but died early from the effects of over-working. He was a bass drummer for many years in the State militia. Our subject got but a little schooling in early years. He has been engaged at canal-boating, saw-milling, etc., but has generally given his attention to farming pursuits. In the fall of 1835, he removed with his parents to Hamilton County, Ohio, and shortly afterward removed to Warren County, same State. In April, 1859, he came to this county, and located on what is called the Monroe farm, and after moving around several times, finally purchased part of his present place, before moving, in the spring of 1877. He has 120 acres in Blissville and 165 in Bald Hill Townships. His first marriage was with Catharine Wheeler, who died in 1859. He was married a second time, to Martha McConnaughey, who bore him seven children, of whom six are living—John, Annie, Georgie, William, David and Sarah.

He married his present wife, Mary E., June 3, 1875; she is a daughter of D. H. and Nancy B. (Hargett) Thomas. This union has given four children—Ettie, Mary, Arthur and Carrie. In the fall of 1864, Mr. Shurtz joined Company G, Thirty-second Illinois Volunteer Infantry. The regiment joined Sherman at Atlanta, and went through the entire campaign with him. Mr. Shurtz came home from St. Louis in June, 1865. He and wife are members of the Free-Will Baptist Church. He has filled many of the offices in his township; is a Republican.

HARRISON M. SMITH, farmer, P. O. Ashley, was born in this county September 2, 1838, to Drury and Rachel (Whitten) Smith, the father a native of South Carolina and the mother of Johnson County, Ill. Drury Smith is a substantial farmer, and now resides in Sullivan County, Mo. He was married a second time, to Widow Howell, who has borne him five children, three of whom are living. Our subject's own parents were blessed with nine children, of whom six survive—Ambrose, Coleman, Harrison M., Nimrod, Meredith and Delilah. Mr. Smith received but a limited education in early life. He has always given his attention to farming pursuits, and at present rents land and engages in mixed farming. He married Elizabeth Flannigan, a daughter of Robinson and Finice Flannigan. Mr. and Mrs. Smith are the parents of eight children, one of whom, Lydia, is deceased; those living are Drury, William, Hulda, Belle, John, Riley and Louvina. Subject and wife are members of the Christian Church. Politically, he is a Democrat.

JOSIAH TUTTLE, farmer, P. O. Ashley, is a native of Guernsey County, Ohio, born August 19, 1823, the eldest child of John A. and Mary A. (Douglas) Tuttle, natives of Maryland. They were the parents of seven children, five of whom are living—Josiah, Henry, John A., J. N. and Mary J., who married David Johnson. Mr. Tuttle's mother died when he was small, and he was raised by his step-mother, who was a Miss Annie Marsh. He was raised on a farm, and has always given his attention to farming pursuits. Since seventeen years of age, he has been a member of the Methodist Church and also of the Quarterly Conference, and for thirty years past he has been a licensed preacher in that church, and is also the local Elder. Mr. Tuttle was first married to Elizabeth Wells, who died in 1844, the mother of one child—Mary A., who died November 27, 1872. She had married John Dasher, by whom she had four children, of whom three survive—Annie, Elizabeth and Phœbe. Mr. Tuttle was married a second time to Phœbe Welch, a sister of Andrew Welch, of this county. This union has been blessed with five children, two of whom are living—Thomas H. and Ann E. Mr. Tuttle came to Jefferson County in 1853. His present property consists of 800 acres of land and some town property in Ashley, Ill. He built a fine residence on the home place in 1871, and is counted as one of Jefferson County's substantial farmers. He is a member of the I. O. O. F., Ashley Lodge, No. 302. In politics, he is a Republican.

SPRING GARDEN TOWNSHIP.

JOSEPH ADCOCK, farmer, P. O. Spring Garden, was born in Hawkins County, Tenn., January 4, 1816, son of John and Ellender (Hicks) Adcock. His father was a native of Rockingham County, Va. Soon after the birth of our subject, the parents separated, the mother taking the custody of the children. She afterward married Solomon Goddard, and in 1828 the family moved to this county, where they settled in Dodds Township. Subject attended subscription schools but very little; but after he came to manhood taught himself. As soon as he was able, he commenced to work around among the farmers of this county, and after two years' work here he went to St. Louis, where he ran on the river from that point to Alton. He remained there some six or seven years, and then returned to this county, just as he was nearing manhood. In this neighborhood, he commenced to farm himself, and first settled on a farm in Dodds Township, but only remained there about eighteen months, and then came to Spring Garden Township, where he settled about one and a half miles from where he now lives. On that farm he resided until 1846, when he came to his present farm, a tract of 100 acres, lying in Sections 9 and 10 of Town 4, Range 3 east. Has eighty acres in cultivation. Mr. Adcock was married in Spring Garden Township, April 2, 1833, to Polly Kimball, a daughter of William and Sarah (Burns) Kimball. The father was a native of Germany. She was the mother of four children, three of whom are living—John H., Eliza J. (wife of R. V. Gibson) and William M., in Marion County. This lady died September 30, 1845, and subject was married the second time, to Sarah Jane Pitts, a native of Virginia, and a daughter of Jesse Pitts, of Pittsylvania County, Va. This marriage resulted in eight children, four of whom are now living—Nancy Ellender (wife of Marion Page), Jesse C. (in Dodds Township), Minerva (wife of John Rines) and Willaby (now at home with his father). This lady also died, on February 5, 1866, and he was married the third time, to Elizabeth Addison, a native of Logan County, Ky., and a daughter of Jonathan and Elizabeth (Grigsby) Addison, the father being a native of North Carolina. Mrs. Adcock is a member of Moore's Prairie Methodist Church. Mr. Adcock is a Democrat in politics.

THOMPSON ANGLEN, saddler and harness-maker, Spring Garden. Subject was born in Rockingham County, N. C., September 15, 1822, was a son of Caleb and Hannah (Powel) Anglen. The father was a native of Pittsylvania County, Va., the mother of North Carolina. Subject was the ninth of thirteen children, and of that number six are now living. In his native county he attended the first school, and in 1831, the father brought his family to Montgomery County, Tenn., where he died in 1856. Subject finished his education in the schools of that county, and then assisted on the home farm until 1849. December 19 of that year, he came to Jefferson County, and settled on a Government improvement, in Pendleton Township, about a mile east of Belle Rive; he, however, only farmed there for four years, and then came to Mt. Vernon, where he clerked in a general store then owned by Thorn D. Balzell; remained with them but one year and then returned to Pendleton Township, and there purchased the home farm. In connection with his farm, he also ran a store for the accommodation of his neighbors in that township; he only remained three years, and then exchanged his farm for a hotel in Mt. Vernon, then owned by a Mr. Thomas. It stood (1858) where Pavy and Allan's building now stands. In that hotel he remained until 1865, when he came to Spring Garden Township. Here he first purchased a half-interest in a flouring mill and still house which then stood about one and one-half miles south of the village, but only remained about a month there, and then came to the village, where he has since resided. His first venture in the town was merchandising, and he followed that for about two years; he then opened his hotel, which he still continues to run; he also turned his attention some to stock trading and engaged in that for about three years. He next purchased a harness shop and commenced following the occupation of a harness-maker. He now carries a stock of about $1,500. Mr. Anglen was married in Montgomery County, Tenn., on June 10, 1846, to Nancy J. Smith, a daughter of Joseph H. and Nancy (Clifton) Smith, natives of that county. This lady was the mother of five children, of whom four are now living, viz.: H. V., in Princeton, Ky.; E. J., in Huron, Dak.; Thomas, in Macon County, Ill., and Lilly, in Princeton, Ky. This lady died February 14, 1864, and subject was married the second time, in Spring Garden Township, May 11, 1865, to Mrs. Nancy F. Williams, a daughter of Joseph Felps, of Robertson County, Tenn. The result of the marriage is one child—Ora Maude. Mr. Anglen has served in numerous county and township offices, among which are Justice of the Peace of Mt. Vernon Township, from 1859 to 1865, and since his arrival in this township he has held the office almost continually ever since. In April, 1872, was appointed School Treasurer, and is still holding that office. Has also served as member of the County Board of Supervisors. Is a member of Williams Lodge, No. 242, I. O. O. F., of Spring Garden. Has held all the offices in that lodge and is now Past Grand. For the past fifteen years has also served as Treasurer of that organization; is a member of the Spring Garden Baptist Church. In politics, is an Independent.

C. M. BROWN, farmer, P. O. Spring Garden, was born in Washington County, Ill., December 24, 1827, and is a son of Stephen and Elizabeth (Spoon) Brown, who came to this State from Guilford County, N. C. Subject was the sixth of eleven children, of whom six are now living. His education was received in the subscription schools of that day. He remained at home with his father until twenty-five, and then started out in life for himself; settled on his present farm, where he now owns 840 acres, which lie principally in Sections 19, 20, 25, 29, 31 and 36. Of the whole, there are about 700 acres under cultivation, about sixteen acres in orchard. Mr. Brown was married, April 9, 1851, in Ewing Township, Franklin County, Ill., to Ann Eliza Foster, a native of Franklin County, and a daughter of E. H. and Cynthia Freeman Foster, natives of Tennessee. This lady is the mother of nine children, of whom five are living—B. F., S. E., Margaret A., Martha F. and Melissa E. Our subject was a soldier in the Mexican war. Enlisted in the Sixth Regiment of Illinois Infantry, Col. Collins, Company A, Capt. James Bowman, in May, 1846, and was out until July, 1847. Has been a member of the County Board of Supervisors, four terms, and is at present serving in that capacity. He also served as School Director of his district for the last twenty-five years. In politics, Mr. Brown is an Independent.

JOSEPH CARROLL, blacksmith, Spring Garden, was born in this county October 26, 1832, and was a son of James and Elizabeth (DeLaney) Carroll, natives of Tennessee, but emigrated to this county about 1829, settling first in Mount Vernon Township, and then moved into Dodds Township, where the father died in 1849, and the mother in 1877. Our subject was the third of eight children, of whom three are now living. His education was received mostly in the schools of Mount Vernon and Dodds Townships. On his father's farm he remained until twenty-two, and then started out in life for himself. He settled in Dodds Township, where he farmed until about 1858. In that year he came to Spring Garden Township. Here he first farmed for about two years, and then came to the village, where he has since carried on the blacksmith trade. In connection with his shop he also carries a stock of plows, wagons, etc., which generally runs on the average to about $1,500. He also owns a farm of 530 acres, part of which is in Section 7 and the rest in 15, of Town 4, Range 3 east. Also owns some in Elk Prairie Township. Of the whole piece, there are about 320 acres in cultivation. Mr. Carroll was married in this county in August, 1854, to Martha Shaffer, a native of Tennessee, and a daughter of David Shaffer. She was the mother of four children, two of whom are now living—Mollie (wife of Harvey Gardner, of Colorado), and Charles H. This lady died about 1866. Our subject was married the second time, in August, 1868, to Mrs. Sibyl Garrison, a daughter of Uriah Crampton, a native of Mississippi. The result of this marriage is four children, two of whom are now living, Willie and Clyde. He is a member of Mount Vernon Lodge, No. 31, A. F. & A. M., and Williams Lodge, No. 242, of Spring Garden. In politics, our subject is a Democrat.

LOGAN FITZGERRELL (deceased) was born in Posey County, Ind., in 1837, and was a son of Michael and Mary (Overton) Fitzgerrell. The parents moved to Jefferson County as early as 1840, and settled on the farm afterward owned by our subject. Our subject was educated in the schools of his county, and at the age of eighteen assumed the responsibilities of life for himself, and settled on the farm which his widow now occupies. Originally, the father gave his son a tract of eighty acres, and that has since been increased until at present the farm contains 336 acres, located in Sections 21, 22, 23, 24 and 27, of Town 4, Range 3 east. Of the whole, there are about 250 acres in process of cultivation. Mr. Fitzgerrell was married twice. The first time in 1855, on the celebration of his eighteenth birthday, to Miss Miranda Johnson, a daughter of George and Elizabeth Johnson, of this county. The result of this marriage was one child—James Michael (now deceased). This lady died only a few years after her marriage, and our subject was married the second time, February 20, 1858, to Nancy Simpson, who was born in Gibson County, Ind., July 12, 1836, and is a daughter of Richard and Elizabeth Simpson, descendants of Old Virginia stock. This lady has been the mother of the following children: Hiram R., Mary, Lucinda (wife of William Harmon), Melissa E. Daniel L., Luther, Miranda S. and Nancy. Our subject was a member of Williams Lodge, No 242, I. O. O. F., of Spring Garden. In his life time, he sought to walk in the retired paths of life as much as possible, and tried to follow out his duty as a citizen good and true. His aspirations did not tend toward public office-seeking, but toward preparing for his family's wants. And thus Mr. Fitzgerrell's life came to a close January 1, 1879. His family was left well provided, and as his neighbors, in words soft and low, paid their respects to the bereaved family, none spoke but to praise him. At present, Mrs. Fitzgerrell, assisted by her sons, is carrying on the farm.

G. W. HAYS, farmer, P. O. Mt. Vernon, was born in Rutherford County, Tenn., July 4, 1840; was a son of John and Rebecca (Maltus) Hays; was the fifth of twelve children, of whom eight are living. When only two months old, his parents moved to Jefferson County, where the father settled in Spring Garden Township, about one mile from where our subject now lives.

but only lived there a short time, and then came to Dodds Township. In that township he held quite a number of offices of trust and profit, and there he died in 1863—the mother in 1862. Our subject attended the subscription schools of his county, and remained on the home place until about twenty. In starting out in life for himself, he first settled in Elk Prairie Township, but only remained there a short time, and then came to his present farm, where he now owns 190 acres in Sections 5 and 6 of Township 4, Range 3 east. There are about 180 acres under cultivation. Mr. Hays was married in the fall of 1865, in Spring Garden Township, to Margaret Howard, a native of Illinois and a daughter of Charles and Jane (Mendenhall) Howard. This lady is the mother of three living children—Lilly, Josie and a baby boy, born April 6, 1883. Our subject enlisted in the Fifteenth Illinois Cavalry, Col. Bacon, Company E, Capt. Hutchins, in the winter of 1861. Was out three years and three months. Was in the engagements of Hickman, Ky., Union City, Tenn., Corinth, Miss., Island No. 10 and many other smaller skirmishes. Mrs. Hays is a member of the Easter M. E. Church of Spring Garden Township. Mr. Hays has held the offices of School Director, Road Supervisor, etc. In politics, he is a Greenbacker.

JAMES JONES, farmer, P. O. Spring Garden, was born in Todd County, Ky., November 9, 1822; is a son of William and Chrissie (Gibson) Jones, natives of Tennessee. Subject was the elder of two children. The father died when the son was about two years old, and when eight years old his mother moved to this county and settled in Spring Garden Township, where she afterward married a man named Nathaniel Morgan. Subject's education was but very meager as far as schooling goes, but after his marriage he managed to teach himself some. He remained at home on his step-father's farm until twenty-one, then started out for himself. He settled about a mile and a half from his first farm, where he lived until 1871, when he came to his present farm. He now owns about 1,000 acres, situated in Sections 11, 12, 14, 15, 19, 20, 22 and 23, of Town 4, Range 3 east. Has about 300 acres in cultivation. Mr. Jones was married in Jefferson County, on January 1, 1845, to Mrs. Elizabeth Allan, a daughter of Mrs. Nancy Cochran, a native of North Carolina. This union has resulted in the following children: Mary E., wife of Martin Knowles, of this township; John, Nathaniel, Chrissie, Josiah and James, and David. Mr. Jones has served in numerous township and district offices; in politics, is a Democrat.

WILEY KNOWLES, farmer, P. O. Spring Garden, was born near Savannah, Ga., April 25, 1809; was a son of Putaman and Patsey (Greer) Knowles. The parents went from Delaware to Georgia, the mother, however, coming over to the former State from Scotland when a child. Subject was the fourth of ten children, of whom only four are living. When two years old, his parents came to Indiana, and settled near Black River, in Gibson County. His schooling was very limited; remained at home with his father until about twenty-two, and then purchased a farm in Owensville Township, Gibson County. On that farm, he remained until the spring of 1845, when he came to Illinois, and settled in Spring Garden Township, Jefferson County, on his present farm, where he now owns 240 acres in Section 16, 130 acres in Section 4, 120 in Section 9, 40 in Section 8, and 10 in Section 10, all of Town 4, Range 3 west. He also has 120 in Dodds Township. Of the whole, there are about 280 acres under cultivation. Mr. Knowles was married in Gibson County, Ind., July 8, 1830, to Minerva Scott, a native of Bullitt County, Ky., being born there in 1811. She is a daughter of Mrs. Mary Scott, who was one of the old pioneer residents of Gibson County. The result of this union was eleven children, ten of whom are now living—William

R., residing in Missouri; Meniecs, wife of Joseph Wilbanks, of Logan County, Ill.; Patsey, wife of George Farrish, of Clackamas County Oreg.; Martin, farming in Spring Garden Township; Asa, in Custer County, Colo.; Ananias, in Moore's Prairie Township, his sketch appearing in that part of the work; Leander, also farming in Spring Garden Township; Francis M., on the home farm; Sarah, wife of Richard Davis, of this township; and Lizzie Caroline, wife of a Mr. Gamber, of Portland, Oreg. Mr. and Mrs. Knowles are members of the Mount Nebo Cumberland Presbyterian Church. Mr. Knowles has been a Democrat, but in the last few years has been voting the Greenback ticket. Francis M., the eighth child of Wiley and Minerva (Scott) Knowles, was born in Spring Garden Township, Jefferson County, September 1, 1848. In his youth, he attended the free schools of his county, and helped on the home place until he married, and then erected a fine country house; has settled down near his father, and now has the management of the homestead. He was married in Moore's Prairie Township, this county, April 17, 1879, to Florence Smith, who was born in this county January 28, 1852, and is a daughter of Jesse H. and Jane Bliss Smith, whose sketches appear elsewhere. This lady is the mother of three children—Norman Smith, Eliza and Wiley H. In politics, Mr. Knowles is at present a Greenbacker, but formerly, like his father, voted the Democratic ticket.

J. W. MARSHALL, farmer, P. O. Spring Garden, was born in Jackson County October 15, 1836. His parents were William and Judith (Minor) Marshall, who came originally from North Carolina. When subject was three years old, his parents came to Franklin County, and settled in Goode Township. There subject was permitted to attend school but slightly, but since coming to manhood's estate he has taught himself. He early commenced to render all possible assistance to his father on the home farm, and remained with the latter until twenty-four, and then on a rented farm near the old homestead he commenced life for himself. There he remained three years, and then came to Spring Garden Township, Jefferson County; he settled on the farm which he still owns, of 120 acres in Section 11, of Township 4, Range 3 east, and of that there are about 110 acres under cultivation. Subject was married, October 25, 1860, in Jefferson County, to Sarah Farlow, a native of Spring Garden Township, and a daughter of John and Frances (Williams) Farlow; the father was a native of Maryland, the mother of Tennessee. This lady is the mother of seven children, and of that number six are now living—W. H., G. B., C. E., Rosa, Lilly B. and Daisy E. Mr. Marshall is a member of the Spring Garden Baptist Church. Has served as Township Trustee, Justice, Collector and School Director. In politics, he is a Greenbacker.

GABRIEL PEAVLER, farmer, P. O. Spring Garden. The gentleman whose name heads this sketch, is probably one of the oldest settlers in this part of the county. He was born on the Holstein River, in Sullivan County, Tenn., January 27, 1813, and is a son of Jacob and Margaret (Steward) Peavler. The parents were both born in Virginia, the father of German parents, the mother of Irish. Our subject was the youngest of four children, of whom two are living—James, in Cooper County, Mo., and Gabriel Peavler. When about seven months old, his father went to Norfolk, Va., where he enlisted in a Virginia regiment being formed to fight the British in the war of 1812. At that time the city of Norfolk itself was threatened, and the regiment was stationed at that point. While serving at his post, the father was stricken with an epidemic which was then raging in that town, and died, as did thousands of his comrades. The mother also died when subject was about five years old, and he was left at the mercy of the world. His half brothers helped him some, however, and at the age of twelve years he was bound out to a man by the name of Allan, at Monticello, Wayne Co., Ky., and under him subject learned the trade of making and laying brick. He remained there until seventeen, and then deciding to follow that occupation for himself, he came to Clark County, Ind., and worked for some time at that point. Next went to Bloomfield, Greene County, and from there to Marion County, when Indianapolis was but a small village, and there he made and laid bricks on the State road leading from that point. The next few years were spent in running around in different points in Indiana working at his trade, and then made Washington County, Ind., his home. In regard to his education, our subject never had a chance to go to school but about a month in his life, but after he had settled down at this point, he first commenced to teach himself, and has since obtained a rather fair education. His first occupation in Washington County was that of farming, and followed that occupation for about two years and then went to Providence, Clark County, and there opened a grocery store which he conducted for nine months, and then sold that out and opened a dry goods store, but after running that store six months at that point, he went to Pekin, Washington County, and there carried on the same business. Here he ran a store for three years, and then turning his attention again to farming, he purchased a farm near that town, which he operated for nine years. In connection with his farm he also ran a store for the accommodation of his neighbors. In 1850, he came to Illinois and first settled in Clark County, where he both farmed and carried on a store. The first year of his residence there he opened up and put under cultivation a farm of 160 acres. In that county he lived six years, and then came to Spring Garden, Jefferson County, and settled on his present farm. Here he now owns about 456 acres in Sections 22, 23, 26 and 27; has about 370 acres in cultivation—about eight acres in orchard. Mr. Peavler was married, November 27, 1834, in Washington County, Ind., to Nancy McKinney, a daughter of Alexander and Susannah (Turner) McKinney, natives of Virginia. This union resulted in twelve children, six of whom are now living—Dr. J. W. (whose sketch appears elsewhere in this work), born July 20, 1840; Mary Jane (wife of J. W. Fitzgerald), born December 31, 1842; Henrietta (wife of William H. Dorr), born September 3, 1844; W. T. C. (now in Huron, Dakota Territory), October 18, 1846; Nancy Frances (wife of George Will), October 20, 1858; and G. N. E., February 18, 1862. Our subject is a member of the Spring Garden Methodist Episcopal Church; also of Williams Lodge, No. 242, I. O. O. F. In politics, is a Republican. Mrs. Peavler is a member of the Cumberland Presbyterian Church.

DR. J. W. PEAVLER. One of the most successful physicians of this county is the gentleman whose name heads this sketch, and who was born in Washington County, Ind., July 20, 1840. Our subject is a son of Gabriel, whose sketch appears elsewhere in this work, and Nancy (McKinney) Peavler. The father was a native of Tennessee, the mother of Washington County, Ind. Subject was the third of twelve children, and of that number six are now living. When two years old, his father came to Clark County, Ind.; there our subject was first permitted to attend school. In 1856, his father came to Jefferson County, and settled in Spring Garden Township, and here subject attended school until eighteen, and then taught for two years in that township. He next went to Mount Vernon, where he read medicine with his uncle, Dr. H. J. Peavler. With this gentleman he remained three years, and then went to the Medical Department of the Michigan State University, located at Ann Arbor, from which institution he graduated in 1864. He immediately located at Knob's Prairie, this county, and there practiced some five years. From that location he went to Chicago, and there practiced for about one year, also attending lectures. He next came to his present location in Spring Garden Township, where he has practiced most of the time since, except in 1878, when he attended the American Medical College at St. Louis, from which he graduated, and in 1879, when he attended the Eclectic Medical College, Cincinnati, and also graduated from that institution. His present practice extends over a large portion of this county and portions of Franklin County. The Doctor is at present a member of the Missouri State Medical Society. Dr. Peavler was married, August 4, 1867, to Victoria Hagle, a daughter of John W. and Mahalia Boswell Hagle. This lady is a native of this county, and is the mother of six children, five of whom are now living—Eugene, Minnie, Mazie, Ethel and Harry. Subject is a member of Williams Lodge, No. 242, I. O. O. F., of Spring Garden, and No. 765, Ewing Lodge, A. F. & A. M. In politics, is a Republican.

DR. J. B. SCARBOROUGH, physician, Spring Garden, was born in Ewing Township, Franklin County, Ill., March 12, 1842, and is a son of Dr. Bennent and Allie (Bennett) Scarborough. The father was a native of Wilson County, Tenn., and came to this State in 1832. The mother is a native of Posey County, Ind. Subject was the third of five children, and was permitted to attend the schools of his county until about twenty, and then the Doctor commenced reading medicine with his father. Remained with him until twenty-four, reading and assisting the elder Scarborough in his practice. Then our subject took up his chosen practice for himself at the town of Macedonia, Franklin County. In that locality he only remained about six months, when he again betook himself to his native county, and there took up the practice of his father, the latter having become too old to attend to it (his death subsequently occurred in 1879), and in that locality our subject remained until 1873. In that year he removed to Ham's Grove, Pendleton Township, this county, and there practiced until October, 1879, when he came to his present location at Spring Garden. In this locality he now has a practice that extends over territory which lies for miles north and east of Spring Garden, and where he has the confidence of the people of that locality, in Pendleton Township. Subject was married, September 20, 1865, to Miss Ada Yates, a native of Providence, R. I., and the daughter of John I. and Hannah (Stewart) Yates, natives of Maine, but settling in Ohio, where the father died, and the mother married Bennett Woodworth, and subsequently the twain came to this county (in 1853), and settled in Moore's Prairie Township, where they have subsequently resided. The result of this union has been three children, two of whom are now living, Lizzie (wife of Edgar Bernard), born October 20, 1866, and Ida May, born July 22, 1870. Alice was born December 17, 1868, and died July 24, 1869. Mr. and Mrs. Scarborough and daughter Lizzie are members of the Methodist Episcopal Church, and he is a member of Ham's Grove Lodge, No. 405, I. O. O. F. In politics, he is a Republican.

BENJAMIN SMITH, farmer, P. O. Spring Garden, is a great-grandson of Alexander and Joanna Smith, who settled in North Carolina. They had the following children born to them in Tyrrell County, that State, viz.: Ann, born February 6, 1771; Joanna, January 23, 1774; Isaac, January 19, 1779; Ananias, December 12, 1780; Zilpha, April 10, 1782; Euphemia, November 1, 1783; Loef, March 2, 1789; Azilla, October 4, 1792; and Jose, February 12, 1797. The third child of this family, Isaac, was the grandfather of our subject. This child grew to manhood in North Carolina, and there married Millie Hassle. The twain came to Tennessee, and settled in Hickman County, where unto them were born nine children, among them Anderson, the father of our subject, who was born February 6, 1811, and Jesse H., whose sketch appears elsewhere in this work. Isaac came to this county with his family about 1829, and settled in Spring Garden Township, near where subject now resides, where he died about 1850. The father of our subject grew to manhood in this county, and married a Miss Elizabeth Hopper, who was born in Middle Tennessee January 28, 1811. She was a daughter of Thomas Hopper, who came to this county in a very early day, probably about 1820. The parents of our subject also settled near where the latter now resides, and there subject was born August 29, 1838. The parents lived in this county until a ripe old age. The mother peacefully passed away March 22, 1870, and the father, who for fifteen years before his death had been Deacon of the Spring Garden Baptist Church, died May 3, 1872. Our subject attended both the subscription and free schools of his county until about twenty-one, and then worked at home about one year, and then located on his present farm, a piece of land that had been entered by his father, and of whom our subject afterward purchased it. He now owns about 400 acres in Sections 1, 2, 3 and 12, of Township 4, Range 3 east; has about 240 under cultivation and thirty in orchard. Mr. Smith was married, January 24, 1860, to Elizabeth Shirley, a daughter of Russell and Jinca (Allan) Shirley. The father was a native of Hamilton County, Ill., and the mother of Macon County, N. C. The result of this union has been twelve children, of whom nine are living—Isaac N., born February 6, 1862; George H., May 19, 1863; Seth T., June 7, 1865; Charles E., March 14, 1869; Judson A., April 6, 1871; Ellis Lee, April 28, 1877; Ollie J., February 17, 1873; Ornie, September 26, 1879; Rado. December 19, 1881. Of the deceased children, William D. was born September 14, 1860, and died September 14, 1867; Mary F., born May 2, 1867, died December 3, 1869; and an infant born April 28, 1877, and died May 5 of the same year. Our subject has been a member of the County Board of Supervisors, also served as Road Commissioner, School Director, etc. Is a member of Ham's Grove Lodge, No. 405, I. O. O. F.; has served in the different offices in that organization, and is now Past Grand; has also been representative two years at the Grand Lodge. In politics, Mr. Smith is a Greenbacker.

A. J. SWEETEN, lawyer and school teacher, Spring Garden, was born in Franklin County, Ill., September 21, 1839, and is a son of Reuben and Jane (Isom) Sweeten. Subject was the second of three children, of whom two are now living—A. J. (our subject) and John R., in Franklin County. When subject was two years old, his father moved to Jefferson County, and settled in Spring Garden Township. Here the father remained only about three years, and then returned to Ewing Township, Franklin County. Subject attended the schools of that township, and in 1857 he attended for a short time the McKendree College, at Carlyle, Clinton County; also attended the high schools of Mt. Vernon and Benton prior to going to the college. In the winter of 1857, he commenced the occupation of teaching; his first school was taught in Ewing Township, and he continued to teach there until 1861. In 1863, he commenced teaching in Elk Prairie Township, this county, and from that time he taught each consecutive year until 1881. He then came to this township and taught one school in the town, and in 1883 he taught in this township. About 1865, Mr. Sweeten commenced the study of law, first under H. M. Williams, of Spring Garden Township, and then attended Judge A. D. Duff's Law School in Benton, Franklin County. March 19, 1870, he was admitted to the bar of Jefferson County, and since that has followed his profession some in this county. In 1864, he purchased a tract of land in Elk Prairie Township, where he farmed until 1881, and then moved to this township, and now owns about eighty acres in Section 18 of Town 4, Range 3 east. Subject was married, August 7, 1864, in Elk Prairie Township to Harriet Jane Kirk, a daughter of James and Phebe Ann (Cook) Kirk, natives of North Carolina. This lady is the mother of six living children—Margaret Ann, Calvin M., Druzailla J., James R. O., Quintilla O. and Arthur C. Subject was a soldier in the late war; enlisted August 15, 1862, in the One Hundred and Tenth Regiment Illinois Volunteer Infantry, Thomas S. Casey, Company T, Capt. S. G. Dewitt, and was out nine months. Was wounded January 1, 1863, at the battle of Stone River, and was subsequently discharged for disability as a supernumerary officer. Mr. Williams is a member of William's Lodge, No. 242, I. O. O. F., of Spring Garden; served in Ewing and Elk Prairie Townships as Justice of the Peace from 1857 to 1867; also has served as Township Collector two terms, and Township Trustee eleven years. In politics, is a Democrat.

DR. S. L. WILLIAMS, physician, Spring Garden, was born in Franklin County, Ill., November 13, 1839. Is a son of S. M. and Frances (Shaw) Williams. The father was born in North Carolina January 28, 1792, and emigrated to Franklin County in 1837, and there died in September, 1875. The mother was also a native of North Carolina, and died in Franklin County in July, 1874. Subject was next to the youngest of a family of fourteen children, and of this number seven are living. Subject's education was received in the schools of Franklin County. Until twenty-four years of age, he remained at home with his father, and then started out in life for himself on a farm in that county. There he remained until 1865, when he went to Cincinnati, and there attended the Physio-Medical College for a short time. From that institution he returned to Franklin County, and commenced the practice of his chosen profession. He only remained there a short time, however, and then came to Spring Garden Township, where he has since built up quite an extensive practice. Since his coming to this county, he has been here all the time, with the exception of 1878 and 1879, when he attended lectures in the St. Louis American College, from which institution he graduated in 1879. The Doctor was married, January 22, 1869, to Miss Margaret J. Arnold, a native of Robertson County, Tenn., and a daughter of James M. and Nancy (Felse) Williams. This union has resulted in four children, of whom three are living—Hugh, Curtis and Alsa. In politics, he is a Democrat.

G. H. WITMER, salesman, Spring Garden. The gentleman whose name heads this sketch was born in Washington County, Md., November 13, 1850, and is a son of Elmer and Charlotte (Huffman) Witmer. Our subject was the youngest of two children. His education was received, first at the public school of Hagerstown, Washington County, and at the age of thirteen he took a preparatory course at the Franklin & Marshal Collegiate Institute, situated at Mercersburg, Penn. After two years' instruction there, our subject taught for a year, after which he went to Fort Whipple, Va., where he attended the United States Signal Service School of Instruction. At that point he remained until summoned to Washington, where, after passing a creditable examination, he was sent to Nashville, Tenn., and there he opened the first Signal Service Bureau ever had at that point. After remaining at that point about five months, he was transferred, upon application, to the active service, and was stationed at the Department of Columbia, with headquarters at Portland, Ore. In the employ of the Government he remained two years, and then applying for a discharge, which was granted, our subject returned to his native county in Maryland, where he again turned his attention to teaching. After teaching one term there, however, he was offered a position on the *Dispatch*, at Commerce, Mo., and, accepting it, went to that point. But owing to sickness, he was, in the course of three or four months, compelled to resign there and then come to this point, where he farmed for a year; but that not suiting his taste, he again betook himself to his native town, where he accepted the position of Waybill Clerk for the Adams Express Company, and then in due course of promotion was transferred to Harrisburg, Penn., where he assumed the duties of Receiving Clerk. He remained connected with that company but about one year, when his health again failed him and he was compelled to resign his position. From that he came to his present location, where, after teaching one term in the schools of Spring Garden, he accepted the position of head salesman for W. H. Barber, in which capacity he is now acting. August 14, 1879, he was married, in Spring Garden, to Miss Rosa Bernard, a daughter of Dr. and Maurice (Hawkins) Bernard, of Spring Garden. This lady is the mother of two children—Edna Earl and Thomas Bernard. Mr. Witmer is a member of Williams Lodge, No. 242, I. O. O. F., of Spring Garden, and is at present serving as Secretary for that organization. Is also a member of the Spring Garden Baptist Church, and in politics, is a Democrat.

B. F. WHISSENHUNT, farmer, P. O. Spring Garden, was born in Middle Tennessee May 21, 1830; is a son of Uriah and Dorcas (Roach) Whissenhunt, natives of that State; the grandparents, however, came from Pennsylvania. Our subject was the only child. When about one year old, his parents came to Marion County, Ill., where they remained about twelve years. In that county our subject attended his first school. In 1843, the family came to Jefferson County and settled on the farm where our subject now lives, where the mother died in 1859, the father in 1860. In this county our subject had but little chance to attend the subscription schools, and consequently his education is very limited. His life for upward of twenty years was spent at home with his father, and then commenced life for himself on a piece of Congress land which his father entered for him. That has since been increased until he now owns about 160 acres in Sections 2 and 3, of Town 4, Range 3 east. Mr. Whissenhunt was married, April 3, 1850, to Susan Book, a native of this county, and a daughter of Thomas and Elizabeth (Shelton) Book. The father was a native of Virginia, the mother of North Carolina. This marriage resulted in nine children, and of that number two are living—Ellen Catherine, wife of George Harveil, and George Washington. Is a member of Moore's Prairie Baptist Church. In politics, he is a Democrat.

GRAND PRAIRIE TOWNSHIP.

JAMES C. BALDRIDGE, farmer P. O. Centralia, was born in Rutherford County, N. C., December 10, 1811, a son of Dornton and Mary (Boggs) Baldridge, both natives of North Carolina. They resided in Rutherford County till November, 1820, when they came to Jefferson County, where they resided until his death, except for a few years across the line in Marion County. He died January 14, 1832, at about forty-five years of age. His wife was afterward married to Matthew Cunningham, an old settler of this county, removing to Marion County, where she died. Mr. Baldridge was the father of twelve children, of whom three sons and two daughters are now living—James C., Joseph and Thomas; Mrs. Jane Porter, widow of William Porter; and Mrs. Sarah Baltzell, wife of George Baltzell. The subject of our sketch was reared in this county, receiving such an education as could be obtained at the schools of that day. July 26, 1832, he was married in Marion County to Margaret Raney, a native of Kentucky and daughter of Matthew Raney. She died October 3, 1845. She was the mother of six children, three of whom are now living—Sally A., wife of Owen Breeze; Mary J., wife of Zadok Jennings; and James C., of Jerseyville, a minister and farmer. Two children died in youth, and one—Samuel R.—died in the army, Company H, Eightieth Illinois Volunteer Infantry. Mr. Baldridge was married again, January 8, 1846, to Mrs. Tabitha Casey, widow of Isaac Casey and daughter of Robert White. Her father was a native of South Carolina, and came to Madison County, Ill., in 1810, and July 10, 1811, Mrs. Baldridge was born in Chamber's Fort. Her mother, Sarah Holt, was a native of North Carolina, but was married in Georgia. Mr. and Mrs. Baldridge have had four children, two of whom are now living, viz., Joseph D. and George P., both farmers in this county. Immediately after his first marriage, Mr. Baldridge settled on his present farm, where he has lived ever since; his occupation has always been that of farming and stock-raising. His farm now consists of over 500 acres. In politics, Mr. Baldridge is Republican, but has taken no part in political life.

C. W. BEAL, farmer, P. O. Irvington, was born in Bavaria, Germany, July 26, 1838, to Jacob and Catherine (Claymann) Beal. He was born in 1801 and died in 1881. In 1840, he came to America with his family and settled in Lehigh County, Penn., where they remained till our subject was about fourteen years of age, when they removed to St. Clair County, Ill., and in 1857, our subject came to this township and has made this his home since. August 15, 1861, he enlisted in Company C, Eleventh Illinois Volunteer Infantry, Capt. George C. McKee, Col. W. H. Wallace. He served in the engagements of Fort Donelson, Shiloh, was in the siege of Vicksburg for forty-seven days, and with Sherman on the Mississippi campaign. After serving three years in the army, he again returned to this county and has been engaged as a farmer since. His farm contains 160 acres. On this he does general farming and fruit growing. On his farm also is a quarry of splendid sandstone. September 30, 1866, he was married in this county to Miss Ellen J. Fry. She was born in this township October 18, 1849, daughter of Henry and Sarah (Dellenger) Fry. He was born in North Carolina in 1806; she in 1818. He died in 1877, April 4, in this county, whither he had moved in 1844; she still survives. Of their family of six children, only three are living, viz., John, Zachariah and Mrs. Beal. Mr. and Mrs. Beal have four children living and one dead, viz., David E., Sadie J., Charles W., Freddie, and Ole, deceased. In politics, Mr. Beal is a Republican.

HENRY BREEZE, farmer, P. O. Irvington, was born in Orange County, Ind., November 23, 1823, to Robert and Margaret (Copple) Breeze, both of whom were natives of North Carolina —he of Orange County, she of Rowan County. He in early life had been apprenticed to a hatter in his native State, but at the age of seventeen ran off and came to Crab Orchard, Ky., and for some years followed the river, but in 1810 was married in Clark County, Ind., to the mother of our subject, and after that, made farming his occupation, being quite successful. He was in the Indian war under Gen. Harrison, and was at the battle of Tippecanoe. In 1827, he moved with his family to this county, and, with the exception of three years he resided in Washington County, made this his home till the time of his death, December 8, 1862, at the age of eighty-four years. She died in 1875, also eighty-four years of age. In politics, he was a Whig and then a strong Union man, and when the war broke out, although over eighty years of age and feeble, he wanted to do his part, so wrote to Col. S. G. Hicks, of the Fortieth, asking if there was not something he could give him to do. While still in Indiana, he and wife joined the Christian Church and were active members of the church till the time of their deaths. At his house, probably the first Christian Church was organized in the county, by Rev. David R. Chance and Rev. William Chaffen, of Marion County. He afterward deeded the land to the church where Little Grove Christian Church now stands. The following are the names of his children: Richard, Jacob (deceased), Elizabeth (deceased), wife of Crittenden Anderson; John (deceased), Owen, Hannah (deceased), wife of Rev. John A. Williams; Robert, Henry, James (deceased), Jonathan, Margaret (deceased), wife of Alexander Bundy; Catherine, wife of George Fouts; Mary, widow of Jacob Sanders; Nancy (deceased), wife of Samuel Bundy (deceased). Our subject remained at home until he was twenty-one years of age, and then came to his present farm and began its improvement. His farm now contains 180 acres in a high state of cultivation. Mr. Breeze has always taken an active part in political matters, and has been honored with various township and county offices. He was one of the committee who attended to the building of the present county court house. Since March 19, 1851, he has served as Justice of the Peace. In 1876, he was nominated by the Greenback party to represent his district in the State Legislature, and carried his own county by a large majority, but was defeated in the district by a few votes. For thirty-two years, Mr. Breeze has been a member of the I. O. O. F., and is also a member of the A., F. & A. M, Irvington Lodge. He is a member of the Christian Church. October 28, 1847, he was married to Catherine Casey, daughter of Samuel Casey, Sr. She died December 8, 1861, and was the mother of eight children, five of whom are still living, viz., Ellen, wife of Jacob Deal; Robert M.; Harriet; Ida, wife of William Jolliff; and Mary. December 11, 1866, he was married to Mrs. Martha J. (Taylor) Wayman, widow of M. Wayman and daughter of James W. Taylor, who was a native of Georgia, but came to Marion County, Ill., in 1818. By her first husband, Mrs. Breeze had four children, viz., Willis, Jasper, Wiley, and Margaret I., wife of Lewis Breeze. By her present husband, she has two children, viz., Samuel H. and Jacob S.

SAMUEL COPPLE, farmer, P. O. Walnut Hill, was born in Jefferson County, Ill., July 16, 1837, a son of William and Abbie (Hanley) Copple. Both were born in Indiana and came to this State at an early date. He died in Walnut Hill Prairie, October, 1875; she is still living on the old homestead. To them eleven children were born, five of whom still survive—Mary, wife of John Due, of Missouri; Levi; Susan, wife of Charles Simmons; Harvey and Samuel. The subject of this sketch was reared and educated in this county, and has made it his home all his life. His occupation has been that of farmer and fruit raiser. August 15, 1861, he enlisted in Company C, Eleventh Illinois Volunteer Infantry, Capt. George C. McKee, Col. W. H. L. Wallace. He served for three years and was mustered out at Vicksburg, August, 1864. He took part in the battle of Shiloh, siege of Vicksburg, and for nine months before his discharge had been doing detail work at ordnance department, Vicksburg. In September, 1882, he came to his present fruit farm of forty-three and one-half acres, besides forty in timber and ten in orchards. He was married, in 1857, to Sarah A. Bradford, daughter of Avery Bradford. She died in July, 1869, leaving two children—Marion and Minnie. He was married, November, 1869, to Luan·a Moore, daughter of Thomas B. Moore, and to them were born three children—Charity E., Wily D. and Ella A. Mr. Copple and wife are members of the Methodist Episcopal Church. In politics, he is a Republican.

EDMUND COPPLE, farmer, P. O. Irvington, was born in Clark County, Ind., October 12, 1828, to David and Lovina (Huckleberry) Copple. He was a native of North Carolina, but came to Indiana when young. She was born in Indiana. Both died in Marion County, Ill., where they had settled in about 1832. They were the parents of twelve children, eleven of whom lived to be grown. He served in the Indian war under Gen. Harrison. Our subject was reared in Marion County, Ill., receiving his education in the common schools. His occupation has been that of a farmer. In 1852, he came to his present farm, which contains 258 acres and is well improved. He was married in Marion County, Ill., in 1853, to Miss Nancy Barcman. She was born in Indiana, daughter of Isaac and Christina (Huckleberry) Barcman, who were the parents of nine children, eight of whom still survive. Mr. and Mrs. Copple are members of the Methodist Episcopal Church, and in politics he is a Greenbacker. Mr. and Mrs. Copple have the following-named children: Lucy L. (deceased), wife of Albert Copple; Mary A., wife of Adolphus Allcorn; Effie J., wife of Alexander West; John W.; Tenie D., wife of Charles Copple, and Isaac W. (twins); Edmund D., Harriet N. and Orrie.

WILLIAM L. FISHER, farmer, P. O. Irvington, was born in Clark County, Ind., September 7, 1830, a son of John and Elizabeth (Fouts) Fisher. She was born in Indiana, a sister of David Fouts, whose sketch appears in this work. John Fisher was a native of North Carolina, but came to Indiana when small. His occupation was that of farming. Both he and his wife died on the old homestead in Clark County, he at eighty years of age, she at fifty-eight. He was a Democrat in politics and took an active part in local affairs. They were members of the Universalist Church. They were the parents of eight children, viz.: William L.; Sarah J., wife of Alexander Work; James L. (deceased), Isabelle (deceased), Jacob H., John A., Andrew M. and Mollie. Our subject was reared on the farm and educated in the common schools of Clark County. He came to this county in 1857, and in 1859 settled on his present farm of 200 acres, which was then unimproved, and has since been engaged in grain and stock raising. He was married, in September, 1859, to Jane Boles, daughter of Hugh Boles. She died in April, 1861, leaving one child—Jennie. He was again married, in 1863, to Margaret Baird, a native of Madison County, Ill., and daughter of Samuel Baird. Seven children are the result of this union—Erman, Cynthia, Ollie, Carrie, Laura, Wilbur and Harland. Mr. Fisher is a member of A., F. &

A. M., Irvington Lodge, No. 650. In politics he is a Republican, and has held various township offices.

DAVID FOUTS, farmer, P. O. Irvington, was born in Clark County, Ind., November 3, 1820, son of Jacob and Mary (Dougan) Fouts, both natives of North Carolina, she being a daughter of Thomas Dougan, a Colonel in the Revolutionary army under Marion. She was born in 1788, and died at Irvington, Ill., 1868. He was born to Quaker parents in 1782, and died in 1860 in Indiana. Mr. and Mrs. Jacob Fouts were married in North Carolina in 1807, and in 1808 landed in the present State of Indiana and settled within one mile of Indian camps. They were the parents of six sons and three daughters, all of whom reached maturity, and six still survive. Our subject was reared on the farm in Clark County, and obtained such an education as the schools then afforded. Till he was twenty-seven years of age, he remained on the farm, but from 1847 till 1855, he was engaged in the mercantile business at New Washington, Ind., but on account of failing health closed out business and came to this county to his present farm of 400 acres. He remained on that farm till 1866, when he moved to Irvington and engaged in the mercantile business, continuing till 1873, when he again came to the farm and has since remained on it. January 3, 1850, he was married in Indiana to Elizabeth J. Gudgel. She is a native of the same county as her husband, and is the daughter of Allen and Rebecca (Robertson) Gudgel. He died when Mrs. Fouts was only about one year of age. Her mother is still living. Mr. and Mrs. Fouts have two children living and two dead, viz.: Jacob O. and Belle R., living; Mary F. (deceased), wife of Charles K. Smith; and Emma J. (deceased). In politics, he is a Republican. He is not a member of any church, but has always lived a moral, upright life.

DAVID P. FOUTS, farmer, P. O. Irvington, was born in Clark County, Ind., February 28, 1845. He is a son of Lemon and Evaline V. (Reid) Fouts, both natives of Indiana. They came to this county in 1846, settling on the farm now occupied by our subject, where his mother died when he was quite small. His father now resides in Irvington, where for years he was Postmaster and in mercantile business, from which he has now retired. In politics, he is Republican, but has never taken part in political life. He organized Company H of the Eightieth Illinois Volunteer Infantry, and was elected Captain, but through exposure at Central City, was taken sick and never went to the field. His family by his first wife consisted of six children, five of whom are still living—Mary D. (wife of Joseph Porter), David P., John H., Evaline V. (wife of John M. Breeze), and Cynthia H. (wife of Joseph D. Baldridge). Our subject was reared on the farm and has made it his home all his life, except one season. He was married in this county, September 9, 1869, to Rebecca E. Baldridge, daughter of Alexander Baldridge and Evaline (West) Baldridge, both deceased. Mr. and Mrs. Fouts have six children living—Lemon A., David A., Cora E., Lula A. and Lela E. (twins), and Daisie I. and one son deceased. Farming and stock dealing has been his occupation. Mr. Fouts is a member of the Christian Church, his wife of the Methodist Episcopal. In politics, he votes the Republican ticket, but takes little part in political life.

WILLIAM M. GALBRAITH, fruit-grower, P. O. Walnut Hill, was born in Mount Vernon, Jefferson County, Ill., December 23, 1826, son of John S. Galbraith, a native of

Tennessee, but came to this county in 1825, and died here in 1868. He was married in Tennessee to the mother of our subject and by her had two sons, viz., James M., of Villa Ridge, Ill., and William M. Mrs. Galbraith died in this county during the infancy of William M. Mr. Galbraith was again married--1833--and had a family of four sons and one daughter. His occupation was that of farmer and horticulturist. He had one of the first budded fruit orchards in Southern Illinois, and to his industry and success as a fruit grower can now be attributed much of the success which this county has attained in fruit growing. He was a stanch Republican, and was one of the stockholders of the first Republican paper in Mount Vernon. He was a member of the Methodist Episcopal Church and a thorough temperance man. Our subject was reared in this county, receiving such an education as the common schools afforded. When twenty-two years of age, he went to Wayne County, and for some years was engaged in the mercantile business at Johnsonville. When the civil war broke out, he responded to his country's call, enlisting in Company I, Forty-eighth Illinois Volunteer Infantry. He was mustered in as Quartermaster Sergeant and was promoted successively to the Second and First Lieutenancy, and then to Quartermaster of the regiment. He remained in the service till August, 1865, when they were mustered out at Little Rock. After returning from the service, he again entered the mercantile business at Johnsonville, continuing in the same for two years. Then for one year was in Cairo, and in 1868 came to his present farm of 136 acres, and began its improvement, it being all growing in brush, etc. He has since been engaged in raising small fruits, apples, etc. July 16, 1865, he was married in this county to Miss Elizabeth M. Casey, daughter of Rev. Abraham T. Casey and Vylinda (Maxey) Casey. This union has been blest with the following children: John and Charles. He and wife have been members of the Methodist Episcopal Church for years. In politics, he is Independent, not voting for the party but for the man. Rev. Abraham T. Casey was born in Barren County, Ky., July 29, 1798, and in infancy came with his parents to Illinois, and in 1817 to Jefferson County, Ill. He was converted when only twelve years of age. August 28, 1824, he was licensed as a local minister, and in 1833 was ordained Elder. In 1819, he was married to Vylinda Maxey, daughter of William Maxey. She was born December 31, 1803. They were the parents of one son—Lafayette--and six daughters—Harriet (deceased), Bell and Catherine (twins), Sarah (deceased), Elizabeth, and Martha (deceased). Mr. Casey carried the first temperance pledge in this county. He died September 14, 1834. Mrs. Casey remained a widow till the time of her death, March 26, 1883.

JOHN W. HAILS, farmer, P. O. Richview, was born in Sumner County, Tenn., March 19, 1823. His parents were Thomas and Sarah (Justice) Hails, his father a native of North Carolina and his mother of Virginia. Previous to their marriage, they had moved to Tennessee, and in 1827 came to Illinois, settling in Jefferson County, near Mount Vernon, where they lived until their death. His occupation was that of farming, making his home on the wild prairie, with Indians camping near. They were the parents of eleven children, six of whom are still living. He was in the war of 1812, and fought with Gen. Jackson at New Orleans. Both were members of the Methodist Episcopal Church and had been since early life. The subject of this sketch was reared on the farm and educated in the log schoolhouses of the day. When he reached his majority, he began life as a farmer, and has followed the same occupation to the present time, being engaged in stock-raising in connection with his farm. When he left the old home, he came to his present farm and began to improve it. He has now a well-cultivated farm of 330 acres, and besides this has deeded to his children 360 acres. In politics, he still holds to the opinions of his fathers. He has held various township offices, and is now filling the position of Highway Commissioner. He and his wife are both members of the Methodist Episcopal Church (South). He was married, August 8, 1848, to Annis M. Casey, daughter of F. S. and grand-daughter of Abram Casey. Mr. and Mrs. Hails have one child, dead, and eleven living—Narcissus C. (deceased), Thomas F., Alfred M., Zadok C., Sarah, Harriet J., Ellen, Ida P., Mary, Charles, John and Samuel T.—all living in the immediate neighborhood.

WILLIAM JOHNSON, farmer, P. O. Centralia, was born in Clark County, Ind., December 4, 1822. He is a son of John and Millie (Bower) Johnson; he was a native of New Jersey, she of North Carolina. They came to Indiana about 1808, where they died, he in 1836, she in May, 1839. They had nine children, eight sons and one daughter, seven of whom are still living. Our subject was reared in Clark County, Ind., and in the fall of 1850 came to this county. In 1847, he enlisted in the Mexican war, Company B, Fifth Indiana Regiment, under Col. James Lane, and served nine months, when the war closed. September 28, 1854, he was married in Indiana to Sarah B. Rogers. She was born in Clark County, Ind., a daughter of Archibald A. Rogers, a native of North Carolina. Mrs. Johnson died April 22, 1858; she was the mother of two children, one of whom is still living, viz., John A., of Nebraska. Mr. Johnson was again married, in 1859, to Susan A. Beadles. She was born in Clark County, Ind., but came to this State when six years of age. She is a daughter of Richard F. Beadles. There is one son—William R.— by this marriage. In the fall of 1854, Mr. Johnson moved to his present farm of 200 acres. He has a splendid rock quarry on his farm, and furnishes stone for different localities. He and his wife are both members of the Methodist Episcopal Church. In politics, he is a Republican.

CHARLES D. KELL, farmer, P. O. Walnut Hill, was born on his present farm, April 24, 1859, son of James and Margaret (Baldridge) Kell, he born in North Carolina and the son of Thomas Kell, one of the early settlers of this county; she a sister of James C. Baldridge, whose sketch appears in this work. They settled the farm now owned by our subject, but both died at Walnut Hill, Marion County, he in 1873, she in 1875. They were the parents of seven children, three of whom still survive, viz., D. D. Kell, of Walnut Hill; Margaret M. (wife of James L. Patton), and Charles D. Kell. For some years his occupation was that of farmer; he then removed to Walnut Hill and engaged in the milling and mercantile business, and in his business was a successful man. In politics, he was a Republican. Our subject was reared in this and Marion Counties, received his education in the common schools of Walnut Hill and in Irvington College. Since embarking in life for himself, he has followed different employments. One year he rented and ran the mill at Walnut Hill; then for two years was in mercantile business, but in 1882 came to this farm, which contains 280 acres of land. In connection with his farming, Mr. Kell also gives some attention to the growing of fruits, and in 1883, from one acre of strawberries, cleared $430. January 13, 1881, he was married to Sarah E. Foust, daughter of Reuben Foust, a successful fruit grower of this county. Mr. and Mrs. Kell have one child—Clara. In politics, he is a Republican.

CHARLES MILLER, farmer, P. O. Irvington, was born in Prussia September 28, 1821. He is the son of Henry Miller, who came to the United States in 1835, settling first in St. Clair County, then in Washington County, where he died in 1856. His first wife died in Germany, and of her children, two daughters and one son, our subject, still survive. Before leaving Germany, Mr. Miller was again married. The subject of our sketch was reared on his father's farm, receiving his education in the schools of his native land, except the English language, which he taught himself. His occupation has always been that of farming, first in Washington County, where he remained until 1867, when he bought his present farm of 300 acres of Owen Breeze, paying $12,000, this being one of the largest sales ever made in the county up to that time. He was married, December 19, 1843, to Hannah McBride, who was born February 23, 1819, a daughter of Hugh and Elizabeth (Rule) McBride. He was a native of Pennsylvania, his wife of Virginia; they were married in Tennessee and came to Washington County, Ill., in the fall of 1837. They were the parents of seven children, Mrs. Miller being the youngest and the only one now living. Mr. and Mrs. Miller have four children living and one dead, viz., Francis M., John Q. M. (died, November 26, 1868), Charles M., William A. and Emeline. F. M. is a farmer in the county; Charles M. is a doctor at Brimfield; William A. is a farmer in Marion County. In politics he is a Republican.

ESSEX PAYNE, farmer, P. O. Richview. Among the most thrifty farmers in Grand Prairie Township, who have made for themselves pleasant homes in the heretofore wilderness, we find the gentleman whose name heads this sketch. He was born near Mount Vernon January 31, 1840, to Joseph and Harriet (Stanford) Payne. They were natives of Smith County, Tenn., and came to Jefferson County, Ill., about 1835, and died in the county, he at the age of seventy-two years, and she at seventy-four. His occupation was that of farming. They reared to maturity a family of seven children, three of whom still survive, viz., J. H., Essex and J. T. They were both members of the Methodist Episcopal Church. In politics, he was Democratic. Our subject's early life was spent on the farm and in attending the common schools of the county. In 1862, he came to his present farm, which then had none of the splendid improvements it now has. His farm contains 240 acres, and on this he does general farming and stock-raising. August 10, 1861, he was married to Miss Margaret E. Casey, daughter of Maj. F. S. Casey (deceased). This union has been blest with five children, viz., Martha, Mary, Horatio, Cora I. and Joseph F. In politics, Mr. Payne is Democratic. He and wife are connected with the Methodist Episcopal Church.

J. W. PORTER, farmer, P. O. Centralia. The subject of this sketch was born in Jefferson County, Ill., March 16, 1838, to James and Sarah (Baldridge) Porter; she is a sister of James C. Baldridge (see sketch). He was a native of North Carolina, but came to this county when small, and died here in 1850. She is still living and is the wife of George Baltzell, of Centralia. Our subject is one of a family of six children, viz., William C., Joseph W., Martha, James M. and Julia. Only the two eldest now survive. James was lost during the battle of Perryville. Mr. Porter's life, with the exception of two years, has been spent in this county. He was educated in the common schools and has always been engaged in farming, except for two years he was in the mercantile business in Walnut Hill, Ill. November 28, 1860, he was married to Mary D. Fouts. She was born in Clark County, Ind., but came to this county when small. Her father, Lemon Fouts, is now a resident of Irvington. Mr. and Mrs. Porter have three children living and one dead, viz., Sherman S., James E., Walter P., and Sarah E. (deceased). Mr. Porter has been on his present farm of 300 acres since marriage, and has always had to depend upon his own energy to make a success. He and wife are members of the Methodist Episcopal Church. In politics, he is a Republican.

THOMAS L. RATTS, farmer, P. O. Irvington, was born in Clark County, Ind., November 27, 1830, to Jacob and Cynthia (Fouts) Ratts. He was born in North Carolina in 1806; she in Indiana in 1810, Jacob being only fifteen years of age when his father went to Indiana. Jacob and wife were married December 25, 1828, and are the parents of seven children, six of whom still survive, viz., Thomas L., David F., Malinda E. (deceased), Mary E., Sarah J., Henry H., Margaret and Evaline. Since going to Indiana, his occupation has been that of farming, but in early life he learned the hatter's trade. In politics, he is a strong Republican. For many years he was a Deacon in the Christian Church, but when about sixty-five years of age changed to the belief of the Universalist Church. Our subject was reared on the farm and received his education in the common schools of the county. He remained at home till his marriage, March 30, 1854, to Miss Sarah E. Grisamore. She was born November 27, 1832, in Clark County, Ind., to John and Rebecca (Henley) Grisamore. He was a native of Pennsylvania, she of North Carolina. Both were born in 1806, and were early settlers in Clark County, Ind., and for some years have been residents of Irvington, Ill. Mr. and Mrs. Ratts are the parents of eight children, seven of whom still survive--Mary E. (deceased), Ida E. (wife of William F. Copple), John H., J. Oscar, David G., Rebecca J., Cynthia E. and Thomas L. In 1854, Mr. Ratts came to this county and settled on his present farm, which now contains 482 acres, 400 of which are in good state of cultivation. He is engaged in farming, stock-dealing and fruit-growing. He is a member of A., F. & A. M., Irvington Lodge, No. 650. He and wife are members of the Methodist Episcopal Church, and have been since before marriage. In politics, he votes with the Republican party. He has held the various township offices, Supervisor, etc.

FIELD TOWNSHIP.

HARDIN BARKER, farmer, P. O. Divide, is a native of St. Clair County, Ill., and was born August 15, 1847. His father, Nelson Barker, was a native of Maine, and came to Illinois with his parents in 1820, when but a child. Our subject attended the common schools of his native county, and has always been a farmer. He has also run a thresher nearly every season since he became grown. He now owns the Belleville Separator and engine, made by Harrison & Co., of Belleville, Ill. This machine does excellent and very rapid work. In one day he threshed 1,003 bushels of wheat with it, and set three times. Mr. Barker was married, first, in 1873, to Emily Sargent, by whom he had three children—Lucy, George and Frank. Mrs. Barker died in 1880, and he again married in December, 1882, this time to Ellen Sledge. Mr. Barker came to this county in 1875, where he has since resided.

WILLIAM CLAYBOURN, farmer, P. O. Dix, was born in Knox County, Tenn., August 27, 1819, and is the son of Ephraim Claybourn, of Knox County, Tenn., afterward of Allen County, Ky., where he died in the summer of 1850. Our subject got his education in DeKalb County, Tenn., and came to this county in the fall of 1840, where he still resides. He was married, September 4, 1838, to Miss Frankie, daughter of Reuben Hawker, of Virginia. Mrs. Claybourn died July 23, 1863, leaving ten children, viz., Catharine, Sarah J., James T., William P., John B., Harriet N., Ephraim S., Reuben C., Joseph M. and Cassius C. February 14, 1865, Mr. Claybourn married Mrs. Elizabeth J. Maxey, daughter of Francis Sterns, of Virginia; by her he had two children—Charles F. and Lucy B. Mrs. Elizabeth Claybourn had five children by her former husband, viz., Melissa V., George W., Laura S., Mary L. and William H. Subject is a member of the Methodist Episcopal Church. He served one year in the army, in Company H, First Illinois Cavalry. James H. and William P., his sons, each served four years in Company H, Eightieth Illinois Cavalry. They were in the battles of Perryville, Lookout Mountain and several others. James was wounded at Atlanta, Ga. John enlisted when seventeen years of age, and William when eighteen years of age. Mr. Claybourn is engaged in farming and stock-raising. He is a Republican in politics.

RUFUS FIELDS, farmer, P. O. Mount Vernon, was born October 1, 1844, in Jefferson County, Ill., and is the son of James Fields, of North Carolina, since then of Jefferson County, Ill. James Fields came here when eighteen years of age, and was married to Elizabeth Hays, daughter of Samuel Hays, of Alabama, afterward of Jefferson County, Ill. Subject had eleven children, seven living, viz., Ruth S., Malinda, Henry P., Rufus, James M., Noah and Priscilla. Rufus was educated in Jefferson County, Ill., and owns 195 acres of land, and is engaged in farming and stock-raising. Politics, Democrat.

WILLIAM J. GARRISON, farmer and stock-raiser, P. O. Divide (commonly known as Dick Garrison), was born in Field Township, this county, June 4, 1837. He was brought up on the farm and received a common school education. He went to California in 1857, remaining in that State and in Oregon until 1869, when he returned to this county. In 1865, on the 2d day of March, while in Oregon, he married Phœbe A. Sweetin, by whom he had five children; but two of these are living—Joel J. and Charles Quincy. Mrs. Garrison died March 5, 1874, and the 20th day of August of the same year he married Rachel Payne, by whom he has six children, viz., Nora, Lucy J., Myrtie E., James H., Millie A. and Myra A. Mr. Garrison owns 320 acres of land, and is a successful stock-raiser. He is a member of the Chapter in the Masonic fraternity. Our subject held the office of Highway Commissioner for three years, has held the office of Supervisor for six years and is the present incumbent. His father, James N. Garrison (deceased), was born near Nashville, Tenn., and died October 14, 1851, aged thirty-nine years eight months and eighteen days, and is a pioneer of this county, who married Milly Wimberly, and by her had nine children, six of whom are living, viz., Joel V.' Martha A., the subject of this sketch, Thomas W., Caroline and James K. The elder Mr. Garrison died.

JOSEPH HAWKINS, farmer, P. O. Dix, was born January 19, 1824, in Fayette County, Ind., a son of John Hawkins, Sr., of Georgia, who came to this county in the fall of 1840, where he died October 22, 1879. Our subject was educated in Fayette County, Ind., and was Justice of the Peace in Jefferson County eleven years, and is a member of the Christian Church. He was married, September 17, 1843, to Miss Millie, daughter of William Whitlow, of Virginia, later of Jefferson County, Ill. William Whitlow died August 7, 1866. Mr. Hawkins has ten children, viz., Malinda J., William J., Nancy S., Rebecca, Moses D., Tiltha, Susan, Pleasant E., Lucy and Joseph A. Our subject owns 160 acres of valuable land and is engaged in farming and stock-raising. He has been Township Treasurer for twenty-one years, and is a Republican.

JOHN HAWKINS, Jr., farmer, P. O. Dix, was born September 8, 1827, in Kentucky. He is a son of Benjamin Hawkins, of South Carolina, who had moved to Kentucky, Indiana, Missouri, and at last settled in Jefferson County, Ill., where he died September, 1880, leaving three children, viz., John, Eliza and Rachel. Our subject came to Jefferson County, Ill., when young, and still resides there. He is a member of the Masonic fraternity, and was educated in Jefferson County. He was in the war with Mexico in 1846, in Company H, Third Illinois Volunteer Infantry. He was married, April 2, 1848, to Miss Julia A., daughter of Elisha Wimberly, of Tennessee, since of Jefferson County, Ill. Our subject is the father of thirteen children, twelve living, viz., Elisha, Benjamin J., Charles, John, Burl, Laura, Maria, Belle, Emma, Ella, Lena and Eva. Mr. Hawkins has been Supervisor one year, Road Commissioner six years, of Field Township. He owns 520 acres of land, and is engaged in farming and stock-raising. Politics, Democratic.

ELISHA HAWKINS, farming, P. O. Dix, was born August 22, 1836, in Fayette County, Ind., son of John Hawkins, of same county. He served three years in the late war in Company H, Eightieth Illinois Volunteer Infantry, and was in the battles of Perryville and Milton Heights, Tenn., and several other skirmishes. He was educated in Jefferson County, Ill., and was married, February 16, 1859, to Miss Susan, daughter of Henry Fields, of Jefferson County, Ill. He has nine children, viz., Richard W., James E., Mary D., Sarah, Lucinda, Emeline, John, Henry and Laura. Our subject owns 110 acres of land, and is engaged in farming and stock-raising. Politics, Republican. Is a member of the Christian Church.

S. L. HAWKINS, farming, P. O. Dix, was born December 5, 1859, in Jefferson County, Ill., son of Jacob Hawkins, of Jefferson County, Ill., and was educated in Jefferson County, where he was married, January 11, 1879, to Rosa, daughter of S. Murphy, of Jefferson County, Ill. Our subject had one child, but it died in 1882. He owns thirty-three acres of land, and is engaged in farming and stock-raising. Politics, Republican.

M. M. HOWARD, farmer, P. O. Dix, was born December 5, 1821, in Kentucky, son of Ignatius Howard, of Tennessee, afterward of Jefferson County, Ill. Our subject went to White County, Tenn., and remained there until 1837, and he afterward moved to Jefferson County, Ill., where he still resides. He is a member of the Methodist Episcopal Church and was married, August 12, 1841, to Miss Censsey J., daughter of Lewis Carpenter, of Marion County, Ill., and has had six children, viz., Hiram, Sarah, Hezekiah F., John W., Nancy A. and Censsey J. Hiram, son of M. M. Howard, served three years in the army. He enlisted in Company C, Twenty-second Illinois Volunteer Infantry. He was in the battles of Mission Ridge, Peach Tree Creek and several other battles. Subject is engaged in farming and stockraising. Politics, Democratic.

JOHN C. McCONNELL, farming, P. O. Dix, was born January 6, 1825, in Jefferson County, Ill., son of Burl McConnell, from Sumner County, Tenn., late of Jefferson County, Ill., deceased. Mr. McConnell is a member of the Masonic fraternity, also a member of the Methodist Episcopal Church. He was in the Mexican war in 1846 and 1847, and was married, August 25, 1847, to Miss Sarah J., daughter of Samuel Cummins, of Jefferson County, Ill., and has had seven children, five living, viz., Samuel F., William H., Harriet, John D. and James W. Mrs. McConnell died April 18, 1879, and he was again married, to Amering Howard, of Saline County, Ill. He was educated in Jefferson County, and owns 480 acres of land, and is engaged in farming and stock-raising.

DR. WILLIAM K. PARKER, physician, Divide, was born in this county March 3, 1851. He was brought up on the farm, and attended the common schools. He farmed until twenty-one years of age, when he began to read medicine and also worked for railroad companies for about four years. He graduated from the College of Physicians and Surgeons of Keokuk, Iowa, in the spring of 1883. He at once began the practice of medicine at his home in Field Township, and is building up a good practice. His father, James T. Parker (deceased), was born in Kentucky in 1824; came to this county with his parents when a child; was married to Mickey A. Hutcherson, by whom he had six children, viz., Mary C., our subject, Elsah E., Nettie V. (deceased), Charles F. and Wincey A. The father died December 14, 1864. He was a member of the Methodist Episcopal Church in good standing, a consistent Christian and a temperance worker.

BENJAMIN F. PRIMM, farmer, P. O. Mount Vernon, was born in Menard County, Ill., November 19, 1841. Subject is the son of Enoch Primm, of St. Clair County, Ill., who was a carpenter by trade, from whom subject learned the use of tools when young, and uses them at leisure. Subject was married, November 14, 1866, to Martha J., daughter of Peter Conover, of Elk County, Kan., by whom our subject had six children, viz., Minnie A., Thomas S., Charlon M., Arthur C., John S. and Benjamin F. Our subject is a member of the Masonic lodge, also a member of the Christian Church. He served three years in the army, in Company K, One Hundred and Sixth Illinois Volunteer Infantry, and was in the siege of Vicksburg and many other engagements. He is engaged in farming and stock-raising, and owns 240 acres of land.

SILAS J. SIMMONS, farmer, P. O. Divide, was born in Sumner (now Macon) County, Tenn., May 28, 1835, and is a son of Joel Simmons, of Marion County, Ill., who was born in Franklin County, Va., January 17, 1804, and who came to Marion County in 1840, and to this county in 1844, where our subject has since resided. Silas J. was married, November 1, 1855, to Prudence E., daughter of Ellis Branson, of Marion County, Ill. They had twelve children, but three of whom are living—Mary J. (Mrs. John Burnett), William F. (see his biography) and Carroll J. The latter is a promising young school teacher, with a bright future prospect.

One daughter—Martha A.—died in her sixteenth year. Mr. Simmons was Postmaster at Divide Post Office from December, 1879, until March, 1883. He owns eighty acres of land. In religion is a Baptist.

WILLIAM F. SIMMONS, teacher and farmer, P. O. Divide, was born in this township, where he still lives, on Section 11, November 19, 1857, and is a son of Silas J. Simmons, whose biography also appears in this work. He was brought up on the old homestead, and is what we would term a self educated man; often "burned midnight oil" in pursuing his studies, and worked hard during the day to assist in supporting the family. He now teaches of winters and farms during the summer seasons, and owns 120 acres of land. He held the office of Clerk of Field Township for two terms, and is Assistant—and at present acting-Postmaster of Divide Post Office, which is kept at his father's house.

CLABORN M. WHITSON, farmer, P. O. Dix, was born in Parke County, Ind., September 13, 1832, and is a son of Stephen Whitson (deceased), a native of Tennessee, born in 1811, and brought his family to Marion County, Ill., in September, 1853. Our subject attended a subscription school in his native county. He came to this county in 1857, where he has since resided. He was married, February 1, 1855, to Mrs. Agnes White, daughter of Michael Collins. They have had six children, four living—Susan F., John, Mary E. and Nancy I. Mrs. Whitson had five children by her first husband, two living—George W. and Samuel White. The last two are in Marion County, Ill. Mr. Whitson has held the office of Justice of the Peace for seven years, and has been School Director for fifteen years. He is a member of the Masonic fraternity and of the Methodist Episcopal Church. He owns eighty acres of valuable land, and resides on Section 21. Mr. Whitson is also a minister of the Gospel.

JAMES J. WILLIAMS, farming, P. O. Dix, was born April 29, 1822, in Bedford County, Tenn., a son of Moses Williams, of Bedford County, Tenn., who moved to Marion County, Ill., in the fall of 1849. Our subject came to Jefferson County in the spring of 1852. He is a member of the I.O.O.F., also of the Methodist Episcopal Church, and has been a local preacher for fifteen years. He was married, January 17, 1852, to Miss Sophronia, daughter of Nathaniel Bryon, of Jefferson County, Ill., and has had eleven children, nine living, viz., W. C., Mary A., Moses N., Sarah E., Sophronia L., Rosa C., Lavada J., Charles H. and James E. Mr. Williams has 140 acres of land, and is engaged in farming and stock-raising. He went to school six weeks only, in Bedford County, Tenn., but he studied of nights at home to obtain an education. Politics, Democratic.

MOORE'S PRAIRIE TOWNSHIP.

IGNATIUS ATCHISSON, farmer, P. O. Opdyke, was born in Georgia July 7, 1802, and was a son of Barton and Prudence (Nill) Atchisson, both natives of Maryland. Our subject was the second of three children who left Georgia with the father when the former was only eight years old. The father settled in Smith County, Tenn., and there subject received his first education. When he was fifteen, the father moved to Jefferson County, and settled near where subject now lives. Again the latter was permitted to attend school, but it was mainly the subscription school. On the home farm, subject remained until about twenty-two, and then started out in life on a Government improvement. There he remained two years, and then came to his present farm. He now owns 167 acres in Section 6, Town 4, Range 4 east, and of that all except about thirty acres is in process of cultivation. Mr. Atchisson was married in 1824 to Philadelphia Hopper, a daughter of Thomas Hopper, a native of Tennessee. This lady is the mother of ten children, six of whom are now living—Samuel (in Oregon), Thomas, Barton and Ignatius, Jr. (all farmers in this township), Winnie (wife of John Allan, of Spring Garden Township), Harriet (wife of James Marlow); this lady died in 1860, and he was married the second time, in August, 1863, to Mrs. Keziah Williams. Our subject has served his township as Justice of the Peace one or two terms. Was out three months in the Spy Battalion, one of the companies that was in the Black Hawk war. Is a Democrat in politics.

JOHN BURCHELL, farmer, P. O. Opdyke. This gentleman was born in Rockingham County, N. C., May 5, 1823, and was a son of John and Ruthie (Grogin) Burchell, both natives of North Carolina. When subject was five months old, his parents moved to Hawkins County, Tenn., and there the former received his education. Subject assisted at home until twenty-one, and then came to Jefferson County. He arrived in Moore's Prairie Township November 7, 1840, and settled down about two miles from where he now lives. After nine years' residence there, he came to his present farm, and now owns 280 acres, most of which is in Section 17, Town 4, Range 4 east. Mr. Burchell was married, November 10, 1852, to Mary Davis, a daughter of Lewis and Sarah Davis, both natives of Tennessee. This lady died June 10, 1855, and he was married the second time, January 25, 1857, to Minerva Jane Bingham, a daughter of David and Melinda Bingham, also of Tennessee. This lady is the mother of ten children—Harriet Alice (wife of Daniel W. Hughey), James F., Artemesia, Isabella (wife of James Adams), Lilly E., George W., John A., Martin L., Dellie J. and Maude. Subject is a member of the Missionary Baptist Church, and a Republican in politics.

G. W. CLARK, farmer, P. O. Belle Rive, was born in Wilson County, Tenn., October 6, 1841, and is a son of J. A. and Margaret (Beard) Clark, both natives of that State. Subject is the oldest of six living children, and obtained his education in the subscription schools of that county. He remained at home with his father until 1862, and then came to this county, and worked for a number of different farmers, among them James Waters. In 1868, he purchased his present property, and now owns 200 acres in Section 15, Town 4, Range 4 east. He has about 160 acres in cultivation, and two acres in orchard. Mr. Clark was married, January 19, 1873, to Jennie McCarver, a daughter of Mrs. Margaret McCarver, and a native of Northern Arkansas. She is the mother of one child now dead. He is a member of the Missionary Baptist Church. He has served as Township Supervisor. In politics, he is an Independent.

WILLIAM COFIELD, farmer, P. O. Moore's Prairie, was born in Wilson County, Tenn., February 12, 1826, and is a son of Willis and Maria (Thomas) Cofield. The father was a native of Virginia, and the mother was born in Kentucky. Subject was the second of five children, and was brought, when a child of six years, to this county, where the father settled in Pendleton Precinct, about a mile east of Belle Rive. In the schools of that township, the son received his education. It was but limited, and our subject is truly what might be called a self-made man. The father having died when subject was about sixteen years old, the latter, together with his two brothers, took charge of the home place. There he remained until twenty, and then started out in life on a purchased farm, about two miles from his present place, and where Thomas Shipley now lives. There he remained twelve months, and then returned to Pendleton Township, and settled on the home farm. After living on that farm eighteen years, he again moved, and then settled on part of the tract of land that Belle Rive now occupies. In 1875, he left that farm and came to his present location, where he now owns a farm of 200 acres, situated in Sections 22, 23 and 27. He has about 190 acres in cultivation, and two acres in orchard. Mr. Cofield was married, on June 22, 1848, to Brunetta Wilky, a daughter of Maxy and Jennie Wilky, one of the oldest families in this county. She was the mother of three children, one of whom is now living—Thomas, now in Clinton County, Ill. This lady died in January, 1854, and our subject was married the second time, to Nancy J. Laird, a native of Pendleton Township, and the daughter of David and Elizabeth (Tumbleson) Laird. This marriage resulted in ten children, six of whom are now living—W. H. (in Ottawa, Kan.), Leaton, Ransom. Charles Hannibal, Isabelle and Charity. He is a member of the Methodist Episcopal Church, and is a Republican in politics.

C. H. JUDD, farmer, P. O. Moore's Prairie. This gentleman was born in Guyandotte, Cabell County, W. Va., December 7, 1835; he was a son of John T. and Doratha M. (Prosser) Judd. The father, who was a mechanic, was a native of New York, the mother, of Prince William County, Va. At the age of eight years, the father moved to Lawrence County, Ohio, where subject attended the free schools until about eighteen, and then attended the Marietta High School; he remained there two years. Then subject came to Jefferson County with his father, and settled in Moore's Prairie Township, where the father erected a saw and flouring mill, the first in this section of the country. When subject became of age, he became a partner in his father's mill, and soon after he assumed the entire charge of the concern. When the father died, in 1858, the estate was divided and the mill fell into the hands of the younger brother, Lewis Judd. Our subject then turned his attention to farming, and first settled on a farm of 120 acres, about two miles from his present location. There he remained about fourteen years. In 1873, he came to his present location. He now owns 300 acres in Section 21, Town 14, Range 14 east. In 1881, he erected what is considered to be the finest house in the county, at a cost of about $4,000. Subject was married, March 4, 1858, to Elizabeth Riddle, a daughter of Charles H. and Harriet (Irvin) Riddle. The mother was one of the daughters of Abraham Irvin, one of the earliest settlers in the southern part of the State. The result of this marriage was ten children, Leota V. (wife of T. N. Woodruff), John T., Nattie L., Dollie L., Lewis C., William T., Samuel C., Quincy A., Gracie E. and Anna P. Mr. Judd has been Justice of the Peace four times, Township Supervisor several times, also Chairman of the County Board of Supervisors. He is a Greenbacker in politics.

A. KNOWLES, farmer, P. O. Belle Rive, was born in Posey County, Ind., September 7, 1844, and is a son of Wiley and Minerva (Scott) Knowles. The father was born in Georgia, and the mother in Ohio. Subject was the seventh of eleven children, and, when two years of age, his father came to this county and settled about one mile from Spring Garden, in that township, where he now resides. Subject received a common school education, within the confines of that township, and afterward remained at home with his father until his twentieth year, when he started out on a trip of pleasure and observation. He was absent two years, and during the interval he visited Iowa, Colorado, Utah, Wyoming Territory, Oregon and California. He was engaged a part of the time as a stockdriver. At San Francisco, he took a steamer, and from there sailed to the Isthmus, and, crossing it again, took a steamer to New York, and from there home again by way of Chicago. Soon after his arrival home, he commenced life for himself on a farm about one and a half miles from Spring Garden. On that farm he remained two years, and then came to his present farm, where he now owns 295 acres, situated in Sections 8 and 9, of Town 4, Range 4 east. Of this there are about 290 in cultivation and 3 acres in orchard. Mr. Knowles was married, February 26, 1867, to Harriet Smith, a native of this township, and a daughter of Jesse H. (whose sketch appears elsewhere in this work) and Jane (Bliss) Smith. The result of this marriage was five children, one only of whom is now living, Gertrude, born in September, 1879. Mr. Knowles is a Greenbacker in politics.

JOHN LOWRY, SR., farmer, P. O. Dahlgren, Hamilton County. One of the oldest residents in this county is the gentleman whose name heads this sketch, born in Warren County, Ky., May 3, 1803, a son of John and Elizabeth (Reese) Lowry. When three years old, his father brought him to what is now Coffee County, Tenn., then Franklin County. There our subject attended the subscription schools but slightly, but in after years he taught himself, and is truly a self-made man. Until he reached manhood's estate, he remained at home assisting some on the home farm and also in his father's cooper shop. January 25, 1824, he came to Hamilton County, this State, where he settled about three miles from his present location, and there he remained about one year. From there he came to his present farm, where he now owns 280 acres in Sections 7, 13 and 18, of Town 4, Range 4 east. Besides this, he also owns 86 acres in Town 4, of Range 5, Hamilton County, 52 acres within the present limits of the town of Dahlgren, Hamilton County, and 15 town lots in that town. Of the whole, he now has about 160 acres in cultivation, and 2½ acres in orchard.

Mr. Lowry was married in Franklin County, Tenn., July 3, 1823, to Nancy Martin, a daughter of Alexander and Nancy (Dabney) Martin, both of whom were natives of Pennsylvania. This lady was the mother of fourteen children, the following of whom are now living, viz.: David, in Washington Territory; John, in this township; Thomas, in Hamilton County; Elisha, in Stoddard County, Mo.; Jefferson, in business in the town of Dahlgren; Sarah, wife of Zachariah Sinks, now in Texas; Elizabeth, wife of Alfred Dees, of Bald Township; and Mary, wife of Gabriel Joins, of Hamilton County. She died November 16, 1880, and he was married the second time, June 9, 1881, to Nancy Willis, a daughter of James and Nancy Willis, both natives of Virginia. One child is the result of this union, Susie, born May 20, 1882. Subject is a member of the Sugar Camp Baptist Church. Has held the offices of Justice of the Peace and Constable, Township Trustee and School Trustee and Director. In the time of the old State Militia, dating from 1832, he was elected to the office of Lieutenant of a company, and held it for about five years. He was a soldier in the Black Hawk war under Beckerstoff. In politics, he is a Democrat.

B. B. PETTYPOOL, farmer, P. O. Opdyke, was born in Rutherford County, Tenn., April 23, 1821, and was a son of Thomas and Mary (Nixon) Pettypool. Subject was the second of six children, and is the only one now living of that number. When he was six years old, his father came to White County, Ill., and settled in Hervel's Prairie Township. There subject was permitted to attend school but slightly, and is what might be truly called a self-made man. Helped on the home farm until eighteen, and then settled near his father's farm, but in the course of a year or two, his father having become old and infirm, he returned to the home place. In 1868, he came to Jefferson County, and settled on his present farm; he now owns about 280 acres, 80 of which are situated in Section 21, 160 in Section 20, and 40 in Section 19. Of the whole piece, 240 acres are in cultivation. He has about six acres in orchard. Mr. Pettypool was married, August 2, 1839, to Celia McGeahey, a daughter of Parent and Jemmima (Pierce) McGeahey, both natives of Tennessee. His lady was the mother of eight children, and of that number six are now living—Thomas, in Effingham County ; Frances, in White County ; Daniel, in White County; Huldah ; Telitha, wife of John Hanley ; Sarah Ellen, wife of William Jones. The lady died January 15, 1856, and he was married, February 28, 1857, to Mrs. Mary Teachenor, a native of New York. She was the daughter of Reuben Catline, of that State, and the mother of five children, three of whom are now living—Joel, in Spring Garden Township; Ezekiel, in Franklin County, Kan.; and Marshall, in Spring Garden Township. His second wife died October 2, 1876, and on July 4, 1877, he was united in marriage to Mary Jones, a native of this county, and a daughter of John and Mahala Jones. She is the mother of three children, Leah, Dora and Hardin. Subject is a Democrat in politics.

DAVID ROTRAMEL, farmer, P. O. Moore's Prairie, was born in Logan County, Ky., April 8, 1814, and was a son of Henry and Keziah (Simpson) Rotramel. When our subject was five years old, his father moved to Wilson County, Tenn., and there the former attended the schools of that county. He remained on the home farm until 1837, and then came to Frankfort, Franklin Co., Ill. He remained in that town until the next spring, and then commenced farming in that township. In 1846, he left Frankfort Township and went to Benton Township, same county, where he remained two years. In 1848, he came to Jefferson County, and first settled about two miles from where he now resides. In the year 1850, he entered a portion of his present farm, but did not move on the place for about seven years afterward. He now owns 200 acres, 120 of which are in Section 21, and eighty in Section 20, Town 4, Range 4 east. Of this all is in cultivation. Mr. Rotramel was married, January 25, 1847, to Mary Myers, a daughter of Christopher and Agnes (Bright) Myers, both natives of Tennessee. This lady was the mother of eight children, and of this number seven are now living—George Alice, wife of Richard Nooner ; Florida, wife of Edward Burkhead ; Henry Olive, wife of William Hunter ; David Washington ; Arilla, wife of Oscar McClure ; William Lincoln and Richard Yates. Our subject is a Republican in politics. Has served as Township Commissioner.

JESSE H. SMITH, farmer, P. O. Opdyke, was born in Hickman County, Tenn., September 14, 1823, and was a son of Isaac and Millie (Hassell) Smith, both of whom were natives of Tyrrel County, N. C. He was the youngest of nine children, and of that number but two are living—Joan, wife of a Mr. Harrell, of Spring Garden Township, and Jesse H., our subject. When he reached the age of six years, his parents moved to Jefferson County, Ill., and settled in Spring Garden Township. In the schools of that county our subject received his education. In 1843–44, at the request of his father, he attended the St. Louis Medical Institute, but never followed the practice of his profession. He came back home and worked on his father's farm until twenty-four, and then settled on a Government improvement in Spring Garden Township, and finally had about forty acres in improvement. After ten years' residence there, he came to his present farm, where he now owns 400 acres lying in Sections 8 and 18, Town 4, range 4 east, and of that 360 acres. are now in cultivation. Mr. Smith was married, March 30, 1847, to Eliza Jane Bliss, a daughter of Noah and Elizabeth (Martin) Bliss, of Vermont. This lady is the mother of ten children, seven of whom are still living—Harriet, wife of Ananias Knowles, of this township ; Florence, wife of Francis Knowles, of Spring

Garden Township; Hubbard S., Cora, Kirby, Elnora and A. C. A son, L. D., died October 14, 1880. Mr. Smith has held numerous offices, among which are those of County Surveyor, County Coroner, Deputy Sheriff, Township Trustee, Supervisor and Assessor, also the different school offices. He is a member of Ham's Grove Grange, No. 1,604. He is connected with the Baptist organization. In politics, he is a Greenbacker.

JAMES WATERS, farmer, P. O. Moore's Prairie, was born twelve miles east of Lebanon, the county seat of Wilson County, Tenn., March 7, 1815, and was a son of Shelleah and Nancy (Turner) Waters, both natives of Maryland. He was next to the youngest of thirteen children, and of that number our subject is the only one now living. After receiving a fair education, he assisted on the home farm until the age of twenty-four, and then came to Jefferson County, Ill. On July 15, 1839, he settled on his present farm, and there remained eight years, and then went back to Wilson County, Tenn. There he remained until August 27, 1860, and then returned to Illinois, and again settled on the farm in this county September 5 of the same year. He now owns 280 acres; 160 are in Section 28, 80 in Section 29, and 40 in Section 33. Of this all is in cultivation except about sixty acres; there are also four acres in orchard. Mr. Waters was married, July 7, 1842, to Sarah Ann Estes, a daughter of John and Dicia M. (Jordan) Estes; the father was one of the oldest settlers in Pendleton Township. To this lady were born three children, one of whom is now living—John Thomas. Mr. Waters is a member of the United Baptist Church; he is a Republican in politics.

JACOB P. WELLS, farmer, P. O. Moore's Prairie, was born in Indiana County, Penn., January 26, 1840, and was a son of James and Elizabeth (Pierce) Wells, both natives of that State. Our subject received his education in the schools of that county, and at the age of eighteen he was apprenticed to a cabinet-maker in the town of Plumville, Penn., and remained with him three years, and then followed that trade for himself. In 1861, he came to Rock Island County, Ill., where he still follows his trade. In the spring of 1866, after the war was ended, he came to Franklin County, and settled there on a farm about six miles from his present location. There he farmed in the summer, and worked at the carpenter's trade in the winter. In the winter of 1871, he came to the place where he now resides, and soon after his arrival there purchased the saw and grist mill of Edward Choicer. This mill was continued in operation until it was destroyed by fire in 1877. Since then Mr. Wells has given his principal attention to farming. He now owns 240 acres, 180 of which are in Sections 26 and 35 of Town 4, Range 4 east, and 60 acres in Franklin County; of the whole, there are about 200 acres in cultivation. Mr. Wells was married, March 1, 1861, to Emily A. Pilson, a native of Pennsylvania, and a daughter of William and Eliza (McCardle) Pilson. This lady is the mother of ten children—Clara (wife of Henry Pickel), Louis C., Elizabeth, James A., Hiley A., Charles T., Lydia A., Jessie W., Nellie R. and Ettie M.; nine of these are now living. At the breaking-out of the war, our subject, who was then at Rock Island, returned to his old home at Plumville, Penn., and enlisted in Company A of the Second Pennsylvania Volunteer Infantry, going out June 7, 1862, and remained in the service until July 13, 1865, when he again returned to Illinois. In politics, Mr. Wells is a Republican.

DR. JAMES HENRY WILKEY, physician and farmer, P. O. Moore's Prairie, one of the oldest native born citizens of this county, is the gentleman whose name heads this sketch, who was born here April 19, 1825, and was a son of Carter and Brunetta (Casey) Wilkey. The father was born in Walker County, Ga., in

1797. His father was a native of Scotland, and Carter in 1818 came to Mt. Vernon. He was a house carpenter by trade, also followed that of the cabinet-maker. In the early history of Mt. Vernon, he assisted in many public enterprises, among which was the erection of the first county court house in Jefferson County. In 1840, he commenced studying for the practice of medicine, and as soon as his course was completed he located where our subject now lives. In that neighborhood he continued in active practice until his death, which occurred April 3, 1876. The mother was the daughter of Isaac Casey, one of the oldest pioneers of this county. Our subject received his education in the schools of Mt. Vernon Township, and at the age of seventeen he commenced reading medicine with his father. He continued his studies until he reached manhood's estate, and then after a year or so's practice with his father, he made his stand in Wayne County. He has since then practiced in Shadville, White County, Benton, Franklin County, Norris City, in White County, and then at Macedonia, in Hamilton County. While practicing, the death of his father occurred, and soon after that he returned to Jefferson County, and took up the mantle that had fallen from the shoulders of his father. He is now the only physician in that section. He practices over the counties of Jefferson, Hamilton and Franklin, and but few fall under the magic touch of his skillful hand, and the care of his watchful brain, but to be improved and to bless the existence of our subject. Besides his practice, the Doctor owns quite a nice farm of about ninety acres, situated in Section 36, Township 4, Range 4 east. He now has about sixty acres in cultivation. The charge of this devolves mainly on the son—Thomas M. Dr. Wilkey was married, February 25, 1847, in Hamilton County, to Lucy Goodwin, a daughter of John Goodwin, a native of Kentucky. This lady was the mother of two children, one of whom is now living—Thomas M., born March 1, 1848. Her death occurred May 6, 1850, and subject was married the second time, in September, 1856, to Mary Ann Houseworth, a daughter of Jonathan and Rebecca Houseworth, both natives of Ohio. She was the mother of four children, and of this number there is also only one living—Peoria, wife of Louis Shelton, of Hamilton County. This lady died in 1863, and he was married the third time, December 2, 1865, to Emily Darnall, a daughter of James H. and Mary (Robenson) Darnall; the father was a native of Tennessee, and the mother of Franklin County, this State. The result of this union was three children, two of whom are now living—James H., Jr., born August 23, 1866, and Carter Wilkey, born March 16, 1876. In politics, subject is a Republican.

ELI R. YATES, farmer, P. O. Dahlgren, was born in Hamilton County, Ill., May 26, 1834, and is a son of Joseph and Nancy Campbell Yates. The father was a native of Kentucky, and the mother of Tennessee. Subject was the oldest of five children, four of whom are now living. He received his education, such as it was, in the subscription schools of that county. When sixteen years old, his father died, and subject roved about for a number of years working for farmers in Wayne, Hamilton and Jefferson Counties, also in several counties in the northern part of the State. In 1859, he settled down on a farm in Wayne County, but only remained there about one year, and then came to this county, where he settled on his present farm. He now owns 110 acres situated in Section 1, Township 4, Range 4 east. Of this, about ninety acres are in cultivation, and about 4 acres in orchard. Mr. Yates was married, January 13, 1859, to Martha Shelton, a native of this county, and a daughter of John W. and Margaret R. (Smith) Shelton. The father was a native of Kentucky. This lady was the mother of seven children, four of whom are now living—Isam Riley, Oley, Edward and Lillie. Our subject is a member of the M. E. Church of Dahlgren, Hamilton County, and a member of Dahlgren Lodge, No. 486, I. O. O. F. He is a Democrat in politics.

CASNER TOWNSHIP.

HUGH L. BLEDSOE (deceased) was born in Blount County, Tenn., in 1821, a son of Philadelphus and Mildred (Kendrick) Bledsoe, both natives of the same State. He was a farmer by occupation, a Democrat in politics, and died in 1863. His wife, who survives him, was born July 9, 1828, but a half mile from where she at present resides, and has lived here ever since, making her the oldest resident of Casner Township. She is the mother of seven children, of whom six are living—William M., Eliza L., Permelia E., Philadelphus M., Thomas H. and James D. Mrs. Beldsoe is a member of the Christian Church. She has a farm of 140 acres, which is given to general farming. P. M. Bledsoe was born December 30, 1855, and was married, March 28, 1883, to Ollie D. Henley, a daughter of James and Mary (Stilly) Henley. He has a farm of twenty-six acres situated in Washington County. He is a member of the I. O. O. F., Ashley Lodge, No. 302, and in politics is a Democrat.

EDWARD BOND (deceased) came from Tennessee and settled in Jefferson County with his parents, Mitchell and Elizabeth Bond, at an early day. He was reared on a farm, and during his life gave his attention to agricultural pursuits. He was a man of quiet and unpretending ways and was held in high esteem and respect by the community in which he humbly toiled for many years. He responded to the country's call for troops for the Mexican war, and also served a year in the late war—in the Thirty-second Illinois Volunteer Infantry. December 11, 1850, he married Elizabeth A. Gill, a daughter of Joseph and Maria (Campbell) Gill. She still survives him, as do also three of their six children—William E., Michael A. and Francis M. Mr. Bond died August 23, 1874, at which time his farm consisted of 240 acres. Although departed, his record is with us, and it is resplendent with achievements which, although humble and unassuming in their nature, are, nevertheless, noble and grand, reflecting great credit to the worth of his character, which was at all times pure and undefiled.

WILLIAM R. CHAMP, farmer, P. O. Woodlawn, is one of the early settlers of Jefferson County, having come here with his parents, who unloaded their small stock of this world's goods in Grand Prairie Township November 9, 1829. He was born November 15, 1828, in Lincoln County, Tenn., to Henry and Delanie (Brown) Champ. The father was a Georgian by birth, was a substantial farmer during life, had filled many offices, and was a man who occupied a high position in popular favor.. He died August 30, 1876, aged nearly seventy-three years, his noble wife having departed this life in 1872. Their union had been blessed with twelve children, of whom five sons and two daughters are still living, our subject being the eldest. His early schooling was extremely limited—to a single spelling book he was indebted for all that he obtained. Farming claimed his attention in early life, and he has since made that his exclusive business. August 5, 1852, he wedded Nancy Bond, a daughter of Mitchell and Elizabeth Bond, and by her raised a family of six children, of whom five survive—Franklin P., William H., Olive M., Benjamin P. and Seymour. Mr. Champ has a farm of 262⅔ acres, mostly in Casner Township. He is a member of the I. O. O. F., Woodlawn Lodge, No. 522. He has filled many offices, including that of Supervisor, Collector, Town Clerk, etc., and is a Democrat in politics. With a possible exception, Mr. Champ is Casner Township's oldest resident at the present time. His success in life is altogether due to his own energy, and it is such characters as these that insure the growth and prosperity of the country.

SPENCER S. EUBANK, farmer and stock-dealer, P. O. Woodlawn, was born in Lincoln County, Tenn., May 13, 1814, a son of John and Susan (Shelton) Eubank, both natives of Georgia (or South Carolina, as they were right on the line), and here they were also married. The father was a carpenter and millwright by trade, which he followed the most of his life. The parents removed to Lincoln County, Tenn., where our subject was born, and after residing in different counties in Alabama and Carroll County, Tenn., they came to Washington County, this State, about 1830. Their marriage had given them fourteen children, five of whom were living at last accounts—Polly, Spencer S., Richard, Margaret and Betsey. Mr. Eubank received but very little early schooling. He has been variously engaged during his long and active life. He made his first crop of corn, and it was a good crop, too, with a grass collar and hickory bark traces, and was the first owner of a "painted" plow in Washington County. With his father, he put up the first frame house in Ashley, and they burned the first lime in the county. Mr. Eubank built several steam mills, one of them the second in the county. For thirty years he was engaged in farming and milling, owning at one time 1,400 acres of land, which he lost in the flouring mill business in Ashley. He has a present farm of 220 acres, mostly in meadow, which is devoted to stock-raising and grazing. He winters large herds of stock in Missouri and Arkansas and disposes of them in the Northern markets. He was married to Sally White, a daughter of Stinson White. She died in 1875, the mother of fourteen children, of whom seven are living—James, Anrow, Emily, Richard, Robert, Susan and Margaret. Politically, Mr. Eubank is a Republican. Although advanced in years, he is still hale and hearty, and engages in active every-day work.

THOMAS J. GASKINS, farmer, P. O. Woodlawn, is a native of Clark County, Ind., born August 23, 1838, a son of Elias and Mary (Bear) Gaskins, he a native of Ohio and she of Indiana. The father was a farmer, and died in 1882, aged nearly seventy-three years; the mother is still living. The married life of the old folks had been blessed with eleven children, seven of whom still survive—Thomas J., Sarah, Harriett, Owen, Mary, Martha and Leah. When Mr. Gaskins was quite small, his parents came to Jefferson County, and here he obtained what little education was afforded by the common schools. He started in life as a tiller of the soil, and has been always thus engaged, having at present a farm of 105 acres, which is devoted to farming in its various branches. March 7, 1861, he married Sarah E. Westcott, born June 4, 1830, a daughter of John D. and Margaret S. (Willis) Westcott, he born September 12, 1803, and died September 29, 1850, and she born August 24, 1804, and died November 30, 1858. Mr. and Mrs. Gaskins have five children—William T., born March 23, 1862; Mary R. E., February 27, 1864; Francis M., November 19, 1866;

Annie S. C., July 7, 1869; and Harriett E. L., February 27, 1872. Our subject and wife are members of the Christian Church. Politically, he is a Democrat.

THOMAS W. HARVEY, farmer, P. O. Woodlawn, was born June 27, 1830, in Hampshire County, Va. (now West Virginia), to Zachariah and Betsey (Ward) Harvey, both natives of Virginia. His father was a farmer by occupation, and was in the war of 1812. The parents had fourteen children, only two of whom are now living— Ann and Thomas W. The latter received what little education the old subscription schools afforded. At the age of five, he removed with his parents to Tazewell County, Ill., where the mother died. Shortly afterward, the father came to Jefferson County, and here our subject has since resided. His present farm consists of 160 acres, which is given to farming in its general branches. He was united in marriage, July 23, 1852, to Catharine Watkins, a daughter of Samuel and Barbara (Bear) Watkins, and the union has been blessed with fourteen children, seven of whom are now living—Mary E. (wife of Simeon L. White), John H., Isaac Z., Elijah B., Leah F., Thomas J. and Barbara L. Mr. Harvey was a member of the I. O. O. F. until his lodge broke up. He and wife are members of the Southern Methodist Church. He has filled the offices of Supervisor, Assessor, Deputy Sheriff and Constable, and in politics gives his support to the Democratic party.

THOMAS KELLY, farmer, P. O. Woodlawn, is a native of County Galway, Ireland, born September 25, 1829, the eldest child of Edward and Mary Kelly, both natives of the same country. His parents had a large family of children, our subject being the only one in America. He spent his early life in Ireland, and in 1849 embarked for the United States, landing in New Orleans. In the spring of 1852, he came to Jefferson County, where he has since resided, with the exception of several years' residence in the adjoining county of Washington. He has been twice married, first to Catharine Hayes, who bore him one child—Ashford—and afterward to Lucinda (Green) Pitts, by whom he has four children, of whom two are living— Hattie C. and Charles W. In January, 1862, Mr. Kelly enlisted in the Forty-ninth Illinois Volunteer Infantry, Col. Morrison, and was in many heavy engagements throughout the Mississippi and Western campaigns. He received a severe wound in the left leg at the battle of Fort Donelson, but served his three years of enlistment and was mustered out at Springfield. He and wife are members of the Baptist Church, in which he is also a licensed preacher. He has been Justice of the Peace for seven years in succession, and has filled many other offices. Politically, he is a Democrat. Although abrupt and decisive in speech, the Squire is, nevertheless, courteous and considerate, and is ever ready to give his support to enterprises calculated for the public good.

JOHN KENDALL, farmer, P. O. Ashley, was born in Scioto County, Ohio, January 5, 1823, the eldest son of William and Christina (Lawson) Kendall, he a native of Pennsylvania, and she of Virginia. The father was first married to a Miss Brown, who bore him seven children, only one of whom survives—Thomas—a resident of Cleveland, Ohio. Of his second marriage, four children are now living—John, Jeremiah, Susan and Louvina. William Kendall was a surveyor and located a great amount of land in Ohio, and also assisted in laying out Portsmouth, that State. He was engaged in the furnace business in Scioto County, and also steamboat building, and built many of the first to run on the Ohio River. He was a member of the State Legislature for many years, and at his death was an honored member of the State Senate. He was a Whig in politics, and during his life was actively identified with numberless popular enterprises of various kinds. He served in the war of 1812. John Kendall, the subject of these lines, obtained a little schooling in his native county, and was raised on the farm. He was in the mercantile and also coal business in Portsmouth, Ohio, and was afterward railroad agent for two years at Jackson, same State, after which he came to Jefferson County and located on his present place, which now consists of 320 acres, with a large orchard and the various attributes of a good farm. He was first married to Louisa Lucas, who died a short time after her marriage. His second marriage was with Louisa J. (Stamper) Martin. Mr. Kendall has filled many minor offices, and is the present School Treasurer of Casner Township. He is a Republican in politics. He holds a high position in popular esteem, and his humble, yet vigorous life, sets but another example that is worthy of emulation by all.

THOMAS B. LACEY, farmer, P. O. Woodlawn, was born February 17, 1827, in St. Clair County, Ill., to Joshua and Malinda (Gooding) Lacey, the father a native of Tennessee and the mother of Kentucky. Joshua Lacey was a tiller of the soil, and came with his father to Illinois Territory about 1807 and settled in what is now Madison County. He served in the war of 1812, as did also several of his brothers. He died in June, 1858, leaving his wife, who is yet living. Their married life had been blessed with ten children, of whom six are living—Annie, Thomas B., J. R., Thompson, Cynthia and Permelia. The early education of our subject was limited to what little was obtainable in the early schools of his native county. In 1848, he came to Jefferson County and taught two terms of school at Jordan's Prairie. He returned to St. Clair County, and was there married to Eliza McCulley, a daughter of John and Matilda (Nelson) McCulley, and the union has been blessed with twelve children, of whom there are now living—John O., Laura A., Matilda J., Joshua V., Charles A., Hugh B., Thomas M., Myrtle Belle, Lillian and Lorenzo D. Mr. Lacey is a member of the I. O. O. F., Woodlawn Lodge, No. 522, in which he was a charter member also. He belongs to the Methodist Church; has filled many minor offices, including that of Supervisor, Justice of the Peace, etc., and in politics votes the Republican ticket. He has a good farm and residence in Casner Township.

THOMPSON LACEY, farmer, P. O. Woodlawn, is a native of St. Clair County, Ill., born September 1, 1834, a son of Joshua and Malinda (Gooding) Lacey. (See sketch of T. B. Lacey elsewhere.) He obtained his early education in the schools of his native county, and started in life as a farmer. He was united in marriage to Nancy Reed, a daughter of Bird and Emily Reed, and the union has been blessed with eight children—America, Lucinda, Charles S., Robert L., Logan B., Permelia, Frederick and Emma. Mr. Lacey came to Jefferson County in 1858, and has resided here ever since, with the exception of returning to St. Clair County for a few months. He has a farm of eighty acres, and engages in general farming. He is a member of the I. O. O. F., Woodlawn Lodge, No. 522, and, with his wife, of the Methodist Church. He votes the Republican ticket.

DAVID ROACH (deceased) was born in Ireland and came to America when small. He was a son of Frank Roach. In early life he learned the trade of shoe-making, and was thus engaged for several years, mostly in Boston, Mass. Here he was united in marriage to Mary A. Riley, who still survives him. She is a daughter of James and Margaret Riley. In February, 1856, Mr. Roach came West and located in Jefferson County, and at first boarded hands, then working on the railroad. Shortly afterward, he purchased the place his widow now lives on, which consists of 191 acres, which is devoted to farming in its various branches. Mr. Roach died in 1881, leaving a widow and seven children—Frank P., Sarah M. and David R. (twins), Annie, Louisa, Isabelle and Charles. Mr. Roach was a highly respected citizen of Jefferson County. He gave liberally to church and school purposes, and his material assistance was forthcoming for the aid of all enterprises calculated for the good of the community, his generosity ofttimes exceeding his actual means. The grim hand of death cannot blot out, but only brightens with a perpetual glow the footprints of such noble lives, the thoughtful study of which tends to the edification and enlightenment of all mankind.

JOHN M. SEVERS, farmer, P. O. Ashley. Abram Severs was born in Indiana. He was a farmer in early life, but in later years engaged in the saw mill business in Jefferson County, being the owner of several different mills. He married Rebecca C. Dubrise, a native of Tennessee, and raised a family of thirteen children, eight of whom are now living—John M., Eliza J., Joel F., William A., Abraham L., Nancy R., Dora B. and Laura A. John M., the subject of these lines, was born May 26, 1846, in this county, in which he obtained his early education, and which he has always made his home. He has been a farmer all his life, his present farm consisting of eighty acres, which is devoted to farming in its various branches. In February, 1865, he enlisted in the One Hundred and Sixtieth Ohio Volunteer Infantry, Col. Stevenson, and was at Tullahoma and Memphis, at which latter place he was mustered out at the close of the war. He was united in marriage, January 7, 1872, to Cansada McMillion, a daughter of Meredith S. and Caroline (Carter) McMillion. This union has been blessed with five children, two of whom are living—Emery E., born December 12, 1874; and Frank M., May 21, 1880. Politically, Mr. Severs is a Republican.

JAMES WOOD, farmer, P. O. Woodlawn, was born in Saline County, Ill., March 30, 1817, a son of Alfred and Mary (Jackson) Wood, he a native of Tennessee and she of South Carolina. The father was a son of William Wood, who was known throughout the country as "Roaring Billy." Alfred Wood was a farmer by occupation; was in the war of 1812, and was accidentally killed when our subject was small, by a limb striking him while felling a bee tree. The parents were blessed with six children—James, and Leonard, who resides in Texas, being the only ones now living. James received but a very limited schooling, his parents being in poor circumstances. There were no winter schools at that time, and his father needed his assistance in the summer in making the crops. He has always given his attention to farming pursuits, his present property consisting of 320 acres, and he has given largely to his children. He was married to Margaret A. Dyer, a daughter of Martin Dyer, and by her had a family of nine children, of whom six still survive—Francis, John, Pierce, Rodum, Isaac and Annie. Mr. Wood has filled many minor offices. Politcially, he has always been a Democrat. He is one of Casner Township's respected citizens, and, although advanced in years, is still actively engaged in every-day farm work.

WILLIAM A. WRIGHT, farmer, P. O. Richview, is a native of Rockingham County, N. C., born July 14, 1827, to George W. and Susan A. (Wrion) Wright, both of the same State. His father was a farmer; was in the war of 1812; was a strong Democrat of the Jacksonian type, and was identified with many popular enterprises. He died in 1846. His noble wife still survives him, at the advanced age of eighty-nine years. The venerable lady has lived in this vicinity for upwards of fifty years, and is still quite hale and vigorous, the hand of time having touched her lightly. Their marriage was blessed with seven children, of whom three are now living—James M., William A and George W. Mr. Wright's parents moved to Marion County, this State, when he was about four years old. His father was in poor circumstances, and was unable to give his children an adequate schooling. After several years' residence in Marion County, our subject removed to Washington County, and about two years later to Jefferson County, which has since been his home. He has a farm of 120 acres, and engages in general farming. October 11, 1848, he wedded Mary A. Martin, a daughter of James M. and Mary (McCracken) Martin, and they have one child—Sarah A.—wife of Amos Downs, of Casner Township. Mr. Wright, his wife and his aged mother are all members of the Christian Church. In politics, he is a Democrat. Mr. Wright's reputation is above the slightest reproach. He is recognized as a humble and honest man, always seeking opportunities to do good, and of such men the people feel justly proud.

FARRINGTON TOWNSHIP.

CHARLES S. BURKE, farmer, P. O. Pigeon, was born in Jefferson County January 31, 1854, and is a son of Joseph F. Burke, of this township. Our subject was brought up on the farm and has always been a farmer. He was married, in 1876, to Miss Mary E. Hutcherson, by whom he had two children, viz., Augustus C. and Mary E. Mrs. Burke died November 10, 1881, and on the 15th of March, 1883, Mr. Burke married Miss Ruannah J. Fults, daughter of Isaac Fults, of Allen County, Ind. Mr. Burke owns eighty acres of valuable land and resides on Section 35.

WILLIAM A. DALE is a native of Smith County, Tenn., born February 17, 1814. His father, William Dale, was born in Maryland. Our subject came to this county in March, 1839, where he has since resided. He was married, in 1834, to Martha Johnson, by whom he had ten children; of these but two are living, viz., James and Nancy. Mrs. Dale died November 2, 1864, and he again married, September 30, 1865, to Mrs. Sarah White. She had three children by her first husband, one living, viz., Frances. Mr. Dale is a member of the Baptist Church. He was Captain of the militia company that used to drill at Moore's Prairie.

PETER DAMITZ, farmer, P. O. Logansville, is a native of Prussia, and was born April 8, 1840. His father, Ernst Damitz, brought his family to Warren County, Ill., in 1847, where he died in February, 1883, at the age of seventy-nine years. Our subject went to California in 1862, where he learned the stone mason's trade. He worked at his trade also in Nevada, Utah, Montana and Idaho. He traveled through Colorado, and returned to Illinois in 1866. The next year he went to Lynn County, Kan., where he followed his trade and farmed. Mr. Damitz has built enough stone fence to reach half way from Mount Vernon to St. Louis. In 1876, he married Mrs. Sarah A. Wagner, who died when on their way to Colorado in 1878. Mr. Damitz again married, in February, 1880, Mary A., daughter of Lewis Cooper. They have one child—Lewis E.

ROBERT FRENCH, farmer and stock-raiser, P. O. Pigeon, was born in Harrison County, Ind., February 13, 1832, and is a son of Mason French (deceased) a native of Virginia. Mr. French was brought up on the farm and attended a subscription school in a log cabin and sat on a slab bench. He came to Jefferson County in March, 1854. He was married to Eliza J. Matheney, by whom he had fourteen children, nine living —Samantha A., Sarah D., M. Hamilton, John N., Albion T. and Albert C. (twins), Viola B., Robert W. and Agnes M. Mr. French was Constable of this township two years. He owns 280 acres of land. Has been a member of the United Brethren Church for forty years.

SAMUEL GREENWALT, farmer, P. O. Logansville, was born in Wayne County, Ill., April 18, 1841, and is a son of David Greenwalt (deceased), a native of Kentucky, who came to Wayne County about 1820. Our subject was brought up on the farm and educated in the common schools. He was married, March 13, 1865, to Ellen Harvey, by whom he has had eleven children, eight living—Martha C., Olive R., Annie E., Margaret, George S., Bertha, Frederick and Walter. Mr. Greenwalt came to this county in the fall of 1865. He was a soldier in the late war for Uncle Sam three years in Company K, Forty-ninth Regiment Illinois Volunteer Infantry, and participated in the battles of Fort Donelson, Pittsburg Landing, Tupelo, Little Rock, Pleasant Hill, La., Fort Derusa, La., Nashville, and others. He owns 240 acres of valuable land, and is engaged in farming and stock-raising. He held the office of Highway Commissioner for three years.

DR. L. B. GREGORY, farmer and stock-raiser, P. O. Logansville. The subject of this sketch was born in Simpson County, Ky., February 19, 1826, and is a son of Benjamin Gregory (deceased), a native of North Carolina, who brought his family to this county in 1832, where our subject has since resided, except a short time in Missouri. He was reared on the farm and educated in a subscription school, in a log cabin with dirt floor, split pole seats or benches, and no window—just a large door. He graduated from the Cincinnati Medical College in 1856. He at once began the practice of medicine in his neighborhood, and built up a large practice. He has been trying to give up his practice, but has frequent calls from friends. The Doctor began life without a dollar; he educated himself, and is therefore a self-made man. He now owns 1,400 acres of valuable land, and is extensively engaged in farming and stock-raising and dealing in stock. He also has a general store, in which he does a good business. His land is divided into seven farms. He married Eliza Cochran, by whom he has had eight children, seven living—Charley, Mary E., Leander M., Sophronia, Lenna B., Ida and Leona. The Doctor also has the post office, name Logansville. He is the present Supervisor for Farrington Township; resides on Section 24.

NOAH HYRE, farmer, P. O. Logansville, was born in Montgomery County, Ohio, July 15, 1844, and is a son of Absalom Hyre (deceased), a native of the same county. Our subject was brought up on a farm, and has been a farmer for the most part all his life. He is also a carpenter by trade, and carries that on in connection with farming. He was married, December, 1866, to Caroline Hackett, by whom he has had eight children; of these six are living—Flora B., Harriet J., Charles W., John P., Maud R. and James V. Mr. Hyre owns forty acres of land.

JOHN W. JOHNSON, farmer and mechanic, P. O. Pigeon, is a native of Nashville, Tenn., and was born July 17, 1831. His father, William B. Johnson (deceased), was also a native of Nashville, and brought his family to this county in the fall of 1831, when the wolves were howling, and panthers, bears and wild cats were roaming at will through the dense forests of this then wilderness. Our subject attended a subscription school in a log cabin with puncheon floor, clapboard door, stick chimney, greased paper over a crack in the wall for a window. He was married in June, 1854, to Caroline Payne, a daughter of Joseph Payne (deceased). They had seven children, five living, viz., Mary (Webb), Joseph L. (in Arizona), Emma D., Hattie O. and Laura. Mrs. Johnson died in March, 1871. She was a member of the Methodist Church, as also are Mr. Johnson and the most of his family. Mr. Johnson is also a Mason in good standing. He owns 320 acres of land and is engaged in farming, stock-raising and blacksmithing. He also owns a set of buhrs for grinding corn, which is propelled by steam power. These buhrs were cut from a large bowlder in this county by a Frenchman from St. Louis in 1817. They were used many years in an ox-tread mill; then they lay idle for about thirty years. They do first-class work, are fifty inches in diameter and grind faster than any other set of stones in Jefferson County.

PERRINGTON T. MAXEY (deceased). The subject of this sketch was born in this county September 10, 1822, and was a son of Elihu Maxey (deceased), a native of Tennessee, and a pioneer of Jefferson County. Mr. Maxey was brought up on a farm and educated in the old-fashioned subscription school (for a description of the pioneer schoolhouses see biographies of John W. Johnson and Dr. Gregory of this township). He was married, February 19, 1846, to Harriet E., daughter of William B. Johnson (deceased), and a sister of the well-known John W. Johnson, of this township. They had eight children, five living—Frances M., Ellen M., Emma L., Horace T. and Franklin M. Mr. Maxey was a blacksmith by trade; also carried on the farm. He died April 13, 1865, leaving his family a farm of 160 acres on Section 29, where his widow and son Franklin still reside. Mr. Maxey was a worthy member of the Methodist Episcopal Church.

DANIEL E. MILNER, farmer, P. O. Hickory Hill, was born in Wayne County, Ill., February 21, 1849, and is a son of John Milner (deceased) a native of Grayson County, Ky. Our subject was brought up on the farm and received his education in the common schools and the High School of Xenia, Ill. He went to Missouri in 1876, where he engaged as sawyer for four years. In June, 1881, he came to this county, was married January 27, 1881, and has one child—Leola V. He owns eighty acres of land.

WILLIAM WILSON, farmer, P. O. Logansville, was born in Licking County, Ohio, August 12, 1812, and is a son of James Wilson (deceased). Our subject came to this township in 1851, among the deer and wolves. He married Susan Boudinot, a great niece of the eminent and philanthropic Hon. Dr. Boudinot, of Colonial Congress fame. They have had nine children, seven living—Caroline, Horace, William E., Harriet (Coyle), Mary (Stonesifer), Kate (Ellis), and Ann L. (Pearce). Mr. Wilson was eleven months in the late war in Company I, Forty-eighth Regiment Illinois Volunteer Infantry. He was disabled and discharged from duty. He now draws a pension; he owns 120 acres of land.

WILLIAM L. YOUNG, farmer and merchant, P. O. Pigeon, was born in White County, Tenn., December 24, 1843, and is a son of Robert S. Young (deceased), a native of Kentucky, who brought his family to this county in 1854. Our subject was reared on the farm and educated in the common schools. He is a farmer and merchant at Farrington. He married Laura C. Byard, by whom he has had seven children, six living —John G., James E., Cora C., Adda R., and infant boy and girl (twins). Mr. Young established his store in July, 1880, keeps a general stock and does a good business. He owns 120 acres of land, is a member of the Masonic order. Mr. Young has held several offices of trust.

JAMES B. YOUNG, farmer, P. O. Pigeon, was born in White County, Tenn., March 27, 1852, and is a son of Robert S. Young (deceased). Mr. Young was brought to this county by his parents in 1854; he was brought up on the farm and educated in the common schools. He taught school for five winters. Since that time Mr. Young has devoted all his time and attention to the farm. He was married, December 9, 1880, to Miss Lydia Brewer, a daughter of Jacob Brewer (deceased). They have one daughter —Maud. Mr. Young and wife own 160 acres of land. He is a member of the United Brethren Church. He was Assessor for Webber Township one year, and is present Clerk of Farrington Township.

ELK PRAIRIE TOWNSHIP.

J. H. CROSNO, farmer, P. O. Elk Prairie, was born in McClellan Township, Jefferson County, November 16, 1832, a son of R. S. and Mary (Wells) Crosno. The father was a native of Smith County, Tenn., and came to this county in an early day, first settling in McClellan Township, where he resided until 1836, when he moved to Elk Prairie Township. Here he remained until 1865, and then moved to Washington Territory, where he lived until his death, which occurred in 1867. The mother was a native of Giles County, Tenn. Subject was the oldest of eight children, of whom four are now living. His education was received from the subscription schools, but he afterward taught one of the first free schools of the county. He remained at home with his father until about twenty-two, and then purchased a farm in the south part of Elk Prairie Township. On that place he resided until after his father's death, when, buying the interests of the remaining heirs, he returned to the old homestead, on which he now resides. He has at present 300 acres in Sections 1, 2 and 14, of which about two hundred and fifteen acres are under cultivation. Mr. Crosno was married, June 29, 1854, to Lorinda Howard, a daughter of Charles and Jane Howard, early settlers of McClellan Township, coming from Tennessee to this county. This union resulted in the following children, all of whom are living: Pueblo K. (on a farm in McClellan Township), Peoria K. (wife of O. P. Duncan, of McClellan Township), Florida (wife of Lucius Johnson, of Spring Garden Township), Rosa, Willie, Charles R., R. H., S. J., A. O. and Hardin W. Our subject has served as Township Assessor, Justice of the Peace and member of the County Board of Supervisors. In politics, is a Greenbacker.

WILLIAM S. DODDS, farmer, P. O. Laur, born on the farm where he now resides, in Elk Prairie Township, Jefferson County, on December 21, 1849; was a son of John and Lucy (Keller) Dodds. The father was also a native of this county, being born near Mount Vernon, and died in Elk Prairie Township October 8, 1879. The grandfather, Joseph Dodds, however, came from South Carolina to this county in a very early day. Subject was the second of seven children, of whom five are now living—Maggie (wife of T. H. Mannen), William S., Susan (wife of Sydney T. Hirons), David and Neal. Subject attended the free schools of this county. He remained on the home farm until his father's death, and after the division of the estate, subject acquired 140 acres. Mr. Dodds was married, September 8, 1880, to Mary McConnel, a native of Rome Township, this county, and a daughter of John C. and Sarah Jane (Cummings) McConnel. The result of the union was one child—Bertha, born June 11, 1882. This lady died February 15, 1883, and was buried in the McConnel Cemetery, in Rome Township. Mr. Dodds has served as Township Assessor three terms. In politics, Mr. Dodds is a Democrat.

J. J. FITZGERRELL, P. O. Fitzgerell, probably one of the foremost and most extensive farmers in Jefferson County, the gentleman whose name heads this sketch, was born about three miles from Owensville, Gibson Co., Ind., January 25, 1815. He was a son of James and Elizabeth (Roy) Fitzgerrell, who were among the early pioneers of that region. The father was born near Fredericksburg, Va., and the mother near Lancaster, Garrett Co., Ky. Subject was the third of fourteen children, of whom seven are now living. His education was received in the subscription schools of his county. When eighteen, his father moved to Posey County, Ind., to which place the son accompanied him, and with whom the latter made his home until twenty-two, and then commenced life for himself on a farm in that county. There our subject remained until 1839, and then came to Jefferson County. Here he remained only ten weeks, but in that time he fenced eighty acres and entered about two hundred acres more of his present farm. He then returned to Posey County, Ind., and there remained until the spring of 1840, and then came again to this county, where he has since resided and where he stands to-day as one of the largest land owners of the county. In connection with his farming, Mr. Fitzgerrell was also, until about four years ago, one of the most extensive stock-raisers of the county. In the last few years, owing to sickness, he has decreased somewhat in that line. Our subject was married in Posey Co., Ind., March 24, 1837, to Patsey Ann Martin, a native of Gibson County, Ind., and a daughter of James and Sarah (Williams) Martin, who were, probably, originally from Kentucky, and among the earliest settlers of Gibson County. Twelve children blessed this marriage, of whom six are now living—William

L., born August 18, 1839; Evans, born November 10, 1844; Sylvester, born February 6, 1850; Elzina J., April 9, 1852, wife of Dr. I. G. Gee, whose sketch appears elsewhere in this work; Sarah E., born December 9, 1851, and now the wife of Dr. J. H. Mitchel, of Mount Vernon; and Eliza B., born November 3, 1859, wife of A. Q. Mitchel, of Franklin County. Of the deceased ones, Bailey was born January 13, 1838, died May 20, 1840; John S., born March 1, 1841, died August 11, 1862; Andrew, born November 10, 1842, died November 15, 1847; Easter M., born October 26, 1854, died April 1, 1864; J. J., born April 8, 1857, died August 11, 1864; Patsey, born March 4, 1862, died July 4, 1862. Mrs. Fitzgerrell passed away March 31, 1862, and our subject was joined in wedlock, in Franklin County, on July 19, 1862, to Sarah M. Whitlow. This lady was born in Franklin County July 22, 1840, and was a daughter of Thomas and Elizabeth (Tompkins) Whitlow, natives of Hardin County, Ky. The parents came to Jefferson County about 1827, and settled in Moore's Prairie Township, and there lived until 1839, when they moved to Franklin County, where the father died April 12, 1846, and the mother August 17, 1854. The result of this union has been seven children, all of whom are now living—Robert C., born May 3, 1863; Mary C., born August 23, 1865; Daniel G., February 10, 1868; Edgar Lee, born February 6, 1872; Euterpe W., born May 11, 1874; Elnora R., born November 27, 1877; Catharine M., April 14, 1880. Mrs. Fitzgerrell is a member of the Union Baptist Church of Elk Prairie Township. In his lifetime, our subject has kept free from office-seeking and political strifes, and has devoted himself mainly to his business. In politics, he has been a lifelong Democrat.

DR. I. G. GEE, physician and farmer, P. O. Fitzgerell. The gentleman of whose life this is a brief sketch is at present one of the leading physicians of Jefferson County, and was born in Simpson County, Ky., September 19, 1841. He is a son of William and Melinda (Billingsly) Gee. The father was born about 1810, in Barren County, Ky., his father having come from Virginia, and the mother was born Februray 24, 1816, in Warren County, Ky. In October, 1852, the parents came to Illinois and settled in Perry County, near Tamaroa, and here subject received his education. In the spring of 1863, he commenced reading medicine with Dr. W. Sims, of Tamaroa. After reading with that gentleman six months, he went to the Eclectic Medical Institute, where, except for a short time, he attended lectures until February, 1865, when he graduated from that institution and returned to Illinois, where he settled in Elk Prairie Township, Jefferson County. Here he has since remained in the practice of his chosen profession, which now extends over parts of Jefferson, Perry and Franklin Counties. The Doctor also finds time to give considerable attention to farming, and at present owns 80 acres in Section 26, 80 in Section 29, 515 in Section 30, 65 in Section 35, of Township 4, Range 2, 160 acres in Perry County and 240 acres in Franklin County. Our subject was joined in the holy bonds of matrimony to Elzina J. Fitzgerrell on December 26, 1867. This lady is a native of this county, and is a daughter of J. J. Fitzgerrell, whose sketch appears elsewhere in this work. The result of this union has been five children, of whom three are now living—Harl, Earl and Knox. Subject has served as Township Clerk, Highway Commissioner and School Treasurer; is a member of Goode Lodge, No. 744, A., F. & A. M., of Franklin County, and of H. W.

Hubbard Chapter, No. 160, Royal Arch Masons, of Mount Vernon.

JAMES LOMAN, farmer, P. O. Elk Prairie, was born in Madison County, Ky., May 28, 1831, a son of Isaac and Phœbe (Davenport) Loman, who were natives of North Carolina. Subject was the oldest of seven children, and when eleven years old his father died. The former, however, remained at home with his mother and assisted on the farm. In the winter time, however, he found time to attend the subscription schools of his county some. When subject was eighteen, his mother married a Mr. Coffman, but Mr. Loman, however, made his home with his step-father until he became of age, and then, in the fall of 1852, he removed to Illinois and settled in Gallatin County, where he remained six years. From there he came to Jefferson County, and settled on his present farm in Elk Prairie Township. Here he now owns about one hundred and seventy acres, located in Sections 23, 24 and 26, of Township 4, Range 2 east. Of this, there are about one hundred and forty-two acres in cultivation and two acres in orchard. Mr. Loman was married, July 1, 1850, to Miss Sarah J. McClaine, a native of Hopkins County, Ky., and a daughter of Mrs. Lurenna McClaine. This marriage has resulted in seven children, of whom five are now living—Mary (wife of William Hester), William, Vienna (wife of Newton Wells), I. B. and Leota. Subject enlisted in the Thirty-first Illinois Volunteer Infantry in October, 1864, and remained in service until August, 1865. Among the campaigns in which his regiment participated was that of Sherman's famous march to the sea. Mr. Loman has served in many places of trust in his township, having been Justice of the Peace sixteen years. He is at present filling the office of School Trustee. He is a member of the Elk Prairie Christian Church, and in politics is at present connected with the Greenback party; formerly, however, he affiliated with the Democratic party.

JOHN MARTIN, deceased, was born in Gibson County, Ind., August 14, 1813. He was a son of James and Sarah (Williams) Martin, and was the third of six children, of whom two are living. His education was received in the schools of that day, and was somewhat meager, his father having died when subject was a mere boy. The latter rendered what service he could to his mother, and remained at the home farm until he was twenty-seven. Then, starting out in life, he married and settled down on a farm in that county, where he remained until 1847, and then came to Jefferson County, where he settled in Elk Prairie Township, on the farm now occupied by his widow. His first purchase of 200 acres had been partially cleared. By careful saving and frugality he added to that until at the time of his death he owned about nine hundred acres, which have since been divided among his heirs. In Gibson County, Ind., February 11, 1841, Mr. Martin was wedded to Julia Ann Armstrong, who was born in Wayne County, Ill., April 2, 1822, and is a daughter of Elsberry and Elizabeth (Landers) Armstrong, who were probably originally natives of Indiana. Nine children have come to bless this union, of whom seven are now living, viz., Elsberry, born November 11, 1841; Melissa, born January 1, 1845, wife of Harry H. Hartley; Sarah E., born November 29, 1847, wife of J. J. Pierce, of Franklin County; Mary J., born November 25, 1849, wife of J. A. Allen; Nancy E., born February 24, 1852, wife of M. M. Fitzgerrell; Martha A., wife of Elijah Webb; John B., born June 23, 1862. Two infants were born April 23, 1855, and died the same day. It was the nature of our subject to remain aloof from political struggles and strifes, and was in no way an office seeker and holder, but bent all of his energies to the amassing of a considerable competence, which his heirs now enjoy. As far as his political opinions and principles went, however, he gave his support to the Democratic party. Mr. Martin, in his lifetime, was a true and faithful member of the Baptist Church, and at his death, August 17, 1875, he was buried in the cemetery of that church in Elk Prairie Township. His widow and the unmarried children now remain on the farm.

WILLIAM WELLS, farmer, P. O. Elk Prairie, was born in Giles County, Tenn., September 16, 1813, a son of William and Elizabeth (Livingston) Wells. The father was a native of Pennsylvania, and came to Tennessee in a very early day; the mother was a native of Kentucky. Subject was the third of nine children. In 1819, his father went, with his family, to Lauderdale County, Ala., and there William attended subscription school some. In 1825, the father again moved, this time to Jefferson County, and settled in Mount Vernon Township. He was one of the first settlers in that neighborhood, where he, however, remained only about three years, and then moved to Wolf's Prairie, McClellan Township, where he resided until his death, which occurred in June, 1865. The father, in his day, was one of the foremost men of the township in which he resided, and served in numerous township offices. After subject came to this county, he also attended the subscription schools of his township. His first teacher was old Ned Maxey. Another teacher was a young man of the name of Bee, who afterward was County Judge. Our subject remained at home most of the time until he was twenty-five, and then, starting out in life for himself, immediately settled on his present farm. The place was at first a piece of Government land, entirely unimproved. He owns at present 180 acres in Sections 1 and 12, 40 in Section 14, 120 in Sections 22 and 23 of Township 4, Range 2 east; also 160 in Section 25 and 73 in Sections 14 and 23 of McClelland Township. Of the whole, there are about 350 acres in cultivation, about four acres in orchard. Mr. Wells was married, in Jefferson County, February 14, 1838, to Lucy Farthine, a native of Madison County, Ky., and a daughter of William and Sarah Farthine. The father was one of the earliest settlers in McClellan Township. This union has resulted in ten children, of whom eight are living—Elizabeth (wife of Joseph Dial, of Spring Garden Township), Thomas (in McClellan Township), John (in Elk Prairie Township), Harvey, Mary (wife of Thos. Puckett, of Blissville Township), Newton Edward and Jonathan, all at home with their father, and Joseph, in Spring Garden Township. Mrs. Wells is a member of the Elk Prairie Campbellite Church. Mr. Wells has served as Justice of the Peace eight years, Road Supervisor, School Director, etc. In politics, he is Democratic.

JOHN WILBANKS, farmer and banker, P. O. Mount Vernon, is a descendant of an old and prominent family of Jefferson County—a family who came here when the country was an almost unbroken wilderness, with danger lurking everywhere. In its subjection to civilized life, they bore an active and important part, and the education, wealth and refinement by which we are to-day surrounded attest the labors of these and other pioneers of the county. The grandfather of our subject was a native of the Spartansburg District, S. C., where he was born June 15, 1770. He grew up to manhood there, and married Miss Jane Thomas, a native of the same district, a union which resulted in the birth of nine children—Joseph (father of subject, born July 2, 1795), John (born October 22, 1796; he was a carpenter in South Carolina, and never came West), Thomas (was born December 11, 1798, and was a saddler by trade; he came to St. Louis when a young man, where he lived for some years, and was afterward drowned), James (was born march 19, 1801; he came West, and after living in this county a few years removed to Benton, Franklin County, where he lived until his death; his daughter, Rozella, is the wife of William Jones, the present Sheriff of that county), William (born March 19, 1803, was the first one of the family to come to this county and settled in Moore's Prairie Township first, where he remained some years and then moved to a farm in Spring Garden Township, where he died in an early day), Robert A. D. (born in 1805, the father of the present Clerk of the Appellate Court)–Robert Wilbanks (who is appropriately mentioned in another part of the work), "Peggy" (as she was called, was born in South Carolina, came West in 1823 with her parents and August 10, 1824, was married to James Black, a native of Washington, D. C., the twain settling down in the south part of Moore's Prairie Township; at the breaking out of the Black Hawk war, he enlisted in it, and was killed at the battle of Kellogg's Grove in 1832, and in 1837 his widow was married to Uriah Campbell), Judith (was born August 13, 1813, and was married, November 19, 1839, to John Robertson), Daniel P. (was born May 13, 1817, came West and settled in Gallatin County, Ill., where he married Margaret Campbell March 7, 1841; Mr. Wilbanks lived in that county for a number of years, was Circuit and County Clerk and finally moved to Arkansas; in 1854, while returning East on a visit, he died from fever on a steamboat at Memphis. The grandfather came West about 1828, and settled on the old Wilbanks farm in Moore's Prairie Township. There he lived until his death. In 1827, the great-grandmother, Judith Wilbanks, came out from South Carolina to pay her son and her grandchildren a visit, and died at the old homestead January 11, 1829, aged eighty years. Joseph, the father of our subject, came West soon after the close of the war of 1812, and first settled in Madison County, Ill., where he married Candace Pickering October 14, 1819. The mother was a native of Broome County, N. Y., and came West about 1815. They resided in Madison County until about 1826, and then came to Jefferson County, where the father settled in Mount Vernon and commenced merchandising. He was afterward elected to the position of Sheriff. At that time the county was not very thickly settled, his vote being thirty-five and his two opponents receiving thirty-four and thirty-three respectively. Also served as Postmaster. To them were born four children, three boys and one girl—John (our subject), Luke (deceased, was a soldier in the late rebellion, serving as Captain in the Sixtieth Illinois Volunteer Infantry, and while in the service contracted disease from which he afterward died), Q. A. (lives at present in Belle Rive, Pendleton Township), Margaret (married Alexander Moore and died in Mount Vernon about 1853). The father, who was consumptive, thinking a change of climate would help him, went to South Carolina about 1828, and there died from the effects of the disease January 7, 1829. The mother afterward married Stinson H. Anderson, who, in 1838, was elected Lieutenant Governor and served one term; his death occurred in 1853. When subject was about six years old, his step-father moved to Elk Prairie Township. Here subject attended the subscription schools of his day and helped on the home farm until he reached manhood. In 1843, he commenced farming on a piece of unimproved Congress land. In 1849, he entered eighty acres, and soon afterward forty acres more, which he had cultivated. He at present owns 422 acres in Sections 10 and 11; about five acres in orchard. He has given, in past years, a good deal of attention to stock-raising, but in the last few years he has turned his attention more to agriculture. In June, 1873, he embarked in the general banking business, with G. W. Evans, in Mount Vernon, Ill., under the firm name of Evans & Wilbanks. Mr. Wilbanks was married, December 9, 1849, to Elizabeth Evaline Newby, a daughter of Capt. H. B. and Nancy (Brown) Newby, who were among the earliest settlers in Mount Vernon Township. This union has resulted in eight children, five of whom are now living—Vanwert, born October 27, 1852, Cashier of Evans & Wilbanks' Bank; Florence, born December 11, 1854; Nannie C., born July 26, 1859; Frank A., born August 18, 1863; Robert Lee, born June 25, 1866. Of the deceased ones, Euterpe was born August 16, 1850, died May 28, 1874; Joliet, born February 13, 1857, died March 19, 1875; Newby, born February 24, 1861, died April 18, 1862. Mr. Wilbanks served in the Mexican war. He enlisted in June, 1846, in the Third Regiment, and remained in the service for twelve months—the time for which he enlisted. He participated in the battle of Cerro Gordo, and experienced during his term all the hardships of a solider's life, and the dangers and exposures incident to being in an enemy's country. In 1848, he was elected Circuit Clerk of Jefferson County, served one term, and was then (in 1852) elected to represent his county in the State Legislature. In both of these important positions he discharged his duties faithfully, and to the full satisfaction of his constituency. He is at present Commissioner of Highways. Politically, he is a Greenbacker, but has formerly been identified with the Democratic party. He is a member of Marion Lodge, No. 13, I. O. O. F, at Mount Vernon.

McCLELLAN TOWNSHIP.

JOSEPH BRADLEY, farmer, P. O. Mount Vernon, was born May 9, 1809, in Maryland. His father, Purnell Bradley, was also a native of Maryland, and a large farmer; he died there. The mother of our subject, Sinah Tull, was a native of Delaware; she came to this county, where she died. Her father, James Tull, was also a farmer, and a highly respected member of society; he died in Hancock County, Ill. Our subject was educated in Delaware. He has farmed all his life, and now owns a farm of 199 acres of good land in Wolf's Prairie. He was married twice. His first wife, Mary Van Cleave, was the mother of eight children, of whom four are now living, viz.: Sarah P. Downer, Mary A. Langley, Parthenia M. Williams and Eliza E. Gilbert. His present wife, Mrs. Ellen L. Rahm, born August 30, 1820, in Cincinnati, Ohio, and is the daughter of James and Sarah (Decourcey) Kirby. She is the mother of Anna C. Lawrence. Mr. and Mrs. Bradley are members of the United Brethren in Christ Church. His son-in-law, Louis Lawrence, is a minister in that church. In politics, he has been identified with the Democratic party till Greeley was run; of late years he has been independent in politics. Mrs. Ellen L. Bradley's children by her first husband, John Rahm, of Pittsburgh, Penn., were—George A. Rahm, James K. Rahm, Alice L. Rahm, wife of Mr. Joseph Meritt, of Salem, Ill.

ELIJAH COLLINS, farmer, P. O. Mount Vernon, was born April 18, 1846, in Rush County, Ind. His father, Charles Collins, was a native of Pennsylvania, born October 5, 1802; he was a farmer by occupation, and came to this county in the fall of 1865; he was well known and highly respected in this county, where he died April 13, 1872. His father, Ephraim Collins, was a native of Pennsylvania. The mother of our subject, Agnes Johnson, was born July 22, 1815, in Bullitt County, Ky., daughter of Moses and Rebecca (Irons) Johnson; her father, Jonathan Irons, was the discoverer and owner of what is now called the Shepersville Salt Works, and was scalded to death in one of the kettles. Mrs. Agnes Collins is the mother of seven children now living, viz.: Charles, Isaac, Elijah, Anna Morgan, Susan Keaton, John W. and Isabella Gray. Our subject was educated mostly in Brown County, Ind. He has made farming his vocation, having a farm of sixty acres. He has filled the offices of Constable and Highway Commissioner, and now holds the office of Township Supervisor. In politics, he is a Democrat. He was married, July 25, 1867, to Sarah M. Downer, born December 29, 1846, in Jefferson County, Ill. She is a daughter of John and Sarah M. (Neil), very old settlers. She is the mother of six children, viz.: Jennie, Agnes, Walter, Mary C. (deceased), Ethel M. and Louie. Mr. and Mrs. Collins are members of the Christian Church, of which he is an Elder.

WILLIAM A. DAVIS, farmer, P. O. Mount Vernon, was born January 16, 1846, in McClellan Township, Jefferson County, Ill. His father, Clinton S. Davis, was a native of Tennessee, and a farmer, who came to this county in or about 1838; he is yet living, aged sixty-three years. His father, Alfred Davis, was a native of North Carolina. The mother of our subject, Susan (Wells) Davis, was born June 11, 1811, is yet living, and the mother of seven children; her parents were William and Elizabeth (Levingston) Wells. Our subject was educated in this county, and here he was joined in matrimony, November 29, 1870, to Nancy G. Davis, born May 29, 1852, in Smith County, Tenn. She is a daughter of Joseph M. and Rebecca (Roister) Davis. Mrs. Nancy G. Davis is the mother of four children, viz.: Susan R., born October 20, 1870; C. Clinton, born November 8, 1873; N. Norman, born January 8, 1879; W. Willis, born August 16, 1881. Mr. and Mrs. Davis are connected with the Christian Church. He is a member of the A. F. & A. M., Mount Vernon Lodge. He has served the people in the capacity of Township Clerk for one year, as Township Supervisor five years, and for the last seven years he has been Justice of the Peace, filling the office with tact and ability. He has a farm of 260 acres, and in politics has been identified with the Democratic party.

J. G. HOWE, farmer, P. O. Woodlawn, was born February 17, 1827, in Davis County, Tenn. His father, Samuel Howe, was a native of Maryland, and died here, he being the son of William Howe, a native of Scotland. The mother of our subject, Anna Berry, was a native of Tennessee. She was the mother of ten children, of whom only Eliza Rightnowar and James G., our subject, are now living. He went to school but little in this county. He has farmed all of his life, and now owns a farm of 180 acres, which he made all himself. He supported his mother from 1838 till 1863, when she died. He married Margaret Cameron, born September, 1828, in this county. She is a daughter of Stephen and Elizabeth Cameron, old settlers, and she is the mother of five children, viz.: Mary F., William W. (deceased), Samuel S., Sarah A. (deceased), and Margaret H. Mr. and

Mrs. Howe are members of the Christian Church. He is a member of the Odd Fellows fraternity, Woodlawn Lodge, No. 522. In politics, he has been identified with the Democratic party. His grandmother, whose maiden name was Sela Gorden, was married three times, and all three husbands were killed by the Indians in Tennessee.

D. C. JONES, farmer, P. O. Mount Vernon, was born August 1, 1812, in Virginia, son of George Jones, also a good farmer. The mother of our subject, Prudence Keith, was the mother of eight children. Our subject, D. C. Jones, was reared in Jackson County, Ind., but was married in Jennings County, where also all of his children were born. His wife, Susan M. Prather, was born August 8, 1811, in Clark County, Ind. She is a daughter of William and Lettice (McCarroll) Prather, highly respected people, who reared a large family, and who became useful members of society, and were all members of the Methodist Episcopal Church. Mrs. Susan M. Jones reared seven children, viz.: Maria J., Marinda A. Meredith, Cyrena P. Montgomery, Lettia A. Titsworth, Calvin L., Margaret R. Mills and Irena Bell Klein, deceased. Mr. Jones farmed many years in Indiana, and finally, in 1863, he came to Jefferson County, where he has farmed ever since, owning now almost 300 acres of land, and is a good farmer and manager. His past life is worthy of imitation and ought to be recorded in these pages, which will serve as a guide post to the coming generations. In politics, Mr. Jones has been a Democrat.

SAMUEL LACEY, farmer, P. O. Woodlawn, was born April 13, 1825, in St. Clair County, Ill. His father, Thomas Lacey, the old United States Mail carrier, was a native of Kentucky, born February 9, 1800; he died here in 1879. He came to Illinois Territory in 1806, with his father, Liner Lacey, a native of Virginia. They settled in what is now called St. Clair County. He was a pioneer in Kentucky, as well as Illinois. The mother of our subject, Lucinda (Greathouse) Lacey, was the mother of three children, of whom our subject is the only one living. He was educated in Belleville, Ill., and early turned his attention to farming. He now owns 160 acres of land. His wife, Jane A. (Caulk) Lacey, was born March 27, 1832, in Carlinville, Ill. She is the mother of eight children, viz.: Thomas M., deceased; Mary M., Emma B., James H., Edward S., Charles G. Jenette D. and Anna M. Mr. and Mrs. Lacey are connected with the Methodist Episcopal Church. He is a member of the Masonic fraternity, Mount Vernon Lodge, No. 31. He has been Highway Commissioner, and in politics is identified with the Republican party. His son, James H., born February 2, 1857, is a graduate of the St. Louis Medical College. His preceptor was Dr. H. S. Plummer, of Mount Vernon.

ADAM RIGHTNOWAR, farmer, P. O. Woodlawn, was born March 29, 1824, near Elizabethtown, in Hardin County, Ill., son of George Rightnowar, a native of Pennsylvania; he was a farmer, and came here in an early day. The mother of our subject, Jerusha (Rose) Rightnowar, raised ten children. Our subject never went to school three months, all told, in his life. He has followed farming all his life, and owns 280 acres of land, having given about 200 acres to his five children, now married. He was married, March 8, 1849, to Eliza Howe, born August 26, 1829, in this county, daughter of Samuel and Anna E. Howe. She is the mother of eight children, viz., Francis (who married Harriett Giles), Elizabeth Rutherford, Anna Mandrel, Levina Wells, George (who married Sarah Mayberry), Eliza E. (born August 28, 1861), Mary D. (born December 30, 1863), and Adam D. (born October 18, 1866). Mrs. Rightnowar is connected with the Christian Church. Mr. Rightnowar is identified with the Democratic party. He is a man who started out in the world with nothing, but has done well without an education, his example in life being worthy of imitation.

DANIEL STURGIS, farmer, P. O. Mount Vernon, was born February 14, 1832, in Hamilton County, Ohio, son of Daniel Sturgis, Sr., a native of New Jersey; he was a blacksmith, and died in Ohio, his father being Moses Sturgis. The mother of our subject, Mary McKee, was a native of Ohio; she was a daughter of Samuel McKee, a native of Ireland; she was the mother of eleven children, and died in Mount Vernon. Our subject was educated in Ohio. In early life he was a mechanic, and followed it for many years in Mount Vernon; for the last four years, he has been a farmer, owning a farm of 120 acres. He was joined in matrimony twice. His first wife, Anna A. Mayhew, was the mother of four children now living, viz., Martha Hiserman, Viola, Charley and Albert. His present wife, Mrs. Sarah Kelly, born November 6, 1841, in Brown County Ohio, was a daughter of William and Mary A. (Guthrie) Edgington, natives of Ohio. She is the mother of four children, viz., William, Delilah, Mary A. and Daniel. Mr. and Mrs. Sturgis are both church members. He is identified with the Republican party, of which he was an ardent supporter during the war, in which he served about one year, enlisting in the One Hundred and Fifty-first Indiana Volunteers, Company D, serving till close of war, when he was honorably discharged.

BALD HILL TOWNSHIP.

R. W. MANNEN, farmer and stock-raiser, P. O. Laur, was born in Bald Hill Township, Jefferson County, July 5, 1851; is a son of Sydney S. and Eliza A. (Walton) Mannen. The parents were originally from Mason County, Ky., and came to this county about 1844. They settled on the farm now occupied by subject, where the father died in 1872. The mother is still living. Subject was the fifth of nine children, of whom eight are living. In childhood and youth, he attended the free schools of his township, and worked on the home place until the father's estate was settled. And when the estate was divided, subject inherited the part that he now occupies. At present, he owns 220 acres in Sections 1 and 10, of Town 4, Range 1, eighty acres in Section 6, of Town 4, Range 2, and eighty acres in Section 33, of Town 3, Range 1. Of the whole farm, there are about 240 acres in cultivation. He also pays some attention to stock-raising, having about 130 head of cattle, and some sheep and hogs.

Mr. Mannen was married, December 31, 1879, to Amanda E. Dodds, a native of Shiloh Township, Jefferson County, and daughter of William and Anna (Hall) Dodds. The father was born in this county, his parents having come here from South Carolina. The mother was a native of Gallatin County, Ill. The father in his day was one of the foremost men of this county, and served as Circuit Judge, County Clerk, and other responsible positions. He died in 1870. The mother is still living, in Elk Prairie Township. This marriage has resulted in one child—Walton Dodds, born March 13, 1881. In politics, Mr. Mannen is a Democrat.

SIDNEY S. MANNEN, farmer, P. O. Laur, was born October 31, 1853, a son of Sidney S. and Eliza A. (Walton) Mannen. (See sketch of T. H. Mannen, in Blissville Township.) He obtained what little schooling this county afforded in his younger days, and has, during his life, devoted his attention to the prosecution of farming industries. His present place consists of about 200 acres of land, and also a good residence, which he erected in 1880. Mr. Mannen married Eliza S. Stewart, a daughter of Peter Stewart, now deceased. Two children have blessed this union, one of whom is living— Lelia. Politically, Mr. Mannen gives his support to the interests of Democracy.

J. W. PHILP, farmer, P. O. Laur, was born in Bracken County, Ky., October 10, 1833, a son of Thomas and Elizabeth (Baltzell) Philp— the father being a native of England, the mother of Gallipolis, Ohio. Our subject was the sixth of eight children, of whom six are now living. When six years old his parents moved to Illinois and settled in Mt. Vernon, Jefferson County. There the family only remained about six months, and then moved to Bald Hill Township and settled about a mile and a half from where our subject now resides. There the father resided until the spring of 1854, when he moved to Central City, Ill., where he died in 1856, and the mother in 1872. The subscription schools of this county afforded our subject his means of education. He remained at home with his father until of age, and then commencing life for himself, settled on his present farm, where he now owns about 400 acres situated in Sections 1, 2 and 11, of Town 4, Range 1 east, and of that there are about 240 acres in cultivation. Mr. Philp was married, April 6, 1856, to Augusta Kinne, a native of Posey County, Ind., and a daughter of George N. Kinne. This union has resulted in eight children, six of whom are now living—Ida E., wife of Ichabod Newell, of Blissville Township; Emma F., wife of Wilburn Dodds, of McClellan Township; Charles T., James W., Henry O. and Maggie. He is a member of the Williamsburg Universalist Church. Has served his township as Justice of the Peace, Township Trustee and School Director. He enlisted in the Thirty-second Illinois Volunteer Infantry in October, 1864, and was mustered out in June, 1865. He was taken prisoner at the battle of Bentonville, N. C., but was exchanged at Richmond nine days after being taken. He is a Republican in politics.

PETER W. STEWART (deceased). Mr. Stewart came from Abbeville District, S. C., where he was born February 18, 1806, a son of John and Ann (Stewart) Stewart. During his life, he was mostly engaged in farming pursuits. He was first married in South Carolina, to Jane Crawford, and moved to Illinois, locating in Monroe County. She died about 1859. This marriage gave three children, all of whom died in infancy. In 1862, Mr. Stewart married the lady who now survives him. She was Hester A. Upton, a daughter of David and Margaret (Carmichael) Upton. This union was blessed with nine children, of whom there are three who are probably living—Jennie A., Eliza S. and Ida L. Mrs. Stewart had been previously married to Jeremiah Carmichael, by whom she had one child, who was living at last accounts. His son, Hiram S., is now living with his grandmother. The Stewart place consists of about 208 acres of land.

JOHN B. WARD, farmer, P. O. Fitzgerell, is a native of Hampshire County, Va., born September 28, 1820, to Lloyd and Catharine (Wilson) Ward, both of whom were natives of the same State. The father was a farmer. He was a son of Lloyd Ward, who served in the Revolutionary war. The parents of our subject were blessed with ten children, of whom there are six living—Sarah A., John B., William, Edward, Ruth and Lloyd S. Mr. Ward obtained but a meager education in the old-fashioned schools, and at the age of nearly fourteen, came with his parents to McLean County, Ill., where they resided about two years, and removed to Jefferson County, where our subject has since made his home. He has a farm of 460 acres which he devotes to farming in its various branches. He was united in marriage in 1845 to Prudence Reeves, a daughter of

Barnes Reeves. This union has given ten children, eight of whom survive—James S., Lewis D., William E., Franklin P., Rachel, Lucy A., Mary E. and Richard M. The oldest son, James S., served in the late rebellion, a member of the Eighty-first Illinois Volunteer Infantry, Col. Dollins. Mr. Ward has served as Justice of the Peace and Supervisor for many years. In political affairs, he casts his lot within the Democratic ranks.

Sketch received too late for insertion in proper place.

HON. CHARLES T. STRATTON, railroad and warehouse commissioner, Mount Vernon, Ill. We have in the character of this sketch a representative man, whose earnest efforts have won for him a position of high merit, and whose genial, pleasant manners have not failed to leave an impress on the minds of all with whom he has become acquainted of genuine regard. He was born May 1, 1855, in Wilmington, Ohio. He removed with his father, Stephen T., to Mercer County, Ill., in 1855, and in 1857 to Mount Vernon. He attended the Mount Vernon Seminary and awhile at McKendree College, two years at Washington University, at St. Louis, and two years he spent at the Wesleyan University, at Delaware, Ohio, finishing his school course there in 1873. In 1872, he returned home from Delaware, and being in poor health he was advised by the family physician to teach a term of school some distance in the country. This he did, taking a school at $30 per month, and rode on horseback a distance of five miles from his home and return daily. By the close of his school, he was able to resume his studies at the university, of Delaware, Ohio. In 1874, the authorities of the Mount Vernon High School wisely chose him as Principal. One year later, he accepted the Principalship of the high school at Nashville, Ill. Here he had the chance to show his worth, having the advantage of one of the finest school buildings in Southern Illinois and a large number of enterprising students. He subsequently withdrew from this place, much to the regret of the citizens of Nashville, and took charge of the schools of Edwardsville, this State. In the fall of 1878, he was invited to take a position in Washington University, at St. Louis, which he accepted, and his services were much appreciated in the academic department for two years. During the time he was here, his time was not all consumed at teaching, and he studied law. In the spring of 1880, he was admitted to the bar, and in the same year was nominated and elected from the Forty-sixth District to the Thirty-second General Assembly of the State of Illinois. In 1882, he was the Republican nominee for State Superintendent of Public Instruction, but was defeated. Although beaten at the polls, he made a noble fight for the nomination, having as competitors several of the best teachers of the State. In the fall of 1882, he resumed the practice of law at Mount Vernon, and on March 9, 1883, he was appointed by Gov. Hamilton as one of the three Railroad and Warehouse Commissioners for the State of Illinois, to succeed Hon. William H. Robinson, of Fairfield, Ill. This position he now occupies. The record of Mr. Stratton's life is a history of earnest and faithful work; of the actions and employments of one who has done thoroughly and well whatever he undertook to do, and whose life will—imperceptibly, perhaps, but not the less surely—exercise an influence for good on those with whom he was brought in contact.

ADAMS, William T. 73
ADCOCK, Joseph 102
ALLEN, John R............3
ANDERSON, William B. 3
ANGLEN, Thompson 102
ARNOLD, John H. 87
ATCHISSON, Ignatius ...123
BAKER, Charles A. 45
BALDRIDGE, James C. ...111
BALTZELL, R.B. 78
BARKER, Hardin 119
BARRETT, Amos B. 46
BAUGH, C.N. 88
    John W. 3
BAWDEN, William 4
BEAL, C.W. 112
    Lewis N. 4
BITTROLFF, George H. 4
BLEDSOE, Hugh L. 130
BLUM, Robert 5
BOGAN, John S. 5
    S.B. 79
BOGGS, W.A. 79
BOLES, Joseph 79
BOND, Edward 130
    Rufus J. 6
BRADLEY, Joseph 144
BREEZE, Henry 112
BRESACHER, Phillip 88
BROOKMAN, Christopher ...73
BROUGHER, J.W. 46
BROWN, C.M. 103
    Russell 47
BRUCE, Leonard W. 74
    M.D. 80
BUCK, Tobias K. 62
BUMPUS, William S. 88
BURCHELL, John 124
BURKE, Charles S. 135
CALHOUN, John E. 47
CARPENTER, S.W. 80
CARROLL, Joseph 103
CASEY, Clinton M. 62
    Isaac 81
    Thomas S. 7

    R.F. 81
    W.B. 7
CATRON, Jesse M. 48
CHAMP, William R. 130
CLARK, G.W. 124
    Joseph F. 74
CLAYBOURN, James H. 62
    William 120
COFIELD, William 124
COLLINS, Elijah 145
COOK, Andrew J. 74
COPPLE, David 82
    Edmund 113
    Samuel 113
    Riley 81
CORRELL, John F. 82
COWGER, A.D. 88
    William C. 7
CROSNO, J.H. 138
CULLI, Adam 89
CUMMINS, G.L. 83
CUNIO, Lawrence 89
CUNNINGHAM, John R. 83
DALE, William A. 135
DAMITZ, Peter 135
DAVENPORT, L.D. 48
DAVIS, William A. 145
DEES, Jesse A. 94
DEWEY, Russell 7
DODDS, William S. 139
DOWNER, John 89
    Silas 8
DRIVER, James R. 63
ESMAN, Britten D. 75
ESTES, James W. 49
    John 49
    John W. 90
EUBANK, Spencer S. 131
EVANS, George W. 8
FAIRCHILD, Eli 95
FERGERSON, John I. 64
FERGUSON, J.E. 9
FIELDS, Rufus 120
FISHER, William L. 114
FITZGERRELL, J.J. 139

Logan 104	HILLIARD, Samuel H. 75
FOSTER, Jared 49	**HINMAN**, Robert N. 15
FOUTS, David P. 115	**HITCHCOCK**, Edward 15
FRENCH, Robert 136	James 16
GALBRAITH, William M. .115	**HOBS**, Thomas H. 17
GARRISON, George W. 50	**HOLLAND**, Thomas G. 52
Isaac 90	**HOLTSCLAW**, Henry J. 65
J.W. 91	**HOWARD**, M.M. 121
William C. 91	**HOWE**, J.G. 145
William J. 120	**HUDSON**, Thomas 17
GASKINS, Thomas J. 131	**HUDSPETH**, John B. 18
GASTON, J.M.B. 84	**HUGHEY**, W.A. 52
GEE, I.G. 140	**HUNTER**, William H. 53
GIBSON, John 10	**HUTCHISON**, H.H. 84
Samuel 91	**HYRE**, Noah 137
GILBERT, Alvin 96	**JOHNSTON**, Noah 18
Cyrus 95	**JOHNSON**, A.C. 19
Menzis 96	James D. 18
S.B. 64	John A. 92
GRANT, Angus McNeil 10	John W. 137
GREEN, Barnett 97	Samuel 97
Edwin 96	Thomas C. 66
Willis Duff 11	William 117
GREENWALT, Samuel 136	**JONES**, ALONZO 54
GREGORY, L.B. 136	D.C. 146
GRIMES, S.F. 50	F.C. 55
GUTHRIE, S.C. 51	J.D. 55
HAILS, John W. 116	James 105
HAM, Orland M.D. 51	James K. 19
HARLOW, Bluford 11	Sarah J. 54
Robert 12	William A. 20,53
William J. 12	**JUDD**, C.H. 125
HARMON, John Q. 12	**KELL**, Charles D. 117
HARPER, C.B. 65	**KELLER**, Willis A. 20
HARVEY, Thomas W. 132	Columbus A. 21
HAWKINS, Elisha 121	**KELLY**, Thomas 132
John 121	**KENDALL**, John 132
Joseph 121	**KNOWLES**, A. 125
S.L. 121	Wiley 105
HAYNES, George M. 12	**KOONS**, C. 22
HAYS, G.W. 104	**LACEY**, Samuel 146
HERDMAN, W.H. 13	Thomas B. 133
HERMANN, F.W. 13	Thompson 133
HICKS, Stephen G. 15	**LAIRD**, Jesse 55
William 97	Lanson K. 75

LATHAM, Samuel K. 22	PATTON, Charles H. 26
LAUR, Joseph 98	PAVEY, C.W. 27
LINDLEY, C.W. 22	PAYNE, Essex 118
LINDSEY, C.B. 23	J.H. 68
James William 92	PEAVLER, Gabriel 106
LISENBEY, John P. 23	J.W. 107
LIVESAY, Lorenzo M. 75	PEERY, Cornelius 93
LOCK, John W. 24	PETTIT, J.N. 68
LOMAN, James 141	PETTYPOOL, B.B. 126
LOWRY, John 126	PHILP, J.W. 148
MANNEN, R.W. 147	PIERCY, Sherwood 68
Sidney S. 147	PIGG, John C. 28
Thomas H. 98	PLACE, Sidney 99
MARLOW, Abram 75	PLUMMER, Hiram S. 29
MARSHALL, J.W. 106	POLLOCK, James M. 30
MARTIN, John 141	PORTER, J.W. 118
Samuel G. 76	PRIMM, Benjamin F. 122
MAXEY, Charles Hardy ...24	PULLIAM, Oscar J. 77
Harvey M. 76	RATTS, Thomas L. 119
James C. 76	REED, John A. 69
Jehu G.D. 66	REID, George William ...31
Perrington T. ...137	RENTCHLER, James W. 57
Samuel T. 25	RIGHTNOWAR, Adam 146
MAXFIELD, B.P. 85	ROACH, David 133
McCONNELL, John C. 122	ROBINSON, Isaac W. 100
McMILLIAN, William A. ..85	John A. 31
METZ, Jacob 56	ROGERS, Silas 93
MILBURN, Newton 86	ROSS, W.R. 58
MILLER, Charles 118	ROTRAMEL, David 127
Ed 56	RYAN, R.E. 31
MILNER, Daniel E. 137	SANDERS, John 86
MITCHELL, J.H. 25	SATTERFIELD, John R. ...32
MONTGOMERY, M.V.B. 57	SCARBOROUGH, J.B. 108
MOORE, Alexander 77	SEVERS, John M. 134
Thomas F. 76	SEWARD, Lewis S. 69
MORRISON, Rufus A. 26	SHARP, J.F. 69
MOSS, John R. 67	SHIELDS, Henry A. 58
NORMAN H. 26	SHORT, Joshua 32
Thomas L. 66	SHURTZ, Andrew J. 100
NATON, William A. 77	SIDES, William 70
NEWELL, George 99	SIMMONS, Silas J. 122
NEWTON, Joseph H. 77	William F. 123
NORRIS, O.P. 99	SIMONDS, Thomas H. 33
PACE, S.T. 92	SMITH, Benjamin 108
PARKER, William K. 122	Harrison M. 101

      Jesse H. 127
      John T. 70
STEWART, Peter W. 148
STONE, William 77
STONEMETZ, Jacob 59
STRATTON, Charles T. ..149
STURGIS, Daniel 147
SUMMERS, W.H. 33
      John W. 33
SWEETEN, A.J. 109
TAYLOR, Jeremiah 34
      A.F. 34
      S.G.H. 35
TANNER, Allen C. 36
TELFORD, John 86
TIPTON, John 93
TUTTLE, Josiah 101
TYLER, J.C. 71
VARNELL, George H. 37
VOYLES, Thoams S. 78
WARD, John B. 148
      Joseph V. 71
WATERS, James 128
      Lewis Campbell ...59
WATSON, Albert 42
      J.H. 71
      Joel F. 39
      S.H. 40
      Walter 41
WEBB, W.C. 72
WELLS, Jacob P. 128
      William 142
WESTCOTT, T.E. 42
WHISSENHUNT, B.F. 111
WHITE, John N. 72
      W.N. 43
WHITSON, Claborn M. ...123
WILBANKS, John 142
      Robert A.D. 43
      Q.A. 60
WILKEY, James Henry ...128
WILLIAMS, Elisha R. 44
      James J. 123
      S.L. 110
      William T. 43

WILLIAMSON, Patrick 61
WILSON, William 137
WIMBERLY, B.F. 87
WISE, David H. 43
WITMER, G.H. 110
WOLF, James T. 94
WOOD, James 134
WLECKE, Henry 43
WRIGHT, J.W. 61
      William A. 134
YATES, Eli R. 129
YOUNG, James B. 138
      Robert S. 78
      William L. 138

www.ingramcontent.com/pod-product-compliance
Lightning Source LLC
Chambersburg PA
CBHW030223100526
44585CB00012BA/184